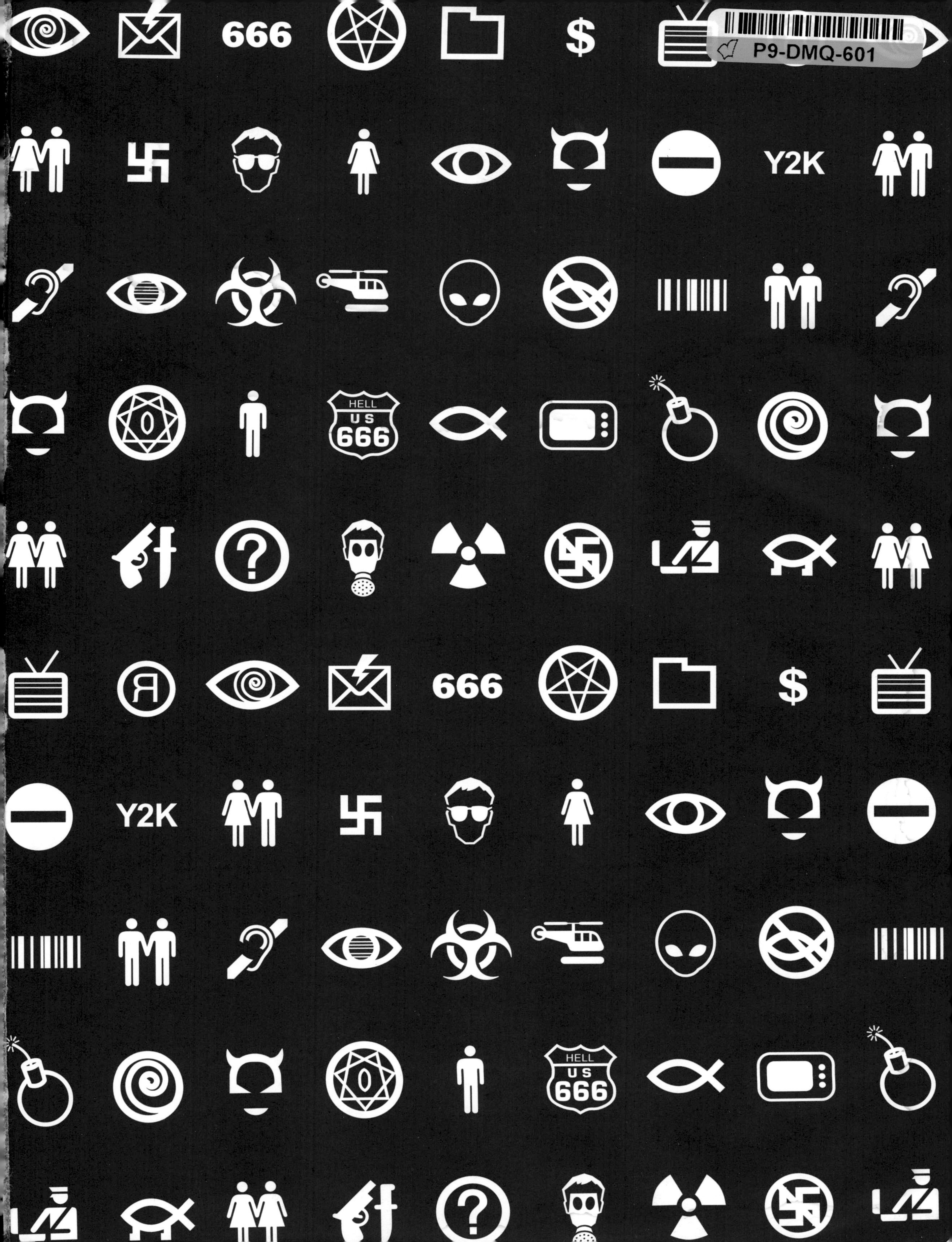
666
$
P9-DMQ-601
Y2K
HELL
US
666
666
$
Y2K
HELL
US
666

Published by The Disinformation Company Ltd.
163 Third Avenue, Suite 108
New York, NY 10003
Tel: 212.529.2330
Fax: 212.387.8152
www.disinfo.com

Editor: Russ Kick

Design and Production: Tomo Makiura and Paul Pollard

Eighth Printing May 2003

Library of Congress Card Number: 00-109281

ISBN 0-9664100-7-6

Printed in China

Distributed by Consortium Book Sales and Distribution
1045 Westgate Drive, Suite 90
St. Paul, MN 55114
Toll Free: 800.283.3572
Tel: 651.221.9035
Fax: 651.221.0124
www.cbsd.com

YOU ARE BEING LIED TO

The Disinformation Guide to Media Distortion, Historical Whitewashes and Cultural Myths

Edited by Russ Kick

disinformation®

ACKNOWLEDGMENTS

To Anne Marie, who restored my faith in the truth.

–Russ Kick

Thanks of a personal nature are due to Anne, Ruthanne, Jennifer, and (as always) my parents, who give me support in many ways. The same goes for that unholy trinity of Billy, Darrell, and Terry, who let me vent and make me laugh.

I'd like to thank Richard Metzger and Gary Baddeley for letting me edit the book line and taking a laissez-faire approach. Also, many thanks go to Paul Pollard and Tomo Makiura, who turned a bunch of computer files into the beautiful object you now hold in your hands. And thanks also head out to the many other people involved in the creation and distribution of this book, including everyone at Disinformation, RSUB, Consortium, Green Galactic, the printers, the retailers, and elsewhere. It takes a lot of people to make a book!

Last but definitely not least, I express my gratitude toward all the contributors, without whom there would be no *You Are Being Lied To*. None of you will be able to retire early because of appearing in these pages, so I know you contributed because you believe so strongly in what you're doing. And you believed in me, which I deeply appreciate.

–Russ Kick

Major thanks are due to everyone at The Disinformation Company and RSUB, Julie Schaper and all at Consortium, Brian Pang, Adam Parfrey, Brian Butler, Peter Giblin, AJ Peralta, Steven Daly, Stevan Keane, Zizi Durrance, Darren Bender, Douglas Rushkoff, Grant Morrison, Joe Coleman, Genesis P-Orridge, Sean Fernald, Adam Peters, Alex Burns, Robert Sterling, Preston Peet, Nick Mamatas, Alexandra Bruce, Matt Webster, Doug McDaniel, Jose Caballer, Leen Al-Bassam, Susan Mainzer, Wendy Tremayne and the Green Galactic crew, Naomi Nelson, Sumayah Jamal–and all those who have helped us along the way, including you for buying this book!

–Gary Baddeley and Richard Metzger

ABOUT DISINFORMATION®

Disinformation® is more than it seems. Literally. From early beginnings almost a decade ago as an idea for an alternative 60 Minutes-type TV news show to the book that you are now holding, Richard Metzger and Gary Baddeley have taken a dictionary term and given it secondary meaning to a wide audience of hipsters, thinkers, anti-establishmentarians, and the merely curious.

The Disinformation® Website <www.disinfo.com> went live on September 13, 1996 to immediate applause from the very same news media that it was criticizing as being under the influence of both government and big business. The honeymoon was short—some three weeks after launch, the CEO of the large US media company funding the site discovered it and immediately ordered it closed down. Needless to say, Metzger and a few loyal members of his team managed to keep the site going, and today it is the largest and most popular alternative news and underground culture destination on the Web, having won just about every award that s ever been dreamed up.

Disinformation® is also a TV series, initially broadcast on the UK s Channel 4, a music imprint in the US in a joint venture with Sony Music s Loud Records, and a huge counterculture conference, the first of which was held shortly after the turn of the millennium in 2000. By the time this book rests in your hands, Disinformation® will probably have manifested itself in other media, too.

Based in New York City, The Disinformation Company Ltd. is a vibrant media company that Baddeley and Metzger continue to helm. They still look for the strangest, freakiest, and most disturbing news and phenomena in order to balance the homogenized, sanitized, and policed fare that is found in the traditional media.

INTRODUCTION

You Are Being Lied To. It takes some nerve to give a book that title, eh? It came to me very early in the process, when this collection was just a germ of an idea. I did pause to wonder if it was too audacious; after all, I didn't want my mouth to write a check that my butt couldn't cash. But after spending several intense months assembling this book, I'm more convinced than ever that the title is the proper one. We *are* being lied to. In many ways.

For the purposes of this book, the definition of "lie" is an elastic one. Sometimes it means an outright falsehood told in order to deceive people and advance the agenda of the liar. Or it can be a "lie of omission," in which the crucial part of the story that we're not being told is more important than the parts we know. Sometimes the lie can be something untrue that the speaker thinks is true, otherwise known as misinformation (as opposed to disinformation, which is something untrue that the speaker *knows* is untrue). In yet other cases, particular erroneous beliefs are so universal—serial killers are always men, the Founding Fathers cared about the masses—that you can't pinpoint certain speakers in order to ascertain their motives; it's just something that everyone "knows." Sometimes, in fact, the lie might be the outmoded dominant paradigm in a certain field. A related type of lie—a "meta-lie," perhaps—occurs when certain institutions arrogantly assume that they have all the answers. These institutions then try to manipulate us with a swarm of smaller individual lies.

Which more or less leads me to my next point: This book doesn't pretend that it has all, or perhaps even any, of the answers. It's much easier to reveal a lie than to reveal the truth. As a wise soul once noted, all you have to do is find a single white crow to disprove the statement, "All crows are black." The contributors to this book are pointing out the white crows that undermine the "black crow" statements of governments, corporations, the media, religions, the educational system, the scientific and medical establishments, and other powerful institutions. Sydney Schanberg may not know the exact truth of the POW/MIA situation, but he sure as hell knows that Senator John McCain does everything he can to make sure that truth will never be known. David McGowan may not know exactly what happened during the Columbine massacre, but he shows us that there are numerous puzzle pieces that just don't fit into the nice, neat version of events that's been presented to us. Judith Rich Harris is still building the case that peers matter more than parents, but she has soundly laid to rest the notion that parenting style is by far the most important influence on who a child becomes. Can we say that a divine hand didn't put a secret code in the Bible? No, not exactly, but David Thomas can show that 1) those "holy" codes also appear in *War and Peace*, *The Origin of Species*, and a Supreme Court decision, and 2) you can find almost any word or name you want to find if you torture the text enough.

There are some cases, though, when it's fairly safe to say that the truth has been revealed. Thomas Lyttle does show us that licking toads will not, indeed can not, get you high, and Michael Zezima definitively reveals that both sides committed atrocities during World War II. Meanwhile, Charles Bufe demonstrates that the founders of Alcoholics Anonymous lifted their ideas wholesale from the evangelical Christian group they belonged to. They even admitted it!

Such cases of positive proof are in the minority, though. Basically, the pieces in this book show that the received wisdom—the common knowledge—is often wrong. Well, then, what's right? That's a much, much more complicated question, and the answers are elusive. Hopefully we'll all spend our lives pursuing them. But the first step is to realize that the "answers" that are being handed to us on a silver platter—or, perhaps more often, shoved down our throats—are often incorrect, incomplete, and usually serve the interests of the people promoting those so-called answers. That's where *You Are Being Lied To* comes in.

So dive in at any point, and you'll see that this book's title is deadly accurate. What you do about it is up to you.

—Russ Kick

A NOTE TO READERS

As you'll notice from the size of this book, my plan (luckily endorsed by Disinformation Books) was to cover a whole lot of ground from various angles. I wanted to bring together a diverse group of voices—legends and newcomers; the reserved and the brash; academics and rogue scholars; scientists and dissidents; people who have won Pulitzer Prizes while working at major newspapers and people who have been published in the (*very*) alternative press. Somehow, it all came together.* The group between these covers is unprecedented.

However, this has led to an unusual, and somewhat delicate, situation. Nonfiction collections typically are either academic or alternative, leftist or rightist, atheistic or religious, or otherwise unified in some similar way. *You Are Being Lied To* rejects this intellectual balkanization, and, in doing so, brings together contributors who ordinarily wouldn't appear in the same book. Some of the contributors were aware of only a handful of others who would be appearing, while most of them didn't have any idea who else would be sharing pages with them. All this means is that you shouldn't make the assumption—which is quite easy to unknowingly make with most nonfiction anthologies—that every contributor agrees with or thinks favorably of every other contributor. Hey, maybe they all just love each other to death. I don't know one way or the other, but the point is that I alone am responsible for the group that appears here. No contributor necessarily endorses the message of any other contributor.

—Russ Kick

* Well, it didn't *all* come together. You'll notice that among the contributors whose politics are identifiable, there is a large concentration of leftists/progressives. I did try to bring aboard a bunch of conservative journalists and writers whose intelligence and talents I respect (in other words, *not* know-nothing propagandists like Rush Limbaugh). However, none of them opted to join the festivities. Some ignored my invitation; some expressed initial interest but didn't respond to follow-ups; and two got all the way to the contract stage but then bailed. So when rightists continue to moan that their voices are excluded from various dialogues, I don't want to hear it. Their ghettoization appears to be self-imposed to a large extent.

CONTENTS

CONDEMNED TO REPEAT IT

TRIPPING

HOLY ROLLING

BLINDED BY SCIENCE

THE BIG PICTURE

KEYNOTE ADDRESS

Reality Is a Shared Hallucination

Howard Bloom

"Being here is a kind of spiritual surrender. We see only what the others see, the thousands who were here in the past, those who will come in the future. We've agreed to be part of a collective perception." —Don DeLillo

"We are accustomed to use our eyes only with the memory of what other people before us have thought about the object we are looking at." —Guy de Maupassant

"After all, what is reality anyway? Nothin' but a collective hunch." —Lily Tomlin

The artificial construction of reality was to play a key role in the new form of global intelligence which would soon emerge among human beings. If the group brain's "psyche" were a beach with shifting dunes and hollows, individual perception would be that beach's grains of sand. However, this image has a hidden twist. Individual perception untainted by others' influence does not exist.

A central rule of large-scale organization goes like this: The greater the spryness of a massive enterprise, the more internal communication it takes to support the teamwork of its parts.[1] For example, in all but the simplest plants and animals only 5 percent of DNA is dedicated to DNA's "real job," manufacturing proteins.[2] The remaining 95 percent is preoccupied with organization and administration, supervising the maintenance of bodily procedures, or even merely interpreting the corporate rule book "printed" in a string of genes.[3]

In an effective learning machine, the connections deep inside far outnumber windows to the outside world. Take the cerebral cortex, roughly 80 percent of whose nerves connect with each other, not with input from the eyes or ears.[4] The learning device called human society follows the same rules. Individuals spend most of their time communicating with each other, not exploring such ubiquitous elements of their "environment" as insects and weeds which could potentially make a nourishing dish.[5] This cabling for the group's internal operations has a far greater impact on what we "see" and "hear" than many psychological researchers suspect. For it puts us in the hands of a conformity enforcer whose power and subtlety are almost beyond belief.

In our previous episode we mentioned that the brain's emotional center—the limbic system—decides which swatches of experience to notice and store in memory. Memory is the core of what we call reality. Think about it for a second. What do you actually hear right now and see? This page. The walls and furnishings of the room in which you sit. Perhaps some music or some background noise. Yet you know as sure as you were born that out of sight there are other rooms mere steps away—perhaps the kitchen, bathroom, bedroom, and a hall. What makes you so sure that they exist? Nothing but your memory. Nothing else at all. You're also reasonably certain there's a broader world outside. You know that your office, if you are away from it, still awaits your entry. You can picture the roads you use to get to it, visualize the public foyer and the conference rooms, see in your mind's eye the path to your own workspace, and know where most of the things in your desk are placed. Then there are the companions who enrich your life—family, workmates, neighbors, friends, a husband or a wife, and even people you are fond of to whom you haven't spoken in a year or two—few of whom, if any, are currently in the room with you. You also know we sit on a planet called the earth, circling an incandescent ball of sun, buried in one of many galaxies. At this instant, reading by yourself, where do the realities of galaxies and friends reside? Only in the chambers of your mind. Almost every reality you "know" at *any* given second is a mere ghost held in memory.

The limbic system is memory's gatekeeper and in a very real sense its creator. The limbic system is also an intense monitor of others,[6] keeping track of what will earn their praises or their blame. By using cues from those around us to fashion our perceptions and the "facts" which we retain, our limbic system gives the group a say in that most central of realities, the one presiding in our brain.

Elizabeth Loftus, one of the world's premier memory researchers, is among the few who realize how powerfully the group remakes our deepest certainties. In the late 1970s, Loftus performed a series of key experiments. In a typical session, she showed college students a moving picture of a traffic accident, then asked after the film, "How fast was the white sports car going when it passed the barn while traveling along the country road?" Several days later when witnesses to the

Individual perception untainted by others' influence does not exist.

The words of just one determined speaker had penetrated the most intimate sanctums of the eye and brain.

film were quizzed about what they'd seen, 17 percent were sure they'd spied a barn, though there weren't any buildings in the film at all. In a related experiment subjects were shown a collision between a bicycle and an auto driven by a brunette, then afterwards were peppered with questions about the "blond" at the steering wheel. Not only did they remember the nonexistent blond vividly, but when they were shown the video a second time, they had a hard time believing that it was the same incident they now recalled so graphically. One subject said, "It's really strange because I still have the blond girl's face in my mind and it doesn't correspond to her [pointing to the woman on the video screen]... It was really weird." In piecing together memory, Loftus concluded that hints leaked to us by fellow humans override the scene we're sure we've "seen with our own eyes."[7]

Though it got little public attention, research on the slavish nature of perception had begun at least 20 years before Loftus' work. It was 1956 when Solomon Asch published a classic series of experiments in which he and his colleagues showed cards with lines of different lengths to clusters of their students. Two lines were exactly the same size and two were clearly not—the dissimilar lines stuck out like a pair of basketball players at a Brotherhood of Munchkins brunch. During a typical experimental run, the researchers asked nine volunteers to claim that two badly mismatched lines were actually the same, and that the real twin was a misfit. Now came the nefarious part. The researchers ushered a naive student into a room filled with the collaborators and gave him the impression that the crowd already there knew just as little as he did about what was going on. Then a white-coated psychologist passed the cards around. One by one he asked the pre-drilled shills to announce out loud which lines were alike. Each dutifully declared that two terribly unlike lines were duplicates. By the time the scientist prodded the unsuspecting newcomer to pronounce judgement, he usually went along with the bogus consensus of the crowd. In fact, a full 75 percent of the clueless experimental subjects bleated in chorus with the herd. Asch ran the experiment over and over again. When he quizzed his victims of peer pressure after their ordeal was over, it turned out that many had done far more than simply going along to get along. They had actually *seen* the mismatched lines as equal. Their senses had been swayed more by the views of the multitude than by the actuality.

Social experience literally shapes critical details of brain physiology, sculpting an infant's brain to fit the culture into which the child is born.

To make matters worse, many of those whose vision hadn't been deceived had still become inadvertent collaborators in the praise of the emperor's new clothes. Some did it out of self-doubt. They were convinced that the facts their eyes reported were wrong, the herd was right, and that an optical illusion had tricked them into seeing things. Still others realized with total clarity which lines were identical, but lacked the nerve to utter an unpopular opinion.[8] Conformity enforcers had tyrannized everything from visual processing to honest speech, revealing some of the mechanisms which wrap and seal a crowd into a false belief.

Another series of experiments indicates just how deeply social suggestion can penetrate the neural mesh through which we think we see a hard-and-fast reality. Students with normal color vision were shown blue slides. But one or two stooges in the room declared the slides were green. In a typical use of this procedure, only 32 percent of the students ended up going along with the vocal but totally phony proponents of green vision.[9] Later, however, the subjects were taken aside, shown blue-green slides and asked to rate them for blueness or greenness. Even the students who had refused to see green where there was none a few minutes earlier showed that the insistent greenies in the room had colored their perceptions. They rated the new slides more green than pretests indicated they would have otherwise. More to the point, when asked to describe the color of the afterimage they saw, the subjects often reported it was red-purple—the hue of an afterimage left by the color green. Afterimages are not voluntary. They are manufactured by the visual system. The words of just one determined speaker had penetrated the most intimate sanctums of the eye and brain.

When it comes to herd perception, this is just the iceberg's tip. Social experience literally shapes critical details of brain physiology,[10] sculpting an infant's brain to fit the culture into which the child is born. Six-month-olds can hear or make every sound in virtually every human language.[11] But within a mere four months, nearly two-thirds of this capacity has been cut away.[12] The slashing of ability is accompanied by ruthless alterations in cerebral tissue.[13] Brain cells remain alive only if they can prove their worth in dealing with the baby's physical and social surroundings.[14] Half the brain cells we are born with rapidly die. The 50 percent of neurons which thrive are those which have shown they come in handy for coping with such cultural experiences as crawling on the polished mud floor of a straw hut or navigating on all fours across wall-to-wall carpeting, of comprehending a mother's words, her body language, stories, songs, and the concepts she's imbibed from her community. Those nerve cells stay alive which demonstrate that they can cope with the quirks of strangers, friends, and family. The 50 percent of neurons which remain unused are literally forced to commit preprogrammed cell death[15]—suicide.[16] The brain which underlies the mind is jigsawed like a puzzle piece to fit the space it's given by its loved ones and by the larger framework of its culture's patterning.[17]

When barely out of the womb, babies are already riveted on a major source of social cues.[18] Newborns to four-month-olds would rather look at faces than at almost anything else.[19] Rensselaer Polytechnic's Linnda Caporael points out what she calls "micro-coordination," in which a baby imitates its mother's facial expression, and the mother, in turn, imitates the baby's.[20] The duet of smiles and funny faces indulged in by Western mothers or scowls and angry looks favored by such peoples as New Guinea's Mundugumor[21] accomplishes far more than at first it seems. Psychologist Paul Ekman has demonstrated that the faces we make recast our moods, reset our nervous systems, and fill us with the feelings the facial expressions indicate.[22] So the baby imitating its mother's face is learning how to glower or glow with emotions stressed by its society. And emotions, as we've already seen, help craft our vision of reality.

Psychologist Paul Ekman has demonstrated that the faces we make recast our moods, reset our nervous systems, and fill us with the feelings the facial expressions indicate.

There are other signs that babies synchronize their feelings to the folks around them at a very early age. Emotional contagion and empathy—two of the ties which bind us—come to us when we are still in diapers.[23] Children less than a year old who see another child hurt show all the signs of undergoing the same pain.[24] The University of Zurich's D. Bischof-Kohler concludes from one of his studies that when babies between one and two years old see another infant hurt they don't just ape the emotions of distress, but share it empathetically.[25]

More important, both animal and human children cram their powers of perception into a conformist mold, chaining their attention to what others see. A four-month-old human will swivel to look at an object his parent is staring at. A baby chimp will do the same.[26] By their first birthday, infants have extended this perceptual linkage to their peers. When they notice that another child's eyes have fixated on an object, they swivel around to focus on that thing themselves. If they don't see what's so interesting, they look back to check the direction of the other child's gaze and make sure they've got it right.[27]

One-year-olds show other ways in which their perception is a slave to social commands. Put a cup and a strange gewgaw in front of them, and their natural tendency will be to check out the novelty. But repeat the word "cup" and the infant will dutifully rivet its gaze on the old familiar drinking vessel.[28] Children go along with the herd even in their tastes in food. When researchers put two-to-five-year-olds at a table for several days with other kids who loved the edibles they loathed, the children with the dislike did a 180-degree turn and became zestful eaters of the dish they'd formerly disdained.[29] The preference was still going strong weeks after the peer pressure had stopped.

At six, children are obsessed with being accepted by the group and become hypersensitive to violations of group norms. This tyranny of belonging punishes perceptions which fail to coincide with those of the majority.[30]

Even rhythm draws individual perceptions together in the subtlest of ways. Psychiatrist William Condon of Boston University's Medical School analyzed films of adults chatting and noticed a peculiar process at work. Unconsciously, the conversationalists began to coordinate their finger movements, eye blinks, and nods.[31] When pairs of talkers were hooked up to separate electroencephalographs, something even more astonishing appeared—some of their brain waves were spiking in unison.[32] Newborn babies already show this synchrony[33]—in fact, an American infant still fresh from the womb will just as happily match its body movements to the speech of someone speaking Chinese as to someone speaking English.

As time proceeds, these unnoticed synchronies draw larger and larger groups together. A graduate student working under the direction of anthropologist Edward T. Hall hid in an abandoned car and filmed children romping in a school playground at lunch hour. Screaming, laughing, running, and jumping, each seemed superficially to be doing his or her own thing. But careful analysis revealed that the group was rocking to a unified beat. One little girl, far more active than the rest, covered the entire schoolyard in her play. Hall and his student realized that without knowing it, she was "the director" and "the orchestrator." Eventually, the researchers found a tune that fit the silent cadence. When they played it and rolled the film, it looked exactly as if each kid were dancing to the melody. But there had been no music playing in the schoolyard. Said Hall, "Without knowing it, they were all moving to a beat they generated themselves...an unconscious undercurrent of synchronized movement tied the group together." William Condon concluded that it doesn't make sense to view humans as "isolated entities." They are, he said, bonded together by their involvement in "shared organizational forms."[34] In other words, without knowing it individuals form a team. Even in our most casual moments, we pulse in synchrony.

Unconsciously, the conversationalists began to coordinate their finger movements, eye blinks, and nods.

No wonder input from the herd so strongly colors the ways in which we see our world. Students at MIT were given a bio of a guest lecturer. One group's background sheet described the speaker as cold; the other group's handout praised him for his warmth. Both groups sat together as they watched the lecturer give his presentation. But

Even in our most casual moments, we pulse in synchrony.

those who'd read the bio saying he was cold saw him as distant and aloof. Those who'd been tipped off that he was warm rated him as friendly and approachable.[35] In judging a fellow human being, students replaced external fact with input they'd been given socially.[36]

The cues rerouting herd perception come in many forms. Sociologists Janet Lynne Enke and Donna Eder discovered that in gossip, one person opens with a negative comment on someone outside the group. How the rest of the gang goes on the issue depends entirely on the second opinion expressed. If the second speechifier agrees that the outsider is disgusting, virtually everyone will chime in with a sound-alike opinion. If, on the other hand, the second commentator objects that the outsider is terrific, the group is far less likely to descend like a flock of harpies tearing the stranger's reputation limb from limb.[37]

Crowds of silent voices whisper in our ears, transforming the nature of what we see and hear. Some are those of childhood authorities and heroes, others come from family[38] and peers.[39] The strangest emerge from beyond the grave. A vast chorus of long-gone ancients constitutes a not-so-silent majority whose legacy has what may be the most dramatic effect of all on our vision of reality. Take the impact of gender stereotypes—notions developed over hundreds of generations, contributed to, embellished, and passed on by literally billions of humans during our march through time. In one study, parents were asked to give their impression of their brand new babies. Infant boys and girls are completely indistinguishable aside from the buds of reproductive equipment between their legs. Their size, texture, and the way in which newborns of opposite sex act are, according to researchers J.Z. Rubin, F.J. Provenzano, and Z. Luria, completely and totally the same. Yet parents consistently described girls as softer, smaller and less attentive than boys.[40]

The crowds within us resculpt our gender verdicts over and over again. Two groups of experimental subjects were asked to grade the same paper. One was told the author was John McKay. The other was told the paper's writer was Joan McKay. Even *female* students evaluating the paper gave it higher marks if they thought it was from a male.[41]

The ultimate repository of herd influence is language—a device which not only condenses the opinions of those with whom we share a common vocabulary, but sums up the perceptual approach of swarms who have passed on. Every word we use carries within it the experience of generation after generation of men, women, families, tribes, and nations, often including their insights, value judgements, ignorance, and spiritual beliefs. Take the simple sentence, "Feminism has won freedom for women." Indo-European warriors with whom we shall ride in a later episode coined the word *dh[=a]*, meaning to suck, as a baby does on a breast. They carried this term from the Asian steppes to Greece, where it became *qu^sai*, to suckle, and *theEIE*, nipple. The Romans managed to mangle *qh^sai* into *femina*—their word for woman.[42] At every step of the way, millions of humans mouthing the term managed to change its contents. To the Greeks, *qh^sai* was associated with a segment of the human race on a par with domesticated animals—for that's what women were, even in the splendid days of Plato (whose skeletons in the closet we shall see anon). In Rome, on the other hand, feminae were free and, if they were rich, could have a merry old time behind the scenes sexually or politically. The declaration that, "Feminism has won freedom for women," would have puzzled Indo-Europeans, enraged the Greeks, and been welcomed by the Romans.

"Freedom"—the word for whose contents many modern women fight—comes from a men's-only ritual among ancient German tribes. Two clans who'd been mowing each other's members down made peace by invoking the god Freda[43] and giving up ("Freda-ing," so to speak) a few haunches of meat or a pile of animal hides to mollify the enemy and let the matter drop.[44] As for the last word in "Feminism has won freedom for women"—"woman" originally meant nothing more than a man's wife (the Anglo-Saxons pronounced it "wif-man").

"Feminism has won freedom for women"—over the millennia new generations have mouthed each of these words of ancient tribesmen in new ways, tacking on new connotations, denotations, and associations. The word "feminine" carried considerable baggage when it wended its way from Victorian times into the twentieth century. Quoth *Webster's Revised Unabridged Dictionary of 1913*, it meant: "modest, graceful, affectionate, confiding; or...weak, nerveless, timid, pleasure-loving, effeminate." Tens of millions of speakers from a host of nations had heaped these messages of weakness on the Indo-European base, and soon a swarm of other talkers would add to the word "feminine" a very different freight. In 1895 the women's movement changed "feminine" to "feminism," which they defined as "the theory of the political, economic, and social equality of the sexes."[45] It would take millions of women fighting for nearly 100 years to firmly affix the new meaning to syllables formerly associated with the nipple, timidity, and nervelessness. And even now, the crusades rage. With every sentence on feminism we utter, we thread our way through the sensitivities of masses of modern humans who find the "feminism" a necessity, a destroyer of the family, a conversational irritant, or a still open plain on which to battle yet

Every word we use carries within it the experience of generation after generation of men, women, families, tribes, and nations, often including their insights, value judgements, ignorance, and spiritual beliefs.

again, this time over whether the word *femina* will in the future denote the goals of eco-feminists, anarcho-feminists, amazon feminists, libertarian feminists, all four, or none of the above.[46]

The hordes of fellow humans who've left meanings in our words frequently guide the way in which we see our world. Experiments show that people from all cultures can detect subtle differences between colors placed next to each other. But individuals from societies equipped with names for numerous shades can spot the difference when the two swatches of color are apart.[47] At the dawn of the twentieth century, the Chukchee people of northeastern Siberia had very few terms for visual hues. If you asked them to sort colored yarns, they did a poor job of it. But they had over 24 terms for the patterns of reindeer hide, and could classify reindeer far better than the average European scientist, whose vocabulary didn't supply him with such well-honed perceptual tools.[48]

All too often when we see someone perform an action without a name, we rapidly forget its alien outlines and tailor our recall to fit the patterns dictated by convention ...and conventional vocabulary.

Physiologist/ornithologist Jared Diamond, in New Guinea, saw to his dismay that despite all his university studies of nature, illiterate local tribesmen were far better at distinguishing bird species than was he. Diamond used a set of scientific criteria taught in the zoology classes back home. The New Guinean natives possessed something better: names for each animal variety, names whose local definitions pinpointed characteristics Diamond had never been taught to differentiate—everything from a bird's peculiarities of deportment to its taste when grilled over a flame. Diamond had binoculars and state-of-the-art taxonomy. But the New Guineans laughed at his incompetence.[49] They were equipped with a vocabulary, each word of which compacted the experience of armies of bird-hunting ancestors.

All too often when we see someone perform an action without a name, we rapidly forget its alien outlines and tailor our recall to fit the patterns dictated by convention...and conventional vocabulary.[50] A perfect example comes from nineteenth-century America, where sibling rivalry was present in fact, but according to theory didn't exist. The experts were blind to its presence, as shown by its utter absence from family manuals. In the expert and popular view, all that existed between brothers and sisters was love. But letters from middle class girls exposed unacknowledged cattiness and jealousy.

Sibling rivalry didn't begin to creep from the darkness of perceptual invisibility until 1893, when future Columbia University professor of political and social ethics Felix Adler hinted at the nameless notion in his manual *Moral Instruction of Children*. During the 1920s, the concept of jealousy between siblings finally shouldered its way robustly into the repertoire of conscious concepts, appearing in two widely-quoted government publications and becoming the focus of a 1926 crusade mounted by the Child Study Association of America. Only at this point did experts finally coin the term "sibling rivalry."

Now that it carried the compacted crowd-power of a label, the formerly non-existent demon was blamed for adult misery, failing marriages, crime, homosexuality, and God knows what all else. By the 1940s, nearly every child-raising guide had extensive sections on this ex-nonentity. Parents writing to major magazines cited the previously unseeable "sibling rivalry" as the root of almost every one of child-raising's many quandaries.[51]

The stored experience language carries can make the difference between life and death. For roughly 4,000 years, Tasmanian mothers, fathers, and children starved to death each time famine struck, despite the fact that their island home was surrounded by fish-rich seas. The problem: Their tribal culture did not define fish as food.[52] We could easily suffer the same fate if stranded in their wilderness, simply because the crowd of ancients crimped into our vocabulary tell us that a rich source of nutrients is inedible, too—insects.

The perceptual influence of the mob of those who've gone before us and those who stand around us now can be mind-boggling. During the Middle Ages when universities first arose, a local barber/surgeon was called to the lecture chamber of famous medical schools like those of Padua and Salerno year after year to dissect a corpse for medical students gathered from the width and breadth of Europe. A scholar on a raised platform discoursed about the revelations unfolding before the students' eyes. The learned doctor would invariably report a shape for the liver radically different from the form of the organ sliding around on the surgeon's blood-stained hands. He'd verbally portray jaw joints which had no relation to those being displayed on the trestle below him. He'd describe a network of cranial blood vessels that were nowhere to be seen. But he never changed his narrative to fit the actualities. Nor did the students or the surgeon ever stop to correct the book-steeped authority. Why? The scholar was reciting the "facts" as found in volumes over 1,000 years old—the works of the Roman master Galen, founder of "modern" medicine. Alas, Galen had drawn his conclusions, not from dissecting humans, but from probing the bodies of pigs and monkeys. Pigs and monkeys *do* have the strange features Galen described. Humans, however, do not. But that didn't stop the medieval professors from seeing what wasn't there.[53] Their sensory pathways echoed with voices gathered for a millennium, the murmurings of a crowd composed of both the living and the dead. For the perceptual powers of Middle Age scholars were no more individualistic than are yours and mine. Through our sentences and paragraphs, long-gone ghosts still have their say within the collective mind.

Endnotes

1. Waller, M.J.C. (1996). Personal communication, May; Waller, M.J.C. (1996). "Organization theory and the origins of consciousness." *Journal of Social and Evolutionary Systems*, 19(1), p 17-30; Burns, T. & G.M. Stalker. (1961). *The management of innovation*. London: Tavistock Publications, pp 92-93, 233-234. **2.** Doolittle, Russell F. "Microbial genomes opened up," p 339-342. **3.** Bodnar, J.W., J. Killian, M. Nagle & S. Ramchandani. (1997). "Deciphering the language of the genome." *Journal of Theoretical Biology*, November 21, pp 183-93; Kupiec, J.J. (1989). "Gene regulation and DNA C-value paradox: a model based on diffusion of regulatory molecules." *Medical Hypotheses*, January, p 7-10; Knee, R. & P.R. Murphy. (1997). "Regulation of gene expression by natural antisense RNA transcripts." *Neurochemistry International*, September, pp 379-92; Sandler, U. & A. Wyler. (1998). "Non-coding DNA can regulate gene transcription by its base pair's distribution." *Journal of Theoretical Biology*, July 7, p 85-90; Hardison, R. (1998). "Hemoglobins from bacteria to man: Evolution of different patterns of gene expression." *Journal of Experimental Biology*, April (Pt 8), p 1099-117; Vol'kenshten, M.V. (1990). "Molecular drive." *Molekuliarnaia Biologiia*, September-October, p 1181-99.; Cohen, Jack & Ian Stewart. (1994). *The collapse of chaos: Discovering simplicity in a complex world*. New York: Viking, 1994, p 73. **4.** Szentagothai, Janos. (1989). "The 'brain-mind' relation: A pseudoproblem?" In *Mindwaves: Thoughts on intelligence, identity and consciousness*. Edited by Colin Blakemore & Susan Greenfield. Oxford: Basil Blackwell, p 330; Douglas, Rodney J., Christof Koch, Misha Mahowald, Kevan A.C. Martin, Humbert H. Suarez. (1995). "Recurrent excitation in neocortical circuits." *Science*, 18 August, p 981. **5.** Caporael, Linnda R. (1995). "Sociality: Coordinating bodies, minds and groups." *Psycoloquy*. Downloaded from <www.ai.univie.ac.at/cgi-bin/mfs/31/wachau/www/archives/Psycoloquy/1995.V6/0043.html?84#mfs>, 95/6/01. **6.** Bower, Bruce. (1994). "Brain faces up to fear, social signs." *Science News*, December 17, p 406; Kandel, Eric R. & Robert D. Hawkins. (1992). "The biological basis of learning and individuality." *Scientific American*, September, pp 78-87; LeDoux, Joseph E. "Emotion, memory and the brain." *Scientific American*, June, pp 50-57; Blakeslee, Sandra. (1994). "Brain study examines rare woman." *New York Times*, December 18, p 35; Emde, Robert N. "Levels of meaning for infant emotions: A biosocial view." In *Approaches to emotion*, edited by Klaus R. Scherer & Paul Ekman. Hillsdale, NJ: Lawrence Erlbaum Associates, p 79; Stein, Kathleen. "Mind reading among the macaques: How the brain interprets the intentions of others." *Omni*, June, p 10. **7.** Loftus, Elizabeth. (1980). *Memory: Surprising new insights into how we remember and why we forget*. Reading, MA: Addison Wesley, pp 45-49; Loftus, Elizabeth. (1992). "When a lie becomes memory's truth: Memory distortion after exposure to misinformation." *Current Directions in Psychological Science*, August, pp 121-123; Loftus, Elizabeth F. (1997). "Creating false memories." *Scientific American*, September, pp 70-75; Roediger, Henry L. (1996). "Memory illusions." *Journal of Memory and Language*, April 1, v 35 n 2, p 76; Roediger III, Henry L. & Kathleen B. McDermott. (1995). "Creating false memories: Remembering words not presented in lists." *Journal of Experimental Psychology*, July, v 21 n 4, p 803. **8.** Asch, Solomon E. (1956). "Studies of independence and conformity: I. A minority of one against a unanimous majority." *Psychological Monographs*, 70, p 9 (Whole No. 416); Raven, Bertram H. & Jeffrey Z. Rubin. (1983). *Social Psychology*. New York: John Wiley and Sons, pp 566-9, 575. **9.** Faucheux, C. & S. Moscovici. "Le style de comportement d'une minorité et son influence sur les résponses d'une majorité." *Bulletin du Centre d"Études et Recherches Psychologiques*, 16, pp 337-360; Moscovici, S., E. Lage, & M. Naffrechoux. "Influence of a consistent minority on the responses of a majority in a color perception task." *Sociometry*, 32, pp 365-380; Moscovici, S. & B. Personnaz. (1980). "Studies in social influence, Part V: Minority influence and conversion behavior in a perceptual task." *Journal of Experimental Social Psychology*, 16, pp 270-282; Raven, Bertram H. & Jeffrey Z. Rubin. *Social Psychology*, pp 584-585. **10.** Eisenberg, L. (1995). "The social construction of the human brain." *American Journal of Psychiatry*, 152(11), pp 1563-1575; Leonard, Christiana M., Linda J. Lombardino, Laurie R. Mercado, Samuel R. Browd, Joshua I. Breier, & O. Frank Agee. (1996). "Cerebral asymmetry and cognitive development in children: A magnetic resonance imaging study." *Psychological Science*, March, p 93; Goldman-Rakic, P. & P. Rakic. (1984). "Experimental modification of gyral patterns." In *Cerebral dominance: The biological foundation*, edited by N. Geschwind & A.M. Galaburda. Cambridge, MA: Harvard University Press, pp 179-192; Pascual-Leone, A. & F. Torres. (1993). "Plasticity of the sensorimotor cortex representation of the reading finger in Braille readers." *Brain*, 116, pp 39-52; Recanzone, G., C. Schreiner, & M. Merzenich. (1993). "Plasticity in the frequency representation of primary auditory cortex following discrimination training in adult owl monkeys." *Journal of Neuroscience*, 13, pp 97-103. **11.** Skoyles; John. (1998). "Mirror neurons and the motor theory of speech." *Noetica*. <psy.uq.edu.au/CogPsych/Noetica/OpenForumIssue9/>. **12.** Werker, Janet F. & Renee N. Desjardins. (1995). "Listening to speech in the 1st year of life: Experiential influences on phoneme perception." *Current Directions in Psychological Science*, June, pp 76-81; Werker, Janet F. (1989). "Becoming a native listener." *American Scientist*, January-February, pp 54-59; Werker, Janet F. & Richard C. Tees. (1992). "The organization and reorganization of human speech perception." *Annual Review of Neuroscience*, 15, pp 377-402; Werker, J.F. & J.E. Pegg. (In press). "Infant speech perception and phonological acquisition." *Phonological development: Research, models and implications*, edited by C.E. Ferguson, L. Menn & C. Stoel-Gammon. Parkton, MD: York Press; Werker, Janet F. (1995). "Exploring developmental changes in cross-language speech perception." In D. Osherson (series editor), *An invitation to cognitive science*: L. Gleitman & M. Liberman (volume editors) *Part I: Language*. Cambridge, MA: MIT Press, pp 87-106. **13.** Eisenberg, L. (1995). "The social construction of the human brain." *American Journal of Psychiatry*, 152 (11), pp 1563-1575. Segall, M.H., D.T. Campbell & M.J. Herskovitz. (1966). *The influence of culture on visual perception*. Indianapolis: Bobbs-Merrill; Shi-xu. (1995). "Cultural perceptions: Exploiting the unexpected of the other." *Culture & Psychology*, 1, pp 315-342; Lucy, J. (1992). *Grammatical categories and cognition: A case study of the linguistic relativity hypothesis*. Cambridge: Cambridge University Press; Berridge, Kent C. & Terry E. Robinson. (1995). "The mind of an addicted brain: Neural sensitization of wanting versus liking." *Current Directions in Psychological Science*, June, p 74; Lancaster, Jane B. (1968). "Primate communication systems and the emergence of human language." *Primates: Studies in adaptation and variability*, edited by Phyllis C. Jay. New York: Holt, Rinehart and Winston, pp 451-453; Emde, Robert N. "Levels of meaning for infant emotions: A biosocial view." *Approaches to Emotion*, p 79; Belsky, Jay, Becky Spritz & Keith Crnic. (1996). "Infant attachment security and affective-cognitive information processing at age 3." *Psychological Science*, March, pp 111-114; Bower, Bruce (1995). "Brain activity comes down to expectation." *Science News*, January 21, p 38; Op cit., Caporael (1995); Nisbett, R. & L. Ross. (1980). *Human inference: Strategies and shortcomings of social judgment*. Englewood Cliffs, NJ: Prentice-Hall; Shweder, R.A. & R.G. D'Andrade. (1980). "The systematic distortion hypothesis." *Fallible Judgment in Behavioral Research. New Directions for Methodology of Social and Behavioral Science*, 4 1980, pp 37-58. For neural plasticity in non-humans, see: Nottebohm, F., M.E. Nottebohm & L. Crane. (1986). "Developmental and seasonal changes in canary song and their relation to changes in the anatomy of song-control nuclei." *Behavioral and Neural Biology*, November, pp 445-71. **14.** Ruoslahti, Erkki "Stretching Is Good For A Cell," pp 1345-1346. **15.** Gould, Elizabeth. (1994). "The effects of adrenal steroids and excitatory input on neuronal birth and survival." In *Hormonal Restructuring of the Adult Brain: Basic and Clinical Perspective*, edited by Victoria N. Luine, Cheryl F. Harding. *Annals of the New York Academy of Sciences*, Vol. 743, p 73. New York: The New York Academy of Sciences; Vogel, K.S. (1993). "Development of trophic interactions in the vertebrate peripheral nervous system." *Molecular Neurobiology*, Fall-Winter, pp 363-82; Haanen, C. & I. Vermes. (1996). "Apoptosis: Programmed cell death in fetal development." *European Journal of Obstetrics, Gynecology, and Reproductive Biology*, January, pp 129-33; Young, Wise, June Kume-Kick & Shlomo Constantini. "Glucorticoid therapy of spinal chord injury." In *Hormonal restructuring of the adult brain: Basic and clinical perspective*, p 247; Nadis, Steve. (1993). "Kid's brainpower: Use it or lose it." *Technology Review*, November/December, pp 19-20. Levine, Daniel S. (1988). "Survival of the synapses." *The Sciences*, November/December, p 51. Elbert, Thomas, Christo Pantev, Christian Wienbruch, Brigitte Rockstroh & Edward Taub. (1995). "Increased cortical representation of the fingers of the left hand in stringed players." *Science*, October 13, pp 305-307. Barinaga, Marsha. (1994). "Watching the brain remake itself." *Science*, Dec, p 1475; Pascual-Leone, A. & F. Torres. (1993). "Plasticity of the sensorimotor cortex representation of the reading finger in Braille readers." *Brain*, 116, pp 39-52. Holden, Constance (1995). "Sensing music." *Science*, 13 October, p 237; Korein, Julius, M.D. (1988). "Reality and the brain: The beginnings and endings of the human being." In *The reality club*, edited by John Brockman. New York: Lynx Books, p 94; Changeux, J.P. (1985). *The biology of mind*. Translated by Laurence Garey. Oxford: Oxford University Press, pp 217-218; Aoki, C. & P. Siekevitz. (1988). "Plasticity in brain development." *Scientific American*, June, pp 56-64; Bagnoli, P.G., G. Casini, F. Fontanesi & L. Sebastiani. (1989). "Reorganization of visual pathways following posthatching removal of one retina on pigeons." *The Journal of Comparative Neurology*, 288, pp 512-527; DePryck, Koen. (1993). *Knowledge, evolution, and paradox: The ontology of language*. Albany: State University of New York Press, pp 122-125; Black, I.B. (1986). "Trophic molecules and evolution of the nervous system." *Proceedings of the National Academy of Sciences of the United States of America*, November, pp 8249-52. **16.** Leonard, Christiana M., Linda J. Lombardino, Laurie R. Mercado, Samuel R. Browd, Joshua I. Breier, & O. Frank Agee. (1996). "Cerebral asymmetry and cognitive development in children: A magnetic resonance imaging study." *Psychological Science*, March, p 93; Scarr, S. (1991). "Theoretical issues in investigating intellectual plasticity." In *Plasticity of development*, edited by S.E. Brauth, W.S. Hall & R.J. Dooling. Cambridge, MA: MIT Press, 1991, pp 57-71; Goldman-Rakic, P. & P. Rakic. (1984). "Experimental modification of gyral patterns." In *Cerebral dominance: The biological foundation*, edited by N. Geschwind & A.M. Galaburda. Cambridge, MA: Harvard University Press, pp 179-192. For brilliant insights on the role of culture in the way the brain is used, see: Skoyles, Dr. John R. (1997). "Origins of Classical Greek art." Unpublished paper. <www.users.globalnet.co.uk/~skoyles/index.htm>. **17.** Without training, guidance, or positive reinforcement, newborns automatically begin to imitate their fellow humans during their first hours out of the womb. (Wyrwicka, W. (1988). "Imitative behavior. A theoretical view." *Pavlovian Journal of Biological Sciences*, July-September, p 125-31.) **18.** Fantz, R.L. (1965). "Visual perception from birth as shown by pattern selectivity." *Annals of the New York Academy of Sciences*, 118, pp 793-814; Coren, Stanley, Clare Porac & Lawrence

Almost every reality you "know" at *any* given second is a mere ghost held in memory.

M. Ward. (1979). *Sensation and perception*. New York: Academic Press, 1979, pp 379-380. **19.** *Op cit*., Caporael. (1995). A baby begins imitating others when it is less than a week old. Bower, T.G.R. (1977). *A primer of infant development*. New York: W.H. Freeman, p 28. **20.** Mead, Margaret. (1977). *Sex and temperament in three primitive societies*. London: Routledge and Kegan Paul. **21.** Ekman, Paul. (1992). "Facial expressions of emotion: an old controversy and new findings." *Philosophical Transactions of the Royal Society of London. Series B: Biological Sciences*, January 29, pp 63-69; Levenson, R.W., P. Ekman & W. Friesen. (1997). "Voluntary facial action generates emotion-specific autonomic nervous system activity." *Psychophysiology*, July, pp 363-84; Ekman, Paul. (1993). "Facial expression and emotion." *American Psychologist*, April, p 384-92. **22.** Hoffman, M.L. (1981). "Is altruism part of human nature?" *Journal of Personality and Social Psychology*, 40(1), pp 121-137; Raven, Bertram H. & Jeffrey Z. Rubin. *Social Psychology*, pp 311-312. **23.** Hoffman, M.L. (1981). "Is altruism part of human nature?" *Journal of Personality and Social Psychology*, 40(1), pp 121-137; *Op cit*., Bertram & Rubin. **24.** Bischof-Köhler, D. (1994). "Self object and interpersonal emotions. Identification of own mirror image, empathy and prosocial behavior in the 2nd year of life." *Zeitschrift fur Psychologie Mit Zeitschrift fur Angewandte Psychologie*, 202:4, pp 349-77. **25.** Hood, Bruce M., J. Douglas Willen & Jon Driver. (1998). "Adult's eyes trigger shifts of visual attention in human infants." *Psychological Science*, March, p 131-133; Terrace Herbert. (1989). "Thoughts without words." In *Mindwaves: Thoughts on intelligence, identity and consciousness*, edited by Colin Blakemore & Susan Greenfield. Oxford: Basil Blackwell, pp 128-9. **26.** Bruner, Jerome. (1986). *Actual minds, possible worlds*. Cambridge, MA: Harvard University Press, pp 60, 67-68; Frith, Uta. (1993). "Autism." *Scientific American*, June, pp 108-114. **27.** Kagan, Jerome. (1989). *Unstable ideas: Temperament, cognition and self*. Cambridge: Harvard University Press, pp 185-186. In the body of psychological literature, the effect we're discussing is called "social referencing." According to Russell, et al., "it is a well-documented ability in human infants." (Russell, C.L., K.A. Bard & L.B. Adamson. (1997). "Social referencing by young chimpanzees (*Pan troglodytes*)." *Journal of Comparative Psychology*, June, pp 185-93.) For more on social referencing in infants as young as 8.5 months old, see: Campos, J.J. (1984). "A new perspective on emotions." *Child Abuse and Neglect*, 8:2, pp 147-56. **28.** But let's not get too homocentric. Rats flock just as madly to the imitative urge. Put them with others who love a beverage that they loathe and their tastes will also change dramatically. (Galef, B.G., Jr, E.E. Whiskin & E. Bielavska. (1997). "Interaction with demonstrator rats changes observer rats' affective responses to flavors." *Journal of Comparative Psychology*, December, pp 393-8.) **29.** Kantrowitz, Barbara & Pat Wingert. (1989). "How kids learn." *Newsweek*, April 17, p 53. **30.** Condon, William S. (1986). "Communication: Rhythm and structure." *Rhythm in psychological, linguistic and musical processes*, edited by James R. Evans & Manfred Clynes. Springfield, IL: C.C. Thomas, pp 55-77; Condon, William S. (1970). "Method of micro-analysis of sound films of behavior." *Behavior Research Methods, Instruments & Computers*, 2(2), pp 51-54. **31.** Condon, William S. (1999). Personal communication. June 10. For information indicating the probability of related forms of synchrony, see: Krams, M., M.F. Rushworth, M.P. Deiber, R.S. Frackowiak, & R.E. Passingham. (1998). "The preparation, execution and suppression of copied movements in the human brain." *Experimental Brain Research*, June, pp 386-98; Lundqvist, L.O. "Facial EMG reactions to facial expressions: a case of facial emotional contagion?" *Scandinavian Journal of Psychology*, June, pp 130-41. **32.** Condon, William S. & Louis W. Sander Louis. (1974). "Neonate movement is synchronized with adult speech: Interactional participation and language acquisition." *Science*, 183(4120), pp 99-101. **33.** Hall, Edward T. (1977). *Beyond culture*. New York: Anchor Books, pp 72-77. Several others have independently arrived at similar conclusions about the ability of shared activity to bond humans. Psychologist Howard Rachlin has called the process "functional bonding," and historian William McNeill has called it "muscular bonding." (Rachlin, Howard. (1995). "Self and self-control." In *The self across psychology: Self-recognition, self-awareness, and the self concept*, p 89; McNeill, William H. (1995). *Keeping together in time: Dance and drill in human history*. Cambridge, MA, p 4.) **34.** Kelley, H.H. (1950). "The warm-cold variable in first impressions of persons." *Journal of Personality*, 18, pp 431-439; Raven, Bertram H. & Jeffrey Z. Rubin. *Social Psychology*, pp 88-89. **35.** Our susceptibility to social input is so powerful it can kill. Knowing someone who's committed suicide can increase your chances of doing yourself in by a whopping 22 thousand percent. The impulse to imitate others sweeps us along. (Malcolm, A.T. & M.P. Janisse. (1994). "Imitative suicide in a cohesive organization: observations from a case study." *Perceptual and Motor Skills*, December, Part 2, pp 1475-8; Stack, S. (1996). "The effect of the media on suicide: Evidence from Japan, 1955-1985." *Suicide and Life-threatening Behavior*, Summer, pp 132-42.) **36.** Eder, Donna & Janet Lynne Enke. (1991). "The structure of gossip: Opportunities and constraints on collective expression among adolescents." *American Sociological Review*, August, pp 494-508. **37.** Psychologist Daniel Goleman calls the family "a conglomerate mind." (Goleman, Daniel, Ph.D. (1985). *Vital lies, simple truths: The psychology of self-deception*. New York: Simon and Schuster, p 167. See also pp 165-170.) **38.** Andersen, Susan M., Inga Reznik & Serena Chen. "The self in relation to others: Motivational and cognitive underpinnings." In *The self across psychology: Self-recognition, self-awareness, and the self concept*, pp 233-275. **39.** Rubin, J.Z., F.J. Provenzano & Z. Luria. (1974). "The eye of the beholder: Parents' views on sex of newborns." *American Journal of Orthopsychiatry*, 44, pp 512-9; Raven, Bertram H. & Jeffrey Z. Rubin. *Social Psychology*, p 512. **40.** Goldberg, P.A. (1968). "Are women prejudiced against women?" *Transaction*, April, pp 28-30; Raven, Bertram H. & Jeffrey Z. Rubin. *Social Psychology*, p 518. **41.** *Webster's Revised Unabridged Dictionary* (G & C. Merriam Co., 1913, edited by Noah Porter), The DICT Development Group <www.dict.org>, downloaded June 1999. **42.** Freda is better known in his Norse incarnation as Freyr. Northern European mythology—that of the Germans, Goths, and Norse—can be confusing. Freyr has a twin sister Freyja. In some stories it is difficult to keep the two straight. Some have suggested that Freyr and Freyja represent the male and female sides of the same deity. (Carlyon, Richard. (1982). *A guide to the gods*. New York: William Morrow, pp 227-9.) **43.** Friedman, Steven Morgan. (1999). "Etymologically Speaking." <www.westegg.com/etymology/>, downloaded June 1999. **44.** Merriam-Webster, Inc. WWWebster.com. <www.m-w.com/netdict.htm>, downloaded June 1999. **45.** n.a. "feminism/terms." Version: 1.5, last modified 15 February 1993, downloaded June 11, 1999. **46.** Bruner, Jerome S. (1995). *Beyond the information given: Studies in the psychology of knowing*, pp 380-386; van Geert, Paul. (1995). "Green, red and happiness: Towards a framework for understanding emotion universals." *Culture and Psychology*, June, p 264. **47.** Bogoras, W. *The Chukchee*. New York: G.E. Stechert, 1904-1909; Bruner, Jerome S. *Beyond the information given: Studies in the psychology of knowing*, p 102-3. **48.** Diamond, Jared. (1989). "This fellow frog, name belong-him Dakwo." *Natural History*, April, pp 16-23. **49.** *Op cit*., Caporael (1995). **50.** Stearns, Peter N. (1988). "The rise of sibling jealousy in the twentieth century." In *Emotion and social change: Toward a new psychohistory*, edited by Carol Z. Stearns & Peter N. Stearns. New York: Holmes & Meier, pp 197-209. **51.** For many examples of similar phenomena, see: Edgerton, Robert B. (1992). *Sick societies: Challenging the myth of primitive harmony*. New York: Free Press. **52.** Boorstin, Daniel J. (1985). *The discoverers: A history of man's search to know his world and himself*. New York: Vintage Books, pp 344-357.

Brain cells remain alive only if they can prove their worth in dealing with the baby's physical and social surroundings.

THE NEWS MEDIA AND OTHER MANIPULATORS

What Makes Mainstream Media Mainstream

Noam Chomsky

From a talk at Z Media Institute, June 1997.

Part of the reason I write about the media is that I am interested in the whole intellectual culture, and the part of it that is easiest to study is the media.

It comes out every day. You can do a systematic investigation. You can compare yesterday's version to today's version. There is a lot of evidence about what's played up and what isn't and the way things are structured.

My impression is that the media aren't very different from scholarship or from, say, journals of intellectual opinion. There are some extra constraints, but it's not radically different. They interact, which is why people go up and back quite easily among them.

If you want to understand the media, or any other institution, you begin by asking questions about the internal institutional structure. And you ask about their setting in the broader society. How do they relate to other systems of power and authority? If you're lucky, there is an internal record from leading people that tells you what they are up to. That doesn't mean the public relations handouts, but what they say to each other about what they are up to. There is quite a lot of interesting documentation.

Those are major sources of information about the nature of the media. You want to study them the way, say, a scientist would study some complex molecule. You take a look at the structure and then make some hypothesis based on the structure as to what the media product is likely to look like. Then you investigate the media product and see how well it conforms to the hypotheses.

Virtually all work in media analysis is this last part—trying to study carefully just what the media product is and whether it conforms to obvious assumptions about the nature and structure of the media.

Well, what do you find? First of all, you find that there are different media which do different things. For example, entertainment/Hollywood, soap operas, and so on, or even most of the newspapers in the country (the overwhelming majority of them) are directed to a mass audience, not to inform them but to divert them.

There is another sector of the media, the elite media, sometimes called the agenda-setting media because they are the ones with the big resources; they set the framework in which everyone else operates. The *New York Times*, the *Washington Post*, and a few others. Their audience is mostly privileged people.

The people who read the *New York Times* are mostly wealthy or part of what is sometimes called the political class. Many are actually involved in the systems of decision-making and control in an ongoing fashion, basically as managers of one sort or another. They can be political managers, business managers (like corporate executives and the like), doctrinal managers (like many people in the schools and universities), or other journalists who are involved in organizing the way people think and look at things.

The elite media set a framework within which others operate. For some years I used to monitor the Associated Press. It grinds out a constant flow of news. In the mid-afternoon there was a break every day with a "Notice to Editors: Tomorrow's *New York Times* is going to have the following stories on the front page." The point of that is, if you're an editor of a newspaper in Dayton, Ohio, and you don't have the resources to figure out what the news is, or you don't want to think about it anyway, this tells you what the news is. These are the stories for the quarter-page that you are going to devote to something other than local affairs or diverting your audience. These are the stories that you put there because that's what the *New York Times* tells us is what you're supposed to care about tomorrow. If you are an editor of a local newspaper you pretty much have to do that, because you don't have much else in the way of resources. If you get out of line and produce stories that the elite press doesn't like, you're likely to hear about it pretty soon. What happened recently at *San Jose Mercury News* (i.e. Gary Webb's "Dark Alliance" series about CIA complicity in the drug trade) is a dramatic example of this. So there are a lot of ways in which power plays can drive you right back into line if you move out. If you try to break the mold, you're not going to last long. That framework works pretty well, and it is understandable that it is a reflection of obvious power structures.

> The real mass media are basically trying to divert people.

The real mass media are basically trying to divert people. "Let them do something else, but don't bother us (us being the people who run the show). Let them get interested in professional sports, for example. Let everybody be crazed about professional sports or sex scandals or the personalities and their problems or something like that. Anything, as long as it isn't serious. Of course, the serious stuff is for the big guys. 'We' take care of that."

There are all sorts of filtering devices to get rid of people who are a pain in the neck and think independently.

What are the elite media, the agenda-setting ones? The *New York Times* and CBS, for example. Well, first of all, they are major, very profitable, corporations.

Furthermore, most of them are either linked to, or outright owned by, much bigger corporations, like General Electric, Westinghouse, and so on. They are way up at the top of the power structure of the private economy, which is a tyrannical structure. Corporations are basically tyrannies, hierarchic, controlled from above. If you don't like what they are doing, you get out. The major media are part of that system.

What about their institutional setting? Well, that's more or less the same. What they interact with and relate to is other major power centers: the government, other corporations, the universities. Because the media function in significant ways as a doctrinal system, they interact closely with the universities. Say you are a reporter writing a story on Southeast Asia or Africa, or something like that. You're supposed to go over to the university next door and find an expert who will tell you what to write, or else go to one of the foundations, like Brookings Institute or American Enterprise Institute. They will give you the preferred version of what is happening. These outside institutions are very similar to the media.

If you go through a place like Harvard, a good deal of what goes on is a kind of socialization: teaching how to behave like a member of the upper classes, how to think the right thoughts, and so on.

The universities, for example, are not independent institutions. There are independent people scattered around in them (and the sciences in particular couldn't survive otherwise), but that is true of the media as well. And it's generally true of corporations. It's even true of fascist states, for that matter, to a certain extent. But the institution itself is parasitic. It's dependent on outside sources of support, and those sources of support, such as private wealth, big corporations with grants, and the government (which is so closely interlinked with corporate power that you can barely distinguish them)—they are essentially the system that the universities are in the middle of.

People within them, who don't adjust to that structure, who don't accept it and internalize it (you can't really work with it unless you internalize it, and believe it)—people who don't do that are likely to be weeded out along the way, starting from kindergarten, all the way up. There are all sorts of filtering devices to get rid of people who are a pain in the neck and think independently.

Those of you who have been through college know that the educational system is highly geared to rewarding conformity and obedience; if you don't do that, you are a troublemaker. So, it is kind of a filtering device which ends up with people who really, honestly (they aren't lying) internalize the framework of belief and attitudes of the surrounding power system in the society. The elite institutions like, say, Harvard and Princeton and the small upscale colleges, for example, are very much geared to socialization. If you go through a place like Harvard, a good deal of what goes on is a kind of socialization: teaching how to behave like a member of the upper classes, how to think the right thoughts, and so on.

I'm sure you've read George Orwell's *Animal Farm*, which he wrote in the mid-1940s. It was a satire on the Soviet Union, a totalitarian state. It was a big hit. Everybody loved it. Turns out he wrote an introduction to *Animal Farm* which wasn't published. It only appeared 30 years later. Someone found it in his papers. The introduction to *Animal Farm* was about "Literary Censorship in England," and what it says is that obviously this book is ridiculing the Soviet Union and its totalitarian structure, but free England is not all that different. We don't have the KGB on our neck, but the end result comes out pretty much the same. People who have independent ideas or who think the wrong kind of thoughts are cut out.

He talks a little, only two sentences, about the institutional structure. He asks, why does this happen? Well, one, because the press is owned by wealthy men who only want certain things to reach the public. His second observation is that when you go through the elite education system, when you go through the proper schools (Oxford, and so on), you learn that there are certain things it's not proper to say and there are certain thoughts that are not proper to have. That is the socialization role of elite institutions, and if you don't adapt to that, you're usually out. Those two sentences more or less tell the story.

When you critique the media and you say, look, here is what Anthony Lewis or somebody else is writing, and you show that it happens to be distorted in a way that is highly supportive of power systems, they get very angry. They say, quite correctly, "Nobody

The press is owned by wealthy men who only want certain things to reach the public.

ever tells me what to write. I write anything I like. All this business about pressures and constraints is nonsense because I'm never under any pressure." Which is completely true, but the point is that they wouldn't be there unless they had already demonstrated that nobody has to tell them what to write because they are going to keep to the rules. If they had started off at the Metro desk and had pursued the wrong kind of stories, they never would have made it to the positions where they can now say anything they like.

The same is largely true of university faculty in the more ideological disciplines. They have been through the socialization system. Okay, you look at the structure of that whole system. What do you expect the news to be like? Well, it's not very obscure. Take the *New York Times*. It's a corporation and sells a product. The product is audiences. They don't make money when you buy the newspaper. They are happy to put it on the World Wide Web for free. They actually lose money when you buy the newspaper. The audience is the product. For the elite media, the product is privileged people, just like the people who are writing the newspapers, high-level decision-making people in society. Like other businesses, they sell their product to a market, and the market is, of course, advertisers (that is, other businesses). Whether it is television or newspapers, or whatever else, they are selling audiences. Corporations sell audiences to other corporations. In the case of the elite media, it's big businesses.

Well, what do you expect to happen? What would you predict about the nature of the media product, given that set of circumstances? What would be the null hypothesis, the kind of conjecture that you'd make assuming nothing further?

The obvious assumption is that the product of the media, what appears, what doesn't appear, the way it is slanted, will reflect the interest of the buyers and sellers, the institutions, and the power systems that are around them. If that wouldn't happen, it would be kind of a miracle.

Okay, then comes the hard work. You ask, does it work the way you predict?

Well, you can judge for yourselves. There's lots of material on this obvious hypothesis, which has been subjected to the hardest tests anybody can think of, and still stands up remarkably well. You virtually never find anything in the social sciences that so strongly supports any conclusion, which is not a big surprise, because it would be miraculous if it didn't hold up given the way the forces are operating.

The next thing you discover is that this whole topic is completely taboo. If you go to the media department at the Kennedy School of Government or Stanford, or somewhere else, and you study journalism and communications or academic political science, and so on, these questions are not likely to appear. That is, the hypothesis that anyone would come across without even knowing anything that is scarcely expressed, and the evidence bearing on it, scarcely discussed. There are some exceptions, as usual in a complex and somewhat chaotic world, but it is rather generally true. Well, you predict that, too.

If you look at the institutional structure, you would say, yeah, sure, that's likely to happen because why should these guys want to be exposed? Why should they allow critical analysis of what they are up to? The answer is, there is no reason why they should allow that and, in fact, they don't.

Again, it is not purposeful censorship. It is just that you don't make it to those positions if you haven't internalized the values and doctrines. That includes what is called "the left" as well as the right. In fact, in mainstream discussion the *New York Times* has been called "the establishment left." You're unlikely to make it through to the top unless you have been adequately socialized and trained so that there are some thoughts you just don't have, because if you did have them, you wouldn't be there. So you have a second order of prediction which is that the first order of prediction is not allowed into the discussion—again, with a scattering of exceptions, important ones.

The last thing to look at is the doctrinal framework in which this proceeds. Do people at high levels in the information system, including the media and advertising and academic political science and so on, do these people have a picture of what ought to happen when they are writing for each other, not when they are making graduation speeches? When you make a commencement speech, it's pretty words and stuff. But when they are writing for one another, what do these people say?

There are several categories to look at. One is the public relations industry, you know, the main business propaganda industry. So what are the leaders of the PR industry saying internally? Second place to look is at what are called public intellectuals, big thinkers, people who write the op-eds and that sort of thing. The people who write impressive books about the nature of democracy and that sort of business. What do they say? The third place to look is the academic sector, particularly that part that has been concerned with communications and information, much of which has been a branch of political science for many years.

So, look at these categories and see what leading figures write about these matters. The basic line (I'm partly quoting) is that the general population are "ignorant and meddlesome outsiders." We have to keep them out of the public arena because they are too stupid, and if they get involved they will just make trouble. Their job is to be "spectators," not "participants." They are allowed to vote every once in a while, pick out one of us smart guys. But then they are supposed to go home and do something else like watch football or whatever it may be. But the "ignorant and meddlesome outsiders" have to be observers, not participants. The participants are what are called the "responsible men" and, of course, the writer is always one of them. You never ask the question, why am I a "responsible man" and somebody else, say Eugene Debs, is in jail? The answer is pretty obvious. It's because you are obedient and subordinate to power and that other person may be independent, and so on.

But you don't ask, of course. So there are the smart guys who are supposed to run the show and the rest of them are supposed to be out, and we should not succumb to (I'm quoting from an academic article) "democratic dogmatisms about men being the best judges of their own interest." They are not. They are terrible judges of their own interests so we have do it for them for their own benefit.

Actually, it is very similar to Leninism. We do things for you, and we are doing it in the interest of everyone, and so on. I suspect that's part of the reason why it's been so easy historically for people to shift up and back from being sort of enthusiastic Stalinists to being big supporters of US power. People switch very quickly from one position to the other, and my suspicion is that it's because basically it is the same position. You're not making much of a switch. You're just making a different estimate of where power lies. One point you think it's here, another point you think it's there. You take the same position.

The first World War was the first time that highly organized state propaganda institutions were developed.

How did all this evolve? It has an interesting history. A lot of it comes out of the first World War, which is a big turning point. It changed the position of the United States in the world considerably. In the eighteenth century the US was already the richest place in the world. The quality of life, health, and longevity was not achieved by the upper classes in Britain until the early twentieth century, let alone anybody else in the world. The US was extraordinarily wealthy, with huge advantages, and, by the end of the nineteenth century, it had by far the biggest economy in the world. But it was not a big player on the world scene. US power extended to the Caribbean Islands, parts of the Pacific, but not much farther.

During the first World War, the relations changed. And they changed more dramatically during the second World War. After the second World War the US more or less took over the world. But after the first World War there was already a change, and the US shifted from being a debtor to a creditor nation. It wasn't a huge actor in the international arena, like Britain, but it became a substantial force in the world for the first time. That was one change, but there were other changes.

The first World War was the first time that highly organized state propaganda institutions were developed. The British had a Ministry of Information, and they really needed it because they had to get the US into the war or else they were in bad trouble. The Ministry of Information was mainly geared to sending propaganda, including fabrications about "Hun" atrocities, and so on. They were targeting American intellectuals on the reasonable assumption that these are the people who are most gullible and most likely to believe propaganda. They are also the ones that disseminate it through their own system. So it was mostly geared to American intellectuals, and it worked very well. The British Ministry of Information documents (a lot have been released) show their goal was, as they put it, to control the thought of the entire world—which was a minor goal—but mainly the US. They didn't care much what people thought in India. This Ministry of Information was extremely successful in deluding leading American intellectuals, and was very proud of that. Properly so, it saved their lives. They would probably have lost the first World War otherwise.

In the US there was a counterpart. Woodrow Wilson was elected in 1916 on an anti-war platform. The US was a very pacifist country. It has always been. People don't want to go fight foreign wars. The country was very much opposed to the first World War, and Wilson was, in fact, elected on an anti-war position. "Peace without victory" was the slogan. But he decided to go to war. So the question was, how do you get a pacifist population to become raving anti-German lunatics so they want to go kill all the Germans? That requires propaganda. So they set up the first and really only major state propaganda agency in US history. The Committee on Public Information, it was called (nice Orwellian title); it was also called the Creel Commission. The guy who ran it was named Creel. The task of this commission was to propagandize the population into jingoist hysteria. It worked incredibly well. Within a few months the US was able to go to war.

A lot of people were impressed by these achievements. One person impressed, and this had some implications for the future, was Hitler. He concluded, with some justification, that Germany lost the first World War because it lost the propaganda battle. They could not begin to compete with British and American propaganda, which absolutely overwhelmed them. He pledges that next time around they'll have their own propaganda system, which they did during the second World War.

More important for us, the American business community was also very impressed with the propaganda effort. They had a problem at that time. The country was becoming formally more democratic. A lot more people were able to vote and that sort of thing. The country was becoming wealthier and more people could participate and a lot of new immigrants were coming in, and so on. So what do you do? It's going to be harder to run things as a private club.

Therefore, obviously, you have to control what people think. There had been public relations specialists, but there was never a public relations industry. There was a guy hired to make Rockefeller's image look prettier and that sort of thing. But the huge public relations industry, which is a US invention and a monstrous industry, came out of the first World War. The leading figures were people in the Creel Commission. In fact, the main one, Edward Bernays, comes right out of the Creel Commission. He has a book that came out a few years afterwards called *Propaganda*, which became kind of a manual for the rising Public Relations industry, in which he was a prominent figure. The term "propaganda," incidentally, did not have negative connotations in those days.

By manufacturing consent, you can overcome the fact that formally a lot of people have the right to vote.

It was during the second World War that the term became taboo because it was connected with Germany and all those bad things. But in this period, the term "propaganda" just meant information or something like that.

So he wrote a book called *Propaganda* in the late 1920s. He explains that he is applying the lessons of the first World War. The propaganda system of the first World War and this commission that he was part of showed, he says, that it is possible to "regiment the public mind every bit as much as an army regiments their bodies." These new techniques of regimentation of minds, he said, had to be used by the "intelligent minorities" in order to make sure that the slobs stay on the right course. We can do it now because we have these new techniques.

This was an important manual of the public relations industry. Bernays was a kind of guru. He was an authentic Roosevelt/Kennedy liberal. He also engineered the public relations effort behind the US-backed coup which overthrew the democratic government of Guatemala.

His major coup, the one that really propelled him into fame in the late 1920s, was getting women to smoke. Women didn't smoke in those days, and he ran huge campaigns for Chesterfield. You know all the techniques—models and movie stars with cigarettes coming out of their mouths, symbolizing the free, liberated modern woman. He got enormous praise for that. So he became a leading figure of the industry, and his book was an important manual.

Another member of the Creel Commission was Walter Lippmann, the most respected figure in American journalism for about half a century (I mean serious American journalism, serious think pieces). He also wrote what are called progressive essays on democracy, regarded as progressive back in the 1920s. He was, again, applying the lessons of propaganda very explicitly. He says there is a new art in democracy called "manufacture of consent." That is his phrase. Edward Herman and I borrowed it for our book, but it comes from Lippmann. So, he says, there is this new art in the practice of democracy, "manufacture of consent." By manufacturing consent, you can overcome the fact that formally a lot of people have the right to vote. We can make it irrelevant because we can manufacture consent and make sure that their choices and attitudes will be structured in such a way that they will do what we tell them, even if they have a formal way to participate. So we'll have a real democracy. It will work properly. That's applying the lessons of the propaganda agency.

Academic social science and political science come out of the same kind of thinking. One of the founders of the field of communications in academic political science is Harold Lasswell. One of his first achievements was a study of propaganda. Writing in an Encyclopedia of Social Science he says, very frankly, the things I was quoting before about not succumbing to "democratic dogmatisms." That comes from academic political science (Lasswell and others).

Again, drawing the lessons from the war-time experience, political parties drew the same lessons, especially the conservative party in England. Their documents from the period, just being released, show they also recognized the achievements of the British Ministry of Information. They recognized that the country was getting more democratized and it wouldn't be a private men's club. So the conclusion was, as they put it, politics has to become political warfare, applying the mechanisms of propaganda that worked so brilliantly during the first World War towards controlling people's thoughts. That's the doctrinal side, and it coincides with the institutional structure.

It strengthens the predictions about the way the thing should work. And the predictions are well confirmed. But these conclusions, also, are not supposed to be discussed. This is all now part of mainstream literature, but it is only for people on the inside. When you go to college, you don't read the classics about how to control people's minds.

When you go to college, you don't read the classics about how to control people's minds.

Just like you don't read what James Madison said during the constitutional convention about how the main goal of the new system has to be "to protect the minority of the opulent against the majority," and has to be designed so that it achieves that end. This is the founding of the constitutional system, but it is scarcely studied. You can't even find it in the academic scholarship unless you look hard.

That is roughly the picture, as I see it, of the way the system is institutionally, the doctrines that lie behind it, the way it comes out. There is another part directed to the "ignorant and meddlesome outsiders." That is mainly using diversion of one kind or another. From that, I think, you can predict what you would expect to find.

Journalists Doing Somersaults

Self-Censorship and the Rise of the Corporate Media State

Norman Solomon

Coverage of Media Mergers: A Window into the Future of Journalism

Four months after the stunning news about plans to combine Viacom and CBS, the year 2000 began with the announcement of an even more spectacular merger—America Online and Time Warner. Faced with these giant steps toward extreme concentration of media power, journalists mostly responded with acquiescence.

Now, as one huge media merger follows another, the benefits for owners and investors are evident. But for our society as a whole, the consequences seem ominous. The same limits that have constrained the media's coverage of recent mergers within its own ranks are becoming features of this new mass-media landscape. For the public, nothing less than democratic discourse hangs in the balance.

"Freedom of the press is guaranteed only to those who own one," A.J. Liebling remarked several decades ago. In 2000, half-a-dozen corporations owned the media outlets that control most of the news and information flow in the United States. The accelerating mergers are terrific for the profits of those with the deepest pockets, but bad for journalism and bad for democracy.

■■■■■■■■■■

When the Viacom-CBS story broke, media coverage depicted a match made in corporate heaven: At more than $37 billion, it was the largest media merger in history. With potential effects on the broader public kept outside the story's frame, what emerged was a rosy picture. "Analysts hailed the deal as a good fit between two complementary companies," the Associated Press reported flatly. The news service went on to quote a media analyst who proclaimed: "It's a good deal for everybody."

Everybody? Well, everybody who counts in the mass-media calculus. For instance, the media analyst quoted by AP was from the PaineWebber investment firm. "You need to be big," Christopher Dixon explained. "You need to have a global presence." Dixon showed up again the next morning in the lead article of the September 8, 1999, edition of the *New York Times*, along with other high-finance strategists. An analyst at Merrill Lynch agreed with his upbeat view of the Viacom-CBS combination. So did an expert from ING Barings: "You can literally pick an advertiser's needs and market that advertiser across all the demographic profiles, from Nickelodeon with the youngest consumers to CBS with some of the oldest consumers."

In sync with the prevalent media spin, the *New York Times* devoted plenty of ink to assessing advertiser needs and demographic profiles. But during the crucial first day of the *Times*' coverage, foes of the Viacom-CBS consolidation did not get a word in edgewise. There was, however, an unintended satire of corporate journalism when a writer referred to the bygone era of the 1970s: "In those quaint days, it bothered people when companies owned too many media properties."

The *Washington Post*, meanwhile, ran a front-page story that provided similar treatment of the latest and greatest media merger, pausing just long enough for a short dissonant note from media critic Mark Crispin Miller: "The implications of these mergers for journalism and the arts are enormous. It seems to me that this is, by any definition, an undemocratic development. The media system in a democracy should not be inordinately dominated by a few very powerful interests." It wasn't an idea that the *Post*'s journalists pursued.

Overall, the big media outlets—getting bigger all the time—offer narrow and cheery perspectives on the significance of merger mania. News accounts keep the focus on market share preoccupations of investors and top managers. Numerous stories explore the widening vistas of cross-promotional synergy for the shrewdest media titans. While countless reporters are determined to probe how each company stands to gain from the latest deal, few of them demonstrate much enthusiasm for exploring what is at stake for the public. With rare exceptions, news outlets covered the Viacom-CBS merger as a business story. But more than anything else, it should have been covered, at least in part, as a story with dire implications for possibilities of democratic discourse. And the same was true for the announcement that came a few months later—on January 10, 2000—when a hush seemed to fall over the profession of journalism.

While countless reporters are determined to probe how each company stands to gain from the latest deal, few of them demonstrate much enthusiasm for exploring what is at stake for the public.

A grand new structure, AOL Time Warner, was unveiled in the midst of much talk about a wondrous New Media world to come, with cornucopias of bandwidth and market share. On January 2, just one week before the portentous announcement, the head of Time Warner had alluded to the transcendent horizons. Global media "will be and is fast becoming the predominant business of the twenty-first century," Gerald Levin said on CNN, "and we're in a new economic age, and what may happen, assuming that's true, is it's more important than government. It's more important than educational institutions and non-profits."

Levin went on: "So what's going to be necessary is that we're going to need to have these corporations redefined as instruments of public service because they have the resources, they have the reach, they have the skill base. And maybe there's a new generation coming up that wants to achieve meaning in that context and have an impact, and that may be a more efficient way to deal with society's problems than bureaucratic governments." Levin's next sentence underscored the sovereign right of capital in dictating the new direction. "It's going to be forced anyhow because when you have a system that is instantly available everywhere in the world immediately, then the old-fashioned regulatory system has to give way," he said.

By happy coincidence, they insisted, the media course that would make them richest was the same one that held the most fulfilling promise for everyone on the planet.

To discuss an imposed progression of events as some kind of natural occurrence is a convenient form of mysticism, long popular among the corporately pious, who are often eager to wear mantles of royalty and divinity. Tacit beliefs deem the accumulation of wealth to be redemptive. Inside corporate temples, monetary standards gauge worth. Powerful executives now herald joy to the world via a seamless web of media. Along the way, the rest of us are not supposed to worry much about democracy. On January 12, AOL chief Steve Case assured a national PBS television audience on *The NewsHour with Jim Lehrer*: "Nobody's going to control anything." Seated next to him, Levin declared: "This company is going to operate in the public interest."

Such pledges, invariably uttered in benevolent tones, were bursts of fog while Case and Levin moved ahead to gain more billions for themselves and maximum profits for some other incredibly wealthy people. By happy coincidence, they insisted, the media course that would make them richest was the same one that held the most fulfilling promise for everyone on the planet.

■ ■ ■ ■ ■ ■ ■ ■ ■ ■ ■

Journalists accustomed to scrutinizing the public statements of powerful officials seem quite willing to hang back from challenging the claims of media magnates. Even when reporting on a rival media firm, journalists who work in glass offices hesitate to throw weighty stones; a substantive critique of corporate media priorities could easily boomerang. And when a media merger suddenly occurs, news coverage can turn deferential overnight.

On March 14, 2000—the day after the Tribune Company announced its purchase of the *Los Angeles Times* and the rest of the Times Mirror empire—the acquired newspaper reported on the fine attributes of its owner-to-be. In a news article that read much like a corporate press release, the *Times* hailed the Tribune Company as "a diversified media concern with a reputation for strong management" and touted its efficient benevolence. Tribune top managers, in the same article, "get good marks for using cost-cutting and technology improvements throughout the corporation to generate a profit margin that's among the industry's highest." The story went on to say that, "Tribune is known for not using massive job cuts to generate quick profits from media properties it has bought."

Compare that rosy narrative to another news article published the same day by the *New York Times*. Its story asserted, as a matter of fact, that, "The Tribune Co. has a reputation not only for being a fierce cost-cutter and union buster but for putting greater and greater emphasis on entertainment, and business."

And so it goes. As the newspaper industry consolidates along with the rest of the media business, the writing is on the virtual wall. The Tribune Company long ago realized that its flagship newspaper, the *Chicago Tribune*, and its other daily papers would need to become merely one component of a multimedia powerhouse in order to maximize growth and profits. Tribune expanded—heavily—into broadcast television, cable, radio, entertainment, and the Internet.

The key is advertising. And now Tribune can offer advertisers a dazzling array of placements in diverse media from coast to coast. Ad contracts will involve massive "penetration" via big newspapers, broadcaster stations, cable outlets, regional Websites, and online services in areas such as Los Angeles, Chicago, New York, and Baltimore. "Synergy" will rule.

Along the way, the new giant Tribune Company will become the country's third-largest newspaper chain—publishing papers with daily circulation of 3.6 million copies—behind only Gannett and Knight Ridder. In addition to putting eleven daily papers under one corporate roof, the new conglomerate will combine the Tribune's current ownership of 22 major TV stations with a range of Times Mirror magazines that claim more than 60 million readers.

For journalists at the *Los Angeles Times*, the signs have been dispiriting for years now. In 1995 corporate parent Times Mirror brought in a CEO, Mark Willes, who had been a whiz at General Mills. He promptly compared selling newspapers to peddling boxes of cereal.

Willes moved quickly to swing a wrecking ball at the walls between the news and advertising departments. Business execs were assigned to each section of the newspaper to collaborate with editors in shaping editorial content. The message was clear: To be fine, journalism must keep boosting the bottom line.

With such an approach it's no surprise that Times Mirror initiated the negotiations with the Tribune Company that led to the $6.46 billion deal. The Chandler family, holding most of the Times Mirror voting shares, was eager to cash out.

■■■■■■■■■■

"It is not necessary to construct a theory of intentional cultural control," media critic Herbert Schiller commented in 1989. "In truth, the strength of the control process rests in its apparent absence. The desired systemic result is achieved ordinarily by a loose though effective institutional process." In his book *Culture, Inc.: The Corporate Takeover of Public Expression*, Schiller went on to cite "the education of journalists and other media professionals, built-in penalties and rewards for doing what is expected, norms presented as objective rules, and the occasional but telling direct intrusion from above. The main lever is the internalization of values."

Self-censorship has long been one of journalism's most ineffable hazards. The current wave of mergers rocking the media industry is likely to heighten the dangers. To an unprecedented extent, large numbers of American reporters and editors now work for just a few huge corporate employers, a situation that hardly encourages unconstrained scrutiny of media conglomerates as they assume unparalleled importance in public life.

The mergers also put a lot more journalists on the payrolls of mega-media institutions that are very newsworthy as major economic and social forces. But if those institutions are paying the professionals who provide the bulk of the country's news coverage, how much will the public learn about the internal dynamics and societal effects of these global entities?

Many of us grew up with tales of journalistic courage dating back to Colonial days. John Peter Zenger's ability to challenge the British Crown with unyielding articles drew strength from the fact that he was a printer and publisher. Writing in the *New York Weekly*, a periodical burned several times by the public hangman, Zenger asserted in November 1733: "The loss of liberty in general would soon follow the suppression of the liberty of the press; for it is an essential branch of liberty, so perhaps it is the best preservative of the whole."

In contrast to state censorship, which is usually easy to recognize, self-censorship by journalists tends to be obscured. It is particularly murky and insidious in the emerging media environment, with routine pressures to defer to employers that have massive industry clout and global reach. We might wonder how Zenger would fare in most of today's media workplaces, especially if he chose to denounce as excessive the power of the conglomerate providing his paycheck.

Americans are inclined to quickly spot and automatically distrust government efforts to impose prior restraint. But what about the implicit constraints imposed by the hierarchies of enormous media corporations and internalized by employees before overt conflicts develop?

"If liberty means anything at all," George Orwell wrote, "it means the right to tell people what they do not want to hear." As immense communications firms increasingly dominate our society, how practical will it be for journalists to tell their bosses—and the public—what media tycoons do not want to hear about the concentration of power in a few corporate hands? Orwell's novel *1984* describes the conditioned reflex of "stopping short, as though by instinct, at the threshold of any dangerous thought...and of being bored or repelled by any train of thought which is capable of leading in a heretical direction."

In the real world of 2000, bypassing key issues of corporate dominance is apt to be a form of obedience: in effect, self-censorship. "Circus dogs jump when the trainer cracks his whip," Orwell observed more than half a century ago, "but the really well-trained dog is the one that turns his somersault when there is no whip." Of course, no whips are visible in America's modern newsrooms and broadcast studios. But if Orwell were alive today, he would surely urge us to be skeptical about all the somersaults.

Break Up Microsoft?... Then How About the Media "Big Six?"

The push by federal regulators to break up Microsoft was big news. Until that point, the software giant seemed untouchable—and few people demanded effective antitrust efforts against monopoly power in the software industry. These days, a similar lack of vision is routine in looking at the media business.

"Circus dogs jump when the trainer cracks his whip," Orwell observed more than half a century ago, "but the really well-trained dog is the one that turns his somersault when there is no whip."

Today, just six corporations have a forceful grip on America's mass media. We should consider how to break the hammerlock that huge firms currently maintain around the windpipe of the First Amendment. And we'd better hurry.

The trend lines of media ownership are steep and ominous in the United States. When *The Media Monopoly* first appeared on bookshelves in 1983, author Ben Bagdikian explains, "Fifty corporations dominated most of every mass medium." With each new edition, that number kept dropping—to 29 media firms in 1987, 23 in 1990, fourteen in 1992, and ten in 1997.

Published in spring 2000, the sixth edition of *The Media Monopoly* documents that just a half-dozen corporations are now supplying most of the nation's media fare. And Bagdikian, a long-time journalist, continues to sound the alarm. "It is the overwhelming collective power of these firms, with their corporate interlocks and unified cultural and political values, that raises troubling questions about the individual's role in the American democracy."

I wonder what the chances are that Bagdikian—or anyone else—will be invited onto major TV broadcast networks to discuss the need for vigorous antitrust enforcement against the biggest media conglomerates. Let's see:

CBS. Not a good bet, especially since its merger with Viacom (one of the Big Six) was announced in the fall of 1999.

NBC. Quite unlikely. General Electric, a Big Six firm, has owned NBC since 1986.

ABC. Forget it. This network became the property of the Disney Company five years ago. Disney is now the country's second-largest media outfit.

Fox. The Fox network is owned by Rupert Murdoch's News Corp., currently number four in the media oligarchy.

And then there's always cable television, with several networks devoted to news:

CNN. The world's biggest media conglomerate, Time Warner, owns CNN—where antitrust talk about undue concentration of media power is about as welcome as the Internationale sung at a baseball game in Miami.

CNBC. Sixth-ranked General Electric owns this cable channel.

MSNBC. Spawned as a joint venture of GE and Microsoft, the MSNBC network would see activism against media monopoly as double trouble.

Fox News Channel. The Fox cable programming rarely wanders far from the self-interest of News Corp. tycoon Murdoch.

Since all of those major TV news sources are owned by one of the Big Six, the chances are mighty slim that you'll be able to catch a discussion of media antitrust issues on national television.

Disney is now the country's second-largest media outfit.

Meanwhile, the only Big Sixer that doesn't possess a key US television outlet—the Bertelsmann firm, based in Germany—is the most powerful company in the book industry. It owns the mammoth publisher Random House, and plenty more in the media universe. Bertelsmann "is the world's third largest conglomerate," Bagdikian reports, "with substantial ownership of magazines, newspapers, music, television, on-line trading, films, and radio in 53 countries." Try pitching a book proposal to a Random House editor about the dangers of global media consolidation.

Well, you might comfort yourself by thinking about cyberspace. Think again. The dominant Internet service provider, America Online, is combining with already-number-one Time Warner—and the new firm, AOL Time Warner, would have more to lose than any other corporation if a movement grew to demand antitrust action against media conglomerates.

Amid rampant overall commercialization of the most heavily-trafficked websites, AOL steers its 22 million subscribers in many directions—and, in the future, Time Warner's offerings will be most frequently highlighted. While seeming to be gateways to a vast cybergalaxy, AOL's favorite links will remain overwhelmingly corporate-friendly within a virtual cul-de-sac.

While seeming to be gateways to a vast cybergalaxy, AOL's favorite links will remain overwhelmingly corporate-friendly within a virtual cul-de-sac.

Hype about the New Media seems boundless, while insatiable, old hungers for maximum profits fill countless screens. Centralization is the order of the media day. As Bagdikian points out: "The power and influence of the dominant companies are understated by counting them as 'six.' They are intertwined: they own stock in each other, they cooperate in joint media ventures, and among themselves they divide profits from some of the most widely viewed programs on television, cable and movies."

We may not like the nation's gigantic media firms, but right now they don't care much what we think. A strong antitrust movement aimed at the Big Six could change such indifference in a hurry.

The Puppets of Pandemonium

Sleaze and Sloth in the Media Elite

Howard Bloom

Everything you've ever heard about pack journalism is true. In fact, it's an understatement. Though journalists pride themselves on their intellectual independence, they are neither very intellectual nor even marginally independent. They are animals. In fact, they operate on the same herd instincts that guide ants, hoofed mammals, and numerous other social creatures.

In 1827, well before the sciences of ethology and sociobiology had even been invented, historian and essayist Thomas Carlyle said that the critics of his day were like sheep. Put a stick in the path as a lead sheep goes by, wrote the sage, and the beast will jump over it. Remove the stick, and each following sheep in line will jump at precisely the same spot...even though there's no longer anything to jump over! Things haven't changed much since then. If the key critics at the *New York Times*, the *Village Voice*, and *Rolling Stone* fall in love with a musical artist, every other critic in the country will follow their lead. On the other hand, if these lead sheep say an artist is worthless, every other woolly-minded critic from Portland to Peoria will miraculously draw the same conclusion.

When I was out on tour with ZZ Top in 1976, I remember sitting at one of the group's concerts between the critics from Minneapolis' two major dailies. At the time, I was also handling a group called Dr. Buzzard's Original Savannah Band. The lead sheep in the press hated ZZ Top, but they loved Dr. Buzzard. So it had been fairly easy to land major features lauding the Original Savannah Band in the *New York Times* and the *Village Voice* during the same week. As I sat between Minneapolis' two finest models of journalistic integrity and independent judgment in the moments before the lights dimmed and ZZ Top hit the stage, one was reading the *New York Times*' article on Dr. Buzzard and the other was reading the *Voice*'s. Both were hungrily snorfing up the latest hints on how they should feel about the music of the month.

From the notes for The Fame Factory: Two Thousand Years of Media Madness*, a book Howard Bloom will probably complete sometime after the year 2010.*

Not surprisingly, when the concert ended and the duo returned to their typewriters, they cranked out copy with identical judgments. ZZ Top, whose music the *Village Voice*, in a blaring headline, had once said sounded like "hammered shit," was roundly panned, despite the fact that both critics admitted grudgingly in print that via some collective descent into tastelessness, the crowd had gone wild. Then both turned their attention to slaveringly sycophantic paeans to Dr. Buzzard, thus echoing the opinions they'd absorbed from their fashionable reading earlier in the evening.

If I sound like I despise such attitudes, it's because I do. An appalling number of the acts the press (and the publicists who fawn over journalistic dictates) dislikes have tremendous validity. I always felt it was my job to do for erring writers what Edmund Wilson, the literary critic, had done for me. When I was a teenager, I couldn't make head nor tails of T.S. Eliot. His poetry utterly baffled me. So I came to the conclusion that Eliot's work was an elaborate hoax, a pastiche of devices designed to fool the pretentious into thinking that if they admitted a failure to understand all of his erudite references, they'd make themselves look like fools.

Then along came Edmund Wilson (or at least one of his books), and gave me the perceptual key that unlocked Eliot's poetry. Now that I finally understood the stuff, I fell in love with it. What's more, I started giving public readings of Eliot's work, and "The Love Song of J. Alfred Prufrock" became one of the biggest influences on my 16-year-old life.

My task as a publicist was to provide similar perceptual keys. It was to read every lyric an artist had ever written, listen to his or her album 20 or 30 times, and immerse myself in his work until I understood its merit. Then my job was to impart that understanding to a hostile press. In other words, my fellow publicists liked riding waves. I preferred the more difficult task of making them happen.

What's more, I felt my job was to act as a surrogate journalist. I studied everything that had ever been written (quite literally) about a new client in English (or sometimes French, my only other tongue), then subjected the artist to an interview that lasted anywhere from six hours to three days. My goal was to find the interesting stories, the things that would amaze, the facts that would make sense out of the music, the angles that would make for unrejectable feature stories,

My fellow publicists liked riding waves. I preferred the more difficult task of making them happen.

and the tales that would give some insight into the hidden emotional and biographical sources of the performer's creations.

After one of these interviews, John Cougar Mellencamp, a natural-born talker, was literally so exhausted that he couldn't croak more than a sentence or two to his wife and fell asleep in his living room chair (we'd been going since ten in the morning, and it was now four in the afternoon).

At any rate, this may explain why it was not Dr. Buzzard's Original Savannah Band—the group with the automatic popularity—that I spent six years working on, but ZZ Top, the band the press either refused to write about altogether or put down with some variation of Robert (*Village Voice*) Christgau's "hammered shit" verdict. It took three years to turn the press around. Creating that about-face involved a process I used to call "perceptual engineering." ZZ Top had authenticity and validity out the kazoo. My task was to do everything in my power to reverse the direction of the herd's stampede and to make the critics see the substance they had overlooked. For the first few years, the press continued to sneer whenever the group's name came up. But gradually, I got a few lead sheep by the horns (do sheep have horns?) and turned them around. The rest of the herd followed. One result: For the next ten years, ZZ Top became one of the few bands of its genre to command genuine, unadulterated press respect.

While millions were being killed in the Soviet Union, Western journalists participated in the cover-up.

Eventually, the group didn't need me anymore. They don't to this day. The press is now ZZ Top's best publicist. Say something nasty at a press party about this band, and those in the know will turn around and snarl, forgetting that over a decade ago they would have growled if you'd even confessed to *listening* to one of the Texas band's LPs.

■ ■ ■ ■ ■ ■ ■ ■ ■ ■

Public relations taught me a good deal more about why facts were not, after all, what a good reporter wanted. He wanted a story that would either titillate his audience, fit his own clique's political prejudices, or replicate a piece of reportage he'd read somewhere else.

If you really want to have your blood curdled, ask for the tale of the day that two members of the paparazzi, using a fast car, chased Michael Jackson's van down a crowded highway, jumped a divider, raced at 60 miles an hour against traffic on a two-way highway, thus endangering lives, then jumped the divider again and spun at a ninety-degree angle, blocking the highway and nearly causing Jackson's van to crash. The photographers exited their vehicle, cameras in hand, smugly thinking they'd cornered Jackson and would get a highly-prized photo. They did not show any identification and could easily have been nut jobs attempting to pull what was threatened in a large pile of daily mail Jackson received—an assassination.

Hence, Jackson's security guards—LAPD officers on leave—exited the van, which had been forced to a screeching halt in mid-highway. Not knowing what they were up against, one of the guards armed himself with a truck iron. Seeing this weapon, one of the photographers (this is not a joke or exaggeration) pulled a gun. Then the two hightailed it to a telephone, called their editor at the *New York Daily News*, and reported that they'd been threatened for no reason by Michael Jackson's bodyguards. The editor then prepared a front-page headline story about the violent way in which Michael Jackson's toughs had just manhandled innocent press folk. It was on its way to press.

I did some quick research (not easy on a Sunday afternoon), found out that the photographer who had waved his firearm had been arrested on two felony charges for similar behavior, got on the phone, pried the paper's publisher from a golf game, and gave him the real details of the story. It took two hours of threatening the man with the nasty facts to convince the publisher to yank the story. On normal occasions there is no one to stop a falsified tale of this nature from hitting the headline of a publication thirsting for tabloid blood.

I suspect a similar race to avoid a pack of rabid paparazzi was in full sprint the night Princess Di was killed in a car crash.

■ ■ ■ ■ ■ ■ ■ ■ ■ ■

That these principles of press misconduct are regularly applied in the world of pop music doesn't really matter much. It will have hardly any effect on the fate of the world. But the same principles at work in the field of politics have wreaked havoc. In fact, they have made the media one of the most egregious collaborators in mass murder throughout the twentieth century.

While millions were being killed in the Soviet Union, Western journalists participated in the cover-up. Walter Durante of the *New York Times*, who was supplied by the People's Government with a luxurious apartment in Moscow and a good supply of caviar, said nothing about Stalin's murderous rampage. Reporting the truth might have endangered his cozy relationship with the Soviet authorities. Hundreds of other journalists visited the Soviet Union without reporting on the slaughter. Lincoln Steffens, an influential American newspaperman, said: "I have seen the future and it works." This didn't fit the facts, but it did fit Steffens' political preconceptions. Writers with similarly idealistic beliefs tried to give the impression that while the West was decomposing, the Soviet Union was showing the way to a brave new world.

More than mere idealism was involved. Writers were determined to remain politically fashionable. They didn't want to be snubbed by their peers. After all, the bright lights of high culture were pro-Soviet. George Bernard Shaw had gone to the Soviet Union and had said it was ushering in a thousand bright tomorrows. He'd read his own dreams into this land of horror. Critic Edmund Wilson had said the death chamber of the Soviet state was "a moral sanctuary where the light never stops shining." Writers who attempted to tell the truth were viciously attacked as enemies of progressive humanitarianism. Meanwhile, shielded by a dishonest Western press, Soviet authorities killed over 25 million men, women, and children—shooting, starving, torturing, or working them to death.

Now the press is doing it again. This time in its coverage of Israel and the Arab states. Several years ago, when the offices of *Omni* magazine were picketed by Arabs for four days because of an article I'd written, I was forced to dive into Jewish issues. I discovered, to my horror, that vast areas of fact were being violently distorted by the media in a subtly anti-Semitic manner, and that no one was getting the truth out.

Only one page on the Lebanese atrocities appeared in the *New York Times* during a four-year period.

Take the following instance. In the early 1970s, the Palestine Liberation Organization had created so much havoc in Lebanon that Jordan's non-Palestinian Hashemite government decided to throw the PLO out.

The PLO moved its operations to southern Lebanon, where the Islamic population welcomed the Organization's members as brothers. But the PLO were not in a brotherly mood. They turned their visit into a military occupation, confiscating Lebanese homes and autos, raping Lebanese girls, and lining up groups of Lebanese who didn't acquiesce quickly enough, then machine-gunning them to death.

The PLO was even harsher to Lebanon's 2,000-year-old Christian population. Using Soviet-supplied heavy artillery, the PLO virtually leveled two Christian cities, Sidon and Tyre, and carried out massacres in smaller Christian villages. Only one page on the Lebanese atrocities appeared in the *New York Times* during a four-year period. No articles whatsoever showed up in *The Times* of London.

Why didn't the press cover any of this? You can infer some of the reasons from the comments on press behavior I mentioned above. For one thing, there's the slavish herd impulse which drives the press (see Evelyn Waugh's brilliant novel *Scoop* for a satirical view of the press at work as Waugh saw it when he was covering the news in Ethiopia). It had become chic among media types to run away from Israel and into the arms of the Arabs. For another, there's the unerring tendency of the press to make the cause of mass murderers politically fashionable. And finally, there's the fact that the PLO had done its best to make sure it got every story covered its own way.

Yasir Arafat's kindly organization killed six Western journalists who strayed from the PLO line. Yasir's boys took an "uncooperative" Lebanese newspaper publisher captive, dismembered him one joint at a time, and sent a piece of the corpse to each of the Beirut foreign press corps with a photo of the man being tortured alive. The message was self-explanatory.

The Associated Press (AP), United Press International (UPI), and the major American newspapers had long been frantic to maintain a foothold in Beirut. After all, Syria, Iraq, and most of the other Arab countries wouldn't let their correspondents in. Beirut was their only toehold in the Arab world. So each outlet bargained sycophantically with the PLO. They promised not to publish stories on PLO atrocities—including the military seizure of southern Lebanon. The major news organizations submitted credentials on all journalists sent to the area for PLO approval. They agreed to headquarter their reporters in a PLO-controlled hotel. And they let the PLO assign a "guide"—that is, a censor, watchdog, and feeder of misinformation—to each writer. Within a short amount of time, only PLO sympathizers were covering Middle Eastern news.

In the early 1980s, Israel sent forces into Lebanon. Every 24 hours or so, the PLO threw a conference at which it rolled out its version of the day's events. The press dutifully printed what it had been given. PLO spokesmen handed out photos of Israeli tanks rolling through the two Christian cities the PLO had leveled several years earlier with captions "explaining" that the PLO-caused damage clearly visible in the pictures had been inflicted by the Israelis. The press printed these distortions as fact.

The PLO distributed photos of a Beirut infant wrapped in bandages with a caption declaring that the baby had been burned over 75 percent of its body by Israeli shelling. Most major newspapers ran the story on page one. President Reagan was so moved that he kept the picture on his desk for days. Later, UPI was forced to issue a retraction. It turned out that the PLO press release accompanying the photos had contained several minor inaccuracies. The child had been injured not by an Israeli shell but by a *PLO* rocket, and 75 percent of the baby's body had not been burned; the infant had suffered a sprained ankle. The PLO had been aware of these facts before it ever wrote up its caption.

But pictures are what counts. No one registered the correction. Everyone remembered the mislabeled image.

By sifting through tens of thousands of pages of information—including ten years' worth of the *New York Times* and *The Times* of London—by digging up some very obscure books, and by working my way through a maze of little-known experts, I found that the Arab countries have a massive campaign of media and press manipulation at work in the United States. They've endowed university chairs from coast to coast to give academic credibility to their spokesmen. One result: When the Ayatollah called for the death of Salman Rushdie in 1989, the head of UCLA's Middle East studies program said he'd be happy to fire the gun himself. So the Middle East "experts" interviewed everywhere from the *Washington Post* to PBS' *Newshour* have an increasing tendency to speak up on the Arab side, defending gross distortions as gospel truths.

In addition, the Arabs pull strings in Washington through top-ranking firms like Bechtel and Aramco. Bechtel, in fact, used its military contacts to obtain top-secret US surveillance photos of Israel's border deployments before the 1948 war of liberation and passed them on to the Saudis. In addition, companies like Ford, General Electric, and numerous other lobbies woo the press actively on behalf of the Arabs under the umbrella of the Arab American Chamber of Commerce.

Meanwhile, journalists like Hedrick Smith shout loudly about the Israeli lobby, while pretending that an Arab lobby dwarfing it in size and resources does not exist.

Meanwhile, journalists like Hedrick Smith shout loudly about the Israeli lobby, while pretending that an Arab lobby dwarfing it in size and resources does not exist.

Until 1948, more Jews than Arabs lived in Baghdad, yet no reporter champions the rights of Baghdad's Jewish refugees. 800,000 Jews fled Arab countries in which their families had lived for centuries—sometimes for millennia—with only the clothing on their backs, yet the press never writes about them. And many of the Palestinian refugees the media are so concerned for are not Palestinians at all. The United Nations Relief and Works Agency for Palestinian Refugees in the Near East was long ago pressured into defining as "Palestinian" any Arab who had lived in Palestine for a minimum of two years.

Yet the press has adopted the slogan, "Land for peace." No Arab country has offered peace. For decades, none talked seriously about stopping the boycott of Israel, which in terms of international law constituted an act of war. Few have offered to drop their official state of war against Israel. And none has ceased the rhetoric in its official newspapers calling for the annihilation of Israel, the genocidal destruction of Israel's citizens, and, in some cases, the elimination of worldwide Jewry.

Just as in the case of Stalin's Soviet Union and Mao's China, the media has chosen sides. And the side it likes the best is that of the mass murderers.

▪▪▪▪▪▪▪▪▪▪▪

In 1964, while writing a position paper on the Viet Nam war for a congressional candidate in Buffalo, NY, I reviewed a tremendous percentage of the material being written on the subject at the time—everything from articles in *Time* and *Newsweek* to the speeches of the President and his leading cabinet members. I turned vehemently against our participation in the bloodbath. It wasn't until 26 years later, while reading a novel by a South Korean who'd participated in the war—an author whose moral stance was neutral and whose work was published by a house whose owners were as much against the war as I had been—that I learned the Viet Cong had regularly enforced discipline in "liberated" villages by tying recalcitrant families—men, women, and children—to kegs of dynamite and blowing them up in the town square as a lesson to anyone else who might disagree with the new form of Viet Cong freedom. Somehow the American and French press—which I'd also followed fairly carefully—was diligent in its reporting of American atrocities. But the atrocities of the Viet Cong were airbrushed out of existence. And my impression these days is that the Viet Cong's outrages were the worst of the two.

▪▪▪▪▪▪▪▪▪▪▪

Print journalists have traditionally been accomplices in mass violence. Television journalists have gone a step further; they have become instigators of violence. Highly respected CBS reporter Daniel Schorr, who started his career with Edward R. Murrow and reported on everything from the Soviets and the CIA to Watergate, confesses that "most of us in television understood, but did not like to think about, the symbiotic relationship between our medium and violence.... In the mid-Nineteen Sixties, covering urban unrest for CBS, I perceived that television placed a premium on violence and the threat of violence. I found that I was more likely to get on the CBS *Evening News* with a black militant talking the language of 'Burn, baby burn!' than with moderates appealing for a Marshall Plan for the ghetto. So, I spent a lot of time interviewing militants like Stokely Carmichael and H. Rapp Brown.

"In early February 1968, the Reverend Martin Luther King Jr. came to Washington to announce plans for a 'poor people's march' on Washington in the Spring. It was envisaged as a challenge to America's social conscience at a time when the Vietnam war was escalating. The civil rights community was sharply divided over whether the campaign should be completely peaceful or resort to disruptive action, like unlicensed demonstrations and blocking the bridges into the capitol. Dr. King was having trouble sustaining his policy on nonviolence. On February 6, the evening before his planned news conference, the civil rights leader expressed his despair to a rally, 'I can't lose hope, because when you lose hope, you die.' Only dimly aware of the pressures on Dr. King, I came to his news conference with a CBS camera crew prepared to do what TV reporters do—get the most threatening sound bite I could in order to insure a place on the *Evening News* lineup. I succeeded in eliciting from him phrases on the possibility of 'disruptive protest' directed at the Johnson Administration and Congress.

"As I waited for my camera crew to pack up, I noticed that Dr. King remained seated behind a table in an almost-empty room, looking depressed. Approaching him, I asked why he seemed so morose. 'Because of you,' he said, 'and because of your colleagues in television. You try to provoke me to threaten violence, and if I don't then you will put on television those who do. By putting them on television, you elect them our leaders. And, if there is violence, will you think of your part in bringing it about?' I was shaken, but not enough to keep me from excerpting the news conference film from the evening news... I never saw Dr. King again. Less than two months later, he was assassinated."[1]

▪▪▪▪▪▪▪▪▪▪▪

Jonathan Swift, the author of *Gulliver's Travels*, was an early pioneer of the kind of not-so-subtle moral corruption of the press that I constantly bumped my nose against during my fifteen years working with journalists. Swift came along at just the time when coffee had been introduced to London. The stuff became a rage and made men unbelievably jumpy and talkative. So they gathered to work off their energies by gossiping in a hot new form of eatery (or drinkery)—the coffeehouse. Out of the coffeehouses and the men who entered them to swap political and economic tidbits came another pair of fashionable new items—the newspaper and the magazine. (The news broadsheet had already been around for nearly 200 years, as had the pamphlet, which Christopher Columbus used to good effect after he got back from America, and which Martin Luther tossed around like dynamite to set off a cultural avalanche in Europe.)

At any rate, Swift made it from Ireland to London just in time to cash in on the power of the newborn press to sway public opinion and to make or break political careers. One of the most influential politicians when Swift arrived was Robert Walpole, First Earl of Orford—a man accustomed to doing things in the old way. He was smooth as a mink at making connections in court circles, but he would by no means lower himself to hobnob with those ghastly writers swamping their stomachs with coffee. So though Walpole met with Swift once, he treated him rather rudely. Swift retaliated by writing a broadsheet filled with phony allegations that ran the man who'd spurned him through the muck and helped to permanently damage his reputation.

On the other hand, Walpole's leading political opponent—Robert Harley, First Earl of Oxford—could see a promising new possibility when it raised its head. He met regularly with Swift, leaked torrents of inside news to him, solicited his advice on major decisions, and made him feel like a co-conspirator, a partner in the process of government. (Of course he also *hid* vast amounts of fact from Swift, something Jonathan never seems to have caught on to.) This swelled Swift's ego like a blimp, and our boy Jonathan wrote reams of prose that made Harley look like an indispensable mainstay of the state.

▪▪▪▪▪▪▪▪▪▪▪

The newspapers of the American colonies weren't any better. They went into fits of hysteria when the British tried to get the colonists to pay part of the costs of the English troops which had been defending Massachusetts, New York, New Jersey, and Pennsylvania against the French and the Indians. Why did the press blow the minor taxes the Brits levied out of all proportion and help precipitate a revolution? Because the method of taxation the English chose raised the cost of paper and shaved a few farthings off publishers' profits.

Meanwhile, one of Benjamin Franklin's first journalistic forays was a virulent attack on Cotton Mather. What was Franklin lacing into Mather for? Advocating a controversial technique for the prevention of the small pox epidemics that continually ravaged the colonial cities. The method Mather favored was an early version of inoculation. Franklin's unresearched diatribes helped kill off thousands of innocents. Nothing much has changed since then. Ah, how heroic is the press in a free society!

Benjamin Franklin's unresearched diatribes helped kill off thousands of innocents.

▪▪▪▪▪▪▪▪▪▪▪

Back in the mid-nineteenth century, when something like eleven newspapers were fighting ferociously for circulation in New York City, a young part-time journalist named Edgar Allan Poe carried out a secret mission for the *New York Sun*. He wrote up a group of British adventurers who had built a propeller-driven balloon, had taken off to cross the English Channel, run into contrary winds, and had been blown across the Atlantic to a beach in Virginia, thus effecting the first aerial transatlantic crossing. This was big news. The *Sun*'s unnamed correspondent was the first to reach Virginia's coast and interview the intrepid airmen about their perilous flight across the ocean.

The *Sun* ran new stories of the balloonist's adventures on the front page every day, and circulation leaped mightily, leaving New York's remaining papers in the dust. So all of them "sent reporters" down to Virginia and began cranking out their own exclusive interviews with the Brits. There was only one small problem: There was no balloon, no balloonists, and no transatlantic crossing. But the papers were no more concerned with truth than they'd been in Ben Franklin's day. They just wanted a hot story, even if they had to make it up by rewriting what had appeared someplace else.

▪▪▪▪▪▪▪▪▪▪▪

When Fidel Castro launched one of his Keystone Comedy-style invasions of Cuba, his rather rusty ship got bogged down in the mangrove roots about a mile offshore, so it was impossible to unload the supplies and ammunition. Castro's men, all 30 or so of them, had to wade 5270 feet in water up to their necks to get ashore, seriously moistening their gunpowder and their weapons in the process. By the time they reached the beach they were exhausted.

Fidel ordered his men to change costumes and identities every hour or two, then report for duty, supposedly as the heads of massive brigades camped out in the neighboring hills.

Then Batista's troops spotted them as they crawled inland and managed to wipe out all but three—Castro and two others. The trio of survivors took refuge in a cane field, but the Batista troops knew they were in there somewhere. So they combed one row of cane after another, while Fidel and his two companions lay still on their bellies and avoided even a belch or a whisper to elude detection. Then the Batista folks got fed up and started to set the fields on fire. Unfortunately for history, they missed the one in which Fidel and his somewhat diminished army of two were ensconced.

That night, when the Batista boys decided to get some sleep, Fidel counted heads—which took about half a second—and inventoried his arsenal. There was one rifle left. The future "savior" of Cuba (poor Cuba) was elated. He spent the rest of the night lecturing his unfortunate duo of followers. The theme of his exuberant, though hushed oration? "We have won the Revolution!!!!" I am not kidding. (Neither was Fidel.) How ironic that this real life Ayn-Randian hero turned out to be a Leninist monster.

But you haven't heard the last of Fidel yet. Once the wily leader had escaped the sugar field, he managed to triple the size of his army—bringing it up to a grand total of seven. Then some of his supporters persuaded the *New York Times* to send a reporter down to the Sierra Madres for a week of interviews. Fidel ordered his men to change costumes and identities every hour or two, then report for duty, supposedly as the heads of massive brigades camped out in the neighboring hills. Each time one of his septet reappeared as a supposedly different member of the revolutionary corps, the entrant would say something like, "Comrade exigente, I have 1000 men stationed three miles away. Do you want me to move them closer to the urinals?"

After seven days of this, the *New York Times* reporter was convinced that the Maximum Leader had roughly 10,000 hard-bitten soldiers salted away among the pine trees, and that the revolutionary force was unbeatable. The scribe wrote this "indisputable fact" up in a highly-touted series on the "Cuban insurrection." Journalists, being an independent-minded lot, immediately scrambled to Cuba to replicate the *Times*' scoop. *Life*, *Look*, and all three networks sent in their best reporters. Fidel repeated the costume-changing trick. The result: Every media outlet in sight parroted the *Times*' conclusion that Fidel and his massive army had practically taken Cuba already. A year later, when Batista finally couldn't stand being made a fool of by the American press anymore, he decamped. Then *The New Yorker* ran a cartoon with a picture of Fidel and the caption, "I got my job in the *New York Times*." I doubt that many people understood the precision of the joke.

▪▪▪▪▪▪▪▪▪▪▪

Watch the weekend talk shows in which Washington "reporters" swap their "insider" data. Note the pools from which their data is gathered: press conferences, not-for-attribution briefings (meaning more press conferences), and "my sources." In other words, each reporter is simply picking up scraps others have gathered for him or her and handed out on a platter. Not a one is reporting (with the exception of Georgie Anne Geyer, who stays out of Washington). None is digging. None is going underground. None is moving from the level of what's offered for official presentation to the level of what's held in secrecy. None is piercing the veil, as I had to when researching my story on the kids of New York's private schools. Okay, granted that my story led to threats of ending my publishing career. The threats were made by some of the wealthiest and most influential men in the Big Apple, the core of the publishing world. The gentlemen using phrases like, "You are putting your head in the noose, Mr. Bloom," were on the boards of New York's most prestigious schools for the elite. But isn't wading your way through threats and attacks part of the job?

Granted that each Washington reporter knows that to retain access to press conferences, briefings, and sources, he or she must abide by a set of unwritten and shamefully unreported rules, rules which seriously constrain what he or she can say. Also granted that without this access, a reporter would no longer have a standard Washington career. But whoever said that journalism is about fol-

None is moving from the level of what's offered for official presentation to the level of what's held in secrecy.

lowing a standard pattern? Isn't reporting all about rule-breaking to pierce the shroud and uncover what's really going on? Isn't it about discovering those well-kept secrets and soaring insights most likely to have an impact on our lives and to explain the hows, whats, whens, wheres, and whys? If not you, as a reporter, then who? And if not now, when?

■ ■ ■ ■ ■ ■ ■ ■ ■ ■ ■

"Karl Marx held that history is shaped by control of the means of production. In our times history is shaped by control of the means of communication." —Arthur Schlesinger, Jr.

"Public sentiment is everything. With public sentiment, nothing can fail. Without it, nothing can succeed. He who molds public sentiment goes deeper than he who executes statutes or pronounces decisions. He makes statutes or decisions possible or impossible to execute." —Abraham Lincoln

"He who molds public sentiment goes deeper than he who executes statutes or pronounces decisions."

■ ■ ■ ■ ■ ■ ■ ■ ■ ■ ■

It's not enough to invent something fantastic, you have to "promote" it.

A nineteenth-century Floridian, John Gory, trying to keep the town of Apalachicola's population from contracting a fever that racked the multitudes every summer. In 1850, Gory invented refrigeration and air conditioning. Alas, the clever tinkerer was better at inventing than at promoting his invention. He was blind to the necessity of creating a climate of belief that gets all the members of a skittish herd moving in the same direction. Normal human beings are afraid of straying from the pack. They are frightened at the thought of finding merit in something they might be ridiculed for championing. Gory and his air conditioners were ridiculed by no less an authority than the writers of the *New York Times*, the lead animals in the herd. So a man whose gizmos could have improved many a Southerner's life died in abject poverty. Air conditioning and refrigeration were denied to mankind until a German inventor more skillful at manipulating the perceptions of the herd came along.

Charles Darwin was far less naïve than Gory. He didn't just theorize and marshal evidence, then leave it at that. Darwin marshaled support, working hard to line up the backing of the top scientists of his day. Darwin already had one herd-head-turner going for him. His family was scientifically illustrious. The famous evolutionary theorist Erasmus Darwin was his grandfather. Anything with the Darwin name on it had an automatic attraction for the scientific sheep of the day. Yet Darwin worked methodically to court the friendship of scientific opinion-makers. When Alfred Russel Wallace showed up in England having already written up ideas Darwin had only penciled in, Darwin's influential friends lined up to support Chuck's prior claim to the concepts. They turned down the claims of Wallace, a stranger to them. When Darwin finally published *On the Origin of Species by Means of Natural Selection* in 1859, he relied on another friend, the famous T.H. Huxley, to publicize his ideas. Said Huxley, "I am sharpening up my claws and beak in readiness." Darwin kept a list of the men he'd have to win over, and methodically checked off each one he was able to "convert." The father of evolution knew that science is more than a struggle for truth, it's a struggle for social influence, a game of manipulating the herd.

Dante was equally savvy. He became known as a great poet through unabashed self-promotion. Thirteenth-century poets were poor, anonymous creatures. But Dante Alighieri lusted after the kind of fame poets had had in the long-lost days of Rome. So he wrote a poem of epic proportions and made himself the hero. Then he structured the plot to leave the impression that the greatest of all earthly poets was, well, who else? Dante Alighieri. Now watch carefully as the Florentine wannabe makes the bunny of renown emerge from a hat. The Roman Virgil was widely acknowledged as the greatest poet who had ever lived. But Dante was a relative unknown. So Dante made Virgil his fictional guide through hell and purgatory, thus putting himself in Virgil's league. When the pair reached heaven, Virgil had to stay behind. Only Dante was allowed in. The implication: that Dante picked up where Virgil had left off, and that the lad from Florence had transcended the old Roman entirely.

This flagrant act of self-promotion worked. In fact, it snowballed. After he died, Florence promoted the theme of Dante as the world's greatest poet. Why? To promote Florence as a leading city of the arts and an all-round admirable town.

■ ■ ■ ■ ■ ■ ■ ■ ■ ■ ■

"The press has become the greatest power within the Western countries, more powerful than the legislature, the executive, and the judiciary." —Aleksandr Solzhenitsyn.

"Hostile newspapers are more to be dreaded than a hundred thousand bayonets." —Napoleon

"The press leads the public." —Japanese saying

"The conscious and intelligent manipulation of the organized habits and opinions of the masses is an important element in democratic society. Those who manipulate this unseen mechanism in society constitute an invisible government which is the true ruling power of our country.... It is they who pull the wires which control the public mind, who harness old social forces and contrive new ways to bind and guide the world." —Edward Bernays

---

We see what we're told is there, not what is. A 1989 survey showed that drug use and crime were on a par in the US and Canada. But Americans ranked drugs as their number-one problem and crime as their third. Canadians saw drugs as insignificant and ranked crime a lowly twentieth on the list of their dilemmas. The facts were the same, but the perceptions were different. Why? Because the headlines in the two countries were different.

Molly Ivins, a highly respected journalist who's worked for the *New York Times*, among other papers, wrote in the *Houston Journalism Review*: "You can find out more about what's going on at the state capitol by spending one night drinking with the capitol press corps than you can in months of reading the papers those reporters write for. The same is true of City Hall reporters, court reporters, police reporters, education writers, any of us. In city rooms and in the bars where newspeople drink you can find out what's going on. You can't find it in the papers."[2]

Then there are the many cases in which the press manufactures or manipulates the news. According to the *New York Times Book Review*, Oliver North "describes being in the office of the Reagan aide, Pat Buchanan, working on an announcement of the capture of the *Achille Lauro* terrorist, when Niles Latham, an editor at the *New York Post*, called to ask Mr. Buchanan to make the President say, 'You can run, but you can't hide,' so the paper could use it as the front page headline. Mr. Buchanan obligingly wrote the line into the President's remarks."[3]

From 1968 to 1988, the average length of a TV news sound bite allotted to a presidential candidate fell from 43 seconds to 9.8. Meanwhile, pictures of the candidates with **none** of his words tripled. This gave the TV producer nearly total power to reshape or distort a candidate's message.

"You can find out more about what's going on at the state capitol by spending one night drinking with the capitol press corps than you can in months of reading the papers those reporters write for."

A 1990 survey showed that an astonishing number of congressmen and other elected officials believed that the pyramids may have been built by aliens. Even worse, one of the groups that came out with the highest levels of general ignorance were newspaper editors. Over 50 percent of these media leaders felt that dinosaurs and humans had inhabited the earth at the same time. (Humans, in fact, didn't show up until some 65 million years after the dinosaurs had abandoned their bones and departed from the scene.) The bottom line: The men and women spooning facts into the brains of most Americans have apparently gotten their scientific education from the Flintstones.

The men and women spooning facts into the brains of most Americans have apparently gotten their scientific education from the Flintstones.

Writes Molly Ivins: "One of the most depressing aspects of reporters as a group is that they tend to be fairly ignorant themselves. There is no excuse for it, and there is a complete cure for it. Read, read, read."[4]

Further muddling the information we receive from overseas is the fact, reported by historian and former *New York Times* journalist Robert Darnton, that "few foreign correspondents speak the language of the country they cover."[5] So-called foreign reporters simply regurgitate preconceptions. English correspondents write of "the England of Dickens" and those in France portray "the France of Victor Hugo, with some Maurice Chevalier thrown in." What justifies this? Says Darnton: "Newspaper stories must fit a culture's preconceptions of news."

Anyone who's been interviewed by the press knows that his so-called quotes will be wild distortions of his original statements, yet writers refuse to check the accuracy of their notes with the source. Why? Says one former investigative reporter: "We don't like to be confronted with our own mistakes." What's more, we "are tired of the story and don't want to do more work."[6]

Writers respond to the world with a kind of herd instinct. They see which direction the animals on either side of them are rushing, and don't bother to notice the real world through which the pack is moving. Yet they pretend to report on the real world. What's worse, they often fool their readers into believing that this is true.

Today, I read 30 different publications, most of them obscure periodicals from both the left and right.

So I am angry at the press. I am angry at its dishonesty. I am infuriated by its moral corruption. I am disgusted with its laziness and lack of intellectual independence. I am sickened by its phony self-image. And I am furious that I was lied to in my youth. I hate *The Reporter* for telling me about Chiang Kai Check's atrocities while hiding Mao's. I hate the *Village Voice* for telling me about My Lai without informing me that the standard Viet Cong procedure for winning the hearts and minds of villagers was to take the most prominent village family—usually a dozen or more grandparents, uncles, aunts, mothers, fathers, children, and infants—tie them to a few canisters of dynamite in the town square, then detonate the charge. I hate the press for turning me into a war protester against Nixon and Johnson when I should have been shouting just as loudly against Ho Chi Minh. And I am disconcerted that the tribe they have slated for the next Cambodian-style annihilation is my own.

Today, I read 30 different publications, most of them obscure periodicals from both the left and right. I never want to be deceived again. And I don't want to see my own people victimized. Though I can't for the hell of me figure out how to stop it.

I could give you numerous other examples from personal experience and subsequent research, but it's a long story and will have to wait for some other time. The surprising part is that just like Jonathan Swift, today's journalists regard themselves as not only the guardians of honesty, morality and truth, but think they're incorruptible. Human nature is so peculiar. In fact, it's a bit worse than that—it's downright dangerous. And the press is among the most dangerous of all.

Well, I see I've put you to sleep. But just remember, all you need is an automatic weapon and a sharp knife and you too can use Yasir Arafat's keys to publicity success. If you handle them properly, the press will fall for anything. Especially if it promises to spill a lot of blood.

Endnotes

1. Schorr, Daniel. Confessions of a newsman. *World Monitor*, May 1992, pp 40-1. **2.** Ivins, Molly. (1991). *Molly Ivins can't say that, can she?* New York: Random House, p 235. **3.** Dowd, Maureen. The education of Colonel North (a review of *Under Fire: An American Story* by Oliver L. North). *New York Times Book Review*, November 17, 1991, p 12. **4.** *Op cit.*, Ivins, p 237. **5.** Darnton, Robert. (1990). *The kiss of Lamourette*. New York: WW Norton & Co, p 92. **6.** Goldstein, Tom. (1985). *The news at any cost: How journalists compromise their ethics to shape the news.* New York: Simon & Schuster, p 204.

The New Rules for the New Millennium

Gary Webb

When the newspaper I worked for in Kentucky in the 1970s, *The Kentucky Post*, took the plunge and hiked its street price from 20 cents to a quarter, the executive editor, Vance Trimble, instructed our political cartoonist to design a series of full-page house ads justifying the price increase. One of those ads still hangs on my wall. It depicts an outraged tycoon, replete with vest and felt hat, brandishing a copy of our newspaper and shouting at a harried editor: "Kill that story, Mr. Editor...or else!"

We were worth a quarter, the ad argued, because we weren't some "soft, flabby, spineless" newspaper. We'd tell that fat cat to take a long walk off a short pier.

"Our readers would be shocked if any kind of threat swayed the editor," the ad declared. "If it happens, we print it. Kill a story? *Never!* There are no fetters on our reporters. Nor must they bow to sacred cows. On every story, the editor says: 'Get the facts. And let the fur fly!' Our reporters appreciate that. They are proud they can be square-shooters."

The newspaper for the most part held to that creed. When the executive editor was arrested for drunk driving, a photographer was dispatched to the city jail and the next day the paper carried a picture of our disheveled boss sitting forlornly in a holding cell. The newspaper had done the same thing to many other prominent citizens, he reminded the stunned staff after his release. Why should he be treated any differently?

Stories that meet every traditional standard of objective journalism are retracted or renounced, not because they are false —but because they are true.

How quaint that all sounds 20 years later. And how distant that post-Watergate era seems. Today, we see corporate news executives boasting not of the hardness of their asses, but of the value of their assets. We witness them groveling for public forgiveness because something their reporters wrote offended powerful interests or raised uncomfortable questions about the past. Stories that meet every traditional standard of objective journalism are retracted or renounced, not because they are false—but because they are true.

The depth of this depravity (so far) was reached the day New York attorney Floyd Abrams decided CNN/Time Warner should retract its explosive report on a covert CIA operation known as Tailwind, which was alleged to have involved the use of nerve gas against American deserters in Southeast Asia in the 1970s. I saw Abrams on a talk show afterwards arguing that the ultimate truth of the Tailwind story was irrelevant to CNN's retraction of it.

"It doesn't necessarily mean that the story isn't true," Abrams insisted. "Who knows? Someday we might find other information. And, you know, maybe someday I'll be back here again, having done another report saying that, 'You know what? It was all true.'"

Stop and savor that for a moment. Let its logic worm its way through your brain, because it is the pure, unadulterated essence of what's wrong with corporate journalism today. Could anyone honestly have dreamed that one day a major news organization would retract and apologize for a story that even it acknowledges could well be true?

For that matter, who could have envisioned the day when a veteran investigative reporter would be convicted of a felony for printing the voicemail messages of executives of a corporation that was allegedly looting, pillaging, and bribing its way through Central America? Yet, like CNN producers April Oliver and Jack Smith, *Cincinnati Enquirer* reporter Mike Gallagher was fired, his work "renounced" as his editors ludicrously wrote in a front-page apology, and he has been uniformly reviled in the mass media as a fabricator for his devastating exposé of Chiquita Brands International. So far, however, no one has shown that his stories contain a single, solitary inaccuracy. Again, the truth seems irrelevant, a sideshow not worthy of serious discussion.

In 1997 Florida television reporters Steve Wilson and Jane Akre, both highly respected journalists, tried to air a series on the dangers of a growth hormone injected into most of Florida's dairy cows to stimulate milk production. After receiving threatening letters from Monsanto, the makers of the growth hormone, Wilson and Akre were ordered to rewrite their script more than 80 times, yet at no time were they told that anything they had reported was inaccurate. Finally, their bosses ordered them to run a watered-down story the reporters felt was misleading, untrue, and heavily slanted towards the chemical giant, and threatened to fire them if they didn't. Instead, they quit and sued the Fox station. In August 2000, Jane Akre won a jury verdict of more than $400,000. Amazingly, the press reports portrayed the verdict as a vindication for Monsanto and the TV station that fired Akre and Wilson.

Astute readers may well wonder what the hell is going on, and the answer is this: The rules are being changed, and they are being changed in such a way as to ensure that our government and our major corporations won't be bothered by nettlesome investigative journalists in the new millennium.

When I started in the newspaper business the rules were simple: Get as close to the truth as you possibly can. There were no hard and fast requirements about levels of proof necessary to print a story—and there still aren't, contrary to all the current huffing and puffing about "journalistic standards" being abused. I worked as a reporter for nearly 20 years, wrote for dozens of different editors, and each had his or her own set of standards. Generally, if you diligently investigated the issue, used named sources, found supporting documentation, and you honestly believed it was true, you went with it. Period. That was the standard that gutsy editors used, at any rate. Some—like Ben Bradlee during Watergate, for example—occasionally went with less because instinct and common sense told them the story was right even if everything wasn't completely nailed down.

The rules are being changed, and they are being changed in such a way as to ensure that our government and our major corporations won't be bothered by nettlesome investigative journalists in the new millennium.

Nervous editors, on the other hand, used different standards. "Raising the bar" was the usual trick they used to avoid printing troublesome news. The squeamish demanded an admission of wrongdoing (preferably written) or an official government report confirming the story's charge.

What that means, of course, is that stories about serious, unacknowledged abuses never get printed, and eventually reporters learn not to waste their time turning over rocks if no one will officially confirm when something hideous slithers out. And once that happens, they cease being journalists and become akin to the scribes of antiquity, whose sole task was to faithfully record the pharaoh's words in clay.

It is this latter standard that was championed by Abrams in the Tailwind case and to some extent by *San Jose Mercury News* editor Jerry Ceppos in the case of my "Dark Alliance" series in 1996. Under these new rules, it isn't enough anymore for a reporter to have on-the-record sources and supporting documentation. Now they must have something called "proof." Investigative stories must be "proven" in order to reach the public; having "insufficient evidence" is now cause for retraction and dismissal.

"Having read all your stuff, as much as I can about this...I can't see where you prove it," CNN commentator Bill Press whined to former CNN producer April Oliver. "None of your sources add up to that."

"What is the standard of proof in a black operation where everyone's supposed to deny, or information is tightly compartmentalized?" Oliver demanded.

Her question, which cuts to the heart of the debate, went unanswered. But judging from Abrams' report, "proof" apparently is a statement no one disagrees with, or something that can be demonstrated, as Ted Turner phrased it, "beyond a reasonable doubt"—the courtroom standard of proof.

Some, including Turner, say this is good for journalism, that it will keep unsubstantiated stories out of public circulation, and there's no doubt about that. But it will also have the same muffling effect on a lot of important stories that happen to be true. Such a standard would have kept Watergate out of the papers. Love Canal, the CIA's mining of Nicaragua's harbors, the El Mozote massacre in El Salvador—all would have been suppressed. Don't believe it? Consider the Iran-Contra scandal. It was only after Ronald Reagan and Edwin Meese held their famous press conference and confessed that something funny had been going on in the White House basement that the Washington press corps felt emboldened enough to start covering the scandal seriously. Until then, the idea of a secret parallel government had been sneeringly dismissed as some left-wing conspiracy theory.

What is devious about these standards of proof is that they sound so eminently responsible. They are doubly handy because they can be applied after publication, when the heat comes down. Then, as CNN/Time Warner did, lawyers and former government operatives can be called in to produce palliative reports bemoaning the lack of "proof," and the bothersome story can be interred without further ado. (Few will question the validity of these reports because, after all, they come straight from the top.)

But somewhere along the way it's been forgotten that journalism was never meant to be held to courtroom standards of proof. As investigative reporter Pete Brewton once put it: "I'm not in the proof business. I'm in the information business." Unlike police and prosecutors, reporters don't have the power to subpoena records or wiretap phone conversations. We can't conduct 24-hour surveillances or pay informants for information. We write what we can find on the public record (which becomes less public all the time). Or at least we used to.

Fortunately, there are still some reporters and editors out there who consider an official denial to be a starting point, rather than the end, of a promising story. It is these men and women who are the true journalists, the ones who will carry on where the giants of yesterday—George Seldes, I.F. Stone, and the late Jonathan Kwitny—left off. Though many of them toil in relative obscurity, for little money and even less appreciation, their work contributes more to our lives than the million-dollar celebrity-correspondents that we see on the nightly news.

Back in 1938, as fascism was sweeping across Europe, George Seldes presciently observed: "It is possible to fool all the people all the time—when government and press cooperate."

Today, such mass deception is possible on a scale that Seldes never could have imagined. That is why it is more important than ever to support the journalists with backbones. If these few bits of illumination should ever sputter and disappear, out of neglect or frustration or censorship, we will be enveloped by a darkness the likes of which we've never seen.

All warfare is based on deception.
—General Sun Tzu, ca. 400BC

If you're not careful the media will have you hating the people who are being oppressed, and loving the people who are doing the oppressing.
—Malcolm X

The Covert News Network

Greg Bishop

As one can imagine, the history of the US intelligence community's relationship to the news media is a long and sordid one. In the halls of the CIA's headquarters in Langley, the corridors of the Pentagon, and the sub-basement strongholds of the National Security Agency, a war of deception is the *raison d'etre*, since the existence of valuable information doesn't depend on whether a war is hot, cold, or even declared. "National Security," in one guise or another, has been used as a cover and excuse for both legitimate intelligence-gathering operations, as well as countless instances of meddling in the internal affairs of sovereign nations and of sovereign citizens at home.

Machiavelli is alive and well in the intel world. In this climate, the end always justifies the means, and ideas like democracy, due process, accountability, and the US Constitution are just recent annoyances in the ancient war of propaganda. Although the last few years and the two generations after the Vietnam war have seen an exponential growth in mistrust of the government, the spin doctors and outright liars who serve as mouthpieces of the covert community plod along. Over 50 years of practice has made them good at their jobs, and they have been able to adapt well to the times. Mention the Branch Davidians in mixed company to see how well the "just a bunch of wackos who deserved what they got" idea has spread.

In April 1967, not even four years after the JFK assassination, the CIA had sent out a memo to their media assets advising them on how to counter any criticism of the magic bullet theory and attendant conspiracy rumors. Headquarters sagely advised that the best methods to attack wacky conspiracy theories were through news features and book reviews. These published pieces would suggest that anyone who questioned the Warren Report was "financially interested," or, "hasty and inaccurate in their research," and that, "No new evidence has emerged." This sort of thing sounds oddly familiar, especially if you've read Gerald Posner's defense of the official line, *Case Closed*. Perhaps this is because the public has been handed so much info-dung for so long that we don't realize the reality that has been manufactured for us over the last 50 years.

JFK, for his part, had a lot of buddies in the press corps, and when wind of the Bay of Pigs invasion reached the staff of the liberal mouthpiece *New Republic*, its editor, Gilbert Harrison, went to his friend Jack Kennedy to ask permission to publish the scoop. He was well aware of the security risks associated with doing so, and Kennedy asked him to scrap the story, which he did. The *New York Times*, long a CIA asset through the cooperation of its publishers like Arthur Hays Sulzberger, was also convinced to severely alter the story from a front-page, four-column banner headliner to a single column that mentioned neither the CIA nor an "imminent" invasion. Kennedy was not, however, a hard-liner on all sensitive operations issues. About a month after this most visible of clandestine policy failures, the President was holding another meeting urging top news editors not to report on security issues, but told a *Times* staffer: "If you had printed more about the [Bay of Pigs] operation, you would have saved us from a colossal mistake." It is not surprising that Kennedy valued a free press as essential to a functioning democracy. Maybe he felt a little better after he branded Allen Dulles the fall guy and fired him for screwing things up.

Dulles was the spymaster extraordinaire who had run the CIA with an iron fist for almost ten years. His experience in covert operations stretched back to at least World War II when he was the Office of Strategic Services station chief in Switzerland. The OSS was the breeding ground for many future movers and shakers in the CIA. After the war, the Machiavellian spirit took over the OSS as the organization arranged for the wholesale US importation of and legal immunity for hundreds of German scientists under Project Paperclip.

With the end of the war came the beginnings of the Central Intelligence Agency. After his appointment as director in 1952, Dulles occasionally contributed articles to the pages of the staid *Reader's Digest*. The *Digest* was such an arm of conservatism and fascist sentiment that in 1942 it was cited by Nazi propaganda minister Joseph "The bigger the lie, the more it will be believed" Goebbels as a "voice in the wilderness" urging the US to stay out of the growing European conflict. During the war, Hitler's 805th Tank Destroyer battalion shot canisters full of reprints from *Reader's Digest* at advancing American troops as a form of low-tech psychological warfare. The *Digest* maintains well-staffed offices in Hong Kong and, before Castro, had another branch in Havana. The owners once distributed American flag stickers to all employees.

Hitler's 805th Tank Destroyer battalion shot canisters full of reprints from *Reader's Digest* at advancing American troops as a form of low-tech psychological warfare.

Dulles recruited OSS alum Edward Hunt to run a worldwide program of pro-capitalist, pro-American propaganda that would eventually be code-named "MOCKINGBIRD." Hunt conceived the program as mind control on the largest scale ever. This project contained the seeds of the "Propaganda Assets Inventory," as it later became known within the Agency. This department's influence became so great that the CIA's first Covert Action Chief, Frank Wisner, egomaniacally christened it "Wisner's Wurlitzer," boasting that the Agency was able to play and sway public opinion anywhere in the world.

Watergate muckraker Carl Bernstein uncovered a list of over 400 reporters and a coterie of publishers and media moguls who had basically been rubber-stamping CIA propaganda since the 1950s.

One of MOCKINGBIRD's most extensive projects was directed through a front called the Congress for Cultural Freedom. The CCF, founded in 1950, funneled millions of dollars to US- and CIA-friendly publications in Britain, South Africa, and Latin America, among others. One magazine, *Encounter*, was so successful that it put most of its competition out of business. This is not surprising, since the competition didn't have Uncle Sam's largesse to fall back on when advertising or subscriptions dwindled. *Encounter* steamrolled over the intellectual life of English-speaking Europeans for 32 years until its dirty secret was discovered by a reporter for *The Observer* newspaper of London, who called the situation a "literary Bay of Pigs." Many reporters and editors working during the Cold War were generally cowed by Red Scare propaganda anyway, which made Dulles and Hunt's job easier.

In Finland, CIA asset Clay Felker edited a publication called *The Helsinki Youth News*. This ostensibly radical, socialist rag attempted to bend the minds of impressionable young leftists toward the cool and benevolent US government. Felker's assistant was none other than former *Playboy* piece of bunnytail Gloria Steinem. After this field training, she returned to the US to found the supposed bastion of modern feminism: *Ms.* magazine. When publisher Random House was about to release a book authored by a feminist group called the Redstockings, charging Felker and Steinem with co-opting the women's movement and steering it on an elitist course, while neutralizing its radical aspects, the two CIA assets—as well as *Washington Post* editor Katherine Graham—protested, and Random caved, deleting the segment from the book. Graham also held a large financial interest in *Ms.* Graham's late husband Philip had been a tested and true friend of the CIA within the pages of the *Post*.

In a 1977 *Rolling Stone* article, Watergate muckraker Carl Bernstein uncovered a list of over 400 reporters and a coterie of publishers and media moguls who had basically been rubber-stamping CIA propaganda since the 1950s. The group included *Life* and *Time* magazines' Henry Luce (the same *Life* magazine that published out-of-sequence stills from the Zapruder film), CBS's William Paley, and the aforementioned Arthur Sulzberger, as well as James Copley of Copley News Service, which owned and supplied reportage to a coven of newspapers like the *San Diego Union* and five major dailies in the Chicago metropolitan area. Bernstein said "at least 23" reporters and editors with Copley were certifiably on the CIA's payroll.

Bernstein interviewed one anonymous Agency official who told him: "One journalist is worth 20 agents." At least one instance of intentional rubber-stamping at the *New York Times* was uncovered by Bernstein: Sulzberger's nephew, C.L. Sulzberger, apparently put his byline on an Agency briefing document and submitted it as one of his daily columns. In *The CIA and the Cult of Intelligence*, authors Victor Marchetti and John Marks described the kowtowing of syndicated columnist Charles Bartlett. In 1970, in the midst of the CIA's campaign to undermine the election of Chilean leftist Carlos Allende, Bartlett received an internal memo from the International Telephone & Telegraph Corporation (ITT) which described efforts "to move in the name of President Nixon...[with] maximum authority to do all possible...to keep Allende from taking power." The American military had pledged its "material and financial assistance," and ITT, for its part, had also promised to forward the funds needed to carry out the operation, which would protect ITT's interests in Chile. Bartlett, instead of breaking the story and launching an investigation, later admitted to

"One journalist is worth 20 agents."

basing his entire column of September 28, 1970, on the ITT memo, "to the point of paraphrase." He apparently never checked out the information with any other independent source before blindly shoveling a heap of bullshit onto his readers.

"Psyops personnel, soldiers and officers, have been working in CNN's headquarters in Atlanta through our program 'Training with Industry.'"

The CIA debriefed foreign news correspondents as they returned, gathering information on diverse ephemera such as railroad and airport traffic, the number of smokestacks on factories, and the personalities of dignitaries and heads of state. In a silent war, every little bit counts. After Bernstein's article was published, the CIA under its director, George Herbert Walker Bush, moved quickly to counter the accusations of the congressionally-appointed Church Committee, stonewalling investigators while promising not to jack around with the media in the future. Bush also later said, "Read my lips: No new taxes."

Once in a while, the hands of other intelligence organizations are caught up Miss Liberty's dress, too. When George Bush became president, he pushed the cover-up program into high gear by drafting a set of press-relations rules for the Department of Defense and its contractor-bitches. The National Industrial Security Program Operating Manual contained a supplement especially designed to handle nosy questions about "black" projects: operations so secret that they don't even appear on any official government budgets. The document, stamped "DRAFT," is dated May 29, 1992, and states:

> Cover stories may be established for unacknowledged programs in order to protect the integrity of the program from individuals who do not have a need to know. Cover stories must be believable and cannot reveal any information regarding the true nature of the contract. Cover stories for Special Access Programs must have the approval of the PSO (Program Security Officer) prior to dissemination.

In an article entitled "Lying by the Book," reporter John Horgan quotes Pentagon spokesperson Sue Hansen's reply to his question about this document: "Whoever sent it to you was unauthorized," and the document was an unapproved draft version that did not "represent the policy of the federal government." Horgan was moved to ask if this reply itself represented a cover story.

During the Kosovo conflict, the Cable News Network (CNN) hired five staffers it referred to as "interns." These interns were working for no pay to learn the intricacies of the daily operations of CNN, presumably to be put to use in their later career paths. The problem is that they had already settled into another career: They were employees of US Army Intelligence. Liberal bastion radio network National Public Radio (NPR) also admitted to hiring interns from Army Intel during the same time period.

The CNN debacle was uncovered by a Dutch newspaper, *Trouw*. A spokesman from the US Army was quoted: "Psyops personnel, soldiers and officers, have been working in CNN's headquarters in Atlanta through our program 'Training with Industry.'" Major Thomas Collins of the US Army Information Service continued: "They worked as regular employees of CNN. Conceivably, they would have worked on stories during the Kosovo war. They helped in the production of news." The military CNN-personnel belonged to the Fourth Psychological Operations Group, stationed at Fort Bragg, North Carolina. One of the main tasks of this group of almost 1200 soldiers and officers is to spread "selected information." When CNN found out about the Dutch newspaper story and a later commentary on the episode by columnist Alexander Cockburn, they dropped the program like a hot potato. Perhaps taking a cue from the Security Program Operating Manual, Susan Binford, the head of CNN public relations, later said: "Is the whole thing embarrassing? Yes. Did it compromise us journalistically? No." What else *could* she say?

The author of the original story, Abe DeVries, also reported on a military symposium on Special Operations that was held behind closed doors in Arlington, Virginia, in February, 1999. A Colonel Christopher St. John said that the cooperation with CNN was a textbook example of the kind of ties the American Army wants to have with the media. Not only do the psychological operations people want to spread hand-picked "information" and keep other news quiet, the Army also wants to control the Internet, to wage electronic warfare against disobedient media, and to control commercial satellites.

Many sources point to a "major media asset" anchor-level news personality who has been a long-time cooperative member of the CIA's stable. Although no one mentions the asset by name, author Alex Constantine writes that Walter Cronkite said, in an unreferenced quote, "My lips have been kind of buttoned for almost 20 years." Herein may lie the plight of the journalist who at least attempts to remain objective on sensitive security issues, and still keep his job.

Despite these leaked revelations and a steady stream of minor scandals, the Agency keeps up its never-ending battle against truth, justice, and the American Way. Dated "20 December, 1991," an internal memo from the "Task Force on Greater CIA Openness" was leaked (or retrieved through an FOIA request—accounts vary) soon after its completion. The report was in response to a request by then-CIA Director Robert Gates for a "Task Force" on suggestions for making the Agency appear more cuddly and user-friendly to the general population. Christic Institute lawyer Daniel Sheehan has a copy of the document and cryptically refers to it in interviews. UFO researcher Robert Dean brought it up in a press conference in Roswell during the fiftieth anniversary festivities. One of the humorous (?) aspects of this document is that a memo on "greater openness" was classified and clamped down upon by CIA censors when they realized what had happened. Perhaps an employee at the Public Affairs Office (PAO) was canned for it, or handed a transfer to Tierra del Fuego.

The text reveals both a self-congratulatory smugness and a paradoxical desire to evolve the image of the CIA as a "visible and understandable" organization. There was obviously a sense that the American public has just about had it with an agency that seems to serve no important purpose in a post-Cold War world.

Reacting to this in an early attempt at spin control, rather than outright stonewalling or lying, the Task Force recommended some changes in the methods that the PAO utilizes to deal with their information conduits (news media, academia, and private sector business). Throughout the document, the Task Force members revealed that they wanted it both ways, as evidenced by this statement: "[T]here was substantial agreement that we generally need to make the institution and the process more visible and understandable rather than strive for openness on specific substantive issues." Viewed in this light, the study recommended no real change in attitude, only in the way that the Agency presents itself to a hostile or at least an indifferent public.

Particularly revealing is a passage that describes CIA "contacts with every major wire service, newspaper, news weekly, and television network in the nation." The memo author goes on to boast that the PAO has been able to change or even scrap stories that were not to the Agency's liking. They had also apparently been able to "turn 'intelligence failure' stories into 'intelligence success stories'" more than once. This appears to indicate that the CIA still controls a portion of the news media through a "carrot-and-stick" relationship with reporters, who boast of their "secret sources" and secretly fear the loss of same if they happen to piss off "Mr. Deep Throat." The document also mentions Oliver Stone's *JFK* by name and reveals that the CIA knew "for some time" that this film was in the works, which may merely indicate that some CIA staffers read *Variety* and *The Hollywood Reporter*.

Particularly revealing is a passage that describes CIA "contacts with every major wire service, newspaper, news weekly, and television network in the nation."

The best way to affect opinion is to make the public and policymakers believe that their conclusions were reached by a fair and balanced judgment of facts. If the "facts" are controlled, the ham-handed coercion practiced in other areas of the world that is feared in a free society never rears its head. The effectiveness of a free press is castrated when the press is compromised, and psychological warfare specialists will always exploit this fact. The CIA long ago overstepped its boundaries as envisioned by Harry Truman, who created the organization by executive order in 1947. The Agency became unsatisfied with merely gathering information, and has obscenely enlarged a loophole in their charter to wage almost continuous covert war for over 50 years. Our friend Sun Tzu said: "When one treats people with benevolence, justice, and righteousness, *and reposes confidence in them*, the army will be united in mind and will be happy to serve their leaders." (Emphasis added.) This time-honored wisdom that allowed a civilization to flourish for over 2,000 years seems to have been forgotten in a country that hasn't passed its third century, and may not see that birthday intact if democracy is continually subverted by a cabal of black-suited control freaks.

Sources and Further Reading

Agee, Philip. (1975). *Inside the Company: CIA diary.* New York: Stonehill Publishing

Constantine, Alex. (1997). *Virtual government: CIA mind control operations in America.* Venice, CA: Feral House.

Hogshire, Jim. (1997). *Grossed out surgeon vomits inside patient!: An insider's look at the supermarket tabloids.* Venice, CA: Feral House.

Horgan, John. "Lying by the book." *Scientific American*, October 1992.

Kauffman, Martin. (1998). "The Manhattan Project to manufacture the first yuppies." *Steamshovel Press* #16.

Marchetti, Victor & John Marks. (1974). *The CIA and the cult of intelligence.* New York: Alfred A. Knopf.

Mosley, Leonard. (1978). *Dulles: The biography of Eleanor, Allen, and John Foster Dulles and their family network.* New York: The Dial Press.

National Insecurity Council. (1992). *It's a conspiracy!* Berkeley, CA: EarthWorks Press.

Richardson, Jeffrey. (1995). *The U.S. intelligence community.* Boulder, CO: Westview Press.

Seldes, George. (1942). *The facts are...: A guide to falsehood and propaganda in the press and radio.* New York: In Fact, Inc.

Vankin, Jonathan & John Whalen. (1998). *The 70 greatest conspiracies of all time.* Seacus, NJ: Citadel Press/Carol Publishing.

Zepezauer, Mark. (1994). *The CIA's greatest hits.* Tucson, AZ: Odonian Press.

Why Does the Associated Press Change Its Articles?

Russ Kick

The Associated Press is a newswire service that sends stories to 1,700 newspapers and 5,000 radio and TV stations in the US, not to mention an additional 8,500 media outlets in over 100 other countries. A non-profit collective owned by 1,550 daily US newspapers, the AP estimates that its news reaches over a billion people every day. Founded in 1848 and currently employing over 3,500 people, the AP describes itself as "the oldest and largest news organization in the world."

The AP often releases two, three, or more versions of one story on its newswire. The changes usually aren't nefarious. Sometimes a story continues to develop, so the AP updates the original story, then re-releases it with the new information. In other instances, they correct a mistake in an earlier version, or the changes can be for more obscure reasons, such as making the story shorter so more newspapers will run it. Overall, the changes are usually made for legitimate reasons.

A few of the changes are highly suspicious and certainly are of benefit to those in power.

But a few of the changes are highly suspicious and certainly are of benefit to those in power. Comparing multiple versions of the same article coming off the AP's wire is a laborious and usually boring process. I was only able do a little bit here and there, but even my very sporadic efforts uncovered some strange goings-on, ranging from changing the phrasing of headlines and key passages all the way to outright deleting damaging information.

When "Threats" Become "Warnings"

The spinning is apparent in an article about Betty Lambuth, a contractor who worked on the White House's email system. Lambuth was told by a member of her team that lots of email—some of it very sensitive—was not being automatically backed up by the system and, thus, was not being searched in response to subpoenas by the Justice Department and Congress. In court papers, Labuth says that when she told White House Office of Administration counsel Mark Lindsay about the problem, he said that she and her staff would be fired, arrested, and jailed if they told anyone.

Labuth's damning testimony was unsealed by a federal court judge, and AP reported on it on March 10, 2000. Two versions of this article appeared—one at 6:47 PM and the second at 10:03 PM. The original, more truthful headline read: "White House Worker Alleges Threats." A few hours later, the headline has become the pathetic, "Warnings Alleged in White House Case." Amazingly the "threats" of termination and jail time had become "warnings" of termination and jail time. Also, notice the way the headline was changed from a strong, active voice to the passive voice. No longer was a White House worker alleging anything—things were being somehow alleged by someone, but we don't know who.

But it wasn't just the headline that changed. Threats also became warnings in the article itself, as we see in the first paragraph:

First version: "In court papers unsealed Friday, a former White House contractor says she was threatened not to reveal a problem with the White House e-mail system that concealed thousands of messages from the Justice Department and congressional investigators."

Second version: "In court papers unsealed Friday, a former White House contractor says she was warned not to reveal a problem with the White House e-mail system that concealed thousands of messages from the Justice Department and congressional investigators."

Here's another change that softens the blow to the White House. First version:

> "I learned that one of the computer e-mail servers, which housed incoming e-mail to much of the Clinton White House staff, approximately 500 individuals, was not being...managed" by the automated records system. The system allows text to be searched in response "to subpoenas and other inquiries," said Lambuth.

Second version:

> "I learned that one of the computer e-mail servers, which housed incoming e-mail to much of the

Clinton White House staff, approximately 500 individuals, was not being...managed" by the automated records system. The system allows text to be searched in response "to subpoenas and other inquiries," said Lambuth, who said the problem stemmed from "an apparent programming error."

The Colombia and/or Disaster Bill

Starting at 8:49 PM on June 29, 2000, AP reporter Alan Fram filed a string of updated articles regarding Congress' passage of a bill that appropriated $11.2 billion for various efforts, including Colombia's alleged struggle against the drug trade, as well as defense spending, disaster relief, and lots of pork projects. By the time the string of articles ended at 5:24 PM the next day, some interesting changes had taken place.

At 2:30 AM, the story was headlined, "Clinton Will Sign Bill For Colombia." At 1:08 PM, it was, "Sen. Passes Colombia, Disaster Bill." Suddenly, it was no longer a bill just about getting involved in an unwinnable civil war in a South American country; it was also about helping victims of disasters. (I suppose you could argue that labeling it a "Colombia, disaster bill" is actually redundant.) By 5:19 PM, the headline was "Congress OKs $11.2 Billion for Colombia, Pentagon, Disasters." This was the same bill, but now the headline proclaimed it was for three things, including national defense.

Not only was the National Security Agency removed from that paragraph, it was removed from the entire article.

The description of what the bill does for Colombia also morphed across the opening sentence of the articles. In the early versions, it was "money for Colombia's drug war;" then it became simply an "emergency measure for Colombia;" before finally it was said to be "financing Colombia's war against drugs."

In the 2:38 AM version—which seems to be least-spun of them all—we find this sentence: "In the end, most members could not resist the election-year largesse it contained for the Long Island Sound's struggling lobster industry, law enforcement along the Arizona-Mexico border, and much in between." That sentence was also in the 1:08 PM version, but it disappeared as of 5:19 PM, being replaced by this sentence: "But legislators also included hundreds of millions for election-year, home-state projects ranging from New York City's proposed Second Avenue subway to the crabbing industry in Alaska, Washington state and Oregon." Of course, this is saying the same thing, but *how* it's said is what's important. The opinionated word "largesse" is gone, as is the slap that "most members could not resist" it. The new, sanitized sentence remained in the final, 5:38 PM version.

The National Security Agency Disappears from an "Alleged" Spy Network

On July 5, 2000, AP released two versions of an article about the European Parliament voting to expand its probe into Echelon, the US-based communications-eavesdropping network that monitors phone calls, faxes, and email worldwide. At 5:33 PM, the headline read, "European Parliament Votes for Wider Probe Into U.S. Spying." The hammer must've come down awfully fast, because when the second version of the article was put on the wire at 6:14 PM, the headline had been softened considerably: "Europe Votes for Wider Probe of Alleged U.S. Spy Network." Ah, so now the spying is merely "alleged." And, more subtly, it's not even US "spying" anymore—it's just a "spy network." They may or may not be actively spying, but the network is there. Allegedly.

The first version starts out: "The European Parliament voted Wednesday to widen a probe into a U.S.-led spy network accused of monitoring billions of phone calls, e-mails and faxes, but denied investigators the right to call witnesses."

But the second version begins: "The European Parliament voted Wednesday to widen a probe into an alleged U.S. spy network that many assembly members say Washington is using to snoop on the businesses of its European allies."

In the second paragraph of the original version, Echelon is identified as "a global satellite eavesdropping service believed to be run chiefly by the U.S. National Security Agency." But in the same paragraph of the second version, Echelon is merely a system "which is believed capable of intercepting billions of phone calls, e-mails and faxes per hour worldwide." Not only was the National Security Agency removed from that paragraph, it was removed from the entire article. People reading the later version of the article—the one that would be picked up by most newspapers—would have no clue as to who might be running Echelon.

Another interesting change occurred regarding the US's acknowledgement of Echelon. In the first version of the article, we learn that, "U.S. intelligence officials have never confirmed its existence, nor do they deny it." But a mere 41 minutes later, the situation had apparently changed: "U.S. intelligence officials have never publicly confirmed the existence of such a system. They have denied eavesdropping on ordinary American and European citizens." Strange, too, that this information was moved from its original place within the eighth paragraph of the article up to the much more prominent position of being the entire third paragraph.

Although the second version of the article is over 30 words shorter than the original, AP was somehow able to find the space to add two exculpatory, completely new paragraphs as a conclusion:

> The motion would have given investigators the power to order witnesses to testify, which the Greens had hoped to use to compel several U.S. officials, including CIA Director George Tenet and Lt. Gen. Michael V. Hayden, head of the National Security Agency, to testify before the committee.
>
> Both have denied reports the United States was involved in spying on Europeans and Americans as part of a satellite surveillance network in testimony to the U.S. Congressional House Intelligence Committee.

Unviewing a Videotape

It registered only a minor blip during the 2000 presidential campaign, but on September 13, 2000, the story broke about a "confidant" of Al Gore who had received documents and a video revealing George W. Bush's debate strategy. The recipient was former congressman Tom Downey, who was helping Gore prepare to debate Bush.

From 3:39 PM to 11:26 PM, the AP released a staggering eight versions of the article on this story. Written by Ron Fournier, the first three versions are headlined "Gore Gets Package of Bush Info." At 6:15 PM, this changes to, "Gore Confidant Gets Bush Package," and it stays this way through the subsequent versions. This isn't a bad thing, since the second headline is more accurate.

The fishy part occurs within the article. All versions of the article contain a timeline of the events from Downey's reception of the package, to his calling his lawyer, to the FBI picking up the package from the lawyer's office. The first five versions contain these sentences:

> He opened the package, which contained a videotape and documents that appeared to relate to the Bush campaign. He played the tape briefly—Miller later said for a few seconds—"which confirmed to Mr. Downey that the materials appeared to relate to Governor Bush's debate preparations." Downey notified Miller...

However, starting with the sixth version (released at 9:00 PM), this admission that Downey watched the tape vanishes:

> He opened the package, which contained a videotape and documents that appeared to relate to the Bush campaign. Downey notified Miller...

The World Bank's Disappearing Sex Slaves

I have come across one case in which there can be absolutely no doubt that a story was changed to protect the powerful. It involves a fairly short article headlined "House Bill Targets Those Involved in International Sex Trade." Published in two versions on May 9, 2000, the article notes that the House of Representatives passed a bill increasing penalties on people who bring foreign women and children into the US and force them into the sex trade.

The article first appeared at 6:49 PM. The whitewashed version appeared at 8:00 PM. Both versions are exactly the same *except* for one portion of a sentence. First, read the eighth paragraph from the original version:

> Smith said he and Rep. Sam Gejdenson, D-Conn., a co-sponsor, recently talked to several women who had been held as "virtual slaves" in the Washington area by foreign diplomats and employees of the World Bank or the International Monetary Fund.

Pretty shocking, eh? This article appeared soon after the big meeting of the IMF and the World Bank in DC in mid-April 2000. According to two US congressmen, women were held against their will and used as sex slaves by the attendees. But that's not what you found out if you read the final version of the article. Here is the complete eight paragraph from the 8:00 PM version:

According to two US congressmen, women were held against their will and used as sex slaves by the attendees.

> Smith said he and Rep. Sam Gejdenson, D-Conn., a co-sponsor, recently talked to several women who had been held as "virtual slaves" in the Washington area.

The phrase, "by foreign diplomats and employees of the World Bank or the International Monetary Fund," was deleted, flushed down the memory hole. That is the one and only change made to the entire article.

What I desperately want to know is: Who called the AP in the intervening hour and got them to yank those fourteen words? Who *really* calls the shots at the AP? Who gets the most prominent print-news organization to change its stories to protect the President, the Congress, the World Bank/IMF, and other powerful parties?

We Distort, You Abide

Diminishing Bisociative Contexts and Expanding Media Technologies

Kenn Thomas

"[Newscaster:] Today, a young man on acid realized that all matter is really energy condensed to a slow vibration, that we are really all one consciousness, there is no such thing as death, life is only a dream, we are the imagination of ourselves. Here's Tom with the weather..."

—*Bill Hicks*

The writer Arthur Koestler coined the phrase "bisociation" as the process by which new insights are gained through correlations between disparate sources. He examined the idea in his magnum opus trilogy: *The Sleepwalkers* (London, 1959), *The Act of Creation* (1964), and *The Ghost in the Machine* (1967). As one example, Koestler used a controversy concerning astronomical measurements in 1796 contributing to the science of neurophysiology, motor and sensory nerve impulses, 50 years later.[1] Robert Anton Wilson pointed out that "electricity and magnetism were two different subjects before James C. Maxwell, whose bisociation into electromagnetism is as basic to modern physics as Einstein's bisociation of space and time into space-time."[2] Koestler identified bisociation with scientific development; students of conspiracy have often used it as a tool to get beyond the compliant media.[3]

Mel Gibson's conspiracy-obsessed character Jerry Fletcher, in the movie *Conspiracy Theory*, demonstrates—rather, parodies—the technique by highlighting a pair of headlines in a newspaper—"Shuttle Launch Set for October" and "President Set to Visit Turkey"—and making a bisociative connection. Fletcher explains later that six major earthquakes in the past three-and-a-half years coincided with Space Shuttle orbits, and speculates that a seismic weapon may be used by the currently orbiting shuttle on the President's plane as it lands on an earthquake during a planned trip to Turkey.[4] At movie's end, Jerry Fletcher finds himself safely in the hands of the intelligence community, the assumed good guys as usual, an irony that underscores the current threat to bisociative learning in parapolitics.

Famous bisociative connections include the subtexts of the biographies of Aristotle Onassis and Howard Hughes. Researcher Bruce Roberts, ostensibly using his own insider information, amassed data suggesting both were high-stakes global manipulators and that Onassis kidnapped Hughes. That theory, called the Gemstone thesis, illuminates what conspiracy students understand about the international mob, and became the subject of a half-dozen books. (See: *Inside the Gemstone File*, by Kenn Thomas and David Hatcher Childress.)

Perhaps the most obvious of bisociations has to do with Lee Harvey Oswald, whose life and career followed the path of the U2 spy plane. He served at the Atsugi airbase in Japan; possibly gave the Soviets information on the U2 that they used to shoot down Gary Powers; and worked at a film-processing lab that handled U2 film before getting a job at the book depository. Those facts, bisociated with what appeared about Oswald in the press, gave the lie to the Warren Commission. It took the bisociative efforts of famed conspiracy researcher Sherman Skolnick to come up with the fact that E. Howard Hunt's wife Dorothy was on the plane that crashed near the Midway airport in 1973 before anyone made the connection to Watergate.

The corporate media, defined less now as television/radio and newspapers/magazines than as the Internet and digital technology, has never offered more than barely rewritten government pronouncements as news and shallow entertainments designed primarily to promote consumer commodities.

The corporate media, defined less now as television/radio and newspapers/magazines than as the Internet and digital technology, has never offered more than barely rewritten government pronouncements as news and shallow entertainments designed primarily to promote consumer commodities. Gibson's movie, like all videos, falls into the latter category, a quick-rental critique of the conspiracy culture that leaves the international cops in firm control. Bill Hicks' example[5] is but a small one of the wide range of reality that goes un- and under-reported by the supposedly all-encompassing and high-powered media. The bisociative idea provides one way to shake

The bisociative idea provides one way to shake loose true informational content from that daily barrage, by shifting contexts and reading between connections.

loose true informational content from that daily barrage, by shifting contexts and reading between connections.

Computer enthusiasts touted the digital environment as another promising way, and the community of conspiracy researchers that joined it enjoyed some success before being thoroughly demonized. The new technology did little to stop the consolidation of corporate control, however, with fewer and fewer corporate entities controlling more and more pseudo-content, all of it seemingly dominated by a global military state. At a time when shifting bisociative contexts should abound, the World Wide Web resembles more the outmoded newsstand, with every magazine reporting the same news from the same angle, or the uniform coverage of the three TV networks in the days before cable. The proliferation of news networks and their accompanying Websites was an expansion of form, not an addition of information and perspective. Despite an underground of researchers and homegrown investigators that continue to struggle mightily on the Internet, the monolith dominates.

That fix is in, and even the slightest examination of developing digital technologies demonstrates that not only has the informed citizen not been given the expected expanded context in which to bisociate, he/she has been given the new burden of a more sophisticated invasive spy technology. The PROMIS software remains in the conspiracy lore as among the best-known of two-way computer systems, sold illegally to police agencies around the world with a backdoor that centralized snooping on those very agencies.[6]

The proliferation of news networks and their accompanying Websites was an expansion of form, not an addition of information and perspective.

Similar backdoor surveillance technologies appeared in everyday computer browsers, reported upon and exposed twice in the mainstream press,[7] and yet according to the conspiracy grapevine still exist.[8] As the confluence of computers and television continues its course, office workers learn on the TV news that employers not only can spy on them through their desktops, but do so and have every legal right. Another measure of that confluence is the common response to the notion that nothing truly subversive can pass through cyberspace: "So what? I never think or do anything subversive on the computer anyway!"

David Burke, editor of an anti-television zine in Britain called *White Dot* and author of a book entitled *SPY TV*, which calls for a boycott of the new interactive digital television,[9] argues against its capacity to create electronic files compiling information about viewers' watching and buying habits. Such information comprises "telegraphics," demographics gathered for the purpose of creating psychographic profiles for the purpose of marketing. Burke quotes one digital television consultant as saying, "What we're trying to do is change or reinforce behavior." This is the language of the Behaviorists, psychologists responsible for the "rat-o-morphic" view of man (in the language of their great critic, Arthur Koestler, in *The Ghost in the Machine*), and is, of course, nothing new to digital TV.[10] Television has always served this function for the advertising industry and society in general.

Burke suggests that the new digital cable, now more commonly available than the cable systems that replaced broadcast television, not only has the previous capacity to transmit subliminals but also to receive feedback from the transmission directly. Burke wants a digital boycott until the industry satisfies six demands for viewer privacy outlined in his book. "They're just the conditions of ownership most viewers thought they were getting anyway." So far any similar effort initiated on behalf of computer users under the same threat to their privacy apparently awaits further convergence of TV and PC technology.

Perhaps more important in preserving future bisociative contexts than the effort to collect information on a docile population (or, alternately, assuring that docility via the threat of constant surveillance) is the massive military intelligence operation to conceal and cover up its criminal past. An executive order signed by Bill Clinton in 1995 (order number 12958) ostensibly requires the declassification of all documents older than 25 years, a US equivalent of the UK's 30-year rule (which is often called the UK's only equivalent of the US's Freedom of Information Act). The order contained the expected exemptions for national security purposes[11] but otherwise held great promise for historical study.

In response, the Army promptly created a new office, the Army Declassification Activity (ADA), hired a private technology services contractor called Kajax Engineering, and by 1999 had dumped 92 million meaningless financial records on the National Archives in College Park, Maryland. Writer Joshua Dean notes that "the remaining documents must be read one by one, because they could reveal information on weapons systems, covert operations or other topics that would hurt national security," precisely the kind of information that students of conspiracy and parapolitics value.

Dean describes the CIA's Image Workflow Automation system, a new digital means to redact documents, replacing the old-fashioned magic-marker approach. "The system has redaction tools that let the declassifiers black out words, sentences, sections or even entire pages.... Once this occurs, the system completely obliterates the text that has been redacted and stores the file to await the next periodic release to the Archives.... The agency has built up its program with technology designed to keep secrets secret."[12] Despite this streamlined destruction of information, by 1999 the CIA had reviewed only 5.2 million documents and released to the archives only 3.4 million from a backlog of 66 million. Intelligence teams work full-time daily making sure nothing of significance is released as part of the declassification process.

Intelligence teams work full-time daily making sure nothing of significance is released as part of the declassification process.

This would be a scandal in a culture with a free press, but if the digital revolution has the corporate media doing anything more than waiting for press releases from the CIA about the documents it does decide to parcel out, it remains hard to tell. As the new competitor to CNN, the Fox News Channel, declaring its ersatz objectivity with the phrase "We Report, You Decide," mimics form and content from the other cable services, although often blending the forms of government-issue news and shallow talk shows. Former CBS broadcaster Paula Zahn, for instance, packages her chatter on Fox as being on *The Edge*, as she calls her show. *Hannity & Colmes* continues the kind of false dialogue of neoconservatism and pseudo-leftism proffered for many years on CNN's *Crossfire*. To make it interactive, each program includes email feedback and has its own Webpage.

Perhaps the Fox Network's worst culprit, however, is Bill O'Reilly. O'Reilly's self-important *O'Reilly Factor* program, named as if the opinions of the host—who has an unfortunate resemblance to the clownish newscaster of the old *Mary Tyler Moore Show*, Ted Baxter—"factored in" on any issue he defines as nationally important. In a rare moment, O'Reilly recently featured writer Jim Marrs, a respected scholar of conspiracy history[13] whose new book, *Rule By Secrecy*, outlines some of the secret fraternal and social groups in US politics. The interview not only reflected Jim Marrs' superb scholarship, but it exposed the extent to which corporate broadcasters such as O'Reilly know about, cover up, and accept as inevitable abusive, conspiracy-dominated power relations:

Bill O'Reilly: What is the purpose of these organizations?

Jim Marrs: To push the same agenda that they're pushing right now, which is globalization.

BO: ...[T]o have everybody to come into a common economy and a common way of thinking. Now, we've heard of the Council on Foreign Relations. Why do you say that's a secret society?

JM: Because you can't just walk off the street and join.

BO: You have to be invited, like any country club.

JM: That's exactly right, and according to the bylaws, you're not supposed to talk about what they discuss. And yes, unlike most country clubs, this is a club made up of people who are shaping the destiny of this country.

BO: They want discretion in the sense that these are powerful people, Henry Kissinger and Alan Greenspan, but we called the Council on Foreign Relations and they say that Al Gore was never a member.

JM: It may be that the material I got referred to Al Gore, Sr...

BO: But you should know that, should you not?

JM: ...[B]ut he's definitely closely connected to all these same people.

BO: You should know whether Al Gore, if you're going to say this in the book, that he was member, you should know whether he was or not, shouldn't you?

JM: It's true. According to the information I have, he was a member before he became a part of the administration.

BO: Again, we'll tell the audience that the Council of Foreign Relations says he is not. Now, even if he was a member of this organization, why is that a bad thing?

JM: It's not necessarily a bad thing. My thing is that they are pushing for this international, global, one-world economy, one-world government, one-world military, being pushed along in secrecy. We don't get to vote on it. I never got to vote on the World Trade Organization.

BO: They're a bunch of old guys sitting around, let's be frank about it, saying all kinds of things they want to say. They have no influence on whether...there's never going to be a one-world military. Let's get to Skull and Bones, because a lot of people have heard of that. This is a Yale thing. We know that George W. Bush and his father, President Bush, were both members. But this is like a fraternity, so what's the big deal here?

"Unlike most country clubs, this is a club made up of people who are shaping the destiny of this country."

JM: That's right. But if you look at the odds of this one fraternity fielding dozens and dozens of high-ranking officials. You go look at any other fraternity and you're not going to find that. This has been styled, and the facts seem to point to it, that it's a stepping stone into this world elite that is in control.

BO: Is there anything wrong with that?

JM: I don't know. My thing is—they say this is the way towards peace and prosperity. I'm not going to argue with that.

BO: It's always been old money that's stuck together. Look, George W. Bush made a lot of money because of his father, President Bush. He had a lot of opportunity, but that's always the way it is! It's the rich guys get richer and the poor guys have to make it on their own! That's America!

JM: But all these rich guys are now pushing for a global economy, a global system of government...

BO: Well, Clinton's pushing for that. He's not a rich guy. The only society he's in is chasing babes.

JM: Where is the guarantee that if they achieve this globalization that some Hitler-like tyrant won't gain control?

BO: Nah. I don't see either of those things as being scary or nefarious.

JM: Just an old boys' network, eh?

BO: Look, you go to Yale, the Yale people take care of you. I'm in the Harvard Club, right? If I need a favor from some guy at Harvard, he's more inclined to do it than if my name is Vinnie and he doesn't know me.

JM: Exactly. That's my point.

BO: But that's America!

JM: But how does this help the guy down in Odessa, Texas?

BO: It doesn't help him.

JM: Well, then, shouldn't we at least point out that they're part of that old-boy network?

BO: I don't mind that you point it out, but I do think that you should have ID'd whether Al Gore was a member of the Council of Foreign Relations or not. But we appreciate you coming in here, Mr. Marrs.

JM: I did check with their material.

Bill O'Reilly's only investigative work here was to call for the official denial by CFR of Al Gore's membership. Such cooperation between the new digital cable TV news apparatus and the old power hierarchies reflects the small extent to which changing technologies alter the flow of information, the potential for adding contexts for bisociative exploration notwithstanding, for the better.

While students of conspiracy no doubt find the expanding media technologies disappointing, they remain phenomena to be studied cautiously, whether manifested as new global surveillance technologies, bloated intelligence bureaucracies feverishly ferreting out and censoring important information from the historic record on a mass scale, or compliant newsmen insisting against all democratic tradition that, "That's America!"[14]

Endnotes

1. Koestler, Arthur. (1964). *The act of creation*. Macmillan, pp 230-231. **2.** Wilson, Robert Anton. (1998). *Everything is under control*. HarperPerennial, p 82. **3.** Chief Executive Bill Clinton proved himself to be one such student. At the height of the Monica Lewinsky scandal, the President compared himself to Rubashov, the protagonist of Koestler's 1940 novel, *Darkness at Noon*. In the novel, Rubashov fell victim of a purge trial by a thinly-disguised, Red-fascist Soviet state he had previously served. When Clinton aide Sidney Blumenthal attempted to spread disinformation to his friend Christopher Hitchens that Lewinsky actually was stalking the President, Hitchens commented, "Sidney's account as given to Starr is the same as I remember except that to me he left out Clinton's breathtaking claim to be the victim and prisoner in Arthur Koestler's *Darkness at Noon*." (Hitchens, Christopher. (May 1999). "I'll never eat lunch in this town again." *Vanity Fair*, pp 72-80.) Bisociatively, Clinton's comparison amounted to a confession, as students of parapolitics have long accepted that he rose to power in part by turning a blind eye to the Reagan/Bush/Ollie North guns-and-drugs operation at the airstrip in Mena, Arkansas. The Lewinsky scandal ended with Clinton's re-funding of the wasteful "Star Wars" missile defense system, a Pentagon pocket-liner, and another remarkable bisociative coincidence. UCLA professor Peter Dale Scott and long-respected researcher John Judge have noted the military intelligence connections of principal players in the Lewinsky affair. If, indeed, Clinton had conspired with extra-electoral forces to gain power, similar forces conspired to constrain that power and permanently tainted his presidential legacy. **4.** Nevertheless, serious speculative research has noted the orbital path of the Shuttle appearing curiously in the airspace above such events as the downing of KAL 007 in 1983 and the plane crash over Gambela, Ethiopia, that killed congressional Black caucus member Mickey Leland during the time of his investigation of CIA-front airlines in 1989. **5.** Bill Hicks was a comic genius on the order of Lenny Bruce. Like Bruce, he still has a small "cult" following despite an early death in 1994. He suffered censorship over a Kennedy assassination joke when Letterman moved his show to CBS, a network notorious for its distortion of that event. Hicks understood his own role in commodifying rebellion (a phenomenon he also shared with Bruce and with rock and roll), remarking in one bit, "I know what all the marketing people are thinking right now, too. 'Oh, you know what Bill's doing? He's going for that anti-marketing dollar. That's a good market. He's very smart.'" **6.** A new edition of the book detailing this history, *The Octopus: Secret Government and the Death of Danny Casolaro* (Feral House, 1996), is currently planned. **7.** See: *The Octopus*. **8.** Cryptographer Andrew Fernandes reported that he found in the security subsystems of the Windows operating system what he described as "a back door for the NSA in every copy of Win 95/98/NT4 and Windows 2000." The back door, an encryption key, was labeled "_NSAKEY", suggesting that Microsoft gives the National Security Agency (NSA), which runs the Echelon satellite super-spy system, access to install surveillance components without the authorization of the user. Microsoft denied the allegation, insisting that the label only indicates that the key "satisfies [NSA] security standards." ("MS denies Windows spy key," Wired News, Sept. 7, 1999.) **9.** Burke, David. (2000). *Spy TV*. Slab-O-Concrete Publications, UK. Burke can be reached at dburke@whitedot.org and has Websites at <www.whitedot.org> and <www.spytv.co.uk>. **10.** These social manipulations do not require advanced technology. The wide array of big-money give-away contests used on television and radio, as well as on much food packaging and in casinos throughout the US, is a form of a phenomenon discovered by the Behaviorists: intermittent reward. Behaviorists discovered that rats run mazes faster when the reward at the end of the maze was not guaranteed. **11.** Protected documents include those that might identify intelligence sources; assist in the development of weapons of mass destruction; impair the use of high-tech weapons systems; harm diplomacy; make it harder to protect the president and vice president; and war plans. **12.** Dean, Joshua. (July 2000). "Assault on the mountain." *Government Executive*, pp 52-60. Dean holds out hope that searches of the recently declassified material may yield new information on the CIA's interest in remote viewing, Nazi assets, and the assassination of JFK. **13.** Marrs' book *Crossfire* provided part of the basis for Oliver Stone's movie *JFK*. **14.** *The O'Reilly Factor*, Fox News, June 2000.

The Media and Their Atrocities

Michael Parenti

For the better part of a decade the US public has been bombarded with a media campaign to demonize the Serbian people and their elected leaders. During that time, the US government has pursued a goal of breaking up Yugoslavia into a cluster of small, weak, dependent, free-market principalities. Yugoslavia was the only country in Eastern Europe that would not dismantle its welfare state and public sector economy. It was the only one that did not beg for entry into NATO. It was—and what's left of it, still is—charting an independent course not in keeping with the New World Order.

Of the various Yugoslav peoples, the Serbs were targeted for demonization because they were the largest nationality and the one most opposed to the breakup of Yugoslavia.

Targeting the Serbs

Of the various Yugoslav peoples, the Serbs were targeted for demonization because they were the largest nationality and the one most opposed to the breakup of Yugoslavia. But what of the atrocities they committed? All sides committed atrocities in the fighting that has been encouraged by the Western powers over the last decade, but the reporting has been consistently one-sided. Grisly incidents of Croat and Muslim atrocities against the Serbs rarely made it into the US press, and when they did they were accorded only passing mention.[1]

Meanwhile, Serb atrocities were played up and sometimes even fabricated, as we shall see. Recently, three Croatian generals were indicted by the Hague War Crimes Tribunal for the bombardment and deaths of Serbs in Krajina and elsewhere. Where were the US television crews when these war crimes were being committed? John Ranz, chair of Survivors of the Buchenwald Concentration Camp, USA, asks: Where were the TV cameras when hundreds of Serbs were slaughtered by Muslims near Srebrenica?[2] The official line, faithfully parroted in the US media, is that Bosnian Serb forces committed all the atrocities at Srebrenica.

Are we to trust US leaders and the corporate-owned news media when they dish out atrocity stories? Recall the 500 premature babies whom Iraqi soldiers laughingly ripped from incubators in Kuwait—a story repeated and believed until exposed as a total fabrication years later. During the Bosnian war in 1993, the Serbs were accused of pursuing an official policy of rape. "Go forth and rape," a Bosnian Serb commander supposedly publicly instructed his troops. The source of that story never could be traced. The commander's name was never produced. As far as we know, no such utterance was ever made. Even the *New York Times* belatedly ran a tiny retraction, coyly allowing that, "[T]he existence of 'a systematic rape policy' by the Serbs remains to be proved."[3]

Bosnian Serb forces supposedly raped anywhere from 25,000 to 100,000 Muslim women, according to various stories. The Bosnian Serb army numbered not more than 30,000 or so, many of whom were involved in desperate military engagements. A representative from Helsinki Watch noted that stories of massive Serbian rapes originated with the Bosnian Muslim and Croatian governments and had no credible supporting evidence. Common sense would dictate that these stories be treated with the utmost skepticism—and not be used as an excuse for an aggressive and punitive policy against Yugoslavia.

The "mass rape" propaganda theme was resuscitated in 1999 to justify the continued NATO slaughter of Yugoslavia. A headline in the *San Francisco Examiner* (April 26, 1999) tells us: "Serb Tactic Is Organized Rape, Kosovo Refugees Say." No evidence or testimony is given to support the charge of organized rape. Only at the bottom of the story, in the nineteenth paragraph, do we read that reports gathered by the Kosovo mission of the Organization for Security and Cooperation in Europe found no such organized rape policy. The actual number of rapes were in the dozens, "and not many dozens," according to the OSCE spokesperson. This same story did note in passing that the UN War Crimes Tribunal sentenced a Bosnian Croat military commander to ten years in prison for failing to stop his troops from raping Muslim women in 1993—an atrocity we heard little about when it was happening.

A few-dozen rapes is a few-dozen too many. But can it serve as one of the justifications for a massive war? If Mr. Clinton wanted to stop rapes, he could have begun a little closer to home in Washington, DC, where dozens of rapes occur every month. Indeed, he might be able to alert us to how women are sexually mistreated on Capitol Hill and in the White House itself.

An Albanian woman crossing into Macedonia was eagerly asked by a news crew if she had been forced out by Serb police. She responded: "There were no Serbs. We were frightened of the [NATO] bombs."

The Serbs were blamed for the infamous Sarajevo market massacre. But according to the report leaked out on French TV, Western intelligence knew that it was Muslim operatives who had bombed Bosnian civilians in the marketplace in order to induce NATO involvement. Even international negotiator David Owen, who worked with Cyrus Vance, admitted in his memoir that the NATO powers knew all along that it was a Muslim bomb.[4]

On one occasion, notes Barry Lituchy, the *New York Times* ran a photo purporting to be of Croats grieving over Serbian atrocities when in fact the murders had been committed by Bosnian Muslims. The *Times* printed an obscure retraction the following week.[5]

The propaganda campaign against Belgrade has been so relentless that even prominent personages on the left—who oppose the NATO policy against Yugoslavia—have felt compelled to genuflect before this demonization orthodoxy, referring to unspecified and unverified Serbian "brutality" and "the monstrous Milosevic."[6] Thus they reveal themselves as having been influenced by the very media propaganda machine they criticize on so many other issues. To reject the demonized images of Milosevic and of the Serbian people is not to idealize them or claim that Serb forces are faultless or free of crimes. It is merely to challenge the one-sided propaganda that laid the grounds for NATO's aggression against Yugoslavia.

The Ethnic Cleansing Hype

Up until the NATO bombings began in March 1999, the conflict in Kosovo had taken 2,000 lives altogether from both sides, according to Kosovo Albanian sources. Yugoslavian sources put the figure at 800. Such casualties reveal a civil war, not genocide. Belgrade is condemned for the forced expulsion policy of Albanians from Kosovo. But such expulsions began in substantial numbers only after the NATO bombings, with thousands being uprooted by Serb forces, especially from areas where KLA mercenaries were operating.

While Kosovo Albanians were leaving in great numbers—usually well-clothed and in good health, some riding their tractors, trucks, or cars, many of them young men of recruitment age—they were described as being "slaughtered."

We should keep in mind that tens of thousands also fled Kosovo because it was being mercilessly bombed by NATO, or because it was the scene of sustained ground fighting between Yugoslav forces and the KLA, or because they were just afraid and hungry. An Albanian woman crossing into Macedonia was eagerly asked by a news crew if she had been forced out by Serb police. She responded: "There were no Serbs. We were frightened of the [NATO] bombs."[7] I had to read this in the *San Francisco Guardian*, an alternative weekly, not in the *New York Times* or *Washington Post*.

During the bombings, an estimated 70,000 to 100,000 Serbian residents of Kosovo took flight (mostly north but some to the south), as did thousands of Roma and others.[8] Were the Serbs ethnically cleansing themselves? Or were these people not fleeing the bombing and the ground war? Yet, the refugee tide caused by the bombing was repeatedly used by US warmakers as justification for the bombing, a pressure put on Milosevic to allow "the safe return of ethnic Albanian refugees."[9]

While Kosovo Albanians were leaving in great numbers—usually well-clothed and in good health, some riding their tractors, trucks, or cars, many of them young men of recruitment age—they were described as being "slaughtered." It was repeatedly reported that "Serb atrocities"—not the extensive ground war with the KLA and certainly not the massive NATO bombing—"drove more than one million Albanians from their homes."[10] More recently, there have been hints that Albanian Kosovar refugees numbered nowhere near that figure.

Serbian attacks on KLA strongholds or the forced expulsion of Albanian villagers were described as "genocide." But experts in surveillance photography and wartime propaganda charged NATO with running a "propaganda campaign" on Kosovo that lacked any supporting evidence. State Department reports of mass graves and of 100,000 to 500,000 missing Albanian men "are just ludicrous," according to these independent critics.[11] Their findings were ignored by the major networks and other national media. Early in the war, *Newsday* reported that Britain and France were seriously considering "commando assaults into Kosovo to break the pattern of Serbian massacres of ethnic Albanians."[12] What discernible pattern of massacres? Of course, no commando assaults were put into operation, but the story served its purpose of hyping an image of mass killings.

An ABC *Nightline* show made dramatic and repeated references to the "Serbian atrocities in Kosovo" while offering no specifics. Ted Kopple asked a group of angry Albanian refugees what they had specifically witnessed. They pointed to an old man in their group who wore a wool hat. One of them reenacted what the Serbs had done to him, throwing the man's hat to the ground and stepping on it—"because the Serbs knew that his hat was the most important thing to him." Kopple was appropriately horrified about this "war crime," the only example offered in an hour-long program.

Unsubstantiated references to "mass graves," each purportedly filled with hundreds or even thousands of Albanian victims, repeatedly failed to materialize.

A widely-circulated story in the *New York Times*, headlined "US Report Outlines Serb Attacks in Kosovo," tells us that the State Department issued "the most comprehensive documentary record to date on atrocities." The report concluded that there had been organized rapes and systematic executions. But as one reads further and more closely into the article, one finds that State Department reports of such crimes "depend almost entirely on information from refugee accounts. There was no suggestion that American intelligence agencies had been able to verify, most, or even many, of the accounts...and the word 'reportedly' and 'allegedly' appear throughout the document."[13]

British journalist Audrey Gillan interviewed Kosovo refugees about atrocities and found an impressive lack of evidence or credible specifics. One woman caught him glancing at the watch on her wrist, while her husband told him how all the women had been robbed of their jewelry and other possessions. A spokesman for the UN High Commissioner for Refugees talked of mass rapes and what sounded like hundreds of killings in three villages, but when Gillan pressed him for more precise information, he reduced it drastically to five or six teenage rape victims. But he had not spoken to any witnesses, and admitted that "we have no way of verifying these reports."[14]

Gillan notes that some refugees had seen killings and other atrocities, but there was little to suggest that they had seen it on the scale that was being reported. One afternoon, officials in charge said there were refugees arriving who talked of 60 or more being killed in one village and 50 in another, but Gillan "could not find one eyewitness who actually saw these things happening." Yet every day Western journalists reported "hundreds" of rapes and murders. Sometimes they noted in passing that the reports had yet to be substantiated, but then why were such unverified stories being so eagerly reported in the first place?

The Disappearing "Mass Graves"

After NATO forces occupied Kosovo, the stories about mass atrocities continued fortissimo. The *Washington Post* reported that 350 ethnic Albanians "might be buried in mass graves" around a mountain village in western Kosovo. They "might be" or they might not be. These estimates were based on sources that NATO officials refused to identify. Getting down to specifics, the article mentions "four decomposing bodies" discovered near a large ash heap.[15]

It was repeatedly announced in the first days of the NATO occupation that 10,000 Albanians had been killed (down from the 100,000 and even 500,000 Albanian men supposedly executed during the war). No evidence was ever offered to support the 10,000 figure, nor even to explain how it was arrived at so swiftly and surely while NATO troops were still moving into place and did not occupy but small portions of the province.

Likewise, unsubstantiated references to "mass graves," each purportedly filled with hundreds or even thousands of Albanian victims, repeatedly failed to materialize. Through the summer of 1999, the media hype about mass graves devolved into an occasional unspecified reference. The few sites actually unearthed offered up as many as a dozen bodies or sometimes twice that number, but with no certain evidence regarding causes of death or even the nationality of victims. In some cases there was reason to believe the victims were Serbs.[16]

On April 19, 1999, while the NATO bombings of Yugoslavia were going on, the State Department announced that up to 500,000 Kosovo Albanians were missing and feared dead. On May 16, US Secretary of Defense William Cohen, a former Republican senator from Maine now serving in President Clinton's Democratic Administration, stated that 100,000 military-aged ethnic Albanian men had vanished and might have been killed by the Serbs.[17] Such widely varying but horrendous figures from official sources went unchallenged by the media and by the many liberals who supported NATO's "humanitarian rescue operation." Among these latter were some supposedly progressive members of Congress who seemed to believe they were witnessing another Nazi Holocaust.

On June 17, just before the end of the war, British Foreign Office Minister Geoff Hoon said that "in more than 100 massacres" some 10,000 ethnic Albanians had been killed (down from the 100,000 and 500,000 bandied about by US officials)."[18] A day or two after the bombings stopped, the Associated Press and other news agencies, echoing Hoon, reported that 10,000 Albanians had been killed by the Serbs.[19] No explanation was given as to how this figure was arrived at, especially since not a single war site had yet been investigated and NATO forces had barely begun to move into Kosovo. On August 2, Bernard Kouchner, the United Nations' chief administrator in Kosovo (and organizer of Doctors Without Borders), asserted that about 11,000 bodies had been found in common graves throughout

The team lugged 107,000 pounds of equipment into Kosovo to handle what was called the "largest crime scene in the FBI's forensic history," but it came up with no reports about mass graves.

Kosovo. He cited as his source the International Criminal Tribunal for the Former Republic of Yugoslavia (ICTY). But the ICTY denied providing any such information. To this day, it is not clear how Kouchner came up with his estimate.[20]

As with the Croatian and Bosnian conflicts, the image of mass killings was hyped once again. Repeatedly, unsubstantiated references to "mass graves," each purportedly filled with hundreds or even thousands of Albanian victims, were publicized in daily media reports. In September 1999, Jared Israel did an Internet search for newspaper articles, appearing over the previous three months, including the words "Kosovo" and "mass grave." The report came back: "More than 1,000—too many to list. " Limiting his search to articles in the *New York Times*, he came up with 80, nearly one a day. Yet when it came down to hard evidence, the mass graves seemed to disappear.

Thus, in mid-June, the FBI sent a team to investigate two of the sites listed in the war-crimes indictment against Slobodan Milosevic, one purportedly containing six victims and the other 20. The team lugged 107,000 pounds of equipment into Kosovo to handle what was called the "largest crime scene in the FBI's forensic history," but it came up with no reports about mass graves. Not long after, on July 1, the FBI team returned home, oddly with not a word to say about their investigation.[21]

Forensic experts from other NATO countries had similar experiences. A Spanish forensic team, for instance, was told to prepare for at least 2,000 autopsies, but found only 187 bodies, usually buried in individual graves, and showing no signs of massacre or torture. Most seemed to have been killed by mortar shells and firearms. One Spanish forensic expert, Emilio Perez Puhola, acknowledged that his team did not find one mass grave. He dismissed the widely publicized references about mass graves as being part of the "machinery of war propaganda."[22]

In late August 1999, the *Los Angeles Times* tried to salvage the genocide theme with a story about how the wells of Kosovo might be "mass graves in their own right." The *Times* claimed that "many corpses have been dumped into wells in Kosovo.... Serbian forces apparently stuffed...many bodies of ethnic Albanians into wells during their campaign of terror."[23] Apparently? Whenever the story got down to specifics, it dwelled on only one village and only one well—in which one body of a 39-year-old male was found, along with three dead cows and a dog. Neither his nationality nor cause of death was given. Nor was it clear who owned the well. "No other human remains were discovered, " the *Times* lamely concluded. As far as I know, neither the *Los Angeles Times* nor any other media outlet ran any more stories of wells stuffed with victims.

In one grave site after another, bodies were failing to materialize in any substantial numbers—or any numbers at all. In July 1999, a mass grave in Ljubenic, near Pec (an area of concerted fighting)—believed to be holding some 350 corpses—produced only seven after the exhumation. In Djacovica, town officials claimed that 100 ethnic Albanians had been murdered, but there were no bodies because the Serbs had returned in the middle of the night, dug them up, and carted them away, the officials seemed to believe. In Pusto Selo, villagers claimed that 106 men were captured and killed by Serbs at the end of March, but again no remains were discovered. Villagers once more suggested that Serb forces must have come back and removed them. How they accomplished this without being detected was not explained. In Izbica, refugees reported that 150 ethnic Albanians were executed in March. But their bodies were nowhere to be found. In Kraljan, 82 men were supposedly killed, but investigators found not a single cadaver.[24]

The worst incident of mass atrocities ascribed to Yugoslavian leader Slobodan Milosevic allegedly occurred at the Trepca mine. As reported by US and NATO officials, the Serbs threw 1,000 or more bodies down the shafts or disposed of them in the mine's vats of hydrochloric acid. In October 1999, the ICTY released the findings of Western forensic teams investigating Trepca. Not one body was found in the mine shafts, nor was there any evidence that the vats had ever been used in an attempt to dissolve human remains.[25]

By late autumn of 1999, the media hype about mass graves had fizzled noticeably. The many sites unearthed, considered to be the most notorious, offered up a few-hundred bodies altogether, not the thousands or tens of thousands or hundreds of thousands previously trumpeted, and with no evidence of torture or mass execution. In many cases, there was no certain evidence regarding the nationality of victims.[26] No mass killings means that the Hague War Crimes Tribunal indictment of Milosevic "becomes highly questionable," notes Richard Gwyn. "Even more questionable is the West's continued punishment of the Serbs."[27]

No doubt there were graves in Kosovo that contained two or more persons (which is NATO's definition of a "mass grave"). People were killed by bombs and by the extensive land war that went on between

A Spanish forensic team was told to prepare for at least 2,000 autopsies, but found only 187 bodies, usually buried in individual graves, and showing no signs of massacre or torture.

Yugoslav and KLA forces. Some of the dead, as even the *New York Times* allowed, "are fighters of the Kosovo Liberation Army or may have died ordinary deaths"—as would happen in any large population over time.[28] And no doubt there were grudge killings and summary executions as in any war, but not on a scale that would warrant the label of genocide and justify the massive death and destruction and the continuing misery inflicted upon Yugoslavia by the Western powers.

In contrast to its public assertions, the German Foreign Office privately denied there was any evidence that genocide or ethnic cleansing was ever a component of Yugoslav policy.

■ ■ ■ ■ ■ ■ ■ ■ ■ ■ ■

We should remember that the propaganda campaign waged by NATO officials and the major media never claimed merely that atrocities (murders and rapes) occurred. Such crimes occur in every war and, indeed, in many communities during peacetime. What the media propaganda campaign against Yugoslavia charged was that mass atrocities and mass rapes and mass murders had been perpetrated, that is, genocide, as evidenced by mass graves.

In contrast to its public assertions, the German Foreign Office privately denied there was any evidence that genocide or ethnic cleansing was ever a component of Yugoslav policy: "Even in Kosovo, an explicit political persecution linked to Albanian ethnicity is not verifiable.... The actions of the [Yugoslav] security forces [were] not directed against the Kosovo-Albanians as an ethnically defined group, but against the military opponent and its actual or alleged supporters."[29]

Still, Milosevic was indicted as a war criminal, charged with the forced expulsion of Kosovar Albanians and with summary executions of a hundred or so individuals—again, alleged crimes that occurred after the NATO bombing had started, yet were used as justification for the bombing. The biggest war criminal of all is NATO and the political leaders who orchestrated the aerial campaign of death and destruction. But here is how the White House and the US media reasoned at the time: Since the aerial attacks do not intend to kill civilians, then presumably there is no liability and no accountability, only an occasional apology for the regrettable mistakes—as if only the intent of an action counted and not its ineluctable effects. In fact, a perpetrator can be judged guilty of willful murder without explicitly intending the death of a particular victim—as when the death results from an unlawful act that the perpetrator knew would likely cause death. George Kenney, a former State Department official under the Bush Administration, put it well: "Dropping cluster bombs on highly populated urban areas doesn't result in accidental fatalities. It is purposeful terror bombing."[30]

In sum, through a process of monopoly control and distribution, repetition, and image escalation, the media achieve self-confirmation, that is, they find confirmation for the images they fabricate in the images they have already fabricated. Hyperbolic labeling takes the place of evidence: "genocide," "mass atrocities," "systematic rapes," and even "rape camps"—camps which no one has ever located. Through this process, evidence is not only absent, it becomes irrelevant.

So the US major media (and much of the minor media) are not free and independent, as they claim; they are not the watchdog of democracy but the lapdog of the national security state. They help reverse the roles of victims and victimizers, warmongers and peacekeepers, reactionaries and reformers. The first atrocity, the first war crime committed in any war of aggression by the aggressors is against the truth.

Endnotes

1. For instance, Bonner, Raymond. (1999). "War crimes panel finds Croat troops 'cleansed' the Serbs." *New York Times*, March 21, a revealing report that has been ignored in the relentless propaganda campaign against the Serbs. **2.** John Ranz in his paid advertisement in the *New York Times*, April 29, 1993. **3.** Anonymous. (1993). "Correction: Report on rape in Bosnia." *New York Times*, October 23. **4.** Owen, David. (1997). *Balkan odyssey*. Harvest Books, p. 262. **5.** Lituchy, Barry. "Media deception and the Yugoslav civil war," in *NATO in the Balkans*, p. 205; see also *New York Times*, August 7, 1993. **6.** Both Noam Chomsky in his comments on Pacifica Radio, April 7, 1999, and Alexander Cockburn in *The Nation*, May 10, 1999, describe Milosevic as "monstrous" without offering any specifics. **7.** Biggs, Brooke Shelby. (1999). "Failure to inform." *San Francisco Bay Guardian*, May 5, p. 25. **8.** *Washington Post*, June 6, 1999. **9.** See for instance, Robert Burns, Associated Press report, April 22, 1999. **10.** For example, *New York Times*, June 15, 1998. **11.** Radin, Charles & Louise Palmer. (1999). "Experts voice doubts on claims of genocide: Little evidence for NATO assertions." *San Francisco Chronicle*, April 22. **12.** *Newsday*, March 31, 1999. **13.** *New York Times*, May 11, 1999. **14.** Gillan, Audrey. (1999). "What's the story?" *London Review of Books*, May 27. **15.** *Washington Post*, July 10, 1999. **16.** See for instance, Gall, Carlotta. (1999). "Belgrade sees grave site as proof NATO fails to protect Serbs." *New York Times*, August 27. **17.** Both the State Department and Cohen's figures are reported in the *New York Times*, November 11, 1999. **18.** *New York Times*, November 11, 1999. **19.** Associated Press release, June 18, 1999. Reuters (July 12, 1999) reported that NATO forces had catalogued more than 100 sites containing the bodies of massacred ethnic Albanians. **20.** Stratfor.com, Global Intelligence Update. (1999). "Where are Kosovo's killing fields?" *Weekly Analysis*, October 18. **21.** Irvine, Reed & Cliff Kincaid. (1999). "Playing the numbers game." Accuracy in Media Website <www.aim.org/mm/1999/08/03.htm>. **22.** *London Sunday Times*, October 31, 1999. **23.** *Los Angeles Times*, August 28, 1999. **24.** *Op cit.*, Stratfor.com. **25.** Richard Gwyn in the *Toronto Star*, November 3, 1999. **26.** *Op cit.*, Gall. **27.** Richard Gwyn in the *Toronto Star*, November 3, 1999. **28.** *New York Times*, November 11, 1999. **29.** Intelligence reports from the German Foreign Office, January 12, 1999, and October 29, 1998, to the German Administrative Courts, translated by Eric Canepa, Brecht Forum, New York, April 20, 1999. **30.** Teach-in, Leo Baeck Temple, Los Angeles, May 23, 1999.

Making Molehills Out of Mountains

How the US Media Downplay and Distort the Conflict in Northern Ireland

Marni Sullivan

When most people think of Northern Ireland, they think of Catholics and Protestants hating each other and of mindless IRA bombings. Most people, especially Americans, seem to believe that a great deal of the trouble comes from religious intolerance. Much of this stereotype results from a lack of understanding of the issues, which in turn results from a lack of information. America's perception of the Northern Ireland conflict is incomplete at best.

The conflict is an extremely complex affair that rarely receives accurate depiction in the media, especially the news coverage that reaches the United States. The most coverage the American people have seen about Northern Ireland started in 1996 when the Canary Wharf bombing ended the 1994 ceasefire, and extends to the present day. During this time period, a lot of information has been misrepresented, omitted, or perhaps just overlooked in US media coverage. Incidentally, the public opinion of what occurs in Northern Ireland is a fairly shallow one. To understand what is actually happening there, one has to know the history of the country and the political agenda of each party involved.

Perhaps the best place to start is with the major parties—who they are and what they actually represent. The key figures are the Unionist (or Loyalist) Party and the Nationalist (or Republican) Party. The Loyalist Party represents those who want Northern Ireland to remain under England's power. The term "Unionist" refers to the party's belief that Northern Ireland should remain united under England's rule. The terrorist arm of this party is the Ulster Volunteer Force (UVF), which gave birth to a more radical splinter group called the Loyalist Volunteer Force (LVF).

The Nationalist Party, also referred to as the Republican Party, represents those who feel that Northern Ireland should be adjoined with the Republic of Ireland. The political group that supports this aim is Sinn Fein, which is often misconstrued as the "political arm of the IRA." The IRA, of course, is the Irish Republican Army—the terrorist group that supports the Nationalist cause. Sinn Fein did have close ties with the IRA back in 1922, when the first faction of the IRA (called the Official IRA) managed to break 26 of Ireland's 32 counties away from England. The Official IRA has more or less become a political party in and of itself. However, in 1969, which marked the beginning of the strife in Northern Ireland (often referred to as "the Troubles"), there was a split in the IRA. Some of the members felt the Official IRA became too political in nature, and they formed the Provisional IRA. This is the group that is referred to as the IRA by the news media. There was quite a bit of distancing between Sinn Fein and the Provisional IRA when these disagreements took place.

Sinn Fein does not know or govern the actions of the IRA, which is something the media overlook time and time again.

In other words, Sinn Fein does not know or govern the actions of the IRA, which is something the media overlook time and time again.

Turning back to the larger viewpoint, it should be pointed out that international affairs receive very little coverage in America in relation to national and local interests. (The only time extensive analysis and examination of international conflicts occur is when the United States has become directly involved.) Televised news offers a very brief and condensed report on such matters. With regard to Northern Ireland, we are only informed of the "major events." An article in the *Los Angeles Times* focused on a program between Northern Ireland and the United States coupling British Protestant teens with Irish Catholic teens to encourage communication and friendship between the two groups. What was interesting was how the article examined the reactions of the participants to the lack of coverage on US television during their stay here:

> The youngsters who spent their summer here say it was strange to watch events in Northern Ireland through the prism of American TV. "You see it here and it seems so big. They only televise the big events," said Joanne McCracken. "At home, it's like we see it every day. Every roadblock, every detail."[1]

Many events are uncovered even where conflict, injury, or death result; they don't draw as much attention as the bombings, since the murders occur on a singular basis. The media seem more interested in reporting those things that result in the death of many people at one time.

Aside from the fleeting five-minute blurbs on major network television news, only five papers in this country offer any direct coverage of the Northern Ireland conflict: the *New York Times*, *Boston Globe*, *Chicago Tribune*, *Los Angeles Times*, and *Washington Post*. This leaves a few major newspapers and the potential biases of their writers as the only source of written documentation on which Americans can form opinions. Furthermore, most of the major Irish newspapers are not readily available on the newsstands in this country. The few that are (such as the *Irish Times*) are not based in Northern Ireland. This means it is very difficult to get direct coverage from the source of the conflict. The Internet offers more availability for international newspapers, but without direct radio or television coverage of foreign affairs, most Americans would not be inclined to research such events on their own.

Lack of coverage is only one of the problems. Misrepresentation and slanted perspectives on the conflict play a big factor in America's confusion on the matter. A large part of this results from language bias, including the repetition of key words that either downplay the importance of a certain factor or indirectly place the blame solely on one party. The consistent use of "Catholics" and "Protestants" in these reports, be they in newspapers or on television, leads the reader to believe that the Northern Ireland conflict is primarily a religious issue, a conclusion that could not be further from the truth. The dissent generated by Catholic and Protestant differences is only a small factor of a much larger problem that has little to do with religion; rather, it deals with country and political alliance. The English gravitate toward the Protestant beliefs, while the Irish are predominantly Catholic. As such, the religious differences help to draw a thicker line between "us" and "them," even though they are largely irrelevant. Thus, it would be better to indicate the parties involved by ethnicity (Irish and British) or by political party (Nationalist and Unionist). Issues between the British (the Unionist/Loyalist parties) and the Irish (the Nationalist/Republican parties) come from a long and bloody history of hostile occupation and struggle for independence.

Kevin Cullen of the *Boston Globe* summed up the adversity between the two factions:

> Catholic nationalists see themselves as the oppressed minority, unfairly cut off from their compatriots in the south by the Anglo-Irish Treaty of 1921 that gave independence to 26 of Ireland's 32 counties. Protestant unionists, whose ancestors were imported to Ireland four centuries ago by a British government determined to install a loyal population, believe they are just as entitled to the land as the settlers who pushed aside Native Americans.[2]

The dissent generated by Catholic and Protestant differences is only a small factor of a much larger problem that has little to do with religion; rather, it deals with country and political alliance.

Since the 1921 treaty, there have been many oppressive measures placed upon the native Irish by the ruling English, and the British immigrants found themselves thrown in the middle.

Perhaps the most intense bias involved in the media's perspective concerns the IRA's responsibility in the terrorist activity in Northern Ireland. When the IRA cease-fire ended with the bombing of Canary Wharf in 1996, a slew of news reports came in stating that the IRA would single-handedly destroy the peace process in Northern Ireland. The *Boston Globe* stated, "Just hours after the IRA announced Friday night that it had abandoned its 17-month cease-fire, the trappings of pre-truce Belfast returned for the first time in more than a year. Police donned bullet-proof vests, security checkpoints sprang up and British soldiers, long confined to barracks, were on the streets again."[3] Within the next five days, the *Washington Post* reported, "a 500 pound IRA bomb killed two people...bringing an abrupt end to a lengthy peace process aimed at negotiating a lasting settlement to 25 years of sectarian strife in Northern Ireland."[4]

This narrow viewpoint on the bombing leaves one with the distinct impression that the IRA, without purpose or concern, just destroyed seventeen months of work toward a worthy cause. This article trivializes, if not completely discounts, the IRA's position. Other articles from Ireland, as well as documentation of meetings regarding the many promises England made leading to the cessation, have shown that the cease-fire ended primarily over "breach of contract." (For example, see *The Nation*, *The Irish Voice*, and Sinn Fein's Website.)

In the United States, I found only one periodical, *The Nation*, that ran an article revealing the failings of the English government to uphold its promises to the Nationalists. When the cessation was declared in 1994, it was instated under the condition that talks between all of the political parties toward a settlement would immediately take place. However, Prime Minister John Major started with a three-month stall because he deemed the IRA's intentions as "untrustworthy," even though the cease-fire had begun. This was just the first of many broken promises. There was a promise that Nationalist political prisoners would be released for the cessation, as well. Not only did Major renege on that promise, he added insult to injury by releasing Clegg, "a British soldier only two years into a life sentence for the murder of a Catholic girl in Belfast."[5]

After several months of prolonged silence on Major's end, coupled by rising tensions within the IRA, the White House got involved and tried to help the process. President Clinton visited Northern Ireland at the end of 1995, thus prompting Major to reschedule talks in February, which also never took place. Impatience rose on the Loyalist side, as well. In January, the head of the INLA (Irish National Liberation Army) was killed in Belfast. The end of the cease-fire was near.

One last-ditch effort was made to fix the rapid deterioration of the peace process, as reported by *The Nation*:

> On February 4, Mitchell warned that continued intransigence from London would lead to a fracture in the IRA's cease-fire consensus. Just hours before the London bomb went off, Irish Foreign Minister Dick Spring was appealing once again for Dayton-style talks to move the peace process forward and again Major wanted none of it.[6]

Many factors could have played into Major's decisions, but *The Nation's* viewpoint took a critical stance on it: "The bombing was an indefensible military response to the corruption and recklessness of a politician who was willing to torpedo the peace to keep his job."[7]

This clearly states that British politics endangered Northern Ireland's chance for peace. However, such concise and precise use of terms is not common. Language bias tends to imply that most or all of the violence in Northern Ireland can be blamed on the IRA, even regarding activities for which it was not responsible. A primary example is the Omagh bombing that took place in August 1998, one of the worst attacks recorded in the history of "the Troubles." This bombing was carried out by a group of dissidents who were not members of the IRA. While it is arguable that the leader of the party was once a member of the IRA, their actions were far more reckless and miscalculated than IRA actions, and resulted in deaths to both Irish and British civilians. However, the group in question was referred to as "an IRA splinter group opposed to the Peace Plan" by the *Washington Post*.[8] Even though the IRA had no involvement in the bombing, this terminology still links the IRA to this action and gives the reader the direct impression that all mayhem in Northern Ireland is ultimately the responsibility of the IRA. This adds further unwarranted stigma to the Nationalist Party.

The strongest example of media bias in the Northern Ireland conflict is best illustrated by the lack of coverage pertaining to the terrorist activities of British Loyalists. When the IRA bomb was released in Canary Wharf, a group of Loyalists retaliated by assaulting a disabled citizen in order to obtain his car. When the man refused to cooperate, the group became more violent. The man fled into his home, and a member of the group fired a shot into his place of residence.[9]

Many shootings have taken place in Northern Ireland by Loyalist groups, but they are rarely covered, since only one to two people may be injured or killed versus many in a bomb blast. The *Boston Globe* reports, "Loyalists have said they are a reaction to the IRA, an assertion that seemed disingenuous in recent years as they began targeting innocent Catholics rather than IRA members or sympathizers. In the three years leading to the cease-fire, loyalists killed more people than the IRA."[10] The fact that Loyalists have a tendency to single out innocent civilians more than IRA affiliates was further brought to light by a tragedy that took place in early July 1998. In a residence in Ballymoney, a suburb of Belfast, Loyalist dissidents had burned three young boys to death by throwing a firebomb into their home while they watched television. The *Atlanta Journal* explained, "Police and neighbors speculate that the boys were targeted because their mother was a Catholic living with a Protestant in a predominantly Protestant housing project." All three of the boys were between the ages of nine and eleven.[11]

Another murder by Loyalists that managed to make it to a US newspaper was the murder of Terry Enwright in Belfast in January 1998. Enwright was an apolitical man who did social work and worked part-time as a doorman at a club. He was respected in his community by both Protestants and Catholics. The reasons for his death were most likely linked to his marriage to the niece of Gerry Adams, president of Sinn Fein. Enwright's death, however, managed to unite a community instead of resulting in further segregation. Both English and Irish residents took part in the funeral procession. The *Washington Post* reported, "Participants said it was the biggest funeral since the 1981 burial service for Bobby Sands, an Irish nationalist who starved himself to death in the Maze prison outside Belfast."[12] This particular murder was probably covered in the US only because of the victim's association with Gerry Adams.

After the Canary Wharf bombing most of the IRA's activities were constrained by negotiations through the Tony Blair Administration. The cease-fire was reinstated in July 1997. The only terrorist act that was recorded afterwards was the murder of Billy Wright, aka King Rat, in December 1997.[13] Unfortunately, a backlash resulted as Loyalists retaliated by shooting at a hotel in a Catholic area, killing one person and injuring three. Once again, we see a pattern where the IRA targeted one of the most dangerous Loyalist dissidents who attempted to undermine the peace process numerous times, and the Loyalists retaliated by killing innocent civilians. In fact, both the Nationalist and the Loyalist parties considered Wright a menace. He was kicked out of the Protestant Ulster Volunteer Force, the largest branch of the Loyalist movement, and later placed under a death sentence by them for renegade activities that jeopardized their stake in the peace process.[14] The Loyalists have proven to be just as dangerous and disruptive, if not more so, than Irish Nationalists, but minimal large-scale coverage is devoted to this factor.

Another crucial factor that is constantly overlooked by the American media is the brutality of the military police in Northern Ireland—the Royal Ulster Constabulary (RUC). There has been no media coverage in the US of RUC brutality, even though Amnesty International has been involved in such cases. One instance involved a youth by the last name of Austin, who had been severely mistreated during interrogation by RUC members. Austin was seventeen years old, living in Belfast. There is a well-known belief held by the RUC that young males are prime candidates for recruitment by the IRA, and as a result, random arrests and interrogations take place in attempts to find Nationalist dissidents. According to Amnesty International, Austin was targeted by the RUC one day upon leaving his school and was taken to the station for interrogation. In an attempt to force him to confess to being a member of the IRA, even though there was no probable cause for him to be singled out, the RUC began to twist his ear. The ear was torn halfway off, and a doctor was called in to stitch the ear back on. Austin was allowed to go home after medical treatment. The very next day, he was picked up again, and most of the stitches were ripped out. His mother immediately petitioned Amnesty International for assistance, and the case—along with those of a group of other parents whose children experienced similar brutality—was brought to the attention of the White House. No newspaper or television coverage was given to this event.

It would surprise most people to know that a substantial percentage of the English populace has been contesting their government's presence in Northern Ireland for years.

A final point to consider is the civilians in England, who are potential targets of IRA bombings. It seems natural to assume that they would support the RUC's measures in controlling the Nationalists, or the Loyalists' retaliations for IRA activity. It would surprise most people to know that a substantial percentage of the English populace has been contesting their government's presence in Northern Ireland for years. A group in England called the "Troops Out Movement" (TOM) is dedicated to this end. The Troops Out newsletter reflects the attitude of English civilians towards the end of the cease-fire in 1996:

> The Irish peace process gave hope that all of those involved had conceded that change was inevitable and that agreement through talks offered a real way to peace. That hope was destroyed not by the IRA bomb in Canary Wharf but by the refusal of the British Government to enter into meaningful negotiations after a cease-fire that lasted over one and a half years.[15]

TOM ran a poll in the spring of 1996 to gauge opinion about the end of the IRA cessation. Upon the end of the cease-fire, they asked the general public if they thought England should start peace talks to salvage the situation. About 73 percent said "yes," with another 7 percent undecided. Upon asking respondents if they felt Britain should leave Northern Ireland, 61 percent said "yes," with 17 percent undecided.

The obvious media bias and tendencies to give leading questions and distort perspectives were made apparent as reporters gathered around the scene of the Canary Wharf bombing. The Troops Out Movement released a newsletter in autumn 1996 reporting that a good number of the casualties resulting from the Canary Wharf bombing was largely attributable to the inept procedures of the British authorities. According to a couple who were evacuated from Cromford Court (one of the buildings on Canary Wharf), they weren't moved until ten minutes before the bomb went off, even though the rescue squads had ample warning of the device's presence. In fact, four people were still in Cromford when the bomb exploded. Furthermore, residents were moved into a building with a glass roof, and when the bomb went off, the backlash of the explosion brought the roof down on the evacuated residents, thus resulting in most of the injuries reported by British and US media.[16]

The important point for all of us to remember is that the prism through which we view the Northern Ireland conflict is narrow and convoluted. Without direct and constant communication within Northern Ireland itself, the United States media will be ill-equipped to bring unbiased and complete coverage of the peace process and insurrection resulting from it. Perhaps America's "special relationship" with England has a lot to do with the tendency of the media to focus primarily on British perspectives of the conflict. The *Boston Globe* appears to take as much interest in the Nationalist perspective as the Unionist perspective, but that is only one paper against many. The best way for the American populace to receive the complete story on Northern Ireland is to make use of all the available resources, such as the Internet and international newspapers (particularly those that are based within Northern Ireland, like *An Phoblacht*). Until the US media can check their own biases and utilize all sources available to them, along with taking an active interest in truth versus what will sell, the American people will need to investigate events for themselves if they want to obtain a clear picture of international affairs.

Endnotes

1. Brown, Jennifer. (1998). "Northern Ireland teens in America leaving their troubles back home: Program unites youths from rival factions to help them dispel fears, misconceptions." *Los Angeles Times*, September 13, p 9. **2.** Cullen, Kevin. (1998). "Reason for hope: Why peace in Northern Ireland now has a chance." *Boston Globe,* December 20, p 71-75. **3.** Cullen, Kevin. (1996). "Toll rises following IRA blast, two dead in London: Peace effort in tailspin." *Boston Globe,* February 11, p 1. **4.** Barbash, Fred. (1996). "IRA intransigent on cease-fire: Second bomb found." *The Washington Post*, February 16, p A23. **5.** Anonymous. (1996). "A major blow." *The Nation,* March 4. **6.** *Ibid.* **7.** *Ibid.* **8.** Reid, T.R. (1998). "Five arrested in bombing that killed 28 in Ulster." *Washington Post,* August 18, p A09. **9.** Cullen, Kevin. (1998). "In an Ulster town, hate still thrives." *Boston Globe,* May 25, p A1. **10.** *Op cit.*, Cullen (1998). **11.** Roughton, Jr., Bert. (1998). "Deaths in N. Ireland strike deep." *Atlanta Journal*, July 25, p B01. **12.** Burgess, John. (1998). "A gentle man is laid to rest in a violent land: Killing unites Northern Irish sects in grief." *Washington Post,* January 15, p A29. **13.** Cullen, Kevin. (1997). "Notorious Loyalist slain in Ulster jail, violence erupts outside Belfast." *Boston Globe,* December 28, p A1. **14.** *Ibid.* **15.** Alderson, David & Louise Purbrick. (1996). "We were used." *Troops Out Movement,* Vol. 19, No. 3. England: Autumn. **16.** *Ibid.*

Why They Hate Oliver Stone

Sam Smith

February 1992. In an hysterical stampede unusual even for the media herd, scores of journalists have taken time off from their regular occupations—such as boosting the Democrats' most conservative presidential candidate, extolling free trade, or judging other countries by their progress towards American-style oligopoly—to launch an offensive against what is clearly perceived to be the major internal threat to the Republic: a movie-maker named Oliver Stone.

Stone, whose alleged crime was the production of a film called *JFK*, has been compared to Hitler and Goebbels and to David Duke and Louis Farrakhan. The movie's thesis has been declared akin to alleged conspiracies by the Freemasons, the Bavarian Illuminati, the League of Just Men, and the Elders of Zion.

Stone, whose alleged crime was the production of a film called *JFK*, has been compared to Hitler and Goebbels and to David Duke and Louis Farrakhan.

The film has been described as a "three hour lie from an intellectual sociopath." *Newsweek* ran a cover story headlined: "Why Oliver Stone's New Movie Can't Be Trusted." Another critic accused Stone of "contemptible citizenship," which is about as close to an accusation of treason as the libel laws will permit. Meanwhile, Leslie Gelb, with best *New York Times* pomposity, settled for declaring that the "torments" of Presidents Kennedy and Johnson over Vietnam "are not to be trifled with by Oliver Stone or anyone."

The attack began months before the movie even appeared, with the leaking of a first draft of the film. By last June, the film had been excoriated by the *Chicago Tribune*, *Washington Post*, and *Time* magazine. These critics, at least, had seen *something*; following the release of the film, NPR's Cokie Roberts took the remarkable journalistic stance of refusing to screen it at all because it was so awful.

Well, maybe not so remarkable, because the overwhelming sense one gets from the critical diatribes is one of denial, of defense of non-knowledge, of fierce clinging to a story that even some of Stone's most vehement antagonists have to confess, deep in their articles, may not be correct.

Stephen Rosenfeld of the *Washington Post*, for example, states seven paragraphs into his commentary:

> That the assassination probably encompassed more than a lone gunman now seems beyond cavil.

If there was more than one gunman, it follows that there was a conspiracy of some sort and it follows that the Warren Commission was incorrect. It should follow also that journalists writing about the Kennedy assassination should be more interested in what actually did happen than in dismissing every Warren Commission critic as a paranoid. Yet, from the start, the media has been a consistent promoter of the thesis that Rosenfeld now says is wrong beyond cavil.

In fact, not one of the journalistic attacks on the film that I have seen makes any effort to explain convincingly what *did* happen in Dallas that day. They either explicitly or implicitly defend the Warren Commission or dismiss its inaccuracy as a mere historical curiosity.

Journalists writing about the Kennedy assassination should be more interested in what actually did happen than in dismissing every Warren Commission critic as a paranoid.

Of course, it is anything but. Americans, if not the *Washington Post*, want to know what happened. And after nearly 30 years of journalistic nonfeasance concerning one of the major stories of our era, a filmmaker has come forth with an alternative thesis, and the country's establishment has gone berserk.

Right or wrong, you've got to hand it to the guy. Since the 1960s, those trying to stem the evil that has increasingly seeped into our political system have been not suppressed so much as ignored. Gary Sick's important new book on events surrounding the October Surprise, for example, has not been reviewed by many major publications. The dozens of books on the subject of the Kennedy assassination, in toto, have received nowhere near the attention of Stone's effort. For the first time in two decades, someone has finally caught the establishment's attention, with a movie that grossed $40 million in the first three or four weeks and will probably be seen by 50 million Americans by the time the videotape sales subside.

It is part of the sordid reality of our times that Hollywood is about the only institution left in our country big and powerful enough to challenge the influence of state propaganda that controls our lives with hardly a murmur from the same journalists so incensed by Stone.

Further, by early January, Jim Garrison's own account of the case was at the top of the paperback bestseller list, and Mark Lane's *Plausible Denial* had made it to number seven on the hardcover tally. Many of Stone's critics have accused him of an act of malicious propaganda. In fact, it is part of the sordid reality of our times that Hollywood is about the only institution left in our country big and powerful enough to challenge the influence of state propaganda that controls our lives with hardly a murmur from the same journalists so incensed by Stone.

Where were these seekers of truth, for example, during the Gulf Massacre? Even if Stone's depiction were totally false, it would pale in comparison with the brutal consequences of the government's easy manipulation of the media during the Iraqi affair.

And, if movies are to be held to the standards set for *JFK*, where are the parallel critiques of *Gone with the Wind* and a horde of other cinemagraphic myths that are part of the American consciousness?

No, Stone's crime was not that his movie presents a myth, but that he had the audacity and power to challenge the myths of his critics. It is, in the critics' view, the job of the news media to determine the country's paradigm, to define our perceptions, to give broad interpretations to major events, to create the myths which guide our thought and action. It is, for example, Tom Brokaw and Cokie Roberts who are ordained to test Democratic candidates on their catechism, not mere members of the public or even the candidates themselves. It is for the media to determine which practitioners of violence, such as Henry Kissinger and Richard Helms, are to be statesmen and which, like Lee Harvey Oswald and James Earl Ray, are mere assassins. It is their privilege to determine which of our politicians have vision and which are fools, and which illegal or corrupt actions have been taken in the national interest and which to subvert that interest. And this right, as Leslie Gelb might put it, is not to be trifled with by Oliver Stone or anyone else.

No, Stone's crime was not that his movie presents a myth, but that he had the audacity and power to challenge the myths of his critics.

Because he dared to step on the mythic turf of the news media, Stone has accomplished something truly remarkable that goes far beyond the specific facts of the Kennedy killing. For whatever errors in his recounting of that tale, his underlying story tells a grim truth. Stone has not only presented a detailed, if debatable, thesis for what happened in Dallas on one day, but a parable of the subsequent 30 years of America's democratic disintegration. For in these decades one finds repeated and indisputable evidence—Watergate, Iran-Contra, BCCI, the War on Drugs, to name just a few—of major politicians and intelligence services working in unholy alliance with criminals and foreign partisans to malevolently affect national policy. And as late as the 1980s, we have documentation from the Continuity in Government program that at least some in the Reagan administration were preparing for a coup d'état under the most ill-defined conditions.

It is one of contemporary journalism's most disastrous conceits that truth can not exist in the absence of revealed evidence. By accepting the tyranny of the known, the media inevitably relies on the official version of the truth, seldom asking the government to prove *its* case, while demanding of critics of that official version the most exacting tests of evidence. Some of this, as in the case, say, of George Will, is simply ideological disingenuousness. Another factor is the unconscious influence of one's caste, well exemplified by Stone critic Chuck Freund, a onetime alternative journalist whose perceptions changed almost immediately upon landing a job with the *Washington Post*, and who now writes as though he were up for membership in the Metropolitan Club. But for many journalists it is simply a matter of a childish faith in known facts as the delimiter of our understanding.

If intelligence means anything, it means not only the collection of facts, but arranging them into some sort of pattern of probability so we can understand more than we actually know.

Thus the elementary school child is inundated with facts because that is considered all that can be handled at that point. Facts at this level are neatly arranged and function as rules to describe a comfortable, reliable world.

Beginning in high school, however, one starts to take these facts and interpret them and put them together in new orders and to consider what lots of facts, some of them contradictory, might mean. In school this is not called paranoia, nor conspiracy theory, but thought.

If intelligence means anything, it means not only the collection of facts, but arranging them into some sort of pattern of probability so we can understand more than we actually know.

Along the way, it is discovered that some of the facts (aka rules) that we learned in elementary school weren't facts. I learned, for example, that despite what Mrs. Dunn said in fifth grade, Arkansas was not pronounced "R-Kansas." Finally, those who go to college learn that facts aren't anywhere as much help as we even thought in high school, for example when we attempt a major paper on what caused the Civil War.

To deny writers, ordinary citizens, or even filmmakers the right to think beyond the perimeter of the known and verifiable is to send us back intellectually into a fifth-grade world, precise but inaccurate, and—when applied to a democracy—highly dangerous. We have to vote, after all, without all the facts. As Benjamin Franklin noted, one need not understand the law of gravity to know that if a plate falls on the floor it will break. Similarly, none of us has to know the full story of the JFK assassination to understand that the official story simply isn't true.

Oliver Stone has done nothing worse than to take the available knowledge and assemble it in a way that seems logical to him. Inevitably, because so many facts are unknown, the movie must be to some degree myth.

To deny writers, ordinary citizens, or even filmmakers the right to think beyond the perimeter of the known and verifiable is to send us back intellectually into a fifth-grade world.

Thus, we are presented with two myths: Stone's and the official version so assiduously guarded by the media. One says Kennedy was the victim of forces that constituted a shadow government; the other says it was just a random event by a lone individual.

We need not accept either, but of the two, the Stone version clearly has the edge. The lone gunman theory (the brainstorm of Arlen Specter, whose ethical standards were well-displayed during the Thomas hearings) is so weak that even some of Stone's worst critics won't defend it in the face of facts such as the nature of the weapon allegedly used (so unreliable the Italians called it "the humanitarian rifle"), the exotic supposed path of the bullet, and Oswald's inexplicably easy return to the US after defecting to the Soviet Union.

In the end, David Ferrie in the movie probably said it right: "The fucking shooters don't even know" who killed JFK. In a well-planned operation it's like that.

I tend to believe that Stone is right about the involvement of the right-wing Cubans and the mobs, that intelligence officials participated at some level, that Jim Garrison was on to something but that his case failed primarily because several of his witnesses mysteriously ended up dead, and that a substantial cover-up took place. I suspect, however, that the primary motive for the killing was revenge—either for a perceived détente with Castro or for JFK's anti-Mafia moves, and that Stone's Vietnam thesis is overblown. The top-level conspiracy depicted is possible but, at this point, only that because the case rests on too little—some strange troop movements, a telephone network failure, and the account of Mr. X—who turns out albeit to be Fletcher Prouty, chief of special operations for the Joint Chiefs at the time.

But we should not begrudge Stone if he is wrong on any of these points, because he has shown us something even more important than the Kennedy assassination: an insight into repeated organized efforts by the few to manipulate for their own benefit a democracy made too trusting of its invulnerability by a media that refuses to see and tell what has been going on.

Just as the Soviets needed to confront the lies of their own history in order to build a new society, so America must confront the lies of the past 30 years to move ahead. Stone—to the fear of those who have participated in those lies and to the opportunity of all those who suffered because of them—has helped to make this possible.

The Martin Luther King You Don't See on TV

Jeff Cohen and Norman Solomon

It's become a TV ritual: Every year in mid-January, around the time of Martin Luther King's birthday, we get perfunctory network news reports about "the slain civil rights leader." The remarkable thing about this annual review of King's life is that several years—his last years—are totally missing, as if flushed down a memory hole.

What TV viewers see is a closed loop of familiar file footage: King battling desegregation in Birmingham (1963), reciting his dream of racial harmony at the rally in Washington (1963), marching for voting rights in Selma, Alabama (1965), and finally, lying dead on the motel balcony in Memphis (1968).

An alert viewer might notice that the chronology jumps from 1965 to 1968. Yet King didn't take a sabbatical near the end of his life. In fact, he was speaking and organizing as diligently as ever. Almost all of those speeches were filmed or taped. But they're not shown today on TV.

In his last months, King was organizing the most militant project of his life: the Poor People's Campaign.

Why?

It's because national news media have never come to terms with what Martin Luther King, Jr. stood for during his final years.

In the early 1960s, when King focused his challenge on legalized racial discrimination in the South, most major media were his allies. Network TV and national publications graphically showed the police dogs and bullwhips and cattle prods used against Southern blacks who sought the right to vote or to eat at a public lunch counter.

But after passage of civil rights acts in 1964 and 1965, King began challenging the nation's fundamental priorities. He maintained that civil rights laws were empty without "human rights"—including economic rights. For people too poor to eat at a restaurant or afford a decent home, King said, anti-discrimination laws were hollow.

Noting that a majority of Americans below the poverty line were white, King developed a class perspective. He decried the huge income gaps between rich and poor, and called for "radical changes in the structure of our society" to redistribute wealth and power.

"True compassion," King declared, "is more than flinging a coin to a beggar; it comes to see that an edifice which produces beggars needs restructuring."

By 1967, King had also become the country's most prominent opponent of the Vietnam War, and a staunch critic of overall US foreign policy, which he deemed militaristic. In his "Beyond Vietnam" speech delivered at New York's Riverside Church on April 4, 1967—a year to the day before he was murdered—King called the United States "the greatest purveyor of violence in the world today."

From Vietnam to South Africa to Latin America, King said, the US was "on the wrong side of a world revolution." King questioned "our alliance with the landed gentry of Latin America," and asked why the US was suppressing revolutions "of the shirtless and barefoot people" in the Third World, instead of supporting them.

In foreign policy, King also offered an economic critique, complaining about "capitalists of the West investing huge sums of money in Asia, Africa and South America, only to take the profits out with no concern for the social betterment of the countries."

You haven't heard the "Beyond Vietnam" speech on network news retrospectives, but national media heard it loud and clear back in 1967—and loudly denounced it. *Time* called it "demagogic slander that sounded like a script for Radio Hanoi." The *Washington Post* patronized that "King has diminished his usefulness to his cause, his country, his people."

In his last months, King was organizing the most militant project of his life: the Poor People's Campaign. He crisscrossed the country to assemble "a multiracial army of the poor" that would descend on Washington—engaging in nonviolent civil disobedience at the Capitol, if need be—until Congress enacted a poor people's bill of rights. *Reader's Digest* warned of an "insurrection."

King's economic bill of rights called for massive government jobs programs to rebuild America's cities. He saw a crying need to confront a Congress that had demonstrated its "hostility to the poor"—appropriating "military funds with alacrity and generosity," but providing "poverty funds with miserliness."

How familiar that sounds today, more than a quarter-century after King's efforts on behalf of the poor people's mobilization were cut short by an assassin's bullet.

As a new millennium gets underway, in this nation of immense wealth, the White House and Congress continue to accept the perpetuation of poverty. And so do most mass media. Perhaps it's no surprise that they tell us little about the last years of Martin Luther King's life.

Sometimes Lying Means Only Telling a Small Part of the Truth

R.U. Sirius with Michael Horowitz and the Friends of Timothy Leary

Frequently the mainstream media lie on behalf of the system by what they don't tell us. A few years ago when the Clinton Administration blew up a pharmaceutical factory in the desperately impoverished Sudan, claiming that it was a chemical warfare factory, it was front-page news for a couple of days. A few days after that, when it was revealed that the administration might have (self-admittedly) been wrong about the factory, it wasn't even in most newspapers. The devastating effect of the loss of that country's only pharmaceutical factory has, of course, received even less coverage still in the mainstream press.

The media don't always feed us vacant pabulum out of a desire to keep us ignorant. Sometimes they're just plain lazy. Back in late June 1999, brief items appeared in papers and newsweeklies across the country telling us that anti-authoritarian counterculturalist Timothy Leary was "an FBI informant." The articles were based on an FBI document released to The Smoking Gun <www.thesmokinggun.com>. Nearly all the pieces that appeared about this were brief, three paragraphs or less. None explored the circumstances that led to Leary's testimonies, and this old news—which was amply covered by the media in the mid-1970s when the testifying was occurring—was treated as a shocking revelation.

The media don't always feed us vacant pabulum out of a desire to keep us ignorant.

As someone who sometimes writes for the mainstream press and knows how their editorial processes work, let me assure you, this was probably not a conscious conspiracy. The mainstream media simply don't think Leary is worth more than three paragraphs. Bringing out the fact that this was old news, or that it involved a complex situation, within three paragraphs would have left too many hanging questions. This final assault on Leary's reputation via oversimplification was a simple matter of word count to the media owners.

I decided that I wouldn't stand still for the slander. With the help of drug historian and Leary archivist Michael Horowitz, I wrote a statement challenging the mainstream media version of the story, and within a couple of weeks we got Winona Ryder, Susan Sarandon, Tom Robbins, and a large group of countercultural luminaries to sign it. We sent it to the media and posted it on Disinformation. Despite the big names attached to it, the media ignored our dissenting view.

This final assault on Leary's reputation via oversimplification was a simple matter of word count to the media owners.

Oh well. At least you can read it.

FBI and Media Kick a Man While He's Dead: An Open Letter from the Friends of Timothy Leary

"Those who want to gnaw on his bones never knew his heart." —Ken Kesey

"He stood up bravely for freedom of speech and behavior and deserves to be remembered for that." —Winona Ryder

Recent media coverage about Timothy Leary's "cooperation" with the FBI brings into focus the Orwellian character of today's tabloid media environment. Focusing on documents selectively released by the FBI, and initially published by the "true crime" Webzine The Smoking Gun, a news story picked up by the Associated Press presented as shocking news the fact that Leary testified about the radical left in 1974 in the hopes of speeding up his prison release. Young readers, or those with a short historical memory, were led to believe that Leary was a secret FBI collaborator, hiding behind a mask of countercultural anti-authoritarianism.

We refer the Associated Press and all other conscientious reporters to newspapers and periodicals from this period. We also refer them to the final chapters (39-41) of Leary's own autobiography, *Flashbacks* (Tarcher/Putnam, 1983). Leary found his interaction with the Feds important enough to make it the closing chapter. He was certainly aware that it was no secret. Trumpeting as "news" the fact that Leary answered the agency's questions is utterly dishonest.

Journalists who wish to investigate this situation further will be rewarded with a complex adventure story of a heroic man whose rights were consistently violated by various government agencies, who served four-and-a-half harsh years in prison and another one-and-a-half years in exile, and who finally evaded several lifetimes' worth of further prison sentences while doing negligible damage to friends and acquaintances.

Here are a few salient facts:

Timothy Leary faced about 100 years in prison. Twenty years were for a total of less than half an ounce of marijuana; another five for escaping from prison. That alone would have put him away for the rest of his life. But in addition, he faced 75 years on some bizarre conspiracy charges around global distribution of LSD. Of his 30 "co-conspirators," 29 were unfamiliar to him, and conspiracy charges were eventually dropped. In contrast, the leaders of the Weather Underground received fines and suspended sentences when they finally turned themselves in, due to the disclosure that the FBI had committed illegal acts against them.

Nobody was seriously injured by Leary's interaction with the FBI, with the exception of a former attorney, who received three months in prison after being set up on a cocaine bust by a girlfriend of Leary working on the outside, not from Tim's testimony. The lawyer has never come forward to express any anger toward Leary. Two other former lawyers of Leary were placed at risk, as were his estranged wife and his archivist, but nothing came of it because of the absence of corroborating testimony from people whom Tim well knew had been underground for years.

The Weather Underground, the radical left organization responsible for his escape, was not impacted by his testimony. Histories written about the Weather Underground usually mention the Leary chapter in terms of the escape for which they proudly took credit. Leary sent information to the Weather Underground through a sympathetic prisoner that he was considering making a deal with the FBI and waited for their approval. The return message was, "We understand."

While in exile, Leary was illegally kidnapped by US agents in Afghanistan (which had no extradition treaty with the US) and brought back to America. On returning to prison, he was thrown into "the hole" in Folsom Prison. His bail was $5 million, the largest in US history. President Richard Nixon had earlier labeled him "the most dangerous man in America."

His bail was $5 million, the largest in US history. President Richard Nixon had earlier labeled him "the most dangerous man in America."

When Leary first agreed to talk to the FBI about those involved in his escape, the agents were so dissatisfied with his testimony that they put him out on the "main line" at a Minnesota prison under the name "Charles Thrush," a songbird. This was a blatant attempt to label him a snitch and get him murdered by prisoners, or at least to scare him into giving the FBI the kind of answers they wanted.

After his testimony, Leary remained in prison for close to two years. His release had as much to do with Nixon's downfall over the Watergate scandal, the fact that the FBI had been exposed for illegal activities against radical groups, and the transition from Ronald Reagan to Jerry Brown as governor of California, as it did with any useful information the FBI might have received from him.

There are lots of FBI files on Tim Leary. The government has released a select number of them, which were clearly chosen to hurt his reputation. The FBI is still doing its best to slow down the release of Leary's full file, according to investigators who have made Freedom of Information Act requests.

> Tim knew he had to make the same sort of rollover when he was in the belly of the beast. He also knew he wasn't telling the Feds anything they didn't already know. And he figured it the same way I did: our true allies and comrades would understand.
>
> I have no need to associate with doubters. When the priests in the Star Chamber promise to stop pouring hot lead in your ear if you'll confess to being in league with Satan, you do what you have to do. Those citizens who think you are being a traitorous coward have never had hot lead poured in their ears.
>
> Tim Leary was a great warrior, funny and wise and clever and, above all, courageous. I judge myself blessed to have battled alongside a revolutionary like this blue-eyed battler. Those who want to gnaw on his bones never knew his heart.
>
> —Ken Kesey

Signed,
The Friends of Timothy Leary:

Howard Bloom
Andrei Codrescu
Michael Horowitz
Ken Kesey
Paul Krassner
Richard Metzger
Cynthia Palmer
Genesis P-Orridge
Tom Robbins
Douglas Rushkoff
Winona Ryder
Susan Sarandon
R. U. Sirius
Larry "Ratso" Sloman
Kenn Thomas
Robert Anton Wilson

Upon Hearing of the Electronic Bogeyman

George Smith

electronic bogeyman: a hacker, instrument of a hacker, or anonymous source portrayed in the mainstream media as a menace to society. The electronic bogeyman must always be quoted making grandiose, unverifiable, or nutty claims (e.g. opening all the automatic garage doors in Anaheim, California, at precisely 2:00 PM) about feats, usually malicious, that can be performed with a computer.

Usage: Reuters interviewed an electronic bogeyman from Taiwan who claimed his computer virus would corrupt data on Japanese computers if that country did not immediately surrender ownership of the Daioyu Islands in the East China Sea.

—from the Crypt Newsletter's Guide to Tech Terminology

The mainstream and very public line regarding the threat to the nation's well-being presented by hackers, electronic terrorists, and unseen cyber-warriors from "rogue states" has been quite clear-cut.

For most of the decade, a large number of intelligence agency officials, representatives of the Department of Defense, and assorted defense industry contractors have gone on the record warning sternly of the vulnerability of the nation to a surprise computerized attack by these electronic bogeymen.

But a shocking amount of the rhetoric is based purely on the equivalent of modern-day ghost stories, exacerbated by the mainstream media's lack of understanding of computer technology and its love for exaggerated sensationalism.

First, let's take a look at one of the more absurd myths propagated by the media: that of menacing hackers stealing nuclear secrets. In June 1998, my Sunday paper brought with it an example of Associated Press' skill in reporting on the matter.

Datelined Washington, the wire service delivered six paragraphs of completely unverifiable news, so fantastic as to appear to be the product of an anonymous psychotic within the organization.

Hackers, intoned AP, had defaced an "Army command's" Website. Computer rebels, the wire service added, claimed to have entered India's national security computer network and stolen sensitive nuclear weapons secrets.

This was linked to yet another alleged nefarious plot in which the anonymous hackers were implied to have used the Army Website as a waypoint in an electronic joyride in which the "nuclear weapons secrets" were seized from networked computers in India.

Yeah, and here at Crypt Newsletter, we're from Missouri. Why? Not because of the defacement of an Army Website or a single hacker penetration. Both were and remain news so regular as to only be notable to the mentally defective. No, instead it was the other "hacker" claims, which, if taken at face value, assumed *a priori* knowledge of the Indian atomic weapons development project: people involved beyond what one could read in general newspaper accounts, physical locations—names—of places where critical development is conducted, and some degree of specialized knowledge on what might be considered sensitive technical information concerning atomic weapons. And that's a tall order—even for an electronic bogeyman.

Consider, for a moment, the history of those who pass nuclear secrets (aka "atom spies"). It is a history remarkable for the fact that all of the famous ones were either genuinely expert inside researchers or those who exploited close connections to such insiders. Two prominent cases, for instance, involved Klaus Fuchs—a scientist involved in the Manhattan Project at Los Alamos—and Israel's Mordechai Vannunu, who worked inside that country's nuclear program at Dimona. They were not publicity-hungry cyberpests and teenagers.

A shocking amount of the rhetoric is based purely on the equivalent of modern-day ghost stories.

In the past several years, this writer has never heard of or met a single mainstream media-type "hacker" or read a single missive from the "computer underground" that seemed to indicate even the slightest real technical knowledge of current atomic weapon design.

In any case, absolutely no proof for the claims in the Associated Press story was presented except for the confused testimony of an Army public relations man who knew almost nothing about what had really happened, if—indeed—anything had.

None of this even begins to address another fact, one that reporters and editors at the Associated Press, as well as their colleagues at other mainstream publications, apparently cannot grasp: Many hackers tend to be reflexive liars.

Like the character Jerry the Bum in *Down and Out in Beverly Hills*, "hackers"—at least the ones found in newspaper and TV news stories—can be counted upon to perform for the listener, telling the gullible just about anything he or she wishes to hear.

The result has been that almost any claim, no matter how nonsensical, has been published.

And over the years there have been plenty of whoppers.

Take the case of Vice Miskovic, another hacker, this time from Croatia, whom Reuters reported had downloaded nuclear secrets from Andersen Air Force Base in Guam.

In February 1996, reporter Laura Lui of the Reuters News Service wrote that Miskovic had accessed "nuclear secrets" at an American military installation in Guam while surfing the Net.

Neither Lui nor Miskovic produced any compelling evidence other than hearsay.

Tellingly, Miskovic was evasive in his claims: "The data are compressed and need to be extracted, so I don't really know everything they contained, but it sure was very interesting," he said.

While Miskovic never produced anything that verified his bold talk, it was very easy for the casual Net surfer to use the popular Dejanews Internet discussion group search engine <www.deja.com> to collect information on this dangerous electronic bogeyman. Yet Reuters did not even do this small bit of research. If it had, editors would have found a search keyed to Miskovic's name returning a mind-rotting number of hits, most of them connected to a get-rich-quick-by-mail scam (known as "Make Money Fast").

At the end of one of his "Make Money Fast" mail scams, the dangerous hacker whom Reuters believed had stolen nuclear secrets pleaded:

> ...it is so expensive to connect to NET here in CROATIA!
> I am spending all MY money on this INTERNET CALL!
> Can U help by sending money 4 me! I'll repay U when
> i EARN money! PLEASE!!!! IF yes mail me to
> virus@openet.freenet.hut.fi I have foreign ADDRESS cause
> it is FREE! If U mail me I'll reply AND send U my ADRESS!

Miskovic then posted his address for all to see, anyway—a domicile in Zadar, Croatia.

"Nuclear secrets" are frequently popular items in alleged cyberthefts, mostly because it's a statement that almost always guarantees a reaction. To Miskovic, whose only real business was getting American journalists to humor him, it must have seemed an easy choice in lies.

Another claim in 1998, equally absurd, was made by "hackers" who defaced Yahoo. Anyone who had accessed Yahoo, they claimed, had received a computer virus the vandals had planted on the company's server. This was supposedly in retaliation for the continued imprisonment of the famous hacker Kevin Mitnick.

Of course, no computers crashed. No virus was found. And Kevin Mitnick stayed in a Los Angeles jail, California corrections officers presumably being somewhat less than impressed by claims of anonymous cyberpests taken seriously by the mainstream media. Hacker publicity stunts aimed at bringing attention to their belief that Mitnick was unjustly imprisoned continued throughout the remainder of the decade. Not one made a lick of difference or abbreviated Mitnick's tenure in a California big-house.

Unfortunately, the media's practice is usually not to run news pieces after the fact indicating that hacker claims proved to be so much rubbish.

Net-joyriding teenagers, however, are not the only source of hacker myths.

Take this example, published in 1998 by the Australian government's Foreign Affairs Defense and Trade Group in a report entitled "Thinking about the Unthinkable: Australian Vulnerabilities to High-Tech Risks":

> A hacker group calling themselves the "Anti-Christ Doom Squad" was involved in attacks against New Zealand and Australia just days after Wellington and Canberra announced troop deployments to the latest Gulf Crisis.... The "Anti-Christ" hackers traversed computer systems worldwide [and once inside] the New Zealand power company's super-computer...accessed a control system commonly used in energy distributions systems to launch their attack....
>
> The "Anti-Christ Doom Squad" then concentrated on manipulating one key choke-point on the outskirts of Auckland.... The 'Doom Squad' altered the temperature within the gas-encased power lines thereby crippling them within minutes.... Simultaneous widespread blackouts across the Australian state of Queensland disrupted businesses, schools and emergency services....

The "Anti-Christ Doom Squad" and its feats of techno-terrorism were a complete fiction.

Julian Assange, Australian moderator of the Legal Aspects of Computer Crime mailing list and a researcher who has written extensively about hackers, states it was a result of "[a typical] paranoia-inducing budget grab" by an Australian advisory group. Although the Foreign Affairs Defense and Trade Group author eventually admitted in the report that the "Anti-Christ Doom Squad" scenario was made-up, the reader had to slog through 100 pages of this thesis before finding this qualifier, buried in its endnotes: "The exact cause of [the power failure] has not been made public... However, as the fictitious news story was attempting to suggest, aggressive attacks are now just as plausible as technical failure."

Plausible? According to whom? A group trying to wring funding from the Australian taxpayer.

Or how about this howler, courtesy of a wannabe Dr. Strangelove at the Pentagon.

In 1998, Arthur Money, an Assistant Secretary of the US Department of Defense, informed journalists at a trade convention on electronic warfare and communications that "hackers" had altered information in a medical database by changing the data on blood types of soldiers.

The "Anti-Christ Doom Squad" and its feats of techno-terrorism were a complete fiction.

Several news sources subsequently reported the story and it immediately became part of the information strata as testimony to the alleged "capabilities" of anonymous hackers.

Congressman Curt Weldon quickly adopted it as part of his speechifying on the dangers of surprise attacks from cyberspace. By 1999, Weldon was delivering the tale of blood-type-tampering hackers as keynote speaker to a variety of information warfare meetings.

However, *none* of it was true. The incident described was not real.

It was merely a *scenario* from a Pentagon wargame. Somewhere along the line, this distinction was apparently lost, and today the story still pops up from time to time as part and parcel of the lore on hacker disruptions. Like most myths connected with the topic, sightings are always characterized by their nonspecificity.

No one ever really knows who did what to whom, when or where, but hackers, cyberterrorists—somewhere, sometime, somehow—diddled military blood-type information.

It's also not always wise to trust the output of colleges or law enforcement agencies. Consider the following:

The December 1996 issue of the FBI's *Law Enforcement Bulletin*, published monthly out of the organization's training academy in Quantico, Virginia, presented an article entitled "Computer Crime: An Emerging Challenge for Law Enforcement." Condensed from a larger paper by two college professors, Andra Katz of Wichita State and David L. Carter of Michigan State, the paper presented a number of computer viruses as tools of hackers.

One of them, the "Clinton" computer virus, wrote Carter and Katz, "is designed to infect programs, but...eradicates itself when it cannot decide which program to infect."

The "Clinton" virus was used to explain the motivations of computer criminals.

Some of them, wrote the authors, introduced such viruses to systems to play with the user. "Some employees could be motivated to infect a computer with a virus simply for purposes of gamesmanship. In these cases, the employees typically introduce a virus to play with the system...as in the case of the 'Clinton' virus," they wrote.

Both authors and the FBI were embarrassed to find there was no such virus as "Clinton"—a trait found with *every* example cited in their report. Unknown to the authors, their examples, instead of being bona fide computer viruses, were all jokes originally published in an April Fool's column of a computer magazine.

Acutely embarrassed over the mistake, the editor of the *Law Enforcement Bulletin* did not initially return phone calls. When a representative of the FBI finally consented to talk about the affair, instead of admitting the errors, the mistakes were compounded. The editor of the FBI publication claimed two anonymous "security experts" had "verified" the jokes were real viruses.

Nevertheless, the damage was done. The FBI magazine had already been sent to 55,000 law enforcement professionals with all the jokes intact. In 2000, I still infrequently run into citations of the FBI work in other research papers that purport to be about cyberterror.

Need more?

The extended tale of the Gulf War virus hoax is an amusingly glaring example of how alleged experts on terrorism, in their zeal to provide examples of cyberweapons for doubting Thomases, grasp at myths.

In 1991 *Infoworld* published an April Fool's column written by reporter John Gantz. The column told of a National Security Agency-developed computer virus smuggled into Iraq from France via the chips inside imported computer printers. In the column, the virus was said to emerge from the printer upon union with the computer network, spread, and disable Iraqi air defense computers by devouring the "windows" opened on PC screens.

US News & World Report subsequently published Gantz's joke almost verbatim in its 1992 book on the Gulf War, *Triumph Without*

The "Clinton" computer virus, wrote Carter and Katz, "is designed to infect programs, but...eradicates itself when it cannot decide which program to infect."

Victory. The joke's publication as a *real story* in *US News* immediately ensured its permanence in the lore on cyberweaponry.

Since then, others have infrequently reported sources—always anonymous, unreachable, or poorly attributed, in the Pentagon or government—repeating the joke, a fairly obvious case of "officials" who have taken their information from gossip evolved from the original joke and laundered through alleged "news" sources. Ironically, it has ensured the tale a longevity and legs well beyond that of a great many real computer viruses.

Here are some of the more recent sightings of the joke:

The May 1, 2000, issue of *New Republic* magazine. For this publication, "professor of defense analysis at the U.S. Naval Postgraduate School and...consultant to the [Rand Corporation]" John Arquilla contributed a piece on the creeping evil of cyber-attack entitled, "Preparing for Cyberterrorism—Badly."

"In the Gulf war, for example, the United States implanted viruses and made other computer intrusions into Iraqi air defenses," wrote Arquilla. Gotcha!

In the March 1999 issue of *Popular Mechanics* magazine, at the end of an article on "information warfare," the publication wrote: "In the days following the Gulf War, stories circulated that [information warfare] weapons had been unleashed on the Iraqi air defense system. According to these accounts, French printers exported to the Iraqi military were intercepted and equipped with special chips developed by the [National Security Agency]. On these chips were programs designed to infect and disrupt the communications systems that linked anti-aircraft missiles to radar installations." No citations given. Gotcha!

The joke's publication as a *real story* in *US News* immediately ensured its permanence in the lore on cyberweaponry.

In 1998 *The Next World War* by James Adams, a book on the threat of cyberterrorists, featured the April Fool's joke as a real-world example of the use of computer viruses as weapons. Adams' citations pointed to the original poisoned entry from *US News*. Gotcha!

At the time, my colleague Rob Rosenberger, a world-renowned expert on computer viruses, commented: "[Adams] gives the story an interesting twist. The virus didn't get a chance to do its job because the U.S. Air Force accidentally bombed the building where Iraq stored the printers!" Adams subsequently started a computer security company, called iDefense. It provides consulting services to the US Department of Defense.

In 1997 the Hudson Institute think tank published an amusingly weird "study" entitled "Russian Views on Electronic and Information Warfare," which dove into the realms of telepathy, the paranormal, and their alleged application in cyber-combat. It, too, included a reference to the old joke: "For example, one cannot exclude the use of software inserts in imported gear used in the Iraqi air defense system..."

And the list of fools goes on.

Today the FBI appears, superficially, to be less vulnerable to disinformation on the topic of cyberterror as it was in the middle of the 1990s. It has built the very well-publicized National Infrastructure Protection Center (NIPC) which specializes in investigation of cyberterror and cybercrime and providing intelligence analyses of the same. NIPC mandarins appear frequently in the US press, generally with news of some type of frightening story. Much of what they have to say is taken very seriously. However, its analysts have also been known to tell whoppers.

In September 1999, a NIPC analyst on loan from the Central Intelligence Agency delivered an intelligence report entitled "Year 2000 Computer Remediation: Assessing Risk Levels in Foreign Outsourcing."

It made the troubling claim that any number of countries—mostly anywhere computer programmers could be found—had the means and motivation to use the process of Y2K remediation as a way to sabotage US computer systems on the rollover.

While everyone dubbed "foreign" could be a potential saboteur, the big players were India, Israel, France, Russia, Taiwan, China, Cuba, Bulgaria, Pakistan, the Philippines, and a host of other nations that routinely appear in the daily news.

"The unprecedented 'trusted' system access given to untested foreign computer software development companies and programmers in the Year 2000 remediation effort has offered a unique opportunity for potential adversaries to implant malicious code in sensitive enterprise or national security information systems," read the analysis at one point.

It also maintained, "Besides stealing data, intruders may use their access as Y2K code developers as an opportunity to insert programs that could deny or disrupt system or network service or corrupt data.

"In general, these illicit activities would begin when remediated software is installed and activated, not necessarily on 1 January 2000."

The publication of this document at a popular computer security convention in northern Virginia immediately touched off paranoid news stories nationwide implying that great calamities from these "activities" could occur on the rollover even though the NIPC analysis did not cite one single, verifiable instance of them in support of its claims.

Where had the programmer-saboteurs gone?

The only proof that was offered was this vague quote: "In one press report, an official of a large US information systems consulting firm involved in Y2K remediation activity stated that the firm had spotted trap doors—illicit portals for continuing access to updated systems and networks—in commercial information systems multiple times during its work."

At the time, the mainstream press also did not inform readers that the analysis had been published on a computer security vendor's Website—sans.org—where it was combined with a thinly-disguised advertisement for the organization's consulting services on detecting Y2K programmer-planted boobytraps and such.

Prior to January 1, there were no sightings of failure due to foreign programmer-saboteurs. On January 1, nothing particularly surprising happened to national computers, either. In the weeks following, it was still all quiet on the electronic front. Where had the programmer-saboteurs gone? There were no answers from the NIPC. The analyst of the report was quietly set aside. The media outlets that had run with uncritical pieces based on the NIPC analysis did not return to the story to question why its claims had been so much in error.

"Jan. 1 has been described as the Super Bowl for virus writers," was one knee-slapping quote proffered by some yahoo for the benefit of *Chicago Sun-Times* readers.

In a related theme, *in addition* to the Y2K Bug, the mainstream media continually promised a computer virus Armageddon in the last quarter of 1999. This threat failed to materialize, too, and the fiasco became known as the Great Y2K Virus Scare.

The Great Y2K Virus Scare contained a number of troubling features: ridiculous disinformation passed off as fact by individuals who stood to benefit from cheap publicity, vendors who used the attention to pump anti-virus software sales, and reporters or editors peddling an entirely hypothetical threat presented as reality in a brainless rush for a sexy scare story to add to Millennial Mania.

The quotes of approaching calamity came in a flood.

"Jan. 1 has been described as the Super Bowl for virus writers," was one knee-slapping quote proffered by some yahoo for the benefit of *Chicago Sun-Times* readers.

Government officials, wrote the *Washington Post* on December 21, were watching for "the stealthy attacks of viruses, worms and other damage-dealing software that already have made their way across the Internet and corporate computer networks. In recent weeks, the warnings have become louder and more fretful."

"Computer experts have been worried for some time about a flood of viruses designed to disrupt the nation's computer systems over the new year," nattered ABC news reader Connie Chung on December 20.

"...The [NIPC] says that malevolent hackers might try to exploit the [Y2K rollover] with viruses timed to multiply on January 1," wrote a Pulitzer-winner for the *New York Times* on December 19.

The FBI's National Infrastructure Protection Center issued a Y2K bulletin on December 31 that listed a number of computer viruses as potential threats. As an example of analytic work, a high school student with passing familiarity of the subject could have done better. Four viruses on the NIPC list—Atomic 1A, Atomic 1B, ARCV-718, and Diogenes—all dated from 1992! All four were simple DOS viruses, three of which (the Atomics and Diogenes) were products of the Virus Creation Laboratory, an antique virus-making kit that pumped out malicious software so non-functional and feeble it became the butt of jokes in the anti-virus community at the *beginning* of the 1990s. Whatever weed the NIPC analysts were smoking when they named 1992 VCL viruses something to be concerned about in Y2K, it was pure skank.

And Reuters continued to insist on deluding itself and readers in spite of a peaceful January 1, reporting, "While a general Y2K crisis appears to have been averted, concerns remain that malicious hackers have planted viruses that will hit in the days ahead when computer users boot up their machines...."

All of it was based on crap.

The media had conveniently forgotten the US anti-virus industry's long and glorious history of cynically hyping end-of-the-computing-world viruses which, somehow, never really seem to cause the end of the world of computing, LoveBug notwithstanding.

In 1989 there was the Columbus Day virus. Never mind that it didn't actually activate on Columbus Day. In 1992 it was Michelangelo. Another flop. In 1994, Junkie. Missed again. In 1995, Boza—"the first Windows95 virus." The virus did not work. In 1996 Hare Krishna was poised to reduce data to cinders. In 1998 it was CIH, set to turn millions of PCs into "useless doorstops." And CIH returned again in the summer of 1998, cynically renamed as Chernobyl so that the same old propaganda on it could be recycled anew.

It should be noted, of course, that the anti-virus industry is not entirely the refuge of mountebanks and dissembling tallywhackers. In fact, quite a few aren't of that ilk, and they tend to be greatly annoyed by the calculating press campaigns waged by competitors. One good example among the realists was Graham Cluley of Sophos, a UK anti-virus company. In November, alarmed by the growing amount of propaganda on the subject, the anti-virus expert took the extraordinary step of trying to halt the stampede. Sophos issued a white paper pooh-poohing the New Year virus panic, and Cluley commented for the UK's *Daily Telegraph*: "Some people are doing the industry a disservice. There is a problem with hype."

As an example of analytic work, a high school student with passing familiarity of the subject could have done better.

As the hysteria from the US spilled over internationally, more were moved to attempt damage control.

On December 23, the Finnish anti-virus firm, DataFellows, which handles the well known F-Prot anti-virus program, released a public memo that read: "[The company's] research shows no increased activity on the part of the virus-writing underground in anticipation of the coming Y2K weekend...."

And Sophos released still another memo on December 24 stating unequivocally that "there [was] simply no evidence that viruses will be any more of a problem on January 1 than any other day of the year."

None of this was reported by the big US media.

Claims of imminent attack by viruses aimed at January 1 were so easy to come by, even windbag politicians with zero expertise in the subject felt moved to jump on the bandwagon.

It should be noted, of course, that the anti-virus industry is not entirely the refuge of mountebanks and dissembling tallywhackers.

Senator Bob Bennett, for instance, was quoted in the December 19 edition of the *New York Times* claiming, "We are seeing evidence that some [hackers] will release viruses that will look like Y2K failures but are not."

But like the closely-related spew of paranoia over foreign programmers working to subvert US systems under the cover of Y2K, real evidence that viruses would make New Year's Day 2000 anything other than another shopping and bowl-watching day was not presented.

Mainstream media coverage of the affair focused on the sensational, completely overlooking the phenomenon of computer viruses over the entire decade to see a more realistic picture.

The common mistake made again and again in the Y2K reporting was in focusing on vendor press releases and the paranoid rantings of government officials about a handful of viruses that only were *said* to be a rising menace. For the layman, it created a superficial image of an unusual number.

The reality was and still is quite different. An average of over 500 computer viruses are discovered per month, according to *Virus Bulletin* editor emeritus Nick FitzGerald. This is ho-hum business to the industry, despite content to the contrary in marketing press releases. So while the number of panicked reports about potential viruses in the media in the space of a few weeks at the end of 1999 seemed quite remarkable, even a trend, it was not. On the contrary, it was the *publicity* surrounding the virus topic that was quite extraordinary. The media had gone virus mad. It would do so again for LoveBug.

The amount of irrationality surrounding the great Y2K virus panic had another rather sad but predictable effect. Large institutions and corporations, even parts of the US military, were buffaloed into disconnecting from the Net or turning off their computers in the mistaken belief that the maneuver would spare them from the black horde of approaching virus locusts.

The Associated Press issued the most certifiably idiotic and internally illogical advice of the entire affair on December 30. It recommended: "Turn off computers if possible..."

Obviously, I have only been able to touch upon a small number of stories here. However, the general trend in the media's coverage of hackers and cyberterror is a history of ludicrous botch-ups, sensationalism for purposes of horrification, and uncritical obeisance to government, Pentagon, and corporate press release.

Before leaving, I will touch upon the recent handling of the LoveBug story. While the virus was certainly real, the media response to it hewed to the news standard for reporting on problems in cyberspace. That is, it was a degenerate, insipid, and predictable routine in which pieties were mouthed and lip-pursing concerns emitted, most of which were worthless. This charade of self-delusion and bewilderment was characterized by the following:

1. Staggering figures of dollar damages due to the virus—all magic numbers—were produced on demand. The media, however, did not inform readers that the anti-virus industry has never had a reliable accounting capability or even a unified epidemiological service, so damages are whatever someone wants them to be.

2. Politicians demanded congressional hearings so that the same experts on viruses could repeat the exact things they always say when called before Congress. "It's a wake-up call"—a certified cliché—was repeated ad nauseam. Among others, Information Technology Association of America (ITAA) president Harris N.

Miller dutifully told a hastily convened House subcommittee, "[the] LoveBug was just one more wake up call..."

3. Justice groups made knee-jerk requests for stronger penalties against hackers. International Computer Security Association director Peter Tippett recommended Congress outlaw virus-writing in the wake of LoveBug hysteria. Tippett has made the recommendation since 1992. The advice is usually ignored as impractical or seen as ineffective.

4. The press loudly announced the FBI's proclamation of a manhunt. But interest rapidly petered out when no one could be quickly and cheaply strung up. After a couple months, no one seemed to care.

5. Two months after the hysteria over the LoveBug virus, Sophos released its list of the most common viruses worldwide. A virus called Kak, even older than LoveBug, was first. As for poor LoveBug, it was a distant third. This was not deemed news.

Today we find ourselves in a world where a great deal of the information we are passed by sources thought to be reliable cannot be trusted at all. Add to this teenagers and college students adept with computers, considered to be wizards by an older generation, not averse to embellishing the truth for a moment of publicity. Leaven with dissembling government or Pentagon officials. Bake slowly in the oven of a clumsy, subservient media. The result is a nasty, unappetizing pie in which most of the material you read about computer hackers and cyberterror is either staggeringly twisted, outright untrue, or presented so far out of context that it is meaningless.

How then can the average citizen detect a rat when confronted with such news?

It started life as a corporate press release or a simple money-making scheme.

A few rules of thumb are helpful. The following should make your bullshit detector buzz should you hear or read of them.

1. Does the story contain pseudonymous hackers? Do the pseudonymous hackers claim membership in a group with a menacing, but actually quite silly name, such as the Association of Really Cruel Viruses, the Internet Liberation Front, the Anti-Christ Doom Squad? Does the news story contain generic anti-corporate, anti-military, or anti-Internet-Service-Provider fist-waving philippics by said hackers?

Yes, yes and yes? Then it's most assuredly predominantly bull of benefit only to the egos successful in getting sucker journalists to bite on it.

2. Does the story contain doom-laden assertions from think tank experts, representatives of the Pentagon, and/or intelligence agency chiefs which seem contrary to common experience? Are the assertions coupled to catchy clichés like "it's a wake-up call," "electronic Pearl Harbor," or "cyber-Chernobyl"? Are the predictions of imminent doom coupled with recommendations for the creation of new government agencies or block funding?

Yes? Consider it more good fiction of benefit only to bureaucrats or representatives of the Department of Defense wishing to justify pet projects blurring the distinction between domestic law enforcement and military operations.

3. Does the story contain references to alarming classified information—news about alleged hacker feats so sensitive it cannot be shared with American citizens?

Yes? This is a common dodge used to protect extremely poor research, the equivalent of Pentagon gossip or blatant military-industrial conflicts of interest.

4. Does the story quote primarily from representatives of companies in the business of providing consulting services, hardware, or software guaranteed to protect computer networks from hackers?

Yes? Classify it as a free advertisement disguised as journalism. It started life as a corporate press release or a simple money-making scheme.

5. Is the story about a computer virus storming the gates of the Internet as corporate America and e-commerce crumble?

Yes? Facts: It will all be over except for the media shouting in a few hours. The Net will seem to be none the worse for wear. Computer viruses have always been a day-to-day problem in networked computing. But they are best classified only as nuisances.

The overly cynical reader may note that all the news reports of hackers and cybertrouble she has read in the past few years fall prey to many of these descriptions. Sadly, that's the truth.

For further related reading: "Electronic Pearl Harbor—Not Likely!" by George Smith, Issues in Science & Technology, *Fall 1998, National Academy of Sciences. <www.nap.edu/issues/15.1/smith.htm>*

School Textbooks

Unpopular History vs. Cherished Mythology?

Earl Lee

One of the most pervasive and yet poorly understood influences on American society is the high school textbook. Thanks to the virtual monopoly of public education, textbook publishers have a wide-ranging power to shape the ideas of young people. In reality, however, textbooks do more to misinform and mislead than almost any other print media. Some of our most basic beliefs, including our conception of ourselves as Americans, are shaped and distorted by the school textbook.

Major textbook publishers will not include content that might offend powerful political and religious constituencies, both national and local.

Looking at the areas of history, literature, and science, it is easy to see how textbooks fail. First, history textbooks typically focus on names, dates, and places, rather than on the conflict of political and economic interests. Second, literature textbooks create a censored and bowdlerized version of our literary heritage. Third, science textbooks present a detail-based version of science that often very deliberately shies away from broader concepts.

The reason for this is obvious. Textbook publishers want to sell textbooks to as many schools as possible. The key to doing this is marketing, which means printing bright, shiny book covers, pages filled with lots of color pictures, and an eye-catching layout. Creating a visually interesting layout is fairly easy and safe—unless you make the mistake, as recently happened, of printing a picture of General Washington in too bright colors, so that his watch fob could be mistaken for an exposed penis—then all hell can break out! At least this is what happened in Muscogee County, Georgia, where school officials, fearful of the "disruptive element" that would be created by fifth-graders who might notice the exposure of General Washington's fob, decided to alter the picture in 2,300 copies of the textbook.[1] Ironically, given the publicity over this picture and knowing the nature of fifth-grade boys, the students will probably draw brand-new cartoon penises on every single copy of the history text, so that within a few years all 2,300 pictures of General Washington will sport an enormous (and anatomically incorrect) "John Thomas" in place of the missing watch fob.

In spite of such occasional errors, the real problem with textbooks is not in the illustrations but in the written content. Major textbook publishers will not include content that might offend powerful political and religious constituencies, both national and local—from the local chamber of commerce to the Church of Christ. Offending these groups could be a serious obstacle to selling books.

Schools go to great lengths to avoid buying books that have dangerous ideas. In some states, a government agency takes over the role of censor by creating lists of "approved" texts. In a state the size of Texas, getting a textbook on the "approved" list means a potential gain of millions of dollars in sales for the publisher. Thus textbook publishers are motivated to search for the lowest possible threshold of political offensiveness.

In some areas, teachers have to select textbooks from a locally-approved list. In these situations, the school board appoints a committee to take over the task of weeding out any textbooks that contain offensive ideas. Also, in recent years a number of organizations have come forward to "help" school boards and state agencies by identifying dangerous textbooks that should be avoided. Controversial ideas must be cut out to avoid offending the feelings not only of the "educators" who select textbooks, but of the parents of students, and even people who have no school-age children but have self-appointed themselves as watchdogs for "community values."

For example, Mel and Norma Gabler, a married couple living in Texas, have had a strong influence on the choice of textbooks for public schools nationwide. For over a decade the Gablers have helped to bring about the rejection, or significant revision, of one-half to two-thirds of the textbooks proposed for use in Texas. Given the economics of textbook publishing, the Gablers have a ripple effect across the country, making them one of the most influential couples in education today. The Gablers include in their guidelines for textbooks that these should "encourage loyalty" and avoid "defaming"

In a state the size of Texas, getting a textbook on the "approved" list means a potential gain of millions of dollars in sales for the publisher.

the nation's founders, and avoid material that might lead students to criticize their parents. In one of his more revealing statements, Mel Gabler criticized textbooks, saying, "Too many textbooks and discussions leave students free to make up their minds about things."[2]

In addition to the Gablers and dozens of other right-wing groups, there are also left-wing groups who lobby textbook publishers, and some of these have been very successful in getting publishers to add more material favorable toward women and minorities, while also getting publishers to cut "expressions containing racial or ethnic statements that might be interpreted as insulting and stereotyping of the sexes, the elderly, or other minority groups or concerns."[3] Of course the word "might" here leaves a hole big enough to drive a truck through. This statement implies that material should be cut that might through some misinterpretation be considered racist. This means bowdlerizing the word "nigger" out of *Huckleberry Finn* and "fixing" the lower-class slang, or, better yet, not teaching the book at all.

Over all, the public-school textbook is designed to avoid controversy and perpetuate ideas that are safe, comfortable, and uncomplicated. To an outsider looking at the goals of public education, it is clear that the primary goal of public schools must be to instill in students conventional and conformist habits of thought. Textbook publishers recognize this fact and do their part to assist in the goal of creating a lazy conformity in students.

There have been a lot of complaints in the media in recent years about the dumbing-down of textbooks. However, most of these complaints point to lower standardized test scores as evidence of a failure in education. In fact, whether or not students can come up with the names of military leaders in the Civil War, the correct location of Lexington on a map, or the date for the passage of amendments to the Constitution, these factoids are of little real importance. It is far more important for students to understand *why* the Civil War started, *why* the Battle of Lexington took place, and *why* the amendments to the Constitution were necessary. But these things are not easily measured on a standardized test. Yet the corporate-controlled media focus almost exclusively on standardized test results when they criticize public education. This philosophy of education is pretty well summed up by Mel Gabler when he said, "Allowing a student to come to his own conclusions about abstract concepts creates frustration. Ideas, situation ethics, values, anti-God humanism—that's what the schools are teaching. And concepts. Well, a concept never will do anyone as much good as a fact."[4]

The possibility that people might view government as an instrument of the public will, much less take up arms to oppose entrenched power, is a dangerous idea that must be squelched on all levels.

In the real world, people tend to remember the things that engage their imagination. People are compelled by the interplay of ideas and personalities, not by the names and dates of historic events. The meaning of the Magna Carta is not in the date when it was signed, but rather in its origins. It has meaning as the result of the conflict that led to its creation and the personalities that brought it into existence. But in the classroom, the significance of the Magna Carta is obscured by factoids and the trivial pursuit of names and dates.

In 1999 when the Kansas State Board of Education voted to remove evolution from state standards, it caused a nationwide furor. Yet when this same Board voted to move away from using essay questions and toward relying on multiple-choice questions in evaluating students, there was virtually nothing said about this. Board members stated that this decision was based on the fact that the results of multiple-choice tests are easier to measure. Clearly the goal of twenty-first-century education is memorization, not understanding.

History

In theory, one of the main functions of public education is to help create a citizenry that understands the functions of government and is able to make informed judgments about how public policy will affect future generations. It is a basic justification for studying history, often repeated by historians, that those who fail to learn about the past are doomed to repeat it. This was certainly the view of many leaders of the American Revolution. We study history in order to understand how humans have responded in the past to different events and situations. As a society, we have a compelling interest in making sure that people understand how government functions, within the context of our history. But, at the same time, there are powerful commercial interests who see an informed citizenry as a direct threat to corporate power. These corporations would rather have a citizenry that is easily influenced to accept whatever message is given them by the corporate-controlled media. For this reason, they find the topics of the American Revolution and the Civil War to be particularly dangerous. The possibility that people might view government as an instrument of the public will, much less take up arms to oppose entrenched power, is a dangerous idea that must be squelched on all levels.

One of the most blatant frauds found in textbooks is the idea of "democracy." All students are taught, from a very early age, that the United States is a democracy and has a democratic form of government. However, anyone who bothers to objectively examine our system of government can quickly see that it is a republic, not a democracy. At the time of the Constitutional Convention, Ben Franklin declared that "we have a republic" and any nineteenth-century schoolboy could have told you this in an instant. This is why we have "The Battle Hymn of the Republic" and not "The Battle Hymn of the Democracy." The United States continued to think of itself as a republic through the end of the nineteenth century. After the Civil War, according to the newly-written Boy Scouts' Pledge of Allegiance, we were well on our way to becoming a homogenized "one nation, indivisible," but the American flag still represented "the republic, for which it stands."

By claiming that we live in a democracy, school textbooks help to deceive us about the basic functions of American government.

Interestingly, "democracy" was not always as cherished a concept as it is today. In the early years of the republic, "democracy" was a dirty word, in part because of its association with Cromwell and the Puritan Revolution in England. Thomas Jefferson, who today is one of the major icons of the Democratic Party, never identified himself as a "democrat" in his speeches or writings. Many other American leaders also avoided the "democratic" label. It wasn't until World War I that the term "democracy" lost its bad associations. During WWI, President Woodrow Wilson began pushing "democracy" as an idea that needed to be defended in Europe.[5] But it is pretty clear that Wilson, and those who followed his lead, used "democracy" as a vague euphemism for Americanism, meaning the Anglo-American form of government.

Thanks to Wilson, following WWI "democracy" stopped being a form of government and became, instead, a vague and loosely-defined expression meaning "The American Way." It is in this sense that the United States began exporting "democracy" to Latin America and other regions worldwide. Since then the history textbooks have reinforced this idea and have helped to homogenize the American federal and state powers into a democracy that isn't one. Today, most people incorrectly use "democracy" in place of "suffrage"—meaning the right of citizens to vote in elections. This confusion over "democracy" makes it easier for politicians to obscure the way our government really functions.

What textbooks do not teach us about government is this: There are very few truly democratic governments in existence in North America, much less the world. Even though politicians claim that the United States is a democracy, espouses democracy and democratic values, and promotes democracy worldwide—this is probably the greatest con game (bait-and-switch) in history. We may claim to be a government "of the people, by the people, for the people," but in fact we are ruled by a government made up of our "legal representatives" who were anointed by the mass media and voted into office with the help of money from lobbyists and PACs. Except for the few states that allow referenda, voters have no direct say in legislative decisions. And this situation is unlikely to change because, in the view of politicians and lobbyists, a republic works much better than a government "of the people," especially since it is very hard to lobby, much less buy off, "the people." By claiming that we live in a democracy, school textbooks help to deceive us about the basic functions of American government.

Looking at the American Revolution and the Civil War, we can see that there are several ideas that are typically obscured, avoided, downplayed, or distorted. A history textbook can easily be judged by how it deals with these problem issues:

1. **How does the textbook deal with the Anti-Federalists and the opposition to the Constitution?**

In some cases the Anti-Federalists are mentioned, though their concerns about the powers granted a new federal government are always dismissed as unfounded. This is the standard view of historians, although a convincing argument can be made that this increased federal power under the new Constitution led to a whole series of terrible consequences, from the extermination of native peoples to the Civil War. But, given the current political climate in this country, no existing school textbook is likely to (1) question the decision to create a new federal power, or (2) clearly explain why banks and other commercial interests strongly supported creating a new centralized federal power. It is worth noting, too, that even though the thirteen colonies had just defeated the most powerful empire on earth, the Federalists still wanted the power to levy federal taxes and establish a powerful federal army. The purpose of this army was clearly stated: to put down internal rebellions, like Shay's Rebellion. And what was the cause of Shay's Rebellion? Heavy taxes and resulting farm foreclosures!

In some cases the Anti-Federalists are mentioned, though their concerns about the powers granted a new federal government are always dismissed as unfounded.

2. **How does the text explain the origins of the Bill of Rights?**

It is common for textbooks to gloss over the Bill of Rights, as if these first ten amendments were a natural outgrowth of the Constitution. In actuality many Federalists did not want a Bill of Rights, and these amendments to the Constitution were passed largely due to the insistence of "old revolutionaries" like Jefferson. Earlier, during the debates over the Constitution, several states agreed to adopt the Constitution with the understanding that a Bill of Rights would be added. Although several dubious methods were used to get the Constitution ratified, not carrying through with the promise of a Bill of Rights would have been a public-relations disaster for the new government, and so passing the Bill of Rights was, grudgingly, supported by many Federalists. It is important for today's students to understand that the passage of the Bill of Rights was not, by any means, a sure thing.

Most textbooks struggle to avoid an honest assessment of Washington's military leadership.

3. How quickly does the textbook gloss over the Alien and Sedition Acts?

The passage of these legislative measures is a touchy point in American history. This was the closest we came, early on, to establishing a monolithic oligarchy. Most textbooks rush to point out that the public reaction against the acts led to Jefferson's election as president. They also often point out that only a few people were actually imprisoned or deported under the acts, which makes as much sense as claiming that the Watergate burglars broke into only one hotel. A comparison with Watergate is an apt one, because the Watergate scandal still creates strong feelings today, and consequently textbooks tend to focus on the reaction and reforms it caused, rather than on what Nixon's men did to cause the scandal.

4. How does the textbook handle George Washington?

Most textbooks struggle to avoid an honest assessment of Washington's military leadership. Washington is often presented as the first person to lead the country (ignoring the earlier leaders of the Continental Congress, like John Hancock and Richard Henry Lee). It would be more honest to say that Washington was the first leader of the new federal government under the Constitution. In spite of the fact that the Continental Congress successfully led us through the Revolution, this body is typically described as weak and ineffective. It is George Washington who is portrayed as the true hero of the Revolution. Additionally, in terms of his military leadership, it is worth noting that the Iroquois knew George Washington as "the destroyer of towns" because his Indian policy was to starve them out by burning their villages and corn fields, rather than fighting them on the battlefield. But this fact will certainly never find its way into textbooks.

5. How does the textbook explain the origins of the Civil War?

Most textbooks focus on slavery as the main issue of the Civil War, even though slavery was really one of several broader political and economic conflicts between North and South. Lincoln himself appeared to have mixed feelings about the issue, as his Emancipation Proclamation freed only the slaves living in the Confederacy, and then only the slaves living in those areas still under control of rebel forces. From a legal point of view, the Emancipation Proclamation was based on the idea that slaves were property used in the act of rebellion and could therefore legally be seized (under the Confiscation Act). Ironically, after the end of the war many newly-freed slaves moved north, becoming a cheap source of labor for Northern factories. As former slaves moved north they often exchanged their former status as chattel slaves for the position of wage slaves in Northern factories. One former slave, years later, described slavery as "a snake pointed south" and emancipation as "a snake pointed north." Of course, this fact is unlikely to find its way into history textbooks, which are more concerned with the effects of Reconstruction.

6. Does the textbook mention the hardships and privations suffered by civilians as the result of the conflict, and especially Sherman's March to the Sea? Does the issue of various "war crimes" come up at all?

Sherman was the first American general to use "total war." By this it is meant that Sherman destroyed food supplies necessary for the survival of many Southerners. People today, who can go to a grocery to buy food, have no idea just how terrible Sherman's March was in its very real consequences for the civilian population of Georgia, white and black. Before this time, American soldiers had not waged this type of war on white civilian populations. Furthermore, in terms of what today we would today call "war crimes," textbooks are very careful about how they deal with various Native American death marches, the most well-known of these being the Cherokee "Trail of Tears."

7. How does the textbook deal with Reconstruction?

Under the influence of Southern states, many of whom had laws requiring the use of the term "War Between the States" rather than "Civil War" in educational materials, textbook publishers have come over the years to adopt a pro-Southern take on this topic. The Reconstruction era is virtually always portrayed as a period when greed and political corruption ran rampant in the South.[6] In reality, though, Reconstruction ushered in an era of relatively honest and fair government.

The effects of Reconstruction can be compared with more recent history to make this process clear. In 1966 when Winthrop Rockefeller was elected the first Republican governor of Arkansas since Reconstruction, his election marked the end of decades of one-party rule, characterized by cronyism, graft, and corruption on a massive scale. For example, when the former governor Orval Faubus left office in 1967 he was able to buy a house worth more than $100,000 even though, as governor, he had only earned $10,000 a year in salary. After taking office, Governor Rockefeller began a massive overhaul of the corrupt state prison system. He did this largely by bringing in experts (i.e. carpetbaggers) from outside of Arkansas to clean up and manage the prisons (as dramatized in the 1980 film *Brubaker*). Of course the locals who lost their jobs (and graft) during Rockefeller's mini-Reconstruction were outraged.

8. How does the textbook deal with race riots, lynchings, and the widespread growth of racial violence in the early part of this century?

This aspect of American history has never been dealt with very well in history textbooks, in large part because textbook authors don't like to write about events where anyone could be blamed for anything. On the one hand, when you write about the Alien and Sedition Acts, it's easy to emphasize that President Adams was hesitant to enforce the legislation, and only a few-dozen people were deported or imprisoned, while the reaction led to Jefferson's election. On the other hand, how do you write about the Tulsa Race Riot of 1921? It is impossible to write about this horrendous event without blaming the white population. It is hard for textbook authors to find a silver lining in an act of pure hatred, when white mobs attacked and burned all the black businesses in the city. And so it is difficult to find the Tulsa Race Riot even mentioned.

Textbook authors don't like to write about events where anyone could be blamed for anything.

On the other hand, the Civil Rights movement of the 1960s does have genuine heroes who can be the main characters of the drama. At the same time, when it is covered in history texts, Civil Rights history is often written so that the whites who opposed integration come off as well as possible, usually as victims of a racist upbringing. The KKK is a handy bad guy, though it is considered bad manners to mention that the KKK was a powerful political force in Northern states, too, from Kansas to Indiana. Typically, in our history books, Martin Luther King, Jr. and Rosa Parks are put center stage, while the lynchings and murders are kept far in the background. After all, in trying to cover American history, textbook publishers have to keep one eye on the large textbook markets in Florida and Texas.

9. How does the textbook deal with the assassination of President McKinley?

History books typically refer to McKinley's assassin, Leon Czolgosz, as an "anarchist." In fact, Czolgosz was a Republican and, like his father and brother, voted in Republican primaries in Cleveland. Newspapers claimed that Czolgosz was an anarchist based on the fact that police found a newspaper story in his coat pocket describing a speech by anarchist Emma Goldman. In truth, Czolgosz was a mentally-disturbed individual who had approached various anarchist groups in the months before the McKinley assassination, talking about violence. These anarchists avoided having anything to do with Czolgosz, believing him to be a police spy or an agent provocateur. They even published warnings, suggesting other anarchists avoid Czolgosz. After the assassination, police arrested Emma Goldman in another city and held her in prison until, after a thorough investigation, they were unable to find any evidence against her.

It is worth contrasting this assassination with the attempted assassination of President Reagan by John Hinckley. Hinckley's ties to the Republican party (his parents knew the Bush family) were barely mentioned in news reports. Instead, reporters universally assumed that Hinckley was a nut-case acting out of his obsession with actress Jodie Foster. Unlike Emma Goldman, Jodie Foster was not arrested and held until proven innocent. Actor Robert De Niro, whose role in *Taxi Driver* supposedly inspired Hinckley, was also not arrested, nor was he questioned about possible ties to Italian anarchist groups.

■ ■ ■ ■ ■ ■ ■ ■ ■ ■ ■

There are literally dozens of other questions one could ask: How does the textbook deal with labor history? Does it mention the struggle for the eight-hour day and the minimum wage at all? Does it mention Eugene Debs, the International Workers of the World (IWW), the Socialist Party, the Haymarket Martyrs, the AFL and CIO, the trials of pacifists in WWI, the women's riots over unsafe factories, etc., etc., etc.?

The problem is, of course, that high school history textbooks tend to give a heavily pro-corporate "consensus" view of history. In this version of history, it is important to develop a cherished mythology rather than an accurate nuts-and-bolts view of historical events. Creating a cherished mythology means that textbooks avoid all the unpopular "revisionist" histories, as textbook publishers particularly dislike the idea of abandoning popular ideas for more pragmatic views of historical events. This resistance to "unpopular" history is also common to public history, meaning the history put forth in museums and public exhibits.

For example, in 1995, when the Smithsonian Institution tried to put on an *Enola Gay* exhibit, the whole project came under considerable criticism from veterans' groups which objected to graphic photographs of the human casualties of the atomic bombing of Hiroshima. Interestingly enough, an earlier exhibit on the use of the V2 bombs by the Nazis, including graphic photographs of the human devastation in London, did not provoke a reaction (although if a similar exhibit were held in a Berlin museum, it would probably have drawn fire). The *Enola Gay* exhibit was quickly withdrawn and replaced by a more politically expedient exhibit. Richard Kurin, in his book *Reflections of a Culture Broker*, says that the curators "naively believed that there is an absolute historical truth." Indeed, many academic historians believe that being historically accurate is a reasonable defense from criticism. The curators at the Smithsonian forgot that the use of the atomic bomb is still a major part of our nation's military capability and should not be criticized by publicly-funded institutions.

It also happens that museum exhibits can be put forward for purely political reasons. In 1998 the Library of Congress opened an exhibit called "Religion and the Founding of the American Revolution." The exhibit was based on a research by James Hutson, chief of the Library's manuscript division. This exhibit went to great lengths to present Jefferson's statement on the separation of Church and State as an empty political exercise, rather than Jefferson's statement of policy. The exhibit opened, interestingly enough, just as the House of Representatives was preparing to vote on the Religious Freedom Amendment, which would do a great deal to cancel recent Supreme Court pro-separation decisions. Additionally, in California, a member of the Academic Standards Commission cited this exhibit in an effort to remove references to Church-State separation from proposed statewide history guidelines for public schools.[7]

Religious history is potentially the most dangerous, politically, for the textbook publishers. And, regrettably, they tend to omit all reference to religion, except in the most broad and general terms. Students do not, for example, know the difference between a Pilgrim and a Puritan. Most don't learn that Thomas Paine, like many of the Founding Fathers, was a deist. Nor do they learn that Teddy Roosevelt once called Paine "a dirty little atheist." They are almost certainly ignorant of the fact that Abraham Lincoln was the first President who thought that politics should be influenced by Christian values. Many areas of the American religious experience are left unexplored—deism, congregationalism, spiritualism, communalism, the origins of various religious denominations in the nineteenth century—most of these are absent from textbooks. Richard Shenkman's popular book *I Love Paul Revere, Whether He Rode or Not* contains more information in one chapter on religion in American history than most schools teach from kindergarten through the twelfth grade.

The goal of history textbooks is to convey a "cherished mythology"—a consensus view of history full of inaccuracies and misrepresentations. In public schools, history becomes what the majority of people think it is. And even though there has been a good deal of progress in terms of expanded coverage of women and minorities, many of the dirty little secrets are left secret.

Literature

As with history, the study of literature often descends into a trivial pursuit of facts and data, things easily measured in multiple-guess questions. This has been true for many years, as I can remember being asked what the Nun ate for dinner in *The Canterbury Tales*, on a test in high-school English. This obsession with trivia hasn't changed in the intervening 30 years.

As with history, the study of literature often descends into a trivial pursuit of facts and data, things easily measured in multiple-guess questions.

Helping students to come to a real understanding of our cultural history is not a goal of public education, largely because there are a lot of dangerous ideas in there. As with history, there are "problems" that textbook editors tend to look at very gingerly, and avoid altogether when possible. In this case, literature anthologies have a decided advantage. It is fairly easy to "select" particular works as essential parts of the established literary canon, while ignoring the more dangerous stuff.

It's not difficult to criticize literature anthologies for not including enough minorities or women. This is an easy (and valid) criticism to make. Recently, some publishers have tried hard to correct this defect. However, it is perhaps more interesting to look at how "major" authors are bowdlerized and distorted in these textbooks. We are all familiar with how Shakespeare is "adapted" for school textbooks, but how is this done for other authors?

For example, most people reading the poetry of Emily Dickinson, as she is anthologized in school textbooks, would assume that she was a nature poet. Her more questionable works are easily omitted. After all, what would a high school student make of her poem "Wild Nights" or, worse yet, "I Held a Jewel"? (Several recent interpretations suggest that Dickinson's "jewel" was, obviously, her clitoris.) The same problem is true of Wordsworth, Byron, Keats, and the other English Romantic poets, as some of their best poetry, like Byron's *Don Juan*, might be considered too erotic for the classroom. Most of these poets were also sympathetic toward the revolutions of the time. But these revolutionary and/or erotic impulses, as well as Shelley's atheism, can easily be omitted from the anthologies.

A good litmus test for a textbook on English literature is to examine how it deals with William Blake. That is, does the anthology include his poetry critical of English society? Does the book deal with his unorthodox religious views? On the other hand, Charles Dickens' *A Tale of Two Cities* is a popular choice for school textbooks, especially since it criticizes the French and the lower classes. But there are a number of land mines, even in popular classics

Swift's *Gulliver's Travels* is the original source for the expression "a piece of ass."

of English literature. For example, Dickens' *Oliver Twist* has a boy called Master Bates who is continually jingling the change in his pocket. And, worse yet, Swift's *Gulliver's Travels* is the original source for the expression "a piece of ass." There are, of course, many texts that will probably never make it into a school textbook. For example, what textbook publisher today would even consider adding selections from De Quincey's *Confessions of an English Opium-Eater*? Or worse yet, selections from anti-authoritarian fiction like *The Loneliness of the Long Distance Runner* by Alan Sillitoe. In fact, any book that celebrates resistance to authority is, like General Washington's penis, a likely candidate for exclusion from school textbooks.

In terms of American literature, a good litmus test involves looking at how the text handles Walt Whitman. Does the anthology include poetry from the first edition of *The Leaves of Grass* or does it use verse from the later versions? The first version of *Leaves* was very powerful, often even erotic (in a nineteenth-century sort of way). Over time Whitman kept rewriting and editing the text, with one eye on his future reputation as a poet. The later versions of *Leaves* are the work of an old man, mainly concerned with becoming a mainstream poet who would be remembered and anthologized, and to that purpose he was very successful. In looking at Whitman, an even more interesting question would be to ask how many school textbooks include Whitman's "A Sun Bath Nakedness" in which he describes going naked near a secluded stream. What high school anthology would dare to make reference to his naturist views, much less to his sexual orientation?[8]

A good deal of the literature that was added in the 1970s because it held echoes with the 1960s generation was removed from textbooks in the 1990s. And there is plenty of material from that era that will never find its way into a textbook. After all, what textbook publisher would consider adding selections from books like *Who Walk in Darkness* by Chandler Broassard, *The Monkey Wrench Gang* by Edward Abbey, or John Holmes' *Go*? These books, along with many others that celebrate the lower classes, environmentalism, and other subcultures—in other words, any work that gives alternatives to the middle-class view of what America should be—are excluded from textbooks.

Like Emily Dickinson, Ralph Waldo Emerson is often included in literature anthologies for his views on nature and his philosophical views on nineteenth-century America. His religious views, however, are too scandalous to be included in any school anthology. Emerson was not anti-Christian, but he was certainly anti-religion, and in his "Divinity School Address" he bluntly said that going to church on the Sabbath was a poor way to get in touch with the divine.

Even more important is Henry Thoreau, especially in terms of his influence on Dr. Martin Luther King, Jr. and Mahatma Gandhi. But although his work "Civil Disobedience" was a major intellectual force in history, it is also problematic in an era where school administrators are obsessed with classroom control. Can a school culture where George Washington's watch fob can be erased as a "disruptive element in the classroom" accommodate Thoreau? This is a case where, although "Civil Disobedience" is too important to be left out of anthologies, one might fairly ask how it is taught.

Looking at the reader *Elements of Literature, Fifth Course* (1993), we find that it includes Thoreau's work, but cut very drastically to remove a number of objectionable passages. This textbook includes his essay complete through the middle of the fourth paragraph—including a strong libertarian statement against government regulation—but cuts a large section beginning, "It is truly enough said that a corporation has no conscience...." It's not hard to see how the editors might have been urged to cut this viewpoint. Shortly after, Thoreau begins a passage that could be viewed as disrespectful of the military, describing marines as "a mere shadow and reminiscence of humanity," mere walking machines without judgment or moral sense. He then expands this description to include "legislators, politicians, lawyers, ministers, and office-holders." This sentiment might have been left intact, satisfying the censors, except for his including ministers in this group.

"It is truly enough said that a corporation has no conscience...."

Then Thoreau is unkind enough to describe his home state of Massachusetts, using the verse:

> A drab of state, a cloth-o'-silver slut,
> To have her train borne up, and her soul trail in the dirt.

This is not exactly the kind of sentiment you'd find engraved on a state commemorative quarter! Thoreau uses this verse to attack the merchants of Massachusetts for profiting from slavery and the war with Mexico. He then follows this with a criticism of voting, saying, "All voting is a sort of gaming, like checkers or backgammon, with a slight moral tinge to it, a playing with right and wrong." This is followed by a damning condemnation of political conventions and men without backbone who live by the principles of what is easy and expedient.

Generally speaking, the editor of this textbook has left the intellectual argument in place, while cutting out the guts of the essay. All that might be objected to has been removed. The people of Massachusetts can sleep safe, knowing that the editors have erased a terrible insult against them. And the people of Massachusetts will, in turn, buy lots of textbooks.

Shortly after the Columbine massacre, a school official claimed that the murders might not have happened if the Ten Commandments had been posted on the wall at Columbine High School. This idea seems laughable to most intelligent people. After all, how could the violent "eye for an eye" ethic of the Old Testament have deterred anyone from committing violence? However, one might seriously ask if the Columbine attack would have happened had Thoreau's "Civil Disobedience," with its principles of non-violent protest, been taught *in its original form* in the English classes at Columbine.

Another popular text that has fairly recently fallen on hard times is Shirley Jackson's story "The Lottery." This story, written at the end of WWII, portrays a rural community where, each year, a person is selected in a lottery and then stoned to death. The community continues this practice because it is traditional and, some residents say, important to the fertility of the crops. The lottery is, obviously, a religious ritual, and the story can also be read as an oblique criticism of the "Red Scare." Although this story was once quite popular in literature anthologies, it has been cut out of recently editions, largely because it associates religion with violence.[9]

On the other hand, you can count on the literary canon to include texts that cover long-dead political controversies. For example, Melville's *Billy Budd* is anthologized fairly often, especially now that sailors are rarely ever whipped or hanged at sea. Similarly, selections from *Moby Dick* are a popular choice, especially as no one today is likely to object to a ship full of whale-killers meeting a watery grave. Like *Rime of the Ancient Mariner*, this novel teaches an exemplary attitude toward animals.

We will never live to see selections from Steinbeck's boldly pro-union *In Dubious Battle* taught in schools.

More problematic are Melville's anti-war poems and his novels *Typee* and *The Confidence Man*. Melville's 1846 novel *Typee* was based on his experiences in the South Pacific, and in the original version, published in England, the novel contains criticism of both missionaries and American imperialism. The revised American edition of *Typee*, published by John Wiley, cut out these references, along with references to the venereal diseases which Americans and Europeans spread among the native population. The expurgated version of *Typee* is still being reprinted, in large part because it renders the novel into a safe "children's adventure story." Similarly, Melville's *The Confidence Man* casts an unfavorable light on American boosterism and commercialism, much like Sinclair Lewis' *Babbitt*, which is also an unlikely choice for a high-school literature anthology. And Lewis' *Elmer Gantry*—don't even think it! His hilarious satire of evangelical Christianity would not go over well in most communities.

Similarly, Upton Sinclair's *The Jungle* is considered a classic novel, but it is rarely taught in schools or included in anthologies. Some of the problems Sinclair describes in the meatpacking industry are still very much alive today—so much so that when a recent unexpurgated version of his novel, called *The Lost First Edition of Upton Sinclair's The Jungle*, was published in 1988, it was quietly suppressed by the meatpacking industry through some backdoor dealings, much the same way they tried to suppress the original 1905 publication. Largely excluded from the literary anthologies, today Sinclair's classic novel has become little more than a footnote in history books.

We are far enough removed from the Great Depression to accommodate *The Grapes of Wrath*, but we will never live to see selections from Steinbeck's boldly pro-union *In Dubious Battle* taught in schools. In fact, although many socialist and pro-union books and novels were published in the early part of this century, very few such books—especially novels—are published today. And virtually no "leftist" material is included in the literary canon or in the literary anthologies. One of the few recent pro-union novels, Kathleen DeGrave's *Company Woman* (1995), even found its way onto the list of Almost Banned Books published by *Counterpoise* magazine. This list is published as a small-press alternative to the so-called "Banned Books" list published each year by the American Library Association.

The lack of fiction dealing with the laboring classes also has another drawback in terms of the literary canon, as many of these working-class novels were written by women, including Meridel Le Sueur, Rebecca Harding Davis, Theresa Malkiel, Agnes Smedley, Mary Heaton Vorse, Catherine Brody, Josephine Herbst, Ruth McKenney, Josephine Johnson, Beatrice Bisno, Leane Zugsmith, and Mari Sandoz.

Science

Science is probably the most difficult area to judge for the layman, especially since most people have a fairly limited understanding of the implications of bad science. It is worth noting that in 2000 the American Association for the Advancement of Science gave its harshest criticism ever of math and science textbooks. They gave unsatisfactory ratings to all ten of the major high school biology textbooks that they reviewed. "At their best, the textbooks are a collection of missed opportunities," according to Dr. Jo Ellen Roseman, director of the study. "While most contain the relevant content on heredity and natural selection, for example, they don't help students to learn it or help teachers to teach it."[10]

Although the books had bright, colorful graphics, they all fell short in terms of four basic ideas: how cells work, how matter and energy flow from one source to another, how plants and animals evolve, and the molecular basis of heredity. The books spent more time on vocabulary words, naming the parts of cells, etc., than on understanding concepts of biology. Generally speaking, the critics claimed that these textbooks were "obscuring with needless detail" the principle ideas of biology. The textbooks did not relate science to everyday life or provide for hands-on experience.

Publishers quickly responded to this criticism by accusing state standards of being responsible for this problem. The people who write the standards, in turn, complained that textbook publishers were not giving them what they asked for. In reality, a major part of the problem is the fact that textbook publishers are desperately trying to avoid being caught up in the creation vs. evolution controversy.

The publisher of *Kansas: The Prairie State Lives* decided to cut the entire first chapter of the textbook, which included references to fossils and the inland sea that once covered what is now Kansas.

Several states are currently involved in that controversy. In August 1999, here in Kansas, the State Board of Education voted to remove references to evolution from state standards, replacing them with standards written with the help of a creationist organization. As a result of this controversy, the publisher of *Kansas: The Prairie State Lives* decided to cut the entire first chapter of the textbook, which included references to fossils and the inland sea that once covered what is now Kansas. The publishers candidly stated that they were concerned about criticism from creationists, most of whom believe that the earth is only a few thousand years old.

■ ■ ■ ■ ■ ■ ■ ■ ■ ■

Mel and Norma Gabler, who are active in criticizing school textbooks, also are supporters of both creationism and home-schooling. Many conservative critics of public schools are supporters of various right-wing causes, including home-schooling and voucher programs. It would be fair to say that they support any changes that would give them more power over the content of education, public and private. Many of these critics approach textbook reform, not as friends of public education, but as enemies who ultimately want to see public education moved to private control. Controlling the content of textbooks in public schools is, in reality, only a temporary position to be maintained until they can get more direct control over education. Controlling textbooks is only one step toward the goal of completely changing public education as it exists today.

Ultimately, in spite of the pressures from these special interests, textbook publishers must take responsibility for producing a bad product. Unfortunately, we probably won't see any mass litigations, as we have with the tobacco industry. But even so, it seems that textbook publishers should take full credit for creating a bad product. And the educators and editors who put together these textbooks should be held accountable for their failures.

Even more importantly, many educational associations and government agencies need to get involved in promoting good textbooks. The National Education Goals Panel, for example, recently sponsored a paper by Harriet Tyson called "Overcoming Structural Barriers to Good Textbooks" and has made the paper available on its Website. Similarly, the Association of Departments of English has promoted research on the censorship of literary texts. These groups can do a great deal to counter the influence of right-wing groups and restore a more balanced and open-minded approach to education.

Endnotes

1. Reed, Kwofi. "Censorship foes: Altering painting of Washington crosses the line." Free! The Freedom Forum Online. <www.freedomforum.org/speech/1999/10/11gawashfobs.asp> **2.** DelFattore, Joan. (Spring 1986). "Contemporary censorship pressures and their effect on literature textbooks." *ADE Bulletin*, pp 35-40. <www.ade.org/ade/bulletin/N083/083035.htm> **3.** *Ibid.* **4.** *Ibid.* **5.** Schenkman, Richard. (1989, c1988). *Legends, lies & cherished myths of American history*. New York: HarperPerrenial, p 22. **6.** Loewen, James W. (1995). *Lies my teacher told me*. New York: New Press, p 149. **7.** Unsigned. (July/Aug 1998). "Library of Congress questions Jefferson's 'wall' letter." *Church & State*, p 18. **8.** see Abrams, Sam. (1993). *The neglected Walt Whitman: Vital texts*. New York: Four Walls Eight Windows. **9.** *Op cit.*, DelFattore. **10.** "Big biology books fail to convey big ideas, reports AAAS's Project 2061." Project 2061 press release, June 27, 2000. <www.project2061.org/newsinfo/press/rl000627.htm>

Additional Works Cited

Elements of literature, fifth course: Literature of the United States. Austin: Holt, Rinehart & Winston; HBJ, 1993.

Shenkman, Richard. (1991). *I love Paul Revere, whether he rode or not*. New York: HarperPerrenial.

Further Reading

Apple, Michael W. & Linda K. Christian-Smith. (1991). *Politics of the textbook*. New York: Routledge.

Crabtree, Charlotte A. (1994). *National standards for United States history: Exploring the American experience*. Los Angeles: National Center for History in the Schools, University of California.

Davis, O. L. (1986). *Looking at history: A review of major U.S. history textbooks*. Washington D.C.: People for the American Way.

Gabler, Norma & Mel. "Scientific weaknesses in evolutionary theory." <www.fni.com/heritage/aug98/evolution.html>

Graves, Patrick K. (May 8, 1999). "Education board honors controversial textbook critics: Five members protest resolution, accuse Mel and Norma Gabler of racism" *Corpus Christi Caller Times*. <www.caller.com/autoconv/newslocal99/newslocal1168.html>

Loewen, James. (1999). *Lies across America: What our historic sites get wrong*. New York: New Press.

McCabe, Joseph. (1947). *The lies and fallacies of the Encyclopedia Britannica*. Girard, KS: Haldeman-Julius Pub.

Nash, Gary B. (1997). *History on trial: Culture wars and the teaching of the past*. New York: Knopf.

Tyson, Harriet. "Overcoming structural barriers to good textbooks." <www.negp.gov/reports/tyson.htm>

The Information Arms Race

Douglas Rushkoff

In any Information War, we human beings lose by definition. For the moment communication becomes information, it is no longer alive. As living beings, when we accept a role in the InfoWar, we also lose the home field advantage—the defensive capability offered any indigenous population.

When we are fooled into believing the battle over information is, in fact, a battle over our reality, we have already lost the war.

Communication Only Occurs Between Equals

Television broadcasting is not communication. Neither are radio news, magazines, or even this little essay. These are all one-way distribution of content. However vital, realistic, or engaging a movie or book, it is not interactive or participatory in any real sense. Unless we can have just as much of an effect on the director, writer, producer, or journalist as he has on us, we are not involved in a communication. We are merely the recipients of programming.

Even the so-called "interactive" media, like computer games and most Websites, simply allow for the user to experience a simulation of free choice. The creator of the simulation is no longer present. If a player creates a sequence of moves that has never been played before, or a reader moves through an interactive story along a path that has never been followed before, this still does not count as communication. It is merely a unique and personalized experience of essentially dead data. Multimedia CD-ROMs are not interactive, because the user is not interacting with anyone.

Even the so-called "interactive" media, like computer games and most Websites, simply allow for the user to experience a simulation of free choice.

This is not so terrible in itself. Stories, movies, and video games are all great storage media. The enduring values of many indigenous cultures are passed down from generation to generation through myths and stories. The artist, philosopher, and scientist alike have published their findings in one form or another for the consumption of others. For centuries, we have willingly submitted to the performances and writings of great thinkers, and have been enriched as result. They are what allow for a cumulative human experience over time, greater than any single life span.

Today, "communications" is the science of influence.

But we should not confuse such experiences with communication. However lifelike it may feel, unless we are in a position to influence the presenter as much as he can influence us, we are not involved in a living exchange. In other words, to be aroused by a pornographic tape is not to make love.

For like lovemaking, communication is a living exchange between equal partners. No matter how much our world's nihilists might like to deny it, there is an energy inherent to such exchanges: a living space of interaction. And this is the zone where change—and all its inherent dangers—can occur.

Just as lovemaking presents the possibility of new genetic combinations, communication initiates the process of cultural mutation. When equals are communicating, nothing is fixed. Honest participation means everything is up for grabs.

Information Wants To Be Preserved

The so-called "Communications Departments" of most major universities would have us believe otherwise. The study of mass media has little to do with mass participation in the design of cultural values. Students do not learn how to foster the living interaction between a society's members. There are few courses in promoting media literacy or creating Usenet groups to solve problems collectively.

Today, "communications" is the science of influence. Mass communication is the study of how governments and corporations can influence their populations and customers—the so-called "masses." The tools they employ are rhetoric, the ancient art of influence,[1] and information, the modern science of control.[2]

But wherever real communication is occurring, there is life. Like the new buds on a tree, the places where communication takes place are the most effective leverage points in a culture from which to monitor and direct new growth. Those hoping to direct or, as is most often the case, stunt the development of cultural change, focus on these points. By imitating the qualities we associate with living communication, and then broadcasting fixed information in its place, the mass media manipulator peddles the worldview of his sponsors.

Anthropology and Religion

Most anthropology is carried out in service of a nation or corporation. The anthropologist is the research half of the "R & D" for cultural manipulation. Historically, the anthropologist is sent to a new territory ripe for commercial, religious, or political colonization. He looks for the gaps or inconsistencies in the culture's mythology, so that these "soft spots" may be hardened with strong, imported data.

For example, sixteenth-century Christian missionaries to the New World first studied the indigenous people in order to appraise their pantheistic belief system, as well as gain their trust. They observed local rituals to learn about particular beliefs associated with each god. Then they converted people by associating local gods with the closest corresponding Catholic saints or deities. The native god for animals, the people were taught, is really just St. Francis. The drinking of chicken's blood is really just a version of the communion. And so on, until a local, hybridized version of Christianity evolved.

In the 1500s, Franciscan brothers studied the language and religion of the people of Tenochtitlàn before choosing to build the hilltop basilica of the Virgin of Guadalupe on the site of an Aztec temple dedicated to the earth goddess Tonatzin. In its new incarnation, the mountaintop church became an homage to Mary, who is pictured stepping on the stars and moon, the symbols of her pagan predecessor. She overlooks what is now called Mexico City. These missions were not generally sponsored by the church, but by the monarchy. As a result, the visiting missionary served the dual role of converter and intelligence gatherer. Ultimately, both functions simply prepared the target population for its inevitable co-option by force.

This is the two-millennium-old process by which Christianity absorbed the rituals and beliefs of the peoples it converted. The Christmas tree began as a solstice ritual practiced by Germans to light the darkest night of the year. Smart missionaries of the time realized that this was the superstitious ritual developed to address the people's fear of the darkness of winter. The missionaries did a fairly advanced job of cultural analysis for the time, keying in on the local people's doubt in the rejuvenation of the coming spring season. The tannenbaum exposed their deepest fear—and most fertile ground for conversion.

By identifying the tree with the rood and the birth of Christ, the missionaries augmented the pagan ritual, and redirected the sense of hope that the ritual fostered away from pagan forces and towards their own messiah. They filled a living ritual with dead information.

Similarly, churches and cathedrals were most often placed on local pagan "power spots" and lay lines—not because the priests believed that these locations offered any magical leverage, but because the people believed they did. What better way to get people into your church than to build it on the same spot where they already did their praying? Ironically, the "black masses" that were conducted illicitly by pagans on church altars were not meant as a statement against Christianity at all. The unconverted people were merely attempting to carry out their pre-Christian ceremonies in the locations where they believed they would work.

In the years preceding World War II, anthropologists studied the cultures of the South Seas so they could more easily be turned to the "Allied" cause against the Japanese once these territories were to become a war zone. Whether or not these well-meaning cultural researchers knew it, the governments funding them had more than pure science in mind when they chose which expeditions to fund.

After World War II, Air Force Brigadier General Edward G. Lansdale emerged as the preeminent "counterinsurgency" strategist for the CIA. Over a period of three decades, he developed a wide range of intelligence and propaganda theories that were employed and refined in the field. His principle strategy was first to engage in qualitative anthropological research to discover a target audience's underlying belief systems, and then exploit these beliefs mercilessly in the pursuit of military gains.

For example, in the 1950s as part of his counterinsurgency campaign against the Huk rebels of the Philippines, Lansdale began by conducting research into local superstitions. He learned that the Huk battleground was believed to be inhabited by an "asuang," or vampire figure. To capitalize on this mythology, his "psywar" units would follow Huk patrols and then quietly ambush the last man on the trail. They would kill the soldier by means of two punctures on the neck, drain him of his blood, and then leave him to be found the next morning. On encountering the victim, the Huks in the area would retreat for fear of further vampire attacks.

Such information campaigns depend on concretizing living myth with fixed data. They invariably mine the most fertile cultural soil for inherent inconsistencies, and then replace them with symbols that can be more easily controlled.

This is the same process by which today's target marketers research and co-opt new cultural strains. Even the language of marketing, in which new populations are called "targets" reveals the war-like precision and hostility with which these marketers attack their new prospects.

When a public relations person reduces a group of human beings to a target market, he has effectively removed himself from the equation. Feedback and user surveys do not put us in communication with anyone; they simply make us the subjects of scrutiny and the victims of an eventual assault. The PR person is the lone gunman at the top of the tower, intentionally isolated so as to get a better shot. When the gun goes off, we panic down in the plaza. Someone is out to get us.

The reticence of the generation formerly known as "X" to belong to anything at all can be traced directly to the corrosive effects of target marketing on our society. In fact, the "slacker" ethic was little more than reaction to the segmentation of a culture based on demographic leanings. No sooner do young people find a new style of music, clothing, or attitude, than marketers sieze on it as a trend to be exploited. The kids rush from style to style, but only stay until they sense the target marketer's sites closing in on them. Then they rush to find something different, and maintain their anomalous behavior until it is recognized and tagged.

The reticence of the generation formerly known as "X" to belong to anything at all can be traced directly to the corrosive effects of target marketing on our society.

When "GenX" adopted the anti-chic aesthetic of thrift-store grunge, for example, it was in an effort to find a style that could not be so easily identified and exploited. Grunge was so self-consciously lowbrow and depressed that it seemed, at first, impervious to the hype and glamour applied so swiftly to trends of the past. But sure enough, grunge anthems found their way onto the soundtracks of television commercials, and Dodge Neons were hawked by kids in flannel shirts saying "whatever." The superstardom and eventual shotgun suicide of Kurt Cobain—lead singer of the seminal grunge group Nirvana—bore witness to the futility of giving chase to the target marketers. Symbolically—at least for his fans—Cobain set his rifle's sites on himself rather than be subjected to the crosshairs of someone else's. Then the kids moved on to other genres.[3]

Advertising as Info-War

The development of advertising throughout this century can best be understood as the process by which marketers find ways to attack our sense of well-being. While advertising may have begun as a way to publicize a new brand or invention, the surfeit of "stuff" with little or no qualitative difference from its competition forced advertisers to find ways of distinguishing their products from that of their competitors.

Advertising quickly became about creating needs rather than fulfilling them. Commercials took the form of coercive teaching stories. We are presented with a character with whom we identify. The character is put into jeopardy, and we experience vicarious tension along with him. Only the storyteller holds the key to our release.

Imagine a man in his office. The boss tells him his report is late. His wife calls to tell him their son is in trouble. His co-worker is scheming to get him fired. What is he to do? He opens his desk drawer: inside is a bottle of Brand X aspirin. He takes the pills and we watch as a psychedelic array of color fills his body. Whether or not we really believe that the aspirin could solve his problems—or cure his headache—we must accept the sponsor's solution if we want to be relieved from tension.

This simple form of programming has been used since Aristotle's day. Create a character, put him in danger, and then choose the method by which he will be saved. The remedy can be Athena or a new brand of sport shoe. The audience must submit.

Because television is not a communicator's medium but the programmer's (why do you think they call the stuff on TV "programming" anyway?), it depends on a passive, captive audience. There is no room for interaction, or the programmer's advantage will be lost.

This is why the remote control has wreaked such havoc on traditional coercive advertising. Although it doesn't allow for feedback, it does allow for escape. A regular television viewer, feeling the rising and uncomfortable tension of a coercive story, would have to walk all the way up to his television set to change the channel. His brain makes the calculation of how many calories of effort this would cost, and instructs the man to sit and bear the momentary anxiety.

A person armed with a remote control, on the other hand, can escape the dilemma with almost no effort at all. One simple click and he's free. The less reverence he feels for the television image, the less hesitation he'll have to click away. Video games help in this regard. The television tube's pixels, which used to be the exclusive province of the programmer, can now be manipulated by the user. Simply moving Super Mario across the screen changes our relationship to the television image forever. The tube is now a playground. It can be changed.

The viewer armed with a remote control becomes an armchair postmodernist, deconstructing images as he sees fit. The shorter his attention span, the less compelled he feels to sit through coercive or tension-inducing media. In fact, Attention Deficit Disorder—an ailment for which millions of parents are now giving their children medication—may just be a reaction to relentless programming. If everywhere you look someone is attempting to program you, you will quickly learn not to look anywhere for too long.

The most skilled viewers have become amateur media semioticians. They maintain an ironic distance from the media they watch so as not to fall under the programmer's influence. Young people watch shows like *Melrose Place* in groups, constantly talking back to the screen. They protect one another from absorption by the image.

Watching television skillfully means watching for the coercive techniques. Watching television with ironic distance means not to watch television at all, but rather to watch "the television." The new entertainment is a form of media study: What are they going to try next? The viewer remains alive and thinking by refusing to surrender to any of the stories he sees.

Unfortunately, it didn't take advertisers long to develop a new set of coercive techniques for their postmodern audience. The state of ironic detachment that young people employ to remain immune to the programming spell is now their greatest liability.

New advertising intentionally appeals to this postmodern sensibility. "Wink" advertising acknowledges its viewers' intelligence. These commercials readily admit they are manipulative, as if this nod to their own coercive intentions somehow immunizes the audience from their effects. The object of the game, for the audience, is to be "in" on the joke.

Sprite commercials satirize the values espoused by "cool" brands like Coke and Pepsi, then go on to insist that, "Image is nothing, thirst is everything." A brand of shoes called "Simple" ran a magazine ad with the copy: "advertisement: blah blah blah...name of company."

By letting the audience in on the inanity of the marketing process, such companies hope to be rewarded by the thankful viewer. Energizer batteries launched a television campaign where a "fake" commercial for another product would be interrupted by their famous pink Energizer bunny marching through the screen. The audience was rescued from the bad commercial by the battery company's tiny mascot. The message: The Energizer Bunny can keep on going, even in a world of relentless hype.

The viewer armed with a remote control becomes an armchair postmodernist, deconstructing images as he sees fit.

Of course the marketers haven't really surrendered at all. What's really going on here is a new style of marketing through exclusivity. Advertisers know that their media-savvy viewership prides itself on being able to deconstruct and understand the coercive tactics of television commercials. By winking at the audience, the advertiser is acknowledging that there's someone special out there—someone smart enough not to be fooled by the traditional tricks of the influence professional. "If you're smart enough to see our wink and get the joke, then you're smart enough to know to buy our product."

Where this sort of advertising gets most dangerous is where there's really no joke at all. Diesel Jeans recently launched a billboard campaign with images designed to provoke a "wink" response, even though no amount of semiotic analysis would allow its audience to "get" the joke. In one print ad, they showed a stylish couple, dressed in Diesel clothing, in a fake billboard advertisement for a brand of ice cream. The advertisement-within-the-advertisement was placed in a busy district of North Korea.

What does this advertisement mean, and why was it placed amongst bicycling North Koreans? Who knows? The meta-advertisement attacks the hip viewer. He must pretend that he understands what's going on if he wants to maintain his sense of ironic detachment. The moment he lies to himself in order to turn the page, he has actually admitted defeat. He has been beaten at his own game by the advertiser, who has re-established himself as the more powerful force in the information war.

The Co-option of Cyberspace

The Internet posed an even greater threat to culture's programmers than channel zappers. For the first time, here was a mass medium that no longer favored broadcasters.

A true communications medium from the start, the Internet was as much about sending as receiving. The early Internet was a text-only technology. Users would send email, join in live chats, or participate in asynchronous discussions on bulletin boards and Usenet groups. For those of us lucky enough to have engaged in this style of contact, we sensed liberation.

The early Internet spurred utopian visions because it was the first time that real people had the opportunity to disseminate their ideas globally. The Internet was less about the information itself than contact. Networked together through wires and computers, the Internet community—and it really was a community—was a living cultural experiment.

To some, it was as if the human race was hardwiring its members together into a single, global brain. People talked about the Internet as if it were the realization of the Gaia Hypothesis—the notion that all living things are part of the same, big organism.[4] Many believed that the fledgling communications infrastructure would allow for the beginning of global communication and cooperation on a scale unimagined before.

Even if these dreams were a bit more fantastic than the reality of an Internet society, they indicated the underlying experience essential to this interconnectivity. The interactive communications infrastructure was merely the housing for a collective project in mutual understanding. It was not about information at all, but relationships. We were not interacting with data, but with one another.

This is why the Internet seemed so "sexy." It was not that pornography was available online. It felt and looked sexy because people and their ideas could commingle and mutate. A scientist sharing his new research would be challenged and provoked. A philosopher posing a new idea would be forced to defend it. Nothing was safe, and nothing was sacred—except, perhaps, the idea that everyone shared an equal opportunity to give voice to his or her opinions.

As more people turned off their TVs and migrated online, the question for influence professionals became clear: How do we turn this communications nightmare into a traditional, dead, and controllable mass medium?

Their great trick was to replace communication with information. The works of futurists like Alvin Toffler were twisted to proclaim that we

Only by killing its communicative function could the Web's developers turn the Internet into a shopping mall.

were on the cusp of the Information Age, forever confusing a revolution in communication with an expansion of the propaganda machine. No, the Internet was not a medium for interpersonal exchange, but data retrieval. And it was tricky and dangerous to use. *Wired* magazine's hip graphics and buzzword-laden text convinced newcomers to the world of "hi-technology" that the Internet was a complex and imposing realm. Without proper instruction (from the likes of *Wired* editors), we would surely get lost out there.

Now that the Internet was seen as a dangerous zone of information, best traveled with the advice of experts, it wasn't long before the World Wide Web became the preferred navigational tool. Unlike bulletin boards or chat rooms, the Web is—for the most part—a read-only medium. It is flat and opaque. You can't see through it to the activities of others. We don't socialize with anyone when we visit a Website; we read text and look at pictures. This is not interactivity. It is an "interactive-style" activity. There's nothing participatory about it.

Instead of forging a whole new world, the Web gives us a new window on the same old world. The Web is a repository for information. It is dead. While you and I are as free to publish our works on the Web as Coke is to publish its advertising or The Gap is to sell its jeans, we have given up something much more precious once we surrender the immediacy of a living communications exchange. Only by killing its communicative function could the Web's developers turn the Internet into a shopping mall.

The current direction of Internet technology promises a further calcification of its interactive abilities. Amped-up processing speed and modem baud rates do nothing for communication. They do, however, allow for the development of an increasingly TV-like Internet.

The ultimate objective of today's communication industry is to provide us with broadcast-quality television images on our computers. The only space left for interactivity will be our freedom to watch a particular movie "on demand" or, better, to use the computer mouse to click on an object or article of clothing we might like to buy.

Promoting the Fixed Reality

Once we have reduced the living exchanges that these new media promise to one side or other in an information war, we have given up the only advantage we really have: to evolve unpredictably.

The enemy of the coercer is change. Coercion and influence are simply the pushing of a fixed point of view. In this sense, the coercer is promoting death. The messy fertility of a living system is the information coercer's greatest obstacle. But it is also our greatest strength as a developing culture.

Finally, the conflict between "them and us" is fictional. The culture war is just a battle between those who see the need for change, and those would hope to prevent it. Those in power, obviously, seek to preserve the status quo. The only time they feel the need to make an adjustment is when they are hoping to absorb a unique new population, or when the populations already under their control have grown immune to the current styles of influence.

And, to be sure, the preservation of certain status quo values is crucial to the maintenance of organized society. Just as there are certain genes in the body with no function other than to resist mutation, there are institutions in our society that work very hard to resist change.

Since the chief agents of change are interaction and communication, these will be the activities that the enemies of evolution will want to keep in check. But when an overwhelming proportion of our world community seeks a referendum on the human project, we must not allow our efforts to be derailed by those who would prevent such a movement by any means necessary.

More importantly, we cannot let ourselves be fooled into thinking that simply having the right to select our data with the click of a computer mouse instead of a TV remote means we have won the Information Arms Race.

Endnotes

1. See Aristotle, 1954. **2.** See Wiener, 1967; see also Chomsky, 1991; Crossen, 1994; Kelly, 1998; Schwartz & Leydon, 1997; Simpson, 1994; Stauber & Rampton, 1995. **3.** For more on the ideas presented in this section, see Carlisle, 1993; Chomsky, 1989; Cialdini, 1993; and Watson, 1978 (which is excerpted at Psywar Terror Tactics Website at <www.parascope.com>). **4.** See Lovelock, 1987.

References

Aristotle. (1954). *Rhetoric* (W. Rhys Roberts, Trans.). New York: The Modern Library.
Carlisle, J. (1993, Spring). Public relationships: Hill & Knowlton, Robert Gray, and the CIA. *Covert Action Quarterly*.
Chomsky, N. (1991). *Media control: The spectacular achievements of propaganda*. Westfield, NJ: Open Magazine Pamphlet Series.
Chomsky, N. (1989). *Necessary illusions: Thought control in democratic societies*. Boston: South End Press.
Cialdini, R. B. (1993). *Influence: The psychology of persuasion*. New York: William Morrow.
Crossen, C. (1994). *Tainted truth: The manipulation of fact in America*. New York: Simon & Schuster.
Kelly, K. (1998). *New rules for the new economy*. New York: Viking.
Lovelock, J.E. (1987). *Gaia : A new look at life on earth*. New York: Oxford University Press.
Schwartz, P. & P. Leydon. (1997, July). The long boom. *Wired*.
Simpson, C. (1994). *Science of coercion: Communication research and psychological warfare, 1945-1960*. New York: Oxford University Press.
Stauber, J. & S. Rampton. (1995). *Toxic sludge is good for you!: Lies, damn lies, and the public relations industry*. Monroe, ME: Common Courage Press.
Toffler, A. (1980). *The third wave*. New York: Morrow.
Watson, P. (1978). *War on the mind: The military uses and abuses of psychology*. New York: Basic Books.
Wiener, N. (1967). *The human use of human beings: Cybernetics and society.* Boston, MA: Avon.

POLITRICKS

The War Secrets Senator John McCain Hides

Former POW Fights Public Access to POW/MIA Files

Sydney Schanberg

This article originally appeared on April 25, 2000, on the APBnews.com Website.

NEW YORK (APBnews.com)—The voters who were drawn to John S. McCain in his run for the Republican presidential nomination this year often cited, as the core of his appeal, his openness and blunt candor and willingness to admit past lapses and release documents that other senators often hold back. These qualities also seemed to endear McCain to the campaign press corps, many of whom wrote about how refreshing it was to travel on the McCain campaign bus, "The Straight Talk Express," and observe a maverick speaking his mind rather than a traditional candidate given to obfuscation and spin.

Literally thousands of documents that would otherwise have been declassified long ago have been legislated into secrecy.

But there was one subject that was off-limits, a subject the Arizona senator almost never brings up and has never been open about—his long-time opposition to releasing documents and information about American prisoners of war in Vietnam and the missing in action who have still not been accounted for. Since McCain himself, a downed Navy pilot, was a prisoner in Hanoi for five-and-a-half years, his staunch resistance to laying open the POW/MIA records has baffled colleagues and others who have followed his career. Critics say his anti-disclosure campaign, in close cooperation with the Pentagon and the intelligence community, has been successful. Literally thousands of documents that would otherwise have been declassified long ago have been legislated into secrecy.

For example, all the Pentagon debriefings of the prisoners who returned from Vietnam are now classified and closed to the public under a statute enacted in the 1990s with McCain's backing. He says this is to protect the privacy of former POWs and gives it as his reason for not making public his own debriefing.

But the law allows a returned prisoner to view his own file or to designate another person to view it. APBnews.com has repeatedly asked the senator for an interview for this article and for permission to view his debriefing documents. He has not responded. His office did recently send APBnews.com an email, referring to a favorable article about the senator in the January 1 issue of *Newsweek*. In the article, the reporter, Michael Isikoff, says that he was allowed to review McCain's debriefing report and that it contained "nothing incriminating"—although in a phone interview Isikoff acknowledged that "there were redactions" in the document. Isikoff declined to say who showed him the document, but APBnews.com has learned it was McCain.

Many Vietnam veterans and former POWs have fumed at McCain for keeping these and other wartime files sealed up. His explanation, offered freely in Senate hearings and floor speeches, is that no one has been proven still alive and that releasing the files would revive painful memories and cause needless emotional stress to former prisoners, their families, and the families of MIAs still unaccounted for. But what if some of these returned prisoners, as has always been the case at the conclusion of wars, reveal information to their debriefing officers about other prisoners believed still held in captivity? What justification is there for filtering such information through the Pentagon rather than allowing access to source materials? For instance, debriefings from returning Korean War POWs, available in full to the American public, have provided both citizens and government investigators with important information about other Americans who went missing in that conflict.

Would not most families of missing men, no matter how emotionally drained, want to know? And would they not also want to know what the government was doing to rescue their husbands and sons? Hundreds of MIA families have for years been questioning if concern for their feelings is the real reason for the secrecy.

Prisoners Left Behind

A smaller number of former POWs, MIA families, and veterans have suggested there is something especially damning about McCain that the senator wants to keep hidden. Without release of the files, such accusations must be viewed as unsubstantiated speculation. The main reason, however, for seeking these files is to find out if there is any information in the debriefings, or in other MIA documents that McCain and the Pentagon have kept sealed, about how many prisoners were held back by North Vietnam after the Paris peace treaty was signed in January 1973. The defense and intelligence establishment has long resisted the declassification of critical records on this subject. McCain has been the main congressional force behind this effort.

The prisoner return in 1973 saw 591 Americans repatriated by North Vietnam. The problem was that the US intelligence list of men believed to be alive at that time in captivity—in Vietnam, Laos, and possibly across the border in southern China and in the Soviet Union—was much larger. Possibly hundreds of men larger. The State Department stated publicly in 1973 that intelligence data showed the prisoner list to be starkly incomplete. For example, only nine of the 591 returnees came out of Laos, though experts in US military intelligence listed 311 men as missing in that Hanoi-run country alone, and their field reports indicated that many of those men were probably still alive. Hanoi said it was returning all the prisoners it had. President Nixon, on March 29, 1973, seconded that claim, telling the nation on television: "All of our American POWs are on their way home." This discrepancy has never been acknowledged or explained by official Washington.

Over the years in Washington, McCain, at times almost single-handedly, has pushed through Pentagon-desired legislation to make it impossible or much harder for the public to acquire POW/MIA information and much easier for the defense bureaucracy to keep it hidden.

"The Truth Bill"

In 1989, eleven members of the House of Representatives introduced a measure they called "The Truth Bill." A brief and simple document, it said: "[The] head of each department or agency which holds or receives any records and information, including live-sighting reports, which have been correlated or possibly correlated to United States personnel listed as prisoner of war or missing in action from World War II, the Korean conflict, and the Vietnam conflict shall make available to the public all such records and information held or received by that department or agency. In addition, the Department of Defense shall make available to the public with its records and information a complete listing of United States personnel classified as prisoner of war, missing in action, or killed in action (body not returned) from World War II, the Korean conflict, and the Vietnam conflict."

Opposed by Pentagon

Bitterly opposed by the Pentagon, "The Truth Bill" got nowhere. It was reintroduced in the next Congress in 1991—and again disappeared. Then, suddenly, out of the Senate, birthed by the Arizona senator, a new piece of legislation emerged. It was called "The McCain Bill." This measure turned "The Truth Bill" on its head. It created a bureaucratic maze from which only a fraction of the available documents could emerge. And it became law. So restrictive were its provisions that one clause actually said the Pentagon didn't even have to inform the public when it received intelligence that Americans were alive in captivity.

First, it decreed that only three categories of information could be released, i.e. "information...that may pertain to the location, treatment, or condition of" unaccounted-for personnel from the Vietnam War. (This was later amended in 1995 and 1996 to include the Cold War and the Korean conflict.) If information is received about anything other than "location, treatment, or condition," under this statute, which was enacted in December 1991, it does not get disclosed.

Second, before such information can be released to the public, permission must be granted by the primary next of kin, or PNOK. In the case of Vietnam, letters were sent by the Department of Defense to the 2,266 PNOK. More than 600 declined consent (including 243 who failed to respond, considered under the law to be a "no").

Hurdles and Limitations

Finally, in addition to these hurdles and limitations, the McCain act does not specifically order the declassification of the information. Further, it provides the Defense Department with other justifications for withholding documents. One such clause says that if the information "may compromise the safety of any United States personnel...who remain not accounted for but who may still be alive in captivity, then the Secretary [of Defense] may withhold that record or other information from the disclosure otherwise required by this section."

Over the years in Washington, McCain, at times almost single-handedly, has pushed through Pentagon-desired legislation to make it impossible or much harder for the public to acquire POW/MIA information and much easier for the defense bureaucracy to keep it hidden.

Boiled down, the preceding paragraph means that the Defense Department is not obligated to tell the public about prisoners believed alive in captivity and what efforts are being made to rescue them. It only has to notify the White House and the intelligence committees in the Senate and House. The committees are forbidden under law from releasing such information.

At the same time, the McCain act is now being used to deny access to other sorts of records. For instance, part of a recent APBnews.com Freedom of Information Act request for the records of a mutiny on a merchant marine vessel in the 1970s was rejected by a Defense Department official who cited the McCain act.

Over the years,
he has regularly vilified any group or person who keeps trying to pry out more evidence about MIAs.

Similarly, requests for information about Americans missing in the Korean War and declared dead for the last 45 years have been denied by officials who reference the McCain statute.

Another Bill Gutted in 1996

And then there is the Missing Service Personnel Act, which McCain succeeded in gutting in 1996. A year before, the act had been strengthened, with bipartisan support, to compel the Pentagon to deploy more resources with greater speed to locate and rescue missing men. The measure imposed strict reporting requirements.

McCain amended the heart out of the statute. For example, the 1995 version required a unit commander to report to his theater commander within two days that a person was missing and describe what rescue and recovery efforts were underway. The McCain amendments allowed ten days to pass before a report had to be made.

In the 1995 act, the theater commander, after receiving the MIA report, would have fourteen days to report to his Cabinet secretary in Washington. His report had to "certify" that all necessary actions were being taken and all appropriate assets were being used "to resolve the status of the missing person." This section was stricken from the act, replaced with language that made the Cabinet secretary, not the theater commander, the recipient of the report from the field. All the certification requirements also were stricken.

"Turn Commanders into Clerks"

"This," said a McCain memo, "transfers the bureaucracy involved out of the field to Washington." He argued that the original legislation, if left intact, "would accomplish nothing but create new jobs for lawyers and turn military commanders into clerks."

In response, the backers of the original statute cited the Pentagon's stained record on MIAs and argued that military history had shown that speed of action is critical to the chances of recovering a missing man. Moving "the bureaucracy" to Washington, they said, was merely a way to sweep the issue under a rug.

Chilling Effect Cited

One final evisceration in the law was McCain's removal of all its enforcement teeth. The original act provided for criminal penalties for anyone, such as military bureaucrats in Washington, who destroy or cover up or withhold from families any information about a missing man. McCain erased this part of the law. He said the penalties would have a chilling effect on the Pentagon's ability to recruit personnel for its POW/MIA office.

McCain does not deal lightly with those who disagree with him on any of these issues or who suggest that the evidence indeed shows that a significant number of prisoners were alive and cached away as future bargaining chips when he came home in the group of 591 released in 1973.

Over the years, he has regularly vilified any group or person who keeps trying to pry out more evidence about MIAs. He calls them "hoaxers" and "charlatans" and "conspiracy theorists." He decries the "bizarre rantings of the MIA hobbyists" and describes them as "individuals primarily who make their living off of keeping the issue alive." Before he died last year of leukemia, retired Colonel Ted Guy, a highly admired POW and one of the most dogged resisters in the camps, wrote an angry open letter to the senator in an MIA newsletter. In it, he said of McCain's stream of insults: "John, does this include Senator Bob Smith and other concerned elected officials? Does this include the families of the missing where there is overwhelming evidence that their loved ones were 'last known alive?' Does this include some of your fellow POWs?"

Sightings Dismissed

McCain has said again and again that he has seen no "credible" evidence that more than a tiny handful of men might have been alive in captivity after the official prison return in 1973. He dismisses all of the subsequent radio intercepts, live sightings, satellite photos, CIA reports, defector information, recovered enemy documents, and reports of ransom demands—thousands and thousands of pieces of information indicating live captives—as meaningless. He has even described these intelligence reports as the rough equivalent of UFO and alien sightings.

In Congress, colleagues and staffers who have seen him erupt—in the open and, more often, in closed meetings—profess themselves confounded by his behavior. Insisting upon anonymity so as not to invite one of his verbal assaults, they say they have no easy way to explain why a former POW would work so hard and so persistently to keep POW/MIA information from coming out. Typical is the comment of one congressional veteran who has watched McCain over many years: "This is a man not at peace with himself."

McCain's Sense of Disgrace

Some McCain watchers searching for answers point to his recently published bestselling autobiography, *Faith of My Fathers*, half of which is devoted to his years as a prisoner. In the book, he says he felt badly throughout his captivity because he knew he was being treated more leniently than his fellow POWs owing to his propaganda value as the son of Admiral John S. McCain II, who was then the CINCPAC—commander in chief of all US forces in the Pacific region, including Vietnam. (His captors considered him a prize catch and nicknamed him the "Crown Prince.")

Also in the book, the Arizona senator repeatedly expresses guilt and disgrace at having broken under torture and given the North Vietnamese a taped confession, broadcast over the camp loudspeakers, saying he was a war criminal who had, among other acts, bombed a school. "I felt faithless and couldn't control my despair," he writes, revealing that he made two half-hearted attempts at suicide. Most tellingly, he said he lived in "dread" that his father would find out. "I still wince," he says, "when I recall wondering if my father had heard of my disgrace."

After McCain returned home, he says he told his father about the confession, but "never discussed it at length." The admiral, McCain says, didn't indicate he had heard anything about it before.

McCain's father died in 1981. McCain writes: "I only recently learned that the tape...had been broadcast outside the prison and had come to the attention of my father."

McCain wasn't alone—it's well-known that a sizeable percentage of prisoners of war will break down under torture. In fact, many of his supporters view McCain's prison travails as evidence of his overall heroism.

He dismisses all of the subsequent radio intercepts, live sightings, satellite photos, CIA reports, defector information, recovered enemy documents, and reports of ransom demands—thousands and thousands of pieces of information indicating live captives—as meaningless.

Fears Unpublished Details?

But how would McCain's forced confession alone explain his endless campaign against releasing MIA/POW information?

Some veterans and other McCain watchers have speculated that McCain's mortification, given his family's proud military tradition (his grandfather was also an admiral), was so severe that it continues to haunt him and make him fear any opening up of information that could revive previously unpublished details of the era, including his own nagging history.

Another question that defies easy explanation is why there has never been any significant public outcry over the POWs who didn't come home or about the machinations of public officials like McCain who carefully wove a blanket of secrecy around this issue. It can only be understood in the context of what the Vietnam War did to the American mind.

Forgetting the Vietnam War

It was the longest war in our history and the only one in which we accepted defeat and brought our troops home. It had roiled the country more than any conflict but the Civil War—to the point where almost everyone, regardless of their politics, wanted to get away from anything that reminded them of this bloody failure. Only a small band of Americans, led by Vietnam veterans and MIA families, kept asking for more information about the missing men and demanding that the government keep its promise to do everything possible to bring them home. Everyone else seemed to be running away from all things Vietnam.

Knowledgeable observers note that it's quite possible that Nixon, leading the country's withdrawal, accepted the peace treaty of January 27, 1973, while telling himself that somehow he would negotiate the release of the remaining POWs later. But when Congress refused to provide the $3 billion to $4 billion in proposed national development reparations that National Security Adviser Henry Kissinger had dangled as a carrot to Hanoi, the prospects for the abandoned men began to unravel.

Observers also point out that over the years that followed, Washington continued to reject paying what it branded as ransom money and so, across six presidencies, including the present one, the issue of POWs left behind remained unacknowledged by the White House and the Pentagon. Hanoi refused to correct the impression that all the prisoners had been returned, and Washington, for its part, refused to admit that it had known about abandoned POWs from the beginning.

Mainstream Press Indifferent

Whether any of these prisoners remain alive to this day is impossible for the outsider to know. Intelligence sources privately express the belief that most of the men had either died or been executed by the early 1990s. Presumably, these sources say, the POWs lost their bargaining value to Hanoi as time passed and ransom dollars never materialized. Eventually Hanoi began seeking another path to the money—the renewal of relations with Washington. Diplomatic ties were restored by President Clinton in 1994, and American economic investment quickly followed.

One factor in the nation's indifference to the POWs was the stance of the national press. From the very start to the present, the mainstream media showed little interest. With just a smattering of exceptions, the journalistic community, like the rest of the country, ran away from the story. During the war, thousands of American journalists poured into Vietnam in shifts; now only a handful cover the country, most of them filing business stories about Nike and other conglomerates opening up factories to avail themselves of the cheap labor.

Even reporters who had covered the war came to view the MIA story, in the years afterward, as a concoction of the far right. Without doing much, if any, first-hand reporting, such as digging into the available documents in the National Archives, nearly all these journalists dismissed the MIA story as unfounded.

At the time of the committee's hearings, the Pentagon had received more than 1,600 firsthand sightings of live American prisoners and nearly 14,000 secondhand reports.

Generated a Hero Aura

In McCain's recently suspended campaign for the presidency, it was almost as if, in the press' eyes, he was to be treated differently and quite gingerly because of the hero aura generated by his POW experience. None of his political opponents ever dared criticize him for his legislative history on withholding POW information, and the press never brought itself to be direct enough to even question him on the issue.

It's not that he didn't give reporters plenty of openings to ask the right Vietnam questions. For one thing, he used his history as a Vietnam prisoner as a constant campaign theme in his speeches. Rarely did he appear without a larger-than-life photo backdrop showing him in battle gear as a Navy pilot before he was shot down over Hanoi in 1967.

Here is a passage typical of the soft, even erroneous, reporting on McCain—this from a March 4 story in the *New York Times*: "His most striking achievement came when he joined with another Vietnam veteran, Senator John Kerry, Democrat of Massachusetts, to puncture the myth that Vietnam continued holding American prisoners." The piece went on to speak with admiration about "his concern over the prisoners-of-war issue"—but, tellingly, it offered no details.

Tepid Veterans' Vote

The press corps, covering the state-by-state primary vote, made an assumption, based apparently on sentiment, that McCain, as the war hero, would capture the significant veterans' vote by stunning margins. Actually, he didn't capture it at all. He carried veterans only in the states that he won, like Michigan and New Hampshire, but was rejected by them in the larger number of states that he lost, like New York, Ohio, and California. Added together, when the states were tallied up, the veterans' vote went to George W. Bush.

The Washington press corps had gone openly soft once before on the prisoner issue, again benefiting McCain. That was in 1991-93, during the proceedings of the Senate Select Committee on POW/MIA Affairs. McCain starred on that committee, working hand in hand with his new ally, Senator John Kerry, the panel's co-chairman, to play down voluminous evidence that sizeable numbers of men were still held alive after the prisoner return in 1973.

One example: At the time of the committee's hearings, the Pentagon had received more than 1,600 firsthand sightings of live American prisoners and nearly 14,000 secondhand reports. The intelligence officers who gathered these reports from refugees and other informants in the field described a large number of them as "credible" and so marked the reports. Some of the informants had been given lie-detector tests and passed.

But the Pentagon's Defense Intelligence Agency, after reviewing all the reports, concluded that they "do not constitute evidence" that men were still alive at the time.

McCain and Kerry endorsed the Pentagon's findings. They also treated both the Pentagon and the CIA more as the committee's partners than as objects of its inquiry. As one committee staff investigator said, in a memo preserved from the period: "Speaking for the other investigators, I can say we are sick and tired of this investigation being controlled by those we are supposedly investigating."

McCain stood out because he always showed up for the committee hearings where witnesses were going to talk about specific pieces of evidence. He would belittle and berate these witnesses, questioning their patriotism and otherwise scoffing at their credibility. All of this is on record in the National Archives.

Confrontation with Witness

One such witness was Dolores Apodaca Alfond, chairwoman of the National Alliance of Families, an all-volunteer MIA organization. Her pilot brother, Captain Victor J. Apodaca, out of the Air Force Academy, was shot down over Dong Hoi, North Vietnam, in the early evening of June 8, 1967. At least one person in the two-man plane survived. Beeper signals from a pilot's distress radio were picked up by overhead helicopters, but the cloud cover was too heavy to go in. Hanoi has recently turned over some bone fragments that are supposed to be Apodaca's. The Pentagon first declared the fragments to be animal bones. But now it is telling the family—verbally—that they came from the pilot. But the Pentagon, for unexplained reasons, will not put this in writing, which means Apodaca is still unaccounted for. Also the Pentagon refuses to give Alfond a sample of the fragments so she can have testing done by an independent laboratory.

Alfond's testimony, at a hearing of the POW/MIA committee November 11, 1992, was revealing. She pleaded with the committee not to shut down in two months, as scheduled, because so much of its work was unfinished. Also, she was critical of the committee, and in particular Kerry and McCain, for having "discredited the overhead satellite symbol pictures, arguing there is no way to be sure that the [distress] symbols were made by US POWs." She also criticized them for similarly discounting data from special sensors, shaped like a large spike with an electronic pod and an antenna, that were air-dropped to stick in the ground along the Ho Chi Minh trail.

These devices served as motion detectors, picking up passing convoys and other military movements, but they also had rescue capabilities. Specifically, someone on the ground—a downed airman or a prisoner on a labor detail—could manually enter data into the sensor pods. Alfond said the data from the sensor spikes, which was regularly gathered by Air Force jets flying overhead, had showed that a person or persons on the ground had manually entered into the sensors—as US pilots had been trained to do—"no less than 20 authenticator numbers that corresponded exactly to the classified authenticator numbers of 20 US POWs who were lost in Laos."

Except for the panel's other co-chairman, Senator Bob Smith (Republican - NH), not a single committee member attended this public hearing. But McCain, having been advised of Alfond's testimony, suddenly rushed into the room to confront her. His face angry and his voice very loud, he accused her of making "allegations...that are patently and totally false and deceptive." Making a fist, he shook his index finger at her and said she had insulted an emissary to Vietnam sent by President Bush. He said she had insulted other MIA families with her remarks. And then he said, through clenched teeth: "And I am sick and tired of you insulting mine and other people's [patriotism] who happen to have different views than yours."

Brought to Tears

By this time, tears were running down Alfond's cheeks. She reached into her handbag for a handkerchief. She tried to speak: "The family members have been waiting for years—years! And now you're shutting down." He kept interrupting her. She tried to say, through tears, that she had issued no insults. He kept talking over her words. He said she was accusing him and others of "some conspiracy without proof, and some cover-up." She said she was merely seeking "some answers. That is what I am asking." He ripped into her for using the word "fiasco." She replied: "The fiasco was the people that stepped out and said we have written the end, the final chapter to Vietnam."

"No one said that," he shouted. "No one said what you are saying they said, Ms. Alfond." And then, his face flaming pink, he stalked out of the room, to shouts of disfavor from members of the audience.

As with most of McCain's remarks to Alfond, the facts in his closing blast at her were incorrect. Less than three weeks earlier, on October 23, 1992, in a ceremony in the White House Rose Garden, President Bush—with John McCain standing beside him—said: "Today, finally, I am convinced that we can begin writing the last chapter in the Vietnam War."

The committee did indeed, as Alfond said they planned to do, shut down two months after the hearing.

"Cannot Discuss It"

As for her description of the motion sensor evidence about prisoners in Laos, McCain's response at the hearing was that this data was in a 1974 report that the committee had read but was still classified, so "I cannot discuss it here.... We hope to get it declassified."

The question to the senator now is: What happened to that report and what happened to the pilots who belonged to those authenticator numbers? Intelligence sources in Washington say the report was never declassified.

It became clear over the months of hearings and sparrings that the primary goal of the Kerry-McCain alliance was to clear the way for normalization of relations with Vietnam. They did it in two ways—first, by regularly praising Hanoi for its "cooperation" in the search for information about the unaccounted-for prisoners and then by minimizing and suppressing the volume of evidence to the contrary that had been unearthed by the committee's staff investigators.

Recasting the Issue

Kerry and McCain also tried, at every opportunity, to recast the issue as a debate about how many men could still be alive today, instead of the real issue at stake: How many men were alive in 1973 after the 591 were returned?

Although much evidence was kept out of the committee's final report in January 1993, enough of it, albeit watered down by the committee's majority, was inserted by the determined staff to demonstrate conclusively that all the prisoners had not come home. Still, if the reader didn't plow through the entire 1,223-page report but scanned just the brief conclusions in the 43-page executive summary at the beginning, he or she would have found only a weak and pallid state-

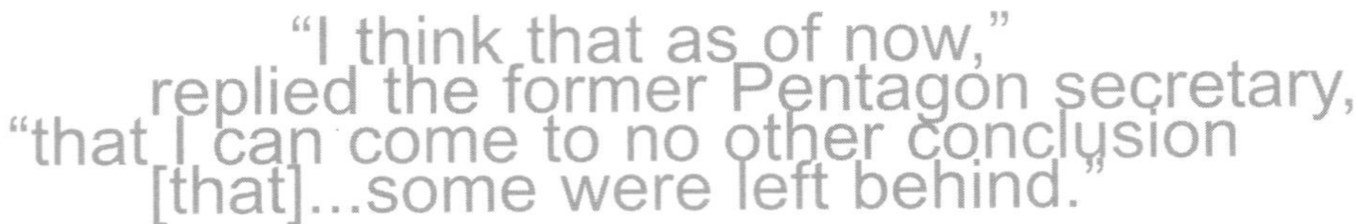
"I think that as of now,"
replied the former Pentagon secretary,
"that I can come to no other conclusion
[that]...some were left behind."

ment saying that there was "evidence...that indicates the possibility of survival, at least for a small number" after the repatriation of 1973. On page 468 of the report, McCain provided his own personal statement, saying that "we found no compelling evidence to prove that Americans are alive in captivity today. There is some evidence—though no proof—to suggest only the possibility that a few Americans may have been kept behind after the end of American's military involvement in Vietnam."

Two Defense Secretaries

And even these meager concessions were not voluntary. They had been forced by the sworn public testimony before the Senate committee of two former defense secretaries from the Nixon Administration, Melvin Laird and James Schlesinger. Both these men testified that they believed in 1973, from strong intelligence data, that a number of prisoners in Vietnam and Laos had not been returned. Their testimony has never been challenged. Schlesinger, before becoming defense secretary, had been the CIA director.

During his committee appearance, Schlesinger was asked why Nixon would have accepted the prisoners being held back in 1973. He replied: "One must assume that we had concluded that the bargaining position of the United States...was quite weak. We were anxious to get our troops out and we were not going to roil the waters..."

Then he was asked "a very simple question. In your view, did we leave men behind?"

"Some Were Left Behind"

"I think that as of now," replied the former Pentagon secretary, "that I can come to no other conclusion [that]...some were left behind."

The press went along once again with the debunkers. The Schlesinger-Laird testimony, which seemed a bombshell, became but a one-day story in the nation's major media. The press never followed it up to explore its implications.

On January 26, 1994, when a resolution ardently backed by McCain and Kerry came up in the Senate calling for the lifting of the two-decade-old economic embargo against Vietnam, some members—in an effort to stall the measure—tried to present new evidence about men left behind. McCain rose to his feet and, offering no rebuttal evidence of his own, proceeded to chide "the professional malcontents, conspiracy mongers, con artists and dime-store Rambos who attend this issue." The resolution passed, 62-38.

"Isolated Personnel"

These days, the Pentagon seems to be moving toward closing its POW/MIA books completely. In recent statements and reports, it has begun describing prisoners not as POWs but as IPs—Isolated Personnel.

And in a 1999 booklet, the Pentagon said: "By the end of the year 2004, we will have moved from the way the US government conducts the business of recovery and accounting [now] to an active program of loss prevention, immediate rescues, and rapid post-hostility accounting." More important, there seems to be no allocation of funds in 2004 for the task force that now conducts POW/MIA investigations, searches for remains, and does archival research.

As for McCain, he continues to stonewall on his own POW records. Through numerous phone calls, faxes, and letters to his office, APBnews.com has been trying since late January to interview the senator and get his permission to view his POW debriefing. The response has been that the senator has been occupied by his campaign schedule.

Call for Openness and Disclosure

During the campaign, McCain, who is chairman of the Senate Commerce Committee, had to address a controversy over queries he had made to the Commerce Department on behalf of a major campaign contributor. To deal with the press interest, he announced he was releasing all of his correspondence with the Commerce Department, not just the letters involving the one case. In addition, to show his full commitment to openness and disclosure, he called on every other government agency to release his communications with them. On January 9 on the CBS program *Face the Nation*, he announced: "Today, we are asking the federal government to release all correspondence that I've had with every government agency."

McCain's staff has acknowledged that this request includes the Pentagon. But the Pentagon says it needs an official document from McCain designating a surrogate before it can show his debriefing report to anyone else.

APBnews.com has repeatedly asked the senator for this waiver. He does not respond.

Benjamin Lesser, APBnews.com reporter, contributed to this report.

Jimmy Carter and Human Rights

Behind the Media Myth

Jeff Cohen and Norman Solomon

Jimmy Carter's reputation has soared in recent years.

Typical of the media spin was a September 1994 report on *CBS Evening News*, lauding Carter's "remarkable resurgence" as a free-lance diplomat. The network reported that "nobody doubts his credibility, or his contacts."

For Jimmy Carter, the pact he negotiated in Haiti was just one achievement in his long career on the global stage.

During his presidency, Carter proclaimed human rights to be "the soul of our foreign policy." Although many journalists promoted that image, the reality was quite different.

Inaugurated thirteen months after Indonesia's December 1975 invasion of East Timor, Carter stepped up US military aid to the Jakarta regime as it continued to murder Timorese civilians. By the time Carter left office, about 200,000 people had been slaughtered.

Elsewhere, despotic allies—from Ferdinand Marcos of the Philippines to the Shah of Iran—received support from President Carter.

In El Salvador, the Carter administration provided key military aid to a brutal regime. In Nicaragua, contrary to myth, Carter backed dictator Anastasio Somoza almost until the end of his reign. In

Carter stepped up US military aid to the Jakarta regime as it continued to murder Timorese civilians.

Guatemala—again contrary to enduring myth—major US military shipments to bloody tyrants never ended.

After moving out of the White House in early 1981, Carter developed a reputation as an ex-President with a conscience. He set about building homes for the poor. And when he traveled to hot spots abroad, news media often depicted Carter as a skillful negotiator on behalf of human rights.

But a decade after Carter left the Oval Office, scholar James Petras assessed the ex-President's actions overseas—and found that Carter's image as "a peace mediator, impartial electoral observer and promoter of democratic values...clashes with the experiences of several democratic Third World leaders struggling against dictatorships and pro-US clients."

From Latin America to East Africa, Petras wrote, Carter functioned as "a hard-nosed defender of repressive state apparatuses, a willing

Carter used his prestige to give international legitimacy to the stolen election.

consort to electoral frauds, an accomplice to US Embassy efforts to abort popular democratic outcomes, and a one-sided mediator."

Observing the 1990 election in the Dominican Republic, Carter ignored fraud that resulted in the paper-thin victory margin of incumbent president Joaquin Balaguer. Announcing that Balaguer's bogus win was valid, Carter used his prestige to give international legitimacy to the stolen election—and set the stage for a rerun in 1994, when Balaguer again used fraud to win re-election.

In December 1990, Carter traveled to Haiti, where he labored to undercut Jean-Bertrand Aristide during the final days of the presidential race. According to a top Aristide aide, Carter predicted that Aristide would lose, and urged him to concede defeat. (He ended up winning 67 percent of the vote.)

Since then, Carter has developed a warm regard for Haiti's bloodthirsty armed forces. Returning from his mission to Port-au-Prince, Carter actually expressed doubt that the Haitian military was guilty of human rights violations.

Significantly, Carter's involvement in the mid-September 1994 negotiations came at the urging of Lieutenant General Raoul Cedras—who phoned Carter only days before the expected US invasion and

"Every time Carter intervenes, the outcomes are always heavily skewed against political forces that want change."

asked him to play a mediator role. (Cedras had floated the idea in an appearance on CNN.)

Carter needed no encouragement. All summer he had been urging the White House to let him be a mediator in dealings with Haiti.

Carter's regard for Cedras matches his evident affection for Cedras' wife. On September 20, 1994, Carter told a *New York Times* interviewer: "Mrs. Cedras was impressive, powerful and forceful. And attractive. She was slim and very attractive."

By then, Carter was back home in Georgia. And US troops in Haiti were standing by—under the terms of the Carter-negotiated agreement—as Haiti's police viciously attacked Haitians in the streets.

The day after American forces arrived in Haiti, President Clinton was upbeat, saying that "our troops are working with full cooperation with the Haitian military"—the same military he had described five days earlier as "armed thugs" who have "conducted a reign of terror, executing children, raping women, killing priests."

The developments in Haiti didn't surprise Petras, an author and sociology professor at Binghamton University in New York. "Every time Carter intervenes, the outcomes are always heavily skewed against political forces that want change," Petras said when we reached him. "In each case, he had a political agenda—to support very conservative solutions that were compatible with elite interests."

Petras described Carter as routinely engaging in "a double discourse. One discourse is for the public, which is his moral politics, and the other is the second track that he operates on, which is a very cynical *realpolitik* that plays ball with very right-wing politicians and economic forces."

And now, Petras concludes, "In Haiti, Carter has used that moral image again to impose one of the worst settlements imaginable."

With much of Haiti's murderous power structure remaining in place, the results are likely to be grim.

All the President's Men

Nazis, the Attempted Assassin, and the Serial Killer

David McGowan

By the time you read this, the 2000 election campaign will have reached a crescendo, and the White House will have a new occupant. This fledgling president will have waged an apparently heated battle for the honor of assuming the throne. He will have exposed himself to attack from his political rivals and from all avenues of the print and electronic media. So much mud will have been flung his way that you will wonder what secrets he could possibly have left to keep. Every detail of his personal and political life will have been scrutinized for the slightest hint of scandal. By all outward appearances, no stone will have been left unturned.

But what if appearances in this instance are—as is so frequently the case—quite deceiving? What if the election process is largely a sham that quickly degenerates into negativity and mudslinging not because it is a true contest between two rivals both intent on winning at any cost and resorting to any means to do so, but because mudslinging is the only way to differentiate between—and create the illusion of conflict between—two nearly indistinguishable candidates? And what if the mud that is being slung is very carefully controlled to insure that the very best mud clods (you know—the ones with the rocks inside that can really do some damage) never get thrown at all?

There is a very strong possibility that the new face in the Oval Office as you read this is that of George W. Bush, a man who in a true democracy—or anything even remotely resembling a democracy, for that matter—would not have had the slightest chance of ascending to that exalted position. Nevertheless, Little George will undoubtedly succeed in his quest to do so; if not now, then in 2004 or 2008 (brief aside: Bush's supporters prefer the nickname "Dubya," while detractors tend to use the equally cute "Shrub." I have a few slightly less endearing nicknames of my own, but will refrain from using them here, opting instead for "Little George").

Regardless of whether Little George emerges victorious from the 2000 race, he will have weathered a blizzard of attack ads. We therefore will have learned everything we need to know about our new (or future) Chief Executive. We will have heard all about his shady financial dealings in Texas, for example. We will have read about his less than stellar academic prowess. We will even have heard the recurrent (albeit muted) rumors of his "youthful" fondness for cocaine and fast women.

But will we really have gotten the straight scoop on Little George? Or are there a few skeletons in the Bush closet that his political "rivals" and the "free" press may have missed? The truth is that the Bush family closet is so jammed with skeletons that it is a wonder that they can still get the door closed. I'm betting that come election day there will be at least three troubling stories that will remain safely locked away there. Any one of these could have posed serious problems for the Bush candidacy; a wide airing of all three would undoubtedly permanently end Little George's political career.

The Nazis

The first is a story that is long overdue for a full public airing—nearly 60 years overdue, in fact. It concerns a particularly unsavory aspect of the Bush family history. Since all is fair in a down-and-dirty election campaign, I see no reason why we shouldn't hold Little George accountable for the sins of his fathers. To do so, we need to look back to the year 1942, admittedly before the current Bush family candidate was even born. But that's OK. Guilt by association is a valid part of any good mudslinging campaign.

Many readers will recall that in 1942 America was in a fully-declared state of war with the Axis powers of Germany, Italy, and Japan. It was in this same year that the United States Alien Property Custodian, acting under authority of the Trading with the Enemy Act, seized the assets of several subsidiaries of the Wall Street powerhouse of Brown Brothers/Harriman. These subsidiaries—including the Union Banking Corporation and the Hamburg-Amerika Line—were declared to be operating as Nazi fronts, which is exactly what they do appear to have been. The problem here for Little George is that two of the principals of Brown Brothers—in addition to Averell Harriman—were none other than Prescott Bush and Herbert Walker. That would be the father and grandfather of former president George Bush (Big George), and therefore the grandfather and great-grandfather of Little George.

This was not, by any means, the only group of bankers and industrialists who were actively trading with and financing the fascist powers of Europe. There were a number of others—most notably the Rockefeller family's Standard Oil. Virtually all of these industrialists and finance capitalists were represented by the Wall Street firm of Sullivan and Cromwell, at the time led by the illustrious Dulles brothers—Allen and John Foster. It was they who facilitated these financial dealings and insured that there would be virtually no public airing of the extensive Nazi/American connections.

It is interesting to note that after the war—as the United States busied itself with the task of persecuting the Rosenbergs for the alleged crime of conspiring with one of our wartime *allies* (the Soviet Union)—these men who actively collaborated with the *enemy* (and not just any enemy, but the most despised—and rightfully so—enemy that America has ever faced in time of war) would ascend to the highest levels of power in the United States government. Nelson Rockefeller, for instance, would become the governor of New York before rising all the way to the office of vice president (and nearly president, if not for the poor aim of Sara Jane Moore and Manson disciple Lynette "Squeaky" Fromme).

John Foster Dulles would emerge as the Secretary of State throughout the coldest days of the Cold War in the 1950s. Little brother Allen, meanwhile, served throughout the same period as the longest-reigning director of the Central Intelligence Agency. Sister Eleanor Dulles busied herself with running the Berlin desk in the State Department, perhaps the most important position within the department in the aftermath of World War II. Between these three siblings, US foreign policy functioned as something of a family-run business for nearly a decade.

None of these men's election campaigns and/or confirmation hearings was ever troubled by questions concerning their unsavory ties to the Third Reich.

Erstwhile partner Averell Harriman would serve in a variety of Cabinet positions and ambassadorships, as well as holding elective office as the governor of New York. And Prescott Bush would become one of the most influential senators in the country as well as serving as a personal adviser to President Eisenhower, working closely with the Dulles triumvirate. He would also father a president—George Herbert Walker Bush—who would in turn father yet another (aspiring?) president—George W. Bush. None of these men's election campaigns and/or confirmation hearings was ever troubled by questions concerning their unsavory ties to the Third Reich.

The Attempted Assassin

Another skeleton in the Bush closet that likely will not be rattled concerns a more recent incident—and one that at least indirectly involved Little George himself. The date was March 30, 1981, and Ronald Reagan had just weeks before assuming occupancy of the White House along with erstwhile sidekick George Bush. But on this day, an assassin's bullet would come perilously close to preempting the Reagan Administration and vaulting Big George into the Oval Office eight years prematurely. Given that Big George arguably had the most to gain from Reagan's assassination, the following story that ran the next day on the Associated Press newswire seems perhaps just a tad bit suspicious:

> The family of the man charged with trying to assassinate President Reagan is acquainted with the family of Vice President George Bush and had made large contributions to his political campaign.... Scott Hinckley, brother of John W. Hinckley Jr. who allegedly shot at Reagan, was to have dined tonight in Denver at the home of Neil Bush, one of the Vice President's sons... The *Houston Post* said it was unable to reach Scott Hinckley, vice president of his father's Denver-based firm, Vanderbilt Energy Corp., for comment. Neil Bush lives in Denver, where he works for Standard Oil Co. of Indiana. In 1978, Neil Bush served as campaign manager for his brother, George W. Bush, the Vice President's eldest son, who made an unsuccessful bid for Congress. Neil lived in Lubbock, Texas, throughout much of 1978, where John Hinckley lived from 1974 through 1980.

It could of course be entirely coincidental that the son of the man just a heartbeat away from the presidency was scheduled to dine with the brother of the man who was *on that very day* attempting to assassinate the one person standing between Big George and the presidency. It is, after all, a small world, but I really don't think it's that goddamn small. The press, though, didn't see anything unusual about these unseemly connections, and chose almost universally not to run the story. And of course no one in Washington felt the need to conduct any sort of an investigation, if for no other reason than to *clear* the Bush family of the *appearance* of guilt.

Of course with no media coverage, there were no appearances to be concerned with. As far as the American people knew then and know now, John Hinckley was just another lone-nut assassin. Little George knows better, though. Shortly after the story aired in the *Houston Post* (from which the AP report was derived), Little George was asked about the connections between the families. Referring to John Hinckley, he acknowledged that: "It's certainly conceivable that I met him or might have been introduced to him."

So there you have it: Little George's social circle may very well have included the man who attempted to assassinate the patron saint of American conservatism. And how do you suppose that would have played at the Republican Convention?

The Serial Killer

A third story that will likely not find its way into the media (despite the persistent efforts of this writer) concerns the application of the death penalty in Texas under the governorship of Little George. Certainly not one to be labeled "soft on crime," Little George now holds the record for presiding over more executions than any other governor in any state in the history of the nation—and this he accomplished after just the first five years of his administration. Now, this does not likely register as a negative with Bush's conservative voter base. They love a guy who is tough on crime. It's not even a negative that some of those executed were mentally impaired and/or mentally ill. Nor that two of them were women—two of only four women executed in the entire country in the last quarter-century.

Most of Bush's core constituents would likewise not be bothered by the fact that some of those executed were convicted of crimes committed as minors. Many would also tend to dismiss—as has Little George—the evidence suggesting that several of those sent to their deaths by Bush had credible claims of innocence. Gary Graham had such a claim. His conviction was based solely on the testimony of a single witness who claimed to have seen the crime for a brief instant in the dark from 30 feet away through the windshield of her car. No physical evidence linked Graham to the crime, and other witnesses who claimed that the perpetrator was someone other than Graham were *not* called by the defense.

Aside from this, Graham was a juvenile at the time of the commission of the crime and at his conviction and sentencing. According to Amnesty International, the United States now stands alone in the world as the only nation known to be carrying out executions of juvenile offenders—the only nation barbaric enough to execute its children. In other words, even if there were no question about his guilt, *no other country on earth* would have executed Gary Graham.

When you add in the fact that his trial was clearly a sham that left serious questions about his guilt, it would appear that Graham was a prime candidate for clemency—for the exercise of Little George's fabled "compassionate conservatism."

Nevertheless, Graham's execution was carried out right on schedule, with the governor never seriously considering intervening. But that's OK. It's good to be tough on crime. When Bill Clinton was running for president, he made a point of running home to Arkansas to sign off on the execution of Ricky Ray Rector, a man so severely retarded that when guards had to interrupt his last meal to lead him to his execution, he assured them that he would just have to finish when they got back. And it was good that Clinton did that. One can never be too tough on crime, even when one is posing as a liberal Democrat.

We all know that showing mercy to "criminals" is the kiss of death for any politician. Most of us probably remember the name Willie Horton, and the effectiveness with which he was used to derail the presidential candidacy of Michael Dukakis in 1988. So it definitely would not do for a conservative Republican presidential candidate to be giving any breaks to America's criminals. Perhaps that is why Little George had no problem sending a great-grandmother in her sixties to her death for the crime of killing her chronically abusive husband. No one, it seems, is worthy of mercy from America's premier hanging governor.

Little George had no problem sending a great-grandmother in her sixties to her death for the crime of killing her chronically abusive husband.

Almost no one, that is. For you see, Little George does not have a perfect score on his execution record. There was one notable occasion, in June 1998, when Bush intervened on behalf of a condemned man. This one man alone—of the nearly 140 men and women whose cases have come before the governor for review as of this writing—was worthy of the governor's compassion. So much so that Little George made the unprecedented move of personally requesting of his State Board of Pardons and Paroles (all of whose members are Bush appointees) that this man's case be reviewed. Eight days later the Board unexpectedly recommended that the execution *not* take place.

The very next day, Bush was only too happy to oblige, sparing the condemned man's life just three days before his scheduled demise. All of which of course begs the question of just who this lucky recipient of the governor's compassionate conservatism was. The answer is, surprisingly enough, Henry Lee Lucas—quite possibly the most prolific, and arguably the most brutally sadistic, serial killer in the annals of American crime. For those not familiar with the life and times of America's premier homicidal maniac, allow me to introduce you to the man whose crimes were immortalized in the movie *Henry—Portrait of a Serial Killer*. Henry has, at various times during his captivity, confessed to as many as *600* cold-blooded murders. While this number is likely inflated, no one denies that Lucas and his erstwhile partner in crime—Ottis Toole—were responsible for literally scores of senseless killings.

This one man alone—of the nearly 140 men and women whose cases have come before the governor for review as of this writing—was worthy of the governor's compassion.

And these were not, mind you, your garden-variety killings. Henry is a necrophile and a torture aficionado, while his partner was a confessed arsonist and cannibal. Their victims were frequently tortured, sexually abused both before and after death, mutilated and dismembered, cannibalized, beheaded, and subjected to any other depraved urges the pair could conjure up. There was an even darker aspect to many of their crimes. Just for kicks, Henry and Ottis liked to bring along Toole's niece and nephew on their killing sprees. The two youngsters, aged just ten and eleven when their forced collaboration began, were made to witness and sometimes participate in the torture, killing, and mutilation of victims.

So if one were to play the devil's advocate in favor of the death penalty, it would be pretty difficult to find a better poster boy for the justness of judicial executions than Lucas. If ever there were a man for whom the ultimate punishment was warranted, Henry would have to be it. If his confessed death toll is accurate, Henry is responsible for wreaking more death and misery on the nation than *all* the other convicts sent to the execution chamber by Governor Bush combined, even assuming that they were all actually guilty of the crimes for which they were convicted.

Speaking before a conference of governors of US/Mexico border states in Brownsville, Texas, Bush attempted to explain his actions: "Henry Lee Lucas is unquestionably guilty of other despicable crimes for which he has been sentenced to spend the rest of his life in prison. However, I believe there is enough doubt about this particular crime that the state of Texas should not impose its ultimate penalty by executing him." As previously noted, though, Bush has had no such reservations about imposing the ultimate penalty on numerous others whose trials showed serious flaws, leaving nagging questions about their guilt.

An independent investigation by the *Chicago Tribune*, published on June 11, 2000, concluded that, "Under Gov. George W. Bush, Texas has executed dozens of Death Row inmates whose cases were compromised by unreliable evidence, disbarred or suspended defense attorneys, meager defense efforts during sentencing and dubious psychiatric testimony." Of the 131 cases reviewed: 23 of the convictions were based at least in part on the testimony of jailhouse informants; 43 involved defense attorneys publicly sanctioned for misconduct; 29 included psychiatric testimony condemned as unethical and untrustworthy by the American Psychiatric Association; and 40 of the condemned men were represented by defense attorneys who either presented no evidence or called but a single witness during the sentencing phase of the trial.

Surely then there must be more to Henry's case than a question of guilt. Fortunately for Little George, he will not be required to provide an explanation so long as no one among his political rivals or from the media chooses to ask the questions. And there are questions here that clearly beg for answers: How does one morally justify sending a juvenile offender to his death despite there being serious doubts about his guilt, while sparing the life of a man who killed his own mother and then proceeded to violate her corpse, and who later killed his underage "common law wife" (actually Toole's niece, whom Henry had been molesting for years) by chopping her body into pieces and scattering them in a field? And why—given that there are a number of other murders for which there is conclusive evidence of Lucas' guilt—has the governor made no effort to seek a new trial for Henry since sparing his life?

How does one morally justify sending a juvenile offender to his death despite there being serious doubts about his guilt, while sparing the life of a man who killed his own mother and then proceeded to violate her corpse?

Why, for that matter, has Lucas not been extradited to any of the other states in which he has confessed to committing murders? And what if Henry was in fact innocent of the crime for which he was convicted, and his innocence was so glaringly obvious that Governor Bush had no choice but to grant him a commutation? What does this say about the Texas criminal justice system and the ease with which it sends innocent men to their deaths? Are we to believe that this was an isolated case and that none of the other condemned men who have put forth similar claims of innocence was likewise falsely convicted?

These are the kinds of questions that cry out for answers from the man who would be king. The irony in the fact that the media have steadfastly avoided asking these questions cannot possibly be overstated. This is the very same media, after all, that gleefully flogged the Willie Horton story just twelve years ago when it was to the benefit of the last George Bush to seek the presidency. With the shoe now on the other foot, the silence of the media is truly deafening. Such is the nature of the American "free" press—or, as many insist on referring to it—the "liberal" press.

Additional Reading

There are a few good books still in print containing information about the ties of the Bush/Dulles/Harriman/Rockefeller crowd to Nazi Germany. The best among them are:

- Higham, Charles. (1995). *Trading with the enemy*. Barnes & Noble Books.
- Lee, Martin. (2000). *The beast reawakens*. Routledge.
- Loftus, John & Mark Aarons. (1994). *The secret war against the Jews*. St. Martins Press.
- Simpson, Christopher. (1995). *The splendid blond beast*. Common Courage Press.

There are several others that are no longer in print but are well worth searching for. For a list of these titles—and help in tracking them down—please visit the author's Website <www.davesweb.cnchost.com>.

Oil Before Ozone
And Other Huge Problems with Al Gore

Russ Kick

Funny thing about Al Gore—both the right and the left hate his guts. This fact was made tangible during the summer of 2000 when two exposés of Gore came out, one written by two conservatives and published by a right-wing house, the other written by two liberals and published by a left-wing house. What could inspire such bipartisan disdain? The answer is complicated, but basically Gore combines the worst traits of the left and the right while at the same time being an ethically bankrupt hypocrite who speaks with a forked tongue.

In the conservative exposé, *Prince Albert: The Life and Lies of Al Gore*, authors David N. Bossie and Floyd G. Brown start with Gore's roots. Though he likes to paint himself as a humble farmboy from Tennessee, Gore is actually part of "a Southern ruling class family." "Gore rarely, if ever, mentions how his relatives distinguished themselves in politics, law, medicine, business, and literature since the seventeenth century." After skillfully avoiding combat in World War II—even though he did everything he could to get the US into the war—Albert Gore Sr. became the protector of communist-capitalist billionaire Armand Hammer, mostly remembered as the owner of oil giant Occidental Petroleum. Hammer was known as "the Godfather of American corporate corruption." Gore Sr. was financially and politically rewarded for aiding this sleazy powerbroker, who laundered money and ran guns for Lenin and Stalin and helped the Soviet Union acquire US military technology. (The younger Al Gore would also do favors for and receive favors from this communist agent.) Gore Sr.'s mostly crummy legacy in Congress has been whitewashed. Though he is now painted as a courageous fighter for racial justice, he admitted in his autobiography that he could not count himself as a hero of civil rights because he "let the sleeping dogs of racism lie as best I could."

Gore combines the worst traits of the left and the right while at the same time being an ethically bankrupt hypocrite who speaks with a forked tongue.

Gore Jr. likes to wax nostalgic about his days on the family farm in Tennessee, but he never publicly waxes nostalgic about the fact that he actually spent three-quarters of his early life in Washington, DC, at a top-floor suite of the swank Fairfax Hotel being groomed for the presidency by a senator (his father) and a UN delegate (his mother). And he didn't exactly attend a one-room schoolhouse in the sticks, instead going to the most elite prep school in Washington (and one of the most expensive in the entire country).

As Vietnam was raging, Gore debated long and hard about how to handle the situation. Thinking that dodging the draft would hurt his political future, he enlisted and was able to get a stateside assignment as a reporter. With seven months left in his two-year tour, Gore was sent to Vietnam, where he was a reporter in the rear echelon, who, unlike the front-line troops, "got to live in safe air-conditioned barracks, take hot showers, eat hot food, and take in Saigon night life..." Despite Gore's 1988 claim that he did guard duty in the bush, "The closest Gore and [his journalist buddy Mike] O'Hara came to combat was to arrive at firebases hours or even days after a firefight."

From 1971 to 1976, Gore plodded along, turning in mediocre performances as a reporter, a divinity student, and a law student (he didn't finish either course of study). He also smoked pot heavily, most witnesses claim, until 1972, although one former friend of his says Gore toked hash and opium-laced pot until he declared his candidacy for the House of Reps in 1976.

Once in the House, Gore purposely made a name for himself by taking on such popular but easy targets as poisonous baby food, toxic waste, and carcinogenic children's pajamas. He was well known among his colleagues for hogging the spotlight and appearing on TV at every opportunity. "His fellow class of '76 Member and rival Richard Gephardt nicknamed Gore 'Prince Albert' for his constant preening before the cameras."

He sat on the fence regarding the events in Nicaragua and El Salvador. It's at this point that the authors' conservative views become apparent. They criticize Gore for not supporting the Contras, which is bad or good depending on your political views. The fact that he tried to play both sides, though, should be troubling (but not surprising) to everyone, no matter where they are on the political spectrum. The authors also take Gore to task for not supporting Reagan's nuclear build-up and SDI, and later they lambaste him for supporting regulation and an end to the ban on gays and lesbians in the military.

Gore's bid for the Democratic presidential nomination in 1988 was bankrolled by "Maryland millionaire real estate developer" Nathan Landow, who had personal and business associations with organized crime figures. Thanks to Gore's dullness and micromanagement, he lost to Michael Dukakis, who then got his ass kicked by George Bush. It's around this time that Gore began to forge his deep, mutually profitable ties to China.

After the Clinton Administration declared war on the tobacco industry in the mid-1990s, Gore suddenly started using his dead sister as a teary-eyed political prop.

During the campaign, Gore bragged to his Southern audiences that he had personally raised and sold tobacco. He told them that he supported tobacco subsidies. He also accepted money from tobacco PACs from 1979 to 1990. All of this despite the fact that his chain-smoking sister died an agonizing death from lung cancer in *1984*. After the Clinton Administration declared war on the tobacco industry in the mid-1990s, Gore suddenly started using his dead sister as a teary-eyed political prop. He's also done the same thing with his son, Albert III, who nearly died after being hit by a car in 1989.

In 2000 Gore declared that he never voted for anti-abortion legislation while he was in Congress, but this is a flat-out lie. In actuality, during his time in the House and Senate he voted against abortion "on 84% of all recorded roll call votes on the issue.... He spoke against abortion in recorded Congressional speeches and wrote against abortion in letters to many constituents." He moved away from his pro-life stance after losing the nomination in 1988, and two weeks after being tapped for VP by Clinton in 1992, Gore miraculously became a full-fledged pro-choice feminist. (Kind of the mirror image of the way George Bush suddenly moved from supporting choice to opposing abortion around the same nanosecond that Reagan made him his running mate.)

Speaking of flip-flops, Gore broke with the Democratic leaders of the Senate to support the Persian Gulf War. In a January 1991 speech, trying to minimize his alienating stance, he declared that the goal of the war should be to expel Iraq from Kuwait, not to invade Iraq and topple Saddam Hussein. However, three months later, Gore started pillorying President Bush for not pressing into Iraq, protecting the Kurds, and overthrowing Hussein. He compared Bush to Stalin for doing exactly what Gore had pushed for that January.

Naturally, Gore is famous for giving lip service to the environment. His actions tell a different story, though. He has been an active proponent of the Tennessee Valley Authority, which has built numerous dams and nuclear reactors. "His Tennessee farm was strip-mined for zinc by three different companies, one of them Armand Hammer's mining subsidiary." He even flails his arms about overpopulation though he and Tipper churned out four kids. But in 1989, Gore suddenly became an eco-warrior, penning *Earth in the Balance*, which completely buys into the myths and failed predictions of Paul Ehrlich's *The Population Bomb* and even compares society's treatment of the earth to the Nazis' treatment of the Jews during the Holocaust. Even into 2000, Gore said he completely stands by what he wrote, including the part about abolishing the internal combustion engine. He never has bothered to renounce his old ways, though. Unfortunately, the authors drop the ball here, failing to show that Gore has continued to help trash the environment *since* 1989. The other Gore exposé, discussed below, does cover this ground.

In 1992 Bill Clinton picked Al Gore as his running mate because Gore at least appeared to be an ethical family man who had experience in Congress and was cherished by important leftist sectors, such as environmentalists who were bamboozled by *Earth in the Balance*. Gore became the most powerful VP in American history. One thing he did with his power was to throw all kinds of support at Russian Prime Minister Victor Chernomyrdin, a corrupt, mobbed-up incompetent who hurt not only Russia but also the US by allowing the Russian Mafia to do whatever it wanted, including stealing money from the IMF and extorting players in the NHL. "Incredibly enough, Gore continues to socialize with Chernomyrdin and to consult him for advice on Russian affairs."

Prince Albert gives a barebones outline of the fundraising scandals (particularly the Buddhist temple shakedown), in which Gore helped Chinese communist agents and high officials give millions of dollars to the Democratic National Committee in exchange for access to the President and the White House, America's military technology secrets, and the President's acquiescence in China's bullying of Taiwan. In China in 1997, Gore raised his glass to toast Prime Minister Li Peng, the man who ordered the Tiananmen massacre, even though Gore had raked George Bush over the coals when two US officials had toasted Peng years earlier.

Likewise, the book quickly sketches some of Gore's other conflicts of interest and potential scandals, such as uranium deals with Russia, the Teamsters election scam, and helping 5,000 felonious

In 2000 Gore declared that he never voted for anti-abortion legislation while he was in Congress, but this is a flat-out lie.

immigrants gain American citizenship so they would vote Democrat. There's also some good info on the dirty dealings of Gore's aforementioned close friend Nathan Landow, who tried to shake down the Cheyenne-Arapaho tribe (whom he called "a bunch of goddamned uneducated Indians") and pressured Kathleen Willey not to testify that Clinton had sexually touched her in the Oval Office. Of course, the authors also look at Gore's defense of Clinton during the whole Lewinsky/impeachment quagmire.

The book ends with a look at the odd cast of characters that Gore brought onboard to run his 2000 campaign: a man who might be criminally indicted for shady dealings, a tobacco industry lobbyist, a race-baiter, people who specialize in slanderous attack ads, and his stealth advisor, Naomi Wolf, who wants to transform Gore into an "alpha male."

"Gore has always used his proficiency with the language of liberalism to mask an agenda utterly in concert with the desires of Money Power."

In the end, *Prince Albert* is a serviceable look at Gore's waffling, lies, and scandals. It suffers from leaden prose, and it should have concentrated on Gore's more recent escapades rather than spreading itself evenly but thinly over his whole life. *Prince Albert* occasionally misses the boat with regard to Gore's unsavory activities. This might be because the authors are conservatives. I have to wonder if, for example, Gore's ties to Big Oil are only given the barest attention because Bush and Cheney are also in Oil's pocket.

No such problems with *Al Gore: A User's Manual*, though. Written by leftist muckrakers Alexander Cockburn and Jeffrey St. Clair—who produce the excellent newsletter *CounterPunch*—this book calls Gore on *all* his bullshit. By doing so, it demonstrates that true, informed leftists also loathe Gore. Some of the brightest lights on the left have lit into Gore and/or Clinton: Christopher Hitchens, Edward Said, Noam Chomsky, James Ridgeway, Sam Smith, Cockburn and St. Clair, *The Nation*, Verso publishing, even Camille Paglia (who oxymoronically calls herself a "libertarian Democrat"). I find this fascinating since it shows such a clear difference between the left and the right. Can you imagine a gallery of prominent conservative commentators and reporters attacking George W. Bush? Can you imagine a conservative publisher putting out an exposé of *Bush* written by two conservatives? It could never happen. Just why the left is willing to do this while the right would never do such a thing, except perhaps under torture, is a topic for another time. Right now, let's look at what the CounterPunchers reveal about Gore.

The first thing I notice is that, as I've come to expect from Cockburn and St. Clair, the prose is smart and the phrasing is snappy. From its chapter titles ("Snaildarter Soup," "Temple of Doom") to its terrific zings ("Tipper raged at him for dumping his family once more and went back to her Prozac bottle."), this is *lively* political writing. And since this book is over 100 pages longer than *Prince Albert*, there is much more juicy detail.

The first chapter provides a concentrated summation of what is wrong with Gore. The main problem is that Gore is yet another corrupt politician who's only loyalty is to the powers-that-be, yet he pretends that he is a visionary progressive who wants to help make the world better. As the authors put it:

> Gore has always used his proficiency with the language of liberalism to mask an agenda utterly in concert with the desires of Money Power. Nowhere is this truer than in his supposed environmentalism, which nicely symbolizes the chasm that has always separated Gore's professions from his performance. He denounces the rape of nature, yet has connived at the strip-mining of Appalachia and, indeed, of terrain abutting one of Tennessee's most popular state parks. In other arenas, he denounced vouchers, yet sends his children to the private schools of the elite. He put himself forth as a proponent of ending the nuclear arms race, yet served as midwife for the MX missile. He offers himself as a civil libertarian, yet has been an accomplice in drives for censorship and savage assaults on the Bill of Rights. He parades himself as an advocate of campaign finance reform, then withdraws to the White House to pocket for the Democratic National Committee $450,000 handed to him by a gardener acting as a carrier pigeon from the Riady family of Indonesia. He and Tipper were ardent smokers of marijuana, yet he now pushes for harsh sanctions against marijuana users.

Cockburn and St. Clair also call attention to the disturbing aspects of Gore's personality. Besides the hypocrisy and lack of ethics noted above:

> Push Gore into any corner and he'll do the wrong thing, which he'll then dignify as the result of an intense moral crisis. Gore is brittle, often the mark of an overly well-behaved, perfect child. When things start to go wrong, he unravels fast....
>
> He is a stretcher in every sense of the word, either with full-blown fibs or the expansion of some modest achievement into impossible vainglory. He claimed to have created the Internet, a ludicrous pretension, although he would have been safe and truthful in describing his early support for federal funding for the Internet.

After examining his use of his sister's and son's tragedies as political props, as well as the hushed-up trouble his own kids have gotten into, this first chapter offers even more penetrating insights into Gore's psyche: "He advertises crisis, depicts an interlude of anguish and claims to have achieved a higher level of moral awareness." "His favorite mode, as adopted in *Earth in the Balance*, is as the herald of catastrophe."

Naturally, Gore's early life is examined, though—as is the case throughout the book—in more detail than *Prince Albert*. In the section on Gore's

> The three books that made the biggest impact on Gore call for reduction in the population of the poor, and one even bemoans the advances in medicine and sanitation that are allowing poor people to live longer.

enlistment in the Army, we find out that it was General William Westmoreland who personally said he would make sure G.I. Gore "will be watched, will be cared for." There's a further drug revelation: John Warnecke claims he and Tipper did mescaline on one occasion.

The authors go into detail about the influences on Gore's environmental outlook. He subscribes heavily to the neo-Malthusian doomsayers who have said for decades that we're just a moment away from global famine and other catastrophes brought about by too many people. The three books that made the biggest impact on Gore hope for a reduction in the population of the poor, and one even bemoans the advances in medicine and sanitation that are allowing poor people to live longer.

During his stint at the *Tennessean* newspaper, Gore and the paper's owners concocted a sting against a black city councilman. Cooperating with the police and TBI, reporter Gore set up the councilman to allegedly take $300 to influence a zoning decision. The politico was acquitted by a second jury after the first one deadlocked. Gore was upset that his hard work at entrapment was for naught.

As a US Representative, Gore refused to help children used as human guinea pigs in radiation experiments at Oak Ridge. This "friend of labor" played a key role in defeating legislation that would've expanded the right of workers to picket. Furthermore, this self-styled "liberal" frequently voted pro-life, pro-gun, pro-nuclear power, pro-nuclear weapon, and pro-US military intervention in foreign affairs. He sided with "B-1" Bob Dornan in trying to protect the tax-exempt status of private schools that bar black children. He likewise aligned himself with Jesse Helms in passing anti-gay legislation and condemning the National Endowment for the Arts for funding Robert Mapplethorpe's exhibit. Gore is a hawk who developed the idea for the "Midgetman" nuclear missile and led the way in guiding the MX missile through the House. Moreover, he has been and continues to be one of the biggest members of the "Israel lobby," and he openly supports the CIA's covert operations, including the overthrow of foreign governments.

Gore was the first to undermine the Endangered Species Act, opening the door for many others to do so. "The way American politics works, it took a reputed environmentalist to destroy America's best environmental law." Of course, this happened before Gore became a full-tilt alleged eco-warrior and wrote *Earth in the Balance*. What happened afterward? As VP, he played a major role in selling NAFTA to the American people, even though 795 out of 800 environmental groups stridently opposed it because it would make a mockery of environmental regulations in Canada and the US. And that was just the beginning. "Over the next six years Clinton and Gore pushed through more than 200 trade agreements and pursued kindred avenues toward unfettered license for corporations to roam the planet, to plunder without hindrance." On a lesser note, as part of his reinventing government project (covered extensively in the book), Gore made the Forest Service charge people to hike in National Forest lands.

A User's Manual also examines Gore's ties to Big Oil, which come chiefly from his close association with Armand Hammer, owner of Occidental Petroleum. In 1996 Gore began engineering the largest privatization in US history—the previously untouchable Elk Hills oil reserves in California were auctioned off. And guess which company won the bidding war. None other than Occidental Petroleum. Coincidentally, since he is the executor of his father's estate, Gore controls up to $1 million in Occidental stock. So much for all the rare and endangered species that inhabit Elk Hills.

And this isn't even touching the full chapter on the other ways VP Gore sold the environment down the river, letting wetlands, coastlines, mountains, whales, giant sea turtles, etc. get crushed under the wheels of "progress." These activities "prompted David Brower, the grand old man of American environmentalism, to conclude that 'Gore and Clinton have done more harm to the environment than Reagan and Bush combined.'"

Gore pushed hard—against the better judgments of Clinton and George Bush—to bomb Iraq because that country had supposedly plotted to whack Bush during a trip to Kuwait City. Gore got his wish, but one third of the missiles missed their targets, instead slamming into apartments, killing numerous people including Iraq's leading artist. At an earlier point when he was asked about the effects of the economic sanctions against Iraq—including 50,000 children dying every year—his response was to laugh. He said he'd address the question later. Of course, he never did.

> VP Gore sold the environment down the river, letting wetlands, coastlines, mountains, whales, giant sea turtles, etc. get crushed under the wheels of "progress."

There's much more dark material gathered in these pages. Among the other topics:

- Gore's (and Al Sr.'s) relationship with Armand Hammer.
- Shafting the poor and labor.
- Pushing for the bombing of Kosovo.
- Destroying Tipper's accomplishments (such as demanding she give up her promising photography career at the *Tennessean* to become a political wife).

- Destroying Jesse Jackson's campaign.
- Plotting to stop Democrats from gaining control of Congress in 1996 in order prevent his rival Dick Gephardt from becoming Speaker of the House.
- Pushing for Police State proposals such as the law requiring telecommunications companies to build wiretap capabilities into their systems, the eavesdropping Clipper Chip, the militarization of the police, and a vast increase in the number of crimes (including some not involving murder) that call for the death penalty.
- Gore's weakness for self-help gurus and pop psychologists.
- Tipper's Puritanical crusade against rock and roll (which was abruptly canned when the Gores realized they need the entertainment industry's money).
- How the depressed Tipper became the leading flack for Prozac.
- Naturally, the book goes into detail about Gore's fundraising scams, devoting an entire chapter to the Buddhist temple, the calls from the White House, using a shill to trick corporations into coughing up money, and Janet Reno's repeated refusals to appoint a special prosecutor to look at Gore's slimy activities.

Dedicated students of political corruption might want to get both books, but if you're only going to read one, *Al Gore: A User's Manual* is more insightful, more detailed, and better written.

Of course, the fun doesn't stop with these two books. More dirt on this supposed Mr. Clean has been turning up. The *Washington Times* reported:

> Rep. Cynthia A. McKinney, in her fourth term from Georgia, said she found out only last week that the Clinton-Gore administration had placed a ceiling on the number of black Secret Service agents who could be assigned to protect Gore, who is the Democratic Party's nominee for president.
>
> "Gore's Negro tolerance level has never been too high," she wrote on her congressional Web site. "I've never known him to have more than one black person around him at any given time. I'm not shocked, but I am certainly saddened by this revelation."
>
> The congresswoman said she learned about the limit of black agents permitted to guard Gore from a group of agents bringing a racial-discrimination suit against the Clinton-Gore Treasury Department, the mother agency of the Secret Service.[1]

If you want an opinion on Gore's alleged environmentalism, just ask the U'wa Indian tribe of Colombia. They're trying to prevent Occidental Petroleum—funny how that name keeps popping up when you read about Gore—from turning their lands into yet another oil-drilling operation. Gore's supporters in the administration have been pushing hard for this plan, and Gore has yet to intercede or even raise an objection. This despite the facts that the tribe is threatening to commit mass suicide and that three children have reportedly died while trying to get away from government troops sent to protect Occidental workers.[2]

One of Gore's many unsavory moments was reported widely in the mainstream press, though they let the story die after just one or two days. In 1995 Democratic officials told Gore to call a trial lawyer who, naturally enough, was opposed to legislation Congress had passed that would limit the financial awards on liability lawsuits. Gore was to call the attorney and ask him to send a $100,000 donation to the DNC before, rather than after, the President vetoed the bill. There's no definitive evidence that Gore made the call, although a memo given to the person who made the call implies that Gore did. The memo suggested the following wording be used during the call: "Sorry you missed the Vice President. I know will give $100K whn the President vetos Tort reform, but we really need it now. Please send ASAP if possible." In the four years following this, the attorney and his firm added $790,000 to the Democrats' trough.[3]

Accuracy in Media has reported a damning story about Gore's maternal uncle, Whit LaFon, a retired Tennessee judge. Gore says that LaFon is a major influence on his life and has helped him at crucial points. Gore appointed LaFon to the national steering committee of Veterans for Gore. LaFon is widely known to be a racist who constantly uses the word "nigger."[4]

"[P]arts of the Indian mounds were being bulldozed into the Tennessee River."

He also owned an island, designated as a national historical site, which contains the remnants of a Native American village and several burial mounds. LaFon sold the island to a real estate developer in March 1999. The developer has begun work on the island, violating environmental regulations. "[P]arts of the Indian mounds were being bulldozed into the Tennessee River."[5]

Written by former *60 Minutes* producer Charles Thompson II and Tony Hays, who won the Tennessee Press Association award for investigative reporting, the Accuracy in Media article states:

> According to state and local officers, a seaplane, allegedly containing narcotics, frequently lands on the water in southern Decatur County, Tenn., near Swallow Bluff Island on the Tennessee River. The drugs are said to be transferred to four-wheelers via motorboats. The four-wheelers then scoot out from LaFon's compound and haul the drugs to delivery points. Federal law enforcement officials have confirmed both the investigation and its targets—retired judge Whit LaFon and Chancery Judge Ron Harmon, a Gore supporter.[6]

The article also delves into the suspicious handling of a case in which LaFon killed a woman:

> On March 3, 1989, a pickup truck driven by Whit LaFon struck 91-year-old Beulah Mae Holmes as she stood by her mail box on a rural Henderson County, Tenn. road with such force that her head went flying in one direction and the rest of her frail body in another. LaFon's vehicle then veered into the oncoming traffic, colliding with an oncoming car. The case file soon disappeared and key parts are still missing today. However, documents from several official sources reveal these violations of procedure that point to a cover-up....
>
> According to his driving record LaFon was a menace on the highway. He was culpable in three accidents, including a hit-and-run involving another judge before killing Mrs. Holmes. Since then he has been involved in five more collisions.[7]

In September 2000 the online news source WorldNetDaily ran a three-part "investigative series on allegations that Vice President Al Gore and his Tennessee associates have thwarted criminal investigations involving friends and family members and have engaged in abuse of power and illegal fund raising." Called "Tennessee Underworld," the series was also written by Thompson and Hays.[8]

The first part covers Gore's uncle Whit and the drug-trafficking investigation focusing on him and Ron Harmon. Part two takes a hard look at Larry Wallace, the Director of the Tennessee Bureau of Investigation, who is alleged to have killed investigations into Gore's friends, family, and fundraisers at Gore's personal request. The final part of the series looks at a specific example of this, in which a drug investigation of two well-connected Gore supporters was suddenly spiked.

After the series ran, a follow-up article reported on the fall-out:

> A representative of Vice President Al Gore's campaign, Doug Hattaway, has been calling media outlets across west Tennessee attempting to stop coverage of last week's series of WorldNetDaily reports detailing allegations of political corruption by Gore and his close friends and supporters in Tennessee.
>
> WMC-TV in Memphis and WBBJ-TV in Jackson, Tenn. both shot interviews with the reporters—and then killed the stories at the last minute with no explanation.
>
> Meanwhile Gore's ally and supporter, Tennessee Bureau of Investigation Director Larry Wallace, is scouring the TBI in an attempt to locate WorldNetDaily.com's sources for its three-part series of reports.[9]

And the hypocrisy just doesn't stop. Gore supports the War on (Some) Drugs and, belatedly, the fight against tobacco, but he has no problem with accepting money from booze merchants.[10] (The alcohol lobby gives as much money to politicians as the tobacco lobby and *more* than the gun lobby.) In September 2000 he urged Clinton to bleed at least 5 million gallons from the nation's oil reserves.[11] Despite the facts that Gore personally received at least $1,500 from Hugh and Christie Hefner and that the Democrats as a whole have raked in a minimum of $105,000 from *Playboy*, Gore forbade Representative Lorretta Sanchez from speaking at a fundraiser at the Playboy Mansion. The sold-out event had already raised over $3 million for Hispanic Unity USA, but Sanchez reluctantly backed out after Gore threatened to cancel her speech at the Democratic National Convention and strip her of her title as Co-chair of the Democratic Party.[12]

Whether you approve or disapprove of Gore's handling of the environment, abortion, Israel, and other issues is going to depend on your politics. We can also debate the importance of his personality and upbringing. But his hypocrisy, exaggerations, outright lies, unethical activities, unsavory associates (including communist spies), and lovey-dovey relationship with big-money interests should upset everyone, regardless of political views.

Books

Prince Albert: The Life and Lies of Al Gore by David N. Bossie and Floyd G. Brown, 2000, ISBN 0-936783-28-1, is published by Merril Press, PO Box 1682, Bellevue WA 98005 <www.merrilpress.com>.

Al Gore: A User's Manual by Alexander Cockburn and Jeffrey St. Clair, 2000, ISBN 1-85984-803-6, is published by Verso, 180 Varick St, 10th Flr, New York NY 10014 <www.versobooks.com>

Endnotes

1. Seper, Jerry. (2000). "Lawmaker questions Gore's racial tolerance." *Washington Times*, Sept 8. **2.** Silverstein, Ken. (2000). "Gore's oil money." *The Nation*, May 22; Sammon, Bill. (2000). "Gore resists calls to halt oil drilling in Colombia," *Washington Times*, June 30. **3.** Yost, Pete. (2000). "Justice Department probes donations." Associated Press, Sept. 14. **4.** Thompson, Charles C., II & Tony Hays. (2000) "Al Gore's embarrassing uncle." Accuracy in Media Website, Sept 12. <www.aim.org/publications/aim_report/2000/08b.html>. **5.** *Ibid.* **6.** *Ibid.* **7.** *Ibid.* **8.** The three-part series "Tennessee Underworld" and the follow-up article can all be accessed at <www.worldnetdaily.com/bluesky_exnews/20000925_xex_gore_rep_tri.shtml>. **9.** *Ibid.* **10.** Hans, Dennis. (2000). "Gore on drugs." The MoJo Wire, Aug 15. <www.motherjones.com/reality_check/goredrugs.html> **11.** Anonymous. (2000). "Gore presses Clinton to tap into oil reserve." UPI, Sept 22. **12.** Ponte, Lowell. (2000). "Gore: Daddy Whore-bucks." FrontPageMagazine.com, Aug 16. <www.frontpagemag.com/archives/ponte/2000/ponte08-16-00.htm>

God Save the President!

How Britain Became the US's Lackey

Robin Ramsay

In the 1980s ideological allies Ronald Reagan and Margaret Thatcher were often pictured together. It's the *Ron and Maggie Show!*. This was followed by the much less impressive successor, starring George Bush and Prime Minister John Major. With the arrival of the Democratic administration, it was the turn of the British Labour Party leaders to head for the White House to have their pictures taken with Bill Clinton. Labour Party officials took How to Win Elections 101 with the Democratic Party pols. And thus we have a kind of transatlantic symmetry: New Labour and new/New Democrats; the *Bill and Tony Show!*. Or so the official Labour version of the Clinton-Blair relationship would have us believe. The truth, of course, is more complex—and more interesting.

Unable to be equal to the United States, the British state wants to be "special" to the United States.

Historical Preamble

Empires come and empires go. The historians differ on when the decline of the British empire began but agree that by the end of WWII it was irreversible. Wars are expensive, and while defeating Hitler ended the Depression for the United States, for the British, defeating Hitler involved a good deal of empire asset realization.

In 1945 the new world top dog was the United States. Not economically damaged by the war, it was producing perhaps half the world's Gross Domestic Product at war's end. With this enormous power, the United States was able to tie a considerable chunk of the world into the new American empire by a series of treaties—of which the most important was NATO—and the creation of American-run international institutions—the IMF and the World Bank and later GATT (now the WTO)—which attempted to regulate the world economy in America's interests. (One of the oddities of the political situation in the United States since the war has been the persistent belief on some sections of the right that the creation of these and similar international institutions are threats to America; when it is these institutions—backed up by force, overt and covert—which have enabled the United States to consume substantially more than its share of the world's energy and minerals.)

Those running the British state resisted acknowledging the loss of top dog status until the 1956 Suez affair when President Eisenhower and US Secretary of State Dulles used the power of the American financial system to attack the pound and thus quickly terminate the British-French-Israeli assault on Nasser's Egypt. The days of independent military action by Britain were over. After Suez, the British state has been wittingly engaged in what has accurately been called the management of decline—while clinging to the United States, and its power, in "the special relationship."

The "Special Relationship"

The Anglo-American "special relationship" is something only the British end of the tandem talks about. Unable to be equal to the United States, the British state wants to be "special" to the United States. Kith and kin; civilization versus the barbarians; Oxford and the Ivy League; white masters of the universe past and present—that is the sort of vaguely racist idea which is the subtext to the British state's use of "the special relationship."

It actually did mean something back in the days between the world wars: Carroll Quigley's thesis on the influence of the Round Table network on Anglo-American foreign policy is demonstrably true in this period; and some of the "allied" spirit generated during WWII did linger on into the post-war period. But as Britain slowly declined in economic and diplomatic significance, while still publicly talked of by US administrations as an ally and a friend, it has been treated rather more like the so-called banana republics of Central America and the Caribbean than its rulers would have us realize.

Britain has been treated rather more like the so-called banana republics of Central America and the Caribbean than its rulers would have us realize.

Britain is covered with US military and intelligence bases. There were 164 facilities in total in the mid-1980s that we are aware of, from nuclear depots downwards.[1] For much of the post-war era when the military game-planned the hypothetical Soviet invasion of Europe—the prevention of which was the formal pretext for NATO's existence—it was clear that US strategy was to resist the Soviet invasion to the last European.

For Britain the "special relationship" has involved remaining the second-biggest contributor to NATO—expenditure which hastened its relative economic decline when compared to other European NATO members spending much less on their military forces; and this relative economic decline has led to slowly decreasing UK military expenditure. By the time of the Gulf War, Britain contributed only 3 percent of the "allied" force against Iraq.

These days, apart from access to its bases in its "unsinkable aircraft carrier" parked off the coast of mainland Europe,[2] Britain is useful to the US chiefly as a figleaf of "international support" and as a proxy, a diplomatic gofer. This does a little to help prevent the US looking entirely like a "rogue state," imposing its will with impunity on the rest of the world.[3] How seriously the United States actually takes Britain was illustrated when, without so much as a phone call to the British government, the US invaded Grenada, a member of the British Commonwealth, whose head of state is formally the Queen.[4]

During the Cold War, the United States embarked on the most ambitious program of world regulation ever seen. Nothing was too small for the US's growing intelligence-gathering services: not even the trade unions in tiny New Zealand (total population less than 2 million), which were reported on all the way down to branch level.[5] Massive propaganda operations were instituted.[6]

In Britain the major potential threat to US dominance was the Labour Party—the party currently led by Bill Clinton's friend, Tony Blair—and its trade union allies. Considerable efforts went into wooing them; hundreds of trade union officials and Labour Party MPs went on US-financed trips to the United States in the 1950s.[7]

Virtually all the Blair faction's leading figures have connections with the United States.

Most of the British Labour Party's leading figures of the 1950s discovered, as did social democrats everywhere, that life was much more comfortable—and occasionally lucrative—if they went along with Uncle Sam. For many this was not a difficult decision: Self-interest coincided with political beliefs. In the early 1950s, to aspiring Labour politicians from grim, war-damaged, ration-bound Britain, the United States must have seemed like the land of milk and honey. And in any case, they were all anti-communists, weren't they?

In the 1950s the Labour Party was led by what became known as the Gaitskellites, named after the party leader, Hugh Gaitskell. The Gaitskellites should now more accurately be called the American tendency. Yes, the CIA was involved—there are a scattering of references to CIA personnel meeting Labour Party figures—but so were other bodies and other sources of American money and propaganda.

With the death of Hugh Gaitskell in 1963,[8] leadership of the American tendency in the Labour Party fell to Roy Jenkins MP, now Lord Roy Jenkins. Jenkins was in the Labour governments of 1964-70 and 1974-6, until his departure for a job with the European Commission in 1976. When he returned from Brussels, the hardcore of the American tendency left the Labour Party and joined the short-lived Social Democratic Party (SDP), formed by Jenkins and three other senior Labour figures—"the gang of four"—in 1981.[9]

This American tendency had three outstanding positions: They were anti-communists and inclined to see reds under all manner of beds; they were pro-NATO; and they were pro-UK membership of the European Economic Community (now the European Union).

Mr. Tony

In a sense the faction of the Labour Party currently led by Prime Minister Tony Blair is a continuation of the Social Democratic Party (SDP). The Blair faction's link with the SDP is visible in the continuing contacts between Prime Minister Blair and Roy Jenkins (now Lord Jenkins of Hillhead), and the role in the Prime Minister's Policy Unit of Roger Liddle, Blair's adviser on Europe and Defence. Liddle's father-in-law is (Lord) George Thomson, Labour Minister in the 1960s, who resigned as an MP to become a European Commissioner in 1973.

Son-in-law Liddle left Labour to join the SDP, and cowrote, with Northern Ireland Minister Peter Mandelson, the most detailed account we have to date of the so-called Blair "project," the Blair Revolution. Liddle's significance to the "project" is suggested by the fact that he survived the so-called "cash-for-access" scandal. This was a piece of routine, low-level political lobbying by American standards: Companies were being offered access to members of the government for money. But for Britain, and especially for a nominally left party like Labour, it was a scandal. Without Prime Ministerial support, Liddle would have had to resign.

Virtually all the Blair faction's leading figures have connections with the United States. What follows are the links that have been made public. In 1986 Tony Blair, then a member of the Campaign for Nuclear Disarmament (CND), went on one of those US-funded trips to America that are available for promising MPs, and came back a supporter of the nuclear deterrent.[10] David Miliband, Blair's head of policy, did a Master's degree at the Massachusetts Institute of

Technology.[11] Gordon Brown used to tell interviewers that he spent his summer holidays in the library at Harvard University; and he seems to have received most of his practical economics education in the US through contacts of Ed Balls, his economics adviser.[12] Balls studied at Harvard University, wrote editorials for the *Financial Times*, and was about to join the World Bank when Brown offered him the job.[13]

Former Northern Ireland Minister Marjorie Mowlam did a Doctorate at the University of Iowa and then taught in the US in the 1970s.[14] Sue Nye, long-serving personal assistant of Chancellor of the Exchequer Gordon Brown, lives with Gavyn Davies, one of Brown's economic advisers, and chief economist with the seriously big-time American bankers, Goldman Sachs.[15] Jonathan Powell, Blair's foreign policy adviser, is a former Foreign and Commonwealth Office (FCO) official whose previous posting was in the British embassy in Washington.[16] Chris Smith, now Heritage Minister, had a US-subsidized stay in the States as a Kennedy Scholar, as did the aforementioned David Miliband and Ed Balls.[17]

When a smooth exit can be found for Foreign Secretary Robin Cook, then Blair's closest ally, Northern Ireland Minister Peter Mandelson, will be appointed Foreign Secretary. In 1976, at the end of his period as a student at Oxford University, Mandelson became Chair of the British Youth Council. This largely invisible organization was a true child of the Cold War, begun as the British section of the World Assembly of Youth (WAY), which was set up and financed by the CIA and the British equivalent, MI6, in the early 1950s to combat the Soviet Union's youth front organisations.[18] By Mandelson's time in the mid-1970s, the British Youth Council was officially financed by the Foreign Office, though that may have been a euphemism for MI6.

Twenty years on, Donald Macintyre, later to write his biography, told us in *The Independent* that Mandelson "is a pillar of the two blue-chip foreign affairs think-tanks, Ditchley Park and Chatham House."[19] Chatham House is perhaps better known to American readers as the Royal Institute for International Affairs, a foreign policy think tank once the axis of the British end of the Round Table network, and the nearest British equivalent of the Council on Foreign Relations. Peter Mandelson looks like an MI6 asset, but there is no evidence to support this view.

Tying the ties that bind the Blair faction to the Americans even tighter, Cabinet Ministers Peter Mandelson; Marjorie Mowlam; George Robertson, Blair's initial Defence Minister and now Secretary General of NATO; Heritage Minister Chris Smith; and junior Foreign Office Minister in the House of Lords, Elizabeth Symons, are all alumni of the British-American Project (BAP), the latest in the long line of American-funded networks which have promoted American interests among the British political elite. The BAP newsletter for June/July 1997 headlined its account of Labour's landslide victory at the May 1997 General Election, "Big Swing to BAP."

NATO's Team

American influence on Labour in the defense field is expressed by the Trade Union Committee for European and Transatlantic Understanding (TUCETU). TUCETU began as the Labour Committee for Transatlantic Understanding (LCTU), which was set up in 1976 by the late Joe Godson, Labour Attaché at the US embassy in London in the 1950s. Currently organized by two officials of the NATO-financed Atlantic Council, TUCETU incorporated Peace Through NATO—the group central to Conservative Defence Secretary Michael Heseltine's Ministry of Defence campaign against the Campaign for Nuclear Disarmament in the mid-1980s—and receives over £100,000 a year from the Foreign Office. TUCETU chair Alan Lee Williams was a defense minister in the Labour Government of 1976-79 before he defected to the Social Democratic Party. In the mid-1980s Williams and TUCETU director Peter Robinson were members of the European policy group of the spook-laden Washington Centre for Strategic and International Studies.[20]

The Atlantic Council/TUCETU network provided New Labour's Ministry of Defence team. The initial Defence Secretary, George Robertson, was a member of the Council of the Atlantic Committee from 1979-90; Lord Gilbert, Minister of State for Defence Procurement, is listed as TUCETU vice chair; and a Ministry of Defence press office biographical note on junior Defence Minister John Speller states that he "has been a long standing member of the Trade Union Committee for European and Transatlantic Understanding."

New Labour and Bilderberg

As well as being thoroughly integrated into the British state's foreign policy apparatus, key members of the Blair government have attended the annual meetings of the Bilderberg group. Running now for over 40 years, Bilderberg is one of several annual meetings at which the European and American political and economic elites explore the issues which affect them and try to arrive at something like a consensus. Because the meetings are held in private and the major media had, until a couple of years ago, complied with the group's request that they not be reported, Bilderberg has acquired an aura of mystery and conspiracy—especially on the American right, where it is suspected of being the decision-making center of the so-called New World Order.

Alas, Bilderberg is not the executive committee of transnational capital, settling the fate of the world at its annual meetings. But it is an important part of the agenda-forming process of world capital and a key interface between politicians and the managers of the transnational corporations. Bilderberg is important, just not as important as some of the American right thinks it is.

The three most important members of the Blair government—Blair, Chancellor of the Exchequer Gordon Brown, and Northern Ireland

The three most important members of the Blair government have attended Bilderberg meetings.

Minister Peter Mandelson—have attended Bilderberg meetings, as has John Monks, an important Blair ally as head of the Trade Union Congress, the British version of the AFL-CIO.[21] But the most significant recent Labour Party connection to Bilderberg was John Smith, erstwhile leader of the Labour Party, whose death in 1994 led to the election of Tony Blair as leader.

In Labour Party memory, John Smith is a genial, whiskey-drinking, hill-walking, honest right-winger. That memory does not include the fact that while Brown, Blair, and Mandelson have attended Bilderberg's meetings (from 1989 until 1992), when he became leader of the Labour Party, John Smith was on the Bilderberg steering committee—the inner group.[22] It was John Smith who, accompanied by Marjorie Mowlam, toured the City of London in 1989-90 assuring the bankers that when he became Chancellor of the Exchequer, Labour would do nothing to reduce their profits or their power. This was the key shift in Labour's policy; this persuaded the financial sector and the major media that the Labour Party could be trusted with a period in office.

Smith was also a lifelong friend of Baroness "Meta" Ramsay, who, before retiring and becoming a Labour member of the House of Lords, had been a career MI6 officer.[23] The sense of undisclosed aspects of Smith's political persona is heightened by the presence of his widow on the board of a company, the Hakluyt Foundation, which, if not a British intelligence front, was set up and is run by senior MI6 officers.[24]

■ ■ ■ ■ ■ ■ ■ ■ ■ ■

The Blair faction is the latest version of the American tendency in the Labour Party. The people around Blair are linked to the United States or to the British foreign policy establishment, whose chief aim—since the end of the Second World War—has been to preserve the Anglo-American "special relationship" to compensate for British long-term economic (and thus military, political, and diplomatic) decline. (And you can rest assured that no matter who the future leaders of Britain and the US happen to be, the countries will continue their "special relationship" of lapdog and master.)

These are the facts—or, at any rate, one selection of the facts—about New Labour. None of this is secret—it just is never pulled together and presented in this light by the British media. If you approve of what is being done by American capital's grip on the world, you may regard all of the above as neither surprising nor disquieting—all hat and no cattle, sound and fury signifying...not much. I do not approve; and it seems to me that the fact that this information is entirely missing from the UK's mainstream political and cultural discourses says a great deal about the all-pervasive influence of the United States on British society.

Endnotes

1. Campbell, Duncan. (1986). *The unsinkable aircraft carrier*. London: Paladin, p 294. This number has reduced with the closure of certain USAF bases, notably that at Greenham Common, the site of the famous women's peace camp. **2.** It is not widely known in the UK that the US bases are sovereign territory, independent of the laws of the UK. **3.** The idea of the US as the world's most important "rogue state" comes from William Blum. See his recent *Rogue State* (Common Courage Press, 1999). **4.** Having defeated an "army" of some 600 Cuban engineers and construction workers, the US military awarded 7,000 medals to the personnel involved in the campaign. Blum, William. (1995). *Killing hope: US military and CIA interventions since World War II*. Common Courage Press, p 277. Boy, they must wear that ribbon with real pride, huh? **5.** "Spies amongst us: How the US embassy saw New Zealand, 1945-69," *Watchdog*, newsletter of the Campaign Against Foreign Control of Aotearoa, No 65. Wellington, New Zealand, October 1990. Aotearoa is the name of New Zealand in the language of the indigenous people. The article is a brief summary of 1,000 pages of declassified State Department documents released under the Freedom of Information Act. **6.** See for example Lucas, Scott. (1999). *Freedom's war: The US crusade against the Soviet Union 1945-56*. Manchester University Press, the first attempt to draw together the various bits and pieces of knowledge of these operations; and Saunders, Frances Stonor. (1999). *Who paid the piper?: The CIA and the cultural Cold War*. London: Granta, a long, wonderfully researched account of the CIA's cultural operations in Europe of the 1950s and 60s centered round the Congress for Cultural Freedom. **7.** For trade union officials and officers, see Carew, Anthony. (1987). *Labour under the Marshal Plan*. Manchester University Press, pp 90, 189. No complete list exists of US-sponsored trips by MPs, but all the leading social democrats of the period took them, including Hugh Gaitskell, Labour Foreign Secretaries George Brown and Anthony Crosland, and Cabinet minister Douglas Jay. **8.** The paranoids in the wing of the CIA led by James Angleton believed—or pretended to believe—that Gaitksell had been assassinated by the Soviet Union. **9.** Some on the Labour Left assumed that the SDP was run or funded by the CIA, but no evidence has ever been forthcoming. I was told in 1987 by Ray Fitzwalter, the then-editor of a major British TV documentary series, that he had got drunk with the late Cord Meyer, founding member of the CIA and London CIA station chief 1973-75. In his cups, Meyer had boasted of the operation the CIA had run to set up the SDP. But despite assigning his best journalists to it, Fitzwalter could find no evidence. **10.** *The Observer*, April 14, 1996. **11.** *The Guardian*, October 3, 1994. **12.** Routledge, Paul. (1998). *Gordon Brown*. London: Simon and Schuster, pp 175-6, 183-4 **13.** *Ibid*. Balls' wife, Yvette Cooper—MP for Pontefract, and now a Junior Minister in the Blair government—also studied at Harvard. **14.** *Who's Who 1992* **15.** *The Sunday Telegraph*, March 24, 1996. Davies was an adviser to the Callaghan government of the 1970s as a member of the Downing Street Policy Unit, headed by Bernard Donoghue (now a Lord). Of Davies' role before the 1997 election, an unnamed "Labour source" said, "Gavyn doesn't write policy, but he is our City sounding board. We draft the ideas and Gavyn tells us what the effect will be on the economy and what the response will be in the markets." This was in a feature on Derek Scott, one of Labour's economic advisers, written by Brian Milton for the *London Financial News*, June 16, 1996, but spiked. I saw a proof copy. **16.** Ken Coates and Michael Barett Brown suggest in their book *The Blair Revelation* (Nottingham: Spokesman, 1996) that Powell's job in the British embassy in Washington concealed a role as the liaison officer between British intelligence and the CIA. Powell's career summary as given in the Diplomatic Service List for 1995 contains nothing from which to definitely infer intelligence connections. He was born in 1956 and joined the FCO (Foreign and Commonwealth Office) in 1979. Since then he was Third later Second Secretary in Lisbon, 1981; Second later First Secretary at the FCO, London; UK delegate to CDE Stockholm, 1986; UK delegate at the CSCE in Vienna, 1986; First Secretary FCO, London, 1989; then First Secretary (Chancery) Washington, 1991. An intelligence role is possible but more evidence is needed. **17.** *The Independent* (Education), July 1, 1989. **18.** On WAY see the scattering of references in Kotek, Joel. (1996). *Students and the Cold War*. London: Macmillan; Smith, Joseph B. (1981). *Portrait of a Cold Warrior*. New York: Ballantine; and Bloch, Jonathan & Patrick Fitzgerald. (1983). *British intelligence and covert action*. London and Dingle [Ireland]: Junction/Brandon. **19.** *The Independent*, July 29, 1995. I have not read the MacIntyre biography of Mandelson which was withdrawn and pulped in 1999 after a libel action, but I am told that this reference to Ditchley and the RIIA (Chatham House) is not included in it. **20.** These paragraphs on TUCETU are taken from David Osler's "American and Tory Intervention in the British Unions since the 1970's" in *Lobster* 33. **21.** Tony Blair refers to the meeting in his Parliamentary declaration of interests. Brown attended the 1991 meeting with then-leader of the party John Smith: A list of those attending was published in the US magazine *The Spotlight*, July 22, 1991, and then posted on the Net. John Monks attended the 1996 meeting in Toronto: The list of those attending appeared in the Canadian media and was posted on the Net. Peter Mandelson attended the 1999 meeting. **22.** Letter to author from M. Banck, Executive Secretary of Bilderberg Meetings. **23.** Most recent sources on Meta Ramsay qua MI6 officer were *Mail*, March 28, 1999, and *Private Eye* (London), April 2, 1999. **24.** "Top firms get secrets from MI6," *Sunday Business*, October 11, 1998, and Osler, David. "Privileged information," *Red Pepper* (London), January 1999.

Choked by almost 800,000 souls, Pristina, Kosovo, a city of tower blocks rising from a parched valley floor, now holds twice as many people as it was built for. The air reeks of exhaust and burning garbage. All day a hot wind blows ghostly airborne litter and clouds of gritty dust from the huge mountain of mine tailings that lies a dozen miles due west. At night one still hears the snap of gunfire and the next day, rumors of another unsolved murder.

Despite the city's hyper-modernist aesthetic (the place was rebuilt from scratch after an earthquake in 1963), Pristina has no public transportation nor any systematic refuse collection. All the most

Water and electrical services are intermittent, but several cybercafes and brothels operate around the clock.

impressive modernist buildings of the downtown now stand as bombed-out relics. Adding to the *Blade Runner* feel of the place are throngs of cellphone-wielding crowds and streams of new Mercedes and Audis that clog the streets below the charred towers. Water and electrical services are intermittent, but several cybercafes and brothels operate around the clock.

Welcome to ground zero of NATO's reincarnation of what Secretary of State Madeline Albright has called "a force for peace from the Middle East to Central Africa."

Billed by almost all media, right-wing and liberal, as the greatest humanitarian intervention since World War II, the UN/NATO occupation of Kosovo doesn't look so noble up close. Rather than a multiethnic democracy, Kosovo is shaping up to be a violent, corrupt, free-market colony erected on the foundation of a massive lie.

Rather than a multiethnic democracy, Kosovo is shaping up to be a violent, corrupt, free-market colony erected on the foundation of a massive lie.

The first fact to establish is this: Despite the shrill and frantic cries about genocide that paved NATO's road to Kosovo, forensics teams from Spain and the FBI found less than 2,500 bodies. As it turned out, this was the total body count from the Serbs' brutal, but hardly genocidal, two-year counterinsurgency campaign against the KLA. A horror and a brutal war fueled by ethnic hatred on all sides? Yes. Genocide? No.

Humanitarian Imperialism

The Albanians here may talk about "their country," but foreign aid workers in official, white SUVs call the shots. After NATO's 78-day bombing—done with radioactive, depleted-uranium-tipped ordnance—the United Nations Mission in Kosovo (UNMIK) was created to act as an "interim administration." The UN in turn has opened Kosovo to a kaleidoscopic alphabet soup of subsidiary governmental and nongovernmental organizations ranging from Oxfam to obscure evangelical ministries. All municipalities and state agencies are run by UN personnel or UN appointees, and deutsch marks are the legal tender.

At the apex of it all sits Bernard Kouchner, the Secretary General's Special Representative in Kosovo. Founder of Médecins Sans Frontiéres and a former socialist, Kouchner took a sharp right in the 1980s when he began to champion the use of Western (particularly American) military intervention to protect human rights. Kouchner's left-wing critics—who correctly point out that American and European corporate and military power are the main causes of human rights violations internationally—see Kouchner as a Clinton-Blair "third way" hypocrite. Meanwhile many mainstream right-wing commentators cast the wiry Frenchman as a publicity-seeking autocrat.

In Kosovo, Kouchner's responsibilities range from censoring the local press when it offends him, to appointing all local government personnel, to unilaterally ditching the Yugoslavian dinar for the mark. Adding muscle to these sorts of executive caprice are about 4,000 so-called UNMIK police, many of whom are transplanted American cops. For the really heavy lifting, Kouchner counts on the 40,000 international soldiers that make up KFOR—the Kosovo Implementation Force.

Along with putting down the occasional ethnic riot, protecting convoys of refugees, and guarding the few small Serb enclaves remaining in Kosovo, KFOR and the UNMIK police occasionally uncover caches of weapons that belong to the officially disarmed Kosovo Liberation Army. Such operations are usual followed up with robust statements by KFOR spokespeople reaffirming their commitment to "building a multiethnic society." Strangely, the ethnic cleansing—this time Albanian against Serb and Roma (Gypsies)—never stops.

"This place is a shithole. All the young people I meet, I tell 'em: Get out! Go to another country."

Violence Still

"This is an amazing place. The people are so resilient, so creative. I've made so many friends," enthuses an American aid worker named Sharon who is helping to set up an Albanian radio station. When asked about the continuing Albanian-on-Serb violence, she chalks it up to the Albanian culture of revenge feuds. It's a typical dismissal, but not all internationals approach the issue with such equanimity.

"This place is a shithole. All the young people I meet, I tell 'em: Get out! Go to another country," booms Doc Giles, a tanned, muscled American cop who speaks in a thick south Jersey accent. A longtime narc-officer from hyper-violent Camden, New Jersey, Giles has spent the last year working homicide in Pristina with UNMIK. The pack on his bike sports a "Daniel Faulkner: fallen not forgotten" button. (Faulkner was the cop that death-row inmate and journalist Mumia Abu Jamal may, or may not, have murdered eighteen years ago in Philadelphia.)

Giles' maggot-eye view of inter-ethnic relations is sobering: "Look, all the perps are oo-che-kaa," says Giles, using the Albanian form for the Kosovo Liberation Army's acronym. "They're fucking gangsters. I don't care what anyone says—they're an organized crime structure. And all the judges are either scared or pro-KLA. They're like: You shot an 89-year-old Serb grandmother? Good for you. Get out of jail."

Of the province's 276 judges, only two are Serb, so Albanian hit squads operate with near total impunity. Among their favorite targets during the last year have been Orthodox churches and monasteries, over 85 of which have been burned, looted, or demolished according to both the UN and a detailed report by the Serbian Orthodox Church.

By the end of one of Giles' rants about fifteen-year-old Maldovan girls "turned out" as prostitutes and KLA thugs ganging-up on their Serb and Roma victims five-to-one, you'll almost agree with his prescription: "What they should've done was put this place under martial law, get a bunch of American cops from cities like Philly, Dallas, and Denver to come in here and just kick the shit out everyone for a few months. Then turn it over to your NGO's, or whatever."

Terrified merchants also tell stories of KLA thuggery. "Ten percent. They take ten percent of everything you make. And you pay or it's kaput," says a hushed and nervous restaurateur in Prizren, an ancient town near the Albanian border. He's a Kosovar Turk whose great-grandparents probably moved here during the twilight of the Ottoman Empire, but when he gets enough money he says he's taking his two children to Canada.

Privatization

While Giles and his comrades recycle Albanian "perps" through a non-working judicial system, the UN's paper-pushers and its partner organizations are hard at work trying to turn Kosovo into a free-market paradise.

"We must privatize so as to secure investment and new technology. There is no alternative," explains Dianna Stefanova, director of the European Agency for Reconstruction's office on privatization, which is working under the auspices of UNMIK and Kouchner.

There's only one problem with this plan: The industries located in Kosovo are not UNMIK's to privatize. Nor does the wording of Security Council resolution 1244—the document defining the UN's role in Kosovo—give UNMIK the power to sell off local industries. And when Kouchner made his pitch for mass privatization to the Security Council in late June, he met stiff opposition from the Russians.

Bizarrely, resolution 1244 recognizes Kosovo as an integral province of Yugoslavia. So technically the dinar should be the currency, trials should proceed according to Yugoslavian law, Yugoslav officials should be free to travel and should control the borders, and Yugoslav state assets shouldn't be sold by the UN.

To get around the awkward parts of resolution 1244, Kouchner has devised a useful bit of legerdemain. The UN isn't actually selling off assets—they are just offering ten- and fifteen-year leases to foreign transnationals. The first industry to go was the huge Sharr Cement factory, leased to the Swiss firm Holderbank. "Sharr could produce all the cement needed for reconstruction and even export to Macedonia," explains Roy Dickinson, a privatization specialist with the European Agency for Reconstruction.

The next assets on the block are a series of vineyards and wine cooperatives, but the ultimate prize is the gargantuan Trepca mining and metallurgical complex that sprawls across northern Kosovo and into the mountains of southern Serbia. Since Roman times, foreign armies have targeted these massive mineral deposits. Hitler took Trepca in 1940, and thereafter the mines—some of the richest in the world—supplied German munitions factories with 40 percent of their lead inputs.

Trepca contains all of Yugoslavia's nickel deposits and three-quarters of its other mineral wealth; during the 1990s the 42 mines and attendant factories were one of Yugoslavia's leading export industries.

"They're like:
You shot an 89-year-old Serb grandmother?
Good for you. Get out of jail."

The Belgrade government and a private Greek bank that has also invested in the mines insist that Trepca shall not change hands. The UN isn't so sure. "The question of who gets what will be settled by a panel of judges that UNMIK is still setting up," says a coy Stefanova. In the meantime UNMIK is drawing up plans to downsize local industries and streamline enterprise so as to make them more attractive to foreign investors. But there's another piece of the equation: Who controls the land above the mines? That of course brings us back to the issue of ethnic cleansing.

Balkan Belfast

The swift and shallow river Ibar, bisecting the town of Mitrovica, is the front line in an unfinished war that pits Albanians against Serbs and Roma. All non-Albanians have been expelled from south of the Ibar, and all Albanians driven from its northern bank. Thus crossing into north Mitrovica is much like entering Serbia: The language, the music, and the beer are all Serbian, and people use the dinar. This is also the heart of the Trepca complex.

Here, despite occupation by French troops, the Belgrade government still pays salaries and pensions and still provides health care. And if even a fraction of UN and KFOR accusations are true, then some of the hard men with mobile phones who lounge at the Dolce Vita Cafe on the banks of the Ibar are probably undercover cops from Serbia (some of whom, you will recall, have been indicted by the International Tribunal on War Crimes at the Hague and could be arrested by KFOR).

"We're in a prison, and under attack. What you see is all we have," says a young Serb Branislav who is hanging out near a north Mitrovica newsstand selling Serbian papers. "If I cross that bridge I'll be killed." This, it seems, is the future: An ethnically "pure" and therefore "stable" Albanian Kosovo in the south, with huge NATO installations like the sprawling 775-acre American base, Bondsteel, which hosts 4,000 GIs on the plains of Kosovo's southeast. While in the north, astride some small part of the Trepca mines, and in a few other spots, Serb and Roma ghettos will remain, possibly as parts of Serbia. In the places where these communities overlap, there will be trouble and therefore "humanitarian work" for NATO troops and, thus, a plausible—and more importantly, palatable—reason for the West to maintain its long-term military presence.

The Truth About Terrorism

Ali Abunimah

The State Department's report, "Patterns of Global Terrorism, 1999," published on May 1, 2000, flatly contradicts the government's statements about terrorism, as well as the general public's perception of the phenomenon.

The Main Conclusions of the Report Are Not Supported by the Data It Provides

The introduction to the report and the conclusion most widely covered states that:

> The primary terrorist threats to the United States emanate from two regions, South Asia and the Middle East. Supported by state sponsors, terrorists live in and operate out of areas in these regions with impunity. They find refuge and support in countries that are sympathetic to their use of violence for political gain, derive mutual benefit from harboring terrorists, or simply are weakly governed.

Yet, the statistics and narrative concerning anti-US attacks and "terrorist" activities in and from these regions tell a different story.

Of the 169 anti-US attacks reported for 1999, Latin America accounted for 96, Western Europe for 30, Eurasia for nine, and Africa sixteen. The Middle East accounted for only eleven, and Asia for six. Most of these attacks were bombings. The report's figures for the total number of terrorist attacks by region indicate that in recent years, Latin America and Europe have each accounted for a greater number of terrorist attacks than the Middle East and Asia combined. 1999 is consistent with this pattern.

Latin America and Europe have each accounted for a greater number of terrorist attacks than the Middle East and Asia combined.

The chapter on the Middle East does not provide any insight into why the report headlines that region as presenting one of the two major threats to the United States today. On the contrary, it details widespread and "vigorous" "counter-terrorism" efforts by Jordan, Algeria, Egypt, Yemen, Israel, and the Palestinian Authority. Although the State Department continues to list Syria, Iran, Iraq, and Libya as "state sponsors" of terrorism, the report does not detail any activity by these states that would support the conclusion that the Middle East region represents one of the two main threats to the United States.

To the extent which the report alleges that "terrorist" activity persists in the Middle East, this is principally directed not at the United States, but at Israel, a country that is illegally occupying the territory of several others. It also categorizes resistance against combatant Israeli occupation forces in Lebanon as terrorism. (This activity is cited in the section on Lebanon, and the section on Iran accuses that country of encouraging Hizballah and other groups "to use violence, especially terrorist attacks, in Israel to undermine the peace process.")

The definition of Hizballah's activities as "terrorist" is at odds with the internationally-recognized right to resist foreign occupation, but it could possibly be justified if it were at least applied in a consistent manner. Yet, while Hizballah is termed a "terrorist" organization, this designation is not used for the Israeli-controlled "South Lebanon Army," a sub-state group that frequently carries out attacks on Lebanese civilians, seizes and tortures noncombatant hostages, and threatens and uses other forms of violence and coercion against Lebanese civilians. In May 2000, Hizballah guerillas succeeded in expelling Israeli occupation forces from Lebanon, after a 22-year occupation.

The continued designation of certain countries as "state sponsors" of terrorism appears to be politically motivated. The report states, for example, "A Middle East peace agreement necessarily would address terrorist issues and would lead to Syria being considered for removal from the list of state sponsors." This may suggest to seasoned observers that Syria's continued designation as a "state sponsor of terrorism" is simply a stick to get Syria to sign an agreement with Israel consonant with US preferences, rather than a designation arising from an objective analysis of that state's policies. This view may be supported by the fact that the report does not allege any activities being planned from Syria and, in fact, says that Syria "continued to restrain" groups operating in Damascus from any but political activities.

The section on Iran claims that that country was "the most active state sponsor of terrorism" in 1999. Yet almost all the alleged activities were directed not at the United States, but were assistance to groups that were fighting the Israeli occupation of southern Lebanon. Iran's other alleged principal activity was assistance to the PKK, the group fighting Turkey's repressive policies against Kurds. Again, none of the reported activities appears to directly threaten the United States.

Furthermore, such violence as occurs is principally related to local political conflicts, not to generalized "hatred of the West" as often portrayed in the media.

None of the other sections on Middle Eastern countries lists any activities by states or groups that would seem to justify the assertion that the Middle East represents a major threat of terrorism to the United States. Certainly this assertion is not borne out by the actual data on terrorist attacks and casualties, which consistent with recent years, shows the Middle East accounting for a relatively tiny number of "anti-US attacks." Historically, attacks have been directed at US interests principally when the United States has intervened directly in the region, as it did heavily in Lebanon in the 1980s. Furthermore, such violence as occurs is principally related to local political conflicts, not to generalized "hatred of the West" as often portrayed in the media. The numbers and descriptions of patterns of violence in the Middle East suggest that as in other regions like Northern Ireland, violence diminishes when broad-based political processes or solutions are set in motion.

As for the assertion that the "locus of terrorism" has shifted from the Middle East to South Asia, and particularly Afghanistan, the entire case seems to rest on assertions that Usama Bin Laden is operating a vast, international terrorism network. It is difficult for observers to evaluate these claims, because the State Department does not publish any substantial evidence or sources, merely assertions. We do know that in cases where the US government has made specific claims, these have often turned out to be exaggerated or false.

Investigative reporting by the *New York Times* and others severely and compellingly questioned the factual basis and process of President Clinton's decision to bomb the Al-Shifa pharmaceutical factory in Khartoum, Sudan, in August 1998. The United States government chose not to contest a lawsuit brought against it by the owner of that factory who sought to recover control of his assets, frozen by the United States on the grounds that he was linked with Mr. Bin Laden. Hence, in the absence of any compelling evidence to the contrary, the US government's past record with regard to claims

By far most of the anti-US attacks occur in Latin America.

about Mr. Bin Laden suggests that a responsible observer should at the very least be deeply skeptical. Some observers have suggested that the threat from Mr. Bin Laden has been deliberately exaggerated to justify limits on civil liberties in the United States, and an expanded US role in the Middle East.

Again, as in the case of the Middle East, the principal events in South Asia, such as the hijacking of an Indian airliner and bombings in India and Pakistan which claimed many lives, were unrelated to the United States, and seemed to be related to local or regional conflicts such as that in Kashmir or Sri Lanka.

Similarly, the vast majority of incidents in Europe are, according to the report, attributable to Basque separatists in Spain, the conflict in Northern Ireland, the Kurdish movement in Turkey, and various anarchist groups in Greece. Middle Eastern or "Islamic" terrorism was not a significant factor in this region, either.

By far most of the anti-US attacks occur in Latin America. Much of this terrorism, which includes bombings and kidnappings, is committed in Colombia and Peru by leftist rebels and right-wing paramilitary groups. American citizens and commercial interests have been attacked partly for ransom money to help finance insurgencies and partly to undermine national economies. But these groups, which commit most of the attacks against Americans and their property abroad, get less attention than groups with Arab or Muslim orientations. Moreover, Colombia and Peru are not designated as a major threat to the United States. The reasoning for this is absent from the report.

The Report Makes Disturbing Assertions That May Fuel Anti-Muslim Prejudice in the United States and Around the World

The report assures the reader:

> Adverse mention in this report of individual members of any political, social, ethnic, religious, or national group is not meant to imply that all members of that group are terrorists. Indeed, terrorists represent a small minority of dedicated, often fanatical, individuals in most such groups. It is those small groups—and their actions—that are the subject of this report.

Yet it appears to do quite the opposite. For example, it states:

> Islamist extremists from around the world—including North America; Europe; Africa; the Middle East; and Central, South, and Southeast Asia—continued to use Afghanistan as a training ground and base of operations for their worldwide terrorist activities in 1999. The Taliban, which controlled most Afghan territory, permitted the operation of training and indoctrination facilities for non-Afghans and provided logistic support to members of various terrorist organizations and mujahidin, including those waging jihads in Chechnya, Lebanon, Kosovo, Kashmir, and elsewhere.

This paragraph appears to cast any Muslim person fighting any battle, for any reason, as an "Islamic extremist." It also uses the Arabic words "jihad" and "mujahidin," which have very specific definitions, as synonyms for terrorism. Is it not possible to imagine that a Muslim in Kosovo or Chechnya could be engaged in a legitimate battle? (I certainly think the United States would have thought so when it provided substantial state sponsorship to groups in Afghanistan and when it designated such people as "freedom fighters," using them to fight against Soviet intervention. Unfortunately the report is silent about US state sponsorship of these groups, so again it is difficult to evaluate how much of the presently observed phenomena is a direct result of United States activities in South Asia over the past two decades. Certainly an objective analysis would have to take this into account.)

Careless references to Islam, "jihad," and "terrorism" are unfortunate and damaging. This report comes in the context of US officials late in 1999 openly linking the Muslim feast of Ramadan with an increased threat of "terrorism" around the world. The threat did not materialize, but the hysteria generated by the government warnings was particularly damaging to Arab Americans and Muslims in the United States who are, despite all the lessons of Oklahoma City, TWA 800, and other incidents, still the first to fall under suspicion and to be victimized by repressive measures such as the use of secret evidence and passenger profiling.

The panic and media sensation created by the arrest of Ahmed Ressam, an Algerian man, at the United States-Canada border in late 1999, allegedly for carrying explosives, reportedly caused an increase of harassment of Arab Americans and Muslims by airlines and others, as well as allegations by law enforcement officials, later retracted, that other Arabs arrested at the border for visa violations were terrorist suspects. For at least two weeks, not a day went by without a reminder of Ressam's name, face, and alleged crimes. The fact that Ressam is Algerian licensed much uninformed speculation about links between Ressam and current US villain Usama Bin Laden, as well as about a global Muslim conspiracy against the US.

The threat did not materialize, but the hysteria generated by the government warnings was particularly damaging to Arab Americans and Muslims in the United States.

On December 28, 1999, however, an American Airlines mechanic was arrested for allegedly having a large arms and explosives cache in his home. This man, with access to commercial aircraft, also allegedly had white supremacist and racist literature in his home. And yet, after brief mentions only on the day of his arrest, the story disappeared. No endless speculation about his motives, no "terrorism experts" pontificating about whether his arrest suggests a wider conspiracy, and so on.

This double standard is strange given that it was Tim McVeigh, a white supremacist who despised the government, who carried out the most deadly terrorist attack ever on US soil. Meanwhile, when the media discussed feared violence by millennialist Christians, say, in Jerusalem where many gathered, they were presented as extremists or loonies, and were not generalized as representatives of "Christian terrorism."

The Definition of "Terrorism" Is Too Narrow

The report states:

> The term "terrorism" means premeditated, politically motivated violence perpetrated against noncombatant targets by subnational groups or clandestine agents, usually intended to influence an audience.

This definition may be overly narrow, since it defines "terrorism" principally on the basis of the identity of its perpetrator rather than by the action and motive of the perpetrator. Hence, if Israel launches a massive attack on Lebanon and deliberately drives several hundred-thousand people from their homes, openly threatens and targets civilians, and states that all of this is intended to pressure the Lebanese or Syrian government—as Israel did in April 1996—it does not fall under the definition of terrorism, solely because the US recognizes Israel to be a state. If, by contrast, Lebanese people organize themselves to resist an internationally condemned foreign occupation of their soil, this is termed "terrorism," even when such people restrict their targets to enemy combatants in occupied territory.

I suggest that the definition of terrorism be broadened to include state terrorism. While terrorism as the report defines it is certainly disturbing, compared with the number of victims of state terrorism, it is a relatively minor concern. If the report included statistics for state terrorism, observers could then objectively evaluate, for example, PKK activities on the one hand against premeditated, politically-motivated violence perpetrated against noncombatants carried out by the Turkish government. Or we could put into perspective a "jihad" by "Islamic extremists" in Chechnya against premeditated, politically-motivated violence perpetrated against noncombatants by the Russian army.

This would provide the public with a fuller picture of the problem, and analysts and policymakers with better information to make policy recommendations which could end the political conflicts, injustices, and occupations which in nearly every case seem to generate the phenomenon known as "terrorism."

You Can't Win

James Ridgeway

Beginning in the early 1980s in Bill Clinton's Arkansas, the American blood supply was poisoned.

Much of the nation's daily political news comes in the form of packaged propaganda, carefully crafted in Washington and dribbled out through TV, newspapers, and the Web. I've been in the Capitol since 1961—and have been covering it for the *Village Voice* since the early 1970s—so I've personally seen this happen countless times. The result of this process is a virtual blackout on news that can affect ordinary people.

Probably the most extraordinary example of the blackout during 1999-2000 was the hair-raising story of how, beginning in the early 1980s in Bill Clinton's Arkansas, the American blood supply was poisoned.

Blood Trail

Surely one of the most unreported news events in Clinton's Washington was a press conference at the National Press Building held by a group of Canadian hemophiliacs. They had traveled to the US to seek help and bring to justice Americans who—while Bill Clinton was President—had sold tainted blood from Arkansas prisons to unsuspecting Canadians, who then contracted hepatitis and other diseases. Many of these people died. Others are fighting for their lives.

"When this case first came to light some fifteen-plus years ago," a White House spokesman said on Canadian TV, "there was no testing being done to detect the AIDS virus. It is impossible to say that the president knew [the danger]. The accusations that President Clinton knew the blood was tainted are wrong."

The international imbroglio has its roots in a program to sell prison blood, which was started two decades ago in Arkansas. In the early 1980s, Clinton's administration awarded a contract for prison medical services to Health Management Associates, a company set up by Francis Henderson, an Arkansas doctor. Later, Leonard Dunn, a friend of Clinton's and a campaign fundraiser, became CEO.

Until then, the Arkansas prisons, as well as prisons in other Southern states, had been making a profit selling inmate blood. But in 1982 the glutted blood market crashed, threatening the program. "I called all over the world," Henderson subsequently told state police investigators, "and finally got one group in Canada who would take the contract."

The "group" was Continental Pharma Cryosan, Ltd., a Canadian company notorious in the blood trade for practices such as importing blood from Russian cadavers and relabeling it as Swedish. Cryosan never checked out the plasma-collecting centers in the US from which it obtained blood, depending instead on the licensing procedures of the Food and Drug Administration. The FDA's procedures were also lax.

Little was known about AIDS during this period, and Cryosan president Thomas Hecht said there was a "strong feeling" that prison plasma was safer than that taken from the population at large. This is hard to believe. Here's how a former inmate, appearing on the Canadian TV program *The Fifth Estate*, described giving blood: "Have sex in the fields on your way going to the plasma, you know, anybody in the dormitory, going to take a quick bath, run and have sex in the showers, then go to plasma. Go shoot up and go to plasma."

In Canada, the tainted blood was turned into clotting factor and sold to the Red Cross. When in 1983 Canadian officals discovered the source of the blood, they canceled the contracts. An international recall followed—blood from Arkansas had gone to Europe and Japan, and in at least one instance was sent back to the US—but it was too late. By then, most of the blood that had been sent to Canada had been used by hemophiliacs.

Unfortunately, the recall didn't stop HMA's prison-blood business, which continued until 1994. According to one prison subcontractor, officials knew that hepatitis was rife in the 1970s, and by 1980 were concerned about a "killer" hepatitis, which became known as hepatitis C. In 1985, there were press reports about AIDS in the prisons. That same year a group of inmates filed suit in federal district court to require AIDS testing.

In 1986 Clinton called for an investigation of HMA after it was accused of negligent care. The investigation eventually cleared HMA of criminal wrongdoing, but a second inquiry, by an independent California firm, concluded that HMA had violated its contract in 40 areas, and put much of the responsibility for its poor performance on state prisons chief Art Lockhart. Asked by reporters whether Lockhart should resign, Clinton said, "No. I do not think that at this time I should ask Mr. Lockhart to resign."

Clinton acknowledged he had been aware of problems with inmate health care when the corrections board renewed HMA's contract the previous year, saying, according to the *Arkansas Democrat-Gazette*, "Everybody in the state knew about them." Clinton said he originally thought the board wouldn't renew the contract. "But then [the chair of the corrections board] called me and said that based on available money and the alternatives, he thought HMA should be given another chance. The only thing I said was that there should be some sort of outside monitor." The contract was renewed.

Waco Noir

No matter what Janet Reno's independent investigator, former Missouri Republican Senator John Danforth, reported to the nation, the legend of Waco won't die easily. After his lengthy study Danforth concluded the government's hands were clean in the siege. A civil case in federal district court in Texas concluded likewise.

Mike McNulty's new, expanded version of his original documentary (*Waco: The Rules of Engagement*), entitled *Waco: A New Revelation*, won't soon be forgotten. In a riveting two hours of documentary footage, taken largely from the government's own archives, the filmmakers make a strong case that the government—far from practicing defensive measures to protect unarmed women and children—mounted an attack using military operators to squash the Davidians. Footage of helicopter machine guns spitting fire into the compound, and sniper pits with empty shell casings in the dirt below gun ports, belie any government claims of defensive fire.

The most powerful sequence shows a tank rolling up to the compound and suddenly disgorging two figures from the underbelly. The figures deploy to the right of the tank, and you see quick muzzle flashes as they apparently shoot into the compound. It was producer Mike McNulty who first brought to light the presence of the Delta Force unit at the Waco compound. The film argues military operators were in the attacking tanks, and the attack described above certainly has the earmarks of a military assault with professional soldiers—certainly not the half-assed, crazy shooting of the BATF agents with which the film begins.

If the military actually ran ground operations at Waco, they did so on command of the Joint Chiefs, who, in turn, were working on orders from—or at least in concert with—the White House. At the screening, the filmmakers passed out declassified Pentagon papers from the Joint Chiefs ordering military units to Waco to "provide the FBI with the requested equipment and two technical operators. The equipment will be used for defensive purposes only (to protect the lives of law enforcement personnel)." The first person who ought to be questioned about this is the then-chairman of the Joint Chiefs, Colin Powell.

As details spilled out, Waco began to look more and more like a training op for the international commando set.

Another major narrative voice in the film belongs to a former CIA official. McNulty asserts the CIA spooks provided a tiny, high-tech multiplexer mixer to electronically sort out all the different bugs, taps, and video shots of the events leading up to and during the fire. Unfortunately, the CIA operatives lost the mixer in the ensuing chaos and had to return the next day to poke around in the charred remnants of Koresh's compound until they found it. It is normally illegal for either the military or the CIA to actively participate in domestic civilian affairs.

As details spilled out, Waco began to look more and more like a training op for the international commando set. Among others present were representatives of Britain's elite Special Air Services, infamous for its counterinsurgency operations in Northern Ireland. In a July 31, 1996, letter to Senator Charles Robb—unearthed recently by the *Irish Echo*—John E. Collingwood, head of the FBI's Public and Congressional Affairs office, revealed that, "two SAS soldiers visiting at Fort Bragg, North Carolina, requested and were granted a courtesy visit. The main purpose...was to experience how the FBI operated its command post. They were shown the relationship of the FBI's command post to the tactical operations center, were allowed a visit to the forward tactical area, and were provided generic briefings regarding the incident. Although the HRT [Hostage Rescue Team] had tactical interface with the SAS during routine practice and training, at no time was the SAS called upon to participate in...the siege."

In his investigation McNulty has discovered that German counterterrorism officials and members of Israel's Directorate of Military Intelligence were present at Waco, in addition to the British Special Air Services. These foreign spook experts liaised with the Army's Delta Force and Navy SEALs, the FBI, and others still unknown.

Back in Washington, US officials trying to figure out what to do about the religious zealots turned to the Russians, who had been doing spy experiments with "White Noise" devices, to see if they couldn't learn something from their techniques. But no luck.

Waco: A New Revelation ought to air on national TV. Politicians and entertainment industry moguls who babble on about violence should see the real stuff. They should see the footage of a man sifting through the Waco rubble, pulling the burned and mangled body of a child from the debris. As he lifts the body, an arm falls off, the spine crumbles. The searcher frantically tries to find some place to put the little body down before it disintegrates.

Sick 'Em

Michael McNulty, whose drop-dead documentary forced the government to reopen the case under the supervision of special counsel (and former Republican senator) John Danforth, raised new questions about the mysterious circumstances under which three key witnesses in the Waco inquiry had fallen ill.

With the Justice Department insisting that government agents didn't fire into the compound, the key to unraveling what occurred may depend on an independent interpretation of the film, which was shot by a hovering government chopper. Central to this endeavor was Carlos Ghigliotti, a videotape analyst for the House Government Reform Committee who was discovered dead in his office in Laurel, Maryland, on April 28, 2000. The coroner ruled that Ghigliotti died of natural causes, but friends and family say he was in good health, and they are mystified at his sudden death just as the Waco investigation was coming to a head.

Now McNulty is raising more questions about a "curious string of coincidences" involving illnesses of important witnesses who, he says, all asked questions about the infrared film and all got sick in late March. Fred Ziegler, an infrared video expert, came down with a serious case of lead poisoning and was rushed to the hospital. About the same time, Dr. Edward B. Allard, the main infrared expert, suffered a stroke that nearly killed him. And finally Mac Cox, a solar geologist who claimed the flashes on the videos were not reflections of sunlight, was hospitalized with a serious renal infection.

Says McNulty: "It's really strange that just these few men involved with this one narrow issue were stricken."

Prison Life

Still mostly hidden from view is the great new prison industry and its effects on America. Do-gooders deplore the death of the family farm and the accompanying poverty, when in fact rural areas throughout the nation are prospering because of the growth of prisons, whose populations have nearly doubled since 1990. Between 1980 and 1990, 213 prisons were constructed in rural communities, and while at first local officials balked at having such facilities constructed amid quiet rural settings, today many of these same officials are soliciting prisons.

Prisons can be a real plus in political terms. First, they help "integrate" the lily-white farm towns of rural American, bringing in blacks and Latinos. Second, since the US has all but dropped the goal of rehabilitation, prisons are now set up to warehouse convicts, which spells long-term growth. In terms of the census, prisoners swell the population, and since most of them are poor, they reduce the overall income level, making communities eligible for federal and state economic aid that they otherwise would not receive. In addition, if a prison operates industry, it can attract related business. Best of all, except in Maine, Vermont, and Massachusetts, inmates can't vote.

Of course, one state's gains in rural prison population are another's lost prisoners—mostly from urban areas. This worries big-city politicians since losing population in inner-city neighborhoods can lead to loss of seats in Congress. "In New York state, for example, while 89 percent of prisoners are housed in rural areas, three-quarters of the inmate population come from seven neighborhoods in New York City," write Tracy Huling and Marc Mauer in the *Chicago Tribune*.

■■■■■■■■■■

The District of Columbia, under court order to improve its prisons, has contracted with Wackenhut Corp. to build a 1,200-inmate facility on the site of one of North Carolina's largest slave plantations. Outraged, Harmon Wray, a D.C. minister, told the *Washington City Paper* that

The feds claimed no real harm resulted from the huge, purposely-set Cerro Grande wildfire, which burned approximately 8,000 acres and nearly overran a plutonium stockpile.

this means "the mostly working-class, poor black descendants of slaves will be making low wages to keep their poor, almost all black brothers and sisters from the ghettos of D.C. locked up in cages."

Cheapskate Nation

Although Americans like to think of themselves as a caring nation, nothing could be further from the truth. A study out in 2000 showed how cheap the US really is.

While protesters have recently focused on the World Bank and the International Monetary Fund for loansharking Third World development projects, the US gives only a pittance of its largesse in foreign aid, according to the Center on Budget and Policy Priorities. US aid now stands at $11.1 billion a year, a mere 0.6 percent of federal expenditures—and it's slated to drop even further.

When ranked among the top 20 industrialized nations, the US is at the bottom. (Although Japan's economy is less than half the size of the US's, it has the largest foreign-aid program in the world.) According to the study, the average US resident "receives 56 times the annual income of residents of the world's low-income countries." Although the US has only 5 percent of the world's population, its economy comprises 27 percent of the world economy.

Los Alamos

The Cold War comes back to kick us in the stomach on a regular basis. Raging forest fires at Los Alamos National Laboratory in New Mexico, and a few weeks later at Hanford nuclear reservation in Washington, raised the prospect of radioactive pollution across wide areas of the nation. But the press quickly skipped over the subject.

The feds claimed no real harm resulted from the huge, purposely-set Cerro Grande wildfire, which burned approximately 8,000 acres and nearly overran a plutonium stockpile, endangering the public health in at least four states. Workers at Los Alamos National Laboratory dug pits to contain runoff from the nuclear lab that might be contaminated with radioactive or hazardous waste. They worry that it could wash into the Rio Grande.

During the 50 years that the lab has built and tested bombs and dumped nuclear waste, large amounts of depleted uranium and similar radionuclides have been dispersed into the area's soil and vegetation. Environmental observers say the lab has 1500 nuclear- and hazardous-waste sites—many in canyon areas that were swept by the fire. Now officials are worried that rains could set off flooding on the fire-ravaged mountain overlooking the lab. Flood waters coming out of the mountain canyons could also sweep contaminants into the Rio Grande system.

According to the *Santa Fe New Mexican*, whose reporters accompanied Senator Jeff Bingaman on a tour of the burned site, some of the most damaged areas in Los Alamos are the most highly secret, including a nuclear facility. The fire also came within a half-mile of a site where hazardous waste is stored in drums under tents atop a mesa—waiting to be moved to underground caverns. Burn trails show it came within a few feet of the high concertina-wire fence that surrounds the lab's plutonium facility, the *New Mexican* said. Results of tests for radioactive chemicals, such as mercury, lead, and beryllium, will take several weeks to process, according to the federal Environmental Protection Agency.

A key problem in fire-ravaged Los Alamos is the fear that depleted uranium and toxic nuclear waste may have worked their way into the atmosphere and become part of the huge plume that has been floating over eastern Colorado.

No one knows for sure what has happened. But in recent years, a lot of testing of high explosives has been done at the plant. It's as a test site for these explosives that various toxic metals may have come into play. Explosives are sometimes bonded with depleted uranium. Los Alamos also manufactures bomb triggers.

The Los Alamos laboratory has disposed of at least 17.5 million cubic feet of hazardous and radioactive waste in 24 areas on the site since 1944, according to the Los Alamos Study Group, an anti-nuclear outfit. The list of contaminants includes lead, beryllium, arsenic, thorium, uranium, plutonium, PCBs, and barium.

■ ■ ■ ■ ■ ■ ■ ■ ■ ■ ■

And then there was Hanford. Reassuring words from Bill Richardson's Department of Energy about the fire that ravaged thousands of acres around the Hanford nuclear complex in eastern Washington didn't work this time around. In 1998, tests picked up more than a dozen radioactive hot spots on the 560-square-mile site along the Columbia River. Investigators found that the radiation was being spread by fruit flies, ants, worms, roaches, and gnats. One report determined that a Hanford worker's trailer was contaminated with radioactivity coming from the garbage can, a cutting board near the sink, and food wrappers. This suggests that even before the fire, radioactive contamination was working its way off the reservation into the surrounding environment.

Quick Cash

The market for body organs proceeds to unravel apace as politicians in Pennsylvania sought to adjust state law so that entrepreneurs can harvest valuable organs like eyes and kidneys from people who have just died in auto or other accidents, and to make it easier to make a market in body parts from others who died of natural causes.

In India, debt-ridden farmers are selling their kidneys to get moneylenders off their backs.

For those who don't make it in a prosperous society, there's always the last resort of selling your body organs. And in the new global economy, body organs have become a booming business. In India, debt-ridden farmers are selling their kidneys to get moneylenders off their backs, according to the *South China Morning Post*. A kidney fetches $8,750 in Andhra Pradesh state, which has been devastated by a severe drought. So far, officials have identified 35 farmers who sold kidneys. Three died after removal of the organs. Previously, moneylenders have demanded farmers' wives as mortgages. Eighteen farmers have committed suicide under the pressure.

Corporate Welfare

While the fair-trade movement has been focusing on stopping the export of US jobs to developing nations, big corporations have been playing another destructive game, pitting states within the US against one another to reduce the cost of labor.

According to an in-depth report in the *Baltimore Sun*, states are providing more than $3 billion each year in incentives to attract companies by doling out grants, tax cuts, and loans. So far, two-thirds of the states either have introduced incentive programs or expanded programs already on the books over the last two years. These deals often are outright scams. Firms cajole, then threaten to leave states when they never have any intention of moving.

As more has been learned about the terms of such incentives and their economic effects, the seeds of political revolt have taken root among unions, citizens' groups, and state and local officials, creating an alliance that binds unionists with Libertarians and liberals like former Illinois governor Jim Edgar and members of the Fed. At the center of this network is Greg LeRoy, director of Good Jobs First, a national clearinghouse on job subsidies. In a recent study, he found that 26 cities, sixteen states, and four counties have moved to attach standards aimed at preserving wages.

After a survey, Minnesota set up new reporting requirements in an effort to ferret out just how much money was being lost in corporate subsidies. In Maine, the most significant findings in a study are that two tax-subsidy programs totaling $25.6 million produced just 95 new jobs at a cost of $269,000 per job. On the other hand, Maine's job-training programs, which cost $1.5 million, yielded 644 new jobs at a cost of $2,300 per job. The findings spurred the creation of a new political coalition of gay, environmental, women's, and community-activist groups called the Dirigo Alliance, which became the force behind five bills in the state legislature. These measures would require that workers in subsidized companies be paid base wages of from $8 to $12 an hour, be guaranteed pension plans, safe workplaces, and health insurance plans under which at least 50 percent of the premiums are paid by the company.

Dam Shame

The Colorado River is America's greatest natural treasure and a symbol of what the environmental movement ought to be fighting for. It begins in the high Rockies and drops 14,000 feet in a wild 1,700-mile torrent to the Pacific Ocean. There is simply nothing else like it. To have been on this river is to have experienced a hallowed moment.

In 1956, horrendous judgment by the government led to the building of the Glen Canyon dam at the Colorado's upper end. The dam created a 300-foot-deep artificial reservoir called Lake Powell, covering the ancient riverbed lands of the Anasazi Indians and their descendants in the Navajo and Ute tribes. The water inundated canyons and tributary streams leading into the main river. So today, instead of the beautiful Glen Canyon, all you see are flotillas of stinking motorboats.

The dam and reservoir have led to the deterioration of the whole river. The reservoir—the second largest in the United States—and the downstream remnants of the Colorado are becoming a toxic sewer, transforming the river and its tributaries into a hazardous waste dump.

Since the dam went up, environmentalists have ranted against it. Edward Abbey dreamed of the day someone would blow it up. Wallace Stegner, the great Western historian, fought it. Environmentalist David Brower at first fought the dam, then gave in as part of a deal to save other natural monuments. Now in his eighties and fighting cancer, he has returned to lead a last effort to dismantle it.

Last December, a group of environmentalists, calling themselves the Glen Canyon Action Network <www.drainit.org>, set up headquarters in Moab, Utah. Their aim is to force the government to decommission the dam, drain Lake Powell, and restore the Colorado River. The group includes river rafters, small business owners, traditional Navajos, and a descendant of Brigham Young. In an era in which the federal government is having second thoughts about big dams—seriously discussing decommissioning three on the Snake River—Brower and his compatriots feel the time is right for a change in policy. For inspiration, there is Barry Goldwater. Shortly before he died, the right-wing Arizona senator was asked which vote he most regretted. "I wish I could take back the vote to put up the Glen Canyon dam," he replied, "and let that river run free."

One Jew = $14.73

Jeff Gates in *The Realist* computes that the payment under discussion for former Nazi slave laborers ($7,500 per survivor) comes down to $14.73 if it had been given in 1945 and invested in an S&P index fund.

License to Spy

Operating through a contractual relationship with a private corporation, the US Secret Service was laying the groundwork until quite recently for a photo database of ordinary citizens collected from state motor vehicles departments. Utilizing the Freedom of Information Act, the Electronic Privacy Information Center (EPIC) discovered that the agency was planning to use the photos, culled by Image Data, for its own activities.

Image Data reportedly got more than $1 million in seed money from the Secret Service for a trial run of its TrueID project in 1997. Marketed as a method of combating check and credit-card identity fraud, TrueID involved the purchase and scanning of photos from participating DMVs. Three states—Florida, Colorado, and South Carolina—participated in the trial run with the Secret Service. But after news disclosures prompted a public outcry, Colorado and Florida halted the transfer of images, and South Carolina filed suit asking for the return of millions of images already in the company's possession.

The US Secret Service was laying the groundwork until quite recently for a photo database of ordinary citizens collected from state motor vehicles departments.

According to EPIC, the Secret Service received regular reports on the trial run and monitored it with a view toward using the photos on a national scale in surveillance against illegal immigration, terrorism, as well as in other law-enforcement activities. Although the files obtained by EPIC show that the Secret Service decided which states would be part of the pilot project and directed the timing of the effort, Image Data downplayed the agency's involvement. A presentation to the government by the company marked "confidential" stressed that pilot projects would "ensure the viability of deploying such service throughout the United States." EPIC said it also discovered that monthly reports were sent to a special agent in the Secret Service's Financial Crimes Division.

In a February 1999 report, Image Data CEO Robert Houvener ridiculed the idea that legitimate privacy issues were at stake. Houvener—who claims he has been a victim of "identity fraud"—says the national photo file is planned to be targeted at "identity criminals" who he estimates cost US businesses billions of dollars a year.

EPIC director Marc Rotenberg characterized the proposal for a national photo database as a threat to basic US privacy safeguards. "This is not a database that people can easily opt out of," he said, noting, "You have to give up your photograph when you get a driver's license."

Thanks for the title of this article go to Jack Black, the small-time criminal from the early 1900s whose autobiography, You Can't Win, *is an all-time classic of subversive lit.*

OFFICIAL VERSIONS

Anatomy of a School Shooting

David McGowan

On May 15, 2000, the Jefferson County Sheriff's Office released the official report on the shooting deaths of fifteen people at Columbine High School in Littleton, Colorado. Not surprisingly, the report confirmed the version of events that had been reported ad nauseam for the past year by the US press.

The official story (for those who are just emerging from a coma or for some other reason inexplicably missed the saturation coverage of this event) goes something like this: Two disaffected teenagers named Eric Harris and Dylan Klebold, acting alone with no assistance in the planning or execution of this crime, entered Columbine High on the morning of April 20, 1999, armed to the teeth, and promptly began shooting up the place, leaving twelve fellow students and one teacher dead before turning their guns on themselves.

"The 20-pound bomb found inside the Columbine High School kitchen suggests the two teenage suspects were aided by others in their plot to blow up the school, police said Thursday."

As with all the "big stories" flogged by the American media, the various avenues of the US press quickly fell in line behind this story, deftly avoiding any evidence that would tend to cast doubt on the official version of events. So while there has been some minor quibbling over insignificant details of the story (e.g. did the gunmen target athletes, blacks, and/or Christians?), few serious journalists have questioned the central thesis that the carnage at Columbine High that day was the work of Harris and Klebold acting alone.

Yet strangely enough, both the *Denver Post* and the *Denver Rocky Mountain News*, the newspapers serving the greater Denver area (of which Littleton is a part), have provided coverage which has been consistently ignored by the media in general.

For the benefit of those living outside the Denver area, presented here you will find a few facts about the tragedy at Columbine of which you may be unaware and which tend to be at odds with the official report. Take, for example, the issue of how long the rampage lasted. One reporter on the scene wrote that: "The bloody rampage spanned four hours... By 3:45 p.m., shots still rang out inside the school (as) more than 200 law enforcement officers and four SWAT teams tried to stop the gunmen and evacuate wounded high school students" [*Denver Post*, April 21, 1999]. Another quoted Jefferson County Sheriff John Stone, one of the first officials on the scene, as saying: "We had initial people there right away, but we couldn't get in. We were way outgunned" [Associated Press, April 20, 1999].

Echoing this sentiment was Terry Manwaring, commander of the Jefferson County SWAT team, who claimed: "I just knew the killers were armed and were better equipped than we were." The SWAT teams, therefore, made no effort to confront the killers [*Playboy*, March 2000].

The official report, meanwhile, contends that the "lunchtime rampage...ended after 45 minutes," and that, "Sometime after noon the killers stood near the library windows and turned their guns on themselves" [*Los Angeles Times*, May 16, 2000]. Strange then that there would be shots ringing out some three-and-a-half hours later.

Stranger still is the notion that two teenagers with limited firearms training and armed only with shotguns and 9mm handguns would be able to outgun a veritable army of law enforcement officers, many with advanced paramilitary training and weapons. And you would think that the fact that the two were already dead would at least have slowed them down a bit.

Then there is the issue of the bombs strategically placed throughout the school prior to the shootings. Some of those involved in the investigation of the case were openly skeptical of the notion that the two boys could have transported and placed all the explosive devices that were found. One report noted that:

> The 20-pound bomb found inside the Columbine High School kitchen suggests the two teenage suspects were aided by others in their plot to blow up the school, police said Thursday. Packed inside a duffle bag with a wired gasoline can—and surrounded with nails and BBs for maximum

> killing power—the propane barbecue tank-bomb points to a wider conspiracy, police said. [*Denver Post*, April 23, 1999]

Likewise, Jefferson County District Attorney Dave Thomas was quoted as saying: "It is obvious to me that they couldn't have carried them all in at the same time, plus the four weapons" [*Denver Post*, May 5, 1999]. And sheriff department spokesman Steve Davis added that: "From day one we've always felt like there was a very good possibility that more people were involved" [Associated Press, May 14, 1999].

Ultimately recovered, according to the final report, were "95 homemade explosive devices," including two bombs fashioned from propane cylinders [*Los Angeles Times*, May 16, 2000]. Picture, if you will, two teenagers strolling unnoticed into a high school, each carrying two firearms, a propane tank-bomb, and some 50 other explosive devices, as well as an abundant supply of ammunition.

Picture them then proceeding to carefully place each of these 95 bombs throughout the school, still unnoticed and undisturbed by faculty or other students. Nothing unusual about that. Just an average day at an American high school. Yet the possibility is clearly there that there may have been more people involved. Many of the witnesses, at any rate, clearly think so:

> Jefferson County Sheriff John P. Stone raised the specter of a third Columbine High gunman anew Tuesday, saying some students have named another suspect. "There was quite possibly one other person shooting," Stone said. "We do have witness statements." The statements came from "students who were witnesses at the scene when this was going down," and they agreed on the third person's identity, he said. [*Denver Post*, May 5, 1999]

In fact, one initial report from Littleton began: "Three young men in fatigues and black trench coats opened fire at a suburban Denver high school Tuesday...," and also noted that a "third young man was led away from the school in handcuffs more than four hours after the attack, and student Chris Wisher said: 'He's one of the ones who shot at us'" [Associated Press, April 20, 1999]. This third suspect has, oddly enough, never been identified or even mentioned again by the press.

In a televised interview, the mother of a student who had escaped the attack quoted her daughter as saying that she "looked up and saw a gunman in a black trench coat with a very huge gun.... He had dark brown hair, thick bushy eyebrows, and was very ugly," a description that clearly did not fit either Harris or Klebold. When asked if the gunman was a student, the mother replied that: "She didn't recognize him as a student. No. Not as a student" [KUSA-TV, April 20, 1999].[1]

Even more disturbing is a report that, "Dozens of witnesses interviewed by police after the crime claimed that from five to eight individuals participated in the shooting that left 15 people dead, including the killers, and more than 20 injured" [*Denver Rocky Mountain News*, July 29, 1999]. Five to eight individuals? Dozens of witnesses? Something definitely seems to be a bit peculiar here.

It is certainly understandable that some witnesses could have trouble recalling some of the details of the attack. In a situation of this nature, extreme levels of fear and confusion can cloud one's recollection. In the ensuing chaos, some witnesses could easily be confused about the number of shooters.

Nevertheless, there is a considerable difference between two gunmen and eight gunmen—the latter being pretty much a small army. Is it really possible for dozens of eyewitnesses to be mistaken about the additional three to six gunmen? This issue could possibly be cleared up by examining the autopsy reports of the various victims. Unfortunately, that isn't likely to happen. It seems that:

> The autopsy reports on the Columbine High School victims will not be released to the public, a Jefferson County judge ruled Friday.... Chief District Judge Henry E. Nieto rejected arguments by 18 news organizations.... The coroner's office, district attorney and the family of killer Dylan Klebold joined the 12 families in getting the documents sealed. [*Denver Post*, May 29, 1999]

Another question that could be cleared up by the release of the autopsy reports is the alleged suicides of the two shooters, seeing as how "Klebold was shot once in the left side of the head, apparently by one of two 9 mm weapons... [T]he wound's location puzzles some investigators. They believe that if the right-handed Klebold had shot himself, the wound should have been on the other side" [*Denver Rocky Mountain News*, June 13, 1999].

Very clever, those investigators. Clever enough, in fact, to come up with an explanation for this anomaly. Some authorities now believe (or claim to, anyway) that Harris shot Klebold before shooting himself. It seems just as likely, however, that a third party shot Klebold, and perhaps Harris as well.

A "third young man was led away from the school in handcuffs more than four hours after the attack, and student Chris Wisher said: 'He's one of the ones who shot at us.'"

Moving on to what is perhaps the most bizarre aspect of the case, we come now to the infamous videotape. You know, the one that was made in 1997, two years before the actual assault, and which "depicts gun-toting, trench coat-wearing students moving through Columbine's halls and ends with a special-effects explosion of the school." The one that was co-produced by "the son of the FBI's lead agent in the investigation" [Associated Press, May 8, 1999].

There's certainly nothing unusual about that. It's actually standard FBI procedure to have your son shoot a training film for a high-school slaughter a couple of years beforehand. It's also standard procedure to have your other son on hand to eyewitness the crime. Which is why "[Agent Dwayne Fuselier's] youngest son, Brian, was in the school cafeteria at the time and managed to escape after seeing one of the bombs explode" [*Denver Post*, May 13, 1999].

It should also be noted that another "student who helped in the production of the film [was] Brooks Brown..." [Associated Press, May 8, 1999]. For those not fortunate enough to be home on the day of the shooting watching the live cable coverage, Brooks Brown was the student enthusiastically granting interviews to anyone who would stick a microphone in his face.

He claimed to have encountered Harris and Klebold as they were approaching the school, and to have been warned away by the pair from entering the campus that day. According to his story, he heeded the warning and was therefore not present during the shooting spree. Fair enough, but let's try to put these additional pieces of the puzzle together.

It's actually standard FBI procedure to have your son shoot a training film for a high-school slaughter a couple of years beforehand.

First, we have the son of the lead investigator, who was obviously a member of the so-called Trenchcoat Mafia, involved in the filming of a pre-enactment of the crime. Then we have a second son of the lead investigator being at ground zero of the rampage. And finally we have a close associate of both the Fuselier brothers and of Harris and Klebold (and a co-filmmaker) being in the company of the shooters immediately before they entered the school, this by his own admission.

And yet, strangely enough, none of them was connected in any way to the commission of this crime, according to official reports. Not even Brooks Brown, who should have, if nothing else, noticed that the pair had some unusually large bulges under their trench coats on this particular day. At the very least, one would think that there might be just a little bit of a conflict of interest for the FBI's lead investigator.

This does not appear to be the case, however, as "FBI spokesman Gary Gomez said there was 'absolutely no discussion' of reassigning Fuselier, 51, a psychologist, in the wake of the disclosures in Friday's *Denver Rocky Mountain News*. 'There is no conflict of interest,' Gomez said" [*Denver Rocky Mountain News*, May 8, 1999]. And as no less an authority than Attorney General Janet Reno has stated: "It has been a textbook case of how to conduct an investigation, of how to do it the right way" [*Denver Post*, April 23, 1999].

So there you have it. There was no conspiracy, there were no accomplices. It was, as always, the work of a lone gunman (OK, two lone gunmen in this case). But if there were a wider conspiracy, you may wonder, what would motivate such an act? What reason could there be for sacrificing fourteen young lives?

Many right-wingers would have you believe that such acts are orchestrated—or at the very least rather cynically exploited—as a pretext for passing further gun-control legislation. The government wants to scare the people into giving up their right to bear arms, or so the thinking goes. And there is reason to believe that this could well be a goal.

It is not, however, the only—or even the primary—goal, but rather a secondary one at best. The true goal is to further traumatize and brutalize the American people. This has in fact been a primary goal of the State for quite some time, dating back at least to the assassination of President John F. Kennedy on that fateful day in Dallas on November 22, 1963.

The strategy is now (as it was then) to inflict blunt-force trauma on all of American society, and by doing so to destroy any remaining sense of community and instill in the people deep feelings of fear and distrust, of hopelessness and despair, of isolation and powerlessness. And the results have been, it should be stated, rather spectacular.

With each school shooting, and each act of "domestic terrorism," the social fabric of the country is ripped further asunder. The social contracts that bound us together as a people with common goals, common dreams, and common aspirations have been shattered. We have been reduced to a nation of frightened and disempowered individuals, each existing in our own little sphere of isolation and fear.

And at the same time, we have been desensitized to ever-rising levels of violence in society. This is true of both interpersonal violence as well as violence by the State, in the form of judicial executions, spiraling levels of police violence, and the increased militarization of foreign policy and of America's borders.

We have become, in the words of the late George Orwell, a society in which "the prevailing mental condition [is] controlled insanity." And under these conditions, it becomes increasingly difficult for the

> On February 14, 2000, two fellow Columbine students were shot to death in a sandwich shop just a few blocks from the school.

American people to fight back against the supreme injustice of twenty-first century Western society. Which is, of course, precisely the point.

For a fractured and disillusioned people, unable to find a common cause, do not represent a threat to the rapidly encroaching system of global fascism. And a population blinded by fear will ultimately turn to "Big Brother" to protect them from nonexistent and/or wholly manufactured threats.

As General McArthur stated back in 1957: "Our government has kept us in a perpetual state of fear...with the cry of grave national emergency. Always there has been some terrible evil at home or some monstrous foreign power that was going to gobble us up if we did not blindly rally behind it...."

Perhaps this is all just groundless conspiracy theorizing. The possibility does exist that the carnage at Columbine High School unfolded exactly as the official report tells us that it did. And even if that proves not to be the case, there really is no need to worry. It is all just a grand illusion, a choreographed reality. Only the death and suffering are real.

Postscript

As the dust settled over Columbine High, other high-profile shootings would rock the nation: at schools, in the workplace, in a church, and—in Southern California's San Fernando Valley—at a Jewish community center where a gunman quickly identified as Buford Furrow opened fire on August 10, 1999. This man, who later would claim that his intent was to kill as many people as possible, had received extensive firearms and paramilitary training, both from the US military and from militia groups.

Shooting in an enclosed area that was fairly heavily populated, Furrow fired a reported 70 rounds from his assault rifle. By design or act of God, no one was killed and only a handful of people were injured, including three children and a teenager. None of the injuries was life-threatening, and all the victims have fully recovered.

With a massive police dragnet descending on the city, Furrow fled, abandoning his rolling arsenal of a vehicle. Not far from the crime scene, he stopped to catch up on some shopping and get a haircut. Along the way, his aim having improved considerably, Furrow killed a postal worker with a single headshot, for no better reason than because he was Asian and, therefore, "non-white."

At about this same time, Furrow car-jacked a vehicle from an Asian woman. Though this woman—besides being obviously non-white—was now a key witness who could place Furrow at the scene and identify the vehicle he had fled in, she was left shaken but very much alive. Having taken great risks to obtain her vehicle, Furrow promptly abandoned it, choosing instead to take a taxi.

In an unlikely turn of events, this taxi would safely transport Furrow all the way to Las Vegas, Nevada. Having successfully eluded one of the most massive police dragnets in San Fernando Valley's history (which had the appearance of a very well-planned training exercise), and having made it across state lines to relative safety, Furrow proceeded directly to the local FBI office to turn himself in. No word yet as to whether Dwayne Fuselier was flown in to head up the investigation.

Meanwhile, in Littleton, Colorado, the death toll continued to mount. On May 6, 2000, the *Los Angeles Times* reported that a Columbine High student had been found hanged. His death was ruled a suicide even though, "Friends were mystified, saying there were no signs of turmoil in the teenager's life." One noted that he had "talked to him the night before, and it didn't seem like anything was wrong."

The young man had been a witness to the shooting death of teacher Dave Sanders. His was the fourth violent death surrounding Columbine High in just over a year since the shooting, bringing the body count to nineteen. Very little information was released concerning this most recent death, with the coroner noting only that: "Some things should remain confidential to the family" [*Los Angeles Times*, May 6, 2000].

On February 14, 2000, two fellow Columbine students were shot to death in a sandwich shop just a few blocks from the school. The shootings, which lacked any clear motive, have yet to be explained. In yet another incident, the mother of a student who was shot and survived "walked into a pawnshop in October, asked to see a gun, loaded it and shot herself to death" [*Los Angeles Times*, May 6, 2000].

Unexplained was why the shopkeeper would have supplied her with the ammunition for the gun. Perhaps she brought her own, though if she had access to ammunition, chances are that she would also have had access to a gun. Such are the mysteries surrounding the still-rising death toll in Littleton, Colorado.

Endnote

1. The KUSA-TV interview was also broadcast on MSNBC. A transcript is posted at the Konformist Website <www.konformist.com/1999/colorado/notstudent.htm>.

How the People Seldom Catch Intelligence

Or, How to Be a Successful Drug Dealer

Preston Peet

For me, one could write about lies from morning till night, but this is the one most worth writing about, because the domestic consequences are so horrible; it's contributed to police brutality, police corruption, militarizations of police forces, and now, as we speak, it contributes to the pretext for another Vietnam War.

—*Peter Dale Scott, July 24, 2000*

Photo: Cele Castillo

Ilopango airbase, El Salvador, where drugs and guns came and went, with the help of the Contra-supporting CIA and NSC.

On May 11, 2000, the US House Permanent Select Committee on Intelligence made public their "Report on the Central Intelligence Agency's Alleged Involvement in Crack Cocaine Trafficking in the Los Angeles Area."[1] The investigation by the HPSCI focused solely on the "implications" of facts reported in investigative reporter Gary Webb's three-part exposé in the *San Jose Mercury News* titled "Dark Alliance." Published on August 18, 19, and 20, 1996, the series alleged that a core group of Nicaraguan Contra supporters formed an alliance with black dealers in South Central Los Angeles to sell cocaine to the Bloods and Crips street gangs, who turned it into crack. The drug-profits were then funneled back to Contra coffers by the Contra supporters.

Approved for release in February 2000, the HPSCI report states the Committee "found no evidence" to support allegations that CIA agents or assets associated in any way with the Nicaraguan Contra movement were involved in the supply or sale of drugs in the Los Angeles area. Utilizing a not-so-subtle strategy of semantics and misdirection, the HPSCI report seeks to shore up the justifiably crumbling trust in government experienced by the American public. But the report is still a lie.

An Eyewitness Strongly Disagrees, Says It's a Lie

The DEA's lead agent in El Salvador and Guatemala from 1985 to 1990, as well as a Vietnam veteran, Celerino Castillo documented massive CIA-sanctioned and -protected drug trafficking, and illegal Contra-supply operations at Illapango Airbase in El Salvador. Asked what he thought of the HPSCI report, Castillo said, "It is a flat-out lie. It is a massive cover-up.... They completely lied, and I'm going to prove that they are lying with the case file numbers... I was there during the whole thing."[2]

Photo: Cele Castillo

Celerino Castillo, Special Agent of the DEA, and Gen. G.C. Walter Amdrade, then-head of Peruvian anti-narcotics police. This photo broke Castillo's cover in Peru.

One would have to intentionally not look in order to miss the copious amounts of evidence of CIA-sanctioned and -protected drug trafficking, even in LA, that exists today in the public record.

One would have to intentionally not look in order to miss the copious amounts of evidence of CIA-sanctioned and -protected drug trafficking, even in LA, that exists today in the public record; the HPSCI succeeds admirably, disregarding sworn testimony and government reports, and ignoring what agents on the ground at the scene have to say.

After participating in the historic CIA-Drugs Symposium in Eugene, Oregon, June 11, 2000,[3] Castillo decided to go back through his notes, journals, and DEA-6's—the biweekly reports he'd filled out at the time—to see just how many times his records didn't match the "not guilty" verdict of the HPSCI report. "I've got them [CIA] personally involved in eight counts of drugs trafficking.... I've got them on three counts of murders of which they personally were aware that were occurring, and...to make a long story short, I [also] came out with money laundering, three or four counts."[4]

Photo: Preston Peet

Cele Castillo at the CIA-Drugs Symposium, June 11, 2000. He is holding the passports of a drug trafficker and his daughter, murdered by US-backed Guatemalan G-2 Intelligence in front of Castillo.

Among the cases Castillo describes in his scathing written response to the HPSCI report—full of DEA case-file numbers and Narcotics and Dangerous Drugs Information System (NADDIS) numbers—is that of drug trafficker Fransisco Rodrigo Guirola Beeche, who has *two* DEA NADDIS jackets, and is documented in DEA, CIA, and Customs files. On February 6, 1985, Guirola flew out of Orange County, California, "in a private airplane with 3 Cuban-Americans. It made a stop in South Texas where US Customs seized $5.9 million in cash. It was alleged that it was drug money, but because of his ties to the Salvadoran death squads and the CIA he was released, and the airplane given back."[5] In other words, the government kept the money, and known drug trafficker Guirola got off with his airplane.

"The CIA's practice of recruiting drug-financed armies is an on-going matter."

In May 1984, Guirola had gone with Major Roberto D'Abuisson, head of the death squads in El Salvador at that time, to a highly secret, sensitive, and, as it turns out, successful meeting with former Deputy Director of Central Intelligence, Vernon Walters. "Walters was sent to stop the assassination of [then] US Ambassador to El Salvador, Thomas Pickering."[6] The CIA knew Guirola, and knew him well. The HPSCI report notes that John McCavitt, a senior CIA official in Guatemala and El Salvador at the time, "rejects forcefully" the idea that there was CIA involvement in trafficking in either country, and that he told the Committee that Illopango Airport in El Salvador hadn't been used as a narcotics trans-shipment point by Contra leaders.[7] However, less than a year after the arrest in South Texas, Castillo documented Guirola flying drugs, cash, and weapons in and out of Illopango Airfield, specifically hangars four and five, which were run respectively by Oliver North and General Richard Secord's National Security Council (NSC) Contra-supply operation, and the CIA.[8] There's no sign of Guirola within the entire 44-page HPSCI report.

The CIA Practice of Recruiting Drug-Financed Armies

Professor Peter Dale Scott also wrote a response to the HPSCI report, in which he says, "this latest deception cannot be written off as an academic or historical matter. The CIA's practice of recruiting drug-financed armies is an on-going matter."[9]

Scott—a professor emeritus at the University of California (Berkeley), a prolific author, and a Canadian diplomat from 1957 to 1961—has spent years studying and reporting on drug-trafficking connections of the CIA and other US government agencies. (His most famous work is *Cocaine Politics: Drugs, Armies, and the CIA in Central America*.) Knowing that the HPSCI report is full of lies and misrepresentations, Scott is at a loss as to how this report could have been authorized for release by the Committee, and he voiced serious concerns about the staff of the HPSCI.

"Well, they were headed by this guy who just committed suicide [Chief of Staff John Millis], who not only was ex-CIA, he'd actually been working with Gulbuddin Hekmatyer in Afghanistan [as part of CIA covert operations assisting in the fight against the Soviets in the late 1970s and early 1980s, while Hekmatyer moved tons of opium and heroin]. He may not have known about the Contra-drug connections, but he certainly knew about some CIA-drugs ties. I don't think it was an accident that they picked someone from that area to sit over the staff either. I mean, this was one of the most sensitive political threats that the CIA had ever faced."[10] John Millis, a nineteen-year veteran of the CIA, was found dead of "suicide" in a dingy hotel room in Vienna, Virginia, just outside of Washington, DC, on June 3, 2000—less than a month after the release of the HPSCI report.

The CIA released its own report, the Hitz Report, in two parts—Volume 1 in January 1998 and Volume 2 in October 1998[11] (within hours of the vote by Congress to hold impeachment hearings over Clinton's lying about a blowjob)—which examined the allegations of

Photo: Preston Peet

Cele Castillo, head DEA agent in El Salvador and Guatemala, shakes hands with George Bush, Jan.14, 1986, at US Embassy reception in Guatemala City. After this photo was taken, Castillo told Bush there were not-so-funny things afoot in El Salvador. Bush walked away.

There were numerous examples contained in the Hitz Report, particularly in Vol. 2, of just how much the CIA really knew about the drug trafficking of its "assets," and *admitted to knowing*.

the CIA protecting, facilitating, and directly participating in drug trafficking. There were numerous examples contained therein, particularly in Vol. 2, of just how much the CIA really knew about the drug trafficking of its "assets," and *admitted to knowing*. But by the time the report was released to the public, the major news outlets—"the regular villains," as Scott calls them—had already denigrated the story for two years, attacking and vilifying Gary Webb, instead of investigating the facts themselves.

"The *Washington Post*, the *New York Times*, and the *Los Angeles Times* all insisted that the Contra-cocaine was minor and could not be blamed for the crack epidemic. As the government investigations [Hitz/CIA and DoJ] unfolded, however, it became clear that nearly every major cocaine-smuggling network used the Contras in some way, and that the Contras were connected—directly or indirectly—with possibly the bulk of cocaine that flooded the United States in the 1980s," wrote one journalist who has covered this story extensively from the very start.[12]

"This has been the case since the beginning," said Scott.[13] "The strategy of how to refute Webb is to claim that he said something that in fact he didn't say. The Committee didn't invent this kind of deflection away from the truth, they just followed in the footsteps of the *New York Times* and the *Washington Post*, and they in turn may have been following in the footsteps of the CIA to begin with, but I don't know. The Committee was originally created to exert Congressional checks and restraints on the intelligence community, in accordance with the spirit of the Constitution. For some time it has operated instead as a rubber stamp, deflecting public concern rather than representing it."[14]

The CIA/DoJ Memorandum of Understanding

Saturday, October 10, 1998. Anyone watching CNN that morning might have caught a brief mention of the release of the Hitz Report, Vol. 2. CNN reported that the CIA acknowledged it knew of at least 58 companies and individuals involved in bringing cocaine into the US and selling cocaine to US citizens in order to help fund the Contra war in Nicaragua, while they were working for the CIA in some capacity.

March 16, 1998. Fred Hitz, then-Inspector General of the CIA, had already told US representatives at the sole Congressional hearing on the first half of this report, Hitz Vol. 1, that the CIA had worked with companies and individuals that it knew were involved in the drug trade.[15] I.G. Hitz went on to say that the CIA knew that drugs were coming into the US along the same supply routes used for the Contras, and that the Agency did not attempt to report these traffickers in an expeditious manner, nor did the CIA sever its relationship with those Contra supporters who were also alleged traffickers.

One of the most important things Hitz testified to was that William Casey, Director of the CIA under President Ronald Reagan, and William F. Smith, US Attorney General at that time, in March 1982 signed a "Memorandum of Understanding," in which it was made clear that the *CIA had no obligation to report the allegations of trafficking involving "non-employees."* Casey sent a private message to A.G. Smith on March 2, 1982, in which he stated that he had signed the "procedures," saying that he believed the new regulations struck a "proper balance between enforcement of the law and protection of intelligence sources and methods...."[16] This was in response to a letter from Smith to Casey on February 11, 1982, regarding President Reagan's new executive order that had recently been implemented (E.O. 12333, issued in 1981), which required the reporting of drug crimes by US employees.[17]

Fred Hitz, then-Inspector General of the CIA, had already told US Representatives at the sole Congressional hearing on the first half of this report, Hitz Vol. 1, that the CIA had worked with companies and individuals that it knew were involved in the drug trade.

With the MOU in place, the CIA, in cooperation with the Department of Justice, changed the CIA's regulations in 1982, redefining the term "employee" to mean only full-time career CIA officials. The result of this was that suddenly there were thousands of people, contract agents, employees of the CIA, who were no longer called employees. Now they were people who were "employed by, assigned to, or acting for an agency within the intelligence community."[18] Non-employees, if you will.

According to a February 8, 1985, memo sent to Mark M. Richard, the Deputy Assistant Attorney General, Criminal Division of the US, on the subject of CIA reporting of drug offenses, this meant, as per the 1982 MOU, that the CIA really was under no obligation to report alleged drug violations by these "non-employees."[19]

Juan Matta Ballesteros and SETCO

It is pure disinformation for the HPSCI to print, "CIA reporting to DoJ of information on Contra involvement in narcotics trafficking was inconsistent but in compliance with then-current policies and regulations. There is no evidence however that CIA officers in the field or at headquarters ever concealed narcotics trafficking information or allegations involving the Contras."[20]

"On April 29, 1989, the DoJ requested that the Agency provide information regarding Juan Matta Ballesteros and 6 codefendants for use in prosecution. DoJ also requested information regarding SETCO, described as 'a Honduran corporation set up by Juan Matta Ballesteros.' The May 2 CIA memo to DoJ containing the results of Agency traces on Matta, his codefendants, and SETCO stated that following an 'extensive search of the files and indices of the directorate of Operations...There are no records of a SETCO Air.'"[21] Matta—whom *Newsweek* magazine described as being responsible for up to a third of all cocaine entering the US[22]—was wanted by the DEA in connection with the brutal 30-hour torture and murder of one of their agents, Enrique Camarena, in Mexico in February 1985. Obviously, Matta was a very well-known trafficker. It is ludicrous to suggest that the CIA *hasn't* covered up evidence of drug trafficking by assets, even from their own investigators.

"I mean, this is different than the MOU, which said the CIA was under no obligation to volunteer information to the DoJ," said Scott. "It never said the CIA was allowed to withhold information from the DoJ. In the case of SETCO, they were asked for the information, and the CIA replied falsely that there was none. The Hitz people tried to find out how this could have happened, and one person said I just didn't know about SETCO, but that is impossible. If people like me knew about SETCO, how could *they* not? Because the SETCO thing was a big thing."[23]

Matta's SETCO airline was one of four companies that, although known by the US government to be engaged in drug trafficking, in 1986 were still awarded contracts by the US State Department with the Nicaraguan Humanitarian Assistance Organization (NHAO). These companies were flying weapons and supplies in to the Contras, then drugs back to the US on the same aircraft, with the knowledge of CIA officials. Matta was protected from prosecution until his usefulness to the Contra efforts came to an end. Then he was arrested, tried, and convicted in 1989, the same year Manuel Noriega was removed from office in Panama by US troops and arrested for trafficking.

The CIA Admits to Shipping a Ton of Cocaine to US Streets

The Contra-CIA drug trafficking was no anomaly, but rather normal operating procedure for US intelligence, particularly the CIA, and for the US government, while they actively perpetuated the War on Some Drugs.

Representative Maxine Waters (D-CA), in a speech in the House of Representatives on March 18, 1997, outlined various reports of CIA drug trafficking complicity. Noting a *New York Times* article dated November 20, 1993, she stated that "the CIA anti-drug program in Venezuela shipped a ton of nearly pure cocaine into the USA in 1990. The CIA acknowledged that the drugs were sold on the streets of the USA.... Not one CIA official has ever been indicted or prosecuted for this abuse of authority." Rep. Waters called it a "cockamamie scheme." She described how the CIA had approached the DEA, who has the authority over operations of this nature, and asked for their permission to go through with the operation, but the DEA said, "No." The CIA did it anyway, explaining later to investigators that this was the only way to get in good with the traffickers, so as to set them up for a bigger bust the next time.[24]

In late 1990, CIA Agent Mark McFarlin and General Ramon Guillen Davila of the Venezuelan National Guard sent an 800-pound shipment of cocaine to Florida, where it was intercepted by US Customs at Miami International Airport, which lead to the eventual indictment of Guillen in 1996 in Miami for trafficking 22 tons of cocaine into the city.[25] Gen. Guillen was the former chief Venezuelan anti-drug cop.

Researcher and author (*Drug War: Covert Money, Power and Policy*) Dan Russell relates, "Speaking from his safe haven in Caracas, Guillen insisted that this was a joint CIA-Venezuelan operation aimed at the Cali cartel. Given that Guillen was a long-time CIA employee, and that the drugs were stored in a Venezuelan warehouse owned by the CIA, the joint part of Guillen's statement is almost certainly true, although the 'aimed at' part is almost certainly false."[26]

"That is the case that has gone closest to the heart of the CIA, because the CIA actually admitted to the introduction of a ton [of cocaine onto US streets]. The man was indicted for 22 tons, and [some people said] that his defense was that the CIA approved all of it," Scott said, recalling the audacity of the case.[27] For the very same *Times* article mentioned in Rep. Waters' speech, "the spin the CIA gave the *Times* was that it was trying to sting Haiti's National Intelligence Service (SIN)—which the CIA itself had created."[28]

In late 1990, CIA Agent Mark McFarlin and General Ramon Guillen Davila of the Venezuelan National Guard sent an 800-pound shipment of cocaine to Florida.

Death Threats Against the Head of the DEA in Haiti

Which brings us to the case of Colonel Michel Francois, one of the Haitian-coup leaders who overthrew democratically-elected Jean-Bertrand Aristide in 1991, helping rule Haiti until 1994. In her impassioned speech, Rep. Waters mentioned a *Los Angeles Times* article (dated March 8, 1997) that reported, "Lt. Col. Michel Francois, one of the CIA's reported Haitian agents, a former Army officer and a key leader in the military regime that ran Haiti between 1991 and 1994, was indicted in Miami with smuggling 33 tons of cocaine into the USA."[29]

"Senior members of the CIA unit committed acts of political terror against Aristide supporters, including interrogations and torture, and in 1992 threatened to kill the local chief of the U.S. Drug Enforcement Administration."

Dan Russell writes, "*New York Times*, November 14, 1993: '1980's CIA Unit in Haiti Tied to Drug Trade—Political terrorism committed against Aristide supporters: The Central Intelligence Agency created an intelligence service in Haiti in the mid-1980's to fight the cocaine trade, but the unit evolved into an instrument of political terror whose officers sometimes engaged in drug trafficking, American and Haitian officials say. Senior members of the CIA unit committed acts of political terror against Aristide supporters, including interrogations and torture, and in 1992 threatened to kill the local chief of the U.S. Drug Enforcement Administration. According to one American official, who spoke on condition of anonymity, "[I]t was an organization that distributed drugs in Haiti and never produced drug intelligence."'

"How shocking to the innocents at CIA, who certainly had expected Haiti's policemen to be above venality. That is, the SIN dealers, led by Brig. Gen. Raoul Cedras and Michel Francois, who overthrew the legally elected populist Jean-Bertrand Aristide in September of 1991, were armed and trained by Bush's CIA. In fact, Bush's CIA Director, Casey's assistant Robert Gates, was actually stupid enough to call Cedras one of the most promising 'Haitian leaders to emerge since the Duvalier family dictatorship was overthrown in 1986.'"[30]

Russell continues, "When the DEA's Tony Greco tried to stop a massive cocaine shipment in May 1991, four months before the coup, his family received death threats on their private number from 'the boss of the man arrested.' The only people in Haiti who had that number were the coup leaders, army commander Raoul Cedras and his partner, Port-au-Prince police chief Michel Francois, 'the boss of the man arrested.' A 1993 U.S. GAO [Government Accounting Office] report insisted that Cedras and Francois were running one of the largest cocaine export rings in the world."[31]

In January 2000, US Customs found five cocaine hauls welded deep within the steel hulls of "Haitian" freighters on the Miami River in Florida. (There have since been many more shipments intercepted.) The mainstream press reported that the drugs had "passed through" Haiti from Colombia. What the mainstream press did not focus on was that the five freighters were registered in Honduras, where Haitian expatriate Michel Francois coincidentally lives. Francois, a graduate of the infamous US Army's School of the Americas, has an extradition request out for him from the DEA.

During the subsequent investigation of this freighter-smuggling by the DEA, two Haitians were arrested in Miami, suspected of masterminding the freighter operation. One, Emmanuelle Thibaud, had been allowed to emigrate to Miami in 1996, two years after Aristide returned to power. When US police searched his Florida home January 29, 2000, "they found documents linking him to Michel Francois."[32] The *Los Angeles Times* quoted an FBI investigator, Hardrick Crawford, saying "it is not a big leap to assume that Francois is still directing the trafficking from Honduras."[33] Although the US requested extradition of Francois in 1997, the Honduran Supreme Court ruled against it. So the CIA-molded and -nurtured Francois continues to surface in these international drug investigations.

Explaining why they feel the US government recertified Haiti again in 2000 as a cooperative partner in the War on Some Drugs—even with the abundance of evidence pointing to Haitian officials' continued involvement in the drug trade—*Haiti Progress*, the leftist Haitian weekly based in New York City, wrote, "Because they need the 'drug war' to camouflage their real war, which is a war against any people which rejects U.S. hegemony, neoliberal doctrine, and imperialism.... Like Frankenstein with his monster, the U.S. often has to chase after the very criminals it creates. Just as in the case of Cuba and Nicaragua, the thugs trained and equipped by the Pentagon and CIA go on to form vicious mafias, involved in drug trafficking, assassinations, and money laundering."[34]

Most Favored Traffickers Receive Overt Support

A case involving the CIA stepping in and crushing an investigation into drug trafficking by CIA assets and favored clients took place in Philadelphia from 1995 to 1996, and continues in the official

"Just as in the case of Cuba and Nicaragua, the thugs trained and equipped by the Pentagon and CIA go on to form vicious mafias, involved in drug trafficking, assassinations, and money laundering."

harassment of the investigating officer in charge. John "Sparky" McLaughlin is a narcotics officer in the Philadelphia, Pennsylvania Bureau of Narcotics Investigations and Drug Control, Office of the Attorney General (OAG/BNI). On October 20, 1995, McLaughlin and two other officers approached Daniel Croussett, who was acting suspiciously. While questioning Croussett, the officers found documents in his car marked "Trifuno '96," which Croussett told McLaughlin's team belonged "to a political party back in the DR [Dominican Republic], and they are running Jose Francisco Pena-Gomez for President in May."[35] This political party was the Dominican Revolutionary Party (PRD).

McLaughlin, in a supplemental report filed January 29, 1996, wrote that "Trifuno '96" was basically a set of instructions on how to "organize the estimated 1.2 million Dominicans who currently reside outside the Dominican Republic to overthrow the present regime in the elections May, 1996."[36] Soon it was obvious that McLaughlin's team had uncovered an enormous drug-trafficking operation, run by a group associated with the PRD, the Dominican Federation, who were supporters of the man most favored to win the Dominican presidency in 1996, and more ominously, most favored by the US government and the Clinton Administration. An informant for McLaughlin told him that if Pena were elected, he was going to make sure that the price of heroin for Dominican supporters fell dramatically.

On October 26, 1995, former CIA operations officer and State Department field observer Wilson Prichett—hired as a security analyst by the BNI—wrote a memo to McLaughlin's boss, BNI supervisor John Sunderhauf, stating he felt that it was time to bring in the CIA as they may already have had a covert interest in the PRD. By December 7, 1995, the CIA was called in to give assistance and to advise the local officers in this case, which had potential international ramifications. On January 27, 1996, Sunderhauf received a memo from Larry Leightley, the CIA Chief of Station in Santo Domingo, Dominican Republic.

"'It is important to note that Pena-Gomez and the PRD in 1995 are considered mainstream in the political spectrum,' Leightley wrote. 'Pena-Gomez currently leads in the polls and has a better than even chance of being elected the next President of the Dominican Republic in May, 1996 elections. He and his PRD ideology pose no specific problems for U.S. foreign policy and, in fact, Pena-Gomez was widely seen as the "U.S. Embassy's candidate" in the 1994 elections given the embassy's strong role in pressuring for free and fair elections and Pena's role as opposition challenger.' Leightley went on to say that on December 11, 1995, Undersecretary of State Alex Watson had a lengthy meeting with Pena-Gomez, whom Leightley stated 'is a well-respected political leader in the Caribbean.'"[37]

By this time, McLaughlin's team had hooked up with DEA investigators in Worcester, Massachusetts, who informed them that the PRD headquarters in Worcester was the main hub of Dominican narcotics trafficking for all of New England. McLaughlin was able to get an informant wearing a wire inside some meetings of the PRD. He taped instructions being given by PRD officials on how to raise money for the Pena-Gomez candidacy by narcotics trafficking. Then the CIA turned ugly and wanted the name of McLaughlin's informant, as well as all memos they had written to the BNI on the matter.

McLaughlin and his team refused to turn the name over, fearing for the informant's life. As this was potentially a very damaging case for the US government, which seemed to be protecting a known group of traffickers, if the informant disappeared, there'd be no more potential problem for the US government. On March 27, 1996, CIA Agent Dave Lawrence arrived for a meeting with McLaughlin and Sunderhauf at BNI headquarters. According to court documents filed in McLaughlin's civil suit against the CIA, the Pennsylvania Attorney General, the United States Attorney in Philadelphia, and the State Department, "CIA Agent Lawrence stated that he wanted the memo that he gave this agency on Jan. 31, 1996, and that BNI shouldn't have received it in the first place. CIA agent Lawrence went on to state that he wanted the identification of the C/I and what province he came from in the Dominican Republic. CIA agent Lawrence was adamant about getting this information and he was agitated when BNI personnel refused his request."[38]

Within two weeks of refusing to turn over the name of his informant to the CIA, all of McLaughlin's pending cases were dismissed as unprosecutable by the Philadelphia D.A., stories were leaked to the press alleging investigations into McLaughlin's team for corruption, and superiors ordered McLaughlin's team not to publicly comment on charges to the press, putting McLaughlin under a gag order.[39] McLaughlin's team broke up, and McLaughlin's civil suit against his employers and the CIA is still pending at the time of writing (July/August, 2000).

"We have uncovered more than sufficient evidence that conclusively shows that the US State Department was overtly —there wasn't anything secret about it— overtly supporting the PRD, and that the PRD had as part of its structure a gang that was dedicated to selling drugs in the United States," said former US Congressman Don Bailey.

"We have uncovered more than sufficient evidence that conclusively shows that the US State Department was overtly—there wasn't anything secret about it—overtly supporting the PRD, and that the PRD had as part of its structure a gang that was dedicated to selling drugs in the United States," said former US Congressman Don Bailey, who is representing McLaughlin in his suit.[40] Bailey said that he suspects the government got the name of the informant anyway, as he cannot find the informant now.

A source close to the case confirms that photographs were taken of Al Gore attending a fund-raising event at Coogan's Pub in Washington Heights in September 1996. The fund-raiser was held by Dominicans associated with the PRD, some of whom—such as PRD officers Simon A. Diaz and Pablo Espinal—even having DEA NADDIS jackets, and several had "convictions for sales of pounds of cocaine, weapons violations and the laundering of millions of dollars in drug money."[41] Why was the Secret Service allowing Vice President Gore to meet with known drug traffickers and accept campaign contributions from them?

In one memorable raid, officers found $136,000 "wrapped and ready" to be shipped to Sea Crest trading, a suspected CIA front company.

Sea Crest Trading and More Dominican Connections

Joe Occhipinti, a senior Immigration and Naturalization Service agent in New York City with 22 years of service—one of the most decorated federal officers in history, with 78 commendations and awards to his credit—began investigating Dominican drug connections in 1989. Occhipinti developed evidence, while solving the murder of a NYC cop by Dominican drug lords, that one of the Dominican drug lords was "buying up Spanish grocery stores, called bodegas, in Washington Heights to facilitate his drug trafficking and money laundering activities."[42] Occhipinti launched what began to turn into the very successful, multi-agency task-force Operation Bodega, netting 40 arrests and the seizure of more than $1 million cash from drug proceeds.

In one memorable raid, officers found $136,000 "wrapped and ready" to be shipped to Sea Crest trading, a suspected CIA front company.[43] Then Occhipinti found himself set up, arrested, tried, and convicted for violating the rights of some members of the Dominican Federation he'd busted during the operation. Sentenced to 36 months in prison in 1991, Occhipinti was pardoned by outgoing President Bush in 1993.

Another investigator who tied Sea Crest trading to the CIA was former NYPD detective Benjamin Jackobson, who began investigating the company for food-coupon fraud in 1994. "According to Justice Department documents obtained by Congressman James Trafficant (D-OH), the Drug Enforcement Administration (DEA) believes that Sea Crest is behind much of the money laundering in New York's Washington Heights area of Manhattan, but that attempts to prosecute the company 'have been hampered and legislatively fought by certain interest groups and not a single case has been initiated.' Jackobson's inquiry led him to conclude that one of those 'interest groups' was the CIA, which, the investigator believes, was using Sea Crest as a front for covert operations, including weapons shipments to *mujahideen* groups in Afghanistan."[44]

"All I can say is," said Occhipinti, "I find it very unusual that dozens of viable federal and state investigations into the Dominican Federation and the activities of Sea Crest Trading company were prematurely terminated... I am not optimistic that this stuff is ever going to really break. They will just simply attempt to discredit the people bringing forward the evidence, and to try to selectively prosecute some to intimidate the rest."[45]

In sworn testimony entered into the Congressional Record by Representative James Trafficant, NYPD Internal Affairs officer William Acosta said, "My investigation confirmed that Sea Crest, as well as the Dominican Federation, are being politically protected by high ranking public officials who have received illegal political contributions which were drug proceeds. In addition, the operatives in Sea Crest were former CIA-Cuban operatives who were involved in the 'Bay of Pigs.' This is one of the reasons why the intelligence community has consistently protected and insulated Sea Crest and the Dominican Federation from criminal prosecution.... I have evidence which can corroborate the drug cartel conspiracy against Mr. Occhipinti."[46]

It should also cause no undue concern among American citizens that the winner of the Dominican presidential race on May 18, 2000, was Hipolito Mejia, who was the vice-presidential running mate of the infamous Pena-Gomez in 1990 and who was the vice president of his party, the PRD, for years before winning the race. The inauguration took place as scheduled on August 16, 2000.[47] Not to mention that Clinton Administration insider and former Chairman of the Democratic National Party, Charles Manatt, accepted the US Ambassadorship to the poverty-stricken Dominican Republic, presenting his credentials on December 9, 1999, to the Dominican government.[48]

The Ninth Circuit Court Has Its Doubts About US Government Drug-Ties Denials

Bringing one of the minor players in Gary Webb's story back into the limelight, on July 26, 2000, the US Ninth Circuit Court of Appeals (the second-highest court in the US) ruled that asylum-seeking Nicaraguan Renato Pena Cabrera—a former cocaine dealer and Fuerza Democratica Nicaraguense (FDN) Contra faction spokesman in Northern California during the early 1980s—should have a judge hear his story in court. Pena is fighting extradition from the US stemming from a 1985 conviction for cocaine trafficking. Pena alleges the drug dealing he was involved in had the express permission of the US government, and that he was told by the prosecutor soon after his 1984 arrest that he would not face deportation, due to his assisting the Contra efforts.

"Pena and his allies supporting the Contras became involved in selling cocaine in order to circumvent the congressional ban on non-humanitarian aid to the Contras. Pena states that he was told that leading Contra military commanders, with ties to the CIA, knew about the drug dealing," the three-judge panel wrote in its decision.[49] Pena's story seemed plausible to the judges, who decided that the charges were of such serious import that they deserved to be heard and evaluated in court. It also means that they probably do not believe the HPSCI report. Perhaps they were remembering the entries in Oliver North's notebooks, dated July 9, 1984, concerning a conversation with CIA agent Duane "Dewey" Clarridge: "Wanted aircraft to go to Bolivia to pick up paste," and, "Want aircraft to pick up 1,500 kilos."[50]

The CIA-created FDN was the best-trained, best-equipped Contra faction, based in Honduras and lead by former Nicaraguan dictator Anastasio Samoza's National Guardsman, Enrique Bermudez. Pena was selling drugs in San Fransisco for one of the main figures in Webb's story, Norwin Meneses, another Nicaraguan who was in turn sending much of that money to the Contras. "It was during October, 1982, that FDN leaders met with Meneses in L.A. and San Fransisco in an effort to set up local Contra support groups in those cities."[51] Pena was arrested along with Jairo Meneses, Norwin's nephew. Pena copped a guilty plea to one count of possession with intent to sell, in March 1985, getting a one-year sentence in a halfway house, partly in exchange for informing on Jairo.

Dennis Ainsworth—an American Contra supporter in San Francisco—told the FBI in 1987 that he was told by Pena that "the FDN is involved in drug smuggling with the aid of Norwin Meneses." Ainsworth also told the FBI that the FDN "had become more involved in selling arms and cocaine for personal gain than in a military effort to overthrow the current Nicaraguan Sandinista government." He went so far as to tell them that he'd been contacted in 1985 by a US Customs Agent, who told him that "national security interests kept him from making good narcotics cases." When Jairo Meneses reached court for sentencing in 1985, in exchange for a three-year sentence he testified against his uncle, claiming to be a bookkeeper for Norwin, but nothing happened. Norwin Meneses continued to operate freely.[52]

Webb's attention was initially directed toward Norwin Meneses' partner, Danilo Blandon Reyes, who turned out to be the supplier for "Freeway" Ricky Ross, described by many as being instrumental in the spread of crack throughout South Central Los Angeles and beyond, beginning in late 1981. By 1983, Ross "was buying over 100 kilos of cocaine a week, and selling as much as $3 million worth of crack a day."[53] Pena, during this same time (1982 to 1984)—according to information in the CIA's Hitz Report, Vol. 2—made six to eight trips "for Meneses' drug-trafficking organization. Each time, he says he carried anywhere from $600,000 to $1,000,000 to Los Angeles and returned to San Fransisco with 6 to 8 kilos of cocaine." Webb speculates that, "Even with the inflated cocaine prices of the early 1980s, the amount of money Pena was taking to LA was far more than was needed to pay for 6 to 8 kilos of cocaine. It seems likely that the excess—$300,000 to $500,000 per trip—was the Contras' cut of the drug proceeds."[54]

Whether Pena's appeal will eventually reach a court is not yet known. Most likely someone in Washington, DC—perhaps even former CIA officer and current Chairman of the HPSCI, Representative Porter Goss himself (R-FL)—is going to pick up the phone and call the Special Assistant US Attorney listed in the court filings, Robert Yeargin, tell him to drop the case, and allow Pena to remain in the US. The CIA and the US government do not want anyone bringing Hitz Vol. 2 into a courtroom and giving it the public hearing that former CIA Director John Deutch promised.

Older Reports, Irrefutable Evidence

The evidence of the CIA working with traffickers is irrefutable. Many Congressional inquiries and committees have gathered massive amounts of evidence pointing to CIA drug connections. Senator John Kerry's (D-Mass) Senate Subcommittee on Narcotics and Terrorism, which released a report in December 1988,[55] explored many of the Contra/CIA-drug allegations. As Jack Blum, former chief counsel to the Kerry Committee, testified in Senate hearings October 23, 1996, "If you ask: In the process of fighting a war against the Sandinistas, did people connected with the US government open channels which allowed drug traffickers to move drugs into the United States, did they know the drug traffickers were doing it, and did they protect them from law enforcement? The answer to all those questions is 'YES.'"[56]

The Kerry Report's main conclusions go directly opposite those of the latest HPSCI report: "It is clear that individuals who provided support for the Contras were involved in drug trafficking. The supply network of the Contras was used by drug trafficking organizations, and elements of the Contras themselves received financial and material assistance from drug traffickers."[57]

Webb's articles resulted in a Department of Justice investigation as well, lead by DoJ Inspector General Michael Bromwich. The DoJ found that indeed the CIA did intervene to stop an investigation into Julio Zavala, a suspect in the "Frogman" case in San Fransisco, in which swimmers in wetsuits were bringing cocaine to shore from Colombian freighters.

Photo: Preston Peet

Contras in San Miguel, El Salvador, after a mission to Honduras.

When police arrested Zavala, they seized $36,000. The CIA got wind of depositions being planned and stepped in. "It is clear that the CIA believed that it had an interest in preventing the depositions, partly because it was concerned about an allegation that its funds were being diverted into the drug trade. The CIA discussed the matter with the U.S. Attorney's Office, the depositions were canceled, and the money was returned."[58]

Since the release of the HPSCI report, there has been a noticeable silence emanating from the office of Representative Maxine Waters, who after the release of Hitz Vol. 1, had called for open hearings. Rep. Waters told the HPSCI in 1998 it was a shame that the CIA either absolutely knew, or turned its head, "at the same time we are spending millions of dollars talking about a war on drugs? Give me a break, Mr. Chairman, and members. We can do better than this."[59]

White House NSC members Oliver North, Admiral John Poindexter, and General Richard Secord were all barred for life from entering Costa Rica by the Costa Rican government in 1989 due to their Contra drug trafficking connections.

There has yet to be a public hearing on Hitz Vol. 2. The HPSCI has released a report that blatantly lies to the American people—who have watched their rights and liberties chipped away a bit at a time in the name of the War on Some Drugs—while certain unscrupulous individuals within the CIA and other parts of the US government, as well as the private sector, have made themselves rich off the war. The investigations into the CIA-Contra-Cocaine connections serve only to focus attention upon one small part of the whole picture, while the HPSCI report narrows the field even further, by insisting on refuting—poorly, one might add—Webb's reporting yet again. "These guys have long ago become convinced that they can control what people believe and think entirely through power and that facts are irrelevant," said Catherine Austin Fitts, former Assistant Secretary of Housing and Federal Housing Commissioner under Bush.[60]

The HPSCI only mentions the most prolific drug smuggler in US history—who used the Contra-supply operations to broaden his own smuggling operation—in passing, relegating Barry Seal to a mere footnote. Mena, Arkansas—Seal's base of operations during the same time then-Arkansas Governor Clinton's good friend Dan Lasatar was linked by the FBI to a massive cocaine trafficking ring—isn't mentioned once. White House NSC members Oliver North, Admiral John Poindexter, and General Richard Secord were all barred for life from entering Costa Rica by the Costa Rican government in 1989 due to their Contra drug trafficking connections, but you won't read that in the HPSCI report.

Then there are the drug-financed armies, such as the Kosovo Liberation Army (KLA), which in 1996 was being called a terrorist organization by the US State Department, while the European Interpol was compiling a report on their domination of the European heroin trade. US forces handed a country to the KLA/Albanian drug cartels, and just over one year later the US is facing a sharp increase in heroin seizures and addiction figures.

Back in the 1960s and 1970s, it was the Hmong guerrilla army fighting a "secret" war completely run by the CIA in Laos. Senator Frank Church's Committee hearings on CIA assassinations and covert operations in 1975 "accepted the results of the Agency's own internal investigation, which found, not surprisingly, that none of its operatives had ever been in any way involved in the drug trade. Although the CIA's report had expressed concern about opium dealing by its Southeast Asian allies, Congress did not question the Agency about is allegiances with leading drug lords—the key aspect, in my view, of CIA complicity in narcotics trafficking," wrote Alfred McCoy, author of the seminal *The Politics of Heroin*, in 1972.[61] Sounds a bit familiar, doesn't it?

Brit Snider, current Inspector General of the CIA, testified before the HPSCI in a closed-door session, May 5, 1999: "While we found no evidence that any CIA employees involved in the Contra program had participated in drug-related activities or had conspired with others in such activities, we found that the Agency did not deal with Contra-related drug trafficking allegations and information in a consistent, reasoned or justifiable manner. In the end, the objective of unseating the Sandinistas appears to have taken precedence over dealing properly with potentially serious allegations against those whom the Agency was working."[62] Yet, somehow the HPSCI felt justified in releasing its utter sham of a report to the American people, assuring us that it "found no evidence to support allegations" that CIA-connected individuals were selling drugs in the Los Angeles area.

Photo: Preston Peet

Cele Castillo holding a picture of himself and CIA agent Randy Capistar in Central America.

Are We About to Commit Another Vietnam, or Has It Already Begun?

US politicians continue hollering for stronger law enforcement tactics and tougher sentencing guidelines. They vote to give the Colombian military $1.3 billion dollars—so it can turn around and buy 68 Blackhawk helicopters from US arms merchants—to assist Colombia in its War on Some Drugs. The lies have a personal effect on our lives. This is not a harmless little white lie—this is costing thousands of

Photo: Cele Castillo

Back from Nicaragua: Contra helicopters landing at Ilopango.

undue, horrible deaths each year, this sham of a war. For US politicians to continue to vote for increased Drug War funding—when the evidence is irrefutable that US intelligence agencies, federal law enforcement agencies, and even some government officials in elected office have actively worked to protect and cover up for the real, major drug lords—the analogies to Vietnam are not so far off the mark.

"When I came to America in 1961, the US was just beginning a program where they were sending advisors [to Vietnam], insisting that they would never be anything more," said Scott. "And [they had] a defoliation program, an extensive defoliation program, which is what we are doing now in Colombia. Only, I think we now have even more advisors in Colombia, and we've graduated to biowarfare in Colombia, which is something we are treaty-bound not to do. Yet we are doing it. The deeper in we get, the harder it will be to get out. So there may still be a chance to get out of this mess, or to change it to a political solution, but it is dangerously like Vietnam."[63]

Colombia is a perfect illustration of the hypocrisy of the War on Some Drugs, when we consider the case of Colonel James Hiett, former head of the US anti-drug efforts in Colombia. Col. Hiett covered up for his wife, Laurie, who in 1998 came under investigation by the US Army for smuggling cocaine and heroin through the US Embassy postal service in Bogata. Laurie gave at least $25,000 in drug profits to her husband to launder for her. The US military put her under investigation, but they told Col. Hiett they did so, giving him time to cover his tracks. The Army performed a perfunctory investigation of the Colonel, cleared him of any involvement in the drug trade, then recommended he get probation. In May 1999 Laurie was sentenced to five years, and in July 2000 Col. Hiett was sentenced to five months of prison (followed by five months of home detention) after pleading guilty to ignoring his wife's illegal activities. Both were sentenced by US District Judge Edward Korman in Brooklyn, New York. Hernan Aquila, the mule that Laurie hired to pick up the drugs in NYC and deliver to the dealers, got a longer sentence than the two Hietts put together—five and a half years. He is Colombian; they are white Americans. He was simply a mule, while Col. Hiett was in charge of all US anti-drug efforts in Colombia, and his wife was one of the masterminds of the operation.

"In the Colombian drug war, denial goes far beyond the domesticated: Col. Hiett turned a blind eye not only to his wife's drug profiteering but to the paramilitaries, to the well-documented collusion of Colombian officers in those death squads and to the massive corruption of the whole drug-fighting enterprise. [Col.] Hiett's sentencing revealed not an overprotective husband, but a military policy in which blindness is the operative strategy—a habit of mind so entrenched that neither Col. Hiett nor the Clinton administration nor the U.S. Congress can renounce it, even as the prison door is swinging shut," wrote one aghast reporter.[64]

Former US Ambassador to Paraguay and El Salvador Robert White said, "Cocaine is now Colombia's leading export," laughing at "the idea that an operation of that magnitude can take place without the cooperation of the business, banking, transportation executives, and the government, civil as well as military."[65]

Will the American people continue to accept the lies and cover-ups? Will the people allow Congress to continue refusing to address the officially-sanctioned and CIA-assisted global trafficking, insisting that it cannot find any evidence that it exists, meanwhile voting ever more cash to support the Drug War? Every American should feel personally insulted that regardless of the facts, their elected representatives choose to yet again foist another lie upon them, but they shouldn't feel surprised. This entire War on Some Drugs is predicated upon the existence of the black market, and to ensure the existence of that black market, the intelligence agencies such as the CIA actively promote and protect the power and wealth of the cartels, and themselves, by creating endless enemies.

Perhaps the suitable way to stop their lies and cover-ups would be to sentence these men and women to ten years of addiction on the streets of America under prohibitionist policies, to suffer the consequences of their actions and give them a taste of their own medicine.

Endnotes

1. House Report: US Congress, House, Permanent Select Committee on Intelligence, "Report on the Central Intelligence Agency's Alleged Involvement in Trafficking Crack Cocaine in the Los Angeles Area," 106th Cong., 2nd Session, Washington: GPO, Feb. 2000 **2.** Interview with Celerino Castillo by Preston Peet, July 23, 2000. **3.** The "CIA-Drugs Symposium" was held in Eugene, Oregon, June 11, 2000, at the Wheeler Pavilion, Eugene Fairgrounds. An all-day event, there were nine speakers and presenters with evidence of CIA and official US-sanctioned drug trafficking, including Catherine Austin Fitts, Mike Ruppert, Didon Kamathi, Kris Milligan, Rodney Stich, Cele Castillo, Dan Hopsicker, and Peter Dale Scott, plus a presentation by Bernadette Armand, an attorney working for teams of attorneys, under the direction of attorneys William Simpich and Katya Kamisaruk, in the ongoing lawsuits filed against the CIA and others for their failure to offer equal protection under the law to everyone in South Central Los

Angeles, Oakland, and elsewhere in California. Anita Belle, a Florida attorney, is handling various class-action suits filed in eight other states around the US along the same lines as the California suits. **4.** *Op cit.*, Castillo interview. **5.** "Written Statement of Celerino Castillo 3rd, (former DEA Special Agent), July 2000, for the House Select Committee on Intelligence," pg 16. **6.** *Ibid.*, p 17; Webb, Gary. (1998). *Dark alliance: The CIA, the Contras, and the crack cocaine explosion*. New York: Seven Stories Press, p 249. **7.** *Op cit.*, HPSCI report, p 18. **8.** *Op cit.*, "Written Statement of Castillo," p 17; *Op cit.*, Webb, pp 249-250. **9.** Scott, Peter Dale, PhD. (2000). *Drug, Contras, and the CIA: Government policies and the cocaine economy—An analysis of media and government response to the Gary Webb stories in the* San Jose Mercury News *(1996-2000).* From The Wilderness Publications, p 47. **10.** Interview with Peter Dale Scott by Preston Peet, July 24, 2000. **11.** "Allegations of Connections Between CIA and the Contras in Cocaine Trafficking to the United States, (96-0143-IG), Volume 1: The California Story," (classified and unclassified versions). January 29, 1998, Office of the Inspector General, Central Intelligence Agency; "Allegations of Connections Between CIA and the Contras in Cocaine Trafficking to the United States, (96-0143-IG), Volume II: The Contra Story," (classified and unclassified versions). October 8, 1998, Office of the Inspector General, Central Intelligence Agency. **12.** Parry, Robert. (1999). "Congress puts Contra-coke secrets behind closed doors." *IF Magazine*, July/August, p 19. Parry was instrumental in breaking the Contra-cocaine connections in the early 1980s, including winning the George Polk Award for Journalism in 1984 for reporting on the CIA assassination/torture manual given to the Contras. He also wrote, along with Brian Barger, the very first published article on Oliver North's connection to the secret Contra-supply operations on June 10, 1985, and the first story linking the Contras to drug running on Dec. 20, 1986, while working for the Associated Press. **13.** *Op cit.*, Scott interview **14.** *Op cit.*, Scott (*Drugs, Contras, and the CIA*). Emphasis added. **15.** Testimony of CIA Inspector General Fredrick P. Hitz, Before the House Permanent Select Committee on Intelligence, On the CIA OIG Report of Investigation, (Hitz) "Vol 1: The California Story," March 16, 1998. **16.** Memo to William French Smith, Attorney General, Department of Justice of the USA, from William J. Casey, Director of Central Intelligence, dated March 2, 1982, obtained at <www.copvcia.com>. **17.** Memo from William F. Smith, Attorney General, Department of Justice of the USA, to William Casey, Director of Central Intelligence, dated February 11, 1982, obtained at <www.copvcia.com>. **18.** As noted in the lawsuit *Lyons v CIA*, Class Action Lawsuit on Behalf of Victims of the Crack Cocaine Epidemic, filed March 15, 1999, in Oakland, CA, and simultaneously in Los Angeles, CA. **19.** Memo to Mark M. Richard, the Deputy Assistant Attorney General of the USA, from A.R. Cinquegrana, the Deputy Counsel for Intelligence Policy, dated February 8, 1985, subject: CIA Reporting of Drug Offenses. **20.** *Op cit.*, HPSCI report, p 42. **21.** Ruppert, Michael C. (1998). "Selected Excerpts With Commentary" from "The Central Intelligence Agency Inspector General Report of Investigation, Allegations of Connections Between CIA and the Contras in Cocaine Trafficking to the United States, Vol. 2: The Contra Story (declassified version)," From the Wilderness Publications. **22.** *Op cit.*, Scott (*Drugs, Contras, and the CIA*), p 7. **23.** *Op cit.*, Scott interview. SETCO was the airline owned by known drug trafficker Juan Mattas Ballestaros, whom *Newsweek* (May 15, 1985) estimated was responsible for up to one-third of all cocaine reaching the US at that time. SETCO was just one of the 58 companies and individuals mentioned by the Hitz report. **24.** Speech of Representative Maxine Waters in the House of Representatives, March 18, 1997. Televised on C-Span. Also see Adams, David. (1997). "Anti-drug mission turns sour." *St. Petersburg Times*, Jan. 26, p A1 **25.** Cockburn, Alexander & Jeffrey St. Clair. (1998). *Whiteout: The CIA, drugs, and the press*. New York: Verso Press, p 96. **26.** Russell, Dan. (1999). *Drug War: Covert money, power, and policy*. Camden, NY: Kalyx.com, p 450. **27.** *Op cit.*, Scott interview. **28.** *Op cit.*, Russell, p 451. **29.** *Op cit.*, Speech of Rep. Maxine Waters. See also Scott, Peter Dale & Jonathan Marshall. (1991). *Cocaine politics: Drugs, armies, and the CIA in Central America*. University of California Press, p vii. **30.** *The Shadow*: April-June 1994: "Haiti's national nightmare." *Los Angeles Times*, March 8, 1997, p A9, as noted in *Op cit.*, Russell, p 451 **31.** *Op cit.*, Russell, pp 451-452. **32.** *Haiti Progres*, Feb. 16-22, 2000. <www.haiti-progres.com/2000/sm000216/Xeng0216.htm>. **33.** Fineman, Mark. (2000). "Haiti takes on major role in cocaine trade." *Los Angeles Times*, March 29. Available at <www.mapinc.org/drugnews/v00/n421/a05.html?200479>. **34.** *Op cit.*, *Haiti Progres*. **35.** Altman, Howard & Jim Barry. (2000). "The Dominican connection," part 1, City Paper (Philadelphia, Pennsylvania), July 27-August 3. <www.citypaper.net/articles/072700/cs.cover1.shtml>; Altman & Barry. (2000). "The Dominican connection, part 2: Shafted." *City Paper* (Philadelphia, Pennsylvania), August 3-10, front page. <www.citypaper.net/articles/080300/cs.cover1.shtml>. See also Ruppert, Michael C. (1999). "Sparky: A case study in heroism and perseverance." From the Wilderness, August 30, pp 7-11. **36.** *Op cit.*, Altman & Barry. **37.** *Ibid.* **38.** *Op cit.*, Ruppert (1999), p 9. **39.** *Ibid.*; interview with Michael C. Ruppert by Preston Peet, August 1, 2000. **40.** Interview with Don Bailey by Preston Peet, July 31, 2000. **41.** *Op cit.*, Ruppert (1999). **42.** House Judiciary Committee, Subcommittee on Commercial and Administrative Law, Sworn Testimony by Joseph Occhipinti, July 27, 2000, testifying in support of H.R. 4105 "The Fair Justice Act of 2000," which would form an agency to investigate alleged misconduct within the Justice Department. **43.** Grigg, William Norman. (1997). "Smuggler's dues." *The New American*, Vol. 13, No. 9, April 28. **44.** Anonymous. (1997). "US grocery coupon fraud funds Middle Eastern terrorism." *The New American*, Vol. 13, No. 5, March 3. **45.** Interview with Joseph Occhipinti by Preston Peet, July 31, 2000. **46.** Sworn Affidavit of William Acosta, entered into the Congressional Record in the ongoing Investigation of Joe Occhipinti, by Hon. James A Trafficant Jr, September 26, 1996, pp E1733-E1734. Also see sworn affidavit of Manuel DeDios, former editor of *El Diario Le Prensa* newspaper, and the first US journalist killed by the Dominican Drug Cartel, the Dominican Federation, same pages of Congressional Record. **47.** Anonymous (2000). "Mejia wins in Dominican presidential race." Associated Press, May 20. **48.** Ruppert, Michael. (2000). "The Democratic National Party's presidential drug money pipeline." From the Wilderness, April 30, p 8. **49.** Egelco, Bob. (2000). "Former Contra wins review of drug ties, fights deportation to Nicaragua, says CIA knew of drug trafficking." *San Fransisco Examiner and Chronicle*, July 27, p A4. **50.** *Op cit.*, Cockburn & St. Claire, p 35. **51.** *Op cit.*, Webb, p 166. **52.** *Ibid.*, pp 168-169. **53.** *Op cit.*, Cockburn & St. Claire, p 7. **54.** *Op cit.*, Webb, pp 166-167. **55.** US Congress, Senate, Subcommittee on Narcotic, Terrorism, and International Operations, "Drugs, Law Enforcement, and Foreign Policy," Committee Staff Report, December, 1988, also known as the Kerry Report. **56.** Testimony and prepared statement of Jack Blum, Chief Counsel for Senator John Kerry's Subcommittee on Narcotics, Terrorism, and International Relations, which released its own report in 1986, testifying before Sen. Arlen Specter's Subcommittee Hearings in 1996. See also *op cit.*, Cockburn & St. Claire, p 304; *op cit.*, Scott, p 6. **57.** *Op cit.*, Cockburn & St. Claire, p 303. **58.** "The CIA-Contra-Crack Cocaine Controversy: A Review of the Justice Department's Investigations and Prosecutions," US Department of Justice, Office of Inspector General, (Michael Bromwich), December, 1997, Executive Summary, Section VIII, Julio Zavala. **59.** Testimony of Rep. Maxine Waters Before the House Permanent Select Committee on Intelligence, on the CIA OIG Report of Investigation, "Vol 1: The California Story," March 16, 1998. **60.** Email correspondence of Catherine Austin Fitts to Preston Peet, August 2, 2000. **61.** McCoy, Alfred W. & Cathleen B. Reed. (1972). *The politics of heroin in Southeast Asia*. Harper & Row, Publishers, Inc. Re-released as *The politics of heroin: CIA complicity in the global drug trade*. Lawrence Hill Books, 1991, p xviii. **62.** *Op cit.*, HPSCI report, p 34. **63.** *Op cit.*, Scott interview. Also see Stevenson, Sharon & Jeremy Bigwood. (2000). "Drug control or biowarfare." Mother Jones online, May 3, updated July 6. <www.motherjones.com/news_wire/coca.html>. Discusses the planned forcing of Colombia by US drug warriors to spray Fursarium Oxysporum, a hideous, mutating, killer fungicide on their coca fields, and hence their land and themselves, in exchange for the $1.3 billion in "anti-drug" aid. The US state of Florida has banned the spraying of Fusarmrium Oxysporum within its borders, yet the drug warriors will export it to Colombia. **64.** Shapiro, Bruce. (2000). "Nobody questions the Colonel." Salon Website, July 15. <www.salon.com/news/feature/2000/07/15/hiett/index.html>. **65.** Stein, Jeff. (2000). "The unquiet death of Jennifer Odom." Salon Website, July 5. <www.salon.com/news/feature/2000/07/05/odom/index.html>.

Col. Hiett covered up for his wife, Laurie, who in 1998 came under investigation by the US Army for smuggling cocaine and heroin through the US Embassy postal service in Bogata.

Reassessing OKC
The Truck-bomb Hoax
Cletus Nelson

Overview

In the blink of an eye, the 1995 Oklahoma City bombing abruptly transformed the United States from an invulnerable superpower to a nation under siege. As grisly images of death and dismemberment invaded the capsular world of our television screens, Americans witnessed the true horror of a large-scale terrorist attack. However, within 48 hours of this senseless tragedy, the Justice Department had broken the case. A disaffected ex-soldier named Timothy McVeigh was the prime suspect and, five years later, after a rather anti-climactic day in court, the taciturn Gulf War veteran now resides in Colorado's notorious "Supermax" federal facility awaiting his impending death. Few will doubt that his conviction along with the life sentence meted out to his confederate, Terry Nichols, has provided an institutional palliative to the mass outrage that followed the homicidal attack. However, although the two appear guilty of attempting to destroy the Alfred P. Murrah federal building, the story is far from over.

From day one, a surfeit of scientific anomalies and inexplicable events have surrounded the allegedly airtight case against the two men. Indeed, despite widespread public belief that the crime has been solved, a number of looming questions remain unanswered. While many would prefer to ignore the shroud of mystery that still envelops this monumental tragedy, to do so would sacrifice perhaps our most valuable commodity: the historical record. In order to better understand why many people remain intractably opposed to the government's "lone bomber" scenario, one must begin by examining the alleged bomb itself.

Was It ANFO?

According to federal prosecutors, McVeigh and co-conspirator Terry Nichols constructed a bomb containing 4,800 pounds of Ammonium Nitrate mixed with fuel oil to create a combustible "slurry" known as ANFO. The destructive device was then placed in a 24-foot Ryder truck and driven to the curb just outside the Alfred P. Murrah building on Fifth Street and detonated at 9:02 A.M., April 19, 1995.[1] With few exceptions, most trial-watchers and members of the establishment press have unquestioningly accepted this version of events. Yet from the outset, the government's conclusions have been called into question by a battery of esteemed experts, particularly those with training and experience with explosives. To these researchers, accepting this dubious interpretation of the bomb's destructive capacity would require a physical and scientific leap of faith that openly contradicts accepted knowledge of the explosive capabilities of Ammonium Nitrate.

The first individual to point out the many glaring inconsistencies in the truck-bomb theory was someone with very little to gain by joining the embattled ranks of OKC conspiracy theorists: Brigadier General Benton K. Partin (USAF ret.). A world-renowned expert in the field of explosives and weapons systems, Partin is well-acquainted with the military capabilities of a variety of destructive charges. His immediate misgivings about the single-bomb theory compelled him to produce a highly technical assessment of the damage sustained by the Murrah building that remains a samizdat document to OKC researchers. His authoritative report certainly makes some startling observations.

"To produce the resulting damage pattern in the building, there would have to have been an effort with demolition charges at column bases to complement or supplement the truck bomb damage," he asserts in his lengthy "Bomb Damage Analysis of the Alfred P. Murrah Federal Building, Oklahoma City, Oklahoma." According to the detailed analysis, it would be physically impossible for an ANFO bomb to have destroyed the many steel-reinforced concrete columns which were situated far from the bomb site, as blast "pressure would have fallen off to about 375 pounds per square inch. That would be far below the 3,500 pound compressive yield strength of concrete."[2]

"To produce the resulting damage pattern in the building, there would have to have been an effort with demolition charges at column bases to complement or supplement the truck bomb damage," asserts Brigadier General Benton K. Partin (USAF ret.).

To substantiate his assertions, the military expert notes that building columns B-4 and B-5, which were in direct proximity to the blast, remained standing, while column A-7, which stood some 60 feet from the Ryder truck, was mysteriously demolished. "The much closer columns...are still standing, while the much larger column A-7 is down...These facts are sufficient reason to know that columns B-3 and A-7 had demolition charges on them," he states confidently.[3]

Partin's skepticism was echoed by Gary McClenny, an Army veteran with years of hands-on experience working with ANFO. In a May 16, 1995 letter to FBI Director Louis Freeh, McClenny adamantly disputed the Bureau's preliminary findings. "Ammonium Nitrate is a poor choice for breaching reinforced concrete...it is a low-level, low velocity (2,700 m/sec by itself, 3,400 m/sec when boosted by a 25% TNT charge) explosive primarily used to remove dirt from drilled holes," he notes.[4]

Sam Groning, a demolitions expert with three decades' worth of experience, also told researcher Jim Keith that after a lifetime spent "using everything from 100 percent Nitrogel to ANFO, I've never seen anything to support that story." In fact, Groning recalls setting off 16,000 pounds of ANFO and alleges he was "standing upright" a mere 300 yards from the blast site.[5]

Few FBI experts have publicly contradicted these damaging observations. In fact, numerous internal government studies soundly debunk allegations that an ANFO bomb destroyed the Murrah building. In his exhaustively researched tome on the bombing, *The Oklahoma City Bombing and the Politics of Terror*, investigative reporter David Hoffman cites a little-known August 1996 study published by the Federal Emergency Management Agency (FEMA), which concluded that "4,800 pounds of ANFO would have been virtually unable to have caused the so-called 30-foot crater in Oklahoma City."[6] Hoffman also discusses a leaked Pentagon study that originally appeared in *Strategic Investment Newsletter,* which reported that, "the destruction of the federal building last April was caused by five separate bombs."[7]

Hoping to counter this obvious threat to the state's case, in 1997 the Air Force conducted the "Eglin Blast Effects Study" in a last-ditch attempt to reconcile the ANFO theory with expert opinion. The plan backfired. The final report, which was never released to the general public, could not "ascribe the damage that occurred on April 19, 1995 to a single truck bomb containing 4,800 pounds of ANFO" and instead suggested that "other factors such as locally placed charges within the building itself" may have been responsible.[8]

Adding yet more weight to this determined opposition is Samuel Cohen, the legendary physicist credited with inventing the neutron bomb. "I believe that demolition charges in the building placed inside at certain key concrete columns did the primary damage to the Murrah Federal Building," he commented three years after the bombing. "It seems to me that the evidence has gotten much stronger in favor of internal charges, while the ammonium nitrate bomb theory has fallen apart." The observations of this scholar echo those of General Partin.[9]

Further imperiling the single-bomb theory are the findings of the Justice Department Inspector General's Office (IGO), which publicly questioned the shoddy practices and overt bias in favor of the prosecution that pervaded the Bureau's investigation of the bombing. Indeed, prior to McVeigh's 1997 trial, a draft report issued by the IGO rebuked the FBI laboratory for engaging in "unsound science" and concluded that "officials...may not know for certain if ammonium nitrate was used for the main charge that killed 168 people and injured more than 850 others."[10]

The Inspector General's Office rebuked the FBI laboratory for engaging in "unsound science" and concluded that "officials...may not know for certain if ammonium nitrate was used for the main charge that killed 168 people and injured more than 850 others."

These well-reasoned critiques of the evidence, steeped in the unambiguous language of hard science, leave little room for politicized or abstract argument. Indeed, the simplistic theory that a home-brewed fertilizer bomb nearly leveled a fortified federal installation becomes downright untenable, especially when considering US Government Technical Manual No. 9-1910, issued by both the Army and Air Force, which implies that ANFO couldn't possibly produce a shock wave capable of mangling the building's concrete supports.[11] This growing body of evidence seems to ominously point toward an alternative scenario involving additional explosives.

Bomb(s)?

Although given little coverage by the mainstream press, eyewitness testimony and other supporting evidence show that undetonated charges were located and defused once rescue efforts were underway. "We got lucky today, if you can consider anything about this tragedy lucky. It's actually a great stroke of luck, that we've got undefused bombs," noted terrorism expert Dr. Randall Heather on Oklahoma's Channel Four after the blast.[12]

At approximately 11:31 EST, on the day of the bombing, KFOR television broadcast the following announcement:

> The FBI has confirmed there is another bomb in the federal building. It's in the east side of the building...We're not sure what floor, what level, but there is definitely danger of a second explosion.[13]

Radio logs and other documentary materials provide transcripts of OKC police and fire department personnel discussing the removal of additional explosives. Reports of up to four bombs have surfaced.[14]

"As reported widely on CNN and TV stations across the nation, up to four primed bombs were found...inside what remained of the Murrah federal building on April 19, 1995," asserts investigative journalist Ian Williams Goddard.[15] Even more revealing: on the day of the bombing, KFOR television also broadcast that as many as two explosive charges had been located that were far more lethal than the *original* charge that nearly toppled the Murrah building.[16] The significance of this statement cannot be ignored as it suggests that highly powerful non-ANFO explosive devices were detected *inside* the building.

Although press flacks for the Bureau of Alcohol, Tobacco, and Firearms (BATF) later claimed these devices were "training bombs," Goddard scoffs at this explanation. He notes that the allegedly non-explosive "practice bombs" were tracked down by dogs trained to sniff for explosives, and if they were indeed deactivated "dummies," as described by BATF spokesmen, there would be little need for the bomb squad to "defuse" them.[17]

There are also a number of witnesses who have testified to distinctly hearing or experiencing two separate blasts. Attorney Charles Watts was in the federal courtroom across the street at 9:02 that fateful morning. He told *Media Bypass* that he heard an explosion that knocked everyone to the floor and, as the Vietnam vet hit the deck, he alleges he felt a second detonation far more powerful than the first. "There were two explosions...the second blast made me think the whole building was coming in," he recalls.[18]

Adam Parfrey's influential essay on the subject, "Oklahoma City: Cui Bono," reveals that Dr. Charles Mankin of the University of Oklahoma Geological Survey found that there were two separate explosions based on his analysis of seismographic data from two facilities. Seismograms show two distinct "spikes" roughly ten seconds apart.[19] "The Norman seismogram clearly shows two shocks of equal magnitude...the Omniplex...depicts events so violent they sent the instruments off the scale for more than ten seconds," reports *New Dawn* magazine.[20]

This substantial body of evidence lends credence to the existence of additional (and deadlier) explosives inside the building, which creates the distinct possibility that other suspects were either ignored or successfully eluded federal law enforcement. This development openly contradicts Attorney General Janet Reno's claim that the bombing investigation would "leave no stone unturned."[21]

"Others Unknown"

Despite the indictment and later conviction of McVeigh and Nichols, many still maintain that other conspirators were selectively ignored by federal investigators. These allegations are not just being voiced in the underground press. In the months leading up to McVeigh's trial, the *Denver Post* also "found evidence that the Oklahoma City Bombing plot involved the assistance of at least one person the government hasn't charged in the case."[22]

This belief that a more far-reaching conspiracy helped facilitate the attack on the Murrah building was shared by the Grand Jury that indicted Timothy McVeigh. The official indictment cites "others unknown," a decision obviously intended by the jury to signify the existence of co-conspirators still not apprehended.[23] Unfortunately, the subsequent convictions of Nichols and McVeigh have led government sources to staunchly assert that the embittered veterans were the sole perpetrators behind the terrorist attack. However, if ANFO is physically incapable of causing the level of damage sustained by the Murrah building, and if evidence shows that more than one explosion occurred on April 19, 1995, one must at least consider the existence of a more far-reaching conspiracy than the one sanctified by the mainstream media.

Another disturbing development that has served to undermine the credibility of the prosecution is the discovery of evidence which seems to indicate that the federal government possessed prior knowledge of an imminent terrorist strike on the Murrah building.

Those Who Knew

In the wake of the blast, rumors immediately began circulating that members of law enforcement received warnings of the bombing which they failed to relay to the public. Edye Smith, whose sons Chase and Colton perished in the blast, brought this issue before the public in the aftermath of the deadly blast. "Where was ATF?" she asked. "Fifteen of seventeen employees survived...They were the target of the explosion...Did they have advance warning?...My two kids didn't get that option," Smith lamented. The distraught mother went on to tell reporters that BATF investigators ordered her to "shut up...don't talk about it," when she demanded to know why only two employees of the embattled agency were in the building at the time of the blast.[24]

In the months leading up to McVeigh's trial, the *Denver Post* "found evidence that the Oklahoma City Bombing plot involved the assistance of at least one person the government hasn't charged in the case."

Soon others began to relate further insights into the possibility of prior government knowledge. Frustrated federal informants Gary

The Executive Secretariat's Office at the Justice Department received a call 24 minutes before the explosion announcing that, "The Oklahoma federal building has just been bombed!"

Cagan and Carol Howe described their repeated attempts to alert federal authorities that various white supremacist groups were planning a major undertaking in the Oklahoma City area, and Judge Wayne Alley later told the *Oregonian* that he was advised to "take extra precautions" by security officials prior to the bombing.[25]

The allegations that various officials were forewarned of the imminent disaster became so widespread that on January 17, 1997, ABC's *20/20* broadcast a story discussing this controversial issue. The results were far from flattering to members of the Justice Department.

One man, his face hidden behind a shadow for fear of BATF reprisal, asserted that he was told by a BATF agent that, "we were tipped off by our pagers not to come into work [that day]." His employer, who overheard the conversation, willingly confirmed this controversial claim. The *20/20* reporters, who spent seven months investigating the "prior knowledge" issue, also located several eyewitnesses who vividly recalled seeing the county bomb-squad truck outside the Murrah building on the morning of the bombing. ABC investigators also provided substantial proof that local fire department officials were instructed by the FBI five days before the blast that "there were some people coming through town they should be on the lookout for."[26]

In perhaps the most startling revelation, the *20/20* investigation uncovered proof that the Executive Secretariat's Office at the Justice Department received a call 24 minutes before the explosion announcing that, "The Oklahoma federal building has just been bombed!" Unfortunately, in an unforgivable sin of omission, authorities failed to notify anyone of this strange call, much less demand the building in question be evacuated.[27] Thus, after numerous warnings of an impending catastrophe, the federal government not only squandered what might have been a last chance to avert this atrocity, but has been far from forthcoming about this knowledge ever since.

Aftermath

When taken together, these disclosures reveal gross negligence on the part of federal investigators and a strange indifference to the possibility of a wider conspiracy in this case. Indeed, the sins of omission committed during the course of the bombing probe have inadvertently created a climate of suspicion and mistrust that has led the more vociferous anti-government activists to compare the Oklahoma City bombing to the Nazi Reichstag Fire of 1933, in which Nazi party activists set fire to the building housing the German legislature to pave the way for a brutal crackdown on communists and other political opponents.

What is perhaps most unsettling is that the latter conclusion is not entirely inconceivable in post-Waco America. Indeed, FBI informant Emad Ali Salem played a crucial and controversial role in the 1993 World Trade Center bombing,[28] and many believe OKC might have been yet another instance of a state-sanctioned operation that went fatally sour. Although this assertion remains speculative, the historical debate on this subject lingers, and one truth has emerged that few will deny: These two events have provided the impetus for a State-sanctioned war against "anti-government" dissent that has produced a chilling effect on certain forms of political activism in this country ever since.

"History tells us to pay attention to the aftermath," Adam Parfrey astutely observes in his essay on the bombing. One need only read the paper to trace the continuation of the OKC epic. Repressive anti-terrorism laws, Internet surveillance, crackdowns on politically suspect dissident groups, and the Clinton Administration's proposal to create a "Homelands Defense Force" that will allow the US military to police the citizenry are but a few of manifestations of the growth of State power that has occurred in the wake of this singular tragedy.

Before we willingly cede our cherished civil liberties under the benign notion of "National Security," and the "lone bomber" theory is inscribed in American history books as the final and everlasting truth of the matter, the victims of this immoral crime deserve nothing less than full explanations for the inconsistencies in the "official version" of events. The public has been offered an alternate reality that simply cannot be reconciled with science and the facts as we know them.

Endnotes

1. Trial transcripts, *United States of America vs. Timothy James McVeigh* (see <www.apb.com>). **2.** Partin, Benton K. "Bomb damage analysis of Alfred P. Murrah Federal Building, Oklahoma City, Oklahoma", pp 1,3. **3.** *Ibid*, p 3. **4.** Keith, Jim. (1995). *OK bomb!: Conspiracy and cover-up*, pp. 94. IllumiNet Press. **5.** *Ibid*, p 93. **6.** Hoffman, David. (1998). *Oklahoma City Bombing and the Politics of Terror*, p 17. Feral House. **7.** *Ibid*, p 16. **8.** *Ibid*, p 17. **9.** Jasper, William. (1998). Proof of bombs and cover-up, *New American*, July 20. **10.** Serrano, Richard. (1997). Faulty testimony, practices found in FBI lab probe, *Los Angeles Times*, April 21. **11.** Parfrey, Adam. Oklahoma City: Cui bono, *Prevailing Winds Research* #2. **12.** Unattributed. Oklahoma City bombing evidence cover-up, World Internet News Distributary Source (WINDS), October 1997 (see <www.thewinds.org>). **13.** *Op cit.*, Keith, pp 14-15. **14.** Goddard, Ian Williams. "Conspiracy Fact vs. Government Fabrication" (see <www.imt.net/~mtpatriot/goddard.htm>). **15.** *Ibid.* **16.** *Op cit.*, Hoffman, p 29. **17.** *Op cit.*, Goddard. **18.** *Media Bypass,* June 1995. **19.** *Op cit.*, Parfrey. **20.** Matthews, Clark. (1995). Behind the Oklahoma City bombing, *New Dawn*, July-August. **21.** *Op. cit.*, Hoffman, p 227. **22.** Wilmsen, Steve and Mark Eddy. (1996). Who bombed the Murrah building, *Denver Post*, December 15. **23.** *United States of America vs. Timothy James McVeigh and Terry Lynn Nichols* (filed August 10, 1995). **24.** Hoffman, David. (1997). A real fertilizer story, *Washington Weekly*, January 27. **25.** Goddard, Ian Williams. Federal government prior knowledge, *Prevailing Winds* #5 (see also <www.eros.com/igoddard/prior.htm>). **26.** Jasper, William. (1996). Evidence of prior knowledge, *New American*, May 13. **27.** *Op. cit.*, Goddard. **28.** DeRienzo, Paul, Frank Morales, and Chris Flash. (1995). Who bombed the World Trade Center?, *The Shadow,* January.

Votescam

Jonathan Vankin

O good voter, unspeakable imbecile, poor dupe...
—Octave Mirbeau, *Voter's Strike!*

On election night, when the three major television networks announce the next president, the winner they announce is not chosen by the voters of the United States. He is the selection of the three networks themselves, through a company they own jointly with Associated Press and United Press International.

That company is called News Election Service (NES). Its address is 212 Cortland Street, New York City. Its phone number is (212) 693-6001. News Election Service provides "unofficial" vote tallies to its five owners in all presidential, congressional, and gubernatorial elections. NES is the only source Americans have to find out how they, as a people, voted. County and city election supervisors don't come out with the official totals until weeks later. Those results are rarely reported in the national media.

NES is the only source Americans have to find out how they, as a people, voted.

The US government does not tabulate a single vote. The government has granted NES a legal monopoly, exempt from antitrust laws, to count the votes privately.

Those are the facts.

NES. The company is a conspiracy theorist's dream—or nightmare.

As mentioned above, NES operates exactly the way most imaginative conspiracy theorists believe all media operate. The ABC, NBC, and CBS networks, together with the AP and UPI, own the company jointly. Associated Press is a nonprofit co-op of a large number of daily newspapers, and UPI serves many of the rest. Local television and radio stations take most of their election returns from network tabulations. NES is a very real "cabal." Every media outlet in the United States acts in concert, at least on election nights.

NES has a full-time staff of fourteen. On election nights, that number swells to approximately 90,000 employees, most of them posted at local precincts phoning in vote totals as they're announced. Others answer the phones and enter these totals into the NES computer. The government has no such computer. Only the privately-held NES counts the votes. I called NES's executive director, Robert Flaherty, and asked him whether his company was run for profit. He wouldn't answer. His only response was, "I don't think that's part of your story."'

The company was conceived in 1964, in part as a cost-saving measure by the three major television networks (it was originally called Network Election Service), but largely to solidify the public's confidence in network vote tallies and projections by insuring uniformity. In the California Republican primary that year, television networks projected Barry Goldwater the winner on election night, while newspapers reported Nelson Rockefeller victorious in their morning editions. The networks themselves could vary widely in their return reports.

"Many television executives believe the public has been both confused and skeptical over seeing different sets of running totals on the networks' screens," the *New York Times* reported.

The networks (the two print syndicates were soon added to the setup) wanted the figures transmitted over their airwaves to be irrefutable. With all the networks—and later the print media—deriving their information from a central computer bank, with no alternative source, how could they be anything but?

"The master tally boards...would probably come to be accepted as the final authority on the outcome of races," the *Times* declared.

The "news media pool" was first tried in the 1964 general election. Most of the 130,000 vote counters were volunteers from civic groups. Twenty-thousand newspaper reporters acted as coordinators. NES central was located at New York's Edson Hotel. Vote-tallying substations were set up in such select sites as an insurance company headquarters and a Masonic temple. When polls closed, the newly-formed system shaved almost 90 minutes off the time needed to count votes in the 1960 election.

Every media outlet in the United States acts in concert, at least on election nights.

News Election Service had its goal circa 1964 to report final results within a half-hour of final poll-closing time. Now, of course, they go much faster than that. In the 1988 election, CBS was first out of the gate, making its projection at 9:17 Eastern time, with polls still open in eleven states. ABC followed just three minutes later.

All of these light-speed results are, naturally, "unofficial." County clerks take a month or more to verify their counts and issue an official tally. Plenty of time for any necessary fudging and finagling. And there may be none needed. Discrepancies are a matter of course throughout the nation's thousands of voting precincts. The major networks rarely bother to report on such mundane matters. So who's going to know?

Discrepancies are a matter of course throughout the nation's thousands of voting precincts.

One rationale behind maintaining a vote-counting monopoly is to insure "accuracy," but in 1968, when Richard Nixon defeated Hubert Humphrey by a margin that could be measured in angstroms, the role of NES became a good deal more shadowy.

At one point in the tally, the NES computer began spewing out totals that were at the time described as "erroneous." They included comedian/candidate Dick Gregory receiving one million votes when, the *New York Times* said, "His total was actually 18,000." The mistakes were described as something that "can happen to anyone."

NES turned off its "erroneous" computer and switched on a backup system, which ran much slower. After much waiting, the new machine put Nixon ahead by roughly 40,000 votes, with just 6 percent of the votes left to be counted. Suddenly, independent news reporters found over 53,000 Humphrey votes cast by a Democratic splinter party in Alabama. When the votes were added to Humphrey's total, they put him in the lead. Undaunted, the Associated Press conducted its own state-by-state survey of "the best available sources of election data" (presumably, NES also makes use of the "best available sources") and found Nixon winning again. And that's how it turned out.

With all the snafus and screwups, the real winner of the 1968 presidential election will never be certain.

What exactly was going on inside the "master computer" at NES? The company's director blamed software, even though the machine had run a twelve-hour test flawlessly just the day before using the same programming. Could the software have been altered? Substituted? Or was the fiasco caused by a routine "bug," which just happened to appear at the most inconvenient possible time? At this point, its more a question of what we can know than what we do know.

With all the snafus and screwups, the real winner of the 1968 presidential election will never be certain. We do know this: Liberal warhorse Humphrey died without fulfilling his dream of becoming president, while Nixon hung around long enough to see his loyal crony George Bush in the White House. (The old, unindicted co-conspirator passed on in 1994.)

Not only does NES keep the election night vote count, but most voters cast their ballots "virtually." Computers tabulate 54 percent of the votes cast in the United States. Sure, paper ballot elections were stolen all the time, and lever voting machines are invitations to chicanery. But there's something sinister about computers. Though most professionals in the field, as one would expect, insist that computers are far less vulnerable to manipulation than old ways of voting, the invisibility of their functions and the esoteric language they speak makes that assertion impossible to accept.

Even executives of computer-election companies will admit that their systems are "vulnerable," although they're reticent to make public statements to that effect. One executive told me, right after asserting that there's never been a proven case of computer election fraud, "there's probably been some we don't know about."

Even if "we" do find out, there's still little chance that the fraud will be prosecuted. A former chief assistant attorney general in California, Steve White, points out that without a conspirator willing to inform on his comrades or an upset so stunning as to immediately arouse suspicion, there's little hope of ferreting out a vote fraud operation.

There are very few elections that qualify as major upsets anymore. Pre-election polling tempers the climate of opinion effectively enough to take care of that. As for turncoat conspirators, if the conspiracy works there are no turncoats. A good conspiracy is an unprovable conspiracy. It remains a conspiracy "theory." To even talk about it is "paranoid."

"If you did it right, no one would ever know," said White. "You just change a few votes in a few precincts in a few states and no one would ever know."

There are several makes of computerized voting machines. One widely used model is the Shouptronic, whose most advantageous feature is the speed with which it tabulates votes. Multiple machines can send results to a central computer instantly over land lines or by satellite.

Shouptronic is essentially an automatic teller machine for voters. All votes are recorded by button pressing. The Shouptronic leaves no physical record of votes. Like all computer vote counters, its programming is top secret.

As solid a source as Robert J. Naegle, author of the federal government's national standards for computerized vote counting, is alarmed by the secrecy masking computer election software.

As solid a source as Robert J. Naegle, author of the federal government's national standards for computerized vote counting, is alarmed by the secrecy masking computer election software.

"They act like it was something handed down on stone tablets,'" he says. "It should be in the public domain."

The Shouptronic is named for its company's owner, Ransom Shoup II. In 1979, Mr. Shoup was convicted of conspiracy and obstruction of justice relating to a Philadelphia election under investigation by the FBI. That election was tabulated by old-fashioned lever machines, which also leave no "paper trail" of marked ballots. Shoup was hit with a $10,000 fine and sentenced to three years in prison, suspended.

Another computer voting company, Votomatic, maker of Computer Election Services (now known as Business Records Corporation Election Services), emerged unscathed from a Justice Department antitrust investigation in 1981. The president of the company quipped, "We had to get Ronald Reagan elected to get this thing killed." The remark was supposed to be a joke. Forty percent of American voters vote on CES systems.

CES machines have been described as relying on "a heap of spaghetti code that is so messy and so complex that it might easily contain hidden mechanisms for being quietly reprogrammed 'on the fly.'" A computer consultant hired by the plaintiffs in a suit against CES described the way a CES computer runs its program as "a shell game."

Votomatic has one especially troubling drawback. On election night 1982 in Miami, Ken and Jim Collier, who spent much of their lives tracking what they describe as a national conspiracy to rig all major elections, captured the problem on videotape. This "Votescam Video" has been the Colliers' Exhibit A ever since. They've showed it to reporters at major television networks, and evangelical talk show host Pat Robertson paid them $2,500 for broadcast rights to the tape. Robertson aired a portion of the tape.

The problem with Votomatic, captured on the Colliers' tape, is something called "hanging chad." The perforated squares on Votomatic computer ballot cards are, for some reason, called "chad." When a voter fails to punch it out completely, it hangs on the card.

To solve this problem and allow the computer to read the cards, election workers routinely remove hanging chad. The registrar of voters in Santa Clara County, California, says that "five percent or less" of all Votomatic cards have hanging chad, and election workers don't pull it off unless it is hanging by one or two corners.

The vision of local ladies from the League of Women Voters deciding how voters have voted, putting holes in perforated ballots with tweezers was an astounding proposition to the Colliers. When they talked their way into the Miami counting room on November 2, 1982, toting video camera with tape rolling, that's exactly what they found. *Prima facie* evidence of tampering, they believed, and Jim started shouting, "Vote fraud! Vote fraud!" for the benefit of the camera. The Colliers were forced out of the room.

Even an average citizen should be a bit unsettled by the prospect of a single consortium providing all the data used by competing news organizations to discern winners and losers in national elections. To Kenneth F. Collier and his equally obsessed older brother James, the possibilities were apocalyptic.

In 1989, the brothers compiled the entirety of their research into 326 pages of manuscript—including a plethora of reprinted memos, clippings, court transcripts, and magazine articles. Their book is called, appropriately enough, *Votescam.* The ordinary person's one chance to take part in democracy, the vote, has been stolen, says the book. Every significant election in the country, the Colliers believe, is fixed. And not by rogue opportunists or even Boss Tweed-style strong-arm "machines," but by a sophisticated web of computer experts, media executives, and political operatives.

Even an average citizen should be a bit unsettled by the prospect of a single consortium providing all the data used by competing news organizations to discern winners and losers in national elections.

The brothers Collier, sons of a Royal Oak, Michigan, businessman, were both journalists. Jim had worked for the *Miami News* (though like so many impoverished reporters, he has already defected to public relations). Ken wrote features for the *New York Daily News.* In 1970 they caught the ear of an editor at Dell Publishing with a book proposal about running a grass-roots political campaign. The main chunk of research, they proposed, would consist of actually running such a campaign. And so Ken decided to take on the venerable Claude Pepper with Jim as his campaign manager and with no fundraising. The whole campaign cost $120 and consisted mainly of gumshoe canvassing, talking to nearly every voter in the eighteenth congressional district.

"It was a random thing that I happened to decide to run in the year 1970," Ken told a radio interviewer in 1988. "But they had never used prognostications like this prior to that time in Florida. And when they did, it seems like we stumbled into the pilot project of the methodology that has since 1970 absolutely, completely, taken over the United States voting system."

The Colliers' revelation came on a date that lives in infamy for them alone: September 8, 1970, in Dade County, Florida.

The events of that day appeared innocent enough. The Democratic party in Dade County held its primary election for the US House seat held by veteran congressman Claude Pepper. Pepper, who remained in Congress up to his death in 1989, was entrenched. He had no Republican opponent. The Democratic primary between Pepper and a hopelessly obscure opponent was *de facto* the final election, and a mere formality even in that regard.

Most voters in Dade County watched the election returns with indifference. There were no big political surprises, least of all in the Claude Pepper race. The dazzling speed and precision of the local stations' projections went largely ignored. Except, of course, by the Colliers, who were mortified.

According to the Colliers, the process used on a limited scale that evening in Miami has been expanded into an Olympian system that allows the three major television networks to "monolithically control"' any election worth controlling—that is, most of them.

"What do they do? They wait 'til the polls close. They announce who's going to win in virtually every race, they announce what percentage these people are going to get. They are virtually *never* wrong. And the key to remember is once you have been named, you can rest assured you will be the winner. And later on, if only these networks can have some sort of mechanism whereby they could make the actual vote turn out the way they projected it nationwide, they would have the same setup they had down in Dade County, where they would announce who won early on, then meddle with the election results later to make sure they turned out that way."

The projections were based on numbers from a single, computerized voting machine.

The shock, to the Collier brothers, came soon after the polls closed at 7:00 PM. Two of Miami's three television news stations projected Pepper the winner almost immediately. Nothing spectacular about that. They could have picked Pepper to win days before the election. What was remarkable were the exact predictions of Pepper's victory margin and of the total voter turnout. At 7:24, one station projected a turnout less than 550 votes away from the eventual count of 96,499. In that same time span, less than half an hour, the stations called several other races on the ballot to within a percentage point of the final totals.

Unbelievable accuracy. But perhaps explainable as a marvel of technology, the genius of statisticians, or at least a mind-boggling stroke of luck. Until a University of Miami professor overseeing the projections announced one other fact: The projections were based on numbers from a single, computerized voting machine. Not one precinct, but one lone machine.

There was a third television station in Miami, but it was reported to suffer a computer malfunction on election night and waited until late in the evening to broadcast election results phoned in from county headquarters. By that time, televisions were off. Dade County received its results not from the courthouse, but from a single machine somewhere. Not even the professor who collected the spewing data knew where that machine was.

Excerpted and adapted from the book Conspiracies, Cover-Ups and Crimes *by Jonathan Vankin (IllumiNet Press, 1996).*

The Rabin Murder Cover-up

Barry Chamish

It took two years before Americans began to suspect that Lee Harvey Oswald did not shoot President Kennedy. It took large sections of the Israeli population less than a week to suspect that Yigal Amir did not shoot the fatal bullets at Prime Minister Yitzhak Rabin. It took me about two hours. Around midnight of November 4, 1995, I asked how Amir could possibly have broken through Rabin's bodyguards to take a clear shot at Rabin's back. My answer was that he couldn't have: unless someone wanted him to.

The next day my suspicions were reinforced by eyewitness testimonies that appeared in the media. After Amir's first shot, one witness after another heard Rabin's bodyguards shout, "They're blanks," "They're not real," and the like. And then, instead of killing Amir on the spot, the same bodyguards let him get off two more rounds. It just didn't add up. The bodyguards are trained to shoot an assassin in less than a second; it would take longer to shout, "They're blanks, they're not real." Why would they think the bullets were duds? Why didn't they kill Amir to save Rabin?

And far more seriously, why did they allow Amir into the so-called sterile security area where only authorized personnel were permitted entrance? The next day, Israel TV broadcast a film clip of Amir being taken away from an anti-Rabin demonstration just two weeks before. Amir was well-known to Rabin's security detail; he was a member of the most extreme anti-Rabin right-wing organization of all, Eyal (an acronym for Jewish Warriors), run by the most extreme right-wing radical of them all, the notorious Avishai Raviv.

Only on November 10, a public accusation was made by (now) Knesset Member Benny Elon that Avishai Raviv was in fact an agent for the General Security Services (Shabak), the very same Shabak charged with protecting Rabin. If people scoffed, it was only for a day. On November 11, respected left-wing journalist Amnon Abramovich broke the truth on Israel's Television One: Raviv was a Shabak officer code-named Champagne, whose duty was to infiltrate groups opposed to the government's peace process and incriminate them in crime. To make his task easier, he created a straw group called Eyal and hyper-radicalized young people, turning legitimate protest into illegitimate outrage. He was the Shabak's chief provocateur.

From that moment on, it was a matter of time before the conspiracy to assassinate Rabin was exposed. The assassin belonged to an organization created by the very Shabak which was charged with protecting Rabin. And that was not all. Amir had spent the spring and summer of 1992 in Riga, Latvia, working with a nest of spies called the Prime Minister's Liaison Office, or Nativ for short. There, the newspapers reported, he had received training from the Shabak.

Yigal Amir was not just a religious kid who got mad one night and shot a prime minister. He had an intelligence background.

Enter: The First Informer

At the time, I was the co-editor of Israel's only intelligence newsletter, *Inside Israel*. My partner was Joel Bainerman. We had both written books, recently published. My book, *The Fall of Israel* (Cannongate Publishers) was about political corruption; his book, *Crimes of a President* (SPI Books), was about the covert and illegal operations that took place during the Bush administration. Combined, we were producing the most honest reporting of Israel's hidden political shenanigans anywhere. We had gained a strong reputation in numerous circles for the exposés of the criminal deceit that lay behind Israel's agreements with the Palestine Liberation Organization (PLO).

And that is why one Moshe Pavlov chose to call me on November 17. His first call was brief: "Watch Channel Two News tonight and you'll see me," he said. "Then I'll call back." He appeared on the news and was described as one of the country's "most dangerous right-wing leaders." Odd, I thought; why hadn't I heard of him before?

The next call wasn't from Pavlov but from my neighbor Joel Bainerman. Though Joel lived in a most obscure location, Pavlov had found his way to Joel's doorstep and appeared unannounced. Joel said, "I don't think we should meet here. I'll see you downtown in ten minutes."

Though he aggressively denies it, all—literally all—of my sources later told me Pavlov is a Shabak agent. In retrospect, there is no other way he could have had the information in his possession if he wasn't an insider. Joel and I sat in a quiet corner of the town square of Bet Shemesh, as a terrified and agitated Moshe Pavlov spewed out reams of, what turned out to be, the truth.

"Amir was supposed to shoot blanks," he insisted. "That's why the bodyguards shouted that he did. He was supposed to. It was a fake assassination. Rabin was supposed to survive the blank bullets, dramatically go back on the podium, condemn the violence of his opponents and become a hero. That's how he was going to save the Oslo Accords. Raviv was supposed to give him the gun with the blanks, but Amir got wind of the plan and changed the bullets."

Pavlov was way off on this point. Later evidence proved beyond doubt that Amir did shoot blanks and that Rabin was shot elsewhere. Pavlov became nearly hysterical. "They're killing people to cover this up, and they're setting me up for a fall. Already one of Rabin's bodyguards is dead."

He gave us the name and details of the bodyguard: Yoav Kuriel. A Yoav Kuriel was reported dead in the media the next day, but of a suicide. It would be another two years before I received his death certificate and spoke with the man who prepared his body for burial. He died of seven bullets to the chest. No one was allowed to identify his remains.

And then Pavlov gave us information that *no one* was allowed to know. To this day, only the man's initials can legally appear in the Israeli media. "The guy behind the operation is Eli Barak, a lunatic. He runs the Shabak's Jewish Department. He is Raviv's superior and set up Amir to take the fall."

He added a fact that was positively unknown at the time. "Barak takes his orders from the head of the Shabak. His first name is Carmi, he lives in Mevasseret Tzion, and that's all I want to say." It took over a year before the Israeli public was to learn the name of the Shabak Chief: Carmi Gillon.

Pavlov was insistent: "You have to publish this and my name. Otherwise I'm finished." Joel and I decided to publish the story in *Inside Israel*. When it came out, I met Pavlov at the Holiday Inn lobby in Jerusalem. We were surrounded by policemen. Wherever he went, they followed. That was good enough proof for me that our faith in Pavlov's version of events was justified.

After Amir shoots, Rabin turns his head in the direction of the shot and keeps walking.

An Assassination Film Emerges

Just under two months after the assassination, to the total shock of the nation, an "amateur" videotape of the murder emerged and was broadcast over Channel Two. Joel taped the film from the television, and we scrutinized it closely. Though we are being petty, to this day we argue over who first noticed the mysterious closing car door.

The story of Rabin's last two hours of life is bizarre now, as it was then. The drive to the hospital should have taken less than a minute. But the driver, Menachem Damti, claimed he became confused, and that's why he got lost and took nine minutes to arrive. After seven minutes driving, he stopped the car and asked a cop, Pinchas Terem, to get in the car and direct him to the hospital. So, only three people were alleged to be in the car until then: Rabin, Menachem Damti (the driver), and Yoram Rubin (the personal bodyguard).

There was a fourth person in the car waiting for Rabin.

In the film all three are clearly outside the vehicle when the right back passenger door was slammed shut from the inside. There was a fourth person in the car waiting for Rabin.

We saw two other shocking moments: The first occurs just before Amir makes his move towards Rabin's back. Rabin's rear bodyguard stops dead in his tracks, turns his head sideways, and allows the "killer" in. The act was deliberate, there was no doubting the film.

And then, after Amir shoots, Rabin turns his head in the direction of the shot and keeps walking. Just like eyewitnesses claimed on the night of the assassination. Rabin was unhurt by Amir's shot to the back. It was a blank bullet after all.

A month later, the government-appointed Shamgar Commission of Inquiry into the Rabin Assassination issued its findings. It concluded that Amir shot twice at Rabin's back, once from 50 centimeters while Rabin was walking, then from about 20 to 30 centimeters after he fell. Very logical, except the film showed that Amir never got anywhere near such close range for the second shot. In fact, he was no closer than six feet away for the second shot.

The contradictions had reached and far surpassed the point of being utterly ridiculous.

The Trial

After the government had already declared him the murderer, Amir stood trial for murder...which lets you know how fair a trial he received. Before the trial began, there was a hearing. When Amir stepped into the courtroom, he shouted to reporters: "The whole system is rotten. If I open my mouth I can bring it all down. The people will forgive me when they know the truth. I didn't think they'd start killing anyone."

After this revealing outburst, he was taken away and never allowed to address journalists again. After a month in Shabak custody, he appeared a different person for his trial: a grinning idiot determined to prove his own guilt. He had been transformed, we surmised, by a combination of threats, promises, sleep deprivation, and drugs.

The trial was barely covered by the media, but what emerged was astounding. Damti and Rubin lied through their teeth. Just for starters, Damti claimed he was opening the door for Leah Rabin (Yitzhak's wife) when the first shot rang out. Then he immediately sat in the driver's seat as he had been trained to do. The truth was that Leah Rabin was 24 feet away and nowhere in sight, and the film showed that Damti did not sit in the driver's seat until Rabin was placed in the car.

And if those statements were mere whoppers, Rubin's version of events was a lollapalooza. He testified that he lay on top of Rabin and that Rabin helped him get up. Then they both jumped headfirst into the car, Rabin landing on the seat, Rubin on the floor. Without elaborating on the depth of the lie, no witnesses saw Rabin jump and the film proves he didn't.

After the trial, I received my first prized secret document—the testimony of Chief Lieutenant Baruch Gladstein of the Israel Police Crime Laboratory, taken from the protocols of Amir's trial. After testing Rabin's clothes scientifically, Gladstein testified that the Prime Minister was shot at point-blank, with the gun's barrel on his skin. He insisted that his conclusion was certain and that the combination of massed gunpowder and an explosion tear on the clothing could only have occurred at zero distance. Even half a centimeter would have been too far.

Amir never, ever shot from point-blank range. He did not kill Rabin. That was enough for me. Gathering the film and the testimonies, I started giving lectures on the Rabin murder conspiracy in Jerusalem, and the crowds who came to hear me were always large.

What liars they were! They broadcast an eight-minute snow job which compared me to a Holocaust denier. And they rebroadcast the show the next night. At first it looked like a disaster for my life. The organizations which had sponsored my lectures were forced to cancel them, cabinet ministers condemned me as a "fascist," and a few threatening crank calls resulted.

However, the program did include the clip of Rabin's car door slamming shut when no one was supposed to be in the car. And a few of my strongest points slipped through loud and clear. Everywhere I went, people congratulated me on my courage. The show boomeranged and ended up encouraging me to carry on.

I was not the only one on the show. A Ramat Gan computer technician named Natan Gefen also appeared briefly with his own proofs. As a result of his appearance, the local Ramat Gan newspaper interviewed him at length about his evidence of a conspiracy behind the Rabin assassination.

One would not believe that Natan Gefen deserves to be recognized as one of the greatest investigators of all time. He doesn't look the part, and by day he operates a computer at a pharmaceutical firm. But Gefen uncovered the most sensitive documents of any political assassination, and here's how he did it.

He made a hundred copies of his interview in the Ramat Gan paper, added his fax number and a request for proof, and placed the package in every corner of the hospital Rabin was taken to, Ichilov. And someone faxed him Rabin's medical records.

What an incredible tale they told! The surgeon who operated on Rabin, Dr. Mordechai Gutman, and his surgical team recorded the following fact: Rabin arrived with two bullet holes in the back, was revived, was shot again, and left with a third bullet which passed through the upper lobe of his right lung from the front and finally shattered dorsal vertebrae five and six.

A researcher on one program told me the idea was to get me on the show to humiliate me, but after reviewing my evidence, she and her fellow researchers concluded that I was right.

Shutting Me Up

In October 1996, I received a phone call from the *Weekend Magazine* program on Channel Two. They had heard about my lectures and also believed there were inconsistencies between the evidence and the Shamgar Commission findings. They wanted to interview me.

The conspiracy was broken. The State Pathologist's report had erased all the wounds the hospital staff reported because Amir never shot from the front and couldn't have. And Rabin could not have had his backbone shattered because the videotape of the murder clearly shows him walking after the only shot to the upper back. Gefen had provided the definitive proof that Amir did not shoot the deadly bullets into Rabin.

Three times, I was invited to appear on major TV programs—once I was even filmed beforehand—and all three times my appearances were cancelled at the last moment. A researcher on one program told me the idea was to get me on the show to humiliate me, but after reviewing my evidence, she and her fellow researchers concluded that I was right. So out I went. On another occasion a producer cancelled not just me, but two other researchers who had reached my conclusions. I was told that someone made a phone call two hours before airtime that turned the tide against us. The third time, the producer called me three hours before showtime with the excuse that he was canceling because no one was willing to debate me. I had no idea until then that a debate was planned.

I have a friend who is a producer for the Voice of Israel, which runs three radio stations. She called me with this message: "You won't believe this. They're distributing a memo at the station forbidding us to ever mention your name. It's from the top. Gotta go, someone's coming."

I have been interviewed by a long list of Israeli journalists who understood my case was right. One after another, their stories and filmed reports were cancelled or badly altered. A case in point: Matti Cohen of Television Two interviewed me for four hours, but his station forbade him to broadcast his findings. So he presented them to Rabin's daughter, now a Knesset member, and she publicly demanded a reinvestigation of her father's murder.

People can't believe it's so easy to control Israel's media. But they're wrong. Perhaps 85 percent of all media influence is in the hands of three families: Nimrodi, Mozes, and Shocken. All have deep intelligence and political ties to the Labor Party and its enforcement arm, the Shabak. News is manipulated on a daily basis. There may be *no* accurate reports about stories of import coming from the Israeli media.

I had to get the true information out, but my lectures were cancelled. Then Joel had a brilliant idea: If your lectures are cancelled, let's rent a hotel auditorium and do one ourselves. On a stormy January night in 1997, over 70 people braved the wet and arrived for the lecture. And Channel One television covered it.

I was back.

Attending the lecture was Brian Bunn, who sat on the Foreign Student's council of the Hebrew University of Jerusalem. He was impressed and booked me to speak at the country's most respected educational institution. This the Shabak could not tolerate, so they organized a violent riot against me. And I must thank them for that because I was front page news for a week in Israel, and the riot was covered worldwide.

Next, a smear campaign was organized against me in the Israeli media, but a few reporters listened to me, read the evidence I had gathered, and wrote long, favorable pieces. And over 300 people contacted me within a week, *all* to congratulate me and some 20 to pass along invaluable information. I was invited to give the same lecture in New York, where I met Jay Sidman, who set up a brilliant Rabin Website for me at <www.webseers.com/rabin>. It turned into a meeting place for an international exchange of ideas and information about the assassination.

A Toronto talk was videotaped and later sold commercially. I was really on that night, and the videotape convinced tens of thousands of people that I was right. And best of all, the publicity led to book contracts, first in America, then in Israel and France. I took care with the book (*Who Murdered Yitzhak Rabin?*), reviews have been excellent, and hundreds of thousands have been swayed by the facts.

Further Vindication

In June 2000, a new book called *Lies: The Rabin Assassination and the Israeli Secret Service* by David Morrison (Gefen Books) lifted the lid off the coffin, and the Israeli media were exposed.

Morrison proves that the Israeli media are in the hands of the Shabak. He does so by referring back to the Bus 300 scandal of 1987. To hide its role in the murder of two shackled terrorists, the Shabak persuaded then-Prime Minister Shimon Peres to call a meeting of the Media Forum—a shadowy organization of media owners—and ordered them to ban release of information about the scandal. All immediately complied. However, a new newspaper, *Chadashot*, was not a member of this cabal and released details of Bus 300. The government ordered the paper shut until its policy changed.

The same tactics and the same personalities are shutting down Rabin murder evidence but are going much further this time around. They are also viciously attacking the advocates of "the conspiracy theory" and deliberately promulgating a fake alternative scenario, one which blames the religious community and its leaders for the murder. Morrison traces and proves this media sub-conspiracy convincingly. And it's about time someone did.

Morrison proves that the Israeli media are in the hands of the Shabak.

He begins by reviewing the only three Rabin conspiracy books available at the time: mine, *Fatal Sting* by Natan Gefen, and *Murder in the Name of God: The Plot To Kill Yitzhak Rabin* by Michael Karpin and Ina Friedman, which was paid for by Peace Now financier David Moshovitz. Of *Fatal Sting*, Morrison regrets that it hasn't been given the notice it deserves. But he has many nice words to say about me:

When this author first heard about Chamish's thesis that Rabin was not killed by Amir, but was killed after he got into the car, he dismissed it out of hand as ridiculous. Who in his right mind would want to believe such a thing? After one examines the data Chamish cites, and verifies that it is, with minor exceptions, accurate, one still does not want to believe it but confronts "difficulties in thought..."

Karpin and Friedman cite Chamish's "convoluted theories" about "the angle of trajectory, the composition of explosives," and those things sound very technical and not very interesting. One could posit that they want to discourage the reader from reading Chamish's book. They do not grapple with the abundance of data cited by Chamish that raises serious questions about the official version of Yitzhak Rabin's murder....

So where is the "plot to kill Yitzhak Rabin?" Karpin and Fiedman do not mention that Carmi Gillon's Shabak agents tortured army officer Oren Edri and a number of other religious settlers and still were unable to uncover any evidence of a religious, right-wing underground....

If we have the whole truth, we may also have proof that Karpin and Friedman and other left-wing, secular elements participated in the cover-up, possibly in an obstruction of justice.

And Morrison is just as good at exposing the lies of a variety of Israeli journalists like Dan Margalit, Yoel Marcus, Hirsh Goodman, and others. The *Jerusalem Report* comes in for special treatment because it actually published a whole cover-up book. *Lies* exposes some of the more blatant falsehoods that the *Jerusalem Report*'s staff must have known about but included anyway, and concludes that only the book's amateurish writing saved it from being accepted as a legitimate account of the Rabin murder.

Morrison's own feeling about the Shabak-orchestrated campaign of lies in the Israeli media is:

The Israeli media will stand exposed as a willing agent of the power structure, or participant in the power structure that has something to hide.

When it does,

Each element of society, each in its own way, will have an opportunity to purge themselves of the corrupt elements in their leadership and choose new leaders to represent them....

One could argue that full disclosure of the truth would only increase the schisms in Israeli society. Another view is that it could have exactly the opposite effect. Instead of exacerbating the splits in Israeli society, it may bring together the many components of the culture. It may unite them together against the common enemy—the elite of all the groups, those with the most to lose if the full truth emerges.

It is hard to say if Morrison's book will lead to media reform, but recently there was an indication of some change. The far-left newsmagazine *Kol Ha'ir* published a three-page article on the phenomenon of an anti-media media determined to get the truth about the Rabin murder out to the nation. It noted that since my book was published, four others reaching similar conclusions have hit the Israeli market. The article noted that lately my work has "become legitimized" by a public seeking new media.

It's small, maybe a one-time fluke, but it's a start. Perhaps the Israeli people, after all, won't permit their mass media to perpetrate a not-believable coverup of the true circumstances of Yitzhak Rabin's murder.

In my next book I may name the culprits: I know who did it. Right now, it's a bit too early for my fellow Jews and Israelis to digest the fact that Rabin was murdered from within his own political circle.

What's Missing from This Picture?

Jim Marrs

Through the years, controversies have continually raged over some of the most painful and traumatic events in United States history.

There have been ongoing arguments over who was behind the assassinations of Abraham Lincoln, John Kennedy, and Robert Kennedy, as well as the truth of what really happened in Waco and Oklahoma City and many more recent events, including the scandals of the Clinton Administration.

The poor public has been buffeted by a barrage of neatly-packaged government pronouncements and by ever-broadening conspiracy theories.

What's missing from this picture?

Only the proof, the hard evidence.

Yes, the information which could prove the truth behind these events has gone missing, and the corporate-controlled news media do not seem overly interested. They appear strangely unable or unwilling to dig into these issues or report them with any clarity. So the public has been left at the mercy of private researchers, many diligent and objective, others less so.

Lincoln

Take the assassination of President Abraham Lincoln, for example. It is an historical fact that Lincoln's death was the result of a large conspiracy involving actor John Wilkes Booth, Confederate agents, a secret society called the Knights of the Golden Circle, and, according to a credible mass of evidence, even persons within Lincoln's own administration.

The body was quickly buried in a prison yard and later sunk in the Potomac River to prevent any possible review.

The facts of this conspiracy may never be fully known since much of the vital evidence in the case went missing. This included the body of the man—identified as Booth—killed in a Virginia barn, as well as eighteen critical pages of Booth's diary.

The body of the man thought to be Booth was hustled to Washington and quickly buried after a physician who had briefly lanced a boil on Booth's neck more than a year earlier first denied the body was Booth but later tentatively made an identification. The body was quickly buried in a prison yard and later sunk in the Potomac River to prevent any possible review.

Booth's diary was taken by Lincoln's Secretary of War, Edwin Stanton, and later released as evidence.

But eighteen pages were missing!

Years later, the missing pages, which incriminated not only Northern Radical Republicans and speculator Jay Gould but Stanton himself, were discovered among Stanton's possessions.

Unfortunately, though, most missing evidence is never found.

Nixon

During the Watergate scandal, it was not eighteen pages but eighteen minutes of recording tape that proved the downfall of President Richard M. Nixon.

"Tricky Dick," as he was being called by his enemies, told a national TV audience, "I am not a crook!" But, after his Oval Office tapes were released, the swear words, racial epithets, and political scheming proved unacceptable to his mainstream supporters. One critical conversation dealing with his foreknowledge of the Watergate break-in was of particular interest to the special prosecutor assigned to this case.

But eighteen minutes on the tape are missing!

Nixon, under threat of impeachment, resigned in disgrace.

Johnson

Missing evidence has become a hallmark of American politics. Apparently the idea is that, circumstances notwithstanding, if there's no proof then there can be no guilt.

An example of this tactic came early in the career of Lyndon B. Johnson, whose entire political life was surrounded by controversy and allegations of criminal behavior.

From the infamous stolen election of 1948 to the murder-for-hire death of a golf pro despised by Johnson for courting his sister, Johnson had come under investigation by several Texas authorities including Frank L. Scofield, then Austin District Collector for the IRS.

Scofield was accused of forcing political contributions from his employees (a minor infraction of the law) just as he had amassed a quantity of evidence against Johnson. Scofield was eventually cleared of this charge, but in the meantime, his replacement placed all of Johnson's files in a Quonset hut in South Austin. Within days, the pre-fab structure mysteriously caught fire and burned to the ground.

Missing evidence has become a hallmark of American politics.

The incriminating evidence became missing!

Johnson, of course, went on to become President upon the assassination of John F. Kennedy.

JFK

The Kennedy assassination, too, is replete with missing data. Not just a few government or intelligence files, but even some of the most vital evidence, including a critical part of Kennedy, is gone.

But Kennedy's brain is missing!

Although Naval Technician Paul O'Connor said Kennedy's cranial cavity was empty when the body arrived at Bethesda Naval Hospital in Washington, autopsy records indicate his brain was routinely sectioned and fixed in formaldehyde. Today, any competent forensic pathologist would be able to determine how many shots penetrated the brain and from which direction they came.

But Kennedy's brain is missing!

Tissue samples from Kennedy's body and color slides of his autopsy, all evidence vital to determining the number and trajectory of the bullets, are also missing. Many files on accused assassin Lee Harvey Oswald and his connection to US intelligence, as well his Civil Air Patrol youth leader and Mafia/CIA pilot David Ferrie, turned up missing. Even a half-dozen frames from the famed Zapruder film of Kennedy's assassination are missing, thus altering the time frame of the film, making it useless as a true timetable of the shooting.

At the time of Kennedy's assassination, nearly his entire Cabinet was high over the Pacific on a flight to Japan. When word came of the Dallas shooting, the powerful passengers onboard dithered for more than an hour while searching for the code book which would have allowed them encrypted communication with Washington.

But the code book was missing!

The Cabinet members finally radioed in using standard open frequencies and were told the situation was under control in Washington.

Newly-released documents from the National Archives, missed by researchers for years, have given the public even further revelations about Kennedy's death.

One of the revelations involved missing words which may have changed the verdict of history. The initial Warren Commission Report stated, "A bullet entered his back at a point slightly below the shoulder to the right of the spine." This statement conformed to both the medical and eyewitness evidence. However, then-Representative Gerald Ford, the only US President appointed to office, directed that the wording be changed to, "A bullet had entered the back of his neck slightly to the right of the spine." This subtle change of wording has allowed champions of the government version of the assassination to argue that a single bullet caused all of Kennedy's body wounds and thus supports the idea that all shots were fired by a lone assassin. This conclusion is untenable when the basic facts behind the report are studied.

In 1999 the National Archives released documents that showed the expensive bronze casket used to transport Kennedy's body from Dallas to Bethesda was unceremoniously and secretly dumped in the Atlantic Ocean in 9,000 feet of water off the Maryland-Delaware coast in early 1966.

The casket had been missing since 1964, and General Services Administration (GSA) officials claimed as late as 1998 that they didn't know what happened to it.

This destruction of evidence reportedly was at the request of the President's brother, Robert. However, the dumping was authorized by then-Attorney General Nicholas Katzenbach, the same person mentioned in an FBI memo from Director J. Edgar Hoover issued just two days after JFK's assassination. The memo read, "The thing I am most concerned about, and so is Mr. Katzenbach, is having something issued so we can convince the public that Oswald is the real assassin." Never mind about a true investigation.

Katzenbach, in a February 11, 1966, letter to the GSA ordering the casket's disposal, stated, "I am unable to conceive of any manner in which the casket could have an evidentiary value nor can I conceive of any reason why the national interest would require its preservation."

One reason might have been that the documents stated the bronze coffin was replaced by a mahogany one because it was damaged.

Damaged? This was a brand-new casket ordered from the Vernon O'Neal Funeral Home in Dallas upon Kennedy's death. After placing the President's body in it at Parkland Hospital, it was loaded into an O'Neal ambulance and taken to Dallas Love Field, where it was carefully loaded onto Air Force One. Upon landing at Dulles Airport, it was lowered to a waiting ambulance by a mechanical lift. When did it become damaged and why?

Another most pertinent reason becomes clear in considering the arguments by many assassination researchers who point to glaring discrepancies in the accounts of JFK's wounds and the disposition of the body between Parkland Hospital in Dallas and the naval hospital where his autopsy was performed by inexperienced military doctors under the close direction of senior military officers.

"I am unable to conceive of any manner in which the casket could have an evidentiary value nor can I conceive of any reason why the national interest would require its preservation."

Parkland witnesses said Kennedy's nude body was wrapped in a sheet and carefully placed in the bronze casket. Several medical technicians at Bethesda said JFK's body arrived there wrapped in a rubber body bag inside a slate-gray military shipping casket.

Through the years, a strong argument has been made for the alteration of Kennedy's wounds while in transit, and the casket could possibly have settled the issue.

But by 1966, the casket, as well as any public discourse on this matter, was missing!

Such missing evidence allowed Ford, today the only surviving member of the Warren Commission, to state repeatedly, "We could find no evidence of conspiracy." It has also allowed various authors, untroubled by this obvious destruction and suppression of evidence, to present a reasonable argument that Oswald acted alone and that any idea to the contrary is simply "conspiracy theory."

RFK

The same pattern of missing evidence was seen in the June 4, 1968, assassination of Robert F. Kennedy, gunned down in the kitchen of Los Angeles' Ambassador Hotel minutes after he had received the California Democratic Primary presidential nomination, which most pundits declared would have cinched his place on the national ticket.

Unlike his brother's assassination, in which no one actually saw Oswald firing a gun, RFK's death was immediately attributed to a nondescript Palestinian named Sirhan Sirhan. Sirhan was in the kitchen firing a .22-caliber pistol and was quickly wrestled to the floor by bystanders including pro football players.

It appeared to be an open and shut case. But then Dr. Thomas T. Noguchi, the world-class county coroner who autopsied RFK, testified under oath that the fatal shot, which entered behind his right ear at a steep upward angle, came from a distance of less than one inch. Sirhan was never closer than about six feet *in front* of the Senator.

However, a private security guard named Thane Cesar was walking by Kennedy's right side. Cesar also was carrying a .22-caliber pistol and according to witness Don Schulman, drew his weapon during the shooting. Cesar's clip-on black necktie apparently was pulled from his shirt as Kennedy fell to the floor and can be seen lying beside the stricken senator in photos.

Cesar, who has admitted drawing his pistol that night but denied shooting RFK, initially said he had sold the .22 pistol shortly before the assassination but later decided he had sold it after the assassination. When the weapon was traced to its new owner, the Arkansas man said it had been stolen in a burglary shortly after Cesar was finally questioned by authorities.

This key piece of evidence is missing!

Other evidence indicated that more than one gunman was involved in the RFK shooting. Sirhan carried an eight-shot revolver. Two slugs were recovered from Kennedy's body, and another five from other victims. An eighth slug passed through ceiling panels. Two additional shots were found in the kitchen's door frame and were actually identified as bullet holes in official LAPD and FBI photos. But LAPD officials, after some foot-dragging, finally admitted they destroyed the door and ceiling panels, and no one could locate records of tests conducted on these extraneous bullet holes.

The evidence is missing!

One news photographer who was in the kitchen had his photos, which might have clarified the matter, confiscated by the LAPD. He fought in court for years to have them returned, fearing they might join an estimated 2,500 RFK-assassination photographs unaccountably destroyed just three months after the event. But when a

When the weapon was traced to its new owner, the Arkansas man said it had been stolen in a burglary.

court ordered his pictures returned, a courier was sent to the state capitol at Sacramento to retrieve them from state archives. They were stolen from his car.

These photos are now missing!

In 1988 Professor Philip H. Melanson surveyed released LAPD files on RFK's assassination and concluded that much of the material, especially that suggesting a conspiracy, had disappeared.

Vietnam

Soon after the assassination of RFK and Johnson's escalation of the Vietnam conflict, the anti-war movement began to gain strength. Its youthful leaders made many attempts to discover from government documents which persons were responsible for the debacle in Vietnam. But, to their chagrin, they found many of the government files detailing our involvement in Southeast Asia, as well as the killing of students by the Ohio National Guard at Kent State, were not available.

They're missing!

Only after Daniel Ellsberg made the Pentagon Papers public did some of the historical holes begin to be filled.

Military Scandals

One stumbling block to investigating military-related issues and scandals was a fire which in 1973 swept through a portion of the National Personnel Records Center in St. Louis, destroying many personnel records. This one fire impeded investigations for years for, while it only affected certain Air Force records, it permitted the federal authorities to plead ignorance of several military whistleblowers.

Their records are missing!

MK-ULTRA

The tactic of disappearing evidence has proved even better than foot-dragging during investigations into government wrongdoing. Former CIA Director William Colby explained that during inquiries into assassination plots during the 1970s, CIA officers warned him that "...Congress could not be trusted with intelligence secrets, that release to it was the equivalent to release to the world at large. And still others...asserted that each item that the investigators requested should be fought over tenaciously and turned over only when there was no alternative."

This "defend the bunker" mentality continued during investigations into the CIA's fatal experiments with mind control.

Carrying forward the work of Nazi psychologists in concentration camps, the CIA's mind control experiments, collectively coded MK-ULTRA, began as far back as 1953. According to author Walter H. Bowart, its purpose was "to devise operational techniques to disturb the memory, to discredit people through aberrant behavior, to alter sex patterns, to elicit information and to create emotional dependence."

Many researchers contend that Sirhan Sirhan is an assassin created by mind control, since he has repeatedly said he cannot remember what happened in the Ambassador Hotel and wrote strange words, including mention of the "Illuminati," in a repetitive manner in his personal notebook. When a horrified public finally learned of the mind-control experiments, some of them fatal to people involved, standard government methodology came into play. Memories faded and filing cabinets were emptied.

Former CIA Director Richard Helms, who admitted not revealing CIA assassination plots to the Warren Commission because he was not asked the right questions, also suffered a lapse of memory regarding mind control. He did recall, however, that a majority of MK-ULTRA documents were destroyed on his orders in an effort to solve a "burgeoning paper problem."

So the crucial documents are missing!

With no paper trail and faulty memories, no one was ever jailed over these criminally harmful experiments.

Pan Am 103

Space does not permit the detailed enumeration of evidence and documentation missing from federal government filing cabinets, safes, and archives.

But one further example would have to be the materials, including a briefcase, recovered by CIA agents following the crash of Pan Am Flight 103 near Lockerbie, Scotland, in December 1988. The agents reportedly were on the crash scene before many rescue workers and firefighters.

Barron's, the mainstream business publication, ran a story in 1990 stating that the flight carried CIA officers and that terrorists had substituted a suitcase-bomb for an identical suitcase containing a CIA-approved heroin shipment. By several reports, as many as eight CIA agents, some of whom reportedly were making an unauthorized return to the United States to blow the whistle on the drug smuggling, were killed in the crash. The story remains in controversy due to lack of evidence.

Of course, the briefcase, reportedly containing proof of the plot, was missing!

TWA 800

In another plane disaster—the crash of TWA Flight 800, which killed 230 people when the Boeing 747 crashed off Long Island on July 17, 1996—missing evidence again became the rule rather than the exception.

Many witnesses said they saw strange lights in the sky and a fiery trail reaching upward from the ground to the plane just prior to the crash. Within 24 hours, Congressman Michael P. Forbes of New York told CNN that the craft's flight data recorder, popularly known as the black box, had been recovered. Federal authorities quickly denied this.

So, during the first critical days, the black box was missing!

Six days later, federal officials acknowledged obtaining the box. But even then, there were signs that data on the device had been altered, according to Kelly O'Meara, a former congressional chief of staff turned journalist.

O'Meara also doggedly sought radar logs for the time of the TWA 800 crash.

Other evidence went missing when FBI agents took pieces of the plane's wreckage to Washington rather than to the National Transportation Safety Board (NTSB), which was charged with investigating the crash.

Officials of the National Transportation Safety Board (NTSB) said the radar data were unavailable—missing!

When the missing data finally turned up, they showed a large number of ships concentrated in the area of the crash, a fact totally contrary to initial government pronouncements that only two military vessels were in the area at the time.

Other evidence went missing when FBI agents took pieces of the plane's wreckage to Washington rather than to the National Transportation Safety Board (NTSB), which was charged with investigating the crash. The families of French passengers killed in the crash hired a lawyer, who argued their belief that US government officials lied about significant facts of the case and were withholding critical documents. Senior NTSB Investigator Henry F. Hughes testified to the Senate Judiciary Committee in 1999 that federal agents and officials tampered with the wreckage, destroyed and altered evidence, mishandled forensic evidence, and failed to establish a chain of evidence in connection with passenger autopsies.

The transcripts containing his statements are missing!

The Senate committee was still withholding transcripts of their hearings as of mid-2000, prompting charges of a cover-up. Even Admiral Thomas H. Moorer, former chairman of the Joint Chiefs of Staff, called for a new investigation, stating, "It absolutely deserves more investigation—a lot more. This time, I wouldn't let the FBI do it. I'd have the NTSB do it. I think Congress certainly should get more answers from the FBI."

Space Photos

Even issues not involving deaths include missing evidence. In May 1963, US astronaut Gordon Cooper became the first human to orbit the Earth an astounding 22 times. In a recent book, he detailed how these early spacecraft carried cameras with telephoto lenses of such high resolution they were capable of taking "some unbelievable close-ups of car license plates." Yet today the low-resolution photos of the notorious "Face on Mars" and anomalies on the moon presented to the public by NASA were made by cameras which cannot seem to focus on anything smaller than the size of a football stadium.

The high-resolution photos are missing!

▪▪▪▪▪▪▪▪▪▪▪

Two events of the 1990s most traumatic to the American public were the 1993 deaths at the Branch Davidian home in Waco and the 1995 deaths caused by the explosion of the Murrah Federal Building in Oklahoma City.

In both instances, the primary evidence should have been the remaining structures, which could have been studied for years by both official and unofficial investigators to determine the truth of those tragedies. But both structures were bulldozed and covered with earth by federal government personnel before any independent probe could be launched. And within hours of the Oklahoma City explosion, work crews were filling in the bomb crater.

The primary evidence became missing!

Waco

The tragically fatal events in Waco began with the February 28, 1993, assault by federal agents on the church home of the Branch Davidian sect near Waco, Texas, and ended with the deaths of 84 persons, including four agents and about 21 children.

The fiery end of a 51-day siege on April 19 followed a full-scale attack, complete with special forces snipers, helicopters, and tanks. Despite repeated claims by the government that the Davidians, under the charismatic leadership of David Koresh, committed suicide and torched their own home, troubling questions continued to be raised for years afterward.

For example, someone—no one seems to know exactly who—ordered the refrigeration unit shut off on the truck containing the

But both structures were bulldozed and covered with earth by federal government personnel before any independent probe could be launched.

burnt corpses of the Davidians. The Texas heat quickly caused such decomposition that it was difficult, if not impossible, for autopsy doctors to determine if bullets, rather than the fire, caused their deaths.

Once again, the best evidence is missing!

The Davidians adamantly charged the federal officers with firing the first shots, while the feds claimed just the opposite. If the feds fired first, then any action taken by the Davidians to protect themselves was permissible under existing law. If the Davidians fired first, then they are guilty of firing on law enforcement personnel in the performance of their duties and arguably brought ruin on themselves. The debate continues to this day, despite the year 2000 seeing a civil court decision and a Justice Department special counsel report absolving the federal government of any responsibility in the deaths.

One item of evidence might have brought out the truth of this issue—one of the bullet-riddled front doors to the Davidian home and church.

But the door is missing!

According to the recent testimony of a Texas state trooper, the door may have been taken by federal agents. Testifying in the wrongful death civil suit brought against the US government by surviving Davidians, Sergeant David Keys testified that he saw an object the size of a door being loaded into a U-Haul truck by federal agents just prior to the crime scene being turned over for security to the Texas Department of Public Safety. The seventeen-year law enforcement veteran also said he saw what appeared to be a body spirited away in a government vehicle and overheard FBI agents telling of a "firefight" at the rear of the home at the time of the fatal fire.

Federal agents have always claimed that no shots were fired at the Davidians after the initial February 28 assault. But then they also claimed that no incendiary devices were used at the time of the fiery destruction of the building. However, after Texas authorities in 1999 announced the presence of pyrotechnic devices in the Waco evidence they were holding for the federal government, the FBI finally acknowledged that "a limited number" of military M651 incendiary rounds were fired during the final assault.

Furthermore, a Texas Rangers report released in 1999 stated that three-dozen spent rifle shell casings were found in an outpost used by federal agents during the siege. Although a government spokesman claimed the casings were left over from the initial assault, others saw the late arrival of this report as suppression of evidence.

Lead Davidian attorney Michael Caddell argued that photographs, some taken by Texas troopers and turned over the FBI, as well as others, could have established who started the fatal fire in the Davidian home.

But the photographs are missing!

"The pattern of the photographs produced [in the civil trial] by the FBI suggests only one thing," said Caddell: "The FBI has turned over only those photographs to the court and the press that the FBI wants the court and the public to see."

Two experts in infrared photography who might have settled the question of whether or not federal agents caused the deaths of the Davidians by pinning them inside the burning home with gunfire were missing from the civil court trial—one stricken by a stroke and the other found dead.

Dr. Edward Allard, who, as a holder of three patents on FLIR (Forward Looking Infrared) technology, had been considered one of the world's leading experts on infrared imaging systems, nearly died from a stroke before he could testify in the Waco civil suit. Allard had analyzed FLIR tapes made by the British Special Air Service (SAS), who taped the final assault while working for the FBI during the 1993 siege. He concluded that the video clearly showed persons firing into the Davidian home/church. He was quoted as saying, "This type of behavior, men running up and down the building, firing automatic weapons into a church is disgusting."

With Dr. Allard out of the picture, the Davidians turned to Carlos Ghigliotti, another infrared expert who had been retained by the US House Government Reform Committee investigating the Waco case.

According to friend and attorney David T. Hardy, Ghigliotti owned Infrared Technologies Corporation and had spent months studying the infrared tapes made by the SAS. Hardy said Ghigliotti had verified nearly 200 gunshots from federal agents on the tape and had said the Waco FLIR would probably be the next Zapruder film.

Someone—no one seems to know exactly who—ordered the refrigeration unit shut off on the truck containing the burnt corpses of the Davidians.

But before the Waco civil case began, Ghigliotti turned up missing!

> "The FBI has turned over only those photographs to the court and the press that the FBI wants the court and the public to see."

Not for long, though. A building manager, concerned that Ghigliotti had not been seen in weeks, notified police in Laurel, Maryland, who discovered Ghigliotti's badly decomposed body in his home, which doubled as his office.

Laurel Police spokesman Jim Collins initially said, "We're investigating it as a homicide." But later, with no signs of a break-in or a struggle, investigators concluded that no foul play had been involved.

There was no apparent foul play either in the sudden death of long-time Waco Sheriff Jack Harwell, one of the only authorities involved in the Davidian siege who offered any sympathy for the religious group. Even while the siege was underway, Harwell consistently stated that he had experienced no problems with David Koresh and his followers in the past. He said whenever he wanted to speak with Koresh, he would call him on the phone and Koresh would come to his office.

According to Clive Doyle, the last Davidian to escape the blazing home, Harwell had called him just prior to the civil trial and said that the death of the Davidian children was starting to weigh on him and asked for a meeting with Doyle to talk about the case and "some other things."

There was no meeting, and the sheriff never testified at the trial. Harwell died of a sudden heart attack.

Whatever he, Ghigliotti, and Allard had to say is now missing!

Washington Times columnist Michelle Malkin summed up the federal government's actions in this case by writing, "They lodged bogus charges of child abuse against Branch Davidians. They denied using incendiary devices during the raid—only to acknowledge having fired at least two flammable tear-gas canisters into the compound. They 'misplaced' audio recordings from infrared footage that demonstrated official government orders to use pyrotechnics. They confiscated—then 'lost'—vital autopsy evidence from the Tarrant County, Texas, coroner's office.

> There was no meeting, and the sheriff never testified at the trial. Harwell died of a sudden heart attack.

"And now they want us to believe that what Mr. Ghigliotti and Mr. Allard separately concluded were gunshots were merely flashes of sunlight and reflections of broken window glass." The major news media dutifully reported the government's version, not realizing that infrared technology measures heat, not light, and that reflected light gives off little heat.

Needless to say, with witnesses dead and hospitalized, as well as documents and some photos and audio recordings missing, it came as no surprise when Federal District Judge Walter Smith in mid-2000 found that while "there may be some indication of mishandling and/or mislabeling by the FBI, there is nothing to indicate that this was the result of anything more than mere negligence."

Judge Smith, after hearing testimony from FBI agents in charge of the infrared taping that clearly indicated tampering with the tapes, decided that an expert hired by the government who disputed this account "was more persuasive."

He also declined to punish the Bureau for failing to hand over documents and other evidence in a timely manner and generally absolved the government of any responsibility in the deaths.

This opinion was echoed about a week later with the release of a preliminary report from John Danforth, who was appointed as a special counsel by Attorney General Janet Reno to investigate the Waco tragedy. While critical of a 1993 Justice Department review of the case stating investigators "went into the project with the assumption that the FBI had done nothing wrong," Danforth nevertheless "fully exonerated" his boss Reno of any wrongdoing in the matter.

Unreported to the public was the fact that Danforth's investigation suffered from the same problem as the others. For example, when a ballistics expert returned to the Tarrant County Medical Examiner's Office to retrieve subpoenaed ballistic records on the Davidians for the Danforth probe, the computer has been emptied.

This crucial evidence is missing!

Nevertheless, at a news conference announcing his preliminary report, Danforth said, "I hope that it lays these questions, the darkest questions relating to Waco, to rest."

But undoubtedly, the many questions raised in this and other cases will not be put to rest by further pronouncements from a government consistently caught in lies and unwilling to take notice of the missing evidence and witnesses.

Oklahoma City

On April 19, 1995, shortly after 9:00 AM a tremendous blast ripped through the Alfred P. Murrah Federal Building, killing 168 people, including many children in the building's day care center, and demolishing one whole side of the structure.

Just 34 days later, over the objections of many people, including Oklahoma Representative Charles Key, Senator James Inhofe, and explosives experts who were already voicing disagreement with the federal government's version of the explosion, the Murrah building was demolished and the rubble hauled away to a guarded, barbwire-enclosed landfill. According to federal officials, it was a "health hazard."

Questions over the destruction of the federal building in Oklahoma City have never been satisfactorily answered.

This is because the best evidence, the building, is missing!

Also missing are the additional bombs reportedly removed from the building just after the initial explosions. In the minutes following the first reports from Oklahoma City, KFOR reported, "The FBI has confirmed there is another bomb in the Federal Building. It's in the east side of the building. They've moved everybody back several blocks, obviously to, uh, unplug it so it won't go off. They're moving everybody back." KWTV also reported another bomb was found in the building and added that a bomb disposal unit had moved into the building. Even Oklahoma Governor Frank Keating told newsmen, "The reports I have is that one device was deactivated and there's another device, and obviously whatever did the damage to the Murrah Building was a tremendous, very sophisticated explosive device."

Keating later would reverse himself, supporting the federal government's contention that one man, Timothy McVeigh, destroyed the building with 4,800 pounds of ammonium nitrate fertilizer and characterizing those who questioned this version as "howling at the moon."

Oklahoma City FBI chief Bob Ricks, who spearheaded the official publicity effort at Waco and was later named head of the Oklahoma State Police by Governor Keating, told the media, "We never did find another device...we confirmed that no other device existed."

Several witnesses, including firemen at the scene, reported two military ambulances were loaded with stretchers containing boxes during the time that spectators and rescue workers were pulled back because, they were told, additional bombs had been found.

Once again, the chief evidence of conspiracy is missing!

Early on, media members talked about the possibility that the bomber or bombers may have been caught on tape by surveillance cameras in the parking lot of a Southwestern Bell office across the street from the Murrah Building. David Hall, manager of TV station KPOC, reported that two Bell employees stated that the tapes showed the Murrah Building shaking before the truck bomb exploded, strong evidence that more than one explosion took place.

The Bell surveillance tapes have never been made available to the public, so are missing from public debate!

The idea that more than one explosion occurred was voiced by several survivors and corroborated by a tape recording made during a conference of the Water Resources Board across from the Murrah Building and by a seismograph at the Oklahoma Geological Survey at the University of Oklahoma. Both recordings indicated large explosions ten seconds apart.

But today this evidence is missing!

The United States Geological Survey released a report stating USGS geologist Dr. Thomas Holzer concluded that the second spike on the seismograph was simply the building's side collapsing. However, Professor Raymond Brown, senior geophysicist at the University of California who studied the seismograph data as well as interviewing victims, argued against the one-bomb theory, saying, "[T]his was a demolition job. Somebody who went in there with equipment tried to take that building down."

Like so many other cases in recent history, foot-dragging and obstructionism on the part of federal authorities prevented any truthful investigation. Representative Key reported that a subsequent federal grand jury was prevented from hearing even one of more than 20 witnesses who saw persons other than McVeigh at the scene of the bombing. "Indeed, the best witnesses who can positively place McVeigh in downtown Oklahoma City that morning, saw him with one or more individuals and are able to describe to some degree what that person or persons looked like. These witnesses were not even allowed to testify at McVeigh's trial," said Key, who added, "...the Federal Grand Jury wanted to interview both the eyewitnesses and the sketch artist who drew John Doe [unknown accomplices] composites but were flatly refused by the federal 'authorities.' Clearly, they were blatantly deprived of their basic constitutional rights as grand jurors. Why?"

The congressman answered his own rhetorical question by stating, "[S]ome in our federal law enforcement agencies (i.e. ATF and FBI) had prior knowledge that certain individuals were planning to bomb the Murrah Federal Building!"

In 1999 Republican Key was defeated by another Republican, and his voice advocating a truthful investigation is now missing.

Danny Casolaro

In the early 1990s one intrepid investigator was on the trail of the conspirators behind many of this nation's recent scandals.

A 44-year-old freelance journalist named Danny Casolaro had been digging into the interlocking nexus of intelligence agencies, arms and drug dealers of the Iran-Contra scandal, the financial criminals of the BCCI bank, Justice Department officials involved in the PROMIS software theft, and connected issues like the October Surprise scandal, covert biological warfare testing, and Area 51. He called this sprawling conspiracy "The Octopus." He told friends that he was close to identifying an international cabal of just a handful of men who were the masterminds behind "The Octopus."

According to close friends, Casolaro kept his "Octopus" files in a large accordion-style file case, which he carried with him at all times. He began growing anxious about his safety, telling his physician brother, "I have been getting some very threatening phone calls. If anything happens to me, don't believe it was accidental."

On the afternoon of August 10, 1991, a cleaning woman found Casolaro's nude body in the bathtub of his Martinsburg, West Virginia, motel room. His wrists had been slashed more than a dozen times. Nearby a scrawled note stated, "Please forgive me for the worst possible thing I could have done."

His death was quickly ruled a suicide, and his body was released to a local mortician, who promptly embalmed the body before contacting the next of kin, an action not only hasty but illegal.

Casolaro's file box, which he took with him to his motel, remains missing!

Vince Foster

On July 20, 1993, the body of President Clinton's friend and attorney Vincent Foster was discovered in Fort Macy Park near Washington, DC. His body was stretched out in a serene posture on a gentle slope. A pistol was still gripped in one hand. He had been shot in the head. Most thought it was a classic suicide pose, although veteran investigators knew that a suicide's muscles flinch with gunshot trauma, and the gun never remains in the victim's hands. However, within days his death was ruled a suicide. But serious questions began to surface until the controversy over Foster's death reached national proportions.

Although his death was attributed to a gunshot wound to the head, an official crime-scene Polaroid seemed to show a small bullet wound in his neck. This was corroborated by Fairfax County EMT Richard Arthur, who worked on Foster's body and claimed to have seen such a hole. Obviously, X-rays of Foster's body would have cleared up this issue.

But X-rays of the body are missing!

Then, perhaps a careful examination of the fatal bullet might shed some light on this case. Investigators and park police conducted an exhaustive search of the park but failed to find any trace of the fatal projectile at the scene or elsewhere.

The bullet is missing!

Investigators turned to the official crime scene photographs, which originally reportedly numbered 30 Polaroids and one roll of 35mm film. Police later listed only thirteen Polaroid photos, only one of which—a close-up of Foster's hand—was later leaked to the public.

The photos are missing!

Park police searched Foster's body and clothing, but his car keys were missing. But in a later search in the morgue, his keys turned up in his pants pocket. In another peculiar circumstance, six days after the death, Associate White House Counsel Stephen Neuwirth discovered a shredded, handwritten "suicide" note in Foster's office briefcase. (His briefcase had already been checked twice before, but no note had been found during those searches.) The FBI lab found no fingerprints on the note despite the fact that it was torn into 27 pieces. Toward the bottom right-hand corner, where one would expect to find a signature, there was a gap.

The critical piece was missing!

Although the FBI concluded the note was genuine, three separate first-class forensic handwriting experts—Reginald E. Alton, Vincent Scalice, and Ronald Rice—all reported that it was a clever forgery.

"Freak things can happen in any violent death. But the laws of nature cannot be suspended and inconsistencies don't range into the dozens, as in this case."

Scalice, formerly a veteran NYPD homicide detective, stated, "Freak things can happen in any violent death. But the laws of nature cannot be suspended and inconsistencies don't range into the dozens, as in this case."

Foster's death was only the beginning of the scandals and improprieties of the Clinton Administration.

Ron Brown

On April 3, 1996, Commerce Secretary Ron Brown and 34 other passengers onboard a T-43 military transport plane died when the craft crashed into the rocky hills of Croatia. With Brown were other government officials, twelve corporate chiefs, a CIA analyst, and a *New York Times* bureau chief.

The major media reported that Brown's plane went down in the Adriatic Sea during "the worst storm in a decade." Yet the Dubrounik Airport, less than two miles from the actual inland crash site, reported only light scattered rain with five miles visibility. Several other planes landed safely immediately before and after Brown's plane crashed.

Brown, at the time of his death, was the object of an investigation by an independent counsel appointed by a three-judge panel in the wake of a lawsuit by Judicial Watch. This case had already uncovered the illegal campaign contributions of John Huang, prompting a minor scandal. According to Judicial Watch head Larry Klayman, "...Brown had told President Clinton days before he was asked unexpectedly to travel to Croatia that he would negotiate a plea agreement with the independent counsel, which would entail telling the independent counsel what he knew about alleged illegalities in the Clinton-Gore administration."

The suspicions over the crash could have been ended by studying the cockpit voice and flight data recorders, the black box. When Prime Minister Zlatko Matesa of Croatia said a voice recorder had been recovered from the tail of Brown's plane and offered to turn it over to US officials, Air Force officials declined, saying that the converted training plane had not carried such equipment.

The black box remains missing!

The White House and the mass media reported that Brown died in the plane crash, but two members of the Armed Forces Institute of Pathology reported that he had a large hole in his head. Air Force Lieutenant Colonel Steve Cogswell and Army Lieutenant Colonel David Hause both said the hole was consistent with a bullet wound. Their conclusion was supported by veteran pathologist Dr. Cyril Wecht. This question of homicide could be resolved by simply checking the photos and X-rays of the body.

Brown, at the time of his death, was the object of an investigation by an independent counsel appointed by a three-judge panel in the wake of a lawsuit by Judicial Watch.

But they're all missing!

White House Email

Illegal campaign finances, Whitewater, Travelgate, Chinagate, Filegate...the list of Clinton Administration scandals goes on and on. How can the investigators of the various ongoing probes get to the truth?

One such probe, the Justice Department's campaign-finance task force, decided to look at White House email for clues and evidence. Congress also wanted the emails. Imagine their surprise when they found that a mysterious malfunction of a critical White House Office email server caused some emails not be to archived.

Robert Haas, a computer contractor from Northrop Grumman assigned to audit the missing email, was among the technicians who discovered that the White House automated archiving system had failed to scan and store email sent to the server by the Executive Office.

Almost a million West Wing emails are missing!

These missing emails, initially reported to number only about 100,000, include messages to prominent White House officials, including President Clinton himself, according to reporter Paul Sperry of WorldNetDaily. Other missing messages came from the Democratic National Committee. Recipients of the lost email include Clinton's secretary Betty Currie, whose email reportedly included 400 to 500 messages from Monica Lewinsky in just one file.

"When I heard the number, I couldn't believe they talked that much," said one of the computer contractors involved. "They must have been busy typing all day long. I don't know if they did any work."

Other investigators were more concerned about serious scandals. Sheryl Hall, a former manager in the White House's Information Systems and Technology Division, said she learned that within the missing email were "smoking guns" to many contentious issues. Hall told WorldNetDaily that "different people...would go to jail. And that there was a lot of stuff out there." This "stuff" involved illegal campaign finances, as well as the involvement of Vice President Al Gore in some of the controversies.

"Every White House aide whose name has popped up during the parade of scandals was on that server," noted one investigator. "And those that helped them do their jobs."

Technicians learned that of the 526 persons whose email went missing, 464 of them worked in the White House Office. Someone suggested that perhaps a study of Gore's email might provide a clue as to why so much information had been lost.

But all of Gore's office email from that period is missing!

The Final Missing Piece

There is enough information available today regarding missing information and evidence to fill an entire book, a sad commentary on justice in America.

The public must summon the will to demand truth and honesty from their elected leaders and from federal authorities who seem to feel they are above the laws and ethics imposed on the rest of us.

But that will seems to be missing!

THE SOCIAL FABRICATION

Don't Blame Your Parents
An Interview with Judith Rich Harris

When *The Nurture Assumption: Why Children Turn Out the Way They Do* was published in 1998, a lot of heads turned quickly. Seemingly out of nowhere, Judith Rich Harris—a former author of psychology textbooks on child development—unleashed a theory that has the potential to change not only the way we view parents and children but also the way we view ourselves. Hers is not an abstract theory. It hits us where we live, because each of us is the child of two parents, and some of us were raised by step-parents, adoptive parents, or grandparents in addition to two, one, or no biological parents. People who are themselves parents get hit with a double whammy, since Harris' revolutionary idea alters their beliefs not only about their own parents but also about their own children.

Psychologists, reporters, and other people couldn't believe that this theorist—who doesn't even have a Ph.D. behind her name—strolled up and told us that almost everything we think we know about parents' effects on their children is wrong. To top it off, she had a lot of evidence to back her up, which she presented with fierce intelligence and a witty writing style. The insular world of child development studies was rocked. The mainstream media caught on, and lots of articles and interviews followed. The *New York Times* listed *The Nurture Assumption* as a notable book. It was nominated for the Pulitzer Prize in nonfiction.

By the time I interviewed Harris via email in August 2000, most of the furor had died down, but the deeper effects of her theory hadn't. No developmental psychologist can legitimately continue researching and theorizing without taking into account her thesis. More importantly to the rest of us, we can no longer whine about how our parents raised us, blaming them for our faults, nor can the parents among us worry themselves sick about whether they're doing everything possible to create the next Florence Nightingale and Albert Einstein rolled into one. No wonder *The Nurture Assumption* shook everybody up!

Russ Kick: I think the best way to start out is by asking you to summarize your groundbreaking thesis (or, judging by the reactions it's triggered, earthquaking thesis) at the heart of your book, *The Nurture Assumption*.

Judith Rich Harris: Most people believe that children's psychological characteristics are formed by a combination of "nature"—meaning their genes—and "nurture"—meaning the way their parents bring them up. The "nature" part of that statement is unquestionably true. It's the "nurture" part I disagree with. The evidence I've put together in my book indicates that parents have little or no long-term effect on their children's personality, intelligence, or mental health. The *environment* definitely has an effect on how children turn out, but it's not the *home* environment. It's not the nurture they do or don't get from their parents.

The evidence I've put together in my book indicates that parents have little or no long-term effect on their children's personality, intelligence, or mental health.

That's the first half of my thesis—what you called the "earthquaking" part. The second half—I call it group socialization theory—is my answer to the question, Well, if it isn't the home environment, what environment is it? My answer: the environment children share with their peers.

Oddly enough, it's the controversial part of my thesis that is well-supported by evidence. The second part, group socialization theory, is much more speculative. It's consistent with the existing evidence but as yet largely untested. It will take new research, using better research techniques, to test it.

RK: So the evidence indicates that parents have no important effects, in the long run, on the way their children turn out? If that's true, why hasn't anyone noticed it before? Why does almost everyone believe that parents do have important effects?

JRH: Several reasons. The primary one is that most children are reared by their biological parents—the same people who gave them their genes. About 50 percent of the variation in personality traits is genetic, which means that for genetic reasons alone, children have many of the same faults and virtues as their parents. Heredity can

> About 50 percent of the variation in personality traits is genetic, which means that for genetic reasons alone, children have many of the same faults and virtues as their parents.

explain why "dysfunctional" parents tend to have "dysfunctional" kids. But the effects of heredity are generally underestimated, and children's successes and failures are assumed to be due to the way they are treated by their parents.

To test that assumption, you have to use research methods that provide a way to control for the effects of genes. When researchers do that, the similarities between parents and children disappear. Adopted children, for example, do not resemble their adoptive parents in personality or intelligence. On the average, once you control for genetic effects, the children of sociable parents are no more (or less) sociable than the children of introverts, and the children of tidy parents are no more (or less) tidy than the children of slobs.

Another reason for the belief in the efficacy of parenting has do with what I call "context effects." According to my theory, children learn separately how to behave in each of their environments. Children don't blindly generalize from one context to another—their behavior is a function of what they've experienced in *that particular context*. If the behavior they learned at home turns out to be inappropriate outside the home—and this is often the case—they drop the home behavior and learn something new.

> In fact, there is very little correlation between how children behave with their parents and how they behave with their peers.

I've never questioned the fact that parents influence how their children behave at home—what I question is that the children take these behaviors with them to school or the day-care center or the playground. In fact, there is very little correlation between how children behave with their parents and how they behave with their peers—a child may be obnoxious with his parents, pleasant and cooperative with his peers, or vice versa. Even more surprising, there is very little correlation between how children behave with their *siblings* and how they behave with their peers.

RK: Let's take an extreme example based on your thesis. Assuming that we could magically control for factors like genetics, time, and location, you're saying that children of Eva Braun, Mother Teresa, Madonna (the pop star), and the Madonna (the Virgin Mary) would all turn out pretty much the same if they had basically the same set of peers?

JRH: Actually, we *can* control for factors like genetics, time, and location, though not, alas, with Madonna (either one). Nature has allowed us to perform exactly the experiment you've suggested, by providing us with identical twins. Identical twins have the same genes; usually they are reared in the same home at the same time; and they have basically the same set of peers (identical twins often belong to the same peer group). And yet there are noticeable differences between them in personality. This is one of the mysteries that inspired me to think up a new theory: not the fact that twins separated at birth and reared in separate homes are so similar, but the fact that twins reared in the *same* home are much less similar than you would expect!

There are personality differences, not due to genes, between twins or siblings reared in the same home, and group socialization theory can explain them. According to my theory, the things that happen within peer groups not only create or increase similarities among the members—they also create or widen certain kinds of differences. The kids become more alike in some ways (due to a process called assimilation) and *less* alike in others (due to differentiation).

Assimilation is the way children are socialized—how they acquire the behaviors and attitudes that are appropriate for their culture. But personality development, I believe, is more a function of differentiation. Groups sort people out. The members of groups differ in status and in the way they are typecast or labeled by the others. This is true even for identical twins who belong to the same peer group: One might be characterized as the bold one, the other as the shy one, for instance. Or the other members might address their comments and questions to one twin rather than the other—a sign that they regard that twin as the dominant one. If such differences in status or typecasting are persistent, I believe they can leave permanent marks on the personality.

So the answer to your question is no. If we could clone the people you named and give them the same set of peers and so on, according to my theory they probably wouldn't turn out the same.

RK: The theory seems so incredibly counterintuitive. Looking at parents and children around me, and thinking back on my own childhood, it seems to go without saying that parents have drastic effects on who children become. Some of this impression is, as you've pointed out, due to genetics and to context effects, but you've also described other factors that contribute to the impression that parents mold their children. An example is what you've called "child-to-parent effects"—the overlooked fact that often it's the children who mold their parents' behavior, rather than vice versa. Please discuss how these effects work.

JRH: Yes, you're right—child-to-parent effects are another reason why the parents are held responsible for the way the child turns out. People notice that children who are treated nicely by their parents tend to turn out better than children who are treated harshly, and they jump to the conclusion that the good treatment caused the good outcome. But it could be the other way around. An amiable, cooperative child is likely to receive affectionate parenting—it's easy to be nice to a child like this. A surly or defiant child, on the other hand, is likely to be treated harshly. The parents find that reasoning with this child doesn't work and end up losing their tempers.

The failure to take account of child-to-parent effects is particularly flagrant among researchers who study adolescents. They've found, for example, that teenagers whose parents monitor their activities get into less trouble than teenagers whose parents fail to keep track of them. Therefore, the researchers conclude, it must be the parents' fault if the teenager gets into trouble—the parents didn't monitor the kid carefully enough. But did you ever try keeping track of the whereabouts of a kid who is determined to outwit your efforts to do so? A kid who wants to do things he knows his parents wouldn't approve of can always find ways to evade parental supervision. The parents of well-behaved teenagers don't realize how much their ability to monitor their kids' activities depends on the kids' willingness to cooperate with them.

Pretty soon these children will be trying to talk to their parents in English, even if their parents continue to address them in Russian or Korean.

The same error is made by the people who advise parents to talk to their kids about drugs and sex, because kids whose parents don't do this—or, more accurately, kids who *tell* researchers that their parents don't do it—are more likely to use drugs and have sex. Aside from the fact that it's always risky to take what respondents tell you at face value, have you ever tried talking to a sullen or contemptuous teenager about the hazards of drugs or sex?

RK: When a friend of mine first told me about your book, I have to say that it basically fried my brain circuits. It was very tough to wrap my head around, although now that I've read the book, I have to admit that I'm quite convinced of your theory. However, after reading your previous responses, there are undoubtedly some readers who are having the same reaction I originally had. Please lay out one or two of the most convincing pieces of evidence that support your theory.

JRH: I think the most convincing evidence comes from the study of language and accents. Most of the behaviors that people observe in children are influenced both by their genes and their experiences, so it's very difficult, without using special methodology, to figure out what's going on. But children don't inherit a tendency to speak English or Russian or Korean, and they don't inherit their accents. So looking at language gives us an easy way to eliminate the effects of genes. The first thing we notice is that most children speak the same language as their parents, which turns out to be another of those misleading observations. It's misleading because most children are reared by parents who speak the same language as everyone else in their community. The children's two environments are in harmony, so you can't tell which one is having the effect. You have to look for cases in which the environment of the home conflicts with the environment outside the home. What happens when children are reared by parents who speak a *different* language from the one that's used outside the home?

What happens is that children learn their parents' language first. Then, when they go outside and encounter other children who are using a different language, they quickly pick up that second language as well. Usually they go through a period where they'll switch back and forth between the two languages, using their parents' language at home and their peers' language outside the home. The interesting thing is that there's no carryover from the home language to the outside-the-home language, no blurring together of contexts. Unless they were past elementary-school age when they encountered their second language, they will speak it without a foreign accent.

What happens next is that the outside-the-home language will gradually supplant the home language. Pretty soon these children will be trying to talk to their parents in English, even if their parents continue to address them in Russian or Korean. English will become their "native" language—the language they'll think in, the language they'll speak as adults.

The example of language shows that parents have a powerful effect on the children's *early* behavior, but in the long run it's what the children experience outside the home—in particular, what they experience in the company of their peers—that determines the ultimate outcome. (I know it's the peers' language that matters, rather than the language of the adults in their community, because there are cases in which the children of a community speak a language that is different from the adults'.)

RK: I think it's important to note that you say parents can and, indeed, do affect their children's behavior and personality when the children are with their parents. But you maintain that how they act with their parents not only doesn't generalize to the rest of the world but it also doesn't affect who they are when they grow up. How can this be?

JRH: I think this is how children were designed by evolution. After all, what's childhood for? It's preparation for the future. Parents aren't the future—parents are the past! In order to be successful as an adult, a child has to figure out what works best in the world that he or she is destined to inhabit in adulthood. They will share that world with their peers, not (at least under the conditions in which our species evolved) with their parents.

The nurture assumption is a creation of the twentieth century.

RK: It's interesting to note that not all time periods and cultures have held the belief that parents are crucial in determining their children's course in life. In fact, most didn't/don't believe that, including America up to the 1930s. What does this tell us about the nurture assumption?

JRH: Quite true: The nurture assumption is a creation of the twentieth century. Freud has a lot to answer for. In other cultures, and in previous generations of our own culture, parents were given condolences, not blame, if their children didn't turn out as hoped.

Consider the changes in child-rearing styles that have occurred just within the past century. I was born in 1938, and when I was growing up it was considered perfectly all right for a parent to strike a child with a weapon such as a belt or a ruler—some parents even kept a suitable object specifically for that purpose! Kisses and hugs were administered sparingly in those days, and declarations of parental love were made only on the deathbed.

A generation later, when I was rearing my children, it was no longer considered all right to strike a child with a belt or a ruler, but it was still okay to give them an occasional swat on the seat of the pants. Hugs, kisses, and declarations of parental love were more common.

Now, another generation later, it's no longer considered okay to hit children at all—my 4-year-old granddaughter has never experienced any kind of physical punishment—and the words "I love you" have become as common as "please" and "thank you."

If the experts were right, wouldn't you think that such drastic changes in child-rearing methods would produce a better product? But there are no signs that children are happier or less aggressive today than they were when I was growing up; there are no signs that they have higher self-esteem. Rates of childhood depression and suicide have gone up, not down, over this period. And yet the experts continue to claim that if parents would only follow their instructions to the letter, their children will turn into happy, well-adjusted people. Happy, well-adjusted, and *smart*!

RK: In your research, you've also studied other factors that are supposed to influence children's development and mold who they become. In particular, can you briefly comment on birth order?

JRH: Birth order is an interesting question, because most people believe that it has important effects on personality. The idea is that firstborns, because of their special place in the family—the fact that they've had their parents all to themselves for a while, the fact that they can dominate their younger siblings—have personality characteristics that differ, on the average, from laterborns. But objective evidence does not support this widespread belief. Studies in which personality tests are given to large numbers of subjects do not show consistent differences in personality as a function of birth order. Similarly, if you look at educational achievement, you find that (contra the usual stereotypes) laterborns are not more likely to be underachievers or dropouts, and firstborns are not more likely to graduate from high school and go to college.

On the other hand, there is no question that birth order influences the way people behave with, and feel about, their siblings and their parents. But this is a context effect—these behaviors and feelings are left behind when people leave home. This is true even in childhood. Research has shown that laterborns who are dominated at home by older siblings are no more likely than firstborns to allow themselves to be dominated by their peers. Which makes sense, from an evolutionary point of view. Why should a child who is dominated by his siblings be handicapped by the notion that he's going to be dominated everywhere he goes? This child might turn out to be the largest and strongest in his age group!

The reason why the belief in birth order effects is so prevalent is that we don't know the birth orders of most of the people we meet—we know the birth orders only of relatives and close friends, and of the children of our friends and neighbors. These are the people we are most likely to see in the presence of their parents and siblings. We see the way they behave with their parents and siblings and assume that they behave that way in other contexts, too. But they don't! Outside of the context of the family they grew up in, firstborns and laterborns are indistinguishable.

RK: Tell me about the reactions your book has caused. What were some of the immediate and longer-term reactions?

JRH: There was quite a lot of response to the book—from the media, from members of the academic world, and from ordinary people who wrote to me in email or postal mail. The mail from the public was overwhelmingly favorable; many people told me that I had made parenting seem less burdensome—less fraught with anxiety—or that I had explained some mystery about their own childhood.

The media response was vigorous but mixed. There were many published essays by writers who absolutely hated what I was saying. They seemed to feel that if people believed my message, it would be

They seemed to feel that if people believed my message,
it would be the end of civilization as we know it.

the end of civilization as we know it. Parents, once they learned that trying hard wouldn't necessarily make their children turn out better, would surely let them die of neglect! Another criticism—usually made by journalists who hadn't actually read the book—was that my theory was an oversimplification and things were really much more complicated than I had made them out to be. But there were also plenty of open-minded journalists who felt that my book was interesting and enlightening, and who approved of my criticisms of the research methods commonly used in the field of child development.

The reception from the academic world was also mixed. In general, social psychologists, evolutionary psychologists, and behavioral geneticists tended to be favorable; clinical psychologists tended to be unfavorable. Developmental psychologists, by and large, were outraged. Not surprising, since I was saying that the entire careers of many of them were built upon a falsehood and that they'd have to start all over from square one. This, coming from a nobody like me, who doesn't even have a Ph.D. or an academic appointment! (I do have some graduate training in psychology, but Harvard kicked me out without a Ph.D. Before I had the idea that led to *The Nurture Assumption*, I spent many years as a writer of textbooks for college courses in child development.)

But aside from their efforts to discredit me by pointing out my lack of credentials, the developmental psychologists have been remarkably ineffectual. Journalists kept interviewing prominent members of the field and asking them what they thought of my book, and they'd say things like, "There are lots and lots of studies that Harris has ignored and that prove she's wrong!" But generally they didn't name specific studies. When specific studies have been named, I've examined them and found them to be full of holes.

Let me give you a couple of examples. Here's a quote from an article in *Newsweek* (September 7, 1998):

> [M]any of the nation's leading scholars of child development accuse Harris of screwy logic, of misunderstanding behavioral genetics and of ignoring studies that do not fit her thesis. Exhibit A: the work of Harvard's [Jerome] Kagan. He has shown how different parenting styles can shape a timid, shy child who perceives the world as a threat. Kagan measured babies at 4 months and at school age. The fearful children whose parents (over)protected them were still timid. Those whose parents pushed them to try new things—"get into that sandbox and play with the other kids, dammit!" lost their shyness. (Begley, 1998, p. 56)

What Kagan is evidently referring to here is a study by one of his students, Doreen Arcus. Arcus reported her results in 1991, in her doctoral dissertation. She followed 24 timid babies (that is, babies whose test results at the age of four months indicated that they might turn out to be timid) to the age of 21 months—not to school age, as reported in *Newsweek*. The mothers who were less indulgent—who held their babies less and who used firmer methods of discipline—had babies who were less likely to be timid at 21 months.

This study has never been published in a peer-reviewed journal. Kagan described it in a 1994 book—a book in which he summarized his fifteen years of research on timid children—but he didn't give the details. It was, by the way, the only evidence he offered in that book to support his belief that the right kind of child-rearing style can prevent a nervous infant from turning into a timid child.

If there have been any follow-ups of these 24 children, to check on whether the results found at age 21 months held up when the children were retested at school age, they haven't been reported in the child-development literature. This is not, by the way, the only case I have found in which evidence used against me turned out to be nonexistent or at least unpublished.

Here's my second example—another quote from the same *Newsweek* article:

> "Intervention" studies—where a scientist gets a parent to act differently—also undercut Harris. "These show that if you change the behavior of the parents you change the behavior of the kids, with effects outside the home," says John Gottman of the University of Washington. (Begley, 1998, p. 56-57)

Well, that worried me, because if it were true it would indeed be very good evidence against my theory. My theory predicts that if you change the behavior of the parents, you can change the way the children behave *at home*, but it won't affect the way the children behave outside the home—in school, for example.

So I did a thorough review of published intervention studies. The conclusion I came to was the same as that expressed by Michelle Wierson and Rex Forehand in an article in a psychology journal. Wierson and Forehand (Forehand is a leading figure in the field of intervention studies) reported that parent training interventions, in which parents are taught better ways of getting their children to listen to them, can improve the way the child behaves in the presence of the parents. "However," the researchers admitted, "research has been unable to show that child behavior is modified at school." Which is exactly what my theory predicts, and quite different from the claim made in the *Newsweek* article.

RK: What's next for you? Are you still concentrating on this theory, or are you tackling something else?

Some developmentalists seem to have the idea that even if what I'm saying is true, the public shouldn't be told about it.

JRH: I've been writing articles for psychology journals—mostly critiques of the work of traditional developmental psychologists. In my next article, I plan to illuminate the defects in developmental research by comparing it to medical research. Over the years, medical researchers have developed elaborate procedures to guard against experimenter bias and other sources of spurious results. These procedures are seldom used in psychology; most developmentalists have never heard of them, and consequently their studies are riddled with methodological errors.

The problem is that no one bothers to question the methodology if the results turn out the way they're expected to. That's why it's so important, in science, to put aside prior assumptions and ideology. There are important questions that require answers based on solid science—for example, if parent training interventions don't make children behave better in school, what kind of interventions do make children behave better in school? One reason there has been so little progress in answering such questions is that most of the research time and money has been spent on futile efforts to confirm the researchers' assumptions.

Worse still, some developmentalists seem to have the idea that, even if what I'm saying is true, the public shouldn't be told about it, because it would be bad for parents to think that what they do for their kids doesn't matter. Well, that's not what I'm saying—I've never said that parents don't matter, only that they don't have long-term effects on their children's personalities. But let's not split hairs. If what I'm saying is true, do the developmentalists have the right to say that people shouldn't be told about it? Do they have the right, or even the knowledge, to decide what's best for people?

References

Begley, S. (1998, Sept. 7). The parent trap. *Newsweek*, pp 52-59.

Wierson, M., & R. Forehand. (1994). Parent behavioral training for child noncompliance: Rationale, concepts, and effectiveness. *Current Directions in Psychological Science*, 5, pp 146-150.

The Female Hard-on

Tristan Taormino

The Lower East Side chicks from Toys in Babeland hosted a big bash a few weeks ago at the feisty dyke club Meow Mix to celebrate the National Masturbate-a-Thon. That's right—instead of walking or running, participants gathered pledges and collected cash for each minute they spent pleasuring themselves. All proceeds from this jack- and jill-off fest and the finish-line party went to From Our Streets With Dignity (FROST'D), a nonprofit that provides health and social services to one of the hardest-working and most overlooked groups of women—sex workers on New York City's streets. As a Toys in Babeland consultant, I had the honor as mistress of ceremonies to welcome local performers, who each did their part to applaud all the folks who "came for a cause."

Instead of walking or running, participants gathered pledges and collected cash for each minute they spent pleasuring themselves.

The evening's festivities culminated with the Fraggle Rock House Band's tribute to songs about self-loving, and I found myself on the dance floor sandwiched between slices of sexy, sweaty, horny girls. As the band belted out a Joan Jett song ("Do you wanna touch? Yeah! Do you wanna touch? Yeah! Do you wanna touch me there? Where?"), girls were bumping and grinding with gusto. Strangers rubbed their drenched bodies up against mine, fingers stroked my flesh from every direction. It was a wild, wild night.

Although I was riding the high that came with the knowledge (and firsthand experience) that sex in the city is thriving, my spirits were slightly dampened when I picked up the recent *Newsweek* with the "Science of Women's Sexuality" cover. Next to a photo of a woman in the throes of passion are the words: "Searching for the Female Viagra: Is It a Mind or Body Problem?" Fueled by the success of Viagra in treating male sexual dysfunction, scientists have turned to the sexual problems of women. But what promised to be an informative article turned out to be a muddled mess that reinforced just how little scientists know about women and sex. I found it especially telling that the report was written by a man.

The bad news is that in the most recent study of the effects of the super blue pill on women, Viagra was no more successful than a placebo in women with a wide variety of sexual dysfunction symptoms. We've given all the men supercharged erections but haven't had any luck when it comes to women's erotic woes. I am tempted to say: Who needs Viagra when we've got Meow Mix? But the truth is that 40 percent of American women experience some form of sexual dysfunction. It's actually a bigger problem than it is for men (30 percent suffer from some form of dysfunction), and yet all the money and research has focused on the boys. In part, this is typical of a

We've given all the men supercharged erections but haven't had any luck when it comes to women's erotic woes.

misogynist industry that has always geared research toward males. But there is another reason that the fairer sex has again gotten the short end of the stick: Men's sexual problems (including erectile dysfunction) just seem much easier to solve than the complex, layered issues surrounding women's sexual dysfunction.

Concerned that medication I was taking was diminishing my libido, I queried my doctor about it. He asked if I could still get turned on and come, to which I replied yes, but I was worried that my sex drive had nearly disappeared. "If you can achieve orgasm, then there is no sexual dysfunction." Gee thanks, doc. I tried to explain that if Tom Cruise walked in with his flight jacket from *Top Gun*, a freshly shaved asshole, and a raging hard-on, I just wouldn't feel anything. Even if Nicole Kidman joined him—with a huge strap-on between her legs, nipples perked up like mini-torpedoes, and a double-ended vibrator with unlimited juice—still nothing. Now, if neither member of this supercouple—nor both—can get my juices flowing, well, something's wrong. Isn't it? According to this doctor (and plenty of others), no.

The doctor's dismissal of my problem is symptomatic of a medical industry that not only is clueless about women's sexual dysfunction, but barely knows what's going on with female sexual *function*. The truth is, there are many different forms of female sexual dysfunction. Some women have little or no desire to have sex. Others have trouble getting aroused or can't get turned on at all. Others cannot achieve orgasm, and others experience pain during sex. Some women have a combination of these symptoms. For me, while on this medication, after we got into it and I had my tongue on Tom's butthole and Nic's slim fingers in my pussy, I'd get into the groove and shoot my load. I'd just have trouble getting revved up in the first place.

How can we expect to figure out how to fix the leak when we don't know how the plumbing works in the first place?

On the subject of the Big O, the *Newsweek* article gets even more infuriating. Pondering the evolutionary benefits of the female orgasm, a pull quote teases—"One possible theory: orgasms in women have no function and are just a developmental vestige, like male nipples." First of all, why are we wasting time, money, and column-width on debating the importance or necessity of the female orgasm? It's just more misogynist bullshit, if you ask me. (And on the subject of male nipples, try telling all the men who appreciate having theirs tweaked and squeezed and clamped that they have no function.)

To understand why some of us have an easy time of it and others don't, we first have to understand sex and girls: female sexual anatomy (folks still can't agree on how big or far-reaching the clitoris is); desire and the experience of arousal and pleasure; the complexities of the female orgasm; plus, the emotional and psychological aspects of sex and how they play a role in arousal and satisfaction. You see, we don't even have the 411 on this stuff, so how can we expect to figure out how to fix the leak when we don't know how the plumbing works in the first place?

I will say it again—we need more research, folks. There are promising options on the table beyond Viagra: other drugs that work for men being tested on women, several creams designed to increase blood flow to the vagina and clitoris, a testosterone patch that seems to increase sex drive but has problematic side effects. The most interesting little item in the *Newsweek* article was a new, recently FDA-approved device called EROS-CTD, designed to pump blood to the clitoris. Reminiscent of a penis pump, which gets blood flowing and pumps up a man's erection, the EROS-CTD is basically a clit pump. It reminds me of a butch dyke I know in San Francisco, sex educator Karlyn Lotney, a/k/a Fairy Butch. Fairy Butch has an innovative technique for clit-pumping in which she employs a penis pump to make her clit (temporarily) the size of two short fingers—her own female hard-on. Whoops, there I go: describing female arousal in men's terms, but the truth is that the tissue is the same, and we do get hard-ons, too. I'm going straight to my HMO in hopes of securing a prescription for this expensive, doctor-approved sex toy. Then I'm gonna take her out for a spin. I'll try to come up with another word for my big clit while I'm at it.

Art and the Eroticism of Puberty

David Steinberg

*The following talk was part of a plenary panel on this subject at the Western Regional meeting of the Society for the Scientific Study of Sexuality (SSSS), April 24, 1999. SSSS is the principal organization of professional sex educators, counselors, and therapists in the US. Other panel members were photographer Jock Sturges (*Radiant Identities*;* The Last Day of Summer*) and author Judith Levine (*My Enemy, My Love: Women, Men, and the Dilemmas of Gender*;* Harmful to Minors: How Sexual Protectionism Hurts Children*, upcoming from the University of Minnesota Press).*

I want to use my portion of this panel to examine some current sex-cultural dynamics that help explain the tremendous emotional charge behind the debate about nude photography of children and adolescents.

What's in need of explanation is not simply the fact that nude photographs of children are considered controversial. This in itself, while a sad commentary on the sexual state of the nation, is hardly surprising. Nudity is still controversial in this country, and nude photography, while accepted as legitimate in the world of fine art, still raises eyebrows in the general population. In addition, we know all too well that any artistic work that treats eroticism or sexuality in a friendly, let alone explicit, way is itself decidedly suspect.

What is surprising about the current controversy is why these predictable aesthetic and ethical disagreements have taken on such intensely loaded meaning and significance over the past several years. By looking at the dynamics behind this particular controversy, we stand to learn a great deal not only about nude photography, but also about how a variety of cultural attitudes relating to both sex and children affect us more generally.

Let me start with a basic observation that I think just about everyone in this room would embrace: That our particular culture still sees sex fundamentally as a dangerous, demonic, potentially chaotic force, a force that requires constant vigilance lest it tear apart otherwise sensible individuals, their primary relationships and, indeed, the very fabric of society. This in contrast, say, to the possibility of relating to sex primarily as a blessing, as a positive, joyous, wholesome, or spiritual part of life, as a way of connecting with other human beings in loving, intimate, creative, and enriching ways.

Because our basic cultural fear and suspicion of sex sets social order in opposition to many forms of natural and common sexual expression, elaborate institutions of social indoctrination and control are required to suppress those forms of sexual behavior and desire that are considered unacceptable. I want to look at two institutions of enforced sexual control that I think animate the extreme reactions we are seeing around the issue of nude photography of children and adolescents.

The first of these is the creation and maintenance of a mythical, idealized class of innocent, supposedly non-sexual, individuals onto which society can project its yearning to escape the conflicts generated by overly-repressed sexual desire. I'm going to call these the "designated innocents."

The second is the creation and maintenance of a parallel mythical, demonized class of subhuman sexual deviants onto which individuals can project their transgressive sexual desires as a way of keeping those desires under control. I'm going to call these the "designated perverts."

While the particular groups assigned these archetypal roles of sexual innocents and sexual deviants has varied, the perception of an ongoing battle between sexual innocence and sexual perversion has been continuous.

If we look back historically, we can see that, while the particular groups assigned these archetypal roles of sexual innocents and sexual deviants has varied, the perception of an ongoing battle between sexual innocence and sexual perversion has been continuous. It is a battle that is represented as being the eternal struggle between good and evil, between God and Satan. Sadly, it is also defined as the battle between asexual purity and the sexual contamination of that purity.

In its current incarnation, this drama pits the imagined asexual innocence of children and adolescents against the imagined perversion

It has thus become more important than ever, among those who see sex as a form of impurity, to insist that children are entirely non-sexual beings.

of anyone who dares acknowledge and respect, let alone appreciate or celebrate, the eroticism or sexuality of anyone who has not crossed the socially-defined threshold into adulthood.

Designated Innocents

The role of designated innocents in the social drama of asexuality and perversion has well-defined requirements. The social function of this group is to posit the existence of a class of people so pure of heart and spirit that they have not been sullied by sex in any form. Traditionally, this role has been filled not only by children but also by women.

As late as the mid-nineteenth century, American women were still presumed to have no natural sexual desire of their own. Indeed, an entire culture developed to enforce asexuality on women, whether they liked it or not. Historian Barbara Goldsmith details one aspect of this culture of asexuality in her book, *Other Powers*. "In 1868," she writes, "American gynecological surgeons began performing clitoridectomies to quell sexual desire in women, which was considered a form of derangement. Upper- and middle-class white women who had been taught that any sexual urges were sinful, willingly surrendered their bodies to these male doctors, who tested them for abnormal arousal by stimulating the breast and clitoris; if there was a response, they surgically removed the clitoris."

Along with the creation of women as an asexual class came the need to protect women from sexual contamination of any form—whether this be from sexual predators (men) or from the corrupting influence of sexual awareness and information—even as we now assume that society must protect its asexual children both from predators and from sexual information.

As women gained social and political power in the twentieth century, they have not surprisingly demanded recognition and respect for the reality of their sexual desires, and for their right to fulfill those desires without being denigrated as insane or immoral. While women's right to sexual expression equal to that of men's is still far from complete, the notion that women are naturally asexual, or that asexuality can be forced on them by social commandments and expectations, is certainly a thing of the past. As a result, the group of innocents presumed to be asexual has been reduced to the children alone. It has thus become more important than ever, among those who see sex as a form of impurity, to insist that children are entirely non-sexual beings.

Since, as we know, children are in fact far from asexual, maintaining this myth—and with it, to some extent, an exaggerated sense of the sexual innocence of adolescent girls—requires both a significant denial system and an elaborate program of societal enforcement. Pat Califia describes this well in her book *Public Sex*. Children, she notes, "are not innocent; they are ignorant, and that ignorance is deliberately created and maintained by parents who won't answer questions about sex and often punish their children for being bold enough to ask. This does not make sex disappear.... Sex becomes the thing not seen, the word not spoken, the forbidden impulse, the action that must be denied."

Designated Perverts

The second role in the drama of innocence and violation is that of the deviant or, more precisely, the pervert. As with the role of designated innocent, requirements for the role of designated pervert are both specific and extreme.

To fulfill the function of the designated pervert it is not sufficient for a form of sexual deviance to simply be disapproved of by those in the sexual mainstream. Nor is it sufficient for the designated pervert to be seen as merely a misguided soul in need of understanding or therapeutic help. The designated pervert must be so loathsome to the general population that the social outrage he generates (designated perverts are usually male) is extreme enough to serve as a warning to all who would deviate from sexual normalcy as to what will happen to them if they do. Designated perverts must be seen as so vile, so subhuman really, that the full venom of social punishment—social ostracism, legal confinement, even violent personal attack—can be visited upon them without any sense of guilt, mercy, or compromise.

As with the designated innocents, the specific incarnation of the designated pervert has varied with changing historical circumstances. In general, the designated pervert of any given era will be whoever most threatens to overturn the prevailing myth of asexual innocence.

Designated perverts must be seen as so vile, so subhuman really, that the full venom of social punishment—social ostracism, legal confinement, even violent personal attack—can be visited upon them without any sense of guilt, mercy, or compromise.

In the late nineteenth century, for example, all that was required to be branded a "Satanic Free Loveist" was believing that women had sexual appetites of their own, and that they should have equal rights with men to choose their sexual partners, in and out of marriage, and equal rights to end their marriages if those marriages were unsatisfactory to them, sexually or otherwise. Those who acknowledged and validated women's sexuality were deemed loathsome perverts because they threatened to desecrate women—the mythical "asexuals" of the day—with the scourge of sex.

The leading "Free Love" spokesperson of the time was Victoria Woodhull, the first woman to run for the office of President of the United States (in 1872). On the issue of women' sexual desire, she was outspoken and uncompromising. "Some women," she declared, "seem to glory over the fact that they never had any sexual desire and to think that desire is vulgar. What? Vulgar?... Vulgar rather must be the mind that can conceive such blasphemy. No sexual passion, say you. Say, rather, a sexual idiot, and confess your life is a failure.... The possession of strong sexual powers [is] a necessary part of human character, the foundation upon which civilization rests."

> In general, the designated pervert of any given era will be whoever most threatens to overturn the prevailing myth of asexual innocence.

Predictably, Woodhull was subjected to the harshest attacks of the church, the press, and those in political power. Because of her sexual beliefs, she was driven out of the Suffragist movement (where she had until that time played a leading role), vilified in the major newspapers of the day, and driven into poverty. She was the first person prosecuted under the then-new Comstock Act, the Federal law that to this day prohibits sending obscene material through the mails.

As it became impossible to maintain the myth of women's asexual nature, it also became impossible to brand as a Satanic act the affirmation of women's sexual desire. As respect for women's sexuality grew in the early twentieth century, the issue lost the absolutist edge required for a true antisexual crusade. A new class of designated perverts was needed, and a new class was found.

The new targets of antisexual hatred and vilification were gays and lesbians. Once again, the full symphony of social loathing was called out to define the new designated perverts as truly subhuman, evil-minded threats to decency and social order. Once again, attacks on the designated perversion were justified by the supposed threat these perverts posed to the sexually innocent. Being a gay man was equated with being a vicious molester of young boys. Being a lesbian was equated with slyly seducing decent women out of their heterosexuality. Once again, the Devil was at the door, and the men and women of the sexual mainstream created a vivid image of vile perversion they could use to keep their own straying desires in check.

The Search for a New Designated Pervert

Recently, however, the horror of homosexuality has also begun to lose its punch. This is not to say that American society has truly embraced or accepted homosexuality, as it obviously has not. But the successes of the Gay Rights movement and the increased visibility of gays and lesbians have diluted the subhuman characterization required of true designated perverts. As more and more heterosexual Americans become aware of homosexuals as human beings instead of archetypes of evil, antisexual society once again needs to find a new class of perverts loathsome enough to serve as the vehicles for the general suppression of sexual deviance.

For a while it seemed that sadomasochists would fill the role quite nicely. S/M was just weird and disgusting enough to mainstream American consciousness to justify full vilification and violent suppression. But just as that wheel began to turn, S/M rather unexpectedly slipped into mainstream American culture as an intriguing, even chic, sexual variation, something altogether different from full-on perversion. Madonna's flawed book, *Sex*, was a significant factor in this rather instantaneous social turnaround, as was the widespread experience with S/M of many media celebrities themselves.

For a while it seemed that transsexuals might arouse sufficient scorn and revulsion to take on the designated pervert mantle but, like S/M, transsexuals have been surprisingly embraced in the past few years both by the mass media and by popular culture—perhaps, as James Green (a leading transgender advocate) points out, because the issue that transsexuals challenge is not sex at all, but gender.

While the precise definition of the new designated perverts is still evolving, it seems clear that it will center on those who acknowledge and affirm the sexuality of young people. The work of photographers like Jock Sturges, David Hamilton, and even Sally Mann happens to fall in the line of fire of this need to find new villains in the ongoing battle against sex itself. I believe this is why the objections to nude photographs of children have been so vicious and impassioned.

The continuing pattern of these attacks suggests that it will not be necessary to be a child molester, or even a pedophile, to be seen as the new pervert. The social need to enforce the non-sexuality of children and the exaggerated sexual innocence of adolescents is so great that the simple act of photographically addressing the eroticism of adolescents in an honest, respectful, and appreciative way has become sufficient to draw the full venom familiar to designated perverts.

While the precise definition of the new designated perverts is still evolving, it seems clear that it will center on those who acknowledge and affirm the sexuality of young people.

Photographic Content

While, in this climate, all nude photographs of young people have become suspect, it is worth noting that some photographs seem to generate more reactive heat than others, and not always in predictable ways. A photograph by Czech photographer Jan Saudek, for example, included in a recent book of his work widely distributed in the US, depicts a young girl passively having intercourse with Saudek himself. Yet, to my knowledge, neither the book nor the photograph have drawn any criticism whatsoever.

On the other hand, two photographs by Robert Mapplethorpe, showing nothing more than a nude and partially-nude young boy and girl, sitting and standing alone, were considered so objectionable that they helped bring the curtain down on Mapplethorpe's scheduled exhibition at the Corcoran Museum and were then seized from the Cincinnati museum that went ahead and exhibited the show.

The art photographs that current antisexual critics are finding most objectionable seem to fall into three categories. First there are the photos that portray the eroticism of their subjects so clearly that they force the viewer to acknowledge this eroticism as well. These portraits are threatening because they so clearly challenge the mythical belief in the complete asexuality of young people. The more successful the portrait—the more deeply and compellingly it captures the full personhood of its subject—the more threatening it becomes.

Second are photographs that generate some level of sexual response, and therefore extreme discomfort, in the people who look at them. These photos are threatening because they force viewers to acknowledge their own attraction, or potential attraction, however mild, to the sexuality and eroticism of young people.

"It is important to realize that sexual fantasies about one's children are normal," therapist and author Lonnie Barbach wrote in 1975, appealing to reason at a time when it was more safe to talk publicly about these things. "Many mothers report having some such fantasies at least occasionally. Children are sexual, warm, cuddly human beings—we can feel turned on and have the fantasies but we don't have to act them out." Yet, despite reassurance from therapists and media professionals that simply having sexual feelings for one's children is natural and almost always harmless, most people still feel intense distress at having any such feelings, and intense anger at any visual stimulus that forces them to acknowledge what they feel, or might potentially feel.

Third are photos that are seen as affronts to innocence whether or not they have anything to do with sexuality, such as the inclusion of the photos of nude children in the Mapplethorpe retrospective. In this case, the mere proximity of photos of childhood innocence to photos of radical sexuality was considered an attack on innocence itself.

In closing, let me emphasize that I strongly believe that protection of the sexual integrity of children and adolescents from the intrusion of adults is a crucial issue of social concern. National attention to the genuine sexual abuse of children is something that has been long overdue. Photography critic A.D. Coleman is correct when he appreciates that our culture is now "in a climate of deep terror over child abuse, and deep concern over the difficulty of catching child abusers. The system and the culture are understandably frustrated about this." But, as Coleman goes on to say, "the problem is that people are taking this frustration out on photographers who have absolutely no intention of contributing to that problem in any way, and whose work, as I read it, does not in any way contribute to that problem."

The current definition of children as a class of non-sexual innocents, and the attack on photographers whose work contradicts that notion, is the latest version of the false dichotomy between asexuality and sexual perversion that has been a long-standing characteristic of American sexual culture. The combination of denying the sexual existence of young people and vilifying those who acknowledge and affirm their sexuality only creates an impossibly conflicted social climate, divorced from sexual reality, that does nothing to support the emotional well-being of children. Indeed, it is the refusal to deal realistically with the sexuality of young people that lies at the heart of our failure to address this social problem effectively. If people like Christian fundamentalist Randall Terry and Operation Rescue truly want to protect children from sexual abuse, they might begin by taking a good, long look at the images of photographers like Jock Sturges and Sally Mann, and take to heart what the faces and bodies looking out at them have to say.

"A World That Hates Gays"

Is There Really a Gay Teen Suicide Epidemic?

Philip Jenkins

Though official statistics can often seem lifeless and overwhelming, some figures emerge with such clarity and power that they can achieve something like scriptural status in public debate, and these memorable numbers can even have the power to drive social policy.

We may remember the much-quoted 1980s figure of "one and a half million missing children," or the claim that serial killers took 5,000 American lives each year. Endlessly repeated, such awe-inspiring numbers presented a knock-down case for the urgency of finding an official response to these obvious menaces, respectively child abduction and repeat homicide. The difficulty is that in each of these cases, the memorable numbers offered were simply bogus, a fact which must raise devastating questions about the legitimacy of the political campaigns which they inspired. The figures were deliberately chosen in order to divert people's attention to the particular issue at hand, to make it seem as serious as possible.[1]

Through the 1990s, it was common to claim that gay victims represented perhaps a third of the teen suicide "epidemic," and this figure became simply a social fact, something that "everybody knows."

Both these instances of misleading statistics are quite well-known in the social science literature, but just as glaring an example of wholly false numbers continues to be cited as undeniably correct. We find this in claims made about the prevalence of "gay teen suicide," that is, the statistics for suicide by young homosexual people. Suicide by teenagers and young adults has for some years been regarded as a particularly grave form of social pathology, and has given rise to numerous official investigations as well as preventive programs by schools and social service agencies. In the 1980s, however, gay social and political groups began to draw attention to a particular aspect of this perceived crisis, namely the high overrepresentation of young gay men and lesbians as victims of these tragic acts.[2] To quote the gay newspaper *The Advocate*:

> Gay and lesbian teenagers are killing themselves in staggering numbers. They are hanging themselves in high school classrooms, jumping from bridges, shooting themselves on church altars, cutting themselves with razor blades and downing lethal numbers of pills. A conservatively estimated 1500 young gay and lesbian lives are terminated every year because these troubled youths have nowhere to turn.[3]

Through the 1990s, it was common to claim that gay victims represented perhaps a third of the teen suicide "epidemic," and this figure became simply a social fact, something that "everybody knows." The phenomenon predictably led to protests about the hostile social environment which caused such emotional turmoil for so many young people. "Each year an estimated fifteen hundred gay youth kill themselves because they cannot continue to live in a world that hates gays."[4]

Gay rights activists continue to use the teen suicide issue as one of their most effective rhetorical weapons, chiefly because of its appeal to audiences who might not normally be sympathetic to liberal views in this area. The theme easily lends itself to moving illustration by stories of specific young people who had killed themselves, the presumption being that homosexuality had been a determining factor in their decisions.[5] Rhetorical lessons drawn from such incidents have been invaluable in debates over the coverage of homosexual issues in the schools, one of the most controversial political issues of the last decade.

In fact, estimates for the level of gay teen suicide are quite misleading and wildly inflated.[6] Advocates citing the figure ignore grave methodological flaws both in the definition and prevalence of homosexuality, and the statistical shortcomings should certainly have been evident to the groups and individuals citing the numbers. Believers in a "crisis" of gay teen suicide employ definitions of the term "gay" that are malleable, dubious, and self-contradictory, while

In fact, estimates for the level of gay teen suicide are quite misleading and wildly inflated.

estimates of the gay population, however defined, rely on statistics that are hopelessly discredited. If we have no idea how many "gay teens" there are, we can conclude nothing about the proportion of suicide victims who meet this criterion.

The claims were based on data and assumptions so profoundly flawed that they can tell us little about the objective realities of suicide. However, the appearance and popularization of these claims in recent years is valuable in its own right as evidence for the development of a social problem, and the means by which an interest group has been able to formulate and publicize claims until they achieved the status of unchallenged social fact.

Crucially, the suicide issue permitted gay rights campaigners to transform the common stereotype of homosexuals from victimizers of the young to young victims themselves: It was gays who should be seen as victims of official neglect, persecution, and even conspiracy. The locus of victimization was thus fundamentally altered, and with it the whole rhetorical direction of the suicide problem.

The phenomenon also offers yet another illustration of a rhetorical tactic that has long distinguished the gay rights movement, namely the use of very high estimates of the incidence of homosexuality to portray as mainstream problems that might otherwise be considered specifically gay issues. Thus redefined and "mainstreamed," issues like gay teen suicide and gay-bashing can successfully seek the attention and sympathy of a substantial majority of the population.

Teen Suicide: Formulating a Crisis

From the late 1970s, the issue of suicides by teenagers and young adults attained general recognition as a serious social problem. (Though standard federal categories studied individuals aged 15 through 24, the problem was generally defined as one of "teen suicide," and that term will be employed here). This perception was founded on a straightforward observation, that suicide rates in this age group had indeed been increasing steadily since the 1950s, and growth in the 1960s and 1970s was quite explosive. Suicide rates for persons aged 15-24 stood at 4.5 per 100,000 in 1950, and 5 in 1960, but subsequently grew to 8.8 in 1970, and 12.4 by 1978-79. Though the rate stabilized somewhat thereafter, the 1990 figure was approaching 13 per 100,000. There was throughout a substantial and growing gender differential, with males outnumbering females by three to one in 1970, five to one by 1980.

Between 1975 and 1990, the average annual total for teen suicides amounted to 5,000 fatalities each year, and this age group was heavily overrepresented in overall suicide statistics. By the early 1980s, suicide even briefly overtook homicide as the second largest killer of teens and young adults, following accidents. Moreover, completed or "successful" suicides were well-known to constitute only a small fraction of suicidal behavior, and estimates for the number of suicide attempts by young people each year ranged from 400,000 to two million.

There is also speculation that the 5,000 known cases of teen suicide might understate the scale of the issue, in that other deaths recorded as "accidents," especially in automobile crashes, might in reality have involved suicidal intent. (While youth suicide rates did increase substantially, it might be noted that rates for this group were still far lower than the rate for those over 65 years of age, customarily around 20 per 100,000 in the late 1980s: If there is a real suicide epidemic in America, this is it.)

Though the sharp rise in teen suicide seemed abundantly documented, the figures have been subject to critical scrutiny based on changing recording practices. The public stigma attached to suicide has often led to undercounting, while correct identification of such an act depends on the conduct of investigators no less than the skill of medical examiners.[7]

Particularly where a juvenile is concerned, police and doctors would be likely to exercise discretion in ways intended to ease the emotional suffering of a family, even to the point of concealing suicide notes. For statistical purposes, this behavior would not be significant if it could be assumed to be constant, but Mike Males and others have suggested, controversially, that the dramatic increases in youth suicide rates since the 1950s were in large measure due to changes in the behavior of medical examiners, and the consequent correction of earlier undercounting. While admitting a rise in suicide rates between about 1964 and 1972, Males views the "epidemic" terminology as quite misleading. In fact, he argues, juvenile rates have not increased much more than those for adults, while rates for both categories have remained relatively constant since the early 1970s.[8]

Even if an authentic rise in suicide rates is acknowledged, the interpretation of this phenomenon is open to much debate. Only a tiny proportion of episodes involving self-directed violence result in an event officially recorded as suicide, perhaps less than 1 percent of the total, with the outcome dependent on a complex array of factors. These include the lethality of the particular means of violence chosen, firearms usually being the most deadly weapon of choice, and also the likelihood of early and effective medical intervention. For both reasons—availability of guns and remoteness of medical facilities—Western states have been marked by the highest youth suicide rates, with rural regions often exceeding urban.

For both reasons—availability of guns and remoteness of medical facilities—Western states have been marked by the highest youth suicide rates, with rural regions often exceeding urban.

We should never assume that the individuals who actually commit suicide constitute a truly representative sample of the youth population at large. Such statistical caveats were rarely noted in the growing concern of these years, in which youth suicide rates were repeatedly employed as an index of juvenile alienation and despair. Few denied that there was a "teen suicide problem," or even a national epidemic. The plight of "kids on the brink" was obviously potent in its ability to attract public and media attention.[9]

Suicides were distributed across all social categories, and some of the most notorious incidents affected better-off or even elite families: The popular media often had occasion to report incidents of this sort affecting celebrities. In addition, whites were overrepresented among the victims, constituting 93 percent of completed suicides.

Throughout the 1980s, teen suicide was the subject of a steady outpouring of books and magazine articles, most of which aimed to provide advice for parents seeking to detect warning signs of suicide within their families, and for schools wishing to implement prevention programs. The theme also appeared regularly in the visual media, in television movies and "after-school specials" aimed at teenagers.

This widely recognized problem offered rich rhetorical opportunities for numerous interest groups and activists of many different ideological perspectives, usually seeking to identify the social dysfunctions which had led to such a tragic loss of young people. The link with suicide was so powerful because the act symbolized utter despair and rejection, and claims that a given behavior or set of social conditions led to suicide were commonly used in these years to highlight the destructive effects of many other types of conduct, including rape. Youth suicide was used to illustrate the social harm caused by divorce and broken families, by child abuse, by drugs and substance abuse, by schoolyard bullying, by rock music, or by young people dabbling in the occult and fantasy role-playing games. Though the rhetorical lessons drawn in such discourse were generally conservative or traditionalist in nature, the issue also lent itself to liberal or radical interpretation, for example in a critique of youth unemployment and shrinking economic opportunities, or of the evils of the traditional patriarchal family.

Youth suicide was used to illustrate the social harm caused by divorce and broken families, by child abuse, by drugs and substance abuse, by schoolyard bullying, by rock music, or by young people dabbling in the occult and fantasy role-playing games.

From both liberal and traditionalist standpoints, public rhetoric and claims-making about youth suicide reached new heights in the mid-1980s, when the theme was often linked to wider concerns about the state of the nation's "threatened children." Responding to this concern was a natural way for political figures to win support from multiple constituencies, and there were inevitably calls for action at federal level. In 1984, Health and Human Services Secretary Margaret Heckler commissioned a prestigious "Task Force on Youth Suicide" to determine means by which the number of deaths might be substantially reduced, with an initial target of reducing the rate to 11 per 100,000 by 1990.

Suicide and Homosexuality

In deciding appropriate areas for study, there was no question that the Task Force would allocate at least some attention to sexual issues, among which homosexuality would certainly feature. At least from the mid-nineteenth century, it was frequently suggested that homosexuals were at greater risk of suicidal behavior, a stereotype epitomized by the title of Rofes' 1983 book, *I Thought People Like That Killed Themselves*. The late Victorian English writer John Addington Symonds expressed the opinion that, "I do not think it far from wrong when I mention that at least half of the suicides of young men are due to this one circumstance." "It is not difficult for anyone familiar with gay literature to name dozens of novels and stories that climax with the suicide of a homosexual."[10] In the cinema, portrayals of gay characters prior to the 1980s almost inevitably concluded with their violent deaths, usually by murder but often by suicide. Gay suicides featured in major 1960s films like *Advice and Consent*, *The Children's Hour*, *The Detective*, and *Victim*.[11]

In these decades, indeed, the clichéd association between homosexuality and suicide occasioned resentment among gay activists, for whom it reflected the common assumption that homosexuals were emotionally disturbed: "that the inherent psychopathology of gay people makes them suicidal."[12] Rofes attacked the "dual myth of homosexual suicide. This myth asserts that lesbians and gay men not only commit suicide at a rate considerably higher than society-at-large, but that somehow a person's homosexuality is itself the source of self-destructiveness."[13]

In fact, the belief that homosexuality increased one's self-destructive tendencies was repeatedly cited in the anti-gay literature produced by religious activists like Tim LaHaye and Anita Bryant. Both claimed that approximately half of all American suicides were the direct consequence of homosexuality, while LaHaye posited a gay suicide rate twelve to fourteen times higher than than for non-homosexuals.[14] Combating such theories had played a crucial role in the struggle during the 1970s to have homosexuality removed from the list of "diseases" acknowledged by the American psychiatric profession.

The suicide issue attracted a substantial scholarly literature, although the value of quantitative studies was repeatedly impaired by methodological issues, which compounded the already substantial difficulties inherent in any research on suicide. Some studies concentrated on suicidal behavior among groups of homosexuals, without attempting to use a control group, while designs that did involve controls were often of limited scale and relied too heavily on institutionalized populations. One 1972 study suggested a high rate for young male homosexuals, but without offering a control sample.[15] Prior to the late 1980s, only a handful of studies used large and well-chosen samples both for homosexual subjects and non-homosexual controls.[16]

By the mid-1980s, cumulative evidence from these and other studies did indeed indicate a higher incidence of suicidal behavior or attempts among the homosexual population, especially among younger men and women.[17] Despite some methodological problems, this increased vulnerability may be taken as a plausible and reasonably well-established trend, and observers were swift to explore its implications. In 1983, Rofes' book on suicide and homosexuality included a groundbreaking chapter on "lesbians and gay youth and suicide," in which he remarks that hitherto, "the relationship between homosexuality and youth suicide has virtually been ignored," and cites examples in which television presentations on the suicide issue were forced to omit reference to sexual orientation.[18] However, the coming years would more than compensate for this gap, and most of the themes discussed in his work would soon become commonplace in the mainstream literature.

By the mid-1980s, cumulative evidence from these and other studies did indeed indicate a higher incidence of suicidal behavior or attempts among the homosexual population, especially among younger men and women.

The Federal Task Force

Research on the homosexual aspect of the teen suicide problem attained national visibility through the work of the federal Task Force, and especially through a number of conferences convened in association with that investigation. In 1986 two important meetings were held, respectively at Oakland, California, and at Bethesda, Maryland, and both heard papers directly arguing for a major link between homosexuality and teen suicide. One of the Bethesda papers, by Professor Joseph Harry, examined the literature relating suicide to "sexual identity issues," a term which included pregnancy, sexual abuse, and venereal disease, but which also presented several pages on homosexuality. Reviewing the admittedly flawed literature, Harry used the Bell-Weinberg and Saghir-Robins studies to argue plausibly that homosexual youth attempted or committed suicide at a rate from two to six times that of non-homosexuals. The author was careful to emphasize that his conclusions affected individuals of definitely homosexual orientation, as opposed to bisexuals, or those with some same-sex experience in their pasts.

This restrained finding was in marked contrast in tone and methodology to a paper presented at the Oakland conference by Paul Gibson, a clinical social worker based at San Francisco's "Huckleberry House" shelter. He argued at length that "gay youth are two or three times more likely to attempt suicide than other people. They may comprise up to 30 percent of completed youth suicides annually."[19] Gibson therefore took a reasonably well-accepted figure for the high prevalence of suicidal behavior among homosexual youth, and added a crucial but dubious statistical extrapolation, which sought to estimate the "gay element" in the overall figures for teen suicides. Though Gibson repeatedly presents anecdotal and survey evidence to show that young homosexuals are likely to contemplate suicide, he never explicitly states how the "30 percent" statistic is derived. The logical process by which this second stage is established seems to develop as follows:

1. Every year, some 5,000 young people commit suicide.

2. Assuming that one tenth of the population is homosexual, we would expect about 500 of these cases to involve gay teenagers and young adults, if homosexuals had a "normal" rate of suicidal behavior.

3. However, homosexuals are approximately three times as likely as heterosexuals to commit suicide, so that the actual number of homosexual suicides in a given year would be closer to 1500.

4. Therefore, the proportion of teen and young adult suicide cases involving homosexuals is about 30 percent of the whole, or approximately one-third.

Gibson's argument, especially in step (2), depends on his estimate of the proportion of the total population that is homosexual, and it is here that we encounter serious difficulties. He evidently accepts a higher figure for the prevalence of homosexuality than would commonly be accepted, in order to reach the conclusion that, "There are far more gay youth than you are presently aware of." This is substantiated by Kinsey's account "of homosexual behavior among adolescents surveyed with 28 percent of the males and 17 percent of the females reporting at least one homosexual experience. He also found that that approximately 13 percent of adult males and 7 percent of adult females had engaged in predominantly homosexual behavior for at least three years prior to his survey. That is where that figure that 10 percent of the homosexual comes from...a substantial minority of youth—perhaps one in ten as one book suggests—have a primary gay male, lesbian or bisexual orientation." (Though not explicitly named, the "one book" probably refers to Ann Heron's 1983 selection of writings by young gay people, entitled *One Teenager in Ten*.) Given the studies of gay tendencies towards suicidal behavior, "this means that 20-30 percent of all youth suicides may involve gay youth."[20] He feels that this is a minimum figure, and notes another study which suggests that gay teen suicides might amount to 3,000 each year, or 60 percent of the whole. If the proportion of gay victims is extended to the problem of suicide attempts rather than completed acts, then each year, the number of homosexual youths who try to kill themselves would perhaps run into the hundreds of thousands.

Gibson's argument makes some dubious assumptions, but the figures for gay suicidal behavior are quite of a piece with other estimates in the paper, which suggest, for example, that "gay male, lesbian, bisexual and transsexual youth comprise as many as 25 percent of all youth living on the streets in this country." This surprising statistic, unsupported by any citation, may well depend on anecdotal evidence of the sort found throughout the paper, which largely derives from grassroots and mutual-assistance organizations and shelters concentrated in major urban centers like San Francisco. The paper achieves its very high estimates for homosexual behavior by extrapolating such atypical characteristics of an urban underclass to the nation at large. In addition, the paper repeatedly refers with little distinction to "gay male, lesbian, bisexual and transsexual youth," which as we will see, raises serious difficulties of definition.

The very different work of Harry and Gibson was acknowledged in the final 1989 report to the extent that homosexuality was noted as a significant risk factor which increased the likelihood of teen suicide, but the report did not accept or explore the far-reaching implications of Gibson's paper. However, it was striking to find such arguments in a document produced under the imprimatur of the federal government, and a conservative Republican administration at that, and the Task Force Report was widely cited. It still appears as the chief source for the claims that lesbian and gay youth may constitute "up to thirty percent of completed suicides annually," and that "homosexuals of both sexes are two to six times more likely to attempt suicide than are heterosexuals."[21]

"One in Ten"

Though Gibson's argument achieved immediate recognition from many researchers and activist groups, its conclusions are suspect, and so are those of the many other articles which rely upon it.[22] His assumptions involve two chief areas of difficulty: first, that cases of youth suicide represent a cross-section of the young adult population; and second, that about 10 percent of the population can be characterized as gay or homosexual. The first argument is questionable for the reasons noted above, that a suicide attempt is far more likely to result in death in some circumstances rather than others, and the social categories likely to kill themselves do not necessarily correlate with those groups likely to have a high incidence of homosexuality. Notably, homosexual populations are likely to be found disproportionately in urban areas, where guns might be less available to teenagers, but where emergency medical facilities are more abundant. Though this is controversial, it can be argued that areas marked by high youth suicide rates are less likely to have substantial homosexual populations.

> Several influential studies in the early 1990s necessitated a further revision of the estimated homosexuality rate for men, down to between 1 and 3 percent.

Much more serious, however, is his estimate of the gay element of the population at large. It is striking that for both Gibson and his many successors, the main cited source for estimating the homosexual population is Kinsey, rather than any of the later revisions of that much-challenged study, or one of the more recent surveys that rely on far superior data-gathering techniques.[23] As is common in gay activist writing on other social issues, the prevalence of homosexuality was estimated at a round but very dubious "one in ten" of the population.

Though Kinsey himself rejected a simplistic "one-in-ten" rate, his study had argued that about 10 percent of men were chiefly or exclusively homosexual for at least three years between the ages of 16 and 55. The original methodology was, however, so flawed as to create grave concern. Problems were numerous, not least the ethical difficulties of reporting children's sexual responses in conditions which have been criticized for violating most accepted standards for the treatment of child research subjects: In fact, conservative critics have denounced the Kinsey project as constituting formalized molestation.[24] Also, the study relied chiefly on volunteer subjects disproportionately drawn from metropolitan areas, and active homosexuals were overrepresented in the sample, as were college-educated individuals. In addition, a substantial number of subjects had institutional backgrounds, generally in jails or prisons. In sum, the study was likely to produce a sizable overrepresentation of subjects who reported same-sex contacts both on a sporadic basis and as a continuing lifestyle. Later scholars were divided over whether the data might usefully be reinterpreted, or if indeed the whole project is beyond salvage.

The numerical issue was sensitive because of its political connotations. For the gay rights movement of the 1970s and 1980s, the "one in ten" figure became a powerful slogan, suggesting as it did that homosexual legal and political rights were a crucial matter for a large portion of the population, and that a very large number of individuals were suppressing their authentic sexual nature for fear of the consequences. The National Gay and Lesbian Task Force claimed to represent "23 million gay and lesbian persons," while some activists even viewed the 10 percent estimate as excessively conservative. Conversely, moral conservatives minimized the number of homosexuals in order to present the condition as "a behavioral oddity, certainly not entitled to special protective status," in the words of Lou Sheldon of the Traditional Values Coalition.[25]

Already by the early 1970s, studies employing methodologies superior to Kinsey's found the number of active homosexuals to be far less than the popular commonplace. In 1972, Gebhard's reevaluation of the Kinsey figures suggested a revised estimate of around 4 percent of men, which long remained the most convincing figure; and which should have been the source employed by the suicide studies of the 1980s. This was in fact the number employed by Harry, though not by Gibson. In 1990, a careful review of past research on American men suggested that "estimated minimums [sic] of 5 to 7 percent report some same-gender sexual contact during adulthood," but even this would soon appear excessively high.[26] The scale of the gay population became an urgent issue during these years because of the need to determine accurately the population at special risk from AIDS. New estimates were far more conservative than the Kinsey figures, and in 1988, the estimated number of gay males in New York city alone was revised downward by some 80 percent.[27]

Several influential studies in the early 1990s necessitated a further revision of the estimated homosexuality rate for men, down to between 1 and 3 percent. In 1993, the Alan Guttmacher Institute reported that between 1.8 and 2.8 percent of men surveyed reported at least one sexual contact with another man in the previous decade, while only about 1 percent had been exclusively homosexual in the previous year. This was in accord with the findings of a national survey recently undertaken in France.[28] In 1994 a University of Chicago study found that 2.8 percent of men and 1.4 percent of women surveyed identified themselves as homosexual or bisexual, with respondents in urban areas reporting same-sex contacts at far higher rates than their counterparts in suburban or rural regions.[29] Whites also reported same-sex behavior at approximately double the rate of blacks. However, of all the groups sampled, only one reported recent homosexual contacts at the "10 percent" level, and that figure was attained by men living in the largest cities.

Contrary to Kinsey's "one in ten," a figure of one in 30 would offer a more accurate assessment of the male population that can be described as homosexual or bisexual; and one in 60 would best represent the exclusively homosexual. The corresponding figures for women reporting sexual contacts with other women are somewhat lower.[30]

Counting Gay Suicides

The "gay teen suicide" problem also depended upon a highly expansive interpretation of the term "gay." Research had shown that "homosexuals" had a greater tendency to attempt suicide, meaning individuals whose sexual orientation is predominantly toward the same sex. However, the suicide figures of Gibson and others concern that "one in ten" element of the population who have "a primary gay male, lesbian or bisexual orientation." This is a substantial leap, even if we set aside the quandary of whether one can in fact refer to a "primary...bisexual orientation." Evidence based strictly on homosexual subjects has been illegitimately extended to cover a poorly-defined "gay" population. This extrapolation may derive from Kinsey's suggestion of a spectrum of sexual preference in which individuals are located in terms of their degree of homosexual or heterosexual orientation. If this model is correct, then terms like "homosexual" and "bisexual" are strictly relative, and the general term "gay" could appropriately be applied to those individuals towards one end of the spectrum, as opposed to a discrete population. However, criticisms of the Kinsey material also raise grave doubts about the accuracy of the whole "spectrum" idea, and thus the use of the term "gay."

Evidence based strictly on homosexual subjects has been illegitimately extended to cover a poorly-defined "gay" population.

For the gay suicide statistics, the difficulty lies not in the original Kinsey research, but in its misapplication. In the original studies, homosexual subjects were located by quite proper techniques, requesting volunteers from homosexual activist or self-help groups, or through gay-oriented newspapers. This produced a sample of self-identified and (usually) overt homosexuals, and we may reasonably assume that findings will reflect the conditions and behavior of a wider population of active homosexuals whose sexual orientation is more or less exclusively focused on others of the same sex. However, Gibson and others imply that the studies are applicable to "gay and bisexual" individuals, the criterion being that a person had had one or more same-sex contacts within the past number of years, even though he or she would not define themselves as actively homosexual.

While it is not impossible that similar emotional problems and suicidal tendencies might be found among this larger population, this assumption would be a quite inappropriate extension of available research findings. It might, for example, be argued that the higher suicide rates recorded for overt homosexuals reflect social ostracism and legal discrimination, which would not apply to a "closeted" homosexual, and still less to someone with an isolated same-sex experience some years in his past. Does one same-sex contact predispose one to suicide? No basis was offered for the link repeatedly drawn between same-sex experience and suicide, still less an established causal relationship. As Erwin notes, "The distinction between behavior and identity raises important questions with respect to the impact of heterosexism on mental health."[31]

And there were other difficulties, such as the inclusion of lesbians in the statistics, with the suggestion that homosexual women also represented "one in ten" of the female population. Even Kinsey claimed to find only 7 percent of the female population meeting his definition of lesbianism, a rate that has never been approached by any subsequent study. Given that girls and women compose a small minority of completed suicides, the number of additional cases supplied by lesbian victims is tiny.

Finally, the whole "gay teen" hypothesis provides no explanation for the sharp rise of youth suicide since the 1950s, and in fact is counterintuitive. According to the "one in ten" theory, the frequency of homosexual tendencies should be more or less constant over time, and should not have changed significantly since the 1950s. What has unquestionably changed since the 1950s is the social environment, which uniformly has altered in directions favoring the overt expression of homosexuality, whether this is measured through the reform or repeal of criminal statutes, hate crime laws penalizing anti-gay violence, or media depictions of homosexuality. Logically, one might expect this to have resulted in a massive decline in the suicide rates of homosexuals, yet this is not suggested in the literature. All in all, the evidentiary foundations of the "gay teen suicide" problem appear fragile in the extreme.

"Death by Denial": The Rhetoric of Gay Teen Suicide

Despite difficulties of evidence, the inflated scale of the issue soon achieved national visibility, a process accelerated by the publication of other research confirming that homosexual teens did indeed appear at high risk of attempting or completing suicide. In 1991, especially, an influential article by Remafedi, *et al.* in the journal *Pediatrics* was reported under dramatic headlines claiming that, "Nearly One-Third of Young Gay Men May Attempt Suicide, Study Suggests."[32] Remarkably, the study did not employ a control group, presumably on the basis that the relative vulnerability of gay youth (however defined) could be taken as a given: Why argue with the obvious?[33] However, this omission did not prevent the "one-third" figure from becoming a public commonplace. Accidental transposition or misunderstanding of the figures during the course of reporting may also have reinforced the popular notion that "one-third of teen suicides involve homosexuals".

Accumulating testimony from the behavioral sciences now provided the basis for a popularization of the issue and for the construction of "gay teen suicide" as a pressing social problem. Initially, the figures were presented in the gay activist press in late 1991 and early 1992, when the suicide issue was prominently stressed in gay publications like *The Advocate* and *Christopher Street*. The theme was used to attack the Republican Bush Administration, then under liberal assault for adopting extremist positions on social issues like abortion and homosexuality in order to appease religious conservatives.

These articles viewed the muted official reaction to the 1989 Task Force as part of a deliberate strategy of anti-gay persecution, or at least "denial." This interpretation was influenced by the vigorous controversy which initially greeted the report. Conservatives denounced its political approach, and California Republican Congressman William Dannemeyer persuaded Health and Human Services Secretary Louis Sullivan to reject any document which undermined family values. Dannemeyer was a notorious enemy of gay causes, who at that time was campaigning against homosexuality and the extension of disability protections to AIDS sufferers, while alleging that gays were infiltrating federal agencies in the interests of promoting tendentious research.[34]

In the activist press, the mythology was that the Task Force as a whole had asserted the particular danger to gays, but the report was rejected or even suppressed entirely due to "pressure from conservative religious and family groups," with Dannemeyer as the prominent villain.[35] In Massachusetts, a state commission on gay and lesbian issues made the incorrect assertion that, "Pressure from anti-gay forces...led to suppression not only of the controversial chapter, but also of the entire report."[36] In this view, the document was simply too incendiary for the administration, and the failure to take account of the Gibson paper thus reflected not methodological concerns, but a craven submission to conservative protests.

There was a systematic and perhaps ingenuous misunderstanding of Gibson's original argument, which has repeatedly been cited as the considered findings of the Task Force as a whole, rather than merely the opinion of one participant that made little impact on the final report.[37] One article in *Education Digest* claimed that, "The U.S. Department of Health and Human Services reported in 1989 that 30 percent of all teens who commit suicide are gay."[38] A recent collection of essays quotes the Task Force findings on gay suicide in its blurb, and continues, "The report was swept aside by the Bush administration, yet the problem didn't go away."[39] The book, *Death by Denial*, reprinted the "alarming and hotly contested" Gibson paper in its entirety, presumably as a definitive statement on the dimensions of the perceived crisis.[40]

Themes of conspiracy, cover-up, and official denial pervaded the activist press. *The Advocate*, for example, examined "The Government's Cover-Up and America's Lost Children."[41] Examining a "conservatively estimated" total of 1,500 gay teen suicides each year, the author argued that the problem arose from cynical neglect by a bureaucracy that had fallen under the influence of right-wing religious fundamentalists. According to Robert Bray of the National Gay and Lesbian Task Force, gay youth suicide was "an unconscionable tragedy that has been ignored by health officials in Washington because of homophobia."[42] Teen suicide was thus but another aspect of official abuse that was also reflected in the lack of progress in stemming the AIDS epidemic. Federal inaction exacerbated an already dangerous situation, and literally cost many young lives.

Finally, the whole "gay teen" hypothesis provides no explanation for the sharp rise of youth suicide since the 1950s, and in fact is counterintuitive.

Christopher Street similarly traced a pattern of malign neglect, arguing that "government officials, scientists, writers, commentators and activists have been criminally silent on the issue" of gay youth suicide, despite its "epidemic proportions." The suicide statistics indicated the "plain fact that...thousands of gay and lesbian youth all over the United States are calling out for help in the face of bigotry, ignorance and hatred."[43] In the *New York Native*, David Lafontaine of the Coalition for Lesbian and Gay Civil Rights estimated "that about one third of the estimated one million teen suicide attempts are committed by gay youth."[44] According to such claims, the pervasive social, political, and emotional crisis afflicting young homosexuals drove hundreds of thousands each year to attempt violence against themselves. Urgent action was demanded to stop the "hidden holocaust."[45]

In these months, the gay suicide issue won an audience outside the activist press, as it received attention in the national news media. In 1991, for example, controversy surrounded an episode of the television series *Quantum Leap*, in which a gay character was depicted wrestling with thoughts of suicide. The following May, the ABC news program *20/20* showed a report on the problem of suicide among gay and lesbian teens, an item criticized as "overheated" for its acceptance of the most extreme claims about the perceived menace.[46] The ideas now permeated the self-help literature directed at young people and parents concerned about suicide prevention.[47] One recent book characteristically notes that "researchers who study gay youth and suicide estimate that about one-third of the young people who attempt or commit suicide are gay or lesbian," but the only citation is to a reprint from the Gibson paper.[48]

Homosexuality and the Young

By this point, the magnitude of the "epidemic" seemed to have been established quantitatively, so that authors could proceed to a wide-ranging social and political analysis of the roots of the problem, and to proposing solutions. The common assumption was that gay teens are killing themselves in very large numbers because of the anti-homosexual attitudes pervading society. These difficulties would certainly include overt violence in the form of "gay-bashing," but homophobia was also reflected in social ostracism, derision, and hostile media stereotypes. Suicide could only be prevented by curing the social climate of homophobia, by providing legal, physical, and emotional protection for homosexuals. To adapt the common slogan of AIDS activists, this is an instance where "Silence = Death," and lives would be saved only by forthright militancy. As Remafedi writes, "to ignore the problem now is a missed opportunity to save thousands of young lives, tantamount to sanctioning death by denial."[49]

Claims-makers in this affair had a number of agendas. In general terms, they were seeking to illustrate the sufferings of the homosexual population and the necessity for official action, in the form of protective laws or proactive government policies. Valerie Jenness has shown how the perceived threat of anti-homosexual violence and "gay bashing" was employed for exactly these ends in this same time period.[50] However, the activist perspective on teen suicide now suggested that the protection of homosexuals as a category directly benefited young people and might actually preserve them from harm or violence. "Gay rights," in short, would save young lives. The significance of this linkage is only apparent when set alongside the long historical association of homosexuality with the exploitation or injury of the young, for many years one of the most powerful weapons in the rhetorical arsenal of homophobia.

Campaigns against pedophiles and sex offenders often have at least a covert anti-homosexual agenda, on the grounds that individuals who might tolerate consensual sexual acts between adults would not be prepared to extend this acquiescence to the exploitation of children. The gay/pedophile association appeared regularly in "gay rights" referenda since the 1970s, when a notorious slogan alleged that "homosexuals aren't born—they recruit."[51] Pedophilia was central to anti-gay rhetoric until the mid-1980s, when it was largely replaced by the still more effective terror weapon of AIDS. However, the pedophile issue has since reemerged in recent attempts to weaken or abolish gay-rights legislation, especially in numerous state referenda through the 1990s.[52]

A perceived homosexual threat against the young gave rise to countless local battles of the early 1990s—for example, over attempts to permit gay couples to adopt children—but public education was the most common arena of conflict. Battles often developed when school boards sought to introduce curricular materials depicting gay relationships in a favorable light, such as the books *Heather Has Two Mommies* and *Daddy's Roommate*. Such texts and materials were widely denounced, and their sponsors accused of promoting homosexuality among underage children. Also at issue were programs which used homosexual speakers in order to address gay issues, and schemes to provide support and counseling services for gay and lesbian students.

Controversies reached a peak in 1989 and 1990, when there was a vigorous struggle in San Francisco, as well as at state level in California. In 1992 New York City encountered ferocious controversy over the proposed "Children of the Rainbow" curriculum, regarded by critics as too sympathetic to gay issues. Opposition to new educational approaches was epitomized by two headlines in the conservative *Washington Times*: "Parents Fear Schools Teach Homosexuality," and, "When Tolerance Becomes Advocacy."[53] Resistance to gay-oriented curricula was a major issue in mobilizing conservative activism on school boards, often providing a vehicle for candidates of the Christian Right.[54]

The new focus on gay teen suicide offered an ideal opportunity to counter such linkages, showing that the introduction of homosexual themes in the classroom or other youth contexts might actually protect young people from physical and emotional harm and even an untimely death.[55] Gay activists thus adopted children's rights' rhetoric, placing themselves in the position of defending the best interests of the young. Conversely, they sought to show that—to quote *The Advocate*—"the government does not have the best interest of children at heart."[56]

The response demanded by the suicide problem would certainly focus on educational issues. Gibson's pioneering paper had argued:

> We need to make a conscious effort to promote a positive image of homosexuals at all levels of society that provide gay youth with a diversity of lesbian and gay adult role models. We each need to take personal responsibility for revising homophobic attitudes and conduct. Families should be educated about the development and positive nature of homosexuality. They must be able to accept their child as gay or lesbian. Schools need to include information about homosexuality in their curriculum and protect gay youth from abuse by their peers to ensure they receive an equal education.[57]

By 1992, the construction of the gay teen suicide problem had become so well-established that the issue could be used as a multifaceted weapon in numerous struggles over gay issues, and not merely in schools and churches.

Similar themes pervaded the writing of the early 1990s. Ciara Torres argued that "gay teens kill themselves more often than other young people simply because their life chances are so limited by social and legal discrimination. Only when this discrimination is eliminated will these shocking statistics change." "Thus young gay individuals realize that they must hide their identity for fear of social and legal consequences which can destroy their lives. Homosexuals can be fired, evicted, kept from their own biological children, restricted from adopting children, and imprisoned for sodomy." "The homosexuality of historical figures has been systematically left out of education in the public schools, giving gay youth the false impression that gays have never affected history in a positive way."[58] The answers were largely to be found in the schools:

> As they recognize that they are different and discriminated against, [gay youth] lose self-esteem and become depressed. Many suicide, out of extreme depression and helplessness. Those who don't suicide live an adolescence of silence and oppression, rarely being able to speak up without being struck down by peers.... Homosexual teen suicide, discrimination from all areas of life, and misunderstanding of homosexuality, both from the heterosexual community and from the homosexual youth who have not had access to information, would greatly reduce, or nearly disappear, if proper education was given in the public schools to combat homophobia."[59]

Though there was no federal response to the questions raised by the Task Force, gay teen suicide proved a powerful issue at state level. In Massachusetts, notably, the discovery of a gay suicide problem led several school districts in 1991 to initiate programs involving support groups for gay and lesbian pupils. Later that year, the socially liberal Republican Governor Weld proposed an advisory body with the goal of developing strategies to stem the "epidemic." This scheme was challenged by legislators who felt that the commission's mandate should extend to all vulnerable students, but the gay focus was retained after activists emphasized the "stunning" fact "revealed" by the Task Force that 30 percent of all youth suicides involved homosexuals. Weld himself asserted that, "Half a million young people attempt suicide every year. Nearly 30 percent of youth suicides are committed by gays and lesbians."[60]

The suicide issue was thus examined by a Commission of Gay and Lesbian Youth, chaired by gay activist David Lafontaine.[61] In 1993 the group's report envisaged far-reaching reforms that would train teachers and families about the problems faced by gay and lesbian youth, promote anti-harassment and anti-discrimination policies, and generally "guarantee gay and lesbian students equal rights to an education and equal access to school activities."[62]

A public crusade against gay youth suicide would also have to combat homophobic attitudes in the churches. This was a significant theme, in view of the central role played by religious groups in movements against homosexual rights, and the related controversies within churches about the toleration or even ordination of gay clergy. For Gibson and others, religious denominations were primary villains in the production of the hostile rhetoric which drove so many teens to their deaths, with Catholics, Baptists, and Protestant fundamentalists singled out for special blame. Gibson explicitly demands that "faiths that condemn homosexuality should recognize how they contribute to the rejection of gay youth by their families, and suicide among gay and lesbian youth."[63]

By 1992, the construction of the gay teen suicide problem had become so well-established that the issue could be used as a multifaceted weapon in numerous struggles over gay issues, and not merely in schools and churches. The suicide "epidemic" was frequently cited as a powerful illustration of the outcome of anti-homosexual prejudice, especially by groups like PFLAG (Parents, Families and Friends of Lesbians and Gays). In Colorado, local media gave dramatic coverage to a gay suicide which allegedly occurred in direct response to the passage of a legal measure restricting homosexual rights. The theme would again be cited during 1993, as the question of allowing homosexuals to serve openly in the US military became a prominent issue in national politics.

From an activist standpoint, homophobic threats, and presumably the consequent dangers of youth suicide, were dramatically increased by specific political events like the 1994 Congressional elections, which so sharply increased the power of visible social conservatives such as Newt Gingrich and Jesse Helms. As one gay rights campaigner wrote, if suicide rates were to be reduced, "then the country must make spaces in which it is safe to come out. This means removing discriminatory statutes in the workplace, real estate, and the political arena. Activists can still hope that this will be the gay '90s, but the battle for legal and social equality must rage on."[64]

I have suggested that the "gay teen suicide" myth was closely linked to the politics of a specific historical moment, namely the intense cultural politics of the early 1990s, but the underlying idea did not simply fade away when that environment changed. Throughout the 1990s, the notion that "one third of teen suicides are gay" continued to be recycled and cited every time young people or teenagers featured in gay rights debates. In 1997 the figure was cited by Diane Sawyer in a television news feature on lesbian actress Ellen DeGeneres, and the following year, the number appeared in a *60 Minutes* report.[65] The prolonged life of the mythology suggests how very valuable it was to its proponents.

Building the Problem

In establishing a problem as serious and worthy of public concern, claims-makers inevitably employ the terminology likely to carry the greatest conviction in a given society. Though in earlier periods this might involve using scriptural or classical references, modern audiences are more generally impressed by the rhetoric of social and behavioral science, so quantitative measures are given great prominence. Statements about a given issue thus tend to begin with estimates about the scale or prevalence of a given behavior, claiming that x thousand children are abused or abducted each year, or that y million Americans have been harmed by a particular drug. These statistics are intended to impress, both by their very large scale and by the suggestion of rapid and uncontrollable growth and ubiquitous threat. In the case of gay teen suicide, the awful (and easily memorable) statistics provided a powerful warrant for the case which activists were making so passionately.

In establishing a problem
as serious and worthy of public concern,
claims-makers inevitably employ
the terminology likely to carry
the greatest conviction in a given society.

Claiming a vast scale for the gay suicide problem was closely related to other themes emphasized by gay activists these years, above all the transformation of homosexuality from a deviant or pathological state to a condition which attracted unmerited persecution. It was all part of a process of constructing gays as victims of social injustice. In the United States especially, modern movements claiming rights for a particular segment of the population have all been influenced to a greater or lesser degree by the rhetoric of the African-American civil rights movement and its emphasis on structural oppression and group victimization. Other groups who viewed themselves as historically oppressed have claimed a parallel victim status, so that feminists stressed the systematic violence inflicted on women in the form of rape and domestic abuse. A claim to collective victim status implied that the group was "unjustly harmed or damaged by forces beyond their control," and that victimization occurred chiefly or solely due to the essential characteristics of that group.[66] On the analogy of civil rights legislation, it was thus the proper role and obligation of government to seek to prevent or compensate for this victimization.

For the gay rights movement, which emerged alongside modern feminism, oppression and persecution manifested themselves most visibly in the form of anti-gay violence, but the same themes were also applied to other dysfunctions where a victimization theme was not initially evident. In the matter of AIDS, notably, it was by no means apparent that blame for the epidemic could be attached to anti-homosexual prejudice, still less to any particular institution or administration. During the 1980s, however, activism over the issue successfully cast the problem as an issue of homophobia, in the sense that anti-gay prejudice prevented the allocation of sufficient resources to find a cure for the disease, while prudery prevented the establishment of public education programs to limit the spread of AIDS.

Teen suicide followed on similar lines, taking a matter that had previously been viewed as one of personal misfortune or dysfunction, and presenting it as the consequence of structural bias and victimization, and even of official conspiracy. The teen suicide issue benefited from a cumulative process, in that AIDS campaigners had already established notions of official neglect and suppression of evidence, which could easily be transferred to the sensitive issue of teen suicide. If so many teenagers killed themselves because they lived in "a world that hates gays," the obvious rhetorical message was that this world should be changed and that reform would have to begin with those institutions and laws which most directly affected the young.

Debates over homosexuality have often revolved around the issue of the victimization of the young. In rhetorical terms, the gay suicide issue succeeded in retaining concerns about exploitation, but transferring the stereotypical role of the homosexual from abuser and molester to victim; from defiler of the young, to young victim. It remains to be seen whether this transformation will endure, but at least in the short term, the political benefits for gay activism have been substantial. The whole affair amply demonstrates the real-world consequences of the recasting of a social problem in a particular ideological direction: And once again, we observe the immense value of potent-sounding statistics.

Endnotes

1. Best, Joel. (1990). *Threatened children.* University of Chicago Press; Crossen, Cynthia. (1994). *Tainted truth.* New York: Simon and Schuster; Jenkins, Philip. (1994). *Using Murder.* Hawthorne, NY: Aldine de Gruyter. **2.** The word "gay" has come to be widely accepted as a descriptive term for homosexuals, though it has achieved varying success in establishing itself in academic writing. This reluctance partly reflects its slang origins, and also its rather disreputable older usage as a euphemism for a prostitute. On the other hand, it is by far the most popular word employed for self-description, and for convenience, the term will here be employed without quotation marks. **3.** Maguen, Shira. (1991). "Teen suicide." *The Advocate*, September 24, p 40. **4.** Galas, Judith C. (1994). *Teen suicide.* San Diego, CA: Lucent Overview, p 60. **5.** See for example Aarons, Leroy. (1995). *Prayers for Bobby.* San Francisco, CA.: HarperSanFrancisco. **6.** Shaffer, David. (1993). "Political science." *The New Yorker*, May 3; Knight, Al. (2000). "Gay suicide studies flawed." *Denver Post*, Apr 9. **7.** Douglas, Jack D. (1967). *The social meanings of suicide.* Princeton University Press. **8.** Males, Mike. (1991). "Teen suicide and changing cause of death certification 1953-1987," *Suicide and Life-Threatening Behavior*, 21(3), pp 245-259. **9.** Holinger, Paul C. (1994). *Suicide and homicide among adolescents.* New York: Guilford Press; Bergman, David B. (1990). *Kids on the brink.* Washington, DC: PIA Press; Cimbolic, Peter & David A. Jobes, eds., *Youth suicide.* Springfield, IL: Thomas; Pfeffer, Cynthia R. (Ed.). (1989). *Suicide among youth.* Washington, DC: American Psychiatric Press. **10.** Symonds is quoted in Tremblay, Pierre J. (1995). "The homosexuality factor in the youth suicide problem." Paper presented at the Sixth Annual Conference of the Canadian Association for Suicide Prevention, Banff, Alberta, October 11-14; Rofes, Eric E. (1983). *I thought people like that killed themselves: Lesbians, gay men and suicide.* San Francisco, CA: Grey Fox, p 11. **11.** Russo, Vito. (1981). *The celluloid closet.* New York: Harper and Row, p 261-262. **12.** Erwin, Kathleen. (1993). "Interpreting the evidence: Competing paradigms and the emergence of lesbian and gay suicide as a social fact," *International Journal of Health Services*, 23(3), pp 437-453. **13.** *Op cit.*, Rofes, 1. **14.** *Ibid.*, 130-132. **15.** Roesler, T. & R.W. Deisher. (1972). "Youthful male homosexuality." *Journal of the American Medical Association*, 219, pp 1018-23. Compare Schneider, Stephen G., Norman L. Farberow & Gabriel N. Kruks. (1989). "Suicidal behavior in adolescent and young adult gay men." *Suicide and Life-Threatening Behavior*, 19(4), p 381-94. **16.** Bell, Alan P. & Martin S. Weinberg. (1978). *Homosexualities.* New York: Simon and Schuster, pp 201-6, 450-7; Saghir, Marcel T. & Eli Robins. (1973). *Male and female homosexuality.* Baltimore: Williams and Wilkins, though neither study was strictly directed at the exact age-group of interest to later research. **17.** *Op cit.*, Erwin; Saunders, Judith M. & S. M. Valente. (1987). "Suicide risk among gay men and lesbians." *Death Studies*, 11, pp 1-23; Kourany, R. F. (1987). "Suicide among homosexual adolescents." *Journal of Homosexuality*, 13 pp 111-7; Jay, Karla & Allen Young. *The gay report.* New York: Summit. **18.** *Op cit.*, Rofes, 36; though the issue had in fact been discussed in some earlier works. **19.** Gibson, Paul (1989). "Gay male and lesbian teen suicide," in Report of the Secretary's Task Force on Youth Suicide, iii, p 110. **20.** *Ibid.*, iii, p 115. **21.** Adams, Jane Meredith. (1989). "For many gay teenagers, torment leads to suicide tries." *Boston Globe*, Jan 3. **22.** Early criticisms are found in *op cit.*, Shaffer; Marco, Tony "Special class protections for self-alleged gays," at <campus.leaderu.com/marco/special/spc-toc.html>. **23.** Kinsey, A., W. Pomeroy & C. Martin. (1948). *Sexual behavior in the human male.* Philadelphia, PA: W.B. Saunders; compare Heron, Ann. (Ed.). *One teenager in ten.* Boston: Alyson Publications; *idem. Two teenagers in twenty.* Boston: Alyson Publications. **24.** Reisman, Judith & Edward Eichel. (1990). *Kinsey, sex and fraud.* Lafayette, LA: Lochinvar/Huntington House. **25.** Schmalz, Jeffrey. (1993). "Survey stirs debate on number of gay men in US." *New York Times*, April 16. **26.** Rogers, Susan M. & Charles F. Turner. (1991). "Male-male sexual contact in the USA: Findings from five sample surveys 1970-1990." *Journal of Sex Research*, 28(4), pp 491-519. **27.** Lambert, Bruce. (1988). "Halving of estimate on AIDS is raising doubts in New York." *New York Times*, July 20; *idem*. (1988). "The cool reaction to New York's good news on AIDS." *New York Times*, July 21. **28.** Dunlap, David W. (1994). "Gay survey raises a new question." *New York Times*, October 18; Barringer, Felicity. (1993). "Sex survey of American men finds one percent are gay." *New York Times*, April 15; Fumento, Michael. (1993). "How many gays?" *National Review*, April 26, pp 28-9. **29.** Laumann, Edward O., et al. (1994). *The social organization of sexuality.* Chicago: University of Chicago Press. **30.** Compare Michael, Robert T. [et al.]. *Sex in America.* Boston: Little, Brown. **31.** *Op cit.*, Erwin, p 447. **32.** Flax, Ellen. (1991). "Nearly one-third of young gay men may attempt suicide, study suggests." *Education Week*, June 12, p 12; compare Proctor, Curtis D. (1994). "Risk factors for suicide among gay, lesbian and bisexual youths." *Social Work*, 39(5), pp 504-13; Schneider, Stephen G. (1991). "Factors influencing suicide intent in gay and bisexual suicide ideators," *Journal of Personality and Social Psychology*, 61(5), pp 776-88. See also the special supplementary issue of the journal *Suicide and Life-Threatening Behavior* on "Research Issues in Suicide and Sexual Orientation," vol. 25 (1995). **33.** Remafedi, Gary, James A. Farrow & Robert W. Deisher. (1991). "Risk factors for attempted suicide in gay and bisexual youth." *Pediatrics*, 87(6), pp 869-75. **34.** Rutten, Tim. (1991). "One congressman's fight against a sexual 'conspiracy'." *Los Angeles Times*, August 9. **35.** Hunt, Scott A. (1992). "An unspoken tragedy." *Christopher Street*, January 6, pp 28-30; *op cit.*, Maguen. **36.** "Making schools safe for gay and lesbian youth," in Remafedi, Gary (1994). *Death by denial.* Boston, MA: Alyson, pp 151-205, at p156. **37.** Hunt,Scott A. (1992). "An unspoken tragedy." *Christopher Street*, January 6, p 29; Remafedi, et al., "Risk Factors for Attempted Suicide in Gay and Bisexual Youth," p 869. **38.** Quoted in Marco, "Special Class Protections for Self-Alleged Gays." **39.** Remafedi, ed. *Death by Denial*, cover. **40.** The description derives from Remafedi, ed., *Death by Denial*, p 10. **41.** *Op cit.*, Maguen. **42.** quoted in *ibid*, p 42. **43.** *Op cit.*, Hunt. **44.** *Op cit.*, Galas, pp 60-1. **45.** *Op cit.*, Marco. **46.** Kastor, Elizabeth. (1992). "Suicide at an early age: *20/20*'s overheated report on gay teens." *Washington Post*, May 8. **47.** See for example Colt, George Howe. (1991). *The enigma of suicide.* New York: Summit, p 259. **48.** Nelson, Richard E. & Judith C. Galas. (1994). *The power to prevent suicide.* Minneapolis: Free Spirit, p 45; compare *op cit.*, Galas. **49.** *Op cit.*, Remafedi, p 13. **50.** Jenness, Valerie. (1995). "Social movement growth, domain expansion and framing processes." *Social Problems*, 42, pp 145-70; *idem*. "Hate crimes in the United States," in *Images of Issues*, 2nd edition, edited by Joel Best. Hawthorne, NY: Aldine de Gruyter, pp 213-37. **51.** Jenkins, Philip. (1998). *Moral Panic.* Yale University Press; Bull, Chris & John Gallagher. (1996). *Perfect enemies: The religious right, the gay movement and the politics of the 1990s* . New York: Crown. **52.** Foster, David. (1993). "Volatile debate often centers on children." AP wire story printed in the *Centre Daily Times*, State College, PA, May 16. **53.** Innerst, Carol. (1989). "Parents fear schools teach homosexuality." *Washington Times*, November 21; Adelman, Ken (1990). "When tolerance becomes advocacy." *Washington Times*, June 18. **54.** Adams, Jane Meredith. (1989). "For many gay teenagers, torment leads to suicide tries." *Boston Globe*, January 3. **55.** Besner, Hilda F. & Charlotte I. Spungin. (1995). *Gay and lesbian students.* Washington, DC: Taylor & Francis; Unks, Gerald. (Ed.). *The gay teen.* New York: Routledge; Harbeck, Karen M. (Ed.). *Coming out of the classroom closet.* New York: Harrington Park Press. **56.** *Op cit.*, Maguen. **57.** *Op cit.*, Gibson, iii, p 110. **58.** Torres, Ciara (1995). "Searching for a way out: Stopping gay teen suicide." Webpage. **59.** Gable, Jenny. "Problems Faced by Homosexual Youth," at <www.imsa.edu/~jgable/lbg/paper.html>. **60.** *Op cit.*, "Making Schools Safe for Gay and Lesbian Youth," p 157. **61.** Locy, Toni. (1991). "Gay activists criticize changes to suicide bill." *Boston Globe*, December 17. **62.** *Op cit.*, "Making Schools Safe for Gay and Lesbian Youth," p 154. **63.** *Op cit.*, Gibson, iii, pp 127-8, 135. **64.** *Op cit.*, Torres, "Searching for a Way Out: Stopping Gay Teen Suicide" **65.** The whole issue of "gay teens" continues to thrive in the media: see for instance Woog, Dan (1995). *School's out: The impact of gay and lesbian issues on America's schools.* Alyson; Bass, Ellen & Kate Kaufman. *Free your mind.* New York: HarperCollins; Ryan, Caitlin & Donna Futterman. (1998). *Lesbian and gay youth.* Columbia University Press. For media citations of the figure, see Ponnuru, Ramesh. (1998). "The new myths." *National Review*, November 9, pp 48-52. **66.** Jenness, Valerie. "Hate Crimes in the United States," p 214. Jenness, Valerie & Kendal Broad. (1997). *Hate crimes: New social movements and the politics of violence.* Hawthorne, NY: Aldine De Gruyter.

Even Kinsey claimed to find only 7 percent of the female population meeting his definition of lesbianism, a rate that has never been approached by any subsequent study.

We don't need no education,
We don't need no thought control.

—*The Wall*, by Pink Floyd

Apt Pupils

Robert Sterling

Almost immediately after fifteen people were tragically gunned down at Columbine High School in Littleton, Colorado, a chorus began screaming a question, over and over again. The chorus grew, treating the shocking mass shooting as though it were some sort of Agatha Christie novel. The question was a rather simple, direct one: "Why?"

"Why?" indeed. Why would two boys, teenagers Dylan Klebold and Eric Harris, decide to go on a mass slaying? What could have inspired such hateful rage, a rage that ultimately led to the destructive murders of thirteen others and their own suicides? Was there some sort of primal cause behind the deaths that we can learn about, hopefully so we can avoid further killings?

Soon, the most popular whipping boy for blame was Marilyn Manson, aka Brian Warner, the industrial goth-rock king and self-proclaimed "Anti-Christ Superstar." There were other cultural targets, including the film *The Matrix* (which included Keanu Reeves and others in a trenchcoat-wearing shooting spree) and violent videogames such as Mortal Kombat and Doom, but ultimately, Manson was just too irresistible for the mainstream media to ignore. Never mind that the sales for Manson's music are dwarfed by crap from the Backstreet Boys and 'N Sync (which leads some to conclude the problem is that not enough kids are listening to Manson's music, but that's another story). Marilyn Manson came to represent a culture of death, and it was this death culture that ultimately led to the Colorado carnage.

Of course, even Mr. Warner himself would admit that a culture of death was a culprit in the murders. Yet he argued persuasively that this culture was a mirror, a mirror for the destructive nature of American society in general.

This led quite nicely to Scapegoat Number Two, namely guns. Easy access to weapons caused the deaths, it was pronounced, fueled by the powerful lobbying muscle of the gun industry and the National Rifle Association. The demonization of the right to bear arms became so intense after Littleton, that "Queen of Nice" talk-show hostess and closeted lesbian Rosie O'Donnell proved herself to be a mean-spirited bitch, after viciously attacking *Magnum P.I.* actor Tom Selleck on her show for being an NRA member. (Some would note the hypocrisy of the obese former K-Mart shill blasting her guest, since the discount department store has long been a cheap and easy supplier of firearms. Oh yeah, and her bodyguard packs heat, too.)

That, in a nutshell, was the choice provided by the corporate media. Behind Door Number One and Door Number Two were the First and Second Amendments, and the choice, whether you were a "conservative" or a "liberal," was basically which fundamental American liberty to sacrifice in the name of security.

Incredibly, these two choices were even better than two other explanations for the murders that were floated. The first to be widely circulated was that the gunmen were homosexuals, and that the attack therefore was a hate crime against heterosexuals. The theory, ironically promoted by Internet gossip-hound Matt Drudge himself, was dubiously based on one posting to an online newsgroup, and alleged claims that Klebold and Harris were taunted as being homosexuals on campus. (Of course, anyone who has the slightest memory of high school knows that calling someone "faggot" has long been a popular slur.) Then there was the right-wing "Christian" political group, the Family Research Council, who insisted the massacre may be linked to pot smoking, and used the tragedy to promote public school-based random drug testing as a solution. (Even William Randolph Hearst wasn't that bold.)

It turned out that neither Klebold nor Harris had marijuana in his body at the time, and they apparently weren't pot-heads. (Those who know the anti-violent tendencies inspired by getting stoned weren't surprised by the revelation.) However, it also turned out that Eric Harris, the leader of the two boys, was taking a prescribed dosage of Luvox, a pharmaceutical prescribed to youth and others for its supposed anti-depressive qualities. According to Dr. Peter Breggin, a noted psychiatrist and author (*Toxic Psychiatry*, *Talking Back to Prozac*, *Talking Back to Ritalin*): "With Luvox there is some evidence of a four-percent rate for mania in adolescents. Mania, for certain individuals, could be a component in grandiose plans to destroy large numbers of other people. Mania can go over the hill to psychosis." This (and the surprising link between mass shootings and gunmen who take drugs such as Luvox, Ritalin, and Prozac) led investigative journalist Jon Rappoport to argue that the rash of teen shootings that climaxed in Columbine was the byproduct of overdependence on often harmful psychiatric drugs.

An even more conspiratorial theory began to circulate on the Internet, primarily courtesy of John Quinn, a cyber-sleuth behind the digital enterprise NewsHawk. In his breathless, excited prose, Quinn proclaimed that Klebold and Harris, like the shooters behind other mass school slayings, were the victims of mind control, and that the real culprit was the CIA-Pentagon, all as part of some diabolical plot to enslave Americans in a New World Order. With his sensationalistic style, Quinn's work was met with skepticism and derision from many, but even critics of Quinn could at best ignore some of the more disturbing facts. (See the article "Anatomy of a School Shooting" by David McGowan, elsewhere in this book, for an incredible presentation of the evidence that the authorities are lying about Columbine.)

Of course, while suppressed explanations such as poisonous pharmaceuticals and Manchurian Candidates are intriguing to contemplate, they aren't the real focus of this article. After all, while they certainly are accurate, such propositions seem to buy into the false notion that somehow the mass murders should be a shocking surprise.

The Onion, a popular online satire magazine, would publish one of its more bleakly hilarious bits in September 1999, with a title which said it all: "Columbine Jocks Safely Resume Bullying." Here are some of the more cruelly amusing segments from the fictional piece, in which local police forces and school authorities aid power cliques in their oppression of social outcasts:

- "We have begun the long road to healing," said varsity-football starting halfback Jason LeClaire, 18, a popular senior who on Aug. 16 returned to the school for the first time since the shooting. "We're bouncing back, more committed than ever to ostracizing those who are different."

- "A school where the jocks cannot freely exclude math geeks, drama fags, goths and other inferiors without fearing for their lives is not the kind of school I want to go to."

- "It's almost as if a helpful 'big brother' is watching us now," homecoming queen Lori Nowell said. "None of the losers can mess with us. Now that the entire school is blanketed by surveillance equipment, the popular kids, like, totally rule the school!"

- "We thought that the systematic cruelties inflicted on our school's desperate, alienated outcasts would be sufficient... Those kids were beaten up, pelted with rocks and universally rejected by their more popular peers, not only because they were smart and computer-literate, but also because of the way they dressed and the music they liked. But the shootings sent a clear message to this school and this community: We hadn't done nearly enough to keep such misfits shunned and in their place."

What made the article so entertaining was that it almost sounded like truth. As Jon Katz eloquently noted in a Slashdot article, "People who are different are reviled as geeks, nerds, dorks. The lucky ones are excluded, the unfortunates are harassed, humiliated, sometimes assaulted literally as well as socially. Odd values—unthinking school spirit, proms, jocks—are exalted, while the best values—free thinking, non-conformity, curiosity—are ridiculed."

If a zero-tolerance policy was instituted against cliquish torment, it would disappear, or at least be seriously curtailed. The continued existence of such malignant social structures and arrangements says all that has to be said about how school authorities view the threat of bullying.

Incredibly, across the country, school authorities even overtly harassed and targeted the outcasts in the days following Littleton. Katz would coin a term for it: Geek Profiling. Katz reported that by email, "teenagers traded countless stories of being harassed, beaten, ostracized and ridiculed by teachers, students and administrators for dressing and thinking differently from the mainstream. Many said they had some understanding of why the killers in Littleton went over the edge."

Pretty powerful words. The actions of school authorities across the country spoke even more strongly, with "suspensions and expulsions for 'anti-social behavior' to censorship of student publications to school and parental restrictions on computing, Web browsing, and especially gaming." Rather than go after those who control a toxic school culture, the usual suspects were fingered for blame and attack.

"Jay in the Southeast" wrote:

I stood up in a social studies class—the teacher wanted a discussion—and said I could never kill anyone or condone anyone who did kill anyone. But that I could, on some level, understand these kids in Colorado, the killers. Because day after day, slight after slight, exclusion after exclusion, you can learn how to hate, and that hatred grows and takes you over sometimes, especially when you come to see that you're hated only because you're smart and different, or sometimes even because you are online a lot, which is still so uncool to many kids.

After the class, I was called to the principal's office and told that I had to agree to undergo five sessions of counseling or be expelled from school, as I had expressed "sympathy" with the killers in Colorado, and the school had to be able to explain itself if I "acted out". In other words, for speaking freely, and to cover their ass, I was not only branded a weird geek, but a potential killer. That will sure help deal with violence in America.

"Dan in Boise" warned:

Be careful! I wrote an article for my school paper. The advisor suggested we write about "our feelings" about Colorado. My feelings—what I wrote—were that society is blaming the wrong things. You can't blame screwed-up kids or the Net. These people don't know what they were talking about. How bout blaming a system that takes smart or weird kids and drives them crazy? How about understanding why these kids did what they did, cause in some crazy way, I feel something for them. For their victims, too, but for them. I thought it was a different point-of-view, but important. I was making a point. I mean, I'm not going to the prom.

You know what? The article was killed, and I got sent home with a letter to my parents. It wasn't an official suspension, but I can't go back until Tuesday. And it was made pretty clear to me that if I made any noise about it, it would be a suspension or worse. So this is how they are trying to figure out what happened in Colorado, I guess. By blaming a subculture and not thinking about their own roles, about how fucked-up school is. Now, I think the whole thing was a setup, cause a couple of other kids are being questioned too, about what they wrote. They pretend to want to have a "dialogue" but kids should be warned that what they really want to know is who's dangerous to them.

Fortunately for a world threatened by the diabolical geek youth menace, a solution has come about: a program called WAVE America. WAVE is an acronym for Working Against Violence Everywhere, and is a private program for public schools created by corporate dick monolith Pinkerton (best noted for teaming up with big business to harass labor unions). WAVE provides a toll-free number for students to call and inform on students who exhibit certain "risk" characteristics. The information is handled by WAVE America itself (i.e. Pinkerton), who coincidentally, as a security firm hired by many major corporations, could benefit from the surveillance information they obtain, by providing clients extensive history reports on prospective employees.

To sell children on WAVE America, the program offers a WAVE Card, which doesn't seem to have much value in selling safety, the supposed purpose of the program. Here is how WAVE America itself has promoted the nifty concept, in a style that seems almost written by The Onion:

WAVE provides a toll-free number for students to call and inform on students who exhibit certain "risk" characteristics.

The incredible WAVE Card is going to make your life very fun. Here's what we have planned—coming soon. We are going to get your favorite restaurants,

clothing stores, computer places and other fantastic retailers to give you discounts and free stuff. Yes, I'm sure it is hard to contain the absolute excitement you are feeling right now upon learning about the benefits of the WAVE Card.

Though WAVE America founders spent enough money to come up with a WAVE Card as part of their marketing campaign, they supposedly didn't do enough research to uncover the fact that the name echoes *The Wave*, a novel based on a real-life social experiment performed by a Palo Alto high school teacher in 1969. The history teacher wanted to show students how easily they could be seduced into joining a fascist Hitler Youth program. Under the banner of "strength through discipline, community, and action," the Wave was introduced to students and faculty, who eagerly embraced it. Soon, Wave cards were introduced, and students and teachers began informing on those opposed to the program. When Ben Ross, the teacher and mastermind of the program, revealed its obvious parallels to Hitler's kiddie army, students and faculty alike were stunned by how easily they were deceived.

Joanne McDaniel, a spokeswoman for the WAVE America program, would claim dubiously that the similarities were "just a coincidence." Incredibly, Todd Strasser, one of the book's coauthors, agreed, and added that the book would prevent an evolution of WAVE America into something sinister, as students and teachers are too wise to be fooled into participating in an overtly fascist program. (Apparently, Strasser missed the point of his own work.)

The program was formed in partnership with the Center for the Prevention of School Violence, founded by North Carolina Governor James B. Hunt, Jr. North Carolina is the home of Fort Bragg, location of the Army's Psychological Warfare division, whose official job is to influence public opinion in enemy territory. In another incredible coincidence, the group's name echoes that of the Center for the Study and Reduction of Violence, created by then-California Governor Ronald Reagan. Its plans were formulated by the late Dr. Louis Jolyon "Jolly" West, who was heavily involved in the CIA's notorious MK-ULTRA mind control program. The Jolly doctor described the program as an attempt to predict occurrences of violent behavior in specific population groups. According to Dr. West, "The major known correlates of violence are sex (male), age (youthful), ethnicity (black), and urbanicity."

Dr. West then discussed a wide variety of treatments, including chemical castration, psychosurgery, and experimental drugs, which were to be coordinated with a California law enforcement program, using computer databases to track "pre-delinquent" youth (i.e. young blacks with no criminal record) for preemptive treatment. The California State Legislature officially dismantled plans for the Center after information regarding the program was leaked to the press.

Coincidentally, in the wake of Columbine, another program, Mosaic 2000, has been designed to anticipate threatening or violent behavior by students, rating children on a computerized violence scale before any crimes have been committed. The program was created by a partnership of a private security consultation firm and the folks at the Bureau of Alcohol, Tobacco and Firearms.

James Neff, at the Sightings Website, stated a rarely pronounced truth:

When I was in high school...when we all were in high school...there was a sick, twisted system long ago established by which the gifted—those who by nature do not meld with the "Borg" of normative society—were trampled, humiliated and slowly beaten down psychologically, and oftentimes physically, until we fit the mold or perished.

Some of you reading this were the instruments of that torment, and you yourselves were guided and manipulated by peer pressures to do so. Adapt or die. And some of you reading this are still struggling with well-disguised and hidden scars from those years. Adapt or die. Others...sloughed it off, burying it deep in the subconscious.

Adapt or die.

But some are not with us anymore. They dropped a load of sleeping pills to escape it; they pulled the trigger on Dad's 12 gauge in the garage seeking that perfect sleep; they wandered off in a fugue state never to be seen or heard from again. All the while the conformers, the normals, the happy-go-lucky cogs of the great Borg went on morally blind to the incredible tragedy surrounding them and in which they blindly—or knowingly—participated. No body count.

Neff would then add the following pronouncement:

The question is, is it deserved? That is not to say did any of these young people in Littleton deserve to die, but rather: Is this war, this "rage against the machine" deserved? I say yes. It has been a long time coming. It is much deserved. Not the deaths, not the tragedy. It's horrific that it has come to this! I have nothing but pity and sorrow for the victims and their families. But on a raw-truth level, this sort of lashing out is utterly predictable and sustained by a system even those parents participate in, regarding it as "normal" and "good." We reap what we sow. And I truly wonder how many of the people closely involved with this debacle have any clue how much they themselves feed the beast. They feed

Could a phenomenon such as social persecution develop independently across nearly every high school in the country without it being a byproduct of some design?

it when they hand their kid a charge card and tell them to go forth and reflect what the many varied cliques demand in clothing, in music, in style. They feed it when they buy into this disturbed system that creates a hierarchy of acceptability and conformity, and in turn demonstrate to their children that the "way things are" is good...right...the "way it should be" because it has always been that way.

The Onion, Jon Katz, and James Neff are hitting as close to the true cause behind the deaths at Columbine as anyone. Frankly, it is remarkable that there aren't more Columbines, that it isn't a weekly occurrence. As Dr. Wilhelm Stekel would put it in *Sadism and Masochism*: "One must be amazed, when one learns of the inner nature of man, that the number of criminals is so small."

The funny thing is, when people do admit that there is something terribly wrong with the high school social structure (something which is fairly self-evident), it is treated as though it is some reality created in a vacuum, that there is neither a cause nor cure for the malady. Such beliefs defy reason: Could a phenomenon such as social persecution develop independently across nearly every high school in the country without it being a byproduct of some design?

Alvin Toffler is perhaps the most important social critic of the last 50 years. In his 1980 masterpiece, *The Third Wave*, he pointed out that the purpose of the schooling system was to train children to become industrial workers. As Andrew Ure would write in 1835, it was "nearly impossible to convert persons past the age of puberty, whether drawn from rural or from handicraft occupations, into useful factory hands." Thanks to the schooling system, youth are trained very early in how they are expected to be useful. While mass education claims to be mainly about reading, writing, and arithmetic, the "covert curriculum," as Toffler puts it, consists "of three courses: one in punctuality, one in obedience, and one in rote, repetitive work. Factory labor demanded workers who showed up on time, especially assembly-line hands. It demanded workers who would take orders from a management hierarchy without questioning. And it demanded men and women prepared to slave away at machines or in offices, performing brutally repetitious operations." Toffler would grimly conclude that the schooling system "machined generation after generation of young people into a pliable, regimented work force of the type required by electro-mechanical technology and the assembly line."

John Taylor Gatto was a New York school teacher for 26 years, and in 1991 he was named New York State Teacher of the Year. In his acceptance speech, he bit the hand that fed him, and attacked the very institution he served, going even further than Mr. Toffler did with his harsh words. He told his stunned audience that teachers aren't employed to develop minds, but to destroy them. Soon afterwards, Gatto would unsurprisingly leave the "educational" system. As he would later put it in a *Wall Street Journal* Op-Ed to explain his decision of retirement: "I teach how to fit into a world I don't want to live in."

As Gatto has plainly presented in his book *Dumbing Us Down*, there are seven universal lessons taught by the mass schooling system:

1. **Confusion**. Teachers teach too many facts and not enough connections. They don't show the larger picture or how things work together.
2. **Class position**. Children are grouped into classes based on "intelligence"—special needs, average, or gifted—and that's where they stay.
3. **Indifference**. Teachers demand that students get highly involved in a lesson for 50 minutes, and when the bell rings, forget about it and go to the next class. "Indeed, the lesson of the bells is that no work is worth finishing, so why care too deeply about anything."
4. **Emotional dependency**. Teachers and higher authorities decide everything for students, from what they are allowed to say to who may use the bathroom.
5. **Intellectual dependency**. Teachers decide what will be taught and when and how it will be taught. "It is the most important lesson, that we must wait for other people, better trained than ourselves, to make the meanings of our lives."
6. **Provisional self-esteem**. Students are constantly judged and evaluated. Their feelings of self-worth depend on how an outsider rates them.
7. **One can't hide**. Students have no private time or private space. They are encouraged to snitch on each other. "I teach students that they are always watched, that each is under constant surveillance by myself and my colleagues."

(As summarized in *Psychotropedia*.)

"I teach how to fit into a world I don't want to live in."

According to Gatto, it only takes around 100 hours to teach the fundamentals of real education to people eager to learn (which children naturally are until the joy of learning is beaten out of them). To learn the seven lessons of the covert curriculum takes a little bit longer, which is why the state imposes a twelve-year educational system. All of which fulfills the wet-dream fantasies of a mighty autocratic state Plato gushed over, as he proposed a mass schooling system to be a prime component for creating his ideal Republic.

One of the greatest tools for the industrial-educational system is the handing out of grades. If, as so many foolishly insist, the purpose of the educational system is to educate, why are students graded rather than the teachers, the people who are getting paid to do the teaching? If a student fails to learn a subject, why is it he or she alone who receives the scarlet F? When teachers clearly fail at the job of teaching, why should they be able to pull a Pontius Pilate and wipe their hands clean of all blame? The essence of teachers' response to failed students is them declaring, "Hey, don't look at me, I had nothing to do with this fuck-up."

The truth is, contrary to popular belief, grades are not handed out to promote real learning. If anything, the grading system kills and maims the inquisitive spirit: Why try to learn something new if the result may be the punishment of being branded a failure? The purpose of grades is to teach kids that they are at the mercy of authorities, who have near absolute power to judge them on their own worthiness. Self-worth must be earned by pleasing the goals and edicts of superiors, and if a student succeeds, he or she will move up the totem with better opportunities provided by the schooling system. As Albert Einstein once put it:

> **It is in fact nothing short of a miracle that the modern methods of instruction have not yet entirely strangled the holy curiosity of inquiry; for this delicate little plant, aside from stimulation, stands mainly in need of freedom; without this it goes to wrack and ruin without fail. It is a very grave mistake to think that the enjoyment of seeing and searching can be promoted by means of coercion and a sense of duty.**

Each student, then, is a direct competitor of his fellow student, in a dog-eat-dog system, with the spoils going to the victorious canine. Or, as Neff put it, "Adapt or die." If some people can't compete in such a system, they will resort to other techniques (bullying and social ostracizing) to punish and hinder those who compete with them. Some will participate in such rituals to provide outlets for frustrations and inferiority complexes, which predictably develop in such a twisted training ground.

The cruel social structure of mass schooling is no accident: It is by design. The purpose of mass schooling is to teach people their place, and it does this quite well. As for actual learning, it is severely lacking. Little surprise that increasing numbers are opting out of the system via homeschooling, a trend which is increasing by 15 percent a year. Even less surprising is that children who are homeschooled—with teachers (i.e. parents) who have a vested interest in their students succeeding and without a grading system—tend to do even better on standardized achievement tests, ironically created to measure mass education output. Median scores for homeschoolers at all grade levels are between the 70th to 80th percentile in most studies.

Perhaps even more surprising to some is that homeschooling doesn't harm the socialization skills of children, a charge often used to justify the unjustifiable system in place. Julie Webb, a researcher who examined the lives of homeschooled students, found that their socialization skills were often better than those of their peers. Her findings were published in 1989 in *Educational Review*, which is hardly a propaganda unit for the homeschooling movement. While such evidence defies conventional wisdom, it does make sense after all: Opting out of a psychopathic school culture does wonders in reducing tensions with peers and adults.

Naturally, politicians of all stripes are loath to discuss the malignant nature of mass schooling, and the masses, like sheep, rarely speak out against it themselves. True, conservatives may complain that God has been taken out of the classroom and offer self-serving solutions like school vouchers. Yes, liberals may criticize the supposed underfunding for schools and the unfair underrepresentation of oppressed groups in history books. Yet, despite such ideological rhetoric, both sides of the debate still buy into the basic fraud that our school system is a boon to mankind. In the end, any discussion of "reforming" it is about as productive as talk of reforming a death camp. When the inherent goal of an institution is fundamentally evil, there is no way to "reform" it for improvement.

Which leads to a final point: the actual original purpose for mass schooling. As can be clearly observed, mass education wasn't introduced to educate children's minds. Still, was it all just to create an industrial economy and corporate state?

The answer, unsurprisingly, is no. As Gatto noted in an interview in *Flatland* magazine, the beginnings of the modern educational system were in 1806, when the French forces of Napoleon kicked the ass of the Prussian State. Considering that the French were a quiche-munching, wine-sipping group of toads led by a midget with a shrunken penis, this was a major blow to the psyche of the Prussian intellectuals. There was a big debate over the mystery of how Prussia

Self-worth must be earned by pleasing the goals and edicts of superiors.

> The true purpose behind the Western schooling system was to transform the young into killers.

could have lost so badly. Soon after, a German philosopher named Johann Gottlieb Fichte delivered his famous "Address to the German Nation," where he laid out his explanation for the debacle, an explanation that soon became national gospel. Simply put, the problem was that the Prussian people were too independent-thinking and weren't committed to important values like being eager to sacrifice oneself for the society.

The answer, therefore, was to come up with a system where people's innate desire for dangerous concepts like freedom and liberty could be effectively squashed. The solution came in 1819, when Prussia founded a compulsory "educational" system. By crushing the insidious independent spirit early on in the little tikes, the Prussian State could easily use the more docile public as the necessary fodder for an effective death machine. All this was perfectly symbolized in the term *kindergarten*, German for *children's garden*. No, it didn't mean that the children were at play in a garden, but rather, that they were like vegetables to be prepared by teachers, with the ultimate goal that they be sliced up by the State in the name of some greater good salad.

It certainly worked: Trained from an early age to deny infantile instincts, the children grew to be good soldiers, and Prussia quickly became one nasty motherfucker. A little over 100 years later, the same ideology of National Socialism that was behind the making of modern education went to the most efficient and successful death machine in history, thanks to the inheritors of the Prussian Empire in Nazi Germany. Hitler's birthday, incidentally, is April 20, the same day as the Columbine tragedy.

The implications of all this are rather startling: The true purpose behind the Western schooling system was to transform the young into killers. That being the case, don't we really have it all backward? Rather than screaming, "Why?" shouldn't we instead be asking, like Timothy Leary did moments before he died, "Why not?"

If the purpose of our schooling system is to make an efficient murder machine, shouldn't we be hoping that more Columbines continue to happen? Shouldn't the educational establishment, rather than paying lip service to spineless politicians squeamish as to what war is really about, trumpet the Columbine massacre as one of its great success stories? Isn't the real tragedy here not that Klebold and Harris killed thirteen other people, but rather that these well-trained gunmen killed themselves as well, before they could replicate their actions on some Third World country whose leader begins defying IMF-World Bank edicts? Indeed, since the whole purpose of the schooling system is to turn children into what they had become, don't both Klebold and Harris deserve posthumous degrees (with honors, no less) for their fine work?

Perhaps to some, such statements are politically incorrect, but this writer, for one, is going to do the patriotic thing and salute these two fine boys. Three cheers for Dylan Klebold and Eric Harris. They obviously learned their lessons well.

Special thanks to John Taylor Gatto and Flatland *editor Jim Martin for their extraordinary ihformation on the history of mass education.*

Sources

From The Konformist <www.konformist.com/1999/colorado.htm>:
"The Littleton conspiracy (or: connect these dots)".
"Beast of the Month - June 1999: Lou Pearlman, bubble gum pop mephistopheles"
"Trenchcoat Mafia: Homosexual group?"
Family Research Council. "Possible April 20 (420) connection to pot smoking sub-culture in Littleton tragedy".
Quinn, John. "The Littleton massacre: The mystery deepens".

From John Taylor Gatto:
Dumbing Us Down (New Society Publishers, 1992).
"I may be a teacher, but I'm not an educator," *Wall Street Journal*, July 25, 1991.
"The six-lesson schoolteacher," *Whole Earth Review*, Fall 1991.
"The origins of compulsory education," John Taylor Gatto interviewed by Jim Martin, *Flatland* #11 (April 1994) <www.flatlandbooks.com/flatmag.html>.

From David M. Bresnahan at WorldNetDaily:
"'Wave' of protest over violence plan"
<www.worldnetdaily.com/bluesky_bresnahan/20000402_xex_wave_protest.shtml>
"Anonymous tip program under fire"
<www.worldnetdaily.com/bluesky_bresnahan/20000330_xex_anonymous_ti.shtml>
"Spying 10"
<www.worldnetdaily.com/bluesky_bresnahan/20000327_xex_spying_101.shtml>

Other sources

Dougherty, Jon. "Computer to identify violence-prone students," WorldNetDaily.
<www.worldnetdaily.com/bluesky_dougherty/19991215_xnjdo_computer_t.shtml>
Fichte, Johann Gottlieb. "Address to the German nation".
Katz, Jon. "Voices from the Hellmouth," Slashdot, April 26, 1999 <slashdot.org>
Kick, Russ. (1998). *Psychotropedia*. Critical Vision (Headpress).
Manson, Marilyn. "Columbine: Whose fault is it?" *Rolling Stone* <www.rollingstone.com>
Neff, James. "The war on individuality comes home: Littleton shootings predictable," Sightings <www.sightings.com/politics2/system.htm>
Policy.com. "Education reform in America: Homeschooling" <www.policy.com>
Rappoport, Jon. "Why did they do it?: An inquiry into the school shootings in America," The Truthseeker Foundation <truthseeker.com>
Strasser, Todd, Harriet Harvey Coffin, & Morton Rhue. (1981). *The Wave*. (Latest edition from Laurel Leaf.
Thompson, E.P. (1966). *The making of the English working class.* Random House.
Toffler, Alvin. *The third wave*.
Unattributed. "Columbine jocks safely resume bullying," The Onion, September 9, 1999
<www.theonion.com/onion3532/columbine_jocks.html>.
WAVE America <www.waveamerica.com>
Yahoo Full Coverage: Columbine High School
<fullcoverage.yahoo.com/Full_Coverage/US/Columbine_High_School>

A Panic of Biblical Proportions over Media Violence

Paul McMasters

August 21, 2000. Two lawyers have asked the German government to place the Bible on the national "not for children list" because it is too violent. This book contains a "gruesomeness difficult to exceed," said lawyers Christian Sailer and Gert-Joachim Hetzel in a letter to Germany's family minister. "It preaches genocide, racism, enmity toward Jews, gruesome executions for adulterers and homosexuals, the murder of one's own children and many other perversities," they wrote.

In these days of panic and political pandering over violence in the media, it's difficult to know whether these lawyers are serious or just trying to make a point.

This is just the latest professional group to trump reason and science with political rhetoric about media violence as a cause of real violence.

Certainly, the American Bar Association's Division for Public Education was serious last week when it announced the publication of a new guide to help teachers address violence in television programs, movies, video games, and the Internet. The division quoted Mary A. Hepburn, professor emeritus of social science at the University of Georgia in Athens, as saying that media violence is "a powerful ingredient" in violent youth behavior. And the ABA group cited "an increasing number of studies linking media violence" and "violence in the classroom."

This is just the latest professional group to trump reason and science with political rhetoric about media violence as a cause of real violence.

Late last month, four major health groups issued a joint statement endorsing the scientifically dubious claim that media cause violence. They announced their conclusions at a political "summit" organized by Senator Sam Brownback, a leading proponent of the idea that violence in the media translates into violence in the streets. (The four groups taking part were the American Medical Association, the American Academy of Pediatrics, the American Psychological Association, and the American Academy of Child and Adolescent Psychiatry.)

Members of the AMA board had not read any of the studies they were citing.

Later, a spokesman for the American Medical Association conceded that (1) the groups issued their joint statement at the request of Senator Brownback, (2) members of the AMA board had not read any of the studies they were citing, and (3) a report on the issue actually hasn't been written yet.

These groups are not the only ones who came to a conclusion before they came to a thorough study of the evidence. In this case, however, it's difficult to understand how they arrived at this particular conclusion when there are so many serious questions about a causal connection between media and violence.

Yet in the joint statement they trot out the tired claim, "At this time, well over 1,000 studies...point overwhelmingly to a causal connection between media violence and aggressive behavior in some children."

It would be most difficult for these groups to produce a list of more than 1,000 studies on media violence. It would be even more difficult to produce a list of 1,000 studies that focus primarily on children and violence. It would be impossible to produce a list of 1,000 studies that state an unequivocally causal link between media and "aggressive behavior" in children, let alone violent acts by children.

Yet this "fact" has been tossed about so often by politicians and activists that even professionals and scholars feel safe in using it. That is just one example of the loopy nature of this debate: Political leaders exaggerate and distort what studies do exist, their rhetoric gets written into legislation as reality, experts adopt and cite the "official" position, and in turn are quoted by political leaders in proposing yet more legislation to solve the problem by limiting expression containing violence.

All of this takes place in an environment where terms are ambiguous and agendas are numerous. Definitions of "violence" as depicted in entertainment media frequently are broad and vary from one pronouncement to another. They conflate all so-called "violent acts" into one negative or harmful category, with little or no regard given to content or context or whether the depiction is fact or fiction, virtual or real.

A few studies do suggest a connection between television violence and "aggressive behavior" in a small percentage of the individuals studied (the causal link for other types of media is generally assumed since few non-TV studies exist). The reality is that there are significant scientific hurdles to overcome in demonstrating that media violence actually causes violence, no matter whether the research takes place in a laboratory study, a field study, a longitudinal study, or a combination or variation of those approaches.

The methodological challenges are nearly insurmountable. Researchers are bound ethically not to produce actual violence among their subjects, so they must rely instead on measuring "arousal" or testing for "aggressive behavior"—responses that often are modeled or sanctioned by the studies or researchers themselves and sometimes cannot be distinguished from the emotional reactions to the medium itself rather than the content of the programming.

The reality is that there are significant scientific hurdles to overcome in demonstrating that media violence actually causes violence.

Those who cite these carefully qualified studies suggesting a connection between media and violence ignore the reality that there is absolutely no way of predicting with certainty whether a so-called violent depiction will produce a positive, negative, or neutral result in a given individual.

They also ignore the word of criminologists, sociologists, biologists, and others that media is not even a significant factor in determining the causes and interventions for violence. The real causes of violence, in fact, are well-known and securely documented: poverty, drugs, gangs, guns, broken families, neglect and abuse, harsh and inconsistent discipline, peer association. These problems, however, don't lend themselves to easy solutions or easy rhetoric.

So the political appeal of the idea of media violence causing real violence is such that many are unwilling to search for real solutions, which would be too complicated and expensive and take too long to yield results.

But policy-makers are not the only ones who should be excoriated for diverting the nation's attention from the real causes of violence and expending time, energy, and resources on false solutions.

There is plenty of blame to go around among:

- Health professionals, for lending their authority and credibility to this delay and denial.
- Child advocacy groups, for letting others hijack their campaigns for addressing children's real needs.
- Scholars, for failing to set the record straight when their studies are misrepresented, exaggerated, and harnessed to a political agenda.
- And the rest of us, for allowing all of that to go on while our children still wait for answers.

There is an inevitable line of logic that must issue from the assertion that media cause violence: We must censor TV, the movies, the Internet, music, and video gámes. Gloria Tristani of the Federal Communications Commission even endorses the idea that violence can be treated as obscenity and banned accordingly.

There is a reason, of course, that violence as obscenity or the concept of "copycat crimes" has not taken hold in the courts, where evidence and reason trump assertions and wishfulness, and where freedom of expression is a constitutional mandate rather than a political irritant.

But it isn't in a court of law where this story is playing out. It is in the court of public opinion, and right now rant and rhetoric are winning out over science and reason. In such an environment, it's only a matter of time before the Bible winds up on the censored list.

Gloria Tristani of the Federal Communications Commission even endorses the idea that violence can be treated as obscenity and banned accordingly.

This article originally appeared on the Freedom Forum <www.freedomforum.org>, where Paul McMasters is the First Amendment Ombudsman.

The Man in the Bushes

Mythkiller Philip Jenkins Deconstructs Serial Killers, Child Molesters, and Other Scary People

Interview with Philip Jenkins

> *"Although a phenomenon may remain more or less unchanged over time, it can be seen as a problem or social fact in one era but not another."*
> *—from* Moral Panic *by Philip Jenkins*

Russ Kick: I was hoping you'd briefly discuss your approach to studying social problems (or, perhaps more accurately, phenomena correctly or incorrectly regarded as problems). You employ social constructionism. Please tell me about that approach.

Philip Jenkins: Any society faces a range of problems and crises, and there are two ways of looking at them. One is to assume that the problem really is there, it is what people believe it to be, and then you have to decide how to combat it. Put in extreme terms, if people are worried about interracial couples having sex, or about witches causing bad weather, then as an expert, your job is to come up with ways of solving these terrible problems. Perhaps you should go out and draw up personality profiles of witches, or find what dreadful mental diseases cause people to have sex across the color line.

In many cases, "no known suspect or motive" just meant the local police could not be bothered to fill in the forms.

A constructionist would ask totally different questions, namely why people are concerned about these particular issues. They would also note that some phenomena are around for a very long time before suddenly being recognized as problems. So what is it about a particular time or place that leads people to imagine that X is a problem? One basic assumption is that there is no necessary link between the objective threat posed by a particular issue and how seriously people take it at any given time.

How Many Serial Killers?

RK: In your book *Using Murder*, you look at the serial killer phenomenon, showing that the danger was blown way out of proportion. For example, the government came up with the oft-quoted statistic that 4,000 people are murdered by serial killers every year. You believe that the number is much lower. What do you think the real number is, and how did you arrive at it?

PJ: How the FBI got to the 4,000 figure was this. They looked at homicide statistics and counted the number of murders without an immediate and obvious suspect, and assumed that this was the number of serial murders. That's ludicrous, especially since in many cases the actual killers were turning up a week or month after the stats were recorded, and were obviously not serial killers.

In many cases, "no known suspect or motive" just meant the local police could not be bothered to fill in the forms—guess what, the NYPD has a vast number of such crimes, because they have such a low opinion of the feds, and don't want to do their paperwork for them. But the figures were very useful for the FBI, which suddenly declared a serial killer menace, and used this to argue for new resources.

I used a couple of different tactics, partly taking all the known serial killers for particular periods, and estimating the number of their victims. Also, I found how many recorded cases could not be explained any other way. That leaves us with between 100 and 300 serial-murder victims each year, which in the 1980s meant around 1 percent of total homicides, really a minuscule fraction of the whole. So the problem was vastly exaggerated and distorted, and any fool should have been able to see that. I am still amazed that the media gave the FBI a free ride on this one.

Oh—and the FBI also stressed that all their imagined killers wandered around to commit their crimes, killed in various cities and states, which the vast majority do not do: Most are homebodies, killing in the same town or even street. But wandering killers fall under federal jurisdiction.

Not Just White Males

RK: You also note that stereotypes of serial killers are highly inaccurate. There's the idea that serial killers are almost always male; there may be a female serial killer or two, but they're basically statistical flukes. Then there's the popular idea that serial killers are white.

PJ: The best breakdown of known American serial-killer cases is by Eric Hickey, who finds substantial numbers of women and minorities as

I would suggest anywhere between a third and a half of all serial killers are women.

serial killers. Also, even his figures are likely to be underestimates, since women kill in ways that are less likely to be detected. If a body is found nude and disemboweled, a police officer does not need to be a genius to deduce that a sex killer is on the loose, and the police will start looking for other unsolved cases. On the other hand, if an old man turns up without obvious signs of violence, police and doctors will not spend too much time looking for foul play, especially in a nursing home or hospital. Women tend to smother, strangle, or poison, so there are likely far more women serial killers than we ever know. I would suggest anywhere between a third and a half of all serial killers are women.

The same is true of black serial killers. Hickey's records show that about 15 percent of known serial cases are black, but again, that's a minimum figure, due to discriminatory police attitudes. Put simply, poor people living in certain high-crime neighborhoods appear to inspire less concern when they die or vanish.

The case of Calvin Jackson is interesting here. When he was arrested in 1974 for a murder committed in a New York apartment building, he confessed with little prompting to a series of other homicides committed in the same building over a six-month period. Before this confession, there had been no suggestion that any of the crimes were linked, or indeed that most of the deaths were caused by anything other than natural causes. The police had not been too concerned, in large part a consequence of the nature of the victims and of the environment in which they died: The building was a single-occupancy hotel, where most of the guests were poor, isolated, and often elderly. In the case of Jackson's victims, foul play was only recorded in cases where victims were killed with conspicuous signs of violence; autopsies were rare. Deaths resulting from smothering were customarily dismissed as the result of natural causes. Where foul play was noted, the police saw no reason to suspect a serial killer, and naturally viewed the crime as part of the interpersonal violence that was endemic in such a transient community.

In other words, whether we are talking about blacks or women, police naturally approach a suspicious death with certain preconceptions that depend both on the nature of the victim and the social environment in which the incident occurs. In some contexts, a sudden death can be explained in many ways without the need to assume the existence of a random or repeat killer, and serial murder activity is thus less likely to be noted. Then we get a cyclical effect: Police and media do not record many serial killers who are blacks or women, so they begin to believe that not many exist; so when a new case does show up involving a black or a woman, there is no conceptual model to fit it into, no convenient profile; and so these cases remain unstudied. In contrast, serial killers who target people for obviously sexual reasons, "rippers" if you like, are easy to spot, and make up a wholly disproportionate amount of the writing on the subject. And to cut a long story short, that's why we think all serial killers are rippers.

> *"Sexually appropriate behavior is a socially constructed phenomenon, the definition and limits of which vary greatly among different societies, and this is epspecially true where children and young people are concerned."*
> *—from* Moral Panic

Changing Concepts of Child Molestation

RK: Please explain the basic premise—the overarching theme—of your book *Moral Panic: Changing Concepts of the Child Molester in America*.

PJ: The idea of child abuse is so deeply ingrained in our society that it seems absolutely obvious that all sensible people, everywhere, will think likewise unless they are deeply sick. To the contrary, even this absolute orthodoxy is in fact very new in historic terms: Even within the US, anti-child abuse movements can be overwhelmingly strong in one year, and nonexistent 20 or 30 years later. My book is both about the history of child abuse as a concept and how society forms its orthodoxies. It is as much about mass amnesia as social learning (i.e. how problems are forgotten and then relearned).

RK: You note that words and phrases such as "pervert," "pedophile," "child molester," and "sex offender" have had different meanings and have been used in different ways at different times. Please elaborate.

Even within the US, anti-child abuse movements can be overwhelmingly strong in one year, and nonexistent 20 or 30 years later.

PJ: There is a long record of people trying to get neutral, objective, nonjudgmental words for different types of conduct that are seen as pathological but not necessarily evil. Through the years, each of these medical words has been annexed by media and law enforcement as a demon word, usually distorting its original meaning. "Molestation" originally meant mild bothering, and people invented it to refer to acts which were trivial compared with rape—yet a "molester" today is the worst thing in the world.

The inflation process is under way right now with "pedophile," which just refers to people sexually interested in kids under the age of puberty. It does not imply violence, and more to the point, it does not refer to sex with older teenagers, "jailbait."

RK: Let's break down the phrase "child molestation" into its two parts and examine each one. First of all, you have "child." Obviously, the notion of what constitutes a child is very fluid. This topic could fill an entire book of its own, but could you briefly discuss how the concept of "child" has been constructed?

In England and America prior to the 1880s, the age of sexual consent was *ten*.

PJ: All societies are likely to limit the sexual activity of kids under the age of puberty, and most do—yet in England and America prior to the 1880s, the age of sexual consent was *ten*, and only gradually did it creep up to fourteen, fifteen. As time has gone by and people have tried to expand the borders of childhood, the age has grown, so that in American child porn legislation makes any sexual depiction of a person under *eighteen* pornographic and illegal, even if taken with his/her own consent. At the same time, the age of puberty has fallen, so we have an ever-wider gap between girls being physically ready for sex, and what the law permits. The scope of criminal law grows proportionately.

RK: Turning to the second part of the phrase "child molestation," the concept of molestation is also up for grabs in various times, locations, and arenas. How has this concept changed? What are some accepted behaviors of the past (or of other current cultures) that most Americans would now define as molestation?

PJ: As I said, molestation originally meant milder acts short of rape—often mutual masturbation. As time has gone by, the concept has extended to acts of voyeurism and fondling, and even taking pornographic pictures. It always pays to ask just what a "molester" is supposed to have done—and what was the age of the "victim." This lack of definition is a basic problem with much sex-offender legislation, since many "sex predators" are in fact guilty of fairly trivial acts, and with willing victims little short of the age of consent.

RK: You've pointed out a double standard regarding the perception and treatment of men who molest girls versus women who molest boys. In fact, it's almost as if child molestation automatically refers to men molesting children of either gender, while the phenomenon of women who molest children of either gender is almost entirely swept under the rug. Please comment on this.

PJ: Well, this does raise the issue of whether we can speak of "molestation" when a 25-year-old woman sleeps with a 15-year-old boy—or vice versa. I honestly don't know. I would say that when we have moved to fifteen or sixteen, we should not be speaking of molestation. Such intergenerational affairs might be ill-advised or destructive, but should they be criminal? Obviously, I am drawing a distinction here with encounters involving pubescent youngsters, or even prepubescent kids: There, we all agree the law has a legitimate protective role to play. But can we really call youngsters of sixteen or so "victims"?

Going in Cycles

RK: You've noted that like many other panics, the molestation panic in America has gone in cycles from approximately 1894 to today. Please give a broad overview of this timetable, explaining what may have caused the upsurges and—just as importantly—the lulls. (Also, according to the cycles, the 1990s should've seen a lull, but saw just the opposite. What happened to explain this?)

PJ: There are "booms" of concern roughly in the mid-1890s, again from 1908-22, 1936-58, and 1977-present. Real peak panic years have occurred in 1915, 1950, and 1985. I think the variables that matter are demographic and gender-related. Gender, because in a society in which women are establishing their own set of issues, they draw attention to sex crime as a particular threat to them, and stress male violence. Demography, because of booms and slumps in the proportion of children in a society: The baby boom of the 1950s was by no means the first of its kind.

Equally, there are troughs of concern, when gender politics lie low and sex crime is seen as trivial, and these too are cyclical. The cycle seems to have come to an end in the 1980s-90s, because the voices of gender politics were no longer struggling to be heard but had now established themselves as a firm part of social orthodoxy, based on women getting firmly ensconced in the workplace and the economic order.

I would say that when we have moved to fifteen or sixteen, we should not be speaking of molestation.

RK: On the question of who represents the gravest danger to children, the pendulum has swung many times from family members to strangers, and back again. Please elaborate.

PJ: Societies with intense gender politics focus on the incest problem because it illustrates problems within the family and gender roles; societies with more of a law enforcement emphasis stress the threat from stranger pedophiles. We have gone back and forth on this issue quite as much as the overall cycle of concern about abuse. In the 1910s, the issue was incest, and again in the 1980s; in the 1940s and 1990s, the focus shifted to stranger pedophiles.

Current Problems

RK: What ill effects have come from these child molestation panics? What ill effects are we currently seeing?

PJ: I think that threats to children serve as stealth justifications for policies that advocates would be afraid to avow openly, including hostility to fringe religions (see the ritual abuse panic of the 1980s), homosexuality (witness every anti-gay referendum), and sexual experimentation by the young. Also, they justify a vast and self-sustaining bureaucracy of social workers and psychologists, whose whole careers and (let's be frank) bank accounts depend entirely on maintaining a level of panic about threats to children.

I think that threats to children serve as stealth justifications for policies that advocates would be afraid to avow openly.

RK: Your book *Priests and Pedophiles* looked at the 1990s brouhaha over men of the cloth molesting children. You found that things were not really as they seemed. Please tell me more.

PJ: The received idea was that Catholic priests were abusing children in large numbers because of frustration resulting from their forced celibacy. In reality, there is no evidence that priests were abusing at a greater or lesser rate than any other religious professionals, or indeed than people in any walk of life. The charges resulted from rhetoric thrown around by rival Catholic factions.

Also, the Catholic church was the easiest and most attractive target of litigation, so we just heard more about Catholic cases. Finally, most priests involved in sex cases were not active with children, but with older teenagers, and should more properly be described as homosexuals.

RK: The murder of a child—especially coupled with that child being sexually attacked by a stranger—is tied to the whole concept of child molestation. You wrote that although we can never know how many children are molested, we can know pretty accurately how many children are murdered by strangers. What are these figures, and what do they tell us?

PJ: The problem here is that any attempt to minimize child murder has to sound callous, because you have to use phrases like "only" x children were murdered. But the picture is very different from what most people think. If we take children below the age of twelve (the age-group of interest to pedophiles), then between 1980 and 1994, 13,600 individuals were murdered in the US, about 900 each year. Of these, over 400 were babies or infants below the age of one, usually killed by parents. Family members killed 54 percent of all child victims. In contrast, strangers accounted for just 6 percent of the annual total, or about 54 children each year. Only about *five* victims per year involved the murder of a child by a stranger in a sexual assault, the classic sort of crime people imagine when they think about homicidal pedophiles.

Questioning Assumptions

RK: There are a lot of people—mainly feminists and Christian conservatives (those odd bedfellows)—who *still* believe that there is a multi-billion dollar child pornography "industry" that spans the globe. Please explain how we know that this is a myth and why it refuses to die.

PJ: In the late 1970s, there were claims about child porn being a billion dollar industry, and estimates just swelled over the years. In reality, the last real child porn entrepreneur was jailed in the early 1980s, and she (it was a woman, incidentally) never made more than a million or two. The Internet has revolutionized matters, and most people trade child porn for free, with money never changing hands.

RK: I'd like to look at some of the currently accepted ideas about child molestation and see what your research has uncovered about them. First up: Abuse is cyclical in nature. An abused child grows up to abuse children.

PJ: The argument is often stated, but it rests on very weak evidence: Of course abusers claim they were abused, since like everyone else who watches TV, they know the "right" answers to give to courts and psychologists.

RK: Sexual contact with adults always scars a child for life.

PJ: Answer as above. There is a good deal of contrary evidence, which publishers are terrified to put out for fear of the backlash.

RK: Child molesters cannot be helped. They will always abuse children, usually lots of them.

PJ: Define "molesters;" define "children;" define "abused;" define "helped."

The Catholic church was the easiest and most attractive target of litigation, so we just heard more about Catholic cases.

RK: You can identify potential child molesters (and other potential sex offenders) early, before they do any serious harm.

PJ: Define "molesters;" define "children." How to identify them? Most sex killers begin their careers by minor sex acts (e.g. voyeurism and exhibitionism). However, if we identify and incarcerate every person guilty of such acts, we had better set up our own Gulag Archipelago for the millions involved—the vast majority of whom will never progress to violent or predatory behavior. We have a lot of evidence on this now, and there is *no* accurate predictor of who will become a sex killer.

RK: There are millions of active pedophiles.

PJ: Define "pedophiles."

RK: One-fourth to one-half of all girls are victims of incest.

PJ: Not according to any survey done by a competent scholar without a major feminist agenda to establish.

The Crystal Ball

RK: What do you see regarding the future of attitudes towards child molestation?

We have a lot of evidence on this now, and there is no accurate predictor of who will become a sex killer.

PJ: The shift in gender politics and the role of women in the economy means that in the foreseeable future at least, we can never go back to the old idea about child abuse not mattering or not harming people: Sex crime will remain in the forefront of moral politics. I wonder, though, as a new baby boomlet comes of age in the next decade, whether they will insist on greater sexual rights like the original boomers did in the 1960s and 1970s.

Panic Inoculation

RK: Finally, what can the reader of this book do to spot panics? In other words, how can we inoculate ourselves against hyped-up dangers? What are some of the telltale signs of a hysteria?

PJ: I always look for anyone claiming an "epidemic" or using impressively round numbers—five million attacks, 50,000 incidents. Also pseudoscientific words like "addict." As you know, 94.5 percent of all social statistics are made up on the spot, without any supporting evidence. And yes, that is a joke.

CONDEMNED TO REPEAT IT

Amnesia in America

Or, The Sociology of Forgetting

James W. Loewen

In colonial times, everyone knew about the great Indian plagues just past. Many citizens were aware that even before *Mayflower* sailed, King James of England gave thanks to "Almighty God in his great goodness and bounty towards us," for sending "this wonderful plague among the salvages [*sic*]." Two hundred years later J. W. Barber's *Interesting Events in the History of the United States*, published in 1829, supplied this treatment on its second prose page:

> A few years before the arrival of the Plymouth settlers, a very mortal sickness raged with great violence among the indians inhabiting the eastern parts of New England. "Whole towns were depopulated. The living were not able to bury the dead; and their bodies were found lying above ground, many years after. The Massachusetts Indians are said to have been reduced from 30,000 to 300 fighting men. In 1633, the small pox swept off great numbers."

Today, however, not one in a hundred of my college students has ever heard of these plagues or any of the other pandemics that swept Native Americans, because most American history textbooks leave them out.

Could this be because they are not important? Because they have been swept aside by developments in American history since 1829 that must be attended to?

Consider their importance: Europeans were never able to "settle" China, India, Indonesia, Japan, or most of Africa, because too many people already lived there. The crucial role played by the plagues in the Americas (and Hawaii and Australia) can be inferred from two historical population estimates: William McNeill reckons the population of the Americas at 100 million in 1492, while William Langer suggests that Europe had only about 70 million people when Columbus set forth. The advantages Europeans enjoyed in military and social technology would have enabled them to dominate the Americas, as they eventually dominated China, India, Indonesia, and Africa, but not to "settle" the hemisphere. For that, the plagues were required. Thus, after the European (and African) invasion itself, the pestilence is surely the most important event in the history of America.

Today, however, not one in a hundred of my college students has ever heard of these plagues or any of the other pandemics that swept Native Americans, because most American history textbooks leave them out.

Nevertheless, our history books leave it out.

Or consider our "knowledge" of the voyages of Christopher Columbus. In 1828 novelist Washington Irving wrote a three-volume biography of Columbus in which he described Columbus' supposed defense of his round-earth theory before the flat-earth savants at Salamanca University. Actually, in 1491 most Europeans knew the world was round. The Catholic Church held it to be round. In eclipses of the moon, it casts a round shadow on the moon. On this side of the Atlantic, most Native Americans saw it that way, too. It looks round. Sailors in particular see its roundness when ships disappear over the horizon, hull first. Nevertheless, *The American Pageant*, a bestselling American history textbook that has stayed in print since 1956 despite the death of its author, still proclaimed as late as 1986, "The superstitious sailors, fearful of sailing over the edge of the world, grew increasingly mutinous." (In the current edition, this sentence has been softened to "fearful of sailing into the oceanic unknown," thus allowing the publisher deniability while still implying the false flat-earth story.)

In reality, Columbus never had to contend with a crew worried about falling off the end of the earth. His crew was no more superstitious than he was, and quite likely less. Again, histories written before 1828 got this right.

Something happens to our historical understanding over time, and it isn't pretty. Moving closer to our own time, consider John Brown, whose brief seizure of Harpers Ferry in 1859 helped lead to the Civil War. The great abolitionist has undergone his own transformation in American history textbooks. From 1890 to about 1970, John Brown was insane. Before 1890 he was perfectly sane, and after 1970 he has slowly been regaining his sanity in most of our textbooks.

Several history books still linger in the former era. *The American Pageant* is perhaps the worst offender: It calls him "deranged," "gaunt," "grim," "terrible," "crackbrained," and "probably of unsound mind," and claims that "thirteen of his near relatives were regarded as insane, including his mother and grandmother." In an unusual retro-action, the newest *Pageant* adds his mother to the list to make Brown even crazier than earlier editions. Still other books finesse the sanity issue by merely calling him "fanatical." No textbook among twelve I studied has any sympathy for the man or takes any pleasure in his ideals and actions.

Thus as white supremacy increasingly pervaded American culture during this era, more even than during slavery, Brown's actions became less and less intelligible. Not until the civil rights movement of the 1960s was white America freed from enough of its racism to accept that a white person did not have to be crazy to die for black equality. In a sense, the murders of Mickey Schwerner and Andrew Goodman in Mississippi, James Reeb and Viola Liuzzo in Alabama, and various other whites in various other Southern states during the civil rights movement liberated textbook writers to see sanity again in John Brown. Observe their impact on the bestselling high-school American history textbook of the period: *Rise of the American Nation*, written in 1961, calls the Harpers Ferry plan "a wild idea, certain to fail," while in 1986 in *Triumph of the American Nation* (the same book, retitled after we lost the Vietnam War) it becomes "a bold idea, but almost certain to fail."

We must recognize that the insanity with which historians have charged John Brown was never psychological. It was ideological.

For the benefit of readers who, like me, grew up reading that Brown was at least fanatic if not crazed, let's consider the evidence. To be sure, some of his lawyers and relatives, hoping to save his neck, suggested an insanity defense. But no one who knew Brown thought him crazy. He impressed people who spoke with him after his capture, including his jailer and even reporters writing for Democratic newspapers, which favored slavery. Governor Wise of Virginia called him "a man of clear head" after Brown got the better of him in an informal interview.

Textbook authors in the period after 1890 didn't rest their judgment of insanity on primary sources. They inferred Brown's madness from his plan for the Harpers Ferry raid, which admittedly was farfetched. Never mind that John Brown himself told Frederick Douglass presciently that the venture would make a stunning impact even if it failed. Nor that his twenty-odd followers can hardly be considered crazed, too. As Brown pointed out in his last speech in court, each "joined me of his own accord." This was true even of his sons.

No new evidence of insanity caused authors to withdraw sympathy from John Brown. Rather, we must recognize that the insanity with which historians have charged John Brown was never psychological. It was ideological. Brown's actions made no sense to textbook writers between 1890 and about 1965. To make no sense is to be crazy. Since Brown himself did not change after his death, his sanity provides an inadvertent index of the level of white racism in our society.

After 1890, as Southern and Border states disfranchised African Americans, as lynchings increased, as blackface minstrel shows dominated American popular culture, white America abandoned the last shards of its racial idealism. White historians lost their ability to empathize with whites who might genuinely believe in equal rights for blacks. John Spencer Bassett's *A Short History of the United States*, published in 1923, makes plain the connection: "The farther we get away from the excitement of 1859 the more we are disposed to consider this extraordinary man the victim of mental delusions."

Not just textbooks change over time. So do historical markers and monuments. Consider this comparison of two Civil War memorials, early and late. A sphinx in Mount Auburn Cemetery in Cambridge, Massachusetts, proclaims, "American Union preserved, African slavery destroyed, by the uprising of a great people, by the blood of fallen heroes." The first two phrases constitute a reasonable statement of the war's immediate outcome. The last two have become cryptic—what uprising? Surely not white Unionists—they hardly "uprose." This seems to be a representation on the landscape of black historian W.E.B. DuBois' claim of a general strike by slaves during the Civil War. Certainly it was true that after mid-1863 slaves across the South bargained for better living conditions, escaped to US lines when possible, and on some plantations stopped work altogether except for their own gardens. Early on, white historians mislaid any understanding of this action, especially as a general phenomenon, and have never rediscovered it.

In contrast, South Carolina's monument at Gettysburg, dedicated in 1965, gives a very different version of what the Civil War was about:

> South Carolina
>
> That men of honor might forever know the responsibilities of freedom, dedicated South Carolinians stood and were counted for their heritage and convictions. Abiding faith in the sacredness of states rights provided their creed here. Many earned eternal glory.

If this monument were in remembrance of South Carolina's 5,500 volunteers to the Union cause, the first sentence might make sense. Those men, almost all African American, took up arms precisely to obtain "the responsibilities of freedom" for themselves and for their friends and relatives who still languished in slavery. Unionist South Carolinians never fought at Gettysburg, however. Nor in 1965, at the height of its white supremacist reaction to the Supreme Court's 1954 school desegregation decree, would South Carolina have erected a monument to black South Carolinians or white Unionists. This monument is an attempt to do the impossible: to convert the Confederate cause—a war to guarantee that 3,950,000 people might never know the responsibilities of freedom—into a crusade on behalf of states' rights.

Again, the original record was clear and the misunderstanding is recent. On Christmas Eve, 1860, South Carolinian leaders signed a document to justify leaving the United States. Their first grievance: "that fourteen of the States have deliberately refused, for years past, to fulfill their constitutional obligations," under Article Four of the United States Constitution. Article Four (Section 2, Paragraph 3) is the fugitive slave clause.

The ideology of progress lets historians sequester repugnant people and events, from racists to robber barons, in the distant past, so we don't have to worry about them now.

"The General Government, as the common agent, passed laws to carry into effect these stipulations of the States," declared the South Carolina Ordinance of Secession, approvingly. "But an increasing hostility on the part of the non-slaveholding States to the institution of slavery, has led to a disregard of their obligations... The States of Maine, New Hampshire, Vermont, Massachusetts, Connecticut, Rhode Island, New York, Pennsylvania, Illinois, Indiana, Michigan, Wisconsin and Iowa, have enacted laws which either nullify the Acts of Congress or render useless any attempt to execute them."

Thus abiding opposition to states' rights when claimed by free states provided South Carolinians' creed here. Since the pro-slavery wing of the Democratic party had controlled the federal government throughout the 1850s, slaveowners favored a strong central power and opposed states' rights. And the delegates went on to condemn Northern states for allowing blacks to vote, refusing to let slaveowners transport slaves through their borders, and even for allowing their residents the freedom of speech to "denounce as sinful the institution of slavery."

South Carolinians in 1965 knew perfectly well that slavery, not states' rights, prompted their state to leave the United States. But in 1965 white supremacists still controlled South Carolina and strove mightily to keep African Americans in separate and unequal institutions. Controlling the past, including how that past is told across the American landscape, helped white supremacists control the future. "States' rights" was just a subterfuge for those who wanted to take away individual rights. Converting the Confederate cause after the fact into a struggle for states' rights in the 1860s helped transmogrify the segregationist cause of the 1960s into a similar struggle for states' rights against an intrusive federal government. Glorifying the Confederacy in Pennsylvania thus had ideological consequences in South Carolina in 1965.

Amazingly, historians do not often admit that history often grows less accurate over time. Instead, they preach just the reverse: that historians today know better than persons in the past who were "too close" to an event to have "historical perspective." On the landscape, historians enforce this notion by requiring petitioners who want to celebrate historical characters to wait "a sufficient length of time" (50 years in Georgia, whose regulations I am quoting) "for their ideas, services, and accomplishments to be placed in accurate historical perspective" so we can phrase a historical marker to do them justice.

It is true that one can sometimes view a building better by stepping back from it, but this is merely an analogy when applied to the past. No such animal as historical perspective exists—not as an outcome of the simple passage of time, at any rate. To claim that it does is itself an example of limited historical vision that we might call chronological ethnocentrism or the myth of progress. It assumes without evidence that we today are more tolerant, more advanced, wiser than the dimwits who preceded us. Actually, as time passes we know less and less about more and more. The ideology of progress lets historians sequester repugnant people and events, from racists to robber barons, in the distant past, so we don't have to worry about them now.

Are Americans more tolerant today of personal idiosyncrasies? Surely we have reached an arresting state of intolerance when the huge Disney organization, founded by a man with a mustache, will not allow one now even on a janitor. Are we more empirical in our health practice, to avoid such notorious practices as bloodletting, that probably killed more people than the maladies for which they were used? Well, yes, but consider our anti-empirical, anti-gravity birthing system, which makes giving birth analogous to a medical operation instead of to an enormous bowel movement, with many unfortunate consequences.

Instead of assuming that the present is so advanced, we need to think about the characteristics of our present society, better to assess its effects on our reconstructions of past events. It follows that we should never take for granted the aphorisms that our schoolbooks and memorials use to sum up the past. Did people get to the Americas across the Bering Land Bridge? We really don't have a clue. Were the Dark Ages "dark?" Maybe not. Why did Europe "win?" The usual answers make no sense. Is the United States a classless society compared to more ossified British and French societies? Not at all.

Our most prudent course is to be suspicious whenever every authority agrees that x happened in the past. Precisely then, x is likely to be a myth for which no one has recently examined the evidence.

Columbus and Western Civilization

Howard Zinn

In the year 1992, the celebration of Columbus Day was different from previous ones in two ways. First, this was the quincentennial, 500 years after Columbus' landing in this hemisphere. Second, it was a celebration challenged all over the country by people—many of them native Americans but also others—who had "discovered" a Columbus not worth celebrating, and who were rethinking the traditional glorification of "Western civilization." I gave this talk at the University of Wisconsin in Madison in October 1991. It was published the following year by the Open Magazine Pamphlet Series with the title "Christopher Columbus & the Myth of Human Progress."

George Orwell, who was a very wise man, wrote: "Who controls the past controls the future. And who controls the present controls the past." In other words, those who dominate our society are in a position to write our histories. And if they can do that, they can decide our futures. That is why the telling of the Columbus story is important.

Let me make a confession. I knew very little about Columbus until about twelve years ago, when I began writing my book *A People's History of the United States*. I had a Ph.D. in history from Columbia University—that is, I had the proper training of a historian, and what I knew about Columbus was pretty much what I had learned in elementary school.

But when I began to write my *People's History*, I decided I must learn about Columbus. I had already concluded that I did not want to write just another overview of American history—I knew my point of view would be different. I was going to write about the United States from the point of view of those people who had been largely neglected in the history books: the indigenous Americans, the black slaves, the women, the working people, whether native or immigrant.

I wanted to tell the story of the nation's industrial progress from the standpoint, not of Rockefeller and Carnegie and Vanderbilt, but of the people who worked in their mines, their oil fields, who lost their limbs or their lives building the railroads.

I wanted to tell the story of wars, not from the standpoint of generals and presidents, not from the standpoint of those military heroes whose statues you see all over this country, but through the eyes of the G.I.s, or through the eyes of "the enemy." Yes, why not look at the Mexican War, that great military triumph of the United States, from the viewpoint of the Mexicans?

And so, how must I tell the story of Columbus? I concluded, I must see him through the eyes of the people who were here when he arrived, the people he called "Indians" because he thought he was in Asia.

Well, they left no memoirs, no histories. Their culture was an oral culture, not a written one. Besides, they had been wiped out in a few decades after Columbus' arrival. So I was compelled to turn to the next best thing: the Spaniards who were on the scene at the time. First, Columbus himself. He had kept a journal.

His journal was revealing. He described the people who greeted him when he landed in the Bahamas—they were Arawak Indians, sometimes called Tainos—and told how they waded out into the sea to greet him and his men, who must have looked and sounded like people from another world, and brought them gifts of various kinds. He described them as peaceable, gentle, and said: "They do not bear arms, and do not know them for I showed them a sword—they took it by the edge and cut themselves."

Throughout his journal, over the next months, Columbus spoke of the native Americans with what seemed like admiring awe: "They are the best people in the world and above all the gentlest—without knowledge of what is evil—nor do they murder or steal...they love their neighbors as themselves and they have the sweetest talk in the world...always laughing."

And in a letter he wrote to one of his Spanish patrons, Columbus said: "They are very simple and honest and exceedingly liberal with all they have, none of them refusing anything he may possess when he is asked for it. They exhibit great love toward all others in preference to themselves." But then, in the midst of all this, in his journal, Columbus writes: "They would make fine servants. With fifty men we could subjugate them all and make them do whatever we want."

Yes, this was how Columbus saw the Indians—not as hospitable hosts, but as "servants," to "do whatever we want."

And what did Columbus want? This is not hard to determine. In the first two weeks of journal entries, there is one word that recurs 75 times: GOLD.

In the standard accounts of Columbus what is emphasized again and again is his religious feeling, his desire to convert the natives to Christianity, his reverence for the Bible. Yes, he was concerned about God. But more about Gold. Just one additional letter. His was a limited alphabet. Yes, all over the island of Hispaniola, where he, his brothers, his men, spent most of their time, he erected crosses. But also, all over the island, they built gallows—340 of them by the year 1500. Crosses and gallows—that deadly historic juxtaposition.

In his quest for gold, Columbus, seeing bits of gold among the Indians, concluded there were huge amounts of it. He ordered the natives to find a certain amount of gold within a certain period of time. And if they did not meet their quota, their arms were hacked off. The others were to learn from this and deliver the gold.

Samuel Eliot Morison, the Harvard historian who was Columbus' admiring biographer, acknowledged this. He wrote: "Whoever thought up this ghastly system, Columbus was responsible for it, as the only means of producing gold for export.... Those who fled to the mountains were hunted with hounds, and of those who escaped, starvation and disease took toll, while thousands of the poor creatures in desperation took cassava poison to end their miseries."

Morison continues: "So the policy and acts of Columbus for which he alone was responsible began the depopulation of the terrestrial paradise that was Hispaniola in 1492. Of the original natives, estimated by a modern ethnologist at 300,000 in number, one-third were killed off between 1494 and 1496. By 1508, an enumeration showed only 60,000 alive.... in 1548 Oviedo [Morison is referring to Fernandez de Oviedo, the official Spanish historian of the conquest] doubted whether 500 Indians remained."

But Columbus could not obtain enough gold to send home to impress the King and Queen and his Spanish financiers, so he decided to send back to Spain another kind of loot: slaves. They rounded up about 1,200 natives, selected 500, and these were sent, jammed together, on the voyage across the Atlantic. Two hundred died on the way, of cold, of sickness.

In Columbus' journal, an entry of September 1498 reads: "From here one might send, in the name of the Holy Trinity, as many slaves as could be sold..."

In Columbus' journal, an entry of September 1498 reads: "From here one might send, in the name of the Holy Trinity, as many slaves as could be sold..."

What the Spaniards did to the Indians is told in horrifying detail by Bartolomé de las Casas, whose writings give the most thorough account of the Spanish-Indian encounter. Las Casas was a Dominican priest who came to the New World a few years after Columbus, spent 40 years on Hispaniola and nearby islands, and became the leading advocate in Spain for the rights of the natives. Las Casas, in his book *The Devastation of the Indies,* writes of the Arawaks: "...of all the infinite universe of humanity, these people are the most guileless, the most devoid of wickedness and duplicity...yet into this sheepfold...there came some Spaniards who immediately behaved like ravening beasts.... Their reason for killing and destroying...is that the Christians have an ultimate aim which is to acquire gold..."

The cruelties multiplied. Las Casas saw soldiers stabbing Indians for sport, dashing babies' heads on rocks. And when the Indians resisted, the Spaniards hunted them down, equipped for killing with horses, armor plate, lances, pikes, rifles, crossbows, and vicious dogs. Indians who took things belonging to the Spaniards—they were not accustomed to the concept of private ownership and gave freely of their own possessions—were beheaded or burned at the stake.

Las Casas saw soldiers stabbing Indians for sport, dashing babies' heads on rocks.

Las Casas' testimony was corroborated by other eyewitnesses. A group of Dominican friars, addressing the Spanish monarchy in 1519, hoping for the Spanish government to intercede, told about unspeakable atrocities, children thrown to dogs to be devoured, newborn babies born to women prisoners flung into the jungle to die.

Forced labor in the mines and on the land led to much sickness and death. Many children died because their mothers, overworked and starved, had no milk for them. Las Casas, in Cuba, estimated that 7,000 children died in *three months.*

The greatest toll was taken by sickness, because the Europeans brought with them diseases against which the natives had no immunity: typhoid, typhus, diphtheria, smallpox.

As in any military conquest, women came in for especially brutal treatment. One Italian nobleman named Cuneo recorded an early sexual encounter. The "Admiral" he refers to is Columbus, who, as part of his agreement with the Spanish monarchy, insisted he be made an Admiral. Cuneo wrote:

> ...I captured a very beautiful Carib woman, whom the said Lord Admiral gave to me and with whom...I conceived desire to take pleasure. I

> wanted to put my desire into execution but she did not want it and treated me with her finger nails in such a manner that I wished I had never begun. But seeing that, I took a rope and thrashed her well.... Finally we came to an agreement.

There is other evidence which adds up to a picture of widespread rape of native women. Samuel Eliot Morison wrote: "In the Bahamas, Cuba and Hispaniola they found young and beautiful women, who everywhere were naked, in most places accessible, and presumably complaisant." Who presumes this? Morison, and so many others.

Morison saw the conquest as so many writers after him have done, as one of the great romantic adventures of world history. He seemed to get carried away by what appeared to him as a *masculine* conquest. He wrote:

> Never again may mortal men hope to recapture the amazement, the wonder, the delight of those October days in 1492, when the new world gracefully yielded her virginity to the conquering Castilians.

The language of Cuneo ("we came to an agreement"), and of Morison ("gracefully yielded") written almost 500 years apart, surely suggests how persistent through modern history has been the mythology that rationalizes sexual brutality by seeing it as "complaisant."

So, I read Columbus' journal, I read las Casas. I also read Hans Koning's pioneering work of our time—*Columbus: His Enterprise*, which, at the time I wrote my *People's History*, was the only contemporary account I could find which departed from the standard treatment.

When my book appeared, I began to get letters from all over the country about it. Here was a book of 600 pages, starting with Columbus, ending with the 1970s, but most of the letters I got from readers were about one subject: Columbus. I could have interpreted this to mean that, since this was the very beginning of the book, that's all these people had read. But no, it seemed that the Columbus story was simply the part of my book that readers found most startling. Because every American, from elementary school on, learns the Columbus story, and learns it the same way: "In Fourteen Hundred and Ninety-Two, Columbus Sailed the Ocean Blue."

How many of you have heard of Tigard, Oregon? Well, I didn't until, about seven years ago, I began receiving, every semester, a bunch of letters, 20 or 30, from students at one high school in Tigard. It seems that their teacher was having them (knowing high schools, I almost said "forcing them") read my *People's History*. He was photocopying a number of chapters and giving them to the students. And then he had them write letters to me, with comments and questions. Roughly half of them thanked me for giving them data which they had never seen before. The others were angry, or wondered how I got such information, and how I had arrived at such outrageous conclusions.

One high school student named Bethany wrote: "Out of all the articles that I've read of yours I found 'Columbus, The Indians, and Human Progress' the most shocking." Another student named Brian, seventeen years old, wrote: "An example of the confusion I feel after reading your article concerns Columbus coming to America.... According to you, it seems he came for women, slaves, and gold. You say that Columbus physically abused the Indians that didn't help him find gold. You've said you have gained a lot of this information from Columbus' own journal. I am wondering if there is such a journal, and if so, why isn't it part of our history. Why isn't any of what you say in my history book, or in history books people have access to each day?"

I pondered this letter. It could be interpreted to mean that the writer was indignant that no other history books had told him what I did. Or, as was more likely, he was saying: "I don't believe a word of what you wrote! You made this up!"

I am not surprised at such reactions. It tells something about the claims of pluralism and diversity in American culture, the pride in our "free society," that generation after generation has learned exactly the same set of facts about Columbus, and finished their education with the same glaring omissions.

A school teacher in Portland, Oregon, named Bill Bigelow has undertaken a crusade to change the way the Columbus story is taught all over America. He tells of how he sometimes starts a new class. He goes over to a girl sitting in the front row, and takes her purse. She says: "You took my purse!" Bigelow responds: "No, I discovered it."

Bill Bigelow did a study of recent children's books on Columbus. He found them remarkably alike in their repetition of the traditional point of view. A typical fifth-grade biography of Columbus begins: "There once was a boy who loved the salty sea." Well! I can imagine a children's biography of Attila the Hun beginning with the sentence: "There once was a boy who loved horses."

Another children's book in Bigelow's study, this time for second-graders: "The King and Queen looked at the gold and the Indians. They listened in wonder to Columbus' stories of adventure. Then they all went to church to pray and sing. Tears of joy filled Columbus' eyes."

I can imagine a children's biography of Attila the Hun beginning with the sentence: "There once was a boy who loved horses."

I once spoke about Columbus to a workshop of school teachers, and one of them suggested that school children were too young to hear of the horrors recounted by las Casas and others. Other teachers disagreed, said children's stories include plenty of violence, but the perpetrators are witches and monsters and "bad people," not national heroes who have holidays named after them.

Some of the teachers made suggestions on how the truth could be told in a way that would not frighten children unnecessarily, but that would avoid the falsification of history now taking place.

The argument about children "not being ready to hear the truth" does not account for the fact that in American society, when the children grow up, they *still* are not told the truth. As I said earlier, right up through graduate school I was not presented with the information that would counter the myths told to me in the early grades. And it is clear that my experience is typical, judging from the shocked reactions to my book that I have received from readers of all ages.

If you look in an *adult* book, the *Columbia Encyclopedia* (my edition was put together in 1950, but all the relevant information was available then, including Morison's biography), there is a long entry on Columbus (about 1,000 words), but you will find no mention of the atrocities committed by him and his men.

The argument about children "not being ready to hear the truth" does not account for the fact that in American society, when the children grow up, they *still* are not told the truth.

In the 1986 edition of the *Columbia History of the World* there are several mentions of Columbus, but nothing about what he did to the natives. Several pages are devoted to "Spain and Portugal in America," in which the treatment of the native population is presented as a matter of controversy, among theologians at that time, and among historians today. You can get the flavor of this "balanced approach," containing a nugget of reality, by the following passage from that *History*:

> The determination of the Crown and the Church to Christianize the Indians, the need for labor to exploit the new lands, and the attempts of some Spaniards to protect the Indians, resulted in a very remarkable complex of customs, laws, and institutions which even today leads historians to contradictory conclusions about Spanish rule in America.... Academic disputes flourish on this debatable and in a sense insoluble question, but there is no doubt that cruelty, overwork and disease resulted in an appalling depopulation. There were, according to recent estimates, about 25 million Indians in Mexico in 1519, slightly more than 1 million in 1605.

Despite this scholarly language—"contradictory conclusions...academic disputes...insoluble question"—there is no real dispute about the facts of enslavement, forced labor, rape, murder, the taking of hostages, the ravages of diseases carried from Europe, and the wiping out of huge numbers of native people. The only dispute is over how much emphasis is to be placed on these facts, and how they carry over into the issues of our time.

For instance, Samuel Eliot Morison does spend some time detailing the treatment of the natives by Columbus and his men, and uses the word "genocide" to describe the overall effect of the "discovery." But he buries this in the midst of a long, admiring treatment of Columbus, and sums up his view in the concluding paragraph of his popular book *Christopher Columbus, Mariner*, as follows:

> He had his faults and his defects, but they were largely the defects of the qualities that made him great—his indomitable will, his superb faith in God and in his own mission as the Christ-bearer to lands beyond the seas, his stubborn persistence despite neglect, poverty and discouragement. But there was no flaw, no dark side to the most outstanding and essential of all his qualities—his seamanship.

Yes, his seamanship!

Let me make myself clear. I am not interested in either denouncing or exalting Columbus. It is too late for that. We are not writing a letter of recommendation for him to decide his qualifications for undertaking another voyage to another part of the universe. To me, the Columbus story is important for what it tells us about ourselves, about our time, about the decisions we have to make for our century, for the next century.

Why this great controversy today about Columbus and the celebration of the quincentennial? Why the indignation of native Americans and others about the glorification of that conqueror? Why the heated defense of Columbus by others? The intensity of the debate can only be because it is not about 1492, it is about 1992.

We can get a clue to this if we look back a hundred years to 1892, the year of the quadricentennial. There were great celebrations in Chicago and New York. In New York there were five days of parades, fireworks, military marches, naval pageants, a million visitors to the city, a memorial statue unveiled at a corner of Central Park, now to be known as Columbus Circle. A celebratory meeting took place at Carnegie Hall, addressed by Chauncey DePew.

You might not know the name of Chauncey DePew, unless you recently looked at Gustavus Myers' classic work, *A History of the Great American Fortunes*. In that book, Chauncey DePew is described as the front man for Cornelius Vanderbilt and his New York Central railroad. DePew traveled to Albany, the capital of New York State, with satchels of money and free railroad passes for members of the New York State legislature, and came away with subsidies and land grants for the New York Central.

DePew saw the Columbus festivities as a celebration of wealth and prosperity—you might say, as a self-celebration. He said that the quadricentennial event "marks the wealth and the civilization of a great people...it marks the things that belong to their comfort and their ease, their pleasure and their luxuries...and their power."

We might note that at the time he said this, there was much suffering among the working poor of America, huddled in city slums, their children sick and undernourished. The plight of people who worked on the land—which at this time was a considerable part of the population—was desperate, leading to the anger of the Farmers' Alliances and the rise of the People's (Populist) Party. And the following year, 1893, was a year of economic crisis and widespread misery.

DePew must have sensed, as he stood on the platform at Carnegie Hall, some murmurings of discontent at the smugness that accompanied the Columbus celebrations, for he said: "If there is anything I detest...it is that spirit of historical inquiry which doubts everything; that modern spirit which destroys all the illusions and all the heroes which have been the inspiration of patriotism through all the centuries."

So, to celebrate Columbus was to be patriotic. To doubt was to be unpatriotic. And what did "patriotism" mean to DePew? It meant the glorification of expansion and conquest—which Columbus represented, and which America represented. It was just six years after his speech that the United States, expelling Spain from Cuba, began its own long occupation (sporadically military, continuously political and economic) of Cuba, took Puerto Rico and Hawaii, and began its bloody war against the Filipinos to take over their country.

That "patriotism" which was tied to the celebration of Columbus, and the celebration of conquest, was reinforced in the second World War by the emergence of the United States as the superpower, all the old European empires now in decline. At that time, Henry Luce, the powerful president-maker and multimillionaire, owner of *Time, Life*, and *Fortune* (not just the publications, but the *things*!) wrote that the twentieth century was turning into the "American Century," in which the United States would have its way in the world.

George Bush, accepting the presidential nomination in 1988, said: "This has been called the American Century because in it we were the dominant force for good in the world.... Now we are on the verge of a new century, and what country's name will it bear? I say it will be another American Century."

What arrogance! That the twenty-first century, when we should be getting away from the murderous jingoism of this century, should already be anticipated as an *American* century, or as any one nation's century. Bush must think of himself as a new Columbus, "discovering" and planting his nation's flag on new worlds, because he called for a US colony on the moon early in the next century. And forecast a mission to Mars in the year 2019.

The "patriotism" that Chauncey Depew invoked in celebrating Columbus was profoundly tied to the notion of the inferiority of the conquered peoples. Columbus' attacks on the Indians were justified by their status as subhumans. The taking of Texas and much of Mexico by the United States just before the Civil War was done with the same racist rationale. Sam Houston, the first governor of Texas, proclaimed: "The Anglo-Saxon race must pervade the whole southern extremity of this vast continent. The Mexicans are no better than the Indians and I see no reason why we should not take their land."

"The Mexicans are no better than the Indians and I see no reason why we should not take their land."

At the start of the twentieth century, the violence of the new American expansionism into the Caribbean and the Pacific was accepted because we were dealing with lesser beings.

In the year 1900, Chauncey DePew, now a US Senator, spoke again in Carnegie Hall, this time to support Theodore Roosevelt's candidacy for vice president. Celebrating the conquest of the Philippines as a beginning of the American penetration of China and more, he proclaimed: "The guns of Dewey in Manila Bay were heard across Asia and Africa, they echoed through the palace at Peking and brought to the Oriental mind a new and potent force among western nations. We, in common with the countries of Europe, are striving to enter the limitless markets of the east.... These people respect nothing but power. I believe the Philippines will be enormous markets and sources of wealth."

Theodore Roosevelt, who appears endlessly on lists of our "great presidents," and whose face is one of the four colossal sculptures of American presidents (along with Washington, Jefferson, Lincoln) carved into Mount Rushmore in South Dakota, was the quintessential racist-imperialist. He was furious, back in 1893, when President Cleveland failed to annex Hawaii, telling the Naval War College it was "a crime against white civilization." In his book *The Strenuous Life,* Roosevelt wrote:

> Of course our whole national history has been one of expansion...that the barbarians recede or

are conquered...is due solely to the power of the mighty civilized races which have not lost the fighting instinct.

An Army officer in the Philippines put it even more bluntly: "There is no use mincing words.... We exterminated the American Indians and I guess most of us are proud of it...and we must have no scruples about exterminating this other race standing in the way of progress and enlightenment, if it is necessary..."

The official historian of the Indies in the early sixteenth century, Fernandez de Oviedo, did not deny what was done to natives by the *conquistadores*. He described "innumerable cruel deaths as countless as the stars." But this was acceptable, because "to use gunpowder against pagans is to offer incense to the Lord."

(One is reminded of President McKinley's decision to send the army and navy to take the Philippines, saying it was the duty of the United States to "Christianize and civilize" the Filipinos.)

Against las Casas' pleas for mercy to the Indians, the theologian Juan Gines de Sepulveda declared: "How can we doubt that these people, so uncivilized, so barbaric, so contaminated with so many sins and obscenities, have been justly conquered."

Sepulveda in the year 1531 visited his former college in Spain and was outraged by seeing the students there protesting Spain's war against Turkey. The students were saying: "All war...is contrary to the Catholic religion."

This led him to write a philosophical defense of the Spanish treatment of the Indians. He quoted Aristotle, who wrote in his *Politics* that some people were "slaves by nature," who "should be hunted down like wild beasts in order to bring them to the correct way of life."

Las Casas responded: "Let us send Aristotle packing, for we have in our favor the command of Christ: Thou shalt love thy neighbor as thyself."

The dehumanization of the "enemy" has been a necessary accompaniment to wars of conquest. It is easier to explain atrocities if they are committed against infidels or people of an inferior race. Slavery and racial segregation in the United States, and European imperialism in Asia and Africa, were justified in this way.

The bombing of Vietnamese villages by the United States, the search and destroy missions, the My Lai massacre, were all made palatable to their perpetrators by the idea that the victims were not human. They were "gooks" or "communists," and deserved what they received.

In the Gulf War, the dehumanization of the Iraqis consisted of not recognizing their existence. We were not bombing women, children,

"To use gunpowder against pagans is to offer incense to the Lord."

not bombing and shelling ordinary Iraqi young men in the act of flight and surrender. We were acting against a Hitler-like monster, Saddam Hussein, although the people we were killing were the Iraqi victims of this monster. When General Colin Powell was asked about Iraqi casualties he said that was "really not a matter I am terribly interested in."

The American people were led to accept the violence of the war in Iraq because the Iraqis were made invisible—because the United States only used "smart bombs." The major media ignored the enormous death toll in Iraq, ignored the report of the Harvard medical team that visited Iraq shortly after the war and found that tens of thousands of Iraqi children were dying because of the bombing of the water supply and the resultant epidemics of disease.

The celebrations of Columbus are declared to be celebrations not just of his maritime exploits but of "progress," of his arrival in the Bahamas as the beginning of that much-praised 500 years of "Western civilization." But those concepts need to be reexamined. When Gandhi was once asked what he thought about Western civilization, he replied: "It's a good idea."

The point is not to deny the benefits of "progress" and "civilization"—advances in technology, knowledge, science, health, education, and standards of living. But there is a question to be asked: Progress, yes, but at what human cost?

Would we accept a Russian justification of Stalin's rule, including the enormous toll in human suffering, on the ground that he made Russia a great industrial power?

I recall that in my high school classes in American history when we came to the period after the Civil War, roughly the years between that war and World War I, it was looked on as the Gilded Age, the period of the great Industrial Revolution, when the United States became an economic giant. I remember how thrilled we were to learn of the dramatic growth of the steel and oil industries, of the building of the great fortunes, of the crisscrossing of the country by the railroads.

We were not told of the human cost of this great industrial progress: how the huge production of cotton came from the labor of black slaves; how the textile industry was built up by the labor of young girls who went into the mills at twelve and died at 25; how the railroads were constructed by Irish and Chinese immigrants who were literally worked to death, in the heat of summer and cold of winter; how working people, immigrants and native-born, had to go out on strike and be beaten by police and jailed by National Guardsmen before they could win the eight-hour day; how the children of the working class, in the slums of the city, had to drink polluted water, and how they died early of malnutrition and disease. All this in the name of "progress."

And yes, there are huge benefits from industrialization, science, technology, medicine. But so far, in these 500 years of Western civilization, of Western domination of the rest of the world, most of those benefits have gone to a small part of the human race. For billions of people in the Third World, they still face starvation, homelessness, disease, the early deaths of their children.

Did the Columbus expeditions mark the transition from savagery to civilization? What of the Indian civilizations which had been built up over thousands of years before Columbus came? Las Casas and others marveled at the spirit of sharing and generosity which marked the Indian societies, the communal buildings in which they lived, their aesthetic sensibilities, the egalitarianism among men and women.

The British colonists in North America were startled at the democracy of the Iroquois—the tribes who occupied much of New York and Pennsylvania. The American historian Gary Nash describes Iroquois culture: "No laws and ordinances, sheriffs and constables, judges and juries, or courts or jails—the apparatus of authority in European societies—were to be found in the northeast woodlands prior to European arrival. Yet boundaries of acceptable behavior were firmly set... Though priding themselves on the autonomous individual, the Iroquois maintained a strict sense of right and wrong..."

In the course of westward expansion, the new nation, the United States, stole the Indians' land, killed them when they resisted, destroyed their sources of food and shelter, pushed them into smaller and smaller sections of the country, went about the systematic destruction of Indian society. At the time of the Black Hawk War in the 1830s—one of hundreds of wars waged against the Indians of North America—Lewis Cass, the governor of the Michigan territory, referred to his taking of millions of acres from the Indians as "the progress of civilization." He said: "A barbarous people cannot live in contact with a civilized community."

The British colonists in North America were startled at the democracy of the Iroquois.

We get a sense of how "barbarous" these Indians were when, in the 1880s, Congress prepared legislation to break up the communal lands in which Indians still lived, into small private possessions, what today some people would call, admiringly, "privatization." Senator Henry Dawes, author of this legislation, visited the Cherokee Nation and described what he found: "...there was not a family in that whole nation that had not a home of its own. There was not a pauper in that nation, and the nation did not owe a dollar...it built its own schools and its hospitals. Yet the defect of the system was apparent. They have got as far as they can go, because they own their land in common...there is not enterprise to make your home any better than that of your neighbors. There is no selfishness, which is at the bottom of civilization."

That selfishness at the bottom of "civilization" is connected with what drove Columbus on, and what is much-praised today, as American political leaders and the media speak about how the West will do a great favor to the Soviet Union and Eastern Europe by introducing "the profit motive."

Granted, there may be certain ways in which the incentive of profit may be helpful in economic development, but that incentive, in the history of the "free market" in the West, has had horrendous consequences. It led, throughout the centuries of "Western Civilization," to a ruthless imperialism.

In Joseph Conrad's novel *Heart of Darkness,* written in the 1890s, after some time spent in the Upper Congo of Africa, he describes the work done by black men in chains on behalf of white men who were interested only in ivory. He writes: "The word 'ivory' rang in the air, was whispered, was sighed. You would think they were praying to it.... To tear treasure out of the bowels of the land was their desire, with no more moral purpose at the back of it than there is in burglars breaking into a safe."

The uncontrolled drive for profit has led to enormous human suffering, exploitation, slavery, cruelty in the workplace, dangerous working conditions, child labor, the destruction of land and forests, the poisoning of the air we breathe, the water we drink, the food we eat.

In his 1933 autobiography, Chief Luther Standing Bear wrote: "True the white man brought great change. But the varied fruits of his civilization, though highly colored and inviting, are sickening and deadening. And if it be the part of civilization to maim, rob, and thwart, then what is progress? I am going to venture that the man who sat on the ground in his tipi meditating on life and its meaning, accepting the kinship of all creatures, and acknowledging unity with the universe of things, was infusing into his being the true essence of civilization."

The present threats to the environment have caused a reconsideration among scientists and other scholars of the value of "progress" as it has been so far defined. In December 1991, there was a two-day conference at MIT, in which 50 scientists and historians discussed the idea of progress in Western thought. Here is part of the report on that conference in the *Boston Globe*:

> In a world where resources are being squandered and the environment poisoned, participants in an MIT conference said yesterday, it is time for people to start thinking in terms of sustainability and stability rather than growth and progress.... Verbal fireworks and heated exchanges that sometimes grew into shouting matches punctuated the dis-

> cussions among scholars of economics, religion, medicine, history and the sciences.

One of the participants, historian Leo Marx, said that working toward a more harmonious coexistence with nature is itself a kind of progress, but different than the traditional one in which people try to overpower nature.

So, to look back at Columbus in a critical way is to raise all these questions about progress, civilization, our relations with one another, our relationship to the natural world.

You probably have heard—as I have, quite often—that it is wrong for us to treat the Columbus story the way we do. What they say is: "You are taking Columbus out of context, looking at him with the eyes of the twentieth century. You must not superimpose the values of our time on events that took place 500 years ago. That is ahistorical."

I find this argument strange. Does it mean that cruelty, exploitation, greed, enslavement, violence against helpless people, are values peculiar to the fifteenth and sixteenth centuries? And that we in the twentieth century are beyond that? Are there not certain human values which are common to the age of Columbus and to our own? Proof of that is that both in his time and in ours there were enslavers and exploiters; in both his time and ours there were those who protested against that, on behalf of human rights.

It is encouraging that, in this year of the quincentennial, there is a wave of protest, unprecedented in all the years of celebration of Columbus, all over the United States, and throughout the Americas. Much of this protest is being led by Indians, who are organizing conferences and meetings, who are engaging in acts of civil disobedience, who are trying to educate the American public about what really happened 500 years ago, and what it tells us about the issues of our time.

There is a new generation of teachers in our schools, and many of them are insisting that the Columbus story be told from the point of view of the native Americans. In the fall of 1990 I was telephoned from Los Angeles by a talk-show host who wanted to discuss Columbus. Also on the line was a high school student in that city, named Blake Lindsey, who had insisted on addressing the Los Angeles City Council to oppose the traditional Columbus Day celebration. She told them of the genocide committed by the Spaniards against the Arawak Indians. The City Council did not respond.

Someone called in on that talk show, introducing herself as a woman who had emigrated from Haiti. She said: "The girl is right—we have no Indians left. In our last uprising against the government, the people knocked down the statue of Columbus and now it is in the basement of the city hall in Port-au-Prince." The caller finished by saying: "Why don't we build statues for the aborigines?"

Despite the textbooks still in use, more teachers are questioning, more students are questioning. Bill Bigelow reports on the reactions of his students after he introduces them to reading material which contradicts the traditional histories. One student wrote: "In 1492, Columbus sailed the ocean blue.... That story is about as complete as Swiss cheese."

Another wrote a critique of her American history textbook to the publisher, Allyn and Bacon, pointing to many important omissions in that text. She said: "I'll just pick one topic to keep it simple. How about Columbus?"

Another student: "It seemed to me as if the publishers had just printed up some glory story that was supposed to make us feel more patriotic about our country.... They want us to look at our country as great and powerful and forever right.... We're being fed lies."

When students discover that in the very first history they learn—the story of Columbus—they have not been told the whole truth, it leads to a healthy skepticism about all of their historical education. One of Bigelow's students, named Rebecca, wrote: "What does it matter who discovered America, really?... But the thought that I've been lied to all my life about this, and who knows what else, really makes me angry."

"What does it matter who discovered America, really? ... But the thought that I've been lied to all my life about this, and who knows what else, really makes me angry."

This new critical thinking in the schools and in the colleges seems to frighten those who have glorified what is called "Western civilization." Reagan's Secretary of Education, William Bennett, in his 1984 "Report on the Humanities in Higher Education," writes of Western civilization as "our common culture...its highest ideas and aspirations."

One of the most ferocious defenders of Western civilization is philosopher Allan Bloom, who wrote *The Closing of the American Mind* in a spirit of panic at what the social movements of the 1960s had done to change the educational atmosphere of American universities. He was frightened by the student demonstrations he saw at Cornell, which he saw as a terrible interference with education.

Bloom's idea of education was a small group of very smart students, in an elite university, studying Plato and Aristotle, and refusing to be disturbed in their contemplation by the noise outside their windows of students rallying against racism or protesting against the war in Vietnam.

As I read him, I was reminded of some of my colleagues, when I was teaching in a black college in Atlanta, Georgia, at the time of the civil rights movement, who shook their heads in disapproval when our students left their classes to sit-in, to be arrested, in protest against racial segregation. These students were neglecting their education, they said. In fact, these students were learning more in a few weeks of participation in social struggle than they could learn in a year of going to class.

What a narrow, stunted understanding of education! It corresponds perfectly to the view of history which insists that Western civilization is the summit of human achievement. As Bloom wrote in his book: "...only in the Western nations, i.e. those influenced by Greek philosophy, is there some willingness to doubt the identification of the good with one's own way." Well, if this willingness to doubt is the hallmark of Greek philosophy, then Bloom and his fellow idolizers of Western civilization are ignorant of that philosophy.

If Western civilization is considered the high point of human progress, the United States is the best representative of this civilization. Here is Allan Bloom again: "This is the American moment in world history.... America tells one story: the unbroken, ineluctable progress of freedom and equality. From its first settlers and its political foundings on, there has been no dispute that freedom and equality are the essence of justice for us..."

Yes, tell black people and native Americans and the homeless and those without health insurance, and all the victims abroad of American foreign policy that America "tells one story...freedom and equality."

It is the guardians of the old stories, the orthodox histories, who refuse to widen the spectrum of ideas, to take in new books, new approaches, new information, new views of history.

Western civilization is complex. It represents many things, some decent, some horrifying. We would have to pause before celebrating it uncritically when we note that David Duke, the Louisiana Ku Klux Klan member and ex-Nazi, says that people have got him wrong. "The common strain in my thinking," he told a reporter, "is my love for Western civilization."

We who insist on looking critically at the Columbus story, and indeed at everything in our traditional histories, are often accused of insisting on political correctness, to the detriment of free speech. I find this odd. It is the guardians of the old stories, the orthodox histories, who refuse to widen the spectrum of ideas, to take in new books, new approaches, new information, new views of history. They, who claim to believe in "free markets," do not believe in a free marketplace of ideas, any more than they believe in a free marketplace of goods and services. In both material goods and in ideas, they want the market dominated by those who have always held power and wealth. They worry that if new ideas enter the marketplace, people may begin to rethink the social arrangements that have given us so much suffering, so much violence, so much war these last 500 years of "civilization."

Of course we had all that before Columbus arrived in this hemisphere, but resources were puny, people were isolated from one another, and the possibilities were narrow. In recent centuries, however, the world has become amazingly small, our possibilities for creating a decent society have enormously magnified, and so the excuses for hunger, ignorance, violence, and racism no longer exist.

In rethinking our history, we are not just looking at the past, but at the present, and trying to look at it from the point of view of those who have been left out of the benefits of so-called civilization. It is a simple but profoundly important thing we are trying to accomplish, to look at the world from other points of view. We need to do that, as we come into the next century, if we want this coming century to be different, if we want it to be, not an American century, or a Western century, or a white century, or a male century, or any nation's, any group's century, but a century for the human race.

Go Out and Kill People Because This Article Tells You To

The Political History of the First Amendment

Nick Mamatas

Black Panthers walked the streets of Oakland, California, with a copy of it written across huge pieces of poster board. The Ku Klux Klan uses it to defend its right to burn crosses. No matter how radical their politics, few Americans understand the true origin of the First Amendment to the Constitution, the little diddy that forbids Congress from making any law interfering with freedom of speech and the free press (among other things). Calls for a return to the original intent of the Founders echo across the political spectrum. It seems that nearly everyone, from pornographers and bomb-throwers, to holy rollers and goose-steppers, are just sure that the secret cabal of wealthy landowners who founded this country would be so eager to read their tracts and pamphlets.

But the Founders were hardly the political idealists that junior-high history books claim they were. Instead, the First Amendment, like much of the rest of the Constitution, was written in flurry of self-interest shot through with compromise. The First Amendment was not designed to make sure you could look at naughty pictures, or read this book, or tell a gaggle of lawyers on the subway, "After the revolution, we'll be strangling our bosses with your entrails! Hear that, motherfuckers? Your entrails!!!" It was designed to make sure that the Federalist and Anti-Federalist wings of America's ruling class had freedom to operate in the public sphere. The notion that anyone else would be able to afford a printing press, or that a newspaper would be something other than the organ of a political faction (or that the people of color and the people of plain ol' no money would be involved in politics, for that matter), was alien to the Founders. The creation of the Bill of Rights and the political economy of the publishing industry at the time tell a more complete story. You were being lied to. In print, even.

When Colonel George Mason first proposed a Bill of Rights at the Constitutional Convention of 1787, the motion was voted down almost unanimously, with zero votes for the Bill.

The Bill of Rights

The inclusion of the Bill of Rights in the Constitution is typically interpreted as a victory of the libertarian Anti-Federalists against the elitist Federalists. The Anti-Federalists were worried that Congress would assume absolute power, while Federalists like Alexander Hamilton claimed that the Constitution gave sufficient protection against dictatorship without the extraneous amendments. The Bill was one of the many compromises between these two factions.

When Colonel George Mason first proposed a Bill of Rights at the Constitutional Convention of 1787, the motion was voted down almost unanimously, with zero votes for the Bill. Even the Anti-Federalist stronghold states voted against the measure, and Massachusetts abstained. No state voted for inclusion of a Bill, including those states which had their own Bills of Rights. Federalist Robert Sherman explained that he, too, was for preserving the rights of the people, but the states could do that just fine. Not surprisingly, these delegates were often the ruling powers of their states; they were land-rich through government grant, they were the leading politicians of their home states, and they had every reason to want the buck to stop at the state legislature, rather than at a distant Congress.

Mason, who is occasionally brushed off and set upright by modern libertarians as an early defender of individual rights, was hardly an idealist himself. He sought protection for Southern shipping interests in the form of a two-thirds majority for commercial legislation, in an attempt to guarantee his own fortune and the continued import of slaves. Back in Virginia, Mason supported limiting the voting franchise to landholders like himself and affirming the freedom to bear arms only within the context of a "well regulated militia," rather than allowing individuals to own their own guns. And this was the one person to initiate discussion of a Bill and one of only three who declined to sign the Bill-less Constitution in 1787.

In spite of this evidence to the contrary, historians continue to insist that the Founders were idealists who were interested in defending individual rights. This apologia includes creating alternative scenarios to explain the near-unanimous antipathy for a Bill of Rights, even up to insisting that it was a very hot summer in Pennsylvania and the delegates just wanted to go home, where they presumably had central air conditioning. It took over two years for the Bill of Rights to be introduced into the Constitution, and even then, it was partially a matter of power politics.

The Anti-Federalists were against a strong central government, not because they felt that such a government would harm the civil rights of the landless and powerless, but because they did not want Congress to have direct authority in raising taxes. This would trump states' rights with federal power through the judiciary, or regulate interstate commerce. "But they found that the more politically popular argument to use against ratification was the Constitution's lack of a Bill of Rights. So they advanced that argument, although it was a smokescreen for their real concerns, to fuel criticism of the Constitution. By dramatically objecting to the absence of a Bill of Rights, the Anti-Federalists hoped to compel revision of the proposed Constitution so as to greatly reduce the powers of the national government or, alternatively, to sponsor a second constitutional convention."[1]

The Founders themselves had no interest in anything more than a class democracy; their meetings were held in secret, and no reporters or information was allowed in or out of the hall during the proceedings.

The Bill of Rights was actually added to the Constitution as a result of struggle from below, and the Founders did all they could to limit the power of the first ten amendments, both in drafting them and in subsequent interpretation. Land seizures by the poor, food riots, and other protests erupted across the United States during and after the 1787 Convention. This convinced even the most libertarian of the Founding Fathers that a strong central government was necessary to preserve their land rights and to challenge the Indian tribes that still occupied most of the continent, while putting limits on the power the ruling elite would grant itself. Radical historian Michael Parenti points out that the Bill of Rights, to the extent that people actually benefit from these rights, is best seen as a product of class struggle against the Founders, rather than as an example of the Founders' interest in the "grand experiment" of democracy. The Founders themselves had no interest in anything more than a class democracy; their meetings were held in secret, and no reporters or information was allowed in or out of the hall during the proceedings. If one wasn't invited, one didn't count.

The Sedition Act of 1798

After ratification, Founding Father John Adams showed that his interpretation of the Bill of Rights didn't actually include the right to disagree with the federal government. The dawn of the 1790s saw a decline in the unity of the ruling elite and the emergence of factionalism. The spirit of compromise that supposedly informed the Constitutional Convention, and which allowed both Southern and Northern landowners to remain rich, faltered almost immediately. Thomas Jefferson and James Madison created a party, the Democratic Republicans, in opposition to the ruling Federalists, in order to head off what was seen as an amalgamation of power by the executive branch. Alexander Hamilton had significant success in arguing for a national bank, a standing army, and excise taxes that transferred wealth to his Northern base. Southerners saw the taxes to support a new treasury loan favoring "pro-British merchants in the commercial cities" as unfairly paid by landowners in the South. The era of Washington was over, and the gloves were off.

After ratification, Founding Father John Adams showed that his interpretation of the Bill of Rights didn't actually include the right to disagree with the federal government.

The Alien and Sedition Acts of 1798 were tools designed to silence Republican opposition and supporters of friendly relations with France. The Alien Act allowed non-citizens to be arrested without evidence during wartime, and the Sedition Act made criticizing the President illegal. These Acts were drafted by contemporaries and political allies of Founders and were passed by a Congress made up of Founders and their allies as well.

The Sedition Act was designed by the Federalists primarily to shut down Republican presses and to maintain power for its own international business practices, which were oriented towards the British. That this bill was politically motivated became obvious when the House voted to extend the act from the originally proposed length of one year to the expiration of John Adams' term, March 3, 1801. Kentucky and Virginia each responded with acts basically nullifying the Congressional act (a tactic which would not work today, given the attenuation of states' rights), but other states accepted Congress' seizure of what had been a state function.

The election of 1803 ended the Alien and Sedition Acts, but not the social relationships that created them. The Sedition Act was powerful in that there were powerful connections between business interests and publishers. Only the wealthy could afford printing presses, and the wealthy had the greatest interest in public policy. There were no "non-partisan" presses, either; they were overwhelmingly owned by members of one faction or the other, and explicitly used as a bully pulpit. Unlike today, where even a relatively small concern can hire a printer to put out a magazine or flyer (and where a nominal independence from political parties is a common conceit among journalists), publishers and printers were formerly one and the same. To attack the press was to attack political opponents, directly. The Sedition Act was not a mistake or the result of a misunderstanding of the First Amendment, but was the result of a very mercenary understanding of the Bill Of Rights. It wasn't *supposed* to mean anything.

Not a Free Press, but an Expensive One

By 1800 there were over 200 newspapers, 24 of which were dailies, and the vast majority of which were political papers, rather than "objective" sources of news. *The Gazette of the United States*, for example, was a Federalist paper, while the cleverly titled *National Gazette* was a Jeffersonian, Anti-Federalist sheet. Political reporting was privileged, while the stuff that fills today's pages (crime reports, news of accidents, unreconstructed press releases, and lifestyle reporting) was nearly nonexistent. The politics were hardly genteel; stinging denunciations and satire were the norm. Advertising, and the need for a mass audience to sell to advertisers, did not exist as we know it. Publishers and printing press owners were one and the same, and they were marketing towards their comrades in the upper classes. Newspapers often cost as much as six cents, a sum that made it impossible for the average working man to keep up on the news, since doing so would actually require buying more than one paper.

The press was vitally important for the founding of the country, as it made up an "internal bulletin" for the ruling elite of post-colonial America. Hamilton and Madison's "Federalist Papers" were printed (anonymously, of course) in *The Independent Journal* and several New York area papers. Anti-Federalist Samuel Bryan published his "Centinel" essays in Philadelphia's *Independent Gazetteer.* In spite of the fact that most papers were totally irrelevant to the average American, the mythology of a press for all from the time of the Founders is still repeated. George Krimsky, the former head of news for the Associated Press' World Services, earned his paycheck with this bit of historical revisionism: "In the wake of America's successful revolution, it was decided there should indeed be government, but only if it were accountable to the people. The people, in turn, could only hold the government accountable if they knew what it was doing and could intercede as necessary, using their ballot, for example. This role of public 'watchdog' was thus assumed by a citizen press, and as a consequence, the government in the United States has been kept out of the news business."

A semblance of objectivity was again required, in order to maximize readership, and to better influence public opinion.

As noted already, very few citizens could even afford to read the "citizen press," much less be a part of it. The 55 attendees to the Constitutional Convention were a strong part of the embryonic publishing and newspaper industry of the United States, and many of them wrote, published, or financed work on politics, economics, and the sciences. The media belonged to the elite, and the First Amendment was nothing more than an attempt to protect that elite from its own legislative excesses. Modern notions of the free press are quite different.

The Trickle-Down Theory of the Free Press

Capitalism happened. Mass production and mass culture emerged hand in hand. The ability to create a large number of commodities also allowed for the creation of large print runs for daily papers. The old political rags of the Founders were for a niche audience—the relatively few Americans who had the voting franchise, large farmers, tradesmen, and proto-capitalists. The new press had to be different, and thanks to mass production, papers could be produced cheaply. Mass production also helped create the final split between "publisher" and "printer." Mass-produced goods needed to be sold, since they were produced for exchange rather than for personal use. Encouraging the purchase of these goods to a nation of relatively poor people who were used to making their own clothing, soap, etc. led to the development of advertising, which could be used to subsidize print runs. The "penny press" was born. The middle classes could found newspapers and sell them to the working and lower classes.

Marketing demanded a change in journalistic principles. Instead of appealing to some segment of the ruling-class niche market, the penny press had to be intellectually accessible to all. Additionally, taking strong political positions could offend the sensibilities of a fickle readership and of the advertisers, so the concept of objective reporting began to be formalized. An examination of most papers of the time wouldn't demonstrate much objectivity, though. By the 1830s, Benjamin Day's *New York Sun* and James Gordon Bennett's *New York Herald* were available on the streets to anyone with a penny. And for a penny, one could read lurid tales of crime, disaster, and later, wars.

New production techniques also inspired the serious press of the ruling classes. These newspapers could also expand into the broader marketplace, and the elite funding these papers could use their huge print runs to cultivate the tastes of the masses through advertising, and the political will of the people through clever reporting. A semblance of objectivity was again required, in order to maximize readership, and to better influence public opinion. A split occurred between the popular press and the more highbrow press; the popular entertained, and the highbrow "informed." The latter only printed "the news that's fit to print."

Michael Schudson, professor of communication at the University of California at San Diego, explains that the *New York Times* "established itself as the 'higher journalism' because it adapted to the life experience of persons whose position in the social structure gave them the most control over their own lives." If the media truly is a "watchdog" or even a distinct part of the polity designed to influence the government, then highbrow papers like the *Times* fulfill the same role as the old political papers of the Founders. They allow a small, elite segment of the population greater influence. As Alexander Hamilton, one of the more brutally honest of the Founders said, "All communities divide themselves into the few and the many. The first are the rich and well-born, the other the mass of the people.... Give therefore to the first class a distinct permanent share in the government." Ironically enough, one of the papers founded by Hamilton, the *New York Post*, has a lot more in common with the penny presses of the urban rabble than the post-colonial gazettes of the ruling elite.

The Supreme Court has flip-flopped, turned backflips, and vibrated itself through walls to manipulate the First Amendment and its protections.

Whose First Amendment? Our First Amendment!

Now what? People in the United States are quite free to publish (if they can afford to) and even freer to read a wider variety of material than most people on the planet. The vision of the Founders was severely shortsighted. The First Amendment and the Bill of Rights are best seen as *realpolitik* maneuvering, not posthumous approval of your assumed right to buy a copy of *D-Cups* at the 7-11. The average daily newspaper had precious little to do with the expansion of First Amendment rights, either. Most of them are designed to deliver the apolitical and economically non-influential segment of the American population (i.e. lots of us) into the hands of advertisers—advertisers who are, of course, busy reading the *Wall Street Journal*, not the *New York Post.*

The Supreme Court has had a lot to say about freedom of speech (and through extension, the press) in the past century. The standard conception of the Supreme Court as an apolitical body puzzling over the Constitution and mysteriously reading between the lines of this living (and sometimes squirming and mewling) document in search of fair-minded decisions is false. The Supreme Court has flip-flopped, turned backflips, and vibrated itself through walls to manipulate the First Amendment and its protections.

The creation of advertiser-friendly "objectivity" in reportage allowed the print media to claim the role of watchdog. In order to protect this role, the laws which allowed the government to control the press via "prior restraint" (blocking a publication before it can be made public) were challenged and struck down. In the first serious challenge to prior restraint, *Near v. Minnesota* (1931), the Supreme Court struck down a Minnesota law that had been used to silence the pro-Klan *Saturday Press*. For the most part, though, radical points of view were not so lucky in this century.

Since the press was now an objective watchdog, polemics, pamphlets, radical newspapers, and articles used to organize dissent and resistance were not considered part of the press at all. Instead, they were merely "speech" and could thus be repressed by the government without upsetting the delicate balance between the power of the state and the public's need for a tame and corporate-owned news industry. Prior restraint precedents protected most mainstream papers and a pro-Klan scandal sheet from censorship, but did not come into play against an entire class of publications which were freely attacked by the government, in spite of the fact that the press as the Founders knew it consisted largely of such polemical pamphlets and news sheets. The middle-of-the-road corporate media were granted the legal protections designed for a revolutionary press, and the State exiled radical thought to the risky hinterlands of seditious speech in a way not dissimilar from the old Sedition Act.

Charles T. Schenck was convicted under the Espionage Act of 1917 for distributing a leaflet urging young men to resist the World War I draft. The Supreme Court upheld the conviction in *Schenck v. US* (1919), claiming that the federal government has the right to suppress speech (though a leaflet is as much a form of press as anything else) if that speech posed a "clear and present danger" to the nation (read: the government). Also in 1919, *Abrams v. US* saw the court uphold the conviction of a Bolshevik immigrant who prepared a leaflet urging resistance to the US's involvement in the Russian Civil War.

The Supreme Court also upheld the conviction of Benjamin Gitlow under New York's old anarchy law, which prohibited people from advocating the overthrow of the government. In *Gitlow v. New York* (1925), the Supreme Court actually developed a looser test for the State's right to ban certain ideas. Instead of a clear and present danger, there only needed to be a "bad tendency" to drive people toward illegal action. By the mid-1920s, the Palmer raids and America's first Red Scare had crippled the power of the radical left. Gitlow's inconsequential pamphlet was easy pickin's for the ruling class in a way that Schenck's and Abram's more influential pieces were not. It is also worth noting that the Court actually offered an expansive interpretation of the First Amendment in this case, ruling that it did apply to states and not just to laws passed by Congress. Didn't help Gitlow any, though.

The Court returned to the "clear and present danger" test two years later in *Whitney v. California* (1927), which found a Communist Labor Party member guilty of breaking California's criminal syndicalism law. It was a law designed to fight organized crime, but it worked just fine against unions and left-wing parties as well.

These laws were rendered largely irrelevant by the Great Depression of 1929 and the civil unrest that followed. The Communist Party saw the circulation of its own paper climb to nearly one million, its power in the union movement increase, and its convention fill Madison Square Garden. The impact of the left on the political culture of the US, and the desperation of Americans workers and the unemployed, was sufficient to guarantee First Amendment rights even under the same conditions where the

Supreme Court had denied they existed. This relative freedom to participate in dissent was brief and informal. The old laws were still on the books, and in 1940, as the Great Depression began to vanish into the build-up to World War II, Congress passed the Alien Registration Act. Also known as the Smith Act, this law made it an offense to support or belong to a group that advocated the violent overthrow of the government. The Smith Act was first used against the Trotskyist Socialist Workers Party, and only then turned against the Communist Party, which benefited from this respite thanks to their ownership of the Stalin franchise in the United States, and the cooperation of the US and the USSR during World War II.

Both the right and the left have their own agendas when they call upon the spirit of the Founding Fathers and the First Amendment.

The 1950s and the rise of the Cold War saw a shrinking of First Amendment rights (yes, the war was that cold). In *Dennis et al v. US* (1951), the Supreme Court upheld the Smith Act, which made membership in the Communist Party illegal, and even reverted to the "bad tendency" test for this case. Communists no longer had to be shown to be dangerous to the US for their speech and press to be repressed. It wasn't until the 1960s and the awakening of a slew of social movements and a resurgent left, that speech on the far ends of the spectrum was found to be protected by the seemingly straightforward First Amendment.

Ironically, it wasn't the Panthers or Students for a Democratic Society (SDS) that won free speech for the fringe—it was the Klan. The Supreme Court overturned Ohio's criminal syndicalism law in *Brandenburg v. Ohio* (1969). Brandenburg was an Ohio Klan leader who held a rally and invited local TV stations to tape it. Even though he promised "revengeance" on the government for anti-white politics, the Court shielded him and his fellow Klansmen from criminal penalties and reversed the old *Whitney* decision. What changed in the 1960s was that the Court "realized" a difference between preaching the moral necessity for violent overthrow of the system and actively organizing for such an overthrow, or actively sparking such violence. And what made the Court come to such a realization? The fact that, by the late 1960s, over a million Americans considered themselves revolutionaries and millions more demanded broad free speech rights for all, no matter how loathsome the speech.

Decades later, the left is once again in shambles and the right on the rise. It is not a surprise to see speech and press once again confused (Webpages, in spite of their similarity to periodicals, leaflets, and books, are often considered "speech") and proscribed limits for publication and speech succeeding more frequently now than in the 1960s. The Founders' real vision of the First Amendment remains in place, in spite of the best efforts of 200 years' worth of insurrectionary pamphleteers and fifty gagillion watts of furious dorm-room discussions about the revolution, man.

Both the right and the left have their own agendas when they call upon the spirit of the Founding Fathers and the First Amendment. The political mainstream attempts to appeal to the ghostly and impossible past of the Founders while slapping together political platforms that are as alien to those old, dead geezers as your collection of pornographic elf comics would be. The left is wrong when it calls for the protection of the mythical First Amendment; it was never designed to protect the rights of the poor and downtrodden against the depredations of the finance state. The fringe-right's frantic seance hasn't made Thomas Jefferson ring a little bell or blow a spirit horn either. The "Founders' intent" interpretation would be as disastrous to corn-pone populists today as it was 200 years ago. Hillbillies and rednecks weren't invited to the Constitutional Convention, nor were they expected to have any part in society. American fascism's call for a return to the spirit of the Founders is just words in the mouth of a pointy-headed sock puppet belonging to the ruling elite.

Neither the politics, nor intent, nor the spirit of the Founders informs modern notions of the First Amendment. If anything, America owes its radicals, malcontents, and revolutionaries its thanks for forcing a free press to develop. Much the same way one can't have a labor union, a strike, or industrial sabotage without a fatcat and a smoke-belching factory in the first place, the modern press is as free as it is in spite of the Founders' vision of a free press. Capital provided the raw material for a society where any cement-head can write a screed on a free Yahoo Website, but it was the opponents of capital who opened the political space for that cement-head to do so. The First Amendment isn't the dream of the dusty corpses of a roomful of lawyers and slaveowners; it is the end result of the hard work of people who want to hang every lawyer with the entrails of every CEO after the revolution comes.

Endnote

1. American Civil Liberties Union. (1997). "A history of the Bill of Rights, ACLU briefing paper number 9." American Civil Liberties Union. <www.wwnet.com/%7Ejcsiler/document/HISTBR.TXT>.

Saving Private Power

The Hidden History of "The Good War"

excerpts from a book by Michael Zezima (aka Mickey Z)

Was World War II a just war? Is the "Good War" fable rooted in reality, false hope, or propaganda? This enduring myth goes well beyond Memorial Day barbecues and flickering black-and-white movies on late-night TV. According to the accepted history, WWII was an inevitable war forced upon a peaceful people thanks to a surprise attack by a sneaky enemy. This war, then and now, has been carefully and consciously sold to us as a life-and-death battle against pure evil. For most Americans, WWII was nothing less than good and bad going toe-to-toe in khaki fatigues.

But, Hollywood aside, John Wayne never set foot on Iwo Jima. Despite the former President's dim recollections, Ronald Reagan did not liberate any concentration camps. And, contrary to popular belief, FDR never actually got around to sending American troops "over there" to take on Hitler's Germany until after the Nazis had already declared war on the US.

WWII was about territory, power, control, money, and imperialism.

American lives weren't sacrificed in a holy war to avenge Pearl Harbor nor to end the Nazi Holocaust, just as the Civil War wasn't fought to end slavery. WWII was about territory, power, control, money, and imperialism. Sure, the Allies won and ultimately, that's a very good thing—but it doesn't mean they did it fair and square. Precisely how unfairly they behaved will be explored in detail herein but, for now, the words of US General Curtis LeMay, commander of the 1945 Tokyo fire-bombing operation, will suffice: "I suppose if I had lost the war, I would have been tried as a war criminal. Fortunately, we were on the winning side."

Myth #1: WWII Was "Good"

When the US entered WWII, patriotism was the watchword and denial was the order of the day. For example, the publicity arm of the American Motion Picture Industry put out a full-page ad in several magazines in 1942. Entitled "Our Morale is Mightier than the Sword," the ad declared that in order to win the war, "[o]ur minds must be as keen as our swords, our hearts as strong as our tanks, our spirits as buoyant as our planes. For morale is a mighty force—as vital as the materials of war themselves...so it is the job of the Motion Picture Industry to *keep 'em smiling*." (Emphasis in original.)

About 25 to 30 percent of wartime casualties were psychological cases.

Indeed, if the folks back home had any idea of what was really going on, few of them would have been *smiling*. That was the true genius of "Good War" propaganda: lies of omission.

Celebrated author John Steinbeck served as a wartime correspondent. "We were all part of the war effort," he later remarked. "We went along with it, and not only that, we abetted it.... I don't mean that the correspondents were liars.... It is in the things not mentioned that the untruth lies." Steinbeck went on to explain that "the foolish reporter who broke the rules would not be printed at home and in addition would be put out of the theater by the command."

"By not mentioning a lot of things," adds author Paul Fussell, "a correspondent could give the audience at home the impression that there were no cowards in the service, no thieves and rapists and looters, no cruel or stupid commanders."

Let's take a look at some of what we weren't told about the "greatest generation," as we just keep *smiling*.

With few exceptions, the Hollywood version of war evokes images of the noble everyman, fighting for freedom and honor without asking any questions. Watching John Wayne or Tom Hanks perform their patriotic duty helps obscure many battlefield realities that would put the "Good War" label in doubt. Some of those realities:

- At least 50 percent of US combat soldiers soiled themselves during battle.
- Ten percent or more of American troops took amphetamines at some time.
- By the war's end, there were roughly 75,000 US MIAs, most of whom, thanks to modern weaponry, "had been blown into vapor."
- Only 18 percent of combat veterans in the Pacific said they were "usually in good spirits."
- The psychological breakdown rate of men consistently in action for 28 days ran as high as 90 percent.
- As of 1994, roughly 25 percent of the WWII veterans still in the hospital were psychiatric cases.
- About 25 to 30 percent of wartime casualties were psychological cases (under severe conditions, that number could reach 70 to 80 percent).
- Mental problems accounted for 54 percent of total casualties in Italy.
- During the battle for Okinawa, 7,613 Americans died and 31,807 sustained physical wounds, while an astounding 26,221 were mental casualties.

▪ ▪ ▪ ▪ ▪ ▪ ▪ ▪ ▪ ▪

For those on the homefront, the good old days don't exactly pan out either. Part of the more recent "Good War" facade is the "greatest generation" hype. This fiction enables the family-values crowd to claim that generation as their own despite the fact that those who lived during the Depression and WWII were no more or less human than the rest of us. There were a record-high 600,000 divorces in 1946. In addition, the divorce rate in 1940 was 16 percent; by 1944, it had jumped to 27 percent. Between 1939 and 1945, illegitimate births in the US rose by 42 percent. The venereal disease rate for girls 15- to 18-years-old in New York City increased 204 percent between 1941 and 1944, while truancy in Detroit jumped 24 percent between 1938 and 1943.

As for the legendary efficiency of homefront war production, the results are mixed. Despite the fable of unquestioned unity, the forces of labor remained focused on the issue of workplace reform. There were some 14,000 strikes involving nearly seven million workers during the war years. "In 1944 alone," says historian Howard Zinn, "a million workers were on strike, in the mines, in the steel mills, in the auto and transportation equipment industries."

As ubiquitous as labor unrest in those days was WWII poster art. Distributed by the US Office of War Information, these colorful single-sheet posters demonized the enemy, canonized "our boys," and helped restore the tattered image of corporate America—all in the name of increasing production, erasing the Depression, and selling the war to a decidedly suspicious public. Representatives from the major advertising firm Young & Rubicam, Inc. argued that the "most effective war posters appealed to the emotions," and must be understood by the "lower third" of the population. Battlefield casualty images were banned, and any labor-management tensions were glossed over. Thus, the consciously fabricated—but effectively unifying—patriotism of the war effort made it harder for labor to mobilize public support for actions against corporations.

WWII poster art also served to define the role of American women in the war effort. "We Can Do It!" said Rosie the Riveter, with "it" meaning following orders on the factory floor until the war was over and then returning to the kitchen.

"This image," says historian Maureen Honey, "both idealized women as a strong, capable fighter infused with a holy spirit and undercut the notion that women deserved and wanted a larger role in public life."

Myth #2: WWII Was Inevitable

To believe this myth, one must accept the rise of fascism as practically a force of nature. By taking a closer look at the decisions made by many of the "good guys," however, one comes away with a new perspective.

When William E. Dodd, US Ambassador to Germany during the 1930s, declared that "a clique of U.S. industrialists is...working closely with the fascist regime[s] in Germany and Italy," he wasn't kidding.

"Many leaders of Wall Street and of the US foreign policy establishment had maintained close ties with their German counterparts since the 1920s, some having intermarried or shared investments," says investigative reporter Christopher Simpson. "This went so far in the 1930s as the sale in New York of bonds whose proceeds helped finance the Aryanization of companies and real estate looted from German Jews.... US investment in Germany accelerated rapidly after Hitler came to power." Such investment, says Simpson, increased "by some 48.5 percent between 1929 and 1940, while declining sharply everywhere else in continental Europe."

One benefactor of Corporate America's largesse was German banker Hermann Abs, who was close enough to *der Führer* to receive advance notice that Germany was planning to seize Austria. Tellingly, upon his death, Abs was judiciously eulogized by the *New York Times* as an "art collector" whose financial career "took off after 1945." The *Times* piece cryptically quoted David Rockefeller as calling Abs "the most important banker of our time."

▪▪▪▪▪▪▪▪▪▪

It wasn't just the Rockefellers who admired Nazi ingenuity. Among the major US corporations who invested in Germany during the 1920s were Ford, General Motors, General Electric, Standard Oil, Texaco, International Harvester, ITT, and IBM—all of whom were more than happy to see the German labor movement and working-class parties smashed. For many of these companies, operations in Germany continued during the war (even if it meant the use of concentration-camp slave labor) with overt US government support.

"Pilots were given instructions not to hit factories in Germany that were owned by US firms," says author Michael Parenti. "Thus Cologne was almost leveled by Allied bombing but its Ford plant, providing military equipment for the Nazi army, was untouched; indeed, German civilians began using the plant as an air raid shelter."

These pre-war business liaisons carried over into the post-war tribunals. "The dominant faction of America's establishment had always opposed bringing Germany's elite to trial," Simpson explained.

Myth #3: The Allies Fought to Liberate the Death Camps

Apologists can pretend that the details of the Holocaust were not known and that if they had been, the US would have intervened, but as Kenneth C. Davis explains, "Prior to the American entry into the war, the Nazi treatment of Jews evoked little more than a weak diplomatic condemnation. It is clear that Roosevelt knew about the treatment of the Jews in Germany and elsewhere in Europe, and about the methodical, systematic destruction of the Jews during the Holocaust. Clearly, saving the Jews and other groups that Hitler was destroying *en masse* was not a critical issue for American war planners."

Indeed, when a resolution was introduced in January 1934 asking the Senate and the President to express "surprise and pain" at the German treatment of the Jews, the resolution never got out of committee.

Indeed, when a resolution was introduced in January 1934 asking the Senate and the President to express "surprise and pain" at the German treatment of the Jews, the resolution never got out of committee.

Such inaction was not reversed even as more specific details began to reach the average American. On October 30, 1939, the *New York Times* wrote of "freight cars...full of people" heading eastward and broached the subject of the "complete elimination of the Jews from European life," which, according to the *Times*, appeared to be "a fixed German policy."

As for the particulars on the Nazi final solution, as early as July 1941, the New York Yiddish dailies offered stories of Jews massacred by Germans in Russia. Three months later, the *New York Times* wrote of eyewitness accounts of 10,000 to 15,000 Jews slaughtered in Galicia. On December 7, 1942, the *London Times* joined the chorus with this observation:

> The question now arises whether the Allied Governments, even now, can do anything to prevent Hitler's threat of extermination from being literally carried out.

The German persecution and mass murder of Eastern European Jews was indeed a poorly kept secret, and the United States and its Allies cannot honestly nor realistically hide behind the excuse of ignorance. Even when the Nazis themselves initiated proposals to ship Jews from both Germany and Czechoslovakia to Western countries or even Palestine, the Allied nations could never get beyond negotiations, and the rescue plans never materialized.

One particularly egregious example was the 1939 journey of the *St. Louis*. Carrying 1,128 German Jewish refugees from Europe, the ocean liner was turned back by US officials because the German immigration quota had been met. The *St. Louis* then returned to Europe where the refugees found temporary sanctuary in France, Great Britain, Belgium, and the Netherlands. "Most of the émigrés were eventually captured by the Nazis after their invasion of the Low Countries in the spring of 1940 and were shipped to death camps," wrote Jerome Agel and Walter D. Glanze.

Myth #4: The Attack on Pearl Harbor Was a Surprise

Especially after the attack on Pearl Harbor, Japan had a reputation of being "treacherous," a tag that justified many war crimes and lasted well past the bombing of Hiroshima and Nagasaki. However, before accepting such a racist stereotype someone should have at least provided some evidence of treachery.

As historian Thomas A. Bailey has written: "Franklin Roosevelt repeatedly deceived the American people during the period before Pearl Harbor.... He was like the physician who must tell the patient lies for the patient's own good."

The diplomatic record reveals some of what Dr. Roosevelt neglected to tell his easily-deluded patients in that now-mythical "Date of Infamy" speech:

December 14, 1940: Joseph Grew, US Ambassador to Japan, sends a letter to FDR, announcing that, "It seems to me increasingly clear that we are bound to have a showdown [with Japan] some day."

December 30, 1940: Pearl Harbor is considered so likely a target of Japanese attack that Rear Admiral Claude C. Bloch, Commander of the Fourteenth Naval District, authors a memorandum entitled, "Situation Concerning the Security of the Fleet and the Present Ability of the Local Defense Forces to Meet Surprise Attacks."

January 27, 1941: Grew (in Tokyo) sends a dispatch to the State Department: "My Peruvian Colleague told a member of my staff that the Japanese military forces planned, in the event of trouble with the United States, to attempt a surprise mass attack on Pearl Harbor using all of their military facilities."

February 5, 1941: Bloch's December 30, 1940, memorandum leads to much discussion and eventually a letter from Rear Admiral Richmond Kelly Turner to Secretary of War Henry Stimson in which Turner warns, "The security of the US Pacific Fleet while in Pearl Harbor, and of the Pearl Harbor Naval Base itself, has been under renewed study by the Navy Department and forces afloat for the past several weeks.... If war eventuates with Japan, it is believed easily possible that hostilities would be initiated by a surprise attack upon the Fleet or the Naval Base at Pearl Harbor.... In my opinion, the inherent possibilities of a major disaster to the fleet or naval base warrant taking every step, as rapidly as can be done, that will increase the joint readiness of the Army and Navy to withstand a raid of the character mentioned above."

February 18, 1941: Commander in Chief of the US Pacific Fleet, Admiral Husband E. Kimmel, says, "I feel that a surprise attack on Pearl Harbor is a possibility."

September 11, 1941: Kimmel says, "A strong Pacific Fleet is unquestionably a deterrent to Japan—a weaker one may be an invitation."

November 25, 1941: Secretary of War Henry L. Stimson writes in his diary that, "The President...brought up entirely the relations with the Japanese. He brought up the event that we're likely to be attacked [as soon as] next Monday for the Japanese are notorious for making an attack without warning."

November 27, 1941: US Army Chief of Staff George C. Marshall issues a memorandum cautioning that, "Japanese future action unpredictable but hostile action possible at any moment. If hostilities cannot...be avoided, the United States desires that Japan commit the first overt action."

November 29, 1941: Secretary of State Cordell Hull, responding to a speech by Japanese General Hideki Tojo one week before the attack, phones FDR at Warm Springs, Georgia, to warn of "the imminent danger of a Japanese attack," and urge him to return to Washington sooner than planned.

Regardless of this record, there were still racists within the US military and government who never imagined that Japan could orchestrate such a successful offensive. Few Westerners took the Japanese seriously, with journalists regularly referring to them as "apes in khaki" during the early months of their conquest of Southeast Asia. The simian metaphor was maintained thereafter. This racist attitude continued as the two sides approached war—with unexpected consequences

"Most American military minds expected a Japanese attack to come in the Philippines, America's major base in the Pacific," writes Kenneth C. Davis. "Many Americans, including Roosevelt, dismissed the Japanese as combat pilots because they were all presumed to be 'near-sighted.'... There was also a sense that any attack on Pearl Harbor would be easily repulsed." Such an attitude appears even more ludicrous in light of the pre-Pearl Harbor record of the Japanese fighter pilots flying the world's most advanced fighter plane, the Mitsubishi Zero.

"The first actual combat test of the Zero occurred in September 1940," reports historian John W. Dower, "when thirteen of the planes downed twenty-seven Chinese aircraft in ten minutes." By August 31, 1941, thirty Japanese Zeros "accounted for 266 confirmed kills in China." Still, the American military planners were somehow shocked by the skill displayed by the Japanese at Pearl Harbor.

It is believed that more people died from fire in a six-hour time period than ever before in the history of mankind.

Shortly after the attack, with the image of a uniquely treacherous enemy spread throughout America, Admiral William Halsey—soon to become Commander of the South Pacific Force—vowed that by the end of the war, "Japanese would be spoken only in hell." His favorite slogan, "Kill Japs, kill Japs, kill more Japs," echoed the sentiments of Admiral William D. Leahy, Chair of the Joint Chiefs of Staff, who wrote that, "in fighting with Japanese savages, all previously accepted rules of warfare must be abandoned."

Myth #5: Only the Axis Nations Committed War Crimes

In the Pacific theater, the aforementioned General Curtis LeMay was head of the Twenty-first Bomber Command. Acting upon Marshall's 1941 idea of torching the poorer areas of Japan's cities, on the night of March 9-10, 1945, LeMay's bombers laid siege on Tokyo, where tightly-packed wooden buildings were assaulted by 1,665 tons of incendiaries. LeMay later recalled that a few explosives had been mixed in with the incendiaries to demoralize firefighters (96 fire engines burned to ashes and 88 firemen died).

One Japanese doctor recalled "countless bodies" floating in the Sumida River. These bodies were "as black as charcoal" and indistinguishable as men or women. The total dead for one night was an estimated 85,000, with 40,000 injured and one million left homeless. This was only the first strike in a firebombing campaign that dropped 250 tons of bombs per square mile, destroying 40 percent of the surface area in 66 death-list cities (including Hiroshima and Nagasaki). The attack area was 87.4 percent residential.

It is believed that more people died from fire in a six-hour time period than ever before in the history of mankind. At ground zero, the temperature reached 1800° Fahrenheit. Flames from the ensuing inferno were visible for 200 miles. Due to the intense heat, canals boiled over, metals melted, and human beings burst spontaneously into flames.

By May 1945, 75 percent of the bombs being dropped on Japan were incendiaries. Cheered on by the likes of *Time* magazine—which explained that "properly kindled, Japanese cities will burn like autumn leaves"—LeMay's campaign took an estimated 672,000 lives.

Radio Tokyo termed LeMay's tactics "slaughter bombing" and the Japanese press declared that through the fire raids:

> America has revealed her barbaric character... It was an attempt at mass murder of women and children.... The action of the Americans is all the more despicable because of the noisy pretensions they constantly make about their humanity and idealism.... No one expects war to be anything but a brutal business, but it remains for the Americans to make it systematically and unnecessarily a wholesale horror for innocent victims.

Rather than denying this, a spokesman for the Fifth Air Force categorized "the entire population of Japan [as] a proper military target." Colonel Harry F. Cunningham explained the US policy in no uncertain terms:

> We military men do not pull punches or put on Sunday School picnics. We are making War and making it in the all-out fashion which saves American lives, shortens the agony which War is and seeks to bring about an enduring Peace. We intend to seek out and destroy the enemy wherever he or she is, in the greatest possible numbers, in the shortest possible time. For us, THERE ARE NO CIVILIANS IN JAPAN.

On the morning of August 6, 1945, before the Hiroshima story broke, a page-one headline in the *Atlanta Constitution* read: "580 B-29s RAIN FIRE ON 4 MORE DEATH-LIST CITIES." Ironically, the success of LeMay's firebombing raids had effectively eliminated Tokyo from the list of possible A-bomb targets—as there was nothing left to bomb.

Myth #6: The Atomic Bombs Dropped on Japan Were Necessary

Although hundreds of thousands of Japanese lives were lost in Hiroshima and Nagasaki, the bombings are often explained away as a lifesaving measure—American lives. Exactly how many lives saved is, however, up for grabs. (We do know of a few US soldiers who fell between the cracks. About a dozen or more American POWs were killed in Hiroshima, a truth that remained hidden for some 30 years.)

In an August 9, 1945, statement to "the men and women of the Manhattan Project," President Truman declared the hope that "this new weapon will result in saving thousands of American lives" by aborting a planned US invasion of the Japanese islands.

"The president's initial formulation of 'thousands,' however, was clearly not his final statement on the matter to say the least," remarks historian Gar Alperovitz. In fact, Alperovitz documents but a few of Truman's public estimates throughout the years:

December 15, 1945: "It occurred to me that a quarter of a million of the flower of our young manhood was worth a couple of Japanese cities..."

Late 1946: "A year less of war will mean life for three hundred thousand—maybe half a million—of America's finest youth."

About a dozen or more American POWs were killed in Hiroshima, a truth that remained hidden for some 30 years.

October 1948: "...in the long run we could save a quarter of a million young Americans from being killed, and would save an equal number of Japanese young men from being killed."

April 6, 1949: "...I thought 200,000 of our young men would be saved..."

November 1949: Truman quotes Army Chief of Staff George S. Marshall as estimating the cost of an Allied invasion of Japan to be "half a million casualties."

January 12, 1953: Still quoting Marshall, Truman raises the estimate to "a minimum one quarter of a million" and maybe "as much as a million, on the American side alone, with an equal number of the enemy."

Finally, on April 28, 1959, Truman concluded: "the dropping of the bombs...saved millions of lives."

Winston Churchill proclaimed that the Allies "now had something in [their] hands which would redress the balance with the Russians." He topped Truman's ceiling by exclaiming how those A-bombs spared well over 1.2 million Allied lives.

Fortunately, we are not operating without the benefit of official estimates.

In June 1945, President Truman ordered the US military to calculate the cost in American lives for a planned assault on Japan. Consequently, the Joint War Plans Committee prepared a report for the Chiefs of Staff, dated June 15, 1945, thus providing the closest thing anyone has to "accurate": 40,000 US soldiers killed, 150,000 wounded, and 3,500 missing.

■ ■ ■ ■ ■ ■ ■ ■ ■ ■ ■

While the actual casualty count remains unknowable, it was widely known at the time that Japan had been trying to surrender for months prior to the atomic bombing. A May 5, 1945, cable, intercepted and decoded by the US, "dispelled any possible doubt that the Japanese were eager to sue for peace." In fact, the United States Strategic Bombing Survey reported, shortly after the war, that Japan "in all probability" would have surrendered *before* the much-discussed November 1, 1945, Allied invasion of the homeland, thereby saving all kinds of lives.

Truman himself eloquently noted in his diary that Stalin would "be in the Jap War on August 15th. Fini [*sic*] Japs when that comes about."

Clearly, Truman saw the bombs as way to end the war before the Soviet Union could claim a major role in Japan's terms of surrender. However, one year after Hiroshima and Nagasaki, a top-secret US study concluded that the Japanese surrender was based more upon Stalin's declaration of war than either of the atomic bombs.

Myth #7: WWII Was Fought to End Fascism

Even before the CIA was the CIA, it was acting an awful lot like the CIA. According to Christopher Simpson—the journalist who has perhaps done more work than any other in the area of US recruitment of ex-Nazis—an August 16, 1983, Justice Department report "acknowledged that a US intelligence agency known as the Army Counterintelligence Corps (CIC) had recruited Schutzstaffel (SS) and Gestapo officer Klaus Barbie for espionage work in early 1947; that the CIC had hidden him from French war crimes investigators; and that it had then spirited him out of Europe through a clandestine 'ratline'—escape route—run by a priest who was himself a fugitive from war crimes charges."

The report went on to state that the CIC agents had no idea at the time what Barbie had done during the war (apparently, having to hide him from French war crimes investigators didn't set off any alarms), and that Barbie was the only such war criminal that the US had protected.

Let's examine the specious claim that the Butcher of Lyon was the only former Nazi welcomed into the American espionage fold.

"The pattern was set," writes Noam Chomsky, "in the first area liberated by US forces, North Africa, where in 1942 the US placed in power Admiral Jean Darlan, a leading Nazi collaborator who was

It was widely known at the time that Japan had been trying to surrender for months prior to the atomic bombing.

the author of the Vichy regime's anti-Semitic laws." Even WWII's official historian, Stephen Ambrose, has admitted:

> The result was that in its first major foreign-policy venture in World War II, the United States gave its support to a man who stood for everything Roosevelt and Churchill had spoken out against in the Atlantic Charter. As much as Goering or Goebbels, Darlan was the antithesis of the principles the Allies said they were struggling to establish.

Darlan was merely the first step in a premeditated program of collaboration with notorious war criminals.

"A US intelligence agency known as the Army Counterintelligence Corps (CIC) had recruited Schutzstaffel (SS) and Gestapo officer Klaus Barbie for espionage work in early 1947."

▪▪▪▪▪▪▪▪▪▪▪

"I am a general and chief of the intelligence department of the High Command of the German Army. I have information of the highest importance for your Supreme Commander and the American government, and I must be taken immediately to your senior commander."

It was with these words that General Reinhard Gehlen, Hitler's notorious eastern front espionage chief, began his relationship with the Office of Strategic Services (OSS) and the budding US intelligence community. As the OSS was transformed into the Central Intelligence Agency (CIA), yet another of many dark alliances emerged.

After surrendering on May 22, 1945, Gehlen, or "Reinhard the Fox," was eventually interviewed by OSS founders "Wild" Bill Donovon and Allen Dulles after flying to Washington in the uniform of a US general. According to his biographer, Leonard Mosley, Dulles recommended that the Nazi superspy be given a budget of $3.5 million and "set up in business as the supplier of Russian and east European intelligence." But the shrewd Gehlen had some conditions:

1. His organization would not be regarded as part of the American intelligence services but as an autonomous apparatus under his exclusive management. Liaison with American intelligence would be maintained by a US officer whose selection Gehlen would approve.

2. The Gehlen Organization would be used solely to procure intelligence on the Soviet Union and the satellite countries of the communist bloc.

3. Upon the establishment of a German government, the organization would be transferred to it and all previous agreements and arrangements cancelled, subject to discussions between the new sovereign authority and the United States.

4. Nothing detrimental or contrary to German interests must be required or expected from the organization, nor must it be called upon for security activities against Germans in West Germany.

Considering that Gehlen was essentially a prisoner of war who could have been brought up on war crimes, these demands were remarkable. Even more remarkable, at first blush, is the fact that the US complied. However, when viewed through the prism of the rapidly escalating Cold War, a Nazi-CIA alliance becomes rather predictable.

With German defeat imminent, Gehlen instructed several members of his staff to microfilm intelligence on the USSR beginning in March 1945. After secretly burying this material throughout the Austrian Alps, Gehlen and his men sought a deal.

Upon his surrender, Gehlen was taken to Fort Hunt, Virginia, where he convinced his US counterparts that the Soviets were planning a westward expansion. Before the end of 1945, Gehlen and most of his high command were freed from POW camps and ready to supply what rabid American cold warriors were dying to hear.

"Gehlen had to make his money by creating a threat that we were afraid of, so we would give him more money to tell us about it," explains Victor Marchetti, formerly the CIA's chief analyst of Soviet strategic war plans and capabilities.

When Allen Dulles became CIA Director in 1953 (brother John was already Eisenhower's Secretary of State by that time), his response to the claim that Gehlen, a known Nazi war criminal, was purposely intensifying the Cold War and influencing American public opinion was:

> I don't know if he's a rascal. There are few archbishops in espionage.... Besides, one needn't ask him to one's club.

Myth #8: The Legacy of WWII Is "Good"

The "Good War" had been won. Now what? Well, besides actively recruiting Nazis and bringing humanity to the brink of nuclear Armageddon, the winners did have a plan. An internal document, written in 1948 by George Kennan, head of the State Department planning staff in the early post-war period, highlights the philosophy behind the US strategy:

> ...we have about 50% of the world's wealth, but only 6.3% of its population.... In this situation, we cannot fail to be the object of envy and resentment. Our real task in the coming period is to

> devise a pattern of relationships which will permit us to maintain this position of disparity without positive detriment to our national security. To do so, we will have to dispense with all sentimentality and day-dreaming; and our attention will have to be concentrated everywhere on our immediate national objectives. We need not deceive ourselves that we can afford today the luxury of altruism and world-benefaction.... We should cease to talk about vague and—for the Far East—unreal objectives [such] as human rights, the raising of living standards, and democratization. The day is not far off when we are going to have to deal in straight power concepts. The less we are then hampered by idealistic slogans, the better.

Thus the post-war era and the age of Cold War propaganda commenced—driven by corporate globalism and virulent anti-communism. The few years spent fighting fascism during WWII were essentially nothing more than a subtle diversion from a larger war to control resources and smash any ideology deemed incompatible with that control. When the dust had cleared, fascism had survived the saturation bombings, the genocide, and the atomic weapons to rise again in a new, more insidious form. The development of the highly unaccountable multinational corporation is one of the saddest legacies of WWII.

The development of the highly unaccountable multinational corporation is one of the saddest legacies of WWII.

Accordingly, Australian scholar Alex Carey has noted the three developments of great political importance that characterize the twentieth century: "...the growth of democracy, the growth of corporate power, and the growth of corporate propaganda as a means of protecting corporate power against democracy." Simply, democratic institutions can hinder the pursuit of capital, so it becomes necessary to create the false arguments discussed earlier. This helps explain how the Department of War was reborn as the Defense Department after WWII.

■ ■ ■ ■ ■ ■ ■ ■ ■ ■ ■

Much of this is possible because the "Good War" myth granted the US the freedom to intervene practically at will across the globe. After all, who could question Uncle Sam's motives when his boys had just saved the world from Hitler? Upon the end of the Cold War and the defeat of yet another evil empire, the Soviet deterrent essentially vanished. This development provided further latitude for the US to frame its military actions as humanitarian, as part of a democratic new world order forged on the battlefields of WWII and affirmed during the Cold War. America is simply defending freedom, we're told, and who could possibly be against freedom?

Saving Private Ryan and *The Greatest Generation* can only serve to reinforce this form of denial by preying upon a citizenry wishing to believe the best about its country. Such books, films, and other forms of pop culture help provide cover for the rich and powerful who seek global dominion through imperialism and warfare while simultaneously keeping much of the general public fragmented and uninformed about alternatives.

However, those who view such manipulation as inescapable, insurmountable, and perhaps even necessary are yet again ignoring the historical record by underestimating the inspirational power of collective human action.

These excerpts represent a fraction of the information exposed in Saving Private Power: The Hidden History of "The Good War" *(published by Soft Skull Press). The book also includes over 300 endnotes and an extensive bibliography. Ask for it at an independent bookstore near you or visit <www.softskull.com> for a 35 percent discount.*

What I Didn't Know About the Communist Conspiracy

Jim Martin

After fifteen years of selling conspiracy books, I took a year off from Flatland in 1999 and concentrated on completing my own book, *Wilhelm Reich and the Cold War.* I had been researching the topic ever since I became aware of the suppressed biography of Reich in 1983. Reich, who died in a US prison in 1957, believed that he was the victim of a communist conspiracy. Little credence was given to this suspicion of Reich's even by his most sympathetic biographers.[1]

After the collapse of the Soviet Union, new evidence about the extent of its espionage apparatus and wide-ranging conspiratorial activities came to light. It will take some years to sort out the data—for a brief time the internal files of the KGB were opened to Western scholars, and everyone is hoping they will become available again, just as we hope for new documents from the US government. In the last few years, a small bookcase of new history books was published in rapid succession, and a picture emerged that requires us to rethink Cold War history. I was certainly surprised by the developments, having known next to nothing about the Cambridge Five, the Silvermaster Ring, the Ware Group, and many other conspirators prior to research for my book.

To make the long story of my book short, Wilhelm Reich underestimated the importance of the role of Soviet intelligence in the suppression of his work, the burning of his books, and his death in prison.

I was predisposed, admittedly, to hear bad things about the Soviet Union. But I was shocked to see exactly what's been going on. After making a survey of about 20 new books on the Cold War, I reached a fundamentally new understanding of post-war history.

Here are a few of the highlights of what I learned:

I have in my hand a list of 349 Americans and US residents who had a covert relationship with Soviet Intelligence agencies during World War II and beyond. No, I didn't find this list rummaging through old "Tailgunner" Joe McCarthy's laundry basket. It's right here in John Earl Haynes and Harvey Klehr's *Venona*, published in 1999 and examining for the first time in detail a set of decoded Soviet cable traffic during the 1940s that reveals hundreds of average citizens, soldiers, government officials, and courtiers to the White House. Each one actively engaged in two jobs: one for the public, and one for a vast, international communist conspiracy directed from Moscow. One recurring phrase in the discussions of the intelligence officers when criticizing agents in the field: "politically incorrect."

The body count. Being politically incorrect in Russia did not earn you a radio show, but only a bullet in the neck. In France, *The Black Book of Communism* appeared in 1997; in 1999 it was translated into English. It's a gut-wrenching book, and it provoked a deep public controversy in France, where many communist politicians were freely elected. The authors, who at one time or another considered themselves as partisans of some variant of communism, make an

They tabulate the number of people killed by communist regimes around the world at just under 100 million.

incredibly detailed survey of the "crimes, terror and repression" of the world communist movement. They tabulate the number of people killed by communist regimes around the world at just under 100 million.[2] Well-researched and tightly documented, *The Black Book of Communism* is worth reading and begs an ongoing question debated today, throughout the world: What are the basic differences between Soviet and Nazi totalitarianism, if any?

Was Stalinism different than Leninism? The historians say, "No." Stalin's reign was a continuation of Lenin's aggressive policies. It's too simplistic to portray Stalin as a madman who corrupted the essentially socialist policies of Lenin. What's more interesting is the overwhelming appeal of the authoritarian program. This appeal wasn't limited to Russia, but gained millions of adherents across the globe.

"I've got a sock full of shit and I know how to use it." So said Senator Joe McCarthy, who never exposed a single Soviet spy during his tenure in Congress. By the time McCarthy was elected to the Senate in 1948, the Army's Signal Intelligence Special Branch had already decoded significant portions of Soviet wartime cable traffic. These messages revealed an extensive Soviet espionage apparatus operating in Washington, New York, and San Francisco throughout the war years. The FBI, working in cooperation with cryptoanalysts at the National Security Agency, had identified many US government officials at a wide range of federal agencies. Most were qui-

These messages revealed an extensive Soviet espionage apparatus operating in Washington, New York, and San Francisco throughout the war years.

etly removed from their positions, and were not prosecuted because the evidence against them was entirely based on the decrypted cable traffic—and the Army intelligence command was loath to reveal its sources. President Truman, along with the American public, was initially unaware of the information from the Army's VENONA Project, but the Soviets knew that their codes had been broken and discontinued many of the spy rings as a result.

The entire McCarthyite spymania was pointless, and could have been cleared up by 1952 if only the results of the decoded VENONA messages had been revealed. The subtext of McCarthy's rant, however, had a large kernel of truth: All Communist Party USA (CPUSA) members were potential spies, insofar as they submitted to "party discipline." Liberal New Deal Democrats were quite supportive of the "Soviet experiment" and protected pro-Soviet conspirators within the Roosevelt Administration. These agents stole sensitive government documents and worked hard at influencing US foreign policy in favor of the USSR. Yet even as McCarthy belatedly railed against the communist conspiracy, the USSR had long since rolled up many of its agents in the US government after the defection of Elizabeth Bentley in 1945. After that time, there was a steep incline in the severity with which the US dealt with the traitors, culminating with the execution of the Rosenbergs. Still, to protect the VENONA secret, they avoided bringing charges against known spies where the decrypts were the only proof.

Liberal New Deal Democrats were quite supportive of the "Soviet experiment" and protected pro-Soviet conspirators within the Roosevelt Administration.

First, the basics. Alger Hiss was a paid, ideologically-committed agent of Soviet intelligence. Whittaker Chambers was a reliable witness. Ethel and Julius Rosenberg were deeply involved with atomic espionage and certainly knew what kinds of risks they had taken. The Manhattan Project was rife with Soviet agents, sources, and sympathizers who designed, built, and deployed a $2 billion superweapon to fight "black" fascism, gave the plans for the atom bomb to the "red" fascists, and then handed the American taxpayer the tab. Aside from the Rosenbergs, most dangerous espionage agents in the US received little retribution or punishment beyond losing high-paying jobs as government bureaucrats.

The Consumers Union: A front group? During the 1930s, the International Communist Movement, as embodied by the Comintern, and directed from the Soviet Union, abruptly changed policy and endorsed cooperation with other social-change organizations after many years of attacking everybody else on the left. The hitch was that Party members should only "work with" organizations insofar as they secretly directed them from within. Thus many "Popular Front Organizations" became home to liberals, socialists, and fellow travelers, many of whom were unaware of the secret leadership.

When I was younger, one of the examples for the McCarthyite excess our history teachers gave us was that the Consumers Union, publisher of the highly popular *Consumers Reports* magazine, had been placed on an official blacklist of organizations with ties to the Communist Party back in the McCarthy Era. We all laughed—imagine that, the stodgy consumers advocate group linked to the communist conspiracy. Well, imagine no more—Consumers Union formed in 1936 as a CPUSA splinter-group after a violent strike against the original group, Consumers' Research, Inc. Enraged by the tactics used by the strikers, the leadership devoted the rest of their organizational lives charting the subversive links of Consumers Union and its leading lights. Much of the documentation was later used by the House Un-American Activities Committee, where former Consumers' Research board member J. B. Matthews served as an advisor and investigator. Matthews, a liberal with a long history in left politics, coined the term "fellow traveler" to describe the non-Party supporters of the Stalinist regime.

The Consumers Union developed into a massive fundraising nonprofit, with enormous influence as a lobby with the FDA and other federal agencies. One employee at the Consumers Union served as an operation-courier in the Soviet assassination of Trotsky in Mexico. Today, an amazing archival trove resides at Rutgers University's special collections library, including detailed files on Ralph Nader. I have yet to see Nader's files, and can't comment on whether Ralph was personally allied with the CPUSA. Without doubt, at least some of the people he worked for in his early career with Consumers Union were covert operators.[3]

The House Un-American Activities Committee—brought to us by an agent of Soviet Intelligence. Samuel Dickstein, who served as US Congressman from New York from 1923 until 1944, was a paid informant and "agent of influence" whose code-name was "Crook" in view of his incessant demands for money from his Soviet handlers.[4] In 1934 he drafted a proposal for Congressional inquiries into subversive activities, and became the vice chairman of what became known as "The Committee" investigating pro-Nazi elements, rather than communist subversion, in America. It was

Had President Franklin Roosevelt died one year earlier than he did, the pro-Soviet Vice President Henry A. Wallace would have become President in 1945.

Dickstein who introduced the concept of ongoing congressional investigations into what he called "slanderous or libelous un-American propaganda." [5]

It almost happened here. Had President Franklin Roosevelt died one year earlier than he did, or had he not chosen Harry Truman as his running mate in 1944, the pro-Soviet Vice President Henry A. Wallace would have become President in 1945. Wallace told reporters at the time that he would consider Harry Dexter White and Laurance Duggan for appointment to Cabinet positions. Both men spent the war providing Soviet agents with sensitive government documents. [6]

Belly up to the beerhall, comrades, this putsch is on the Americans. Harry Dexter White died of a heart attack shortly after testifying before Congress, where he denied charges of "disloyalty." While functioning as a paid Soviet agent within the Department of Treasury, White wrote much of the Bretton Woods Agreement which formed the International Monetary Fund and the World Bank. (How many of our young anti-globalism protesters are aware of this? Most establishment historians have yet to factor in the recent revelations regarding the Soviet conspiracy with postwar internationalist institutions such as the UN, whose first General Secretary was none other than Alger Hiss.)

White's proposal to lend the USSR $10 billion at an annual rate of 2 percent was rejected by the State Department, but no matter; White was able to provide the Russians with the plates, ink, and paper samples for post-war German occupation currency. [7] Cost to the American taxpayer is unknown, but estimated to be in the millions of dollars.

The Al Gores and Armand Hammer. Al Gore, Sr. served as the political bagman for millionaire communist Armand Hammer for a large part of his career. Hammer's father, Dr. Julius Hammer, was one of the earliest American supporters of the Bolshevik regime and a personal friend of Lenin's. Armand Hammer learned how to launder money at the feet of his father, who was the first conduit between Moscow and the CPUSA. Edward Jay Epstein's exposé about Hammer, titled *Dossier*, examines the ingenious techniques of money laundering, and one example remains enshrined in my mind: Armand toured the entire country throughout the 1920s and sold Tsarist collectibles, including vast numbers of Fabergé Eggs, at bargain prices, in every major city's department stores. Of course, many of them were fake. The money went straight to Lenin, whose young dictatorship suffered for hard currency.

While functioning as a paid Soviet agent within the Department of Treasury, White wrote much of the Bretton Woods Agreement which formed the International Monetary Fund and the World Bank.

Armand went on to develop a career as a go-get-'em American capitalist with an uncanny ability to extract complicated yet profitable venture capital deals with the Soviet Union. As the leading proponent of doing business with the USSR, Armand Hammer advised many American Presidents, including Richard Nixon. As time went on, Hammer came to relish his role as a wheeler-dealer and worked more or less independently of his former collectivist masters. It wasn't so much that he was greedy, but his whole life was devoted to covert chicanery, and old habits are hard to break.

Al Gore, Sr. was still on the board of directors of Hammer's Occidental Petroleum in 1997 at the age of 88. Al Gore the younger appeared publicly with his father's patron, Armand Hammer, up until Hammer's death. [8]

Only the poor die young. In 1990 the only surviving member of the original Bolshevik Party, the one that took over Russia in 1917, besides Armand Hammer, was the Russian physicist and musician who, like Prince and Madonna, went by a single name. Theremin invented the first electronic instrument, the one which bears his name and can still be heard in the opening bars of the Beach Boy's "Good Vibrations" and also in bad Cold-War-era sci-fi movies. After a long term in the gulags, Theremin emerged as a darling in the West, and died in his nineties after his apartment was ransacked by thugs in Moscow. All the other old members of the Party who seized the state apparatus in 1918 were dead by then. Both survivors, Hammer and Theremin, died millionaires. [9]

Don't touch that dial. There are uncounted caches of radios and arms protected by booby traps hidden around the US and the rest of the world, placed there decades ago by Soviet agents in anticipation of world revolution. [10]

I have a nightmare. Yuri Modin, former controller of the Cambridge Five spy ring (Philby, Burgess, Blunt, Maclean, and Cairncross), was assigned to conduct "active measures" against Martin Luther King in August 1967, to discredit him in the eyes of the public and bolster the support of pro-Soviet black radicals such as Stokely Carmichael. [11] King was the only American to be the victim of KGB *and* FBI special operations.

Messin' with our heads. Mark Lane, author of the best-selling Kennedy assassination conspiracy book, *Rush to Judgment*, received money and information from the KGB—probably without Lane realizing the true source—while researching his book. The KGB had spent a great deal of money on American conspiracy theorists to promote the idea that Kennedy was assassinated by the CIA and right-wing elements. (The 1970 "Torbitt Document"[12] is undoubtedly one fruit of such efforts.)

In 1975, at the time of the Watergate investigations, the KGB produced a forged letter, purportedly written by Lee Harvey Oswald the night before the assassination, to a "Mr. Hunt"—the KGB intended to implicate E. Howard Hunt, one of the Watergate conspirators. They sent the letter to three "conspiracy buffs"—who, significantly, did not rise to the bait and didn't publish the document. A while later the *New York Times* published the forgery announcing that handwriting experts had confirmed its authenticity. (Conspiracy Buffs: 3, *New York Times*: 0.)

> The targets of the KGB sab-teams included California oil pipelines and radar installations.

The Soviets spent millions of dollars on these kinds of "active measures." The highly popular anti-CIA magazine published in the late 1970s and 1980s, *Covert Action Intelligence Bulletin*, was founded by a defector from the CIA, Philip Agee, and bankrolled by the KGB. I myself was a regular reader of *Covert Action* during the Reagan years, and indeed I wondered where they were getting their information. We know now that V. N. Kosterin from the KGB's Service A (propaganda and disinformation section) had been assigned to keep the journal supplied with material. You can read all about it in Christopher Andrew's *The Sword and the Shield: The Mitrokhin Archive*.[13] Philip Agee's popular book, *Inside the Company*, was written with the support and assistance of both Soviet and Cuban intelligence agencies.

AIDS and biowarfare. Up until 1987, the Soviet press promulgated the theory that AIDS was a bioweapon developed at Fort Detrick. When Mikhail Gorbachev announced that, as a part of *glasnost* and *perestroika*, the Soviets would renounce disinformation tactics, the Soviet officials quietly notified US diplomats in Moscow that they had disowned the AIDS story, and the press campaign abruptly ceased.[14] Of course, this fact doesn't rule out the possibility of some type of relationship between AIDS and biowarfare, as practiced around the globe.

Sandinistas invaded California. As early as 1966, the Sandinista National Liberation Front (FSLN) provided guerrillas for elaborate KGB sabotage teams along the US-Mexico border in cities like Ensenada and Tijuana. The targets of the sab-teams included California oil pipelines and radar installations; they set up networks for smuggling agents and munitions through infiltration of migrant laborers. Recon teams staffed by Sandinistas and coordinated by the KGB crossed the border and identified landing sites and large ammo-dumps along the coast in anticipation of war between the US and the USSR in Europe.[15] Other KGB sabotage and intelligence teams were arrayed along the Canadian border; in 1967 they scouted border crossings and identified targets including Montana's Flathead Dam and hydroelectric systems in New York and Pennsylvania.

▪ ▪ ▪ ▪ ▪ ▪ ▪ ▪ ▪ ▪ ▪

I should stress that the information presented here is based on the best evidence I could find, and that new information is coming in all the time. One of the most time-consuming aspects of the process will be sorting out the river of data and coordinating it with old references published long ago and now forgotten. Even the best historians with the latest information can't foresee the future impact of this incredible material, released from both sides of the former Iron Curtain to a bewildered public.

Let's take one example from the 1930s.

Most books on the Cambridge Five place a man named Arnold Deutsch at the center of the conspiracy to recruit young University students at Cambridge—generally regarded as the most profitable long-term espionage effort in recorded history. Deutsch recruited at least 25 spies in London in the 1930s. Among his pupils: Kim Philby, Guy Burgess, Donald Maclean, Michael Straight, Anthony Blunt, Elizabeth Tudor Hart, Litzi Friedman, and other unnamed agents. Not only did Deutsch originate the plan of seducing well-connected sons of the British establishment for careers in the NKVD, but he accomplished it using Wilhelm Reich's techniques of character analysis, and a promise of a Soviet reality that coincided with Reich's own hopes for a "sexual revolution." Deutsch and several other Viennese radicals played a significant role with USSR intelligence as well as in Reich's "sex-pol" clinics—first organized in 1927 for the education and psychoanalytic treatment of working people at little or no fees. Deutsch was killed in the early 1940s, but serious discrepancies between several stories of his death remain, variants with multiple "witness statements."

Reich repudiated communism between 1931 and 1936. Nobody so far has come clean about the Reich-Deutsch connection. The historians of the "West and East" are silent about these contradictions, for now. I see the story of Wilhelm Reich's relationship—friend, tutor, and coworker—with Arnold Deutsch as a linchpin of any understanding of the Cold War era.

Finally, it's remarkable that so much information has been coming out of the Russian archives, while the US President's Executive Order that the CIA, FBI, and NSA release all documents older than 30 years has largely been ignored.

New Books on Soviet Espionage

Albright, Joseph & Marcia Kunstel. (1997). *Bombshell: The secret story of America's unknown atomic spy conspiracy*. New York: Times Books, 1st edition.
The story of Ted Hall, teenage atom spy.

Andrew, Christopher & Vasili Mitrokhin. (1999). *The sword and the shield: The Mitrokhin archive and the secret history of the KGB*. New York: Basic Books.
Retired KGB officer and archivist Mitrokhin defected from the former Soviet Union, with trunkloads of secret KGB documents dating back to 1918. His notes and copied documents have been verified by independent sources. Andrew is the chair of the History Department at Cambridge University.

Haynes, John Earl & Harvey Klehr. (1999). *Venona: Decoding Soviet espionage in America*. New Haven, CT: Yale University Press.
The VENONA decrypts were released by the National Security Agency and verified by comparison to the Russian originals; a crucial study.

Klehr, Harvey, John Earl Haynes & Fridrikh Igorevich Firsov. (1995). *The secret world of American communism*. New Haven, CT: Yale University Press.
Based on files released in Russia, a detailed account of the Soviet funding for the CPUSA and its role in recruiting spies among Party members.

Klehr, Harvey & Ronald Radosh. (1996). *The Amerasia case: Prelude to McCarthyism*. Chapel Hill, NC: University of North Carolina Press.
First Soviet espionage case predates the end of WWII, sets off the Cold War in 1945.

Schwartz, Stephen. (1998). *From East to West: California and the making of the American mind*. New York: The Free Press.
A quirky and important history of California with special emphasis on the role of California CPUSA members in atomic espionage.

Sudoplatov, Pavel & Anatoli; with Jerrold L. and Leona Schecter. (1994). *Special tasks: The memoirs of an unwanted witness—a Soviet spymaster*. New York: Little, Brown.
How to keep your nose clean when you're up to your eyeballs in blood, by a former Soviet intelligence officer who plotted to kill Trotsky.

Tannenhaus, Sam. (1997). *Whittaker Chambers*. New York: Random House.
They used to say Whittaker Chambers was crazy, queer, and built a typewriter to frame Alger Hiss.

Weinstein, Allen & Alexander Vassiliev. (1999). *The haunted wood: Soviet espionage in America—the Stalin era*. New York: Random House, 1st edition.
Incorporates much of the VENONA documentation, takes an overview of the influence of the USSR's espionage on American history. Probably the most enjoyable read of the bunch.

These books are available at <flatlandbooks.com>.

Endnotes

1. see Sharaf, Myron. (1983). *Fury on earth.* New York: St. Martin's; Greenfield, Jerome. (1974). *Wilhelm Reich vs the USA.* New York: Norton. **2.** Courtois, Stéphan, et al. (1999). *The black book of communism.* Cambridge: Harvard University Press. **3.** Martin, Jim. (2000). *Wilhelm Reich and the Cold War.* Fort Bragg, CA: Flatland, p 279ff. **4.** Weinstein, Allen & Alexander Vassiliev. (1999). *The haunted wood: Soviet espionage in America—the Stalin era.* New York: Random House, p 142. **5.** Goodman, Walter. (1964). *The Committee.* New York: Farrar, Straus and Giroux, p 14. **6.** Haynes, John Earl & Harvey Klehr. (1999). *Venona: Decoding Soviet espionage in America.* New Haven, CT: Yale University Press, p 139. **7.** Andrew, Christopher & Oleg Gordievsky. (1990). *KGB: The inside story.* New York: HarperCollins, p 336. **8.** Epstein, Edward Jay. (1999). *Dossier.* New York: Carroll & Graf. **9.** Radzhinsky, Edvard. (1997). *Stalin.* New York: Anchor. **10.** Andrew, Christopher & Vasili Mitrokhin. (1999). *The sword and the shield: The Mitrokhin archive and the secret history of the KGB.* New York: Basic Books, chapter 22. **11.** *Ibid.*, p 237. **12.** see Thomas, Kenn (Ed.). (1996). *NASA, Nazis & JFK: The Torbitt document & the JFK assassination.* Kempton, IL: Adventures Unlimited Press. **13.** *Op cit.*, Andrew & Vasili, p 233. **14.** *Ibid.*, p 245. **15.** *Ibid.*, p 363.

TRIPPING

Drug War Mythology

Paul Armentano

It's been said that the first casualty of war is truth; the aptly titled US "War on Drugs" is no different. America's Drug War is a $50 billion-per-year[1] boondoggle which thrives on federal lies and distortions, media complicity, and an ill-informed public. Over the course of this battle, bureaucrats and prohibitionists—including the country's top-ranking anti-drug official, Drug Czar Barry McCaffrey—have popularized countless myths to justify and support their endeavor. More often than not these lies go unchallenged and become accepted by the public as truth. Those that are exposed are quickly replaced by even grander sophistry. Let's explore some of the more pervasive myths of America's longest war.

Myth: Law enforcement rarely arrest or jail drug offenders.

"Very few drug-use offenders ever see the inside of a prison cell. It's simply a myth that our prison cells are filled with people who don't belong there."
—Rep. John Mica (R-FL), speaking before Congress, July 1999

Fact: Approximately 25 percent of American inmates are imprisoned on drug charges.
—US Department of Justice, Bureau of Justice Statistics

Drug offenders, often low-level users, comprise the fastest-rising percentage of today's inmates. According to statistics compiled by the Washington, DC Justice Policy Institute, 76 percent of the increase in admissions to US prisons from 1978 to 1996 was attributable to nonviolent offenders.[2] The majority of these were drug violators. Since 1989, the number of drug offenders sent to prison has exceeded the number of violent commitments every year.[3]

There are now more than 450,000 drug offenders behind bars, a total nearly equal to the *entire* US prison population of 1980.

Over the past 20 years, the total number of inmates incarcerated on drug charges in federal and state prisons and local jails has grown over 1,000 percent. There are now more than 450,000 drug offenders behind bars, a total nearly equal to the *entire* US prison population of 1980.[4] Put another way, there are presently 100,000 more Americans imprisoned for drug offenses than total prisoners in the European Union, even though the EU has 100 million more citizens than the US. As a result, nearly one out of every four Americans behind bars is incarcerated for drugs.[5]

The ratio for federal prisoners is even more apalling; drug offenders comprise approximately two out of every three federal inmates.[6]

In 1998 police arrested 682,885 Americans for marijuana offenses, more than the total number of arrestees for all violent crimes combined, including murder, rape, robbery, and aggravated assault.

Punishment for first-time federal drug offenders averages 82.4 months, a sentence longer than those for manslaughter, assault, and sexual abuse.[7]

State prosecutors are sending drug offenders to jail in greater and greater numbers. One recent study found that approximately half of all California prisoners are there on drug charges.[8] A review of 1999 New York State sentencing data revealed that 91 percent of all drug offenders sentenced to prison that year were incarcerated for either drug possession or violating one of the state's three lowest level drug offenses.[9]

The federal drug control budget has escalated at a similarly alarming rate. Today, the federal government spends over $13 billion annually on domestic anti-drug law enforcement alone, a figure that is 800 times larger than the entire federal drug control budget of 1981.[10] Predictably, this increase has led to an unprecedented explosion of drug arrests. Police today annually arrest three times as many individuals on drug charges than they did in 1980. According to FBI crime report figures, approximately 1.6 million Americans were arrested on drug charges in 1998, one of the highest totals ever recorded.[11]

Contrary to prohibitionist rhetoric, the majority of those arrested are low-level offenders charged with drug possession, not sale. Seventy-nine percent of all drug arrests in 1998 were for possession only.[12] Overwhelmingly, those arrested are marijuana smokers. In 1998 police arrested 682,885 Americans for marijuana offenses, more than the total number of arrestees for all violent crimes combined, including murder, rape, robbery, and aggravated assault.[13] Eighty-eight percent of these arrests were for marijuana possession only. This translates into one out of every 25 criminal arrests in the United States.[14] Believe it or not, one in seven drug prisoners is now behind bars for pot![15]

Those drug offenders arrested and sent to prison, typically for lengthy sentences, are citizens not much different than you or I. They are mothers, fathers, and grandparents.[16] They are families like Joane, Gary, and Steve Tucker, together serving 26 years for selling legal hydroponics gardening equipment from their family-owned store. Prosecutors charged and convicted them with conspiracy to manufacture marijuana based on the offenses of a handful of their customers, and the Tuckers' failure to allow DEA agents to install surveillance cameras in their store.

They are patients like Will Foster, sentenced to 93 years by an Oklahoma jury for cultivating marijuana for the purpose of alleviating pain associated with rheumatoid arthritis.

They are grandfathers like Loren Pogue, age 64, presently serving 22 years for conspiracy to import drugs and money laundering. Pogue helped a paid government informant sell a plot of land to undercover agents posing as "investors." The investors, whom Pogue met only once, allegedly were to use the land to build an airstrip for the purpose of smuggling drugs. The fact that there were no actual drugs involved, that Pogue was an upstanding citizen with no prior drug history, and that the airstrip was never built failed to mitigate his virtual life sentence.

These are the faces of America's snowballing drug inmate population, nonviolent offenders that law enforcement and prosecutors are now targeting with frightening regularity. To Drug War hawks, these individuals are simply collateral damage; to the rest of us, they are the unfortunate victims of more than 80 years of lies, propaganda, and political posturing.

Myth: Relaxing anti-drug laws will significantly increase drug use and crime.

"The murder rate in Holland is double that in the United States. The per capita crime rates are much higher than the United States.... That's drugs!"
—US Drug Czar Barry McCaffrey, July 23, 1998

Fact: Jurisdictions that have decriminalized the possession of marijuana and other drugs experience drug use and crime rates equal to or lower than those that have maintained strict criminal penalties.

The Dutch murder rate is 440 percent lower (1.8 per 100,000) than the US murder rate (8.2 per 100,000).
—Dutch Central Planning Bureau of Statistics, 1996, and FBI Uniform Crime Report data, 1998

Drug War proponents argue that any relaxation of anti-drug laws will result in a sharp increase in drug use and associated crime. This assertion is unsupported by epidemiological and survey evidence in America and abroad. In many cases, drug liberalization policies are associated with a reduction in drug use and crime.

Beginning with Oregon in 1973, ten US states removed criminal penalties for the possession of small amounts of marijuana.[17] To date, more than a dozen federal and independent commissions have examined the social and criminal impact of this legislative reform.[18] In short, the available evidence indicates that the decriminalization of marijuana possession has little or no impact on use patterns or individuals' attitudes toward the drug.[19] According to a 1981 US government study investigating the issue, "Overall, the preponderance of the evidence which we have gathered and examined points to the conclusion that decriminalization has had virtually no effect either on the marijuana use or on related attitudes and beliefs about marijuana use among American young people in this age group.... In fact,...states showed a small, cumulative net decline in lifetime prevalence, as well as in annual and monthly prevalence, after decriminalization."[20] A 1999 study by the National Academy of Sciences Institute of Medicine affirmed these conclusions.[21]

There also exists no evidence that decriminalization encourages more prevalent use of other drugs. A 1993 study published in the *Social Sciences Journal* determined: "There is no strong evidence that decriminalization affects either the choice or frequency of use of drugs, either legal (alcohol) or illegal (marijuana and cocaine)."[22] A 1993 examination of drug-related emergency room (ER) cases suggested that decriminalization may reduce recreational demand for hard drugs. It found that incidents of marijuana use among patients were equal in decriminalized states versus non-decriminalized areas, but noted that rates of other illicit drug use among ER patients were substantially higher in states that retained criminal penalties for marijuana.[23]

Since the Dutch government liberalized its marijuana policies, the number of problem hard drug users has fallen steadily.

Research further indicates that decriminalization fails to increase crime, and even reduces criminal justice costs. For example, California saved $958,305,499 from 1976 to 1985 by decriminalizing the personal possession of one ounce of marijuana, according to a study of the state justice department budget.[24] An investigation of the impact of marijuana decriminalization in Maine found that the policy reduced court costs and increased revenue.[25]

International studies of marijuana decriminalization in Australia and elsewhere demonstrate similar results. A 1994 study by the Australian National Drug Research Center reported: "Those jurisdictions which have decriminalized personal cannabis use have not experienced any dramatic increase in prevalence of use."[26] At the same time, those jurisdictions raised significant revenue by issuing instant, non-criminal fines to marijuana users.

In recent years, most Western nations have significantly liberalized their cannabis laws with no ill effects; Germany, Holland, and Switzerland have ceased enforcing criminal penalties against the drug altogether. Spain, Italy, and Portugal have decriminalized the possession of all drugs. Clearly, American drug policy is moving in the opposite direction of the rest of the world.

Unfortunately, American prohibitionists have chosen to malign rather than learn from these examples. They have launched the bulk of their attacks on the Dutch, who have allowed for the public consumption of small amounts of marijuana since the mid-1970s. While on a purported "fact-finding" mission regarding European drug policy in July 1998, Drug Czar Barry McCaffrey publicly charged that the Dutch murder rate is more than twice America's rate.[27] He further purported that three times as many Dutch youth admit trying marijuana than do their US counterparts.[28] McCaffrey said that liberal drug policies were to blame for the higher Dutch figures. As one might expect from the loose-lipped Czar, both charges were absolutely false. Dutch homicide rates and pot use remain far lower than those in America. Official data released by the Dutch government's Central Planning Bureau immediately after McCaffrey's allegations put the country's murder rate for 1996 at 1.8 per 100,000 people, a figure substantially lower than the US murder rate. McCaffrey had falsely claimed that the Dutch murder rate was 17.58 per 100,000.[29]

McCaffrey's charges concerning adolescent marijuana use also proved fallacious. 1996 data recorded by the University of Michigan's Monitoring the Future project determined that 45 percent of America's high school seniors admit having tried marijuana.[30] By comparison, research compiled by the National Institute of Medicine, Health and Addiction in the Netherlands found that only 30 percent of Dutch adolescents have experimented with the drug.[31] McCaffrey falsely stated that only 9.1 percent of American teens had ever experimented with marijuana.

If any cause and effect relationship exists between Dutch drug policy and drug use, it is associated with reducing substance use. Fewer than half as many Dutch adults have tried marijuana as have Americans.[32] Dutch adults also use hard drugs like cocaine and heroin at rates dramatically lower than US citizens.[33] Since the Dutch government liberalized its marijuana policies, the number of problem hard drug users has fallen steadily.[34] Dutch Ambassador to the US Joris M. Vos publicly denounced McCaffey's false allegations. Nevertheless, McCaffrey never apologized or retracted his remarks, and continues to bash Dutch drug policy. Diplomacy has never been his strong suit.

Myth: Marijuana is a "gateway" to the use of hard drugs.

"Statistically speaking, marijuana stands convicted as a gateway drug. Twelve to seventeen year olds who smoke marijuana are 85 times more likely to use cocaine than those who do not."
—Joseph Califano, Executive Director, The Center for Alcohol and Substance Abuse, July 13, 1997

Fact: For every 104 people who have used marijuana, there is only one regular user of cocaine and less than one heroin addict.
—Department of Health and Human Services, National Household Survey on Drug Abuse, 1997.

Since the dawn of drug prohibition, proponents have alleged that experimenting with pot inevitably leads to the use of other illicit substances. Known as the "gateway theory," this notion remains one of the staples of Drug War rhetoric. However, like most prohibitionist arguments, there exist no sound scientific data to support it.

One of the first major studies to explore this issue was commissioned by New York City Mayor Fiorello LaGuardia in 1938. The five-year fact-finding mission was the most comprehensive marijuana study of its era. Released in 1944, the LaGuardia Report concluded: "The use of marijuana does not lead to morphine or heroin or cocaine addiction.... The instances are extremely rare where the habit of marijuana smoking is associated with addiction to these narcotics."[35]

Despite this sound rebuttal, prohibitionists resurrected their hypothesis in the 1960s under a new moniker: "the stepping stone theory." Fortunately, federally-contracted researchers from the National Institute of Mental Health were quick to set the record straight by releasing their pioneering study: *Ganja in Jamaica: A medical anthropological study of chronic marijuana use*.[36] Summarizing its findings in the July 4, 1975, issue of *Science* magazine, Dr. Erich Goode of the State University of New York at Stony Brook wrote: "One of the more interesting findings to emerge from the study relates to the 'stepping stone hypothesis.'... Nothing like that occurs among heavy, chronic, ganja smokers of Jamaica. No other drugs were used, aside from aspirin, tea, alcohol and tobacco. The only hard drug use known on the island is indulged by North American tourists."[37]

Yet another federally-commissioned study rejected the gateway premise in 1982. This study, authored by the National Academy of Sciences Institute of Medicine, determined that: "There is no evidence to support the belief that the use of one drug will inevitably lead to the use of any other drug."[38] A follow-up study released by the IOM in 1999 affirmed this conclusion.[39]

Federal drug use statistics compiled by the US Department of Health and Human Services (HHS) further expose the gateway theory as fraudulent. As self-reported marijuana use increased in the 1960s and 1970s, heroin use declined; while cocaine use rose in the early 1980s, pot use dropped sharply. Conversely, marijuana's rising popularity in the 1990s has not spawned a corresponding increase in the use of cocaine.[40] According to the findings of the 1998 US Government Annual Household Survey on Drug Abuse, although more than 72 million Americans have tried marijuana, only 23 million have ever experimented with cocaine.[41] Less than 4.5 million have ever used crack, and less than 2.4 million have ever tried heroin.[42]

Nevertheless, prohibitionists—most notably the National Center on Addiction and Substance Abuse (CASA) and Drug Czar Barry McCaffrey—continue to tout the gateway theory as fact, and frequently charge that marijuana users are 85 times more likely than nonusers to try cocaine.[43] CASA's misleading calculation is based on cannabis and cocaine prevalence data from 1991.[44] To obtain the 85 times "risk factor," CASA divided the proportion of cannabis users who had ever tried cocaine (17 percent) by the proportion of cocaine users who had never used cannabis (0.2 percent). The "risk factor" is not large because so many cannabis users experimented with cocaine—indeed 83 percent did not—but because very few people try cocaine without trying cannabis first. According to 1998 data, only 21 percent of the 13.6 million estimated current marijuana users also used another illicit substance.[45] For the majority of marijuana users, cannabis is a terminus rather than a "gateway" drug.

Some evidence exists supporting the notion that cannabis may serve as a doorway to the world of illegal drugs, in which adolescents have a greater opportunity and are under greater social pressure to experiment with additional substances. This theory may explain why a minority of cannabis users graduate to other illicit drugs such as cocaine.[46] However, if this is the case, then it is cannabis prohibition which forces users to associate with the illicit drug black market, and not cannabis use alone that influences this pattern of behavior.

Myth: Cannabis has no medical or therapeutic value.

"There is not a shred of scientific evidence that shows that smoked marijuana is useful or needed. This is not science. This is not medical. This is a cruel hoax."
—US Drug Czar Barry McCaffrey, August 16, 1996

Fact: Available scientific research indicates that medical cannabis provides symptomatic relief for a number of serious ailments, and is less toxic and costly than many conventional medicines for which it may be substituted.

"Scientific data indicate the potential therapeutic value of cannabinoid drugs, primarily THC, for pain relief, control of nausea and vomiting, and appetite stimulation.... Except for the harms associated with smoking, the adverse effects of marijuana use are within the range tolerated for other medications."
—Final conclusions of US Institute of Medicine, March 1999

Written references to medical marijuana date back more than 2,000 years. The world's oldest surviving text on medical drugs, the Chinese *Shen-nung Pen-tshao Ching*, specifically cites cannabis' value for reducing the pain of rheumatism and for treating digestive disorders.[47] Western medicine embraced pot's medical properties in the mid-1800s, and by the beginning of the twentieth century, physicians had published more than 100 papers in the Western medical literature recommending its use for a variety of disorders.[48]

Cannabis remained in the United States' pharmacopoeia until the late 1930s when Congress passed the Marijuana Tax Act prohibiting physicians from prescribing it. The American Medical Association was one of the most vocal organizations to testify against the ban, arguing that it would deprive patients of a safe and effective medicine.[49]

Written references to medical marijuana date back more than 2,000 years.

Modern research suggests that cannabis is a valuable aid in the treatment of a wide range of clinical applications.[50] These include pain relief—particularly neuropathic pain associated with cancer, arthritis, and spinal cord damage—nausea, spasticity, glaucoma, movement disorders, and hypertension.[51] Marijuana is also a powerful appetite stimulant, specifically in patients suffering from HIV, the AIDS wasting syndrome, or dementia. Emerging research suggests that pot's medicinal constituents (known as cannabinoids) may protect the body against some types of malignant tumors and are neuroprotective.

Despite overwhelming evidence of marijuana's therapeutic value, it remains classified as a Schedule I substance, the most stringent drug classification available under US law. By definition, Schedule I substances have "no accepted medical use in treatment," and physicians may not legally prescribe them. Federal officials have rejected legal challenges ordering pot to be rescheduled—including a 1988 ruling from the Drug Enforcement Administration's own administrative law judge[52]—and ignored pleas from dozens of esteemed medical organizations[53] to lift the ban on medical cannabis. As a result, physicians often recommend pot to their patients clandestinely. A 1991 Harvard study found that 44 percent of oncologists had previously advised marijuana therapy to their patients.[54] Fifty percent admitted that they would do so if marijuana were legal.

Virtually every government-appointed commission to investigate marijuana's medical potential has issued favorable findings. These include the US Institute of Medicine in 1982,[55] the Australian National Task Force on Cannabis in 1994,[56] and the US National Institutes of Health Workshop on Medical Marijuana in 1997.[57]

After a one-year scientific inquiry, members of the United Kingdom's House of Lords Science and Technology Committee found in 1998 that the available evidence supported the legal use of medical cannabis.[58] MPs determined: "The government should allow doctors to prescribe cannabis for medical use.... Cannabis can be effective in some patients to relieve symptoms of multiple sclerosis, and against certain forms of pain.... This evidence is enough to justify a change in the law."[59]

Five months later, US investigators reached a similar conclusion. After conducting a nearly two-year review of the medical literature—at the request of Drug Czar Barry McCaffrey—investigators at the National Academy of Sciences Institute of Medicine affirmed, "Marijuana's active components are potentially effective in treating pain, nausea, anorexia of AIDS wasting syndrome, and other symptoms [including the involuntary spasticity associated with multiple sclerosis]."[60] The authors added that inhaling cannabis "would be advantageous" in the treatment of some diseases, and that the herb's short-term medical benefits outweigh any smoking-related harms for some patients. Nevertheless, McCaffrey and other Washington bureaucrats—none of whom is a doctor—rejected the findings of their own hand-picked expert commission, and continue to publicly assail medical cannabis as "a crock."[61]

Myth: We can attain a drug-free America by 2003.

"We must continue our commitment to deter the demand inside our country, stop the supply on and beyond our borders and increase the accountability within drug fighting programs. We must win the War on Drugs by 2003."
—House Speaker Dennis Hastert (R-Il), February 25, 1999

Fact: We will never become drug-free, only less free.

"For more than a quarter century the United States has been on a rampage, kicking in doors and locking people up in the name of protecting its citizens from illegal drugs. Hundreds of billions of dollars into the Drug War, nobody claims victory. Yet we continue, devoted to a policy as expensive, ineffective, delusional, and destructive as government policy gets."
—Dan Baum, author of *Smoke and Mirrors: The War on Drugs and the Politics of Failure* (Little, Brown & Company, 1996)

The "War on Drugs" has become America's longest and most costly battle. Though casualties remain high, its leaders show no indication of retreating.

Congress passed the first federal law authorizing law enforcement to control individuals' use of specific substances in 1914.[62] It outlawed marijuana in 1937. It introduced mandatory sentences for drug offenders in the 1950s and again in the 1980s. Yet despite Congress' best efforts, Americans continue to use illicit drugs in greater and greater numbers. In 1937, an estimated 60,000

Americans had tried pot;[63] this total rose to 100,000 in 1945,[64] and tops 72 million today.[65] On a per capita basis, more people use cocaine today than when its use was legal.[66] More Americans die today from illicit drug overdoses, often as a result of administering tainted narcotics, than at any time in our nation's history.[67]

On a per capita basis, more people use cocaine today than when its use was legal.

The prohibitionists' response to this stark reality is unthinking and predictable: tougher laws, stricter enforcement, longer jail terms, and greater intrusions into the lives of suspected drug offenders, a category that includes all of us! This latter approach threatens to shred the US Constitution in its wake. In many instances it already has. High school students are now urine-tested without probable cause; law enforcement seize individuals' property and cash based on little or no suspicion; police conduct warrantless searches of people's trash and infrared scans of citizens' homes to look for clues of drug activity; passengers in motor vehicles are frequently stopped and searched; warrants are procured based solely upon the testimony of confidential informants and are executed in "no-knock" raids;[68] drug roadblocks are common. In one shocking Supreme Court decision, Justices "approved a prolonged and humiliating detention of an incomer who was held by customs agents to determine, through her natural bodily processes, whether or not she was carrying narcotics internally," even though probable cause was lacking.[69] In other words, law enforcement forced a woman to defecate even though there was no probable cause to believe she was carrying drugs.

"Zero tolerance" abandons our nation's traditional sense of justice. Judges are forced to sentence drug offenders to lengthy prison terms without considering mitigating factors. Students are expelled for possessing small amounts of pot or, in some cases, legal over-the-counter medications. Tenants are evicted from public housing because of drug offenses committed without their knowledge by friends and family members. College applicants are denied student aid if they have a prior drug conviction. Former House Speaker Newt Gingrich (R-Ga.) supported legislation in the mid-1990s that would have imposed the death penalty for people convicted of importing two ounces or more of marijuana.[70] A 1999 bill introduced by Congress threatened to impose a ten-year felony sentence on anyone who disseminated—by any means—information relating to the manufacture of a controlled substance if that person should have somehow known that a recepient of the information would use it to commit a federal crime.[71]

And so it goes. Politicians continue to beat the Drug War drum and propagandize the enemy in order to justify their failing policies. All the while, it remains prohibition itself that creates the very problems their extreme measures are meant to target. As a result, "victory" in the "War on Drugs" remains unachievable regardless of our leaders' hollow promises and tall tales. Wake up and listen, America: You are being lied to!

Endnotes

1. Congress is requesting $19.2 billion to fight drugs for fiscal year 2001. State and local governments annually spend $33 billion to fund anti-drug activities. McCaffrey, B. "Fight drugs as you would a disease." *Chicago Tribune*, March 31, 1996. **2.** Irwin, J, V Schiraldi, & J Ziedenberg (1999). America's one million nonviolent prisoners. Washington, DC: Justice Policy Institute. **3.** Annual data compiled by the US Department of Justice, Bureau of Justice Statistics. Washington, DC. **4.** Schiraldi, V & J Ziedenberg. (2000). Poor prescription: The cost of imprisoning drug offenders in the United States. Washington, DC: Justice Policy Institute. **5.** DOJ, Bureau of Justice Statistics. Profile of jail inmates, 1996. Washington, DC: US Government Printing Office. **6.** US Federal Bureau of Prisons. (1998). United States federal prisoners profile, 1998. Washington, DC: US Government Printing Office. **7.** US Federal Bureau of Prisons. (1996). Quick facts. Washington, DC: US Government Printing Office. **8.** *Op cit.*, Schiraldi & Ziedenberg. **9.** *Ibid.* **10**. Based on proposed FY 2001 drug control budget data. Congress appropriated $1.5 billion for drug control in 1981. **11.** Federal Bureau of Investigation. (1999). Table 29: Total estimated arrests United States, 1998. **12.** *Ibid.* **13.** *Ibid.* **14.** *Ibid.* **15.** DOJ, Bureau of Justice Statistics. (1999). Substance abuse and treatment, state and federal prisoners. Washington DC: US Government Printing Office. **16.** The following profiles were initially summarized in Norris, M, C Conrad, & V Resner. (2000). *Shattered lives: Portraits from America's Drug War.* El Cerrito, CA: Creative Xpressions. **17.** Alaska, California, Colorado, Maine, Mississippi, Nebraska, New York, North Carolina, Ohio, and Oregon decriminalized the possession of personal-use amounts of cannabis between 1973 and 1977. To date, not one state legislature has reimposed criminal penalties. (Alaska, the only arguable exception, amended their law via ballot initiative.) The fact that these states have stood by their policy despite pressure from federal anti-drug advocates illustrates the real-world success of this policy as an alternative to criminal penalties and incarceration. **18.** Commissions include: Australian Institute of Criminology; California State Office of Narcotics and Drug Abuse; Connecticut Law Review Commission; National Academy of Sciences Institute of Medicine; National Drug and Alcohol Resource Centre (Australia); University of Michigan Institute of Social Research; etc. **19.** Conclusions from these commissions are available online at <www.norml.org/recreational/decrim.shtml>. **20.** Johnson, L, P O'Malley, & J Bachman. (1981). Marijuana decriminalization: The impact on youth 1975-1980. Monitoring the Future, Occasional Paper series, paper 13. Ann Arbor: Institute for Social Research, University of Michigan. **21.** Joy, J, S Watson, & J Bensen. (1999). *Marijuana and medicine: Assessing the science base.* Washington, DC: National Academy Press. **22.** Theis, C & C Register. (1993). Decriminalization of marijuana and the demand for alcohol, marijuana and cocaine. *The Social Sciences Journal*, 30. **23.** Model K. (1993). The effect of marijuana on hospital emergency room drug episodes: 1975-1978. *Journal of the American Statistical Association,* 88: 737-747. **24.** Aldrich, M & T Mikuriya. (1988). Savings in California marijuana law enforcement costs attributable to the Moscone Act of 1976. *Journal of Psychoactive Drugs*, 20: 75-81. **25**. Kopel, D. (1991). Marijuana jail terms. Independence Institute Issue Paper. Golden CO, as cited by Conrad, C. (1994). *Hemp: Lifeline to the future.* Los Angeles: Creative Xpressions. **26.** National Drug and Alcohol Research Centre. (1994). Patterns of cannabis use in Australia. Monograph Series No. 27. Canberra: Australian Government Publishing Service. **27.** He also charged that the Dutch crime rate is 40 percent higher than America's. "US Drug Czar bashes Dutch policy on eve of visit." Reuters News Wire. July 13, 1998. **28.** "McCaffrey takes his charge to officials in the Netherlands." *Washington Times*. July 15, 1998. **29.** Lucassen, C. "Dutch rebuke US drug advisor." Reuters News Wire. July 14, 1998. **30.** Johnston, L, P O'Malley, & J Bachman. (2000). Table 1A: Trends in Lifetime Prevalence of Use of Various Drugs for 8th, 10th, 12th Graders, 1991-1999. Ann Arbor: Institute for Social Research, University of Michigan. **31.** Letter from Dutch Ambassador to the United States Joris Vos to the *Washington Times*, July 20, 1998. **32.** 32.9 percent of Americans have tried marijuana versus 15.6 percent of Dutch citizens. Center for Drug Research. (1999). Drug use in the population of 12 years and older in the USA and the Netherlands. University of Amsterdam. **33.** 10.5 percent of Americans have tried cocaine versus 2.1 percent of Dutch citizens. 0.9 percent of Americans have tried heroin versus 0.3 percent of Dutch citizens. *Ibid.* **34.** Drucker, E. (1995.) Harm reduction: a public health strategy. *Current Issues in Public Health*, 1: 64-70. **35.** Mayor's Committee on Marihuana. (1944). The marihuana problem in the City of New York: Sociological, medical, psychological, and pharmacological studies (aka The LaGuardia Report). Lancaster, PA: Jacques Cattel Press. **36.** Rubin, V & L Comitas. (Eds.). (1975). *Ganja in Jamaica: A medical anthropoligical study of chronic marijuana use.* The Hague: Netherlands: Moulton & Company. **37.** Goode, E. (1975). Effects of cannabis in another culture. *Science,* July: 41-42. **38.** Institute of Medicine. (1982). *Marijuana and health.* Washington, DC: National Academy Press. **39.** "In the sense that marijuana use typically precedes rather than follows initiation into the use of other illicit drugs, it is indeed a gateway drug. However, it does not appear to be a gateway drug to the extent that it is the cause or even that it is the most significant predictor of serious drug abuse; that is, care must be taken not to attribute cause to association. The most consistent predictors of serious drug use appear to be the intensity of marijuana use and co-occuring psychiatric disorders or a family history of psychopathology (including alcoholism)." Joy, J, S Watson, & J Benson. (1999). *Marijuana and medicine: Assessing the science base*. Washington, DC: National Academy Press. **40.** Summary of annual findings of the Substance Abuse and Mental Health Services Administration's (SAMHSA) National Household Survey on Drug Abuse, as cited by Zimmer, L & J Morgan. (1997). *Marijuana myths, marijuana facts: A review of the scientific evidence*. New York: The Lindesmith Center. **41.** SAMHSA Office of Applied Studies. (1999). Table 3A: Estimated Number (in Thousands) of Lifetime Users of Illicit Drugs, Alcohol and Tobacco in the US Population Aged 12 and Older: 1979-1998. Rockville, MD: US Department of Health and Human Services. **42.** *Ibid.* **43.** National Center on Addiction and Substance Abuse at Columbia University. (1994). *Cigarettes, alcohol, and marijuana: Gateways to illicit drugs*. New York: CASA. **44.** As compiled by the US Department of Health and Human Services. **45.** SAMHSA Office of Applied Studies. (1999). Summary Findings from the 1998 National Household Survey on Drug Abuse. Rockville, MD: US Department of Health and Human Services. **46.** Researchers at the Netherlands Institute of Medicine, Health and Addiction maintain that separating cannabis from the illicit drug market is an essential step in preventing marijuana users from experimenting with hard drugs. "As for a possible switch from cannabis to hard drugs, it is clear that the pharmacological properties of cannabis are irrelevant in this respect. There is no physically determined tendency towards switching from marijuana to harder substances. Social factors, however, do appear to play a role. The more users become integrated in an environment ('subculture') where, apart from cannabis, hard drugs can also be obtained, the greater the chance that they may switch to hard drugs. Separation of the drug markets is therefore essential." The Trimbos Institute. (1997). Netherlands alcohol and drug report: Fact sheet 7: Cannabis policy: Update. Utrecht: Netherlands. **47.** Zimmerman B, N Crumpaker, & R Bayer. (1998). *Is marijuana the right medicine for you?: A factual guide to medical uses of marijuana*. New Canaan, CT: Keats Publishing. **48.** Mikuriya, T. (Ed.) (1973). *Marijuana: Medical papers 1839-1972*. Oakland: Medi-Comp Press. **49.** AMA Legislative Counsel William C. Woodword testified before Congress on July 12, 1937, against the Marihuana Tax Act. He said: "We cannot understand...why this bill should have been prepared in secret for two years without any initiative, even to the profession, that it was being prepared.... The obvious purpose of and effect of this bill is to impose so many restrictions on the medicinal use [of cannabis] as to prevent such use altogether.... It may serve to deprive the public of the benefits of a drug that on further research may prove to be of substantial benefit." **50.** Several books explore this issue in further detail. These include: Grinspoon, L, & J Bakalar. (1999). *Marihuana: The forbidden medicine* (second edition). New Haven: Yale University Press; Zimmerman, B, N Crumpacker, & R Bayer. (1998). *Is marijuana the right medicine for you?: A factual guide to medical uses of marijuana*. Keats Publishing; Conrad, C. (1997). *Hemp for health: The medicinal and nutritional uses of Cannabis Sativa*. Rochester VT: Healing Arts Press; and Mechoulam, R. (Ed.). (1986). *Cannabinoids as therapeutic agents*. Boca Raton: CRC Press. **51.** A comprehensive literature review by the author on the use of medical cannabis to mitigate these and other indications is available online from the GW Pharmaceuticals Website <www.medicinal-cannabis.org>. Indications explored are: AIDS wasting syndrome, Alzheimer's disease, arthritis, asthma, brain injury/stroke, Crohn's disease, depression and other mental illnesses, eating disorders, epilepsy, fibromyalgia, glaucoma, gliomas, hypertension, migraine, Multiple Sclerosis, nausea, neuropathic pain, schizophrenia, spinal cord injury, Tourette's syndrome and other movement disorders, and ulcerative colitis. **52.** After conducting two years of hearings, DEA Administrative Law Judge Francis Young ruled on September 6, 1988, that cannabis met the legal requirements of a Schedule II drug. He affirmed: "Based upon the facts established in this record and set out above, one must reasonably conclude that there is accepted safety for the use of marijuana under medical supervision. To conclude otherwise, on this record, would be unreasonable, arbitrary and capricious." The DEA refused to implement Young's decision. **53.** These include the AIDS Action Counsel, the American Public Health Association, and *The New England Journal of Medicine*. The author recently compiled a list of these organizations and their supporting statements for the National Organization for the Reform of Marijuana Laws (NORML). It may be accessed online at <www.norml.org/medical/mjorgs.shtml>. **54.** Doblin, R & M Kleiman. (1991). Marijuana as anti-emetic medicine: A survey of oncologists attitudes and experiences. *Journal of Clinical Oncology*, 9: 1275-1280. **55.** "Cannabis and its derivatives have shown promise in a varieties of disorders. The evidence is most impressive in glaucoma,...asthma,...and in [combating] the nausea and vomiting of cancer chemotherapy.... Smaller trials have suggested cannabis might also be useful in seizures, spasticity, and other nervous system disorders." Conclusion of the National Academy of Sciences Institute of Medicine. (1982). *Marijuana and health*. Washington, DC: National Academy Press. **56.** "First, there is good evidence that THC is an effective anti-emetic agent for patients undergoing cancer chemotherapy.... Second, there is reasonable evidence for the potential efficacy of THC and marijuana in the treatment of glaucoma, especially in cases which have proved resistant to existing anti-glaucoma agents. Further research is...required, but this should not prevent its use under medical supervision.... Third, there is sufficient suggestive evidence of the potential usefulness of various cannabinoids as analgesic, anti-asthmatic, anti-spasmodic, and anti-convulsant agents." Hall, W, N Solowij, & J Lemon. (1994). The health and psychological consequences of cannabis use: Monograph prepared for the National Task for on Cannabis. Canberra: Australian Government Publishing Service. **57.** "Marijuana looks promising enough to recommend that there be new controlled studies done. The indications in which varying levels of interest was expressed are the following: appetite stimulation/cachexia, nausea and vomiting following anti-cancer therapy, neurological and movement disorders, analgesia [and] glaucoma." Conclusions of the National Institutes of Health. (1997). Workshop on the medical utility of marijuana: Report to the director. Bethesda: National Institutes of Health. **58.** House of Lords Select Committee on Science and Technology. (1998). Ninth report: Cannabis: The scientific and medical evidence. London: The Stationary Office. **59.** "Lords say, legalise cannabis for medical use." (1998). House of Lords Select Committee on Science and Technology Press Office. **60.** Joy, J, S Watson, & J Benson. (1999). *Marijuana and medicine: Assessing the science base*. Washington, DC: National Academy Press. **61.** Speaking at a national conference on addictions on March 3, 2000, Drug Czar Barry McCaffrey told reporters: "Ask a doctor if he really wants a big blunt stuck in a patient's face as treatment. A lot of this is a crock." **62.** The Harrison Narcotics Act **63.** Herer, J. (1991). *The emperor wears no clothes*. Van Nuys, CA: HEMP Publishing. **64.** "Army study of marijuana smokers." *Newsweek*. January 15, 1945. **65.** See footnote 41. **66.** Ostrowski, J. (1989.) *Thinking about drug legalization*. (CATO Policy Analysis No. 121). Washington, DC: The CATO Institute. **67.** Less than 2,500 deaths were attributable to illicit drugs in 1985. By 1995, total deaths rose to almost 10,000. Drucker, E. (1999). Drug prohibition and public health: 25 years of evidence. *Public Health Reports*, 114: 14-27. **68.** Often with deadly results. See Armentano, P. "A man's home once was his castle." *Ideas on Liberty*, October 2000. **69.** *People v. Luna*, 1989 WL 13231 (N.Y. Court of Appeals, 1989), discussing, *US v. de Hernandez*. 473 US 531 in Ostrowski. **70.** Gingrich introduced H.R. 4170, "The Drug Importer Death Penalty Act of 1996," on September 25, 1996. The bill failed to gain majority support in Congress. **71.** This language was included in the Senate's "1999 Anti-Methamphetamine Proliferation Act" (S.R. 486), but was later removed by the House.

The federal government spends over $13 billion annually on domestic anti-drug law enforcement alone, a figure that is 800 times larger than the entire federal drug control budget of 1981.

Toad-Licking Blues

Thomas Lyttle

"Toad licking" or "toad smoking" are the terms that newspaper reporters attached to the ingestion of *Bufo* venom by users of illicit drugs. This was (and is) done with the intent purpose of getting stoned or high, or going into a trance in a shamanic manner. (It is important to note that bufotenine—a minor constituent of all *Bufo* toad venoms—is *not* hallucinogenic.) In light of this, politicians and the courts stepped in to attempt to control this perceived drug-misuse problem.

In 1967 the Food and Drug Administration placed bufotenine in Schedule 1 of the Controlled Substances Act. Schedule 1 maintains that a drug (or plant or substance) shows no redeeming medical value, is too dangerous for human research, and has a high potential for abuse.

Bufo toads are well known as part of shamanic rituals. No mention of the oral ingestion of toad venom exists in classic shamanic literature, however, because the bufotenine present in the venom does not cause trance or mystical experiences, and both bufotenine and the hallucinogenic 5-MeO-DMT are inactive orally.[1] Also, 5-MeO-DMT is present in only one species of *Bufo* toad, *Bufo alvarius*.

It is important to note that bufotenine —a minor constituent of all *Bufo* toad venoms— is *not* hallucinogenic.

Toxic reactions in human and lower animals are common, however, and include death (in animals) from oral toad venom ingestion.[2] Toad smoking and toad licking should be profiled and studied as two distinct activities. This is an important consideration, especially when studying media reports about toad licking, which involves the oral ingestion of the venom only.

The subject of these clandestine or cult-like uses of *Bufo* toads presents an interesting dilemma for researchers. The very nature of such activity makes open data-gathering troublesome. Anecdotal or word-of-mouth descriptions often prove invaluable for building a tentative profile of any illegal drug activity or a legal but persecuted drug activity. This case involves alleged illegal bufotenine use and misuse, and legal but persecuted 5-MeO-DMT misuse.

From all this (but usually with little concern for scientific facts), the media continue to print "psychedelic toad" articles, thus continuing and sensationalizing age-old *Bufo* toad mythologies, including the myth that bufotenine is hallucinogenic. The focus of these many popular articles is on *Bufo* toads and getting high from bufotenine and its analogs. This is confusing, as only one of the analogs (not bufotenine) causes hallucination.

Bufo Toad Smoking

In the late 1960s, LSD evangelist Art Kleps founded a psychedelic church called the Neo-American Church. The church's newsletter was called "Divine Toad Sweat".[3] In 1984, *Bufo* toad evangelist Albert Most revealed his Church of the Toad of Light with his publication of the book *Bufo Alvarius: Psychedelic Toad of the Sonoran Desert*. (The Sonoran Desert is in New Mexico.) This small booklet details how to use the *Bufo* toad for ritual and pleasure, as well as how to catch the *Bufo alvarius* toad, extract or "milk" the glandular secretions, dry them, and "enjoy the smoked venom." Most's book claims that 5-MeO-DMT (5-methoxy-N, N-dimethyltryptamine) is the active hallucinogen, not bufotenine. He is correct, as 5-MeO-DMT is the O-methylated version of bufotenine.[4] Again, it is important to mention that 5-Me0-DMT is present in only one of the more than 200 types of *Bufo* toads.

Bufotenine is illegal to possess in the United States because it is a Schedule 1 drug, even though it is not psychoactive; 5-MeO-DMT is unscheduled and legal to possess, even though it is psychoactive. This makes 5-MeO-DMT potentially illegal in the US as an analog of bufotenine or DMT, by application of the 1987 drug analog act. Possession of only one type of *Bufo* toad (the type that contains both substances in endogenous forms) for the purpose of getting "stoned or high" or for sacramental use remains in legal limbo, pending legislative debate, which is ongoing at the time of this writing. Although seemingly farfetched, conspiracy to possess a (certain type of) *Bufo* toad may someday be a civil violation or a crime in the United States.

In contrast, a letter to the author talks about the introduction of "hallucinatory toad venom" to well-known American Indian artist Christobal. This letter details Christobal's "yarn art" (a stylized shamanic art form, based loosely in traditional Huichol yarn art).

5-MeO-DMT is present in only one of the more than 200 types of *Bufo* toads.

One of Christobal's artworks was based on his ritually taking *Bufo* toad venom. Letter writer Jacaeber Kastor stated that "the colors are very subdued in the Polaroid. They are vibrant and fluorescent in the yarn painting, etc. This piece has to do with Leo [Mercado] turning Christobal on to the *Bufo* toad secretions and Christobal incorporating the desert toad into his technology-iconography, etc....a very interesting mixology."[5] Kastor is the owner of an art gallery in New York City called Psychedelic Solution. Leo Mercado, at the time, was a deacon in the Peyote Way Church of God in Arizona. In a note to author Bartlett J. Ridge, Kastor stated that "the *Bufo* toad is in their [Huichol] cosmology, but I don't think any of the elders have tried smoking it."[6]

Although seemingly farfetched, conspiracy to possess a (certain type of) *Bufo* toad may someday be a civil violation or a crime in the United States.

Christobal's actual description of the *Bufo* toad-venom "visions" is as follows:

> The symbol of brother toad and the mushroom, which are Gods...to give wisdom of the shamanism, and how to study; how to be able to communicate and be able to receive direction. And encounter the sacred spaces that exist. Because not all (places) serve for that which one wants to know.
>
> For the Gods say in which place, one can ask for that; which a person "living in reality" wants to know. To be able to learn here, is when the shaman are in the sacred places with their candles, praying to wait for the hour when God arrives...to be able to communicate for their powers and ask for luck for their shamanism. And when that hour arrives, they see the candles surge...the life-force appears, as if it explodes.... And from the sparks, the force which comes out is seen, and that is the way it is, where the transformation occurs. It is power which the brother toad and the mushrooms have. Because in this way...the Gods speak.[7]

A more recent anecdotal account showing *Bufo* toad-venom use comes from the *Village Voice* in July 1990. Author G. Trebay described art critic Carlo McCormick's sojourn with the hallucinogenic *Bufo* toad: "the group drank tincture of Peyote, chewed dried Peyote buttons and smoked the dried secretions of a desert toad whose toxins produce...'an effect'"[8]

There is anthropological literature to support *Bufo* toad smoking among New World tribes and shamans. Part of this literature is riddled with confusion, based on hearsay and poor research. The excellent paper "Identity of a New World Psychoactive Toad"[9] sums up parts of the research problems: "When Dobkin de Rios asserts that 'Bufotenine' is an hallucinogenic drug which has dangerous cardiovascular effects in man and is usable only in low doses (1974:149) she not only ignores pharmacological evidence (Holmstedt & Lindren 1967; Turner & Merfis 1959) but she also appears to be confusing the physiological effects of the cardioactive steroid in the venom, with the purported activity of bufotenine on the central nervous system...."

The paper goes on to dispel research myths "created by experts": "When LaBarre (1970:146) refers to bufotenine as a 'violently hallucinogenic drug' he mistakenly attributes the psychoactivity of the South American vegetable snuffs to bufotenine (5-OH-DMT) when it has already been well established that the compound responsible was not bufotenine but rather 5-MeO-DMT (Holmstedt & Lindgren 1967)." These authors also clearly understand the many confusions. They have shown that it may be a mistake to cite secondary as opposed to primary sources when establishing a profile of the pharmacological action of a little-known drug like bufotenine or 5-MeO-DMT.

Bufo Toad Licking

The first wave of news reports regarding toad licking occurred in the early 1980s in the popular press, and have continued to the present.[10] Although highly sensationalized in the media, this story is developing still, and holds implications for serious social pharmacologists, sociologists, and legal experts, not to mention animal-rights activists.

These toad-licking stories are usually reported in English-speaking regions (South America and Central America, Canada, the United States, and Australia) where the *Bufo* toad is either indigenous or where it has been introduced from its indigenous environment and bred. Reports have also appeared where the *Bufo* toad has been artificially introduced into an ecosystem for reasons of "pest control."[11]

The practice of toad licking seems to have developed out of the legendary and mythological uses of *Bufo* toads throughout history. For example, Christopher Columbus carried *Bufo* toads aboard his ships on his return trip from "discovering" America.[12] And both *Lancet* and *Discover* magazines reported that "classic German violinists used to handle [*Bufo*] toads before their performances because the toxins reduced the sweat on their palm."[13]

In the mid-1980s, *Discover* reported that Australian "hippies" were forsaking "traditional illegal drugs for *Cane* toads, which they boil for a slimy, potentially lethal cocktail."[14] A later corresponding report described "the drug squad in Brisbane (Australia) as having...a Heinz Baby-Food jar which carried the label 'Venom Cane Toad: Hallucinogenic; Bufotenine'."[15]

In 1986 a report by Hitt and Ettinger[16] described a five-year-old boy licking (by accident) a live *Bufo* toad. Profuse salivation and seizures were reported, and the boy was admitted to the University of Arizona Medical Center. Within fifteen minutes of licking the toad, severe complications developed; the child survived.

A few months later, a "Dr. Inaga" gave a lecture in Baltimore in which he "comically" mentioned the Australian report, and the "phenomena [of toad licking]."[17] Almost simultaneously Dr. Alex Stalcup, then of the Haight-Ashbury Free Medical Clinics, gave this statement to reporters: "[I]t is amazing the lengths that people will go to, to get high."[18] He was referring to the many recent toad-licking articles starting to circulate in the media.

The media interest regarding *Bufo* toads was the topic of discussion at a 1989 conference on crack cocaine misuse in San Francisco.[19] Police Chief R. Nelson of Berkeley, California, was there, and commented that "[toad-licking]...is a problem that comes up from time to time," legitimizing the rumors. Pressed at a news conference, Robert Sager, head of the Drug Enforcement Administration's (DEA) Western regional laboratory, said "[*Bufo* toad venom/bufotenine]...is in the same legal category as LSD and heroin."[20] This further confused the issue through incomplete comparisons. While all three are in the same legal category, only LSD and heroin are widely misused drugs; and bufotenine is not psychoactive, regardless of the DEA's beliefs.

A New York City DEA spokesman also stated to the press that "we have heard of it [toad licking or smoking]...but have yet to make an arrest," implying that there was some sort of an active problem.[21] The rumors now circled back to the Haight-Ashbury Free Medical Clinics. In response to the *Bufo* toad press releases, the Clinic stated that "ironically...the DEA's actions have inspired a few people to try licking live toads."[22]

Reporters now pressed anyone they could find to investigate these fantastic but apparently "legitimate" stories. In Australia, Glen Ingram—a herpetologist at Queensland Museum—told the press "it [*Bufo* toad venom] gives them a kick like alcohol." This and other wire-service stories led some Australians to react with "panic" according to *Scientific American*.[23] Alarmed at the latest "drug craze" and the infestation of *Cane* toads (which also occasionally poison pets, especially dogs that cannot leave them alone), people in Australia formed "toad eradication leagues."[24] Back in California a probation officer stated to the media that "we hear of youngsters who do this frequently [lick live *Bufo* toads]...it's not as strong as LSD, but it's free."[25]

At this point little in the way of actual names, precise locations, witnesses to events, hospital reports, or deaths appeared in the legitimate press surrounding these stories. The press had repeatedly quoted "experts" in related drug-misuse fields. These quotes fueled rumors, hyperbole, and a lot of fantastic misinformation. As well, most of the press reports surrounding *Bufo* toad misuse lacked the solid primary sources needed for tracing facts.

Later in 1990, after a bulk of fantastic literature had been created, this started to change. The press grew even bolder. Reports naming "P. Cherrie and R. Murphy" appeared in the *Albany Times Union*. These stories reported that "Paul Cherrie saw a TV show about 'toad-licking' and decided to experiment. They scraped some [*Bufo*] toad secretions from the back of the *Cane* toads in Cherrie's collection and spread it on a cracker."[26] Murphy, 21, said that after an hour of "deep hallucinations" that he "awoke...'bam!'...in the hospital. Both men suffered from severe vomiting." This story was amended a few days later in the tabloids, which reported that "Murphy had killed himself after being prematurely released from the hospital."[27]

"In a resolution introduced Monday, apparently with a straight face, Rep. Beverly Langford... called on the General Assembly to look into the 'extreme dangers of toad licking becoming the designer drug of choice in today's sophisticated society..."

Stanton Geer was named next, awaiting trial in Columbia after being arrested on "toad licking" charges. He faced a sentence of "two years and a $10,000 fine, if convicted of drug misuse."[28] Other names also started appealing in press releases.

During all of this, Dr. Alex Stalcup of the Haight-Ashbury Free Medical Clinics in San Francisco complained that "we were getting calls from all over the world—Germany, England, South America, etc.—from reporters wondering about this new high."[29] According to Dr. Sager of the DEA, Australian journalists were now studying the situation in the US "to see if there was a *Cane* toad problem in California."[30]

According to *Scientific American*, the main problem with substantiating these original and then these later reports was "that they are all based in other reports...and that there is no evidence to support them."[31] Journalist Edeen Uzelac said "that this is a case of media feeding on media."[32] Words like "urban legend," a term coined by professor and author Jan Brunvand *(The Choking Doberman,* etc.), were now being used along with other explanations for this media circus. Around this time, the popular television show *LA Law* even did a segment about a man charged with using *Bufo* toads to illegally get high.

In all this confusion, a number of legislators were convinced that where there was smoke there must be fire. Not to be beaten to the punch so far as solutions to this new so-called drug epidemic, Georgia State Representative Beverly Langford (D - Calhoun) introduced legislation to the State General Assembly regarding toad licking: "In a resolution introduced Monday, apparently with a straight face, Rep. Beverly Langford...called on the General Assembly to look into the 'extreme dangers of toad licking becoming the designer drug of choice in today's sophisticated society... The [Assembly] has been very diligent in finding and proposing a legitimate solution to every conceivable type of drug problem....'"[33] South Carolina Representative Patrick P. Harris also introduced similar legislation that same year (1990), finding the practice of toad licking "repulsive but amusing" and suggested sentencing offenders to "60 hours of public service in a local zoo."[34]

The next legislative attempt to curb this new drug menace appeared in Vancouver, British Columbia (Canada). This report stated that "...Vancouver police today said that they want the Canadian government to ban imports of the potentially lethal giant toad blamed on the deaths of several Australian drug users.... Cpl. John Dragoni said the city police force is applying to Ottowa to prohibit ownership of...the toads...by outlawing them under the Federal Narcotics Control Act."[35] Amid this hysteria, legislators in New South Wales, Australia, also passed laws against psychoactive toad use, making bufotenine a Schedule 2 Controlled Substance under the Queensland Drug Misuse Act of 1986,[36] which again is ironic as bufotenine is not hallucinogenic.

Trying to lend credibility to what was becoming an embarrassing flurry of misinformation, medical anthropologist George Root—a former administrator at SP Labs in Miami, Florida—had this to say: "[T]here has been much speculation in the anthropological literature regarding the possible hallucinogenic uses of *Bufo*. This debate is largely based on the fact that *Bufo* is a common representation in the art of some Meso American peoples...and the fact that *Bufo* skeletal remains have been discovered at archaeological sites.... Speculations aside...there is a very good reason why licking toads will not get you high. The toxic compounds are likely to kill you before you could possibly consume enough bufotenine to have any hallucinogenic effect (if there is an hallucinogenic effect)."[37] The author's academic article "Misuse and Legend in the Toad Licking Phenomena"[38] also capsulized a lot of this data, as well as the media "comedy of errors" created in part by quotes from legitimate but misinformed scholars.

Calavaras County, California, has also been the site of a highly-publicized *Bufo* toad seizure and arrest. In early 1994, Bob and Connie Shepard were arrested for breeding *Bufo* toads for psychoactive uses. Four toads were impounded and the couple was charged with possession of bufotenine, called "toad missionaries," and Bob Shepard was placed on a special form of probation called PC-1000 (of the California Drug Diversion Act for first-time, nonviolent offenders) after a highly-publicized media circus.[39]

James Kent's short article "The Truth About Toad Licking"[40] talked about "smoking the chopped skins" of the toad and "coming on almost instantly...you will feel a buzzing head-rush, and notice a profound change in light and color perception. Acute closed-eye visual hallucinations...and heart palpitations...are commonly reported." Kent also mentioned a graduate thesis by David Spoerke, M.S., R.Ph., in this area. This thesis gives a lot of detailed information regarding emergency-room treatments of humans and animals poisoned by toad venom.

High Times magazine also ran a brief review of the psychedelic toad myths, mentioning that the MTV show "Beavis and Butt-Head" was touting toad licking in one episode, although a bullfrog, not an actual toad, was shown.[41] "The show reflects what is going on in the youth culture" said a spokesman for the TV show.[42] *High Times* has periodically run articles following the *Bufo* story, with seven articles appearing between 1974 and 1995.

■■■■■■■■■■■

Science often supports myth, but sometimes science is overtaken, creating or re-creating newer and more complex myths. There is no doubt that the *Bufo* toad has been and is central to humankind's medicines, mythologies, and religions since ancient times. Part of this connection is based in psychology, part in pharmacology, and a good part remains a mystery. Future researchers must recognize that there is a considerable confusion regarding this subject, but that it is possible to turn a toad into a prince with correct and accurate information.

Endnotes

1. Root, G. (1990). "First, the bad news, toad licking will not get you high." [Letter]. *New Times* (Miami, Florida); Horgan, J. (1990). "*Bufo* abuse—A toxic toad gets licked, boiled, tee'd up and tanned." *Scientific American* 263 (2), pp 26-7; McKim, W. (1986). *Drugs and behavior: An introduction to behavioral pharmacology*. New Jersey: Prentice Hall. **2.** Chem, M.S., C.Y. Ray, & D.L. Wu. (1991). "Biologic intoxication due to digitalis-like substance after ingestion of cooked toad soup." *American Journal of Cardiology* 67 (5), pp 443-4; Uzelac, E. (1990). (Reprinted from the *Baltimore Sun*). "A desperation high: Crack? Coke? Croak!" *Seattle Times*, Jan. 30; Anonymous (1986). "It could have been an extremely grim fairy tale." *Discover* 7 (8), p 12; McLeod, W.R. & B.R. Sitaram. (1985). "Bufotenine reconsidered." *Acta Psychiatrica Scandinavica* 72, pp 447-50. **3.** Kleps, A. (1971). *The boo-hoo bible*. San Cristobal, New Mexico: Toad Books. **4.** Shulgin, A.T. (1988). *The Controlled Substances Act*. Lafayette, California: privately published; Marki, F., J. Axelrod, & B. Witkop. (1962). "Catecholeamines and methyl transferases in the South American toad, *Bufo marinus*." *Biochimica et Biophysica Acta* 58, pp 367-9; Gessner, P.K., P.A. Khairallah, & W.M. McIsaac. (1961). "Pharmacological actions of some methoxyindolealkylamines." *Nature* 190, pp 179-80. **5.** Lyttle, T. (1989a). Letter from Jacaeber Kastor. Personal communication. **6.** Lyttle, T. (1989b). "Drug-based religions and contemporary drug taking." *Journal of Drug Issues* 18 (2), pp 271-84. **7.** Christobal. (1989). One-page handwritten note describing *Bufo* visions. (From the collection of Thomas Lyttle.) **8.** Trebay, G. (1990). "Mexican standoff: Carlo McComick's bad trip." *Village Voice*, July 10, pp 19. **9.** Davis, W. & A.T. Weil. (1992). "Identity of a New World psychoactive toad." *Ancient Mesoamerica* 3 (1), pp 51-9. **10.** Chamakura, R.P. (1994). "Bufotenine—a hallucinogen in ancient snuff powders of South America and a drug of abuse on the streets of New York City." *Forensic Science Review* 6 (1), pp 1-18; *Op cit.*, Davis & Weil. **11.** Anonymous. (1990). "Australia's investment in cane toads." *Chicago Tribune*, April 19, section 1, p 14a; Lewis, S. & M. Lewis. (1989). *Cane toads: An unnatural history*. (Based on a film by Mark Lewis.) New York: Dolphin, Doubleday; Ebert, R. (1988). "Hungry toads raising cane." (Review of Lewis & Lewis, *Cane toads*.) *New York Post*, October 1, p 2. **12.** Davis, W. (1985). *The serpent and the rainbow*. New York: Simon & Schuster. **13.** *Op cit.*, Anonymous (1986). **14.** *Ibid.* **15.** *Op cit.*, Lewis & Lewis. **16.** Hitt, M. & D.D. Ettinger. (1986). "Toad toxicity." *New England Journal of Medicine* 314, p 1517. **17.** *Op cit.*, Lewis & Lewis. **18.** Carillo, C. (1990). "Toads take a licking from desperate druggies." *New York Post*, Jan. 31, p 4. **19.** Presley, D. (1990). "Toad licking poses threat to youth of America." *Weekly World News*, July 11, p 5; Seligman, K. (1989). "The latest high—warts and all—thrill seekers risk death to lick toads." *San Francisco Examiner*, May 29, pp A1, A10. **20.** *Op cit.*, Seligman. **21.** *Op cit.*, Carillo. **22.** *Ibid.* **23.** *Op cit.*, Horgan. **24.** *Ibid.* **25.** Montgomery, C. (1990). "Druggies find new way to get high: They lick toads." *Weekly World News*, Oct. 28, p 6. **26.** Anonymous. (1990b). "Toad lickers gamble with death." *Sea Frontiers* 36 (May/June), p 5-6. **27.** Alexander, J. (1990). "Toad licker kills himself." *Weekly World News*, Oct. 2, p 21. **28.** Street, M. (1990). "Toad licker busted." *Weekly World News*, March 13, p 9. **29.** Dorgan, M. (1990). "Nobody, but nobody licks toads in California." *Albany Sunday Times Union*, February 18, p A24. **30.** *Ibid.* **31.** *Ibid.* **32.** *Ibid.* **33.** Secrest, D.K. (1990). "Bill gets hopping on way to lick toad drug problem." *Atlanta Journal and Constitution*, Feb 13, p D1f. **34.** Richards, B. (1994). "Toad smoking gains on toad licking among drug users." *Wall Street Journal*, March 7, pp A1, A8. **35.** Anonymous. (1991). [Reuters News Service.] "Drug addicts licking giant toads to get high." *Palm Beach Post*, July 31, p 9a. **36.** *Op cit.*, Chamakura. **37.** *Op cit.*, Root. **38.** Lyttle, T. (1993). "Misuse and legend in the 'toad licking' phenomena." *International Journal of the Addictions* 28 (6), pp 521-38. **39.** Bancroft, A. (1994). "Couple who smoked toad venom avoid jail." *San Francisco Chronicle*, April 29, p B5; Boire, R.G. (1994). "Criminalizing nature and knowledge." *The Entheogen Law Reporter* 2, pp 1-3; De Korne, J. (1994). "Toadal confusion." *The Entheogen Review*, Summer, pp 10-1; Reed, D. (1994). "Man gets high on toad, narcotics agents are not amused." *San Francisco Chronicle*, Jan. 29, pp A17, 122. **40.** Kent, J. (1994). "The truth about toad licking." *Psychedelic Illuminations*, Winter. **41.** Wishnia. (1995). "Dances with toads." *High Times*, January, pp 21, 34. **42.** *Op cit.*, Richards.

Poppycock

Truth and Lies about Poppies, Opium, and Painkilling Drugs

Jim Hogshire

Thomas Jefferson was a drug criminal. But he managed to escape the terrible swift sword of justice by dying a century before the DEA was created to stamp out that sort of thing. In 1987 agents from the Drug Enforcement Agency showed up at Montecello, Jefferson's famous estate. They must have known the Founding Father was dead, but his crime was alive and well.

Jefferson had planted opium poppies in his medicinal garden, and opium poppies are currently illegal. Now, the trouble was the folks at the Montecello foundation, which preserves and maintains the historic site, were discovered flagrantly continuing Jefferson's crimes in the name of "history."

The government has rewritten history more than once to fight the Demon Poppy.

The agents were blunt: The poppies had to be immediately uprooted and destroyed or else they were going to start making arrests, and individuals from the foundation would soon be facing a ten-year stretch in prison.

The story sounds stupid now, perhaps, but the threat was real, and it scared the hell out of the people at Montecello, who immediately waded into the garden and started yanking out poppies. A DEA man scanning the wares in the giftshop noticed the store was selling packets of the poppy seeds, "Thomas Jefferson's Montecello Poppies." The seeds had to go, too. While poppy seeds might be legal, it is never legal to plant them. Not for any reason. So, selling packets of seeds intended for planting was promoting a felony. Better not have these around anymore.

Employees even gathered the store's souvenir T-shirts—with a picture of Montecello poppies silk-screened on the chest—took them out...and burned them.

Nobody told them to do this, but, under the circumstances, it didn't seem so unusual.

Jefferson's poppies are gone without a trace now. Nobody said much at the time, nor are they saying much now. Visitors to Montecello don't learn how the Founding Father cultivated poppies for their opium. His use of opium and cultivation of the plant may as well never have existed.

The memory hole is alive and well in the USA.

▪▪▪▪▪▪▪▪▪▪▪

The American War on Drugs started with opium and continues with opium to this day. The government has rewritten history more than once to fight the Demon Poppy.

Deception is key to this kind of social control—along with the usual mayhem and threats of mayhem. Such a comprehensive disinformation campaign like the one waged against poppies can be so effective that there is no need for violence. Ever since the passage of the Harrison Act made opium America's first "illicit substance" 85 years ago, propaganda has proved itself most effective in the war on poppies. This has not been done so much by eradicating the poppy plant from the nation's soil as by eradicating the poppy from the nation's mind.

Prosecutions for crimes involving opium or opium poppies are rare. But that has less to do with the frequency of poppy crimes and everything to do with suppressing information about the opium poppy. A trial is liable to get out of hand and publicize information at odds with what everybody "knows" about poppies and opium. That might pique interest in the taboo subject and, worse, undermine faith in the government.

Along with the usual tactics of propaganda (outright lies, disinformation, etc.), the United States government battles the poppy by creating and enforcing a sort of deliberate ignorance about opium, opium poppies, and everything connected with them. This strategy has done a remarkable job. The memory of opium poppies has been all but erased, and remaining bits of information still floating around are quickly suppressed by any of numerous techniques. The escapade at Montecello exemplifies one tactic. The poppies were removed swiftly and without fanfare; sotto voce threats ensured no one would talk about it afterwards. Nobody goes to jail, because, ideally, nothing happened.

Nobody goes to jail, because, ideally, nothing happened.

Today's visitors to the famous estate do not learn anything about poppies that aren't there. They won't look at an opium poppy and hear its name. They surely won't learn anything about the plant's value or why Jefferson planted it.

That's the point of suppressing thought—without knowledge of a thing it's tough to think about it and almost impossible to talk about it. Knowledge not disseminated is knowledge in danger of extinction. In the case of poppies, the government has been thorough, removing the tiniest scrap of true information about poppies and replacing it with disinformation meant to confuse and discourage. Although the job is done now, vigilance is still important. Situations like Montecello can crop up without notice. When they do, the establishment dispatches its men to terminate the threat and suppress the information. Just a few years ago, there were almost no books on the subject of opium or opium poppies—certainly none in print. Anyone interested in opium would have to be dedicated indeed to find much of value.

A DEA agent tells a reporter that the process of getting opium from opium poppies (accomplished by slitting the pod with a small knife) is so complex and dangerous, "I don't even think a person with a Ph.D. could do it."

Disinformation about poppies has been spread far and wide. Some of it is fairly subtle—like when the *New York Times* talks about people growing "heroin poppies." Some of it is so bald-faced that it stuns the listener into silence, as when a DEA agent tells a reporter that the process of getting opium from opium poppies (accomplished by slitting the pod with a small knife) is so complex and dangerous, "I don't even think a person with a Ph.D. could do it."

This enforced ignorance reduces the chances of anyone even accidentally discovering true information about poppies. Poring through back issues of pharmaceutical industry news from Tasmania might yield a motherload of cutting edge poppy science—from genetically altered poppies that ooze double-strength opium to state-of-the-art machines producing "poppy straw concentrate." Tasmania provides around a third of the world's narcotic needs. But how many people know that Tasmania is home to the largest, most modern opium industry in the world?

Ignorance about opium and the opium poppy is augmented by widespread but false beliefs, chief among them the belief that it is extremely difficult if not flat-out impossible for the plant to grow anywhere in the United States. Opium poppies require special climatic conditions, don't they? They're found on remote mountainsides in the Golden Triangle, and growing them is a secret art known only to indigenous people there...who jealously guard the seeds to stop the competition.

Not true, as we will see. Opium poppies grow nearly everywhere but the North and South Poles.

The second prong of the strategy is the copious propaganda demonizing opium and opiates. At times this has been brazenly racist, catering to the xenophobic American mind at the beginning of the twentieth century. Later propaganda linked opium with the despised German "Hun" who ate babies and (it was reported in the *Times*) had been mixing narcotics into children's candy and women's face powder in a diabolical plot to weaken the nation from the inside. Later, Germans were replaced by communists, who also shipped narcotics to America's youth to weaken and enslave us. This was the authoritative word from Harry Anslinger, the first Commissioner of the Federal Bureau of Narcotics.

Another example of false history is the mythical "soldier's disease" or "army disease" that supposedly plagued the land after the Civil War. According to the story, opium and morphine were used so extensively during the war as a painkiller for wounded soldiers (especially those requiring amputation), the inevitable result was opium (and morphine) addiction. As a result, crowds of broken-down men roamed the countryside, ramming themselves full of holes with their crude syringes, having been made into dope slaves by the good intentions of doctors.

This is a perfect example of anti-drug propaganda. It sounds so damned possible, few ever question it. And it has worked well for the Drug Warriors from its beginning (the legend appeared just before the Harrison Act was passed). And it's lived on long after researchers discovered that this yarn had been invented. As great a cautionary tale as it may be, there is no documentation of any mass addiction after the Civil War. And the phrase "soldier's disease" (or its variants) did not appear for decades afterward. Yet the story is so appealing! It fits the approved stereotype perfectly by portraying opium and morphine as so powerful and so addicting that it could take over the soul of anyone, even against their will. Nobody was ever, it seems, immune to this instantly addicting and frequently deadly substance.

Opium poppies grow nearly everywhere but the North and South Poles.

But it is the propaganda's installation of certain key misbeliefs about opium poppies that best ensures people will never get their hands on the the valuable drug.

Being brought up on falsehoods almost inoculates a person against true information. If you know for sure that opium poppies do not grow in the US, you could not recognize a poppy if you were staring directly at it. "Hidden in plain sight" is a phrase that comes to mind. Likewise, if you believe that the federal government made it a high priority to keep this poisonous substance from our pristine shores (and surely they are powerful enough to do it!), you'd be forgiven if you doubted you knew anyone who had really seen an opium poppy in this country.

So, the idea of making opium tea from dried flowers purchased at K-Mart is patently ridiculous. C'mon! If it were that easy, the rationale goes, everybody would be doing it.

Maybe so. But the establishment would rather not test it. The ramifications of people having control over their own lives, let alone something as important as medicine (especially pain relief!) just does not sit well with tyrants.

The government and its allies in the military-narcotic complex have gone to great lengths to set things up as they are now, and opium poppies are smack in the middle of it. Losing control of poppies would be a nightmare for them. A shift in control like that would affect sales of narcotic drugs (licit and illicit), poppy seeds, and other things made from *Papaver somniferu*; the reaction is just too great to consider. In a market the size of America, nothing is too insignificant to generate a lot of money. And the opium poppy is hardly insignificant.

If you know for sure that opium poppies do not grow in the US, you could not recognize a poppy if you were staring directly at it.

Just How Important Is the Opium Poppy, Anyway?

In an economy that can support competing brands of Kiwi juice, it's instructive to consider the humble poppy seed. A half-gram of them dotting the top of a bagel gets multiplied in a hurry. Americans consume literally tons of poppyseed, all of it imported—some of it from Tasmania.

Of course the poppy's most important product is narcotic drugs. They are the only drugs that can adequately control severe pain. They do a bang-up job on mild and moderate pain, too, but the severe pain of a gunshot wound or surgery, most kinds of cancer, and all the rest can be quenched only by opioid drugs. Without these drugs, modern medicine and modern warfare would be impossible. That is to say, modern civilization could not exist without them.

Demand for the morphine and other alkaloids found in opium is what economists call "inelastic." There is no other source for morphine, for codeine, or for any of the other opiates used to control pain. Another opium alkaloid, papverine, is the precursor for a couple of heart medications and can still be used by itself for that same purpose. Of course, "inelastic" is something of an understatement when describing the intense demand created by the nation's heroin users and the billion-dollar industry they support. And technological advances have failed to outdo the poppy when it comes to making narcotics.

The total synthesis of morphine was not accomplished until 1952 (codeine would take another 30 years), and it did little more than confirm the molecule's structure. Total synthesis of morphine is so cumbersome, so costly, that it's a pharmaceutical chemistry party trick.

True, there are synthetic opioids that do not require morphine or any other poppy alkaloid to manufacture, but most synthetics have pharmacological problems that make them inferior choices as medicine, and all of them lack morphine's nearly 200-year record of safety and efficacy. Synthetics, like methadone or meperidine (Demerol), are expensive to make, too, requiring specialized equipment and skilled workers. A few acres of land and a single farmer can produce far more and far better narcotic material than the most efficient drug factory—at a fraction of the cost.

Harvesting the Truth About Poppies

Understanding the history of opium in America is an exercise in separating truth from lies.

Once identified, the lies can be examined for the reasoning behind them. Once the lies are exposed, it also becomes possible to evaluate the true results of such a program of enforced ignorance and its effects on the population. An examination of the truth is its own reward, of course, especially about opium poppies.

Critical thinking—or any kind of thinking—about opium, poppies, or poppy seeds is not encouraged. A good example of this: Although it is widely known that poppy seeds which Americans swallow daily by the pound-per-capita cause "false positives" in urine tests for opiates—this doesn't usually lead to the realization that it's because they are opium poppy seeds! Even when the connection is made, it's common to wrongly assume the seeds have been sterilized or are from a variety of opium poppy that produces little or no "dope."

Of course, most people are surprised to learn the opium poppy can be grown anywhere in the United States. In the 1930s, the barely-hatched Bureau of Narcotics surveilled the kitchen gardens of Czech immigrants growing poppies—in Minnesota! Minnesota is a land of open plains devoid of remote mountainsides, and their winters couldn't be more unlike anything found in the tropics.

The truth is: There is no state where the poppy cannot grow. There is probably no state where opium poppies are not growing right now. The US government itself has grown poppies in such diverse states as Montana, Arizona, Maryland, and Washington.

The seeds on sale in grocery stores are indeed opium poppy seeds, which are more than 90 percent viable. And chances are very good that they come from poppy cultivars that produce some of the strongest opium in the world! Good seeds equal good opium. So far, no one has found a way to breed the poppy to produce more and better seeds without also making more and better morphine (and other alkaloids) in the opium. In the future, perhaps, the government will mandate that seeds be sterilized, or they might mandate that we use seeds from some other poppy with edible seed. That is doubtful, though, and not just because the seeds would have a different taste.

For a time in the 1970s there was talk of growing the so-called "safer poppy"—*Papaver bracteatum*. This species does not manufacture morphine, it is said. It produces thebaine, however, which is very similar to morphine in structure but without any of the sought-after effects. Its real value is as starting material for some of the most potent semi-synthetic opiates available. Dilaudid is one of them.

The program never got off the ground. A few test plots were planted, and there was a lot of talking at meetings, but, in the end the DEA withdrew its original support for the idea, then killed it. Perhaps it was a fear that *Papaver bracteatum* might hybridize with *somniferum* or otherwise begin producing morphine. Or perhaps it was killed because *P. bracteatum*, like a number of other *Papaver* species, has been known to produce morphine on more than one occasion.

Vigorous eradication measures like those carried out against marijuana are not possible with poppies. Such measures are too high-profile and would call attention to the poppy. Besides, unlike cannabis growing in ditches or in plots, this flower is most commonly cultivated in gardens all over the country—a favorite of decorators and "little old ladies." Targeting these people for poison spray would be bad PR.

The Poppy Rebellion

No, to control a plant that is already growing literally everywhere, the last thing to do would be to talk about it or otherwise call attention to it, even during what the US government called the "Poppy Rebellion," staged during the 1940s by California farmers trying to increase their earnings by domestically producing the poppy seeds whose import had been cut off by the war. Prices had risen manyfold, to around 50 cents a bushel, and represented opportunities for profit and to fulfill a crying need among American citizens.

By this time, the federal government had cajoled and threatened every other farmer in the country, even going so far as to dictate the editorial policy of Oregon and Washington newspapers to suppress poppy information and to paint those farmers who insisted on growing the crop as just this side of traitorous.

Vigorous eradication measures like those carried out against marijuana are not possible with poppies.

Yet, California State officials—who had repeatedly shown their desire to cooperate with any legitimate federal policy concerning opium-poppy production—continually failed to grasp the central lie of every federal "plan." For instance, if the federal law banning poppy cultivation provided for "permits" to qualifying farmers, it apparently didn't dawn on California officials that the "permit" language was a ruse; the federal government never had any intention of issuing even a single permit. In an agricultural state like California, this was symptomatic of insanity.

In the end, nine farmers, then seven, stood up to the government, challenging its right to dictate state agricultural policy. The feds, predictably, vowed prison for each of the farmers for their impudence. The matter went to court, and an injunction saved the crop. The crops ripened, and a final verdict was handed down.

In a unanimous vote, a three-judge panel certified the Anti-Opium Poppy Act of 1942 as constitutional inasmuch as it was explicitly grounded in the treaty-making powers of the executive branch, which took precedence over all other laws in the country. This law was not repealed until the introduction of the Uniform Controlled Substances Act of 1970.

The farmers, who could have taken their case to the Supreme Court, mysteriously and suddenly agreed to drop their case right there. One might speculate as to why they would come so far, face so much, expend so much, then seemingly "give up," but one thing is certain: Government threats to prosecute and punish the farmers melted away just as mysteriously.

Non-Enforcement of Poppy Laws

There is a tacit policy of not enforcing the laws against opium poppies. "We're not going into Grandma's garden and start taking samples," reassures an anonymous DEA agent in Seattle. His counterpart at the DEA's office in Indianapolis said he had not the slightest interest in poppies grown in someone's flower garden.

"We wouldn't even walk around the corner for that," he sniffed. As recently as 1996, officials of the DEA have admitted in public that the agency had a general policy of non-enforcement of the poppy laws, preferring "voluntary cooperation" from within the community instead. They don't mention that they get cooperation scarcely and grudgingly.

Although there is always the tacit threat of prosecution, the truth is that anything beyond a warning is fairly remarkable. Even when Customs targeted for intensive inspection nearly every package from certain foreign countries in an operation called "Opium Blitz," the goal was not to fill the jail cells. Such efforts are meant to send a discrete and focused message to a specific group—generally immigrants from opium-using areas of the world. Recipients of the opium are contacted (usually when they come to pick up their packages) and told, in essence, "We know you're bringing in opium; we know how you do it and why you do it, but you must stop or go to jail."

As recently as 1996, officials of the DEA have admitted in public that the agency had a general policy of non-enforcement of the poppy laws, preferring "voluntary cooperation" from within the community instead.

In the 1980s Seattle police discovered thousands of opium poppies being deliberately cultivated by what seemed to be Hmong refugees. No arrests were made. No prosecutions were undertaken or even threatened. Later, in the summer of 1997, when it was pointed out to state cops that more than a quarter-acre of opium poppies was obviously being cultivated on state land (no less) within the city of Seattle, investigators dispatched to the scene reassuringly declared that the poppies were being grown for "non-narcotic purposes," although they never did say just why they thought that. The poppies were not destroyed.

Looking at the statistics, it appears impossible to get busted for poppies. Even if you are warned straight-up that you're doing something illegal and might wind up in jail, you can call their bluff. Lots of people have done it, but it helps if you're rich, or at least famous. One such flagrant violator is Martha Stewart, who grows opium poppies in her garden and dismisses fears about narcotics as "silly."

■ ■ ■ ■ ■ ■ ■ ■ ■ ■ ■

In response to "reports" coming out of the Northwest that people were "misusing the pods" in early 1995, the DEA launched a very low-key investigation into the matter and—lo and behold—it was true! Poppies, dried and fresh, were being purchased by drug users, who then skittered home to drink tea made from the powdered pods. This was not the first time the practice had been discovered, though. Besides being a generally-known home remedy for many centuries all over Europe and the rest of the world, it was once practiced by regular Joes in the United States.

Like other unremarkable and fairly mundane facets of Anybody's Life, it wasn't much-discussed. Poppy tea does make a cameo appearance in the original script to *Night of the Iguana* (where the brew is used to calm a distraught character), but that seems to be the extent of its cultural impact before the surveillance state got to it. After that, poppies and opium were identified as a "clear and present danger" to national security, and it was impossible to treat the stuff with anything less than breathless concern. From the beginning of a federal "drug enforcement" agency, throughout the 1930s, 1940s, and 1950s, federal narcotics enforcers have made references to "poppy tea" and its potential use as a drug. In 1959, Harry Anslinger himself discussed the lurking danger posed by even a few unsupervised plants. Tea made from ornamental poppies would provide the run-of-the-mill junkie with "a rich source of crude narcotics."

In Seattle, "wild" opium poppies grow through cracks in the sidewalk!

Then, as now, the "problem" was tiny, more theoretical than anything else. The only time the potential danger was mentioned was in support of existing or proposed laws controlling poppies in the US. Of course, the irony is that even as the laws forbidding poppies got stricter and stricter, police became less and less willing to really enforce any of the laws. To do so would require extensive and exceedingly obnoxious intrusions into people's lives. Because the typical poppy-grower really is a "little old lady" or some other form of otherwise law-abiding citizen, it would mean—at the very least—a sustained campaign of threats against people who were doing no harm.

To make matters worse, for every poppy that is deliberately planted by a little old lady, there are countless others springing up here and there as "volunteers"—products of the plant's highly-evolved system of self-sowing. In this way, poppies have established themselves across the country. In Seattle, "wild" opium poppies grow through cracks in the sidewalk! Volunteer poppies sprout up as single plants, in groups of three or four or five or, sometimes, blossom as good-sized "patches" anyplace that will have them. The area alongside the well-drained berming that flanks the nation's interstate highways is one particularly beckoning home to poppies.

In the end, serious efforts to enforce anti-poppy laws—to really act as if anyone believed the scare stories about the danger posed by poppies—are neither possible nor desirable. Every time federal cops are cornered on the question of enforcement, they admit they have never enforced the laws and have no plans to do so in the future.

This is, of course, almost a textbook definition of a bad law, one that should be repealed out of respect for law itself.

Subversive Nurseries and Florists

To keep the status quo, the DEA targets the knowledge of poppies, seeking to keep it submerged and undisseminated. To do this, agents visited nurseries and florists across the country, "educating" them with abrupt appearances and pointed suggestions that the proprietor pull all such stock and destroy it. Those who didn't merit a personal visit got letters written by the man in charge of this investigation, Larry Snyder—a senior DEA official working out of DEA headquarters in Washington, DC—whose task it was to quell this latest outbreak of knowledge.

Snyder's letter was (per his request) reprinted in various trade journals and newsletters urging cooperation. This DEA intrusion into a publication's editorial policy was necessary "before this situation adds to the drug-abuse epidemic."

Florists were urged to stop selling poppies or poppyseed immediately. It did not matter how much money anyone was making off the dried ornamentals or the seeds for garden cultivation. It didn't even matter if anyone had detected any criminal activity. The trade had to stop. The cops were very clear on the subject: The plant was illegal, and selling it or its seeds was a crime that could cause violators to be prosecuted. Many people called to plead with the DEA to make exceptions, at least to lighten up a bit, but they were all met with the same unyielding hardline to ditch the poppies pronto.

A Sacrificial Lamb

Something of an increase in the war had happened by summer of 1996, when a rural Georgia man was arrested for growing poppies from commercially available seeds, which let the DEA draw a plausible link between the companies and the criminal. Among the potentially-prosecutable seed companies was international giant Thompson & Morgan. The striking difference in the way the poor boy in Georgia was targeted—as opposed to those companies which had been previously warned, then warned again *explicitly* that they were in danger of prosecution—is striking.

The Georgia man, Wesley Allen Moore—32-years-old, married, and with absolutely no criminal history—lost his trailer home, his young wife, and baby son. He was thrown into the hell of the Georgia prison system for *two full decades* without chance of parole. Moore's life was systematically destroyed and gutted mercilessly in a sickening exception to the no-prosecute rule. In his case an "example" was to be made out of him from the beginning. This was obvious when Georgia Narcotics officers arrived at Moore's trailer-side patch of scrawny poppies by shimmying down ropes dangling beneath hovering helicopters, rather than just driving up in their cars like the press was invited to do. Moore was unarmed and posed no danger, and the local, state, and federal police had had him under surveillance ever since a relative narced on him days before. The whole circus surrounding his daring apprehension was as fundamentally mendacious as the outright lies told by the cops.

Each one of the golf-ball-sized seedpods on the plants could produce a kilogram of pure heroin, said the local sheriff, in a comment so flagrantly stupid it requires the suspension of the laws of physics to be believed.

Each one of the golf-ball-sized seedpods on the plants could produce a kilogram of pure heroin, said the local sheriff, in a comment so flagrantly stupid it requires the suspension of the laws of physics to be believed. In truth, a head may yield 80 grams of opium, of which eight grams will be (theoretically) morphine. At best, this will produce no more than eight grams of diacetylmorphine: heroin.

Other cops on the scene—local, state, and federal—fed lie after lie to the gullible reporters, who dutifully reported as fact things they had never witnessed and had no way to verify on their own. It never once happened that any reporter raised the timidest question to test the statements of these cops. Did Moore even have the requisite knowledge to make heroin? Did he have the chemicals? Is there any evidence he wanted to do that or planned to? In other words, if you're going to condemn this man to a living death within the penal system, could we have some proof beyond baseless assertions that he did anything wrong?

Of course, this never happened. Moore is doing his twenty. His life is destroyed. Anyone following the story in the newspaper learned all sorts of lies: The poppies Moore grew "could not grow in the USA, and were imported," and the poppies in grandma's yard might *look* just the same, but they're different—they're "ornamental."

Perhaps the authorities thought such a feeding frenzy and public display of sadism would catch the attention of those more powerful people they meant to intimidate. Along with the gruesome spectacle of one of their fellow citizens being eaten alive before them, these companies were told in no uncertain terms to cease the sale of poppy seeds. It was a violation of the law and would not be tolerated.

The response by the companies has been to ignore the threat. The Georgia man was crucified with a 20-year prison term and, so far, nothing has been done to the seed companies. This is especially strange since the seed companies are in the business of selling what amount to little felony kits, encouraging its customers to commit crimes with the kits. Should the customer be arrested, the company will deny all knowledge and watch poker-faced as the goon squad destroys its prey.

The Results of the Latest Program

Five years after seed companies, florists, and nurseries were alerted to the budding "national epidemic," poppies are still out there. Their price has gone up considerably, however (a bunch of ten to twelve heads could once be purchased for as little as $1.25—now they cost closer to $12.00). But this was to be expected when merchants realized what the new breed of flower enthusiast was willing to pay. Dried poppies are frequently the first- or second-bestseller among those who sell dried flowers. Business is booming. There is no evidence that any of the probably thousands of florists who so cheekily violate the ban have gone to jail or been punished in any way.

This threat seems to have gone right over Madi Heller's head. Heller is the president of the American Association for the Dried and Preserved Floral Industry. She had a personal meeting with Snyder during which they discussed what she could do for him. He gave her a letter of warning, meant to notify florists that the opium poppy is illegal, and they can be sent to prison for selling it. So stop it, the little press release says.

She printed exactly what he told her to print.

There was an "us and them" quality to the DEA's enforcement of this non-problem, something not lost on Heller.

"Perhaps if they made a big public relations thing and it got attention in the media, it would give more people the idea to go after this substance and use it illegally," she said.

Apparently, despite the impending "epidemic," no one could describe the plant she was supposed to be helping to suppress. As for Heller, with all her years of experience and background, she confesses, she does not know what an opium poppy looks like!

"If my life depended on it, I couldn't identify one [opium poppy]," she says cheerfully.

Even after Synder's visit and the warning Heller published for him, the association continued to promote the use of dried poppy heads.

Some poppy purveyors sought to placate the government by craftily renaming their plants. In place of the illegal *Papaver somniferum*, "new" species suddenly appeared. One of the most popular was dubbed *P. giganthemum*. It's a simple trick that seemingly would fool no one, but—in an interview with a reporter for *Harper's* magazine—Larry Snyder himself extolled the virtues of this "new" sort of poppy. He told the reporter that he had one in his hand right at that moment, and in his opinion the head was larger than a *somniferum* head, so he didn't see why this new "*giganthemum*" species might not be considered the perfect replacement!

In a further show of unfamiliarity with the subject, Snyder solemnly informed the reporter that there were some 2,500 other species of *Papaver* besides the evil *somniferum*, and he was sure that among them were even more good substitutes. Snyder may have been confused on the number here, since the true estimate of *Papaver* species is only around 250. However, his confusion is instructive. If the man whose full-time job is understanding the genesis and mechanics of a nation-threatening "drug epidemic" cannot recognize his foe, or even understand certain basics of botany, is it justice to have him decide who shall be treated with kid gloves and who shall be torn apart?

Meanwhile, his men were busy threatening people with prosecution for possession of a plant not even their boss could recognize.

The truth is, it appears that no one in charge of eradicating the supposed menace of opium poppies in America can identify an opium poppy or demonstrates any interest in learning how to do so. They show a shocking indifference to the damage to human life they cause by their asinine jobs. Not the smallest damage being the results of the lies they tell and the oppressive surveillance state they support.

Opium Poppy Law

More than 80 years of the government's imposition of silence about poppies has accomplished an astonishing degree in changing what Americans "know" about opium and opium poppies, as well as how they feel about them. The lies and fears surrounding opium and poppies were duly incorporated into society's most revered alternate reality: the law.

In his article "The Historical Shift in the Perception of Opiates: From Medicine to Social Menace,"[1] J.P. Hoffmann examines the laws prohibiting the use of opiates in the US. These laws, he says, were more cause than effect with regard to public perception of the drugs:

> Historically perceived as efficacious medicines, this perception has shifted to the point that contemporarily the opiates are commonly thought of as a social menace.
>
> This perception now outweighs the efficacious medicine perception to a substantial degree. A historical analysis indicates that this shift occurred not so much because the hazardous potential for addiction and overdose was discovered, nor because recreational use became widespread; rather, this shift was greatly influenced by underlying national economic conditions and concerns.

Hoffman's study correctly identifies the true reasons for the suppression of opiates in the US (those "national economic conditions and concerns"), and highlights the profound effect of "authority" on public opinion. People are reluctant to disagree with authority figures like doctors, religious leaders, and "statesmen" and find it even tougher to disagree with prevailing opinion—especially the opinions of a peer group. The effects of authority and "everybody else" drove a different—and very successful—propaganda campaign during the same time that anti-poppy propaganda got underway. Propaganda directed by President Woodrow Wilson (who had campaigned for the office on an explicit vow not to bring America into war) transformed a population dead-set against war into jingoistic soldiers begging to take part in the Great War.

What have been the effects of the opium ban and its resulting alterations in US jurisprudence and civilization?

• We can see that laws promulgated for unspoken and even hidden aims are bound to promote a perverse "justice" if ever they are applied in any fashion. They will be grossly destructive of civil liberties whenever vigorously or extensively enforced, and they will promote contempt for anyone involved with law enforcement. Of course, any time the State deprives a citizen of his life, property, or any inalienable right by using shaky legal mechanisms, we have a situation ripe for the wholesale violation of the rights of the accused (perhaps the very heart of the Bill of Rights).

• Laws enacted under false pretenses, aiming only to oppress certain people not otherwise susceptible to criminal charges, are the worst and most repulsive example of evil posing as justice. This is easily seen when the law itself is so poorly understood. Poppy laws are uniformly and persistently misunderstood by the very people who write them. When cops or other such government agents use force to obtain obedience to laws that they themselves cannot understand, they necessarily turn a blind eye to justice.

• The way the poppy laws are written makes them impossible to understand, and the extreme paucity of enforcement calls into question the sincerity (or at least ability) of those who write them. This inevitably results in making each prosecution a textbook example of selective or malicious prosecution. Such practices are forbidden by American law and negate the poppy laws *a priori*.

The stunning ignorance of judges, cops, and lawyers tasked with upholding these laws cannot help but set the stage for the imposition of rank injustice. A look at those few "poppy prosecutions" that have shown up in the written record are sad stories of political repression masquerading as some lofty crusade to keep the nation "pure."

Appendix: The Role of Pain in Freedom

The poppy's central and indispensable position in our civilization makes access to it as important as you might expect, so the forbidding of the people's access to the poppy is staggeringly cruel. Ceding control of opiates means ceding control of pain relief to the State...which has shown a truly morbid interest in inflicting pain and denying its relief in order to effect social change. This is not a power a free people should give up without a fight.

To overlook the deep significance of pain relief would be a big mistake. Pain, after all, is the threat behind all threats, the power behind any negative reinforcement, the stick in the carrot-and-stick dichotomy. All too often it is used to modify human behavior all by itself. The awful thing is: It works.

Pain is the archetypal "scourge of mankind" and is what makes tyranny possible. Even without the participation of human evil, pain is the terrible price we pay when we violate the laws of nature.

All by itself, pain can kill you. And it is an affliction that has dragged mankind into misery without sign of letup.

Even the many diseases that science has "conquered" still cause serious pain. Our modern lives are no freer from pain than that of the sclerotic, twisted figure deformed by stoop labor or worse. "Modern" pain is every bit as excruciating as the rack. Ever spoken to someone with carpal tunnel syndrome (RSI)? Advanced cancer? And perhaps worst of all, burn victims? For these last people, even the most powerful opiates are not enough. They normally beg to die.

It is not particularly funny to consider that Dr. Kevorkian once saved a patient from a lifetime of hell simply by agreeing to help her die. When her own doctor discovered how serious she was, she was given the pain medication that was available from the beginning. And yet we are encouraged to perceive the opium poppy and its derivatives as *evil*.

It is obvious that God has provided for mankind an astonishing abundance of medicines to cure or treat disease, including pain. The opium poppy does that better than the best-equipped, most dedicated scientist can do. Opium is so easy to cultivate, so miraculously useful in so many ways, it is mind-blowing to view it as evil. In fact, given the reality of the situation, opium is a blessing and a boon for the poor and oppressed.

The ability to vanquish pain is something of a prerequisite for civilization. People in pain are unproductive, tend to spread their misery by complaining, and it's a matter of biological fact that pain, especially chronic pain, is itself a kind of disease. Whatever else is wrong with you, guaranteed the addition of pain will make it worse.

So the government's control of opiates—and its larger effort to deprive anyone of truly effective pain relief (unless they get the government's permission)—is a stunningly crude method of social control. Pain avoidance is a powerful motivator.

We all know about the rat pressing the bar so often to get a jolt to the pleasure center of his brain, pressing till he keels over from exhaustion. How about the rat that leaps back and forth over a short wall to avoid an electric shock from the screen-floor? A light signaling the impending shock (quickly) teaches the rat to jump immediately. That's bad enough, but when the jerks running the experiment stop linking the warning light with the jolt and just randomly shock the poor rodent, he begins to deteriorate faster than the sickest skid-row bum. He becomes ultra-nervous, develops neurotic behaviors, and is obviously in constant anxiety in anticipation of the pain he cannot avoid.

Ceding control of opiates means ceding control of pain relief to the State.

The power to relieve pain is even greater than the power to inflict it.

In psychological parlance, the rat is the victim of "learned helplessness" and begins to display all of the traits commonly associated with "depression." His life on earth becomes unpleasant and short. In other words, he gets mean and dies.

Yet a single dose of morphine can reverse this learned behavior. What took so much time and sadistic dedication to destroy is healed within minutes. What does this tell us, then?

The power to relieve pain is even greater than the power to inflict it.

Social control and economic control—in a broad sense—are obvious motivations behind the government's "opiate policy." Tightly restricting the creation and dispensation of pain medication concentrates a lot of money into a few hands, and these individuals scratch each others' backs. Besides the money being more-or-less fully controlled, this system makes it possible to increase profits to almost any extent (due to the inelastic demand for opiates).

It also allows a system of surveillance over the segment of the population that seeks painkillers. That is to say, the majority of people, or better still, all people.

The ramifications of controlling pain are huge. At bottom, every organism responds most predictably and most constantly to pain. No police state could exist without the ability to dole out pain. And pain comes in so many forms! The pain of torture from the sting of a whip is only academically different than the more psychic pain of incarceration.

If anyone doubts the power of pain as a tool to control people's behavior, they need only look to the experiments done by Nazis, later duplicated by academics at Yale and other such universities. Enough pain will make you shock your own mother, will make you shock a stranger to death with electricity.

At that point, it isn't really the pain so much as the threat of pain that evokes such obedient responses. At that point, it is relief from pain that is used by the controller to assure compliance.

Even greater than the power to inflict pain is the power to relieve it.

Every tyrant knows that a person in pain will also reliably respond to the "positive" reinforcement of relief from pain. The ability to offer that—an escape from agony—is a power no amount of money can buy.

Endnote

1. In *The Journal of Psychoactive Drugs* 22: 53-62 (1990).

There are probably more myths and misconceptions about Alcoholics Anonymous, America's most sacrosanct institution, than there are about any other mass organization in our country. Neglecting how this came to be,[1] the primary misconceptions regarding AA are that:

1. **AA is the most effective (or the only) way to deal with an alcohol problem.**
2. **AA existed from the start as an independent organization.**
3. **AA's co-founder, Bill Wilson, independently devised AA's "program," its 12 steps.**
4. **AA is "spiritual, not religious."**
5. **AA is a completely voluntary organization—AA works by "attraction, not promotion."**
6. **AA has nothing to do with "outside enterprises" or "related facilities."**
7. **AA takes no position on matters of "public controversy."**

AA's Effectiveness

AA's supporters commonly trumpet AA as the best, if not the only, way to deal with alcohol problems. To back their claims, they cite anecdotal evidence and uncontrolled studies; but they ignore the best scientific evidence—the only available controlled studies of AA's effectiveness, as well as the results of AA's own triennial surveys of its membership.

There have been only two controlled studies (with no-treatment comparison groups) of AA's effectiveness. Both of these studies indicated that AA attendance is no better than no treatment at all.

The first of these studies was conducted in San Diego in 1964 and 1965, and its subjects were 301 "chronic drunk offenders."[2] These individuals were assigned as a condition of probation to attend AA, to treatment at a clinic (type of treatment not specified), or to a no-treatment control group. All of the subjects were followed for at least a year after conviction, and the primary outcome measure was the number of rearrests during the year following conviction. The results were that 69 percent of the group assigned to AA was rearrested within a year; 68 percent of the clinic-treatment group was rearrested; but only 56 percent of the no-treatment control group was rearrested. Based on these results, the authors concluded: "No statistically significant differences between the three groups were discovered in recidivism rate, in number of subsequent rearrests, or in time elapsed prior to rearrest."[3]

The second controlled study of AA's effectiveness was carried out in Kentucky in the mid-1970s, and its subjects were 260 clients "representative of the 'revolving door' alcoholic court cases in our cities."[4] These subjects were divided into five groups: one was assigned to AA; a second was assigned to nonprofessionally-led Rational Behavior Therapy; a third was assigned to professionally-led Rational Behavior Therapy; a fourth was assigned to professionally-led traditional insight (Freudian) therapy; and the fifth group was the no-treatment control group. The individuals in these groups were given an outcome assessment following completion of treatment, and were then reinterviewed three, six, nine, and twelve months later.

The results of this study were revealing: AA had by far the highest dropout rate of any of the treatment groups—68 percent. In contrast, the lay RBT group had a 40 percent dropout rate; the professionally-led RBT group had a 42 percent dropout rate; and the professionally-led insight group had a 46 percent dropout rate.

In terms of drinking behavior, 100 percent of the lay RBT group reported decreased drinking at the outcome assessment; 92 percent of the insight group reported decreased drinking; 80 percent of the professionally-led RBT group reported decreased drinking; and 67 percent of the AA attendees reported decreased drinking, whereas only 50 percent of the no-treatment control group reported decreased drinking.

But in regard to bingeing behavior, the group assigned to AA did far worse than any of the other groups, including the no-treatment control group. The study's authors reported: "The mean number of binges was significantly greater ($p = .004$)[5] for the AA group (2.37 in the past 3 months) in contrast to both the control (0.56) and lay-RBT group (0.26). In this analysis, AA was [over 4] times [more] likely to binge than the control [group] and nine times more likely than the lay-RBT [group]. The AA average was 2.4 binges in the last 3 months since outcome."[6]

It seems likely that the reason for this dismal outcome for the AA group was a direct result of AA's "one drink, one drunk" dogma, which is drummed into the heads of members at virtually every AA meeting.

It seems very likely that this belief all too often becomes a self-fulfilling prophecy, as it apparently did with the AA attendees in this study. The third significant piece of evidence regarding AA's effectiveness is that provided by AA's triennial membership surveys. In 1990 or 1991, AA produced an analysis of the previous five membership surveys, "Comments on A.A.'s Triennial Surveys."[7] This document revealed that 95 percent of those coming to AA drop out during their first year of attendance.[8] Even if all those who remain in AA stay sober (which often is not the case), this is still a poor success rate, even in comparison with the rate of spontaneous remission.

There have been many studies of spontaneous remission (sometimes called spontaneous recovery), and one meta-analysis of such studies indicates that between 3.7 percent and 7.4 percent of individuals with alcohol problems "spontaneously" recover in any given year.[9] In comparison with this, AA's 5 percent retention rate is not impressive. And that 5 percent rate might be optimistic—it was derived from surveys conducted during a period of very high growth in AA membership. In contrast, since the mid-1990s—a time when over one million Americans per year were, and still are, being coerced into AA attendance—AA's US membership has been essentially flat, hovering around 1.16 to 1.17 million persons for the last few years.[10] Even taking into account dropouts with "time" (from this "program for life"), this means that AA's current new-member retention rate could well be *under* 5 percent.

As for AA being the *only* way to beat an alcohol problem, it has been known for decades that alcoholism (alcohol *dependence*—as contrasted with mere alcohol abuse) disappears faster than can be explained by mortality after the age of 40.[11] Also, a very large Census Bureau-conducted study in the early 1990s found that over 70 percent of the formerly alcohol-dependent individuals surveyed (over 4,500 in all) had recovered without participating in AA or attending treatment of any kind, and that those who had not participated in AA or attended treatment had a *higher* rate of recovery than those who had.[12]

As well, in contrast to AA and treatment derived from it (the dominant mode in the US), there are several types of treatment that are well-supported by the best available scientific evidence (studies with random assignment of subjects and no-treatment control groups, and/or comparison groups using standard 12-step treatment). Among the best-supported therapies are those known as the community reinforcement approach, social skills training, motivational enhancement, and brief intervention.[13] All of these well-supported therapies are low-cost, cognitive-behavioral approaches in which alcohol abusers are reinforced in the belief that they have power over their own actions, and are responsible for them. (This is in direct contrast to the 12-step approach, which teaches alcohol abusers that they are "powerless.") Unfortunately, none of these effective, low-cost therapies is in common use in the United States, in which the 12-step approach dominates.

Finally, over the last quarter-century a number of "alternative" (non-12-step) recovery groups have arisen in the US, and many, many individuals have recovered through them. The four largest are SMART Recovery, Women for Sobriety, Moderation Management, and Secular Organizations for Sobriety.[14] Between them, they have hundreds of meetings scattered across the country, and all are easy to contact via the Internet.[15]

In sum, those who trumpet AA as the best (or only) way to deal with an alcohol problem do so only by ignoring well-supported alternative therapies, the widespread "alternative" self-help groups, the best available scientific evidence, and the evidence generated by AA itself.

AA as an Independent Organization

One of the most widespread myths concerning AA is that it has existed as an independent organization from day one, from the day in 1935 that Bill Wilson met AA's other co-founder, Bob Smith, in Akron, Ohio. When they met, Smith and Wilson were both members of a Protestant evangelical group called the Oxford Group Movement (OGM). Convinced that Oxford Group principles were the key to overcoming alcohol abuse (and all other problems in life), they devoted themselves to carrying the Oxford Group message to other alcoholics.[16] What they called "the alcoholic squadron of the Akron Oxford Group" remained as part of the Oxford Group Movement until 1939, and the group Bill Wilson founded in New York remained as part of the Oxford Group Movement until late 1937.

The reasons that AA parted ways with the Oxford Group Movement had nothing to do with differences over ideology; rather, they had to do with personality conflicts, the fear that Catholics would be forbidden to join what was to become AA as long as it was part of a Protestant organization, and, quite possibly, embarrassment over OGM founder Frank Buchman's statements in a 1936 *New York World Telegram* interview, in which he said, "Thank heaven for a man like Adolf Hitler," and in which he pined for "a God-controlled Fascist dictatorship."[17]

One reason that this link between AA and the Oxford Group Movement is not more widely known is that during the years following the adoption of the name Alcoholics Anonymous, AA never credited the Oxford Group Movement for anything—even though AA took its central beliefs, program, and practices almost unaltered from the OGM. For instance, there is not a single acknowledgment of the Oxford Groups in *Alcoholics Anonymous*, AA's "Big Book." It wasn't until the late 1950s, in *Alcoholics Anonymous Comes of Age*, that Bill Wilson and AA (partially) acknowledged AA's debt to the Oxford Groups. Even today, most AA members know little if anything about the AA/OGM connection—and the few who are well-acquainted with it tend not to talk much about it.[18]

AA took its central beliefs, program, and practices almost unaltered from a Protestant evangelical group called the Oxford Group Movement.

The Origin of the 12 Steps

A common myth—even within AA—is that AA co-founder Bill Wilson wrote the 12 steps entirely independently, that they were completely his own invention. A closely-related myth common in AA is that Bill Wilson wrote the 12 steps directly under divine guidance. Neither myth has any but the scantiest relation to reality.

The author of AA's 12 steps and the text portion of AA's bible, the "Big Book" (though not the personal stories in it), Bill Wilson, was a dedicated Oxford Group member who was convinced that the principles of the Oxford Group Movement were the only route to recovery for alcoholics, and the 12 steps he included in the "Big Book" are a direct codification of those principles. Indeed, in *Alcoholics Anonymous Comes of Age*, Wilson directly credits the OGM as the source of the teachings codified in the 12 steps.[19] In a letter to former OGM American leader Sam Shoemaker, Wilson stated:

> The Twelve Steps of A.A. simply represented an attempt to state in more detail, breadth, and depth, what we had been taught—primarily by you [Rev. Shoemaker]. Without this, there could have been nothing—nothing at all.[20]

Wilson also stated publicly:

> Where did early AA's...learn about moral inventory, amends for harm done, turning our wills and lives over to God? Where did we learn about meditation and prayer and all the rest of it?... [S]traight from Dr. Bob's and my own early association with the Oxford Groups....[21]

To be more specific, the Oxford Group principles of *personal powerlessness* and the necessity of *divine guidance* are codified in steps 1, 2, 3, 6, 7, and 11. The principle of *confession* is embodied in steps 4, 5, and 10. The principle of *restitution* to those one has harmed is embodied in steps 8 and 9. And the principle of *continuance* is embodied in steps 10 and 12.

There is not a single original concept in the 12 steps. They all came directly from the Oxford Group Movement.[22]

AA as a Religious, Not Spiritual, Organization

Members of AA routinely assert that AA is "spiritual, not religious," though even a cursory glance at AA's practices and official ("conference approved") publications reveals just the opposite to be true.

As for AA's practices, most meetings open with a prayer to God—the Serenity Prayer ("God grant us the serenity to accept the things we cannot change, the courage to change the things we can, and the wisdom to know the difference"). Most also feature reading (and often discussion) of the 12 steps, with their exhortations to pray and to turn one's life and will over to God. And almost all AA meetings close with a reading of a specifically Christian prayer, the Lord's Prayer.

> 1. We admitted we were powerless over alcohol—that our lives had become unmanageable.
> 2. Came to believe that a Power greater than ourselves could restore us to sanity.
> 3. Made a decision to turn our will and our lives over to the care of God *as we understood Him.*
> 4. Made a searching and fearless moral inventory of ourselves.
> 5. Admitted to God, to ourselves, and to another human being the exact nature of our wrongs.
> 6. Were entirely ready to have God remove all these defects of character.
> 7. Humbly asked Him to remove our shortcomings.
> 8. Made a list of all persons we had harmed, and became willing to make amends to them all.
> 9. Made direct amends to such people wherever possible, except when to do so would injure them or others.
> 10. Continued to take personal inventory and when we were wrong promptly admitted it.
> 11. Sought through prayer and meditation to improve our conscious contact with God *as we understood Him*, praying only for knowledge of His will for us and the power to carry that out.
> 12. Having had a spiritual awakening as the result of these steps, we tried to carry this message to alcoholics, and to practice these principles in all our affairs.

AA's 12 steps, the backbone of its "program," are even more revealing: It's noteworthy that alcohol is mentioned only in the first step, which strongly implies that alcoholics *cannot* overcome their problems on their own. The remainder of the steps implore alcohol abusers to engage in religious activities (prayer, confession) and to "turn [their] will[s] and [their] lives over to the care of God."

Much of the rest of the "Big Book" is just as religious, if not more so, than the 12 steps. In his comments immediately preceding the 12 steps, Bill Wilson exhorts the reader: "Remember that we deal with alcohol—cunning, baffling, powerful! Without help it is too much for us. But there is One who has all power—that one is God. May you find Him now!"[23] Wilson also devotes an entire chapter in the book (chapter 4, "We Agnostics") to attacking atheists and agnostics as "prejudice[d]" or crazy, and to presenting belief in God as the only way to restore "sanity." Wilson also recommends that AA members "work" the seventh step through prayer, and even provides the wording for a prayer to "My Creator."[24] It's also worthy of note that the "Big Book" is saturated with religious terms. There are well over 200 references to God, capitalized masculine pronouns ("He," "Him"), or synonyms for God ("Creator," "Father," etc.) in its 164 pages of text—and this doesn't even take into account such terms in the personal stories that make up the bulk of the book.

AA is a very anti-intellectual organization, in which questioning and skeptical attitudes are viewed as "disease symptoms."

AA's second—and second-most important—book, *Twelve Steps and Twelve Traditions*, also written by Wilson, is just as religious as the "Big Book." For instance, the nine pages devoted to "working" step 2 contain at least 30 references to God, synonyms for it, or capitalized masculine pronouns referring to it. Wilson also repeatedly exhorts the reader to pray, noting in one place that, "Those of us who have come to make regular use of prayer would no more do without it than we would refuse air, food, or sunshine."[25] And in his discussion of step 4, making "a searching and fearless moral inventory," Wilson makes a truly extraordinary recommendation: that the list of one's "moral defects" be based on "a universally recognized list of major human failings—the Seven Deadly Sins[!] of pride, greed, lust, anger, gluttony, envy, and sloth."[26] Contrary to Wilson's assertion, these are *not* "a universally recognized list of major human failings," rather, they are a specifically Christian list of sins as enumerated by Pope Gregory the Great in the sixth century. (Even ignoring their origin, one wonders why this "universally recognized list" would omit such obvious "defects" as cruelty, intrusiveness, dishonesty, hypocrisy, and sanctimoniousness.) That Wilson would make such an extraordinary recommendation underlines the Christian origins of AA and its program.

Indeed, the religious nature of AA and its "program" is so obvious that in the late 1990s four appeal-level courts (the Second and Seventh Federal Circuit Courts of Appeal and the state high courts in New York and Tennessee) ruled that government-coerced attendance at AA and NA (Narcotics Anonymous—a clone of AA) is unconstitutional in that it violates the "Establishment Clause" of the First Amendment because AA is obviously religious in nature.[27] There have been no contrary rulings on the appeal level, but there is as yet no national precedent because the Supreme Court has not ruled on the issue.

Given all this, it seems amazing that AA members routinely and vehemently assert that AA is "spiritual, not religious." There are two primary reasons that they do this. The first is that AA is a very anti-intellectual organization, in which questioning and skeptical attitudes are viewed as "disease symptoms," and in which great emphasis is placed upon unquestioning acceptance of revealed wisdom. Three of the most common AA slogans embody this anti-intellectualism: "Utilize, don't analyze;" "Let go and let God;" and "Your best thinking got you here." So, in a milieu which demands blind acceptance and denigrates critical thought, AA members hear that AA is "spiritual, not religious" and repeat it in parrot-like fashion.

AA members who own treatment facilities and/or work in them have an additional incentive to repeat the "spiritual, not religious" assertion: money. Over 93 percent of treatment facilities in the United States are 12-step facilities,[28] and treatment is a $10 billion-a-year industry.[29] If 12-step members who work in and own treatment facilities would honestly admit that their approach is religious in nature, that river of government and insurance-industry cash would dry up in short order.

AA as a "Voluntary" Organization

AA apologists routinely paint AA as a lily-white, all-volunteer group offering its "spiritual" program on a take-it-or-leave-it basis, and that AA operates on the principle of "attraction, not promotion." This is about as far from the truth as maintaining that people "voluntarily" pay taxes.

That AA depends heavily upon coercion for "attracting" new members can be seen even in AA's promotional "Alcoholics Anonymous [insert year] Membership Survey" brochure. The brochure describing the 1996 survey, for instance, reveals that 16 percent of AA members were originally "introduced" to AA by the courts or penal system. Taking other avenues of coercion into account, such as threats of job loss and coercion by treatment centers,[30] the statistics published in AA's "Membership Survey" brochures strongly suggest that the total percentage of AA's active members who were originally coerced into attendance exceeds 40 percent.[31]

When one considers that these figures apply only to those *currently attending* AA, it becomes clear that in all likelihood a significant majority of newcomers to AA are coerced into attendance—and then leave as quickly as they can through AA's "revolving door." To cite but one example, in a great many jurisdictions throughout the United States it is routine for the courts to sentence DUI defendants to attend AA (and often 12-step treatment as well).

The statistics published in AA's "Membership Survey" brochures strongly suggest that the total percentage of AA's active members who were originally coerced into attendance exceeds 40 percent.

That most such coerced persons leave AA as quickly as they can, can be seen in AA's sky-high dropout rate (discussed above), and in the fact that AA's membership has been flat for the past several years[32] (which means that either experienced members from this "program for life," or the at least one million coerced newcomers per year—who are routinely threatened with "jails, institutions, or death," should they leave AA—are dropping out in droves).

Groups of AA members have set up "educational" and "medical" front groups to promote AA and its core beliefs.

Further confirmation of AA's dependence upon coercion for recruitment of new members can be seen in the vast numbers of individuals who are coerced annually into 12-step (AA-based) treatment. There are approximately 15,000 treatment centers in this country treating approximately 2,000,000 persons annually (with "alcohol only" and "alcohol with secondary drug" clients making up 48 percent of the total),[33] and a recent national survey indicates that 93 percent of treatment facilities are 12-step facilities.[34] Given that virtually all 12-step facilities require that clients attend AA (or its clone, NA) and "work the steps," and that discharge before completion of treatment often means imprisonment, loss of employment, loss of professional certification (for doctors, nurses, and lawyers), loss of child custody, loss of organ transplant candidacy, etc., etc., for the majority of the clients in such treatment centers (that is, coerced clients),[35] this means that the vast majority of newcomers to AA are coerced into attending not only 12-step treatment, but also AA, the program which allegedly works through "attraction, not promotion."

AA and "Outside Enterprises"

Yet another common myth is that AA, the ultra-independent "voluntary" organization, has no connection with "outside enterprises" or "related facilities."

AA's sixth tradition (the traditions are to AA groups and AA as a whole as the 12 steps are to individual AA members) states that, "An AA group ought never endorse, finance, or lend the AA name to any related facility or outside enterprise, lest problems of money, property, and prestige divert us from our primary purpose." Thus AA members keep to the letter (though not the spirit) of this tradition by endorsing, organizing, financing, and staffing "related facilit[ies]" and "outside enterprise[s]" as individual AA members or groups of individual AA members, not as self-declared AA groups.

This is most obvious in the case of 12-step treatment facilities, which as we saw above constitute 93 percent of the total. The percentage for inpatient facilities reported by the National Treatment Center Study investigators is even higher: 96 percent.[36] A great many of these facilities were founded by AA members, are owned by AA members, are staffed (often entirely—down to cooks and janitors) by AA members, have the 12 steps as the centerpiece of their "treatment," force clients to "work" the first three to five steps (depending on the facility and length of stay), and the primary purpose of these programs is to expose clients to AA and to induce them to attend AA meetings for the rest of their lives. Indeed, one pro-AA MD states in a professional journal that a primary goal of 12-step treatment is that, "The patient is indoctrinated into the AA program and instructed as to the content and application of the 12 steps of the program."[37] He then goes on to note that, "followup usually consists of ongoing support by the treatment facility as well as participation in community self-help groups such as AA, NA, OA, and the like."[38, 39]

Yet AA members routinely claim that 12-step treatment has "nothing to do with AA."

AA and "Matters of Public Controversy"

Groups of AA members have set up "educational" and "medical" front groups to promote AA and its core beliefs (especially the disease concept of alcoholism and the absolute necessity of abstinence for anyone who has ever abused alcohol). This allows AA to maintain its pristine, above-the-fray image, while its hidden members and allies do its dirty work. (AA members in these front groups and in other media hide behind AA's tradition of "anonymity" while they promote AA, the disease concept, and the abstinence-only approach, and attack critics of AA and those who promote, study, or practice non-12-step approaches to addictions, many of which are much better supported scientifically than AA and 12-step treatment).[40] Indeed, the hidden members in AA's front groups have moved beyond merely attacking those they disagree with, and have worked actively to suppress alternative modes of treatment.[41]

The two prime examples here are the National Council on Alcoholism and Drug Dependence (NCADD, AA's educational front group—formerly the National Council on Alcoholism [NCA]) and the American Society of Addiction Medicine (AA's medical front group, which was a part of the NCADD for over a decade—like NCADD it promotes the disease model of addiction, preaches the necessity of abstinence, and promotes AA).[42] The connection between AA and the NCADD was obvious from the first, as the group was founded by PR flack Marty Mann, the first female AA member who maintained sobriety for any length of time, and as the full names of AA's cofounders, Bill Wilson and Bob Smith appeared on the group's letterhead. (This caused a great deal of controversy in AA, not because AA members saw anything wrong in the setting up of front groups, but because Wilson and Smith had "broken anonymity" by allowing their full names to be used.)

The primary purpose of the NCADD, in addition to promoting AA and its core beliefs, is to act as AA's spokesman (indeed, enforcer) on "outside issues" and "matters of public controversy;" and the NCADD has indeed been instrumental in helping to maintain adherence to 12-step orthodoxy. This is most obvious in the matter of treatment approaches. There's good evidence that controlled-drinking approaches work at least as well as abstinence approaches in the treatment of problem drinkers,[43] yet the NCADD has virulently attacked controlled-drinking researchers and clinicians over the years in an attempt to limit treatment options in the United States to abstinence-only approaches. To cite but one example, the Rand Report on controlled drinking, Don Cahalan, a well-known alcoholism researcher, reports that, "After valiant year-long attempts by prominent NCA members to have the report suppressed altogether or drastically revised in its findings, it was finally released by Rand in June 1976."[44] When the report was released, 12-step spokespersons denounced it with dire warnings that "some alcoholics have resumed drinking as a result of [the report],"[45] and admonitions that, "After all, people's right to know does not mean the people's right to be confused—especially when it is a matter of life and death."[46]

To cite a more recent example of NCADD attempts to vilify controlled-drinking advocates, on March 25, 2000, Audrey Kishline, founder of the group Moderation Management (MM—a controlled-drinking self-help group), drank herself blind (to a blood-alcohol level of .26—roughly three times the legal limit), climbed into her truck, drove the wrong way on a freeway, and got in a head-on crash with another pickup, killing its driver and his 12-year-old daughter.

The NCADD's response? In late June, after the incident was reported first in the *Seattle Times* and later in the national media, the NCADD, under the signature of its president, Stacia Murphy, issued a press release which strongly implied that the crash was one of the "consequences of 'moderation management'." The NCADD went on to piously implore that, "As a society we must finally accept that abstinence offers the safest and most predictable course for the treatment of alcohol and other drug-related problems and we must do everything we can to break through the denial of those who are actively addicted."

AA's supporters in the media were also quick to exploit the Kishline tragedy. The *San Francisco Chronicle*, *Indianapolis Star,* and other newspapers ran editorials decrying the moderation approach, while making no mention of Kishline's AA involvement either before or after her involvement with MM. *Time* magazine and Scripps-Howard news service each ran a story on the incident which also failed to mention Kishline's AA involvement. One strongly suspects, but cannot prove, that many of the stories and editorials attacking MM and the moderation approach were written by AA members hiding behind AA's "anonymity" stricture.

What the NCADD and AA's media supporters (with almost no exceptions) didn't mention—and this was something that they almost certainly knew—was that on January 20, Audrey Kishline had announced on the MM email list that she was abandoning her attempt to drink moderately, and was instead returning to AA and the abstinence approach! (One self-proclaimed AA member, Caroline Knapp, wrote a lengthy story for Salon <salon.com>, which was very pro-AA and very condemnatory of the moderation approach; deep in the story Knapp included a short, dismissive mention of Kishline's AA involvement immediately prior to the crash. Her piece was later reproduced in the *Los Angeles Times.*)

As well, the NCADD and literally *all* of AA's media supporters did not mention that Audrey Kishline had learned to binge drink during years of AA membership and following participation in an intensive, 28-day, 12-step inpatient program. In her book, *Moderate Drinking: The New Option for Problem Drinkers*, Kishline noted that she had "attended literally hundreds of AA meetings in 10 different states.... The result of all this 'treatment'? At first my drinking became far worse. Hospital staff members had told me that I had a physical disease that I had no control over... I kept hearing 'one drink, one drunk'... In possibly the most defenseless and dependent stage of my entire life, I began to fulfill some of these prophecies. I became a binge drinker..."[47]

Given this, it seems entirely possible that Kishline's 12-step-induced binge drinking had more to do with her criminal actions than the moderation program she was no longer even attempting to follow. But AA's front group, the NCADD, and AA's supporters in the media, saw fit not to mention this. Their only interest was in attributing the fatal crash to the moderation approach which Kishline had abandoned.

Summary

In contrast to what you've heard over and over again in the media (and from AA's often-hidden spokespersons) this is the truth about AA:

1. AA is not only far from the only way to deal with an alcohol problem, but the best available scientific evidence indicates that it is ineffective.
2. AA began its life—for its first several years—as part of the Protestant evangelical group, the Oxford Group Movement, not as an independent organization.
3. AA's co-founder, Bill Wilson, did not independently devise AA's "program," its 12 steps; instead, he merely codified the central Oxford Group Movement beliefs.
4. AA is religious, not spiritual; this is so obvious that even several appeal-level courts have ruled that this is so.
5. AA relies upon coercion to bring it a majority of its new members, and AA members take an active part in much of that coercion.
6. 12-step treatment is essentially institutionalized AA.
7. AA employs front groups and hidden members in the media to do its dirty work for it on matters of "public controversy."

Endnotes

1. See *Alcoholics Anonymous: Cult or cure? (second edition)*, Chapter 8 ("AA's Influence on Society"), pp 105–124. Tucson, AZ: See Sharp Press, 1998. **2.** Ditman, KS, GC Crawford, WE Forgy, H Moskowitz, & C MacAndrew. (1967). A controlled experiment on the use of court probation for drunk arrests. *American Journal of Psychiatry*, 124(2), pp 64–67. **3.** *Ibid.*, p 64. **4.** Brandsma, JM, MC Maultsby, & RJ Welsh. (1980). *Outpatient treatment of alcoholism: A review and comparative study.* Baltimore: University Park Press. **5.** Meaning that the possibility of this outcome being due to random chance was only 1 in 250. **6.** *Op cit.*, Brandsma et al., p 105. **7.** "Comments on A.A.'s Triennial Surveys." New York: Alcoholics Anonymous World Services, n.d. (This document was apparently produced for internal use, as it's very crudely produced—typewritten xeroxed pages bound in one corner with a staple—and is not part of AA's "conference-approved" literature. Other researchers and I obtained copies of it shortly after it was produced by writing to AA's General Service Office and asking for it.) **8.** *Ibid.*, p 12, Figure C-1. **9.** Smart, RG. (1975/76). Spontaneous recovery in alcoholics: A review and analysis of the available research. *Drug and Alcohol Dependence*, (1), pp 277–285. **10.** Membership information taken from AA's official Website <www.alcoholics-anonymous.org>. **11.** Drew, RH. (1968). Alcoholism as a self-limiting disease. *Quarterly Journal of Studies on Alcohol*, 29, pp 956–967. **12.** Dawson, Deborah. (1996). Correlates of past-year status among treated and untreated persons with form alcohol dependence: United States, 1992. *Alcoholism: Clinical and Experimental Research*, Vol. 20, pp 771–779. **13.** See Hester, Reid & William Miller (Eds.). (1995). *Handbook of alcoholism treatment approaches: Effective alternatives (second edition).* Boston: Allyn & Bacon, for discussion of these and other effective approaches. For a discussion of the evidence supporting various approaches, see Hester & Miller and see also Peele, Stanton, et al. (2000). *Resisting 12-Step coercion: How to fight forced participation in AA, NA, or 12-step treatment*, Chapter 2. Tucson, AZ: See Sharp Press. **14.** I do not include Rational Recovery (RR) here, because at the turn of the year 2000 RR founder Jack Trimpey directed all RR self-help groups to disband. While a significant number of RR groups apparently ignored Trimpey's order, they cannot be considered a part of a national organization. **15.** Their Website addresses are: SMART Recovery <www.smartrecovery.org>, Women for Sobriety <www.womenforsobriety.org>, Moderation Management <www.moderation.org>, and Secular Organizations for Sobriety <www.unhooked.com>. **16.** That message was that individuals are powerless in themselves, that the only route to "sanity" is to turn one's life and will over to God, and that God will remove your shortcomings and direct your life if only asked properly. **17.** The entire text of this August 26, 1936, interview is reproduced in Tom Driberg's *The Mystery of Moral Re-Armament.* New York: Alfred A. Knopf, 1965, pp 68–69. For additional treatment of this matter (and the extremely dishonest manner in which AA treats it in its "conference-approved" Wilson biography, *Pass It On*), see *Alcoholics Anonymous: Cult or cure? (second edition)*, *op cit.*, pp 21–23. **18.** There are some exceptions to this rule, notably AA historian Dick B. who has written several scholarly and reliable books on AA's debt to the Oxford Group Movement. One relevant title is *The Oxford Group & Alcoholics Anonymous: A design for living that works (revised edition).* Kihei, HI: Paradise Research Publications, 1998. See also <www.dickb.com>. **19.** Wilson, W. (1957). *Alcoholics Anonymous comes of age.* New York: Alcoholics Anonymous World Services, pp 58–63, 160–167. **20.** Quoted by Dick B. in *Design for living: The Oxford Group's contribution to early A.A.* Kihei, HI: Paradise Research Publications, 1992, p 10. **21.** Quoted in *The Language of the Heart: Bill W.'s grapevine writings.* New York: A.A. Grapevine, Inc., 1988, p 198. **22.** For further discussion of the 12 steps and AA's debt to the Oxford Groups, see *Alcoholics Anonymous: Cult or cure? (second edition)*, *op cit.*, Chapters 4 and 5, pp 57–76. **23.** Wilson, William. (1939, 1976). *Alcoholics Anonymous.* New York: Alcoholics Anonymous World Services, p 58. **24.** *Ibid.*, p 76. **25.** Wilson, William. (1953). *Twelve Steps and Twelve Traditions.* New York: Alcoholics Anonymous World Services, p 97. **26.** *Ibid.*, p 48. **27.** The cases are *Griffin v. Coughlin* (1996); *Kerr v. Farrey* (1996); *Evans v. Tennessee Department of Paroles* (1997); and *Warner v. Orange County Department of Probation* (1999). **28.** *National Treatment Center summary report*, Paul Blum and Terry Roman principal investigators. Athens, GA: Institute for Behavioral Research, 1997, p 24. **29.** Institute of Medicine. (1990). *Broadening the base of treatment for alcohol problems.* Washington, DC: National Academy Press. **30.** For a fuller discussion of avenues of coercion into AA, other 12-step groups, and 12-step treatment, see *Resisting 12-Step Coercion*, *op cit.*, pp 25–30. **31.** For a fuller discussion of these statistics, see *Resisting 12-Step Coercion, op cit.*, p 27, or see *Alcoholics Anonymous: Cult or cure? (second edition)*, *op cit.*, pp 101f–102f. **32.** According to statistics posted on AA's official Website <www.alcoholics-anonymous.org>, AA membership as of January 1, 1998, was 1,166,000; as of January 1, 1999, it was 1,167,000; and as of January 2000, it was 1,161,000. **33.** *The treatment episode data set (TEDS): 1992–1997 national admissions to substance abuse treatment services.* Rockville, MD: Substance Abuse and Mental Health Services Administration, 1999, p 67, Table 3.4. **34.** *National Treatment Center summary report, op cit.*, p 24. **35.** For a discussion of the percentage of coerced clients in 12-step treatment, see *Resisting 12-Step Coercion*, *op cit.*, pp 28–30. The percentage cited in that work (at least 50 percent) is derived from data gathered and published by the Substance Abuse and Mental Health Services Administration. **36.** Email message to this author from J.A. Johnson, Research Coordinator, Center for Research on Behavioral Health and Health Services Delivery, University of Georgia, November 4, 1998. **37.** Collins, Gregory B, MD. Contemporary issues in the treatment of alcohol dependence. *Psychiatric Clinics of North America*, Vol. 16, No. 1, March 1993, p 35. In the quotation, Collins is paraphrasing G.A. Mann. **38.** *Ibid.* **39.** Note that all three of these are 12-step groups, and that NA and OA borrowed their 12 steps directly from AA, virtually unaltered. **40.** See *Handbook of alcoholism treatment approaches*, *op cit.* See also *Resisting 12-Step coercion*, *op cit.*, and *Alcoholics Anonymous: Cult or cure? (second edition)*, *op cit.* **41.** See *Alcoholics Anonymous: Cult or cure? (second edition)*, Chapter 8, "Suppression of Dissent" subsection, *op cit.*, pp 120–123. See also, Peele, Stanton. (1986). Denial—of reality and freedom—in addiction research and treatment. *Bulletin of the Society of Psychologists in Addictive Behaviors,* Vol. 5, No. 4, 1986, pp 149–166. **42.** To appreciate just how disease-model-, abstinence-, and 12-step-oriented these organizations are, see their Websites: <www.ncadd.org> and <www.asam.org>. The NCADD site, for example, contains a page specifically advocating coercive "interventions," probably the single most invasive practice in the addictions field. **43.** See *Handbook of alcoholism treatment approaches*, *op cit.* See also *Resisting 12-Step coercion*, *op cit.* **44.** Cahalan, Don. (1987). *Understanding America's drinking problem.* San Francisco: Jossey-Bass, p 135. **45.** Dr. Luther Cloud, quoted by Stanton Peele (1986), *op cit.* **46.** An unnamed "director of the community services department of a large labor union" quoted by Cahalan, *op cit.*, p 135. **47.** Kishline, Audrey. (1994). *Moderate drinking: The new option for problem drinkers.* Tucson, Arizona: See Sharp Press, p 6.

Those who had not participated in AA or attended treatment had a *higher* rate of recovery than those who had.

The Unconscious Roots of the Drug War

Excerpts from *Shamanism and the Drug Propaganda: The Birth of Patriarchy and the Drug War*

Dan Russell

Author of *Shamanism and the Drug Propaganda* and *Drug War: Covert Money, Power & Policy* <www.drugwar.com>

The central sacrament of all Paleolithic, Neolithic and Bronze Age cultures known is an inebriative herb, a plant totem, which became metaphoric of the communal epiphany. These herbs, herbal concoctions and herbal metaphors are at the heart of all mythologies. They include such familiar images as the Burning Bush, the Tree of Life, the Cross, the Golden Bough, the Forbidden Fruit, the Blood of Christ, the Blood of Dionysos, the Holy Grail (or rather its contents), the Chalice (*Kalyx*: 'flower cup'), the Golden Flower (*Chrysanthemon*), Ambrosia (*Ambrotos*: 'immortal'), Nectar (*Nektar*: 'overcomes death'), the Sacred Lotus, the Golden Apples, the Mystic Mandrake, the Mystic Rose, the Divine Mushroom (*teonanacatl*), the Divine Water Lily, Soma, Ayahuasca ('Vine of the Soul'), Kava, Iboga, Mama Coca and Peyote Woman.

Inebriation—ritual, social, alimentary and medical—is basic to all cultures, ancient and modern.

They are the archetypal—the emotionally, the instantaneously understood—symbols at the center of the drug propaganda. A sexually attractive man or woman is an archetypal image, the basis of most advertising. A loaf of bread is an archetypal image. The emotional impact of the sacramental herbal images, or, rather, the historical confusion of their natural function, is central to the successful manipulation of mass emotion and individual self-image.

Jung: "An image which frequently appears among the archetypal configurations of the unconscious is that of the tree or the wonder-working plant." When people reproduce these dream images they often take the form of a mandala. Jung calls the mandala "a symbol of the self in cross section," comparing it to the tree, which represents the evolving self, the self as a process of growth.[1]

"Like all archetypal symbols, the symbol of the tree has undergone a development of meaning in the course of the centuries. It is far removed from the original meaning of the shamanistic tree, even though certain basic features prove to be unalterable."[2]

"...it is the decisive factors in the unconscious psyche, the archetypes, which constitute the structure of the collective unconscious. The latter represents a psyche that is identical in all individuals.... The archetypes are formal factors responsible for the organization of unconscious psychic processes: they are 'patterns of behaviour.'"[3]

Those patterns of behavior are rooted in our evolutionary biology as surely as is the shape of our body. Inebriative behavior is an oral behavior, related, physiologically and psychologically, to eating and sex. It is as instinctive in people as socializing or music making. I doubt there is a solvent culture on earth in which breakfast isn't accompanied by a traditional herbal stimulant, or in which some herbal inebriant isn't wildly popular.

Inebriation—ritual, social, alimentary and medical—is basic to all cultures, ancient and modern. Traditional cultures don't separate

I doubt there is a solvent culture on earth in which breakfast isn't accompanied by a traditional herbal stimulant, or in which some herbal inebriant isn't wildly popular.

inebriative herbalism from any of the other 'archaic techniques of ecstacy'—dancing, musicalizing, socializing, ritualizing, fasting, curing, ordeal—which are part of the same shamanic behavior complex; nor do they separate medicine from food.

Rome, the last of the great ancient slave states, institutionalized the conquistador ethos of industrial conformity in Western culture. That ethos translates itself today as irrational fear of the shamanic experience; fear, that is, of the unconscious itself and of primitivity in general.

We don't escape the thrall of our dreams. The *psychology* of contemporary politics, 'history,' moves much more slowly than technology, which is a mechanical, not a biological process. We will cease to live in the world of the ancients only when sex, birth, hunger and death become different for us than they were for them. Our dream language, our spectacular automatic creativity, is, of course, archetypal imagery, the evolutionarily-determined picture-language that is the same for all peoples, regardless of culture, just as the human body and emotions are the same.

The artistic level achieved by many Neolithic cultures is extraordinary. The graphite- and gold-painted pottery produced by the Karanovo civilization of central Bulgaria in 4700 BC proves the existence of very sophisticated firing techniques. The Karanovo and Cucuteni cultures traded copper and gold artifacts and precious stones as well as their extraordinary pottery with each other. The largest Cucuteni town in western Ukraine, dating to about 3700 BC, contained 2,000 houses, about 16,000 people.

We will cease to live in the world of the ancients only when sex, birth, hunger and death become different for us than they were for them.

Ceramic workshops were found there in two-story buildings, the top floors of which were apparently temples. The many clay temple models recovered show only women producing pottery in the downstairs temple workshops. Cucuteni pottery, employing the wheel, rivals anything the world produced for the next thousand years. Wheeled vehicles are depicted in both Cucuteni and Karanovo layers from about 4500 BC. A basic element of Cucuteni pottery design was the caduceus, or at least two s-shaped snakes creating an 'energy field,' drawn as floating lines, where their heads met.[4]

The snake, archetypal symbol of earthly regeneration and herbal healing, was a major motif of Neolithic art, both sacred and secular. An 8,000-year-old cult vessel from Yugoslavia has two bird-headed snakes guarding the contents of a ritual bowl.[5] A 6,500-year-old vase from Romania shows snakes encircling the concentric circles of the world, "making the world roll" as Gimbutas says.

Horned snakes, or horned animals in association with snakes, or bird-headed Goddesses wrapped in snakes, or Goddesses with snakes for hair, or schematic snakes, are reproduced on sacred drinking vessels, shrine Goddesses and pottery more frequently than any other imagery, from the Ukraine to Crete, from 8000 to 1500 BC. "The pregnant figurines of the seventh and sixth millennia BC are nude, while the pregnant ladies of the fifth and fourth millennia are exquisitely clothed except for the abdomen, which is exposed and on which lies a sacred snake."[6] At right, a sacramental vase from late Neolithic Greece.

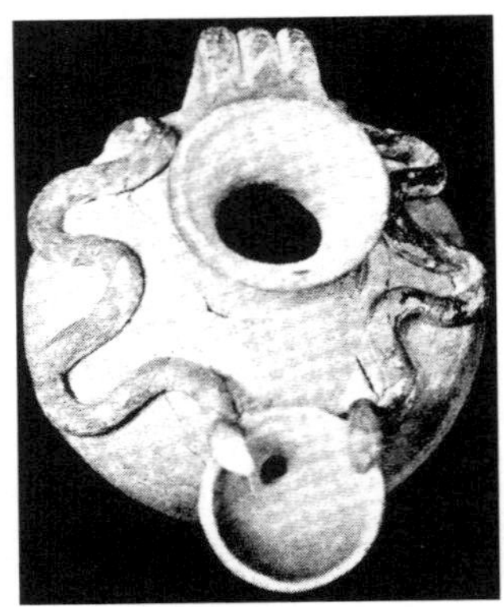

Female Neolithic images, many with the head of a snake or bird, outnumber male images thirty to one.[7] Like the bison-men of the Upper Paleolithic caves, the male god's principal Neolithic manifestation was in the form of a bull or bull-man, the Son of His Mother. The Snake-Bird Goddess, a figure of cthonic transformation and ecstatic resurrection, was the original Creatrix.

Evans: "The Gournia...relics dedicated to the snake cult are associated with small clay figures of doves and a relief showing the Double Axe. These conjunctions are singularly illuminating since they reveal the fact that the Snake Goddess herself represents only another aspect of the Minoan Lady of the Dove, while the Double Axe itself was connected with both. Just as the celestial inspiration descends in bird form either on the image of the divinity itself or on that of its votary...so the spirit of the Nether World, in serpent form, makes its ascent to a similar position from the earth itself."[8] The Double Axe, then, cuts both ways.[9]

Jung: "Archetypes are systems of readiness for action, and at the same time images and emotions. They are inherited with the brain structure—indeed, they are its psychic aspect. They represent, on the one hand, a very strong instinctive conservatism, while on the other hand they are the most effective means conceivable of instinctive adaptation. They are thus, essentially, the cthonic portion of the psyche, if we may use such an expression—that portion through which the psyche is attached to nature, or in which its link with the earth and the world appears at its most tangible. The psychic influence of the earth and its laws is seen most clearly in these primordial images."[10]

Primary among them, the snake, archetypal image of ecstatic creativity and the life force, of herbal magic and evolutionary adaptation, in all Neolithic cultures known. Gimbutas: "The snake is a transfunctional symbol; it permeates all themes of Old European symbolism. Its vital influence was felt not only in life creation, but also in fertility and increase, and particularly in the regeneration of dying life energy. Combined with magical plants, the snake's powers were potent in healing and creating life anew. A vertically winding snake symbolized ascending life force, viewed as a column of life rising from caves and tombs, and was an interchangeable symbol with the tree of life and spinal cord."[11]

The snake, the phallus, the mushroom and the bull, of course, aren't really separable images, as both Neolithic art and contemporary dreams suggest. Gimbutas: "The whole group of interconnected symbols—phallus (or cylinder, mushroom and conical cap), ithyphallic animal-masked man, goat-man and the bull-man—represents a male stimulating principle in nature without whose influence nothing would grow and thrive.... The 'bisexualism' of the water-bird divinity is apparent in the emphasis on the long neck of the bird symbolically linked with the phallus or the snake from Upper Paleolithic times and onwards through many millennia.... The image of a phallic Bird Goddess dominates during the seventh and sixth millennia in the Aegean and the Balkans. Sometimes she is a life-like erect phallus with small wings and a posterior of a woman, which, if seen in profile, is readily identifiable as a bird's body and tail.... 'Bisexualism' is reflected in bird-shaped vases with cylindrical necks and...in representations of hermaphroditic figurines of the Vinca culture having male genital organs and female breasts." (Parenthesis hers.)

"The 'Fertility Goddess' or 'Mother Goddess' is a more complex image than most people think. She was not only the Mother Goddess who commands fertility, or the Lady of the Beasts who governs the fecundity of animals and all wild nature, or the frightening Mother Terrible, but a composite image with traits accumulated from both the pre-agricultural and agricultural eras.... Throughout the Neolithic period her head is phallus-shaped suggesting her androgynous nature, and its derivation from Paleolithic times...divine bisexuality stresses her absolute power."[12]

Marshack reproduces a 20,000-year-old lunar counting bone which is simply a phallic head with two pendulous breasts. A 16,000-year-old lunar counting baton from France is a phallic bone with a vulva. A Goddess figure from Hungary, c.5400 BC, is shaped like a penis and testicles.[13] Just as it was obvious that life came from the womb or egg, so it was obvious that the conjunction of the sexes produced a numinous power. Respect for the power of the Bull was in no way contrary to respect for the Goddess, who bore the Bull.

Many of the magical signs found on Old European pottery from 6000 to 4000 BC are direct descendants of Upper Paleolithic symbols, such as the V sign, used to indicate the Goddess' pubic triangle on 19,000-year-old ivory figurines from the Ukraine. The inverted V sign was used to indicate the cap of sacred mushrooms. Snakes, flowers, eyes, ears, waves, chevrons and x's are equally ancient. These signs evolved into linguistic magical signs, consistently found in all Old European cultures. They include moon-counting lines and circles, triangles, meanders, v's, m's, n's, squares, s's, diamonds, arcs, y's, +'s, tridents, bidents, swastikas, bird's feet, concentric circles, houses and numerous other geometric and schematic patterns.[14]

The 'sacral' ivy-leaf, a standard device of Cretan potters for millennia, became a letter in both Linear A and B.[15] Gimbutas, organizing linguistic work that began with Evans, has graphed 68 Old European signs that can be shown to be identical to either Cretan Linear A or Classical Cypriot syllabic phonemes, the two great island survivals of this Old European, pre-Indo-European, language.[16] This script, which predates the earliest evolved temple-palace script of Old Sumer by 2,000 years, isn't a bureaucratic device designed to manage the tax rolls, as in Sumer, but magical script, produced only on religious items. The Near Eastern scripts, of course, also originated in their predecessor Neolithic communities, thus the evolution is contemporaneous.

The Egyptian name for their hieroglyphs, originally used only for sacral purposes, was 'speech of the gods.'[17] We have 8,000-year-old stamp seals from Macedonia designed to leave their geometric impressions in wet clay, that is, moveable type. We also have Macedonian cylinder seals, designed to be rolled over the wet clay. This script is found only on figurines, thrones, temple models, altars, communion vases, sacred bread models, pendants, plaques and spindle whorls found in temples. Its purpose was to trigger magical communication, automatic speech, not accounting. Spindle whorls were often used as temple ornaments since the Goddess, like the Spider, the Wasp and the Bee, was a weaver of, and carried the sting of, magical plants. At right is a Queen's pendant, Knossos, c.2000 BC.

The Cretan Queens of Knossos were consistently portrayed, for thousands of years, as winged wasps or bee-headed women surrounded by floating eyes and snakes. They were also depicted as bare-breasted shamans, in a flounced skirt, with a flower crown and outstretched arms holding a cobra in each hand.[18] They cast spells. Their flower crowns were sometimes capped by the image of a panther, the premier transformation beast.[19] At left, the image from a Cretan signet seal, worn as a ring by a royal woman.

The throne of the Queen of Knossos was found in its original position against the north wall of the Throne Room. It was flanked by intensely colorful frescoes of huge eagle-headed lions, wingless griffins sprouting peacock plumes to indicate their benevolent character. They are couchant amongst the sacramental papyrus reeds. At their heart, near their lion's shoulder blade, are spiraliform rosettes, symbolic entheogens.[20]

In most ancient cultures, including Mesoamerican and Hellenic, the butterfly represents the soul; a common Greek word for butterfly is *psyche*, soul.[21] Many contemporary Mazatecs and Cretans alike still regard butterflies as the souls of the departed. Some clay seal impressions from Knossos show the dots in the wings of a butterfly actually transformed into floating eyes.[22]

In both cultures the butterfly is equated with the bee. Like the wasp, the power of the bee's sting came from the power of the plants it pollinated. A Mycenaean gem of Minoan workmanship, below, c.1400 BC, pictures a large sacred plant growing from horns of consecration, supported by a chalice. The plant is ceremonially flanked by two lion-headed satyrs in bee skins, that is two shamans, each holding aloft, directly over the plant, a jug of sacramental drink.[23] The bees not only made honey for the honey-beer, but pollinated the magical flowers the mead was spiked with, thus transforming the shamans themselves into buzzing lion-headed bees.

The horse, the tarpan, was first tamed as an engine of war and high-speed travel by fierce nomadic pastoralists from the Ukraine and Kazakhstan about 5300 BC, using antler-tine bridles. Their economy was based on very large horse herds used for milk, meat, hide and sinew, which they didn't hesitate to drive into new territory. Since they relied on conquest, their mobile society was militarized and hierarchical, and their mythology stressed the role of the warrior as Creator. They carried bows and arrows, spears, long daggers and, later, short metal swords.

Since they left barrow or tumulus graves, individual pits covered by a low cairn or mound, *kurgan* in Russian, Gimbutas adopted this as the general name for the various steppe peoples sharing this culture. Kurgan hordes flooded Old Europe in three successive waves, c.4400 BC, c.3500 BC and c.3000 BC. These are the 'Proto-Indo-European' speakers whose language became the basis of the Greek, Celtic, Germanic, Italic, Albanian, Slavic, Armenian, Iranian and Indic language groups.[24]

Kurgan warriors could travel at least five times faster than the sedentary competition, and soon controlled the trade routes over vast areas of Southeastern Europe. For the first time, rich male graves, replete with weapons and horse-head sceptres, appear in Europe, indicating chieftancy and patriarchal organization. Over the centuries Europe's Neolithic villages became socially stratified, with the bulk of the Mediterranean-type population ruled by a warrior-elite of Kurgan, proto-Europid type. Hilltop forts appear, along with a pastoral economy, signs of violence, and patriarchal religious symbols emphasizing the sun. For the first time, throughout the Alpine valleys, Bulgaria, Romania, the Black Sea region and the Caucasus, heavily-armed male gods appear on stone stelae along with their solar symbolism.

By 3500 BC the official solar symbolism replaced the beautifully executed sacred script on Cucuteni pottery. The building of Cucuteni temples, the making of graceful communion vessels and the writing of the Old European script came to an end. Trade in metals and metal weaponry burgeoned. Daggers, shaft-hole axes and flat axes of arsenic bronze are found throughout the Pontic region, along with metal workshops containing clay bivalve molds. Northwest Yugoslavia, southwest Hungary, Slovenia and Slovakia yield an impressive chain of hill forts, where most of the metallurgy took place.[25]

The well-established Neolithic cultures of Old Europe didn't just die out overnight; those that remained unconquered adapted to the new environment. Sacred monarchy, a military institution, was born. As the ecology militarized, the loving Mother-Queen found herself managing constant warfare. She became a Mother-Terrible, a *SHE* Who Must Be Obeyed, as H. Ryder Haggard put it. As the Bull's blood once was, so the Warrior's blood became—the source of life for the tribe. More and more authority devolved to the war shamans, as their responsibility for the survival of the tribe increased. They still ruled by deputizing for the Queen, for the Mother remained the Source of life. It was She, and her Priestesses, who sacrificed the Bull, or the Warrior-Bull, at the solstices.

Since initiation is mock death and resurrection, and since plants became 'plant-man' and bulls became 'bull-man,' the 'sacrifice' would have been symbolic or entheogenic in most cases, since, most often, the Queen and her entourage would be 'killing' the old year and bringing in the new, as in the Bull sacrifice on the Cretan Hagia Triada sarcophagus, c. 1500 BC, below.

Island Crete, however, until the Mycenaean-Dorian age, was militarily secure. Times of terror came to mainland Europe much earlier. And in such times, extreme unction was demanded, one way or the other, of the war shaman, as it was among Paleolithic tribes. The first conception of a 'king' was as the sacrificial servant of the people, the war shaman who would lay down his life. Like the ritual Bull and the *pharmakon* which were traditionally consumed together, the king would sacrifice himself for the common good. The *pharmakos*, the sacrificial king, replaced the *pharmakon* more and more often as competition for the land increased. The Paleolithic Bull became a Warrior sacrificed to an emerging ethos of warfare, to an ecology of territorial competition and functional specialization—to a glorification of servitude and sacrifice that would have been alien to most Neolithic communities, except in extreme circumstances. The evolution, then, was from tribal to theacratic, to theocratic, to militaristic.

The evolution, then, was from tribal to theacratic, to theocratic, to militaristic.

All the great originary city-states of Mesopotamia, China, Mesoamerica, Peru, Africa, India and Europe ended up 'militaristic,' that is, completely absorbed in internecine warfare. Cultural anthropologists classify the stages in the development of early civilizations as Incipient Farming, Formative, Florescent, Theocratic Irrigation-Trade State, and Militaristic State. Although there are regional and sub-regional differences—irrigation, for instance, was less important in some areas than in others—the pattern of creative, matristic, tribal, egalitiarian Neolithic villages enslaved by warrior tribes, or transfixed by internecine warfare, holds throughout. 'Militaristic' is used as a *synonym* for 'historical' by cultural anthropologists. This is not merely a function of the nastiness of those darn men, since increased agricultural efficiency itself produces intense population pressures and competition for resources. The resultant internecine warfare automatically produces the need for an effective defense.

Braidwood and Reed estimate 0.125 people per square mile in Late Paleolithic Iraq, c.10,000 BC.[26] Flannery estimates zero to one person per square kilometre in southwestern Iran, bordering Iraq, in the Late Paleolithic, growing to more than six people after large-scale irrigation appears, c.3000 BC—a sixty-fold increase.[27] Agriculture, then, is a cybernetic engine, creating its own pressure for increased production and territorial expansion. This was the exact opposite of the Neolithic process, which stressed the powerful hearth skills of women. The Bronze Age process stressed the confrontational skills of the warrior.

Furthermore, humans have an inherently carnivorous psychology. Even the tribal Neolithic communities lived by hunting and practicing animal sacrifice, which they uniformly associated with religious epiphany. Animal sacrifice, as the Cretan rite illustrates, was a major function of Neolithic priestesses. Blood was considered nourishing, entheogenic, and the entheogenic or curative sap of plants was regarded as their 'blood.' Wealth-managing bureaucracies, of course, which the Neolithic communities lacked, were careful to generate reasons for acquiring more wealth. In this sense, Early Bronze Age city-states can be seen as military institutions.

Iahu, the Sumerian Exalted Dove, was the daughter of Tiamat, the primeval waters. As the renowned linguist Professor John Allegro, Secretary of the Dead Sea Scrolls Fund and one of the original translators of the Scrolls, teaches, IA, in Sumerian, means 'juice' or 'strong water.' The root idea of U, according to its usage in words like 'copulate,' 'mount,' 'create,' and 'vegetation,' is 'fertility,' thus 'Iahu' means 'juice of fertility.'[28] That is the name of an entheogen, the fruit of 'the menses of Eileithyia.' The Sumerian Goddess was also called Inanna. 'Ishtar,' the Akkadian-Babylonian name, is derived from the Sumerian USh-TAR, 'uterus' in Latin. 'Dove,' *peristera* in Greek, also means 'womb,' as does its Semitic cognate *yonah*, Jonah.

The Akkadian era of Lower Mesopotamia (southern Iraq) was founded by Sargon of Agade or Akkad, c.2360 BC. Bab-ilu, 'the Gate of God,' Hammurabi's capitol city, inherited the political ascendancy about 600 years later. In Hammurabi's Babylon, the Exalted Dove was cut in two by Marduk. "You, Marduk, are the most revered of the awesome gods. Your fiat is unequalled, your dictate is Anu. From this day forward your pronouncements shall be unalterable. Your hands shall have the power to raise up or bring down. Your word shall be prophetic, your command shall be unrivalled. None of the gods shall be above you!"

"Let any downtrodden man with a cause present himself to my statue, for I am the king of justice. Let him read my inscribed words carefully, and ponder their meaning, for these will make his case clear to him, and give peace to his troubled mind! 'He is Hammurabi, the King, a father to all the people. He has heard the word of Marduk, his lord, and thus has guaranteed the prosperity of the people forever, leading the land into righteousness'—let my supplicant proclaim this, praying with his whole heart and soul for me!"[29]

Enuma Elish, 'When on High,' has the unrivalled Marduk creating order out of the corpse of Tiamat, the Primordial Ocean-Woman, specifically called a woman in the myth and portrayed as an enraged shaman, like Hera, creating poisonous monsters for self-protection. Marduk, Tiamat's son, volunteers to rescue the rest of her rebellious progeny from the enraged Goddess: "He looked toward the enraged Tiamat, with a spell on his lips. He carried a magical plant to ward off her poison.... After slaying Tiamat the lord rested, pondering what to do with her dead body. He resolved to undo this abortion by creating ingenious things with it. Like a clam, he split her in two, setting half of her to form the sky as a roof for our earthly house."[30]

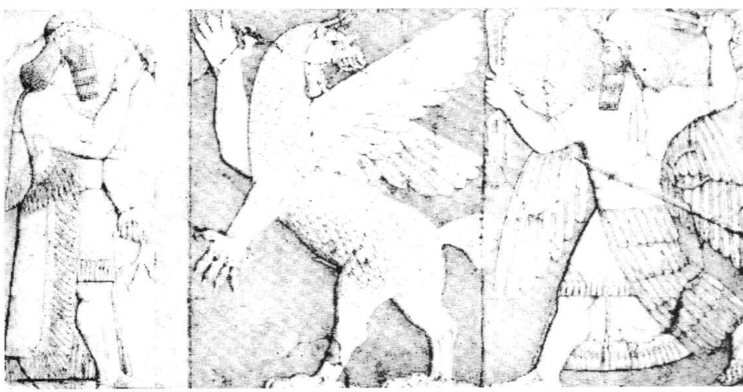

Tiamat, above center, became the *Tehom* of Genesis. 'Firmament' means 'what is spread out,' and is a reference to the body of Tiamat. Marduk is Yahweh to Tiamat's Tehom.[31] Marduk, or his hero Gilgamesh, was craftily portrayed as a winged shaman bringing the herb of immortality from heaven to earth, thus usurping the function of Tiamat's daughter Iahu, the original Yahweh, the Exalted Dove. Gilgamesh brings magical opium poppies to earth on the relief below, from the palace of Ashurnasirpal II, c. 875 BC. Marduk's rite involved ceremoniously cutting a dove in two at the Spring Equinox, an enormously powerful image for a culture that understood the meaning of the dove. Henceforth the wings belonged to Marduk, who proved as useful to Nebuchadnezzar in 600 BC as to Hammurabi in 1700 BC.[32]

Like the Mycenaeans before them, the Dorians, mounted pastoralists, entered the Peloponnese as conquerors. Their three main tribes were divided into 27 phratries, patrilinear brotherhoods, some of the names of which were found at Argos inscribed on water-pipes.[33] The native population of 'Helots' were enslaved as hereditary community property by the pipe-smoking brothers.

Their military hierarchy tolerated no social dissent. By 800 BC Sparta controlled all Laconia, and, along with Argos, Corinth and Megara, all the Peloponnese except the mountains of Arcadia. Attica went through the same process of military consolidation under the Ionians, as did the northern regions under the Aeolians, Boeotians and Thessalians.

The demand for metal, and slaves to work the mines, played a major role in the founding of overseas trading colonies. Archaic Greek states, 800-500 BC, founded hundreds of colonies throughout Europe and North Africa.[34] The enslavement of the locals was standard colonization procedure. Slaves were at a premium since most children never saw fifteen; rare was the woman who lived past 30 or the man who lived past 40.

The canonical Boeotian Hesiod dated the ages of man by the precious metals mined by the slaves: the original golden race of the orchard garden, whose spirits "roam everywhere over the earth, clothed in mist and keep watch on judgements and cruel deeds, givers of wealth"; the matriarchal silver race destroyed by Zeus for refusing to recognize him; the flesh-eating bronze race "sprung from ash trees...terrible and strong," who destroyed themselves in warfare; the founding fathers of Mycenae and Troy who dwell "untouched by sorrow in the islands of the blessed"; and their descendants of iron, who "never rest from labor and sorrow."[35]

In the *Works and Days*, when Pandora "lifts the great lid of the *pithos*" all the misfortunes of mortality fly out. Hesiod, the official mythologer of the Greek warrior class, thus equates the Mystery of the Spring Resurrection with death itself, as the Israelis did in their complex Passover legend. The winged 'All-giver,' Pandora, originally, on Crete, from whence the festival comes, instigated the rebirth of the world, not its woes.[36]

Life comes from Eleusis, 'the place of happy arrival,' from Delphi, 'the womb,' but to acknowledge that would be to acknowledge the primacy of *Thea*. Not Zeus, or his Only Begotten Son Apollon, nor Elohim or his Only Begotten Son *Moshiy'a*/*Yehoshu'a*/Jesus, but the Saviour Persephone, as she was called, the *Arrhetos Koura*, 'the ineffable maiden,' the Only Begotten Daughter, as she was called, first.

Persephone, the winged Snake Nymph Korykia, was inseparable from her herbal magic. Apollonius: "Thereupon the handmaids were making ready the chariot; and Medea meanwhile took from the hollow casket a charm which men say is called the charm of Prometheus. If a man should anoint his body therewithal, having first appeased the Maiden, the only-begotten, with sacrifice by night, surely that man could not be wounded by the stroke of bronze nor would he flinch from blazing fire; but for that day he would prove superior both in prowess and in might. It shot up first-born when the ravening eagle on the rugged flanks of Caucasus let drip to the earth the blood-like ichor of tortured Prometheus. And its flower appeared a cubit above ground in color like the Korykian crocus, rising on twin

stalks; but in the earth the root was like newly-cut flesh. The dark juice of it, like the sap of a mountain-oak, she had gathered in a Caspian shell to make the charm withal, when she had first bathed in seven ever-flowing streams, and had called seven times on Brimo, nurse of youth, night-wandering Brimo, of the underworld, queen among the dead,—in the gloom of night, clad in dusky garments. And beneath, the dark earth shook and bellowed when the Titanian root was cut; and the son of Iapetos himself groaned, his soul distraught with pain. And she brought the charm forth and placed it in the fragrant band which engirdled her, just beneath her bosom, divinely fair. And going forth she mounted the swift chariot..."[37]

Pandora-Korykia-Persephone is the Greek equivalent of Eve, and is similarly manipulated. Eve is the Hebrew equivalent of Ishtar, whose Babylonian legend is a virtual duplicate of the legend of Persephone, as is the legend of Ishtar's Sumerian mother Inanna or Iahu, dug up at ancient Nippur. Ishtar is smitten in the underworld with 60 diseases, stopping all reproductive life on earth. Ea, the Babylonian Prometheus, extracts a magical flagon from Ereshkigal, the Babylonian Hecate, the water from which enables Ishtar to rise to the surface. Reunited with Tammuz (Dionysos), they perform the sacred rites for the dead, who restore life to the upper world as the two make love.

But shamanic spirituality becomes a threat to slavers bent on conquest.

During 'cups,' through entheogenic and erotic ecstacy, the dead earth was brought back to life. By dancing with the ghosts, ancient Eros, the fructifying power, was reborn. After 'cups' came *Chytroi*, 'pots for the food of the dead'—gifts to encourage the ghosts to return once again to their homes underground.[38]

'Death' was a state that could be visited, one could be 'abducted' to the realm of the dead, hence the sacramental identity of Greek women with Persephone; they regularly *became* Persephone. Explains Ishtar: "On the day when Tammuz comes up to me,/When with him the lapis flute and the carnelian ring come up to me,/When with him the wailing men and the wailing women come up to me,/May the dead rise and smell the incense."[39] (Nippur, c.1800 BC.)

This archetypal imagery is brought to life by pharmaco-shamanic rites in tribal cultures, and those rites are criminalized and coopted by their industrial conquerors.

Eliade: "It certainly seems that the chief function of the dead in the granting of shamanic powers is less a matter of taking 'possession' of the subject than of helping him to become a 'dead man'—in short, of helping him to become a 'spirit' too."[40]

But shamanic spirituality becomes a threat to slavers bent on conquest. Almost every significant government from the Late Bronze Age to the nineteenth century has been a theocratic slave state in which the official rituals of the culture reinforced mass servitude. The sacred fire of the Mother City which the colonists so treasured on their arduous voyage of conquest was meant to replace that of their hosts. "Conquering gods their titles take/From the foes they captive make."

Propaganda works by way of true myth, imagery which instantly affects our emotions. This archetypal imagery is brought to life by pharmaco-shamanic rites in tribal cultures, and those rites are criminalized and coopted by their industrial conquerors. The solar monotheism, the Aten of Akhenaten, served the same purpose as the Apollo of the Delphian powers, or the Juppiter Maximus of Caesar, or the Jesus Invictus of Constantine and Charles V. The Imperial Icon facilitated the efficient management of the conquered by requiring the replacement of their culture with the Imperial syncretism. This cultural genocide effectively turned once independent people into farm animals—*andrapoda*, as the Greeks put it, 'human-footed stock.'

The archetypal matristic imagery remained an organic if diminished part of classical Olympian mythology because the Greeks remained more decentralized than either the Israelis or the Romans. King David organized all the women of royal blood into a royal harem, thus making the 'matrilineal' throne of Israel the exclusive province of the King and his line. This device was adopted in Rome on the founding of the Vestal College, but, because there was no central Greek government, and because the canonical Hesiod, early on, had, as Herodotus put it, "given the deities their titles and distinguished their several provinces and special powers,"[41] absolute theological patriarchy never reached Greece, although Olympian tradition is certainly warrior-based.

As Graves puts it, "The institution of patriarchy ends the period of true myth; historical legend then begins and fades into the light of common history."[42] That is, true myth, the archetypes of consciousness evoking evolutionary, that is behavioral, realities, instinct, the stuff of dreams, is more easily discerned through the fog of Greek legend than Israeli or the much later Roman. As Homer put it, "Two gates for ghostly dreams there are: one gateway/of honest horn, and one of ivory./Issuing by the ivory gate are dreams/of glimmering illusion, fantasies,/but those that come through solid polished horn/may be borne out, if mortals only know them."[43]

Graves says that all true poetry celebrates the thirteen lunar months of the ancient year, the birth, life, death and resurrection of the God of the Waxing year, who is the son, lover and victim of the threefold Goddess, the Muse of all true poets. "Her names and titles are innumerable. In ghost stories she often figures as 'The White Lady,' and in ancient religions, from the British Isles to the Caucasus, as the 'White Goddess.' I cannot think of any true poet, from Homer onwards who has not independently recorded his experience of her. The test of a poet's vision, one might say, is the accuracy of his portrayal of the White Goddess and of the island over which she rules. The reason why the hairs stand on end, the eyes water, the throat is constricted, the skin crawls and a shiver runs down the spine when one writes or reads a true poem is that a true poem is necessarily an invocation of the White Goddess, or Muse, the Mother of All Living, the ancient power of fright and lust—the female spider or the queen-bee whose embrace is death."[44]

Human industry is to the ecosphere what individual consciousness is to the collective unconscious. Just as sensitivity to the ineffable ecosphere must be our teacher if we are to survive the effects of our own technology, so must sensitivity to our own ineffable logosphere, our collective unconscious, be our teacher if we are to survive the politics that technology has generated.

Jung: "Just as the day-star rises out of the nocturnal sea, so, ontogenetically and phylogenetically, consciousness is born of unconsciousness and sinks back every night to this primal condition. This duality of our psychic life is the prototype and archetype of the Sol-Luna symbolism."[45] "Luna is really the mother of the sun, which means, psychologically, that the unconscious is pregnant with consciousness and gives birth to it."[46] "The foundation of consciousness, the psyche *per se*, is unconscious, and its structure, like that of the body, is common to all, its individual features being only insignificant variants."[47]

The loss of connection to the ecstatic processes, the loss of an easy bridge between the conscious and the unconscious, is the beginning of neurosis, the loss of connection to the Holy Mother, the irrational voice of our emotions, the fountainhead of our genius. The last thing Greek slaves needed was genuine inspiration, so, for them, the contents of the Jug became taboo. We have all become Greek slaves. The Mycenaeans, conquerors and transmitters of Cretan culture, were themselves absorbed by the southerly march of the Dorians and Ionians. Their Classical Greek imagery was then transformed by the Romans into the Orthodox Christianity which became the mandatory religion of the late Roman slave states, of all the medieval European slave states, and the theological underpinning of the Euro-American industrial theocracy.

We have all become Greek slaves.

Kannabis, as the Greeks called it, sacred mushrooms, coca leaf, Peyote and the other ancient herbal sacraments are among the most easily accessible doorways to the proprioceptive and oracular available. They are fountainheads of creativity and earth-consciousness industrial culture desperately needs. Without institutionalized, or at least legalized shamanism, a Paleolithic adaptive technique, human political culture risks domination by the suicidally robotic, as our repeated acts of genocide and our virtually institutionalized ecocide tend to indicate. It is the tribal, the mammalian, the creative part of our psyche that is sensitive to our biological relationship to the earth. Is global political culture successfully dealing with the industrial destabilization of the ecosphere? Unmitigated industrial values are a path to evolutionary suicide.

The ancient shamanic bridges need to be rebuilt; the familial tribal cultures need to be listened to very carefully. Humanizing the evolved industrial polity will be every bit as difficult as healing the damaged ecosphere and rendering human industry ecological. "The Teleut shaman calls back the soul of a sick child in these words: 'Come back to your country!...to the yurt, by the bright fire!...Come back to your father...to your mother!...' ...It is only if the soul refuses or is unable to return to its place in the body that the shaman goes to look for it and finally descends to the realm of the dead to bring it back."[48] Hence historiography.

The central sacrament of Incan culture, coca leaf, a medicinal chew and tea leaf, was determined to be *un delusio del demonio* by Pizarro's priests, who proceeded to save Incan souls by working them to death as beasts of burden under the lash.

There is nothing whatever dangerous about whole coca leaves; they are as harmless as orange pekoe tea. Cocaine, which wasn't isolated until 1860, comprises about one-half of 1 percent of the weight of a coca leaf. It takes a ton of coca leaves to make 5 to 20 pounds of cocaine. There are far more dangerous compounds in potatoes, tomatoes, celery and fava beans, all of which are perfectly safe to eat.

Traditional sacramental plant-foods can't be equated with poisons, and poisons can't be equated with naturally-occurring plant isolates. Some plants are poisonous, and some plant isolates are as safe to use as corn. This Drug War is largely the political history of that intentional confusion, a confusion rooted in the *unconscious* contents of our political culture. That is, in the planted axiom that "the drug problem" can be discussed in terms of modern politics.

There is nothing whatever dangerous about whole coca leaves; they are as harmless as orange pekoe tea.

The Drug War can't be separated from the cultural compulsion of our conquistador history. Nor can it be separated from the evolutionary function of inebriative behavior. The industrial process has been as successful in burying conscious knowledge of the archaic techniques of ecstacy as it has been in burying the wolf, and those that understood it. Unconscious knowledge, on the other hand, is a tad more difficult to manipulate, as the neurotic lurching of so many of our public figures demonstrates; "just say no," after all, was promulgated by an alcoholic.

We are no longer overtly racist, in our public laws at least, but we are still brutally anti-tribal, in many ways institutionally unloving, structurally violent, to millions of our children, our tribal primitives, and to our shamanic adults. This is a *psychological* inheritance from our conquistador past, as well as a legal one.

This internalized industrial fascism, this proscription, *causes* drug problems, in the same way that violent sexual puritanism causes sexual problems. The ancient tribal wisdom prevents them. There are many cultures, both tribal and industrial, the Vicosinos of Peru and the Dutch, for instance, that don't have anything like our current disaster, and they all apply prescription rather than proscription.

Endnotes

1. Jung, Carl. (1956). *The collected works, volume 13: Alchemical studies*, p 253. Princeton University Press. **2.** *Ibid.*, p 272 **3.** Jung, Carl. (1956). *The collected works, volume 8: The structure and dynamics of the psyche*, p 436. Princeton University Press. **4.** Gimbutas, Marija. (1982). *The goddesses and gods of old Europe*, p 95. University of California Press. Gimbutas, Marija. (1989). *The language of Goddess*, pp 282, 293. HarperCollins Publishers. **5.** *Op cit.*, Gimbutas (1982), p 101. **6.** *Ibid*, p 201. **7.** *Op cit.*, Gimbutas (1989), p 175. **8.** Evans, Sir Arthur. (1921). *The palace of Minos at Knossos, volume 3*, p 508. Macmillan & Company. **9.** *Ibid.*, p 438-440 **10.** Jung, C. (1956). *The collected works, volume 10: Civilization in transition*, p 31. Princeton University Press. **11.** *Op cit.*, Gimbutas (1989), p 121. **12.** *Op cit.*, Gimbutas (1982), pp 216, 135, 152, 196. **13.** *Op cit.*, Gimbutas (1989), pp 231, M-292 **14.** Gimbutas, Marija. (1991). *The civilization of the Goddess*, p 308. HarperCollins Publishers. **15.** Evans, Sir Arthur. (1921). *The palace of Minos at Knossos, volume 2*, p 284. Macmillan & Company. **16.** *Op cit.*, Gimbutas (1991), p 320. evans, 1-134, 1:2:641 **17.** Hawkes, Jacquetta (1993). *The atlas of early man*, p 62. St. Martin's Press. **18.** Palmer, Leonard R. (1965). *Mycenaeans and Minoans*, plate 14. Alfred A. Knopf. **19.** Evans, Sir Arthur. (1921). *The palace of Minos at Knossos, volume 1*, pp 501-507. *Op cit.*, Evans, Vol 2, p 748. **20.** Evans, Sir Arthur. (1921). *The palace of Minos at Knossos, volume 4*, pp 910ff. *Op cit.*, Palmer, plate 11. **21.** Wasson, R. Gordon, with Stella Kramrisch, Jonathan Ott & Carl A.P. Ruck. (1989). *Persephone's quest*, p 189. Yale University Press. **22.** *Op cit.*, Evans, Vol 2, p 789. **23.** *Op cit.*, Evans, vol 4, p 453. *Op cit.*, Gimbutas (1982), p 184. **24.** Crystal, David. (1987). *The Cambridge encyclopedia of language*, p 299. Cambridge University Press. **25.** *Op cit.*, Gimbutas (1991), pp 352-400. **26.** Struever, Stuart (Ed.). (1971). *Prehistoric agriculture*, p 304. The Natural History Press. **27.** *Ibid.*, p 75 **28.** Allegro, John. (1970). *The sacred mushroom and the cross*, pp 20, 91. Doubleday & Company. **29.** Finegan, Jack. (1959). *Light from the ancient past*, p 59. Princeton University Press. **30.** Pritchard, James B. (Ed.). (1971). *The ancient Near East*, pp 33-35. Princeton University Press. *Op cit.*, Finegan, p 64. **31.** Gordon, Cyrus H. (1965). *The common background of Greek and Hebrew civilization*, p 91. W.W. Norton & Company. **32.** *Op cit.*, Finegan, p 224 **33.** *The Cambridge ancient vistory, vol 3:1: The prehistory of the Balkans, the Middle East, and the Aegean*, p 714. Cambridge University Press. **34.** *The Cambridge ancient history, Vol 3:3: Expansion of the Greek world, eighth to sixth centuries BC*, p 160. Cambridge University Press. **35.** Hesiod. Hugh G. Evelin-White, translator. (1914). *The collected works, the Homeric hymns and Homerica*, pp 110-200. G.P. Putnam's Sons. **36.** *Op cit.*, Palmer, p 137 **37.** Apollonius Rhodius. R.C. Seaton, translator. (1921). *The Argonautica*, p 843. G.P. Putnam's Sons. **38.** Kerenyi, Karl. (1976). *Dionysos*, p 304. Princeton University Press. **39.** *Op cit.*, Pritchard, p 85. *Op cit.*, Gordon, p 90. **40.** Eliade, Mircea. (1974). *Shamanism*, p 85. Princeton University Press. **41.** Herodotus. David Grene, translator. (1987). *The history*, p 53. University of Chicago Press. **42.** Graves, Robert. (1959). *The Greek myths*, p 20. George Braziller, Inc. **43.** Homer. Robert Fitzgerald, translator. (1963). *The odyssey*, p 560. Doubleday & Company. **44.** Graves, Robert. (1959). *The white goddess*, p 11. Vintage Books. **45.** Jung, C. (1956). *The collected works, volume 14: Mysterium coniunctionis*, p 97. Princeton University Press. **46.** *Ibid.*, p 177. **47.** *Op cit.*, Jung, vol 13, p 347. **48.** *Op cit.*, Eliade, p 217.

HOLY ROLLING

The Truth About Jesus

Is He a Myth?

M.M. Mangasarian

Let me now give an idea of the method I propose to follow in the study of this subject [whether Jesus is a myth]. Let us suppose that a student living in the year 3000 desired to make sure that such a man as Abraham Lincoln really lived and did the things attributed to him. How would he go about it?

A man must have a birthplace and a birthday. All the records agree as to where and when Lincoln was born. This is not enough to prove his historicity, but it is an important link in the chain.

Neither the place nor the time of Jesus' birth is known. There has never been any unanimity about this matter. There has been considerable confusion and contradiction about it. It cannot be proved that the twenty-fifth of December is his birthday. A number of other dates were observed by the Christian church at various times as the birthday of Jesus. The Gospels give no date, and appear to be quite uncertain—really ignorant about it. When it is remembered that the Gospels purport to have been written by Jesus' intimate companions, and during the lifetime of his brothers and mother, their silence on this matter becomes significant.

The selection of the twenty-fifth of December as his birthday is not only an arbitrary one, but that date, having been from time immemorial dedicated to the Sun, the inference is that the Son of God and the Sun of heaven enjoying the same birthday, were at one time identical beings. The fact that Jesus' death was accompanied with the darkening of the Sun, and that the date of his resurrection is also associated with the position of the Sun at the time of the vernal equinox, is a further intimation that we have in the story of the birth, death, and resurrection of Jesus, an ancient and nearly universal Sun-myth, instead of verifiable historical events.

We have in the story of the birth, death, and resurrection of Jesus, an ancient and nearly universal Sun-myth, instead of verifiable historical events.

The story of Jesus for three days in the heart of the earth; of Jonah, three days in the belly of a fish; of Hercules, three days in the belly of a whale; and of Little Red Riding Hood, sleeping in the belly of a great black wolf, represent the attempt of primitive man to explain the phenomenon of day and night. The Sun is swallowed by a dragon, a wolf, or a whale, which plunges the world into darkness; but the dragon is killed, and the Sun rises triumphant to make another day. This ancient Sun myth is the starting point of nearly all miraculous religions, from the days of Egypt to the twentieth century.

The story which Matthew relates about a remarkable star, which sailing in the air pointed out to some unnamed magicians the cradle or cave in which the wonder-child was born, helps further to identify Jesus with the Sun. What became of this "performing" star, or of the magicians and their costly gifts, the records do not say. It is more likely that it was the astrological predilections of the Gospel writer which led him to assign to his God-child a star in the heavens. The belief that the stars determine human destinies is a very ancient one.... The prominence, therefore, of the Sun and stars in the Gospel story tends to show that Jesus is an astrological rather than an historical character.

That the time of his birth, his death, and supposed resurrection is not verifiable is generally admitted. This uncertainty robs the story of Jesus, to an extent at least, of the atmosphere of reality....

Of course, it is immaterial on which day Jesus was born, but why is it not known? Yet not only is the date of his birth a matter of conjecture, but also the year in which he was born. Matthew, one of the Evangelists, suggests that Jesus was born in King Herod's time, for it was this king who, hearing from the Magi that a King of the Jews was born, decided to destroy him; but Luke, another Evangelist, intimates that Jesus was born when Quirinus was ruler of Judea, which makes the date of Jesus' birth about fourteen years later than the date given by Matthew. Why this discrepancy in an historical document, to say nothing about inspiration? The theologian might say that this little difficulty was introduced purposely into the scriptures to establish its infallibility, but it is only religious books that are pronounced infallible on the strength of the contradictions they contain.

Again, Matthew says that to escape the evil designs of Herod, Mary and Joseph, with the infant Jesus, fled into Egypt; Luke says nothing about this hurried flight, nor of Herod's intention to kill the infant Messiah. On the contrary, he tells us that after the 40 days of purification were over, Jesus was publicly presented at the temple, where Herod, if he really, as Matthew relates, wished to seize him, could have done so without difficulty. It is impossible to reconcile the flight to Egypt with the presentation in the temple, and this inconsistency is certainly insurmountable and makes it look as if the narrative had no value whatever as history.

"Good Friday" falls not before the spring equinox, but as soon after the spring equinox as the full moon allows, thus making the calculation depend upon the position of the Sun in the Zodiac and the phases of the moon.

When we come to the more important chapters about Jesus, we meet with greater difficulties. Have you ever noticed that the day on which Jesus is supposed to have died falls invariably on a Friday? What is the reason for this? It is evident that nobody knows, and nobody ever knew, the date on which the Crucifixion took place, if it ever took place. It is so obscure and so mythical that an artificial day has been fixed by the Ecclesiastical councils. While it is always on a Friday that the Crucifixion is commemorated, the week in which the day occurs varies from year to year. "Good Friday" falls not before the spring equinox, but as soon after the spring equinox as the full moon allows, thus making the calculation depend upon the position of the Sun in the Zodiac and the phases of the moon. But that was precisely the way the day for the festival of the Pagan goddess Oestera was determined. The Pagan Oestera has become the Christian Easter. Does not this fact, as well as those already touched upon, make the story of Jesus read very much like the stories of the Pagan deities?

The early Christians, Origen, for instance, in his reply to the rationalist Celsus who questioned the reality of Jesus, instead of producing evidence of a historical nature, appealed to the mythology of the Pagans to prove that the story of Jesus was no more incredible than those of the Greek and Roman gods. This is so important that we refer our readers to Origen's own words on the subject. "Before replying to Celsus, it is necessary to admit that in the matter of history, however true it might be," writes this Christian Father, "it is often very difficult and sometimes quite impossible to establish its truth by evidence which shall be considered sufficient." This is a plain admission that, as early as the second and third centuries, the claims put forth about Jesus did not admit of positive historical demonstration. But in the absence of evidence Origen offers the following metaphysical arguments against the skeptical Celsus: 1. Such stories as are told of Jesus are admitted to be true when told of Pagan divinities; why can they not also be true when told of the Christian Messiah? 2. They must be true because they are the fulfillment of Old Testament prophecies. In other words, the only proofs Origen can bring forth against the rationalistic criticism of Celsus is that to deny Jesus would be equivalent to denying both the Pagan and Jewish mythologies. If Jesus is not real, says Origen, then Apollo was not real, and the Old Testament prophecies have not been fulfilled. If we are to have any mythology at all, he seems to argue, why object to adding to it the myths of Jesus? There could not be a more damaging admission than this from one of the most conspicuous defenders of Jesus' story against early criticism.

There could not be a more damaging admission than this from one of the most conspicuous defenders of Jesus' story against early criticism.

Justin Martyr, another early Father, offers the following argument against unbelievers in the Christian legend: "When we say also that the Word, which is the first birth of God, was produced without sexual union, and that he, Jesus Christ, our teacher, was crucified, died, and rose again, and ascended into heaven, we propound nothing different from what you believe regarding those whom you esteem sons of Jupiter." Which is another way of saying that the Christian myths are very similar to the Pagan, and should therefore be equally true. Pressing his argument further, this interesting Father discovers many resemblances between what he himself is preaching and the Pagans have always believed: "For you know how many sons your esteemed writers ascribe to Jupiter. Mercury, the interpreting word and teacher of all; Aesculapius...to heaven; one Hercules...and Perseus;...and Bellerophon, who, from mortals, rose to heaven on the horses of Pegasus." If Jupiter can have, Justin Martyr seems to reason, half a dozen divine sons, why cannot Jehovah have at least one?

Instead of producing historical evidence or appealing to creditable documents, as one would to prove the existence of a Caesar or an Alexander, Justin Martyr draws upon Pagan mythology in his reply to the critics of Christianity. All he seems to ask for is that Jesus be given a higher place among the divinities of the ancient world.

To help their cause the Christian apologists not infrequently also changed the sense of certain Old Testament passages to make them support the miraculous stories in the New Testament. For example, having borrowed from Oriental books the story of the god in a manger, surrounded by staring animals, the Christian fathers introduced a prediction of this event into the following text from the book of Habakkuk in the Bible: "Accomplish thy work in the midst of the years, in the midst of the years make known, etc." (Hebrews iii, 2). This Old Testament text appeared in the Greek translation as follows: "Thou shalt manifest thyself in the midst of two animals," which was fulfilled, of course, when Jesus was born in a stable. How weak must be one's case to resort to such tactics in order to command a following! And when it is remembered that these follies were deemed necessary to prove the reality of what has been claimed as the most stupendous event in all history, one can readily see upon how fragile a foundation is built the story of the Christian God-man.

Who were John, Peter, Judas, and Mary? There is absolutely no evidence that they ever existed.

Let us continue: Abraham Lincoln's associates and contemporaries are all known to history. The immediate companions of Jesus appear to be, on the other hand, as mythical as he is himself. Who was Matthew? Who was Mark? Who were John, Peter, Judas, and Mary? There is absolutely no evidence that they ever existed. They are not mentioned except in the New Testament books, which, as we shall see, are "supposed" copies of "supposed" originals. If Peter ever went to Rome with a new doctrine, how is it that no historian has taken note of him? If Paul visited Athens and preached from Mars Hill, how is it that there is no mention of him or of his strange Gospel in the Athenian chronicles? For all we know, both Peter and Paul may have really existed, but it is only a guess, as we have no means of ascertaining. The uncertainty about the apostles of Jesus is quite in keeping with the uncertainty about Jesus himself.

The report that Jesus had twelve apostles seems also mythical. The number twelve, like the number seven, or three, or 40, plays an important role in all Sun-myths, and points to the twelve signs of the Zodiac. Jacob had twelve sons; there were twelve tribes of Israel; twelve months in the year; twelve gates or pillars of heaven, etc. In many of the religions of the world, the number twelve is sacred. There have been few god-saviors who did not have twelve apostles or messengers....

That the "Twelve Apostles" are fanciful may be inferred from the obscurity in which the greater number of them have remained. Peter, Paul, John, James, Judas, occupy the stage almost exclusively. If Paul was an apostle, we have fourteen, instead of twelve. Leaving out Judas, and counting Matthias, who was elected in his place, we have thirteen apostles.

It is impossible to explain why the contemporaries of Jesus, the authors and historians of his time, do not take notice of him.

The number 40 figures also in many primitive myths. The Jews were in the wilderness for 40 years; Jesus fasted for 40 days; from the resurrection to the ascension were 40 days; Moses was on the mountain with God for 40 days. An account in which such scrupulous attention is shown to supposed sacred numbers is apt to be more artificial than real. The biographers of Lincoln or of Socrates do not seem to be interested in numbers. They write history, not stories.

Again, many of the contemporaries of Lincoln bear written witness to his existence. The historians of the time, the statesmen, the publicists, the chroniclers—all seem to be acquainted with him or to have heard of him. It is impossible to explain why the contemporaries of Jesus, the authors and historians of his time, do not take notice of him. If Abraham Lincoln was important enough to have attracted the attention of his contemporaries, how much more Jesus. Is it reasonable to suppose that these Pagan and Jewish writers knew of Jesus, had heard of his incomparably great works and sayings, but omitted to give him a page or a line? Could they have been in a conspiracy against him? How else is this unanimous silence to be accounted for? Is it not more likely that the wonder-working Jesus was unknown to them? And he was unknown to them because no such Jesus existed in their day....

▪ ▪ ▪ ▪ ▪ ▪ ▪ ▪ ▪ ▪ ▪

The following admissions by Christian writers themselves show the helplessness of the early preachers in the presence of inquirers who asked for proofs. The church historian, Mosheim, writes that, "The Christian Fathers deemed it a pious act to employ deception and fraud." Again, he says: "The greatest and most pious teachers were nearly all of them infected with this leprosy." Will not some believer tell us why forgery and fraud were necessary to prove the historicity of Jesus?

Another historian, Milman, writes that, "Pious fraud was admitted and avowed" by the early missionaries of Jesus. "It was an age of literary frauds," writes Bishop Ellicott, speaking of the times immediately following the alleged crucifixion of Jesus. Dr. Giles declares that, "There can be no doubt that great numbers of books were written with no other purpose than to deceive." And it is the opinion of Dr. Robertson Smith that, "There was an enormous floating mass of spurious literature created to suit party views." Books which are now rejected as apocryphal were at one time received as inspired, and books which are now believed to be infallible were at one time regarded as of no authority in the Christian world. It certainly is puzzling that there should be a whole literature of fraud and forgery in the name of an historical person. But if Jesus was a myth, we can easily explain the legends and traditions springing up in his name.

The early followers of Jesus, then, realizing the force of this objection, did actually resort to interpolation and forgery in order to prove that Jesus was an historical character.

One of the oldest critics of the Christian religion was a Pagan, known to history under the name of Porphyry; yet, the early Fathers did not hesitate to tamper even with the writings of an avowed opponent of their religion. After issuing an edict to destroy, among others, the writings of this philosopher, a work, called *Philosophy of Oracles*, was produced, in which the author is made to write almost as a Christian; and the name of Porphyry was signed to it as its author. St. Augustine was one of the first to reject it as a forgery. A more astounding invention than this alleged work of a heathen bearing witness to Christ is difficult to produce. Do these forgeries, these apocryphal writings, these interpolations, freely admitted to have been the prevailing practice of the early Christians, help to prove the existence of Jesus? And when to this wholesale manufacture of doubtful evidence is added the terrible vandalism which nearly destroyed every great Pagan classic, we can form an idea of the desperate means to which the early Christians resorted to prove that Jesus was not a myth. It all goes to show how difficult it is to make a man out of a myth.

Books which are now rejected as apocryphal were at one time received as inspired, and books which are now believed to be infallible were at one time regarded as of no authority in the Christian world.

■ ■ ■ ■ ■ ■ ■ ■ ■ ■ ■

Stories of gods born of virgins are to be found in nearly every age and country. There have been many virgin mothers, and Mary with her child is but a recent version of a very old and universal myth. In China and India, in Babylonia and Egypt, in Greece and Rome, "divine" beings selected from among the daughters of men, the purest and most beautiful to serve them as a means of entrance into the world of mortals. Wishing to take upon themselves the human form, while retaining at the same time their "divinity," this compromise—of an earthly mother with a "divine" father—was effected. In the form of a swan Jupiter approached Leda, as in the guise of a dove, or a Paracletug, Jehovah "overshadowed" Mary.

A nymph bathing in a river in China is touched by a lotus plant, and the divine Fohi is born. In Siam, a wandering sunbeam caresses a girl in her teens, and the great and wonderful deliverer, Codom, is born. In the life of Buddha we read that he descended on his mother Maya, "in likeness as the heavenly queen, and entered her womb," and was born from her right side, to save the world. In Greece, the young god Apollo visits a fair maid of Athens, and a Plato is ushered into the world.

There have been many virgin mothers, and Mary with her child is but a recent version of a very old and universal myth.

In ancient Mexico, as well as in Babylonia, and in modern Korea, as in modern Palestine, as in the legends of all lands, virgins gave birth and became divine mothers. But the real home of virgin births is the land of the Nile. Eighteen hundred years before Christ, we find carved on one of the walls of the great temple of Luxor a picture of the annunciation, conception, and birth of King Amunothph III, an almost exact copy of the annunciation, conception, and birth of the Christian God....

Not only the idea of a virgin mother, but all the other miraculous events, such as the stable cradle, the guiding star, the massacre of the children, the flight to Egypt, and the resurrection and bodily ascension toward the clouds, have not only been borrowed, but are even scarcely altered in the New Testament story of Jesus....

Nearly every one of the dogmas and ceremonies in the Christian cult were borrowed from other and older religions. The resurrection myth, the ascension, the eucharist, baptism, worship by kneeling or prostration, the folding of the hands on the breast, the ringing of bells and the burning of incense, the vestments and vessels used in church, the candles, "holy" water, even the word "Mass," were all adopted and adapted by the Christians from the religions of the ancients. The Trinity is as much Pagan, as much Indian or Buddhist, as it is Christian. The idea of a Son of God is as old as the oldest cult. The Sun is the son of heaven in all primitive faiths. The physical Sun becomes in the course of evolution, the Son of Righteousness, or the Son of God, and heaven is personified as the Father on High. The halo around the head of Jesus, the horns of the older deities, the rays of light radiating from the heads of Hindu and Pagan gods are incontrovertible evidence that all gods were at one time—the Sun in heaven.

■ ■ ■ ■ ■ ■ ■ ■ ■ ■ ■

Only the uninformed, of whom, we regret to say, there are a great many, and who are the main support of the old religions, still believe that the cross originated with Christianity. Like the dogmas of the Trinity, the virgin birth, and the resurrection, the sign of the cross or the cross as an emblem or a symbol was borrowed from the more ancient faiths of Asia. Perhaps one of the most important discoveries which primitive man felt obliged never to be ungrateful enough to forget, was the production of fire by the friction of two sticks placed across each other in the form of a cross. As early as the Stone Age we find the cross carved on monuments which have been dug out of the earth and which can be seen in the museums of Europe. On the coins of later generations as well as on the altars of prehistoric times we find the "sacred" symbol of the cross. The dead in ancient cemeteries slept under the cross as they do in our day in Catholic churchyards.

In ancient Egypt, as in modern China, India, Korea, the cross is venerated by the masses as a charm of great power. In the Musee Guimet, in Paris, we have seen specimens of pre-Christian crosses. In the Louvre Museum one of the "heathen" gods carries a cross on his head. During his second journey to New Zealand, Cook was surprised to find the natives marking the graves of their dead with the cross. We saw, in the Museum of St. Germain, an ancient divinity of Gaul, before the conquest of the country by Julius Caesar, wearing a garment on which was woven a cross. In the same museum an ancient altar of Gaul under Paganism had a cross carved upon it.

Let it be further noted that it was not until 800 years after the supposed crucifixion that Jesus is seen in the form of a human being on the cross.

That the cross was not adopted by the followers of Jesus until a later date may be inferred from the silence of the earlier disciples, Matthew, Mark, and Luke, on the details of the crucifixion, which is more fully developed in the later Gospel of John. The first three evangelists say nothing about the nails or the blood, and give the impression that he was hanged. Writing of the two thieves who were sentenced to receive the same punishment, Luke says, "One of the malefactors that was hanged with him." The idea of a bleeding Christ, such as we see on crosses in Catholic churches, is not present in these earlier descriptions of the crucifixion; the Christians of the time of Origen were called "the followers of the god who was hanged." In the fourth Gospel we see the beginnings of the legend of the cross, of Jesus carrying or falling under the weight of the cross, of the nail prints in his hands and feet, of the spear drawing the blood from his side and smearing his body. Of all this, the first three Evangelists are quite ignorant.

Let it be further noted that it was not until 800 years after the supposed crucifixion that Jesus is seen in the form of a human being on the cross. Not in any of the paintings on the ancient catacombs is found a crucified Christ. The earliest cross bearing a human being is of the eighth century. For a long time a lamb with a cross, or on a cross, was the Christian symbol, and it is a lamb which we see entombed in the "holy sepulchre." In more than one mosaic of early Christian times, it is not Jesus, but a lamb, which is bleeding for the salvation of the world....

■ ■ ■ ■ ■ ■ ■ ■ ■ ■ ■

In all historical matters, we cannot ask for more than a reasonable assurance concerning any question. In fact, absolute certainty in any branch of human knowledge, with the exception of mathematics, perhaps, is impossible. We are finite beings, limited in all our powers, and, hence, our conclusions are not only relative, but they should ever be held subject to correction. When our law courts send a man to the gallows, they can have no more than a reasonable assurance that he is guilty; when they acquit him, they can have no more than a reasonable assurance that he is innocent. Positive assurance is unattainable. The dogmatist is the only one who claims to possess absolute certainty. But his claim is no more than a groundless assumption. When, therefore, we learn that Josephus, for instance, who lived in the same country and about the same time as Jesus, and wrote an extensive history of the men and events of his day and country, does not mention Jesus, except by interpolation, which even a Christian clergyman, Bishop Warburton, calls "a rank forgery, and a very stupid one, too," we can be reasonably sure that no such Jesus as is described in the New Testament, lived about the same time and in the same country with Josephus. The failure of such an historian as Josephus to mention Jesus tends to make the existence of Jesus at least reasonably doubtful.

Few Christians now place any reliance upon the evidence from Josephus. The early Fathers made this Jew admit that Jesus was the Son of God. Of course, the admission was a forgery. De Quincey says the passage is known to be "a forgery by all men not lunatics." Of one other supposed reference in Josephus, Canon Farrar says: "This passage was early tampered with by the Christians." The same writer says this of a third passage: "Respecting the third passage in Josephus, the only question is whether it be partly or entirely spurious." Lardner, the great English theologian, was the first man to prove that Josephus was a poor witness for Christ.

In examining the evidence from profane writers we must remember that the silence of one contemporary author is more important than the supposed testimony of another. There was living in the same time with Jesus a great Jewish scholar by the name of Philo. He was an Alexandrian Jew, and he visited Jerusalem while Jesus was teaching and working miracles in the holy city. Yet Philo in all his works never once mentions Jesus. He does not seem to have heard of him. He could not have helped mentioning him if he had really seen him or heard of him. In one place in his works Philo is describing the difference between two Jewish names, Hosea and Jesus. "Jesus" he says, means Savior of the people. What a fine opportunity for him to have said that, at that very time, there was living in Jerusalem a savior by the name of Jesus, or one supposed to be, or claiming to be, a savior. He could not have helped mentioning Jesus if he had ever seen or heard of him....

■ ■ ■ ■ ■ ■ ■ ■ ■ ■ ■

We pass on now to the presentation of evidence which we venture to think demonstrates with an almost mathematic precision, that the Jesus of the four Gospels is a legendary hero, as unhistorical as William Tell of Switzerland. This evidence is furnished by the epistles bearing the signature of Paul. He has been accepted as not only the greatest apostle of Christianity, but in a sense also the author of its theology. It is generally admitted that the epistles bearing the name of Paul are among the oldest apostolical writings. They are older than the Gospels. This is very important information. When Paul was preaching, the four Gospels had not yet been written. From the epistles of Paul, of which there are about thirteen in the Bible—making the New Testament largely the work of this one apostle—we learn that there were in different parts of Asia, a number of Christian churches already established. Not only Paul, then, but also the Christian church was in existence before the Gospels were composed. It would be natural to infer that it was not the Gospels which created the church, but the church which produced the Gospels. Do not lose sight of the fact that when Paul was preaching to the Christians there was no written biography of Jesus in existence. There was a church without a book.

In comparing the Jesus of Paul with the Jesus whose portrait is drawn for us in the Gospels, we find that they are not the same persons at all. This is decisive. Paul knows nothing about a miraculously born savior. He does not mention a single time, in all his thirteen epistles, that Jesus was born of a virgin, or that his birth was accompanied with heavenly signs and wonders. He knew nothing of a Jesus born after the manner of the Gospel writers. It is not imaginable that he knew the facts, but suppressed them, or that he considered them unimportant, or that he forgot to refer to them in any of his public utterances. Today, a preacher is expelled from his denomination if he suppresses or ignores the miraculous conception of the Son of God; but Paul was guilty of that very heresy. How to explain it? It is quite simple: The virgin-born Jesus was not yet invented when Paul was preaching Christianity. Neither he, nor the churches he had organized, had ever heard of such a person. The virgin-born Jesus was of later origin than the apostle Paul.

Let the meaning of this discrepancy between the Jesus of Paul, that is to say, the earliest portrait of Jesus, and the Jesus of the four evangelists, be fully grasped by the student, and it should prove beyond a doubt that in Paul's time the story of Jesus' birth from the virgin-mother and the Holy Ghost, which has since become a cardinal dogma of the Christian church, was not yet in circulation. Jesus had not yet been Hellenized; he was still a Jewish Messiah whose coming was foretold in the Old Testament, and who was to be a prophet like unto Moses, without the remotest suggestion of a supernatural origin. No proposition in Euclid is safer from contradiction than that, if Paul knew what the Gospels tell about Jesus, he would have, at least once or twice during his long ministry, given evidence of his knowledge of it. The conclusion is inevitable that the Gospel Jesus is later than Paul and his churches. Paul stood nearest to the time of Jesus of those whose writings are supposed to have come down to us; he is the most representative, and his epistles are the first literature of the new religion. And yet there is absolutely not a single hint or suggestion in them of such a Jesus as is depicted in the Gospels. The Gospel Jesus was not yet put together or compiled when Paul was preaching.

Once more, if we peruse carefully and critically the writings of Paul, the earliest and greatest Christian apostle and missionary, we find that he is not only ignorant of the Gospel stories about the birth and miracles of Jesus, but he is equally and just as innocently ignorant of the teachings of Jesus. In the Gospels Jesus is the author of the Sermon on the Mount, the Lord's Prayer, the Parable of the Prodigal Son, the Story of Dives, the Good Samaritan, etc. Is it conceivable that a preacher of Jesus could go throughout the world to convert people to the teachings of Jesus, as Paul did, without ever quoting a single one of his sayings? Had Paul known that Jesus had preached a sermon, or formulated a prayer, or said many inspired things about the here and the hereafter, he could not have helped quoting, now and then, from the words of his master. If Christianity could have been established without a knowledge of the teachings of Jesus, why then, did Jesus come to teach, and why were his teachings preserved by divine inspiration? But if a knowledge of these teachings of Jesus is indispensable to making converts, Paul gives not the least evidence that he possessed such knowledge.

But the apostle Paul, judging from his many epistles to the earliest converts to Christianity which are really his testimony, supposed to have been sealed by his blood, appears to be quite as ignorant of a Jesus who went about working miracles—opening the eyes of the blind, giving health to the sick, hearing to the deaf, and life to the dead—as he is of a Jesus born of a virgin woman and the Holy Ghost. Is not this remarkable? Does it not lend strong confirmation to the idea that the miracle-working Jesus of the Gospels was not known in Paul's time, that is to say, the earliest Jesus known to the churches was a person altogether different from his namesake in the four Evangelists? If Paul knew of a miracle-working Jesus, one who could feed the multitude with a few loaves and fishes—who could command the grave to open, who could cast out devils, and cleanse the land of the foulest disease of leprosy, who could, and did, perform many other wonderful works to convince the unbelieving generation of his divinity—is it conceivable that either intentionally or inadvertently he would have never once referred to them in all his preaching?

What would we say of a disciple of Tolstoy, for example, who came to America to make converts to Count Tolstoy and never once quoted anything that Tolstoy had said? Or what would we think of the Christian missionaries who go to India, China, Japan, and Africa to preach the Gospel, if they never mentioned to the people of these countries the Sermon on the Mount, the Parable of the Prodigal Son, the Lord's Prayer—nor quoted a single text from the Gospels? Yet Paul, the first missionary, did the very thing which would be inexplicable in a modern missionary. There is only one rational explanation for this: The Jesus of Paul was not born of a virgin; he did not work miracles; and he was not a teacher. It was after his day that such a Jesus was—I have to use again a strong word—invented.

The Bible Code

Scientific, Statistical Proof of God? Or Just Another Lie?

David Thomas

We've all seen the tabloid headlines...for example, "Code in Bible Predicts Date of Christ's Return," or, "Bible Predicts Killer Storms This Winter." But there is, in fact, a serious effort by several mathematicians and scientists to show that the Bible actually *does* contain a hidden code which can be substantiated with advanced statistical methods. Code proponents point with pride to an article by Doron Witztum, Eliyahu Rips, and Yoav Rosenberg of Hebrew University in Israel, entitled "Equidistant Letter Sequences in the Book of Genesis." This article was published in the respected journal *Statistical Science* in 1994, and is claimed to provide compelling proof that details of modern people and events are indeed encoded in the ancient symbols of the Torah. A key claim of the code proponents is that, using the exact same methods, the secret codes found in the Bible can *not* be found in mundane texts such as Tolstoy's *War and Peace*.

However, there is a problem with the Bible code claims—they are lies.

In the Beginning

The Bible code has been under development in various forms for a few decades. It didn't really attract serious attention until Witztum and Rips' 1994 paper. In June 1997, a sensational book entitled *The Bible Code*, by journalist and Howard Hughes biographer Michael Drosnin, appeared. It occupied the bestseller lists for months and was enthusiastically pumped on the talk-show circuit. Drosnin appeared on the Oprah Winfrey show in June, and his Bible code prediction of a possible Californian earthquake in 2008 was enough to prompt host Oprah to swear she would move away from California before then.

Drosnin's technique is heavily based on that of the Israeli mathematicians Witztum and Rips (Rosenberg did the computer programming for the work). Like them, Drosnin arranges the 304,805 Hebrew letters of the Bible into a large array. Spaces and punctuation marks are omitted, and words are run together one after another. A computer looks for matches to selected names or words by stepping to every nth letter in the array. One can go forward or backward; and for each value of "step distance," ***n***, there are ***n*** different starting letters. Drosnin's "assassination prediction" match for "Yitzhak Rabin" had a step value ***n*** equal to 4,772. In other words, there were *4,771* letters between each letter in Rabin's name.

Both Rips and Drosnin work with the original Hebrew characters, which are said to have been given by God to Moses one character at a time, with no spaces or punctuation, just as they appear in "the code." The code is considered to exist *only* in the Hebrew Bible, not in translations or any other books. The code concept, however, can be easily demonstrated with English characters. Consider the following single verse from the King James Version (KJV) of the Book of Genesis:

31:28 And hast not suffered me to kiss my sons and my daughters? thou hast now done foolishly in so doing.

If you start at the R in "daughters," and skip over three letters to the O in "thou," and three more to the S in "hast," and so on, the hidden message "Roswell" is revealed! This message has a step value of four, as shown below.

daughte**R**sth**O**uha**S**tno**W**don**E**foo**L**ish**L**yinsodoing.

Once a name or word match is located for a given step value ***n***, a common practice is to rearrange the letters into a huge matrix (which Drosnin calls a "crossword puzzle"). The matrix is typically ***n*** letters wide, and inside this puzzle, the letters for the "hidden message" line up together vertically. (Sometimes, a slightly different value of ***n*** is used to make the hidden word run diagonally, every other row, and so forth.) The analyst or the computer can then look for more keyword-related "hits" around the given hidden word. Secondary matches can be picked off vertically, horizontally, or diagonally. Drosnin found the word "Dallas" (connected with keywords "President Kennedy") in one of his puzzles by starting at a D, and then picking the next letters by moving one space over to the right and three spaces down several times.

An example of such a matrix, or "crossword puzzle," for the "Roswell" mentioned in KJV Genesis appears below. The letters of "Roswell" now appear vertically at the center of the puzzle. The actual matrix of unique letters is only four characters wide here (dashed box), but I took the liberty of showing extra letters for context. A companion hidden message—"UFO"—is indicated within circle symbols. This "UFO" is itself a hidden message with a step value of twelve. Drosnin accepts *any* such messages, even words running horizontally (i.e. the actual words of the Bible strung together). If either "Roswell" or

"UFO" had been found encoded in the Hebrew Bible, Drosnin would not have hesitated to use words from the direct text as a "match" (for example, the words "thou hast now done foolishly.")

```
S A N D M Y D A U G H T E R S T H O U H
M Y D A U G H T E R S T H O U H A S T N
U G H T E R S T H O U H A S T N O W D O
E R S T H O U H A S T N O W D O N E F O
H O U H A S T N O W D O N E F O O L I S
A S T N O W D O N E F O O L I S H L Y I
O W D O N E F O O L I S H L Y I N S O D
N E F O O L I S H L Y I N S O D O I N G
O L I S H L Y I N S O D O I N G I T I S
H L Y I N S O D O I N G I T I S I N T H
```

The unusual pairing of "Roswell" and "UFO" is as stunning as any described in Drosnin's book—yet no one claims that the Bible code would have translated gracefully over to the KJV Genesis. Drosnin claims mathematical proof that "no human could have encoded the Bible in this way." He says, "I do not know if it is God," but adds that the code proves "we are not alone."[1]

Some believe that these "messages" in the Hebrew Bible are not just coincidence—God put them there deliberately. But if someone finds a hidden message in a book, a song played backwards, funny-looking Martian mesas, or some other object or thing, does that prove someone else put the message there intentionally? Or might the message exist only in the eyes of the beholder (and in those of his or her followers)? Does perception of meaning prove the message was deliberately created?

Or is this phenomenon related mainly to the determination and skill of the person looking for a special message? *Any* special message?

For example, there are dozens of books about Nostradamus. In one, the authors find hidden predictions by scrambling the seer's quatrains (in French, no less), and then decoding according to an extremely complicated and mysterious formula.[2] The back cover prominently displays one such unscrambled prediction: "1992—George Bush re-elected." (Wrong.) The authors should have known that it's much safer to find hidden predictions of events that have already happened.

Some critics of Drosnin say the journalist is just "data mining." Mathematician Brendan McKay of Australian National University and his colleagues searched Hebrew texts besides the Bible. They found 59 words related to Chanukah in the Hebrew translation of *War and Peace*. But McKay doesn't think someone engineered this remarkable feat for his or anyone's benefit. Since then, McKay has responded to the following challenge Drosnin made in *Newsweek*: "When my critics find a message about the assassination of a prime minister encrypted in *Moby Dick*, I'll believe them."[3]

McKay found assassination "predictions" in *Moby Dick* for Indira Gandhi, Rene Moawad, Leon Trotsky, Rev. Martin Luther King, and Robert F. Kennedy.

Hidden Names in KJV Genesis and *Edwards v. Aguillard*

In one of my first investigations of the Bible code in 1996, I carried out a study on finding hidden names in both the KJV Genesis and the US Supreme Court's 1987 ruling on *Edwards v. Aguillard* (a well-known ruling on creationism, hereafter referred to as simply *Edwards*). I used the same set of rules for both the KJV Genesis (about 150,000 characters) and *Edwards* (about 100,000 characters). I loaded a list of preselected names and let the computer search for each one in turn, for equidistant letter sequences with step distances from two to 1,000, and for every possible starting letter. I searched forward only.

One would expect that special biblical messages hidden in the Hebrew Bible would simply not make it into the King James Version (translated), much less into *Edwards*. And since the Hebrew alphabet doesn't include vowels, it should be *much* harder to find matches in the English texts, because an additional character match is required for each vowel. Drosnin's control was the Hebrew text of *War and Peace*. Drosnin claims that when they searched for words (such as "comet," "Jupiter," etc.) in the Bible, they often found them there, but not in *War and Peace*.

I picked my set of names carefully. The list contained five names of four letters, five of five letters, five of six letters, five of seven letters, and five of either eight or nine letters. I was more whimsical in my choice of subjects, and chose talk show hosts, scientists, and just plain folks as well as political or historical figures.

I found *thousands* of hidden occurrences of these names. It was amazing that so many hidden occurrences were found for the 25 names submitted, for both Genesis and *Edwards*. More matches were found in the former, but it does have 50,000 more letters to work with.

Another important observation was immediately apparent—short names like "Leno" or "Reed" were found much more frequently than long names like "Gingrich" or "Matsumura" ("Matsumura" is Molleen Matsumura of the National Center for Science Education, in Berkeley). "Martin Gardner" was found hidden in *Edwards*, much as Gardner anticipated could happen in his discussion of gematria and the work of Rips and his colleagues.[4]

The results are clear and compelling, and certainly not surprising. It is much easier to find short names than long names. There might be thousands of occurrences of the four-letter name "Rich," for example. But matching "Gingrich" is much harder, since few or none of the thousands of instances of "Rich" will be preceded by "Ging" at exactly the right step locations. But there are 2,554 hidden occurrences of "Newt" in KJV Genesis, so one could imagine that the former Speaker of the House is certainly mentioned copiously.

There is, of course, another factor in the success of hidden word searches. Simply put, some letters are more common than others. If one considers the relative frequencies for the letters in Genesis and *Edwards*, it is apparent that certain letters (such as A, D, E, H, I, N, O, R, S, and T) appear more often than others. Obviously, words made with these "hot" letters (such as "Reed," "Deer," "Stalin," or "Hitler") have a better chance of being found than words containing any "cool" letters like J or Q. "Rosie" had 202 Genesis matches, more than the 49 for "Oprah"—but "Oprah" contains a cool P. (I also searched for "Harpo," which is just "Oprah" backwards, and found 62 hits).

I then derived a formula for how many occurrences of given words you would expect to find in a text of a given number of random letters. One must calculate the probability of selection for each letter, which depends on the particular text being examined. This is just the number of occurrences of the letter divided by the total number of letters. Typically, the probability for getting an E is above 0.1 (better than 10 percent, or 1 chance in 10), while that for a Q can be just 0.005. For a given word like "Roswell," you multiply the chances for an R with that for an O, then an S, and so on. The final product is multiplied by the total possible number of equidistant letter sequences for the word, which is roughly the square of the number of letters in the entire text divided by one less than the number of letters in the candidate hidden word.

This formula works very well. I estimated that I would find 18.7 occurrences of "Clinton" in *War and Peace*, Book 1 (212,000 characters, 7.5 billion possible seven-letter equidistant sequences); the actual number was 21. I estimated I would find 128.1 matches for the name "Apollo"—and got 129. With each additional letter in candidate words, the chance for a match on a single try falls, because you must multiply your product by another number invariably less than one. And rare letters reduce the expected matches greatly. But the sheer number of possible skip sequences is so large as to often make the overall chances of obtaining matches very reasonable.

How well does this estimation work in the Torah itself? Very well, indeed! I had to adapt my English-based code problems to Hebrew, which I did by using the Michigan-Claremont transliteration scheme for converting Hebrew into English and vice versa. I also developed a method for showing my new puzzles in the Hebrew characters. I calculated the expected number of matches for "Clinton" in the Torah.

In Modern Hebrew, "Clinton" appears as follows, reading from right to left: Quf, Lamed, Yod, Nun, Tet, Vav, and Nun:

Just as in English, some characters are more common than others. Lamed is popular (7 percent) of the Torah's characters are Lameds), as is Yod (10 percent) and Vav (10 percent), but Tet is rare in the Torah (only half of a percent). The odds of finding an exact match for "Clinton," for a single pick of seven equidistant letters in the Torah, is incredibly small: It works out to less than one in a billion. But there are a great many ways of selecting valid seven-letter equidistant sequences from a text. In fact, the number of possible seven-letter sequences in the Torah vastly outnumbers the count of letters in the Torah itself. While there are just over 300,000 characters to work with in the entire Torah, the number of valid seven-letter equidistant sequences is over 15 ***billion***. And the computer lets the Bible code researcher look at each and every one of these sequences. Even though the chances for any given sequence to be a match are small (less than one in a billion), there are so many sequences to look at that the expected number of matches turns out to be reasonable. Thus, I expected to find around two "Clinton" matches in the Torah; the actual number is four (i.e. very close to what I expected).

How Unusual Are Paired Messages?

Drosnin and others sometimes admit that finding isolated hidden names or messages can be the product of random chance. But they claim that finding linked pairs or triples of names or words is so improbable that doing so proves the supernatural, divine, or alien origin of the "message." In Drosnin's words:

> Consistently, the Bible code brings together interlocking words that reveal related information. With Bill Clinton, President. With the Moon landing, spaceship and Apollo 11. With Hitler, Nazi. With Kennedy, Dallas. In experiment after experiment, the crossword puzzles were found only in the Bible. Not in *War and Peace*, not in any other book, and not in ten million computer-generated test cases.[5]

Perhaps there was a bug in Drosnin's computer program. Or perhaps he didn't really want to find hidden message pairs outside of the Hebrew Bible. I don't know if Drosnin was lying on purpose, but I do know the above statement is a lie. I was able to easily produce complex hidden messages in all the texts I worked with. I developed a computer program that takes various words already located as hidden codes (such as "Hitler" and "Nazi") and plays them against each other to find the best-linked pairs. The starting letters and equidistant steps provide all the necessary information, provided one learns how to manipulate it.

I then used this approach to develop many puzzles in many texts having direct coded linkages of "Hitler" and "Nazi." These puzzles are striking counterexamples of Drosnin's claims.

I found an English translation of Tolstoy's epic novel *War and Peace* on the Internet and downloaded the first 24 chapters of Book 1, giving me about 167,000 characters. By the time I got to steps of just 750, I already had found more than half a dozen excellent puzzle linkages of "Hitler" and "Nazi." The best of these appears below: This entire puzzle text spans just five paragraphs (or just 244 words, using 1,083 characters) of the second chapter of Book 1 of Tolstoy's novel.

```
PLOT L=11792,N=69,w=2
W O R D S A W H E R B R I G H T S M I L E A N D T H E C
Y W E R E I N A S P E C I A L L Y A M I A B L E M O O D
W I T H Q U I C K S H O R T S W A Y I N G S T E P S H E
E S S S A T D O W N O N A S O F A N E A R T H E S I L V
H E R S E L F A N D T O A L L A R O U N D H E R I H A V
R B A G A N D A D D R E S S I N G A L L P R E S E N T M
C K O N M E S H E A D D E D T U R N I N G T O H E R H O
P T I O N A N D J U S T S E E H O W B A D L Y I A M D R
W A I S T E D L A C E T R I M M E D D A I N T Y G R A Y
R E A S T S O Y E Z T R A N Q U I L L E L I S E Y O U W
N N A P A V L O V N A Y O U K N O W S A I D T H E P R I
T U R N I N G T O A G E N E R A L M Y H U S B A N D I S
L M E W H A T T H I S W R E T C H E D W A R I S F O R S
I T I N G F O R A N A N S W E R S H E T U R N E D T O S
E L I G H T F U L W O M A N T H I S L I T T L E P R I N
T H E N E X T A R R I V A L S W A S A S T O U T H E A V
A C L E S T H E L I G H T C O L O R E D B R E E C H E S
R O W N D R E S S C O A T T H I S S T O U T Y O U N G M
```

Of special interest is that the match for "Hitler" occurs at the very small step of three, crossing just four words: t**H**e l**I**gh**T** co**L**or**E**d b**R**eeches. The word "Nazi" appears at the larger step of 207. Codes with small steps are much more impervious to slight changes in exact transcriptions than are large-step codes. To alter the "Hitler" above, one would have to change one of the four words involved: "the," "light," "colored," or "breeches." But a change to even ***one*** of the tens of thousands of characters in Drosnin's "Rabin" match (4,772 per letter, over 8 letters) would destroy this match.

Drosnin uses many methods to improve the odds of "impossible-by-chance" linkages. For one, he uses horizontal words taken directly from the original text. For example, when Drosnin found "Clinton" linked to "president," the word "president" was just the Hebrew word for "chief," taken from its actual context in the original Bible. Secondly, Drosnin found some hidden dates referring to the Hebrew calendar; for example, Gulf War activity on January 18, 1991, was found in the words "3rd Shevat." But he found other dates referring to the Gregorian calendar, such as that of the Oklahoma City bombing, which was linked in the Bible by the hidden date "Day 19," and interpreted as a reference to both April 19, 1995, the date of the bombing, and April 19, 1993 (Waco). And finally, Drosnin takes full advantage of the eccentricities of the Hebrew language, in which words can be condensed and letters occasionally dropped.

My study generated several other examples that are just as spectacular and just as unlikely (if not more so) than most of Drosnin's matches. Now, Drosnin and his colleagues would probably say that the "Roswell/UFO" connection in KJV Genesis was just a lucky break and couldn't happen again. But I found 5,812 hidden "UFO"s in Genesis, and dozens of these happen to be flying right around and through the hidden word "Roswell." As the puzzle step is changed, linked matches appear and disappear with astonishing frequency. All that is really happening here is that codes can be engineered—***made*** to happen. You just have to know how to harvest the field of possibilities.

Here is another striking linkage I found in KJV Genesis, 42:18 through 45:21. Here, the name "Regis" appears at a step distance of 808, but also at a step of 810, which makes a nice "X" pattern if the puzzle step is 809. (Perhaps someone should notify Regis Philbin and agents Mulder and Scully).

```
U S A L I T T L E F O O D A N D J U D A H S P A K
E R E D S U R E L Y N O W W E H A D R E T U R N E
N D T H E M E N W E R E A F R A I D B E C A U S E
R A N D T H E Y M A D E R E A D Y T H E P R E S E
E E G Y P T I A N S M I G H T N O T E A T B R E A
B Y I N D E E D H E D I V I N E T H Y E H A V E D
R O U N D A N D J O S E P H S A I D U N T O T H E
E S A I D U N T O M Y L O R D T H E L A D C A N N
A N T S S H A L L B R I N G D O W N T H E G R A Y
```

If you work at any given puzzle for a while, large numbers of unexpected names and words invariably turn up. Consider the large puzzle below. This text is a contiguous rendition of Genesis 41:38-46. This particular puzzle is easy for the reader to verify manually, since it has a relatively small step of 40. The puzzle itself is 41 characters wide, so the rightmost column is a repetition of the leftmost. I used the computer to find several diagonal messages here: "Deer," "Regis," "Nazi," "Leno," "Dole." Many vertical messages were simple enough to be found just by poring over the puzzle: for example, "Oprah," "here," "Leia," "Hale," "sent," "nude," "pure," "hate," "data," "Roe," "Reed," "Meg," "hood," "pins (snip)," "Deion," and "lone."

"Newt" is in there, too, but at an offbeat step that makes for a jilted arrangement. And then, there are all those horizontal words, too!

```
S S E R V A N T S C A N W E F I N D S U C H A O N E A S T H I S I S A M A N I N W
W H O M T H E S P I R I T O F G O D I S A N D P H A R A O H S A I D U N T O J O S
S E P H F O R A S M U C H A S G O D H A T H S H E W E D T H E E A L L T H I S T H
H E R E I S N O N E S O D I S C R E E T A N D W I S E A S T H O U A R T T H O U S
S H A L T B E O V E R M Y H O U S E A N D A C C O R D I N G U N T O T H Y W O R D
D S H A L L A L L M Y P E O P L E B E R U L E D O N L Y I N T H E T H R O N E W I
I L L I B E G R E A T E R T H A N T H O U A N D P H A R A O H S A I D U N T O J O
O S E P H S E E I H A V E S E T T H E E O V E R A L L T H E L A N D O F E G Y P T
T A N D P H A R A O H T O O K O F F H I S R I N G F R O M H I S H A N D A N D P U
U T I T U P O N J O S E P H S H A N D A N D A R R A Y E D H I M I N V E S T U R E
E S O F F I N E L I N E N A N D P U T A G O L D C H A I N A B O U T H I S N E C K
K A N D H E M A D E H I M T O R I D E I N T H E S E C O N D C H A R I O T W H I C
C H H E H A D A N D T H E Y C R I E D B E F O R E H I M B O W T H E K N E E A N D
D H E M A D E H I M R U L E R O V E R A L L T H E L A N D O F E G Y P T A N D P H
H A R A O H S A I D U N T O J O S E P H I A M P H A R A O H A N D W I T H O U T T
T H E E S H A L L N O M A N L I F T U P H I S H A N D O R F O O T I N A L L T H E
E L A N D O F E G Y P T A N D P H A R A O H C A L L E D J O S E P H S N A M E Z A
A P H N A T H P A A N E A H A N D H E G A V E H I M T O W I F E A S E N A T H T H
H E D A U G H T E R O F P O T I P H E R A H P R I E S T O F O N A N D J O S E P H
H W E N T O U T O V E R A L L T H E L A N D O F E G Y P T A N D J O S E P H W A S
S T H I R T Y Y E A R S O L D W H E N H E S T O O D B E F O R E P H A R A O H K I
```

Genesis 41:38 - 41:46, Multiple Matches, Step = 40

I suspect that with diligence, one could find enough matches to make almost all of the characters in the puzzle into parts of hidden words. The puzzle above is literally dripping with additional hidden surprises. Rips himself appears in "spirit" read backwards. "Pour," "Alan," and "sash" run vertically. And diagonal messages of varying complexity lurk everywhere. Can you find the "apes" swinging between "data" and "Reed"? "Love" intersecting with "nude"? How about "Ares," "reel," "deft," "lion," "dogs," "pony," "hard," "diet," "trace," "card," "Poe," and "wart"? They are all in there—and more.

There are dozens of linked messages in the puzzle above. But how are we to know which words are linked by the secretive author? Is the "real" message "Nazi sent pure hate here," or is it, "Deion pins nude Oprah?" All of these hits are authentic, encoded names and words that have lurked inside the text of the King James Version of Genesis for hundreds of years. But the whimsical combinations they appear in show that these surprises are simply lucky breaks, and not authentic messages from above.

What Are the Odds, Really?

Drosnin and his colleagues say that getting linked matches by coincidence is statistically impossible and cite the odds against such coincidences as more than 3,000 to one (and sometimes much more). Using numbers like these, the Bible code promoters try to convince their readers that the existence of God is now proven statistically beyond the shadow of a doubt, simply because they can find linked pairs like "Clinton" and "chief" in the same general area of the Bible.

But their core conclusions are based on severely flawed probability arguments. Drosnin's formulation of the improbability of the occurrence of linked pairs is implicitly based on the assumption that you have only one opportunity to get the match. But, with the help of the computer, Drosnin gets to take advantage of billions of opportunities.

Let's look at Drosnin's approach with a lottery analogy. The probability of winning a lottery with a single ticket is very small, and Drosnin says the probability of getting an improbable match (such as "Clinton" and "president") is also very small. But what happens if you buy more than one ticket?

In the "Powerball" lottery, the odds of winning the $10 million minimum jackpot with just one ticket are about eighty million to one against. With two tickets, the odds plummet, to about forty million to one. If you buy one million tickets, your odds drop to only about eighty to one against. And if you invest $80 million in tickets, the odds become approximately two to one in your favor! Most people can't afford to buy millions of tickets. Those who do have that kind of money usually don't dump it on the lottery, because you almost always end up losing.

But in Drosnin's game, you don't have to win more than you lose. You don't even have to break even. All you need for success is to win every once in a while. And, you can have what amounts to millions of "free lottery tickets" simply by running a computer program, or poring over crossword-puzzle printouts. Drosnin routinely tests billions of letter sequences for matches to selected words or names, and goes to steps of many thousands. By using steps lower than 1,000 only, I limited myself to using only about 3 percent of the potential of Genesis or *Edwards*.

Australian mathematician Brendan McKay (in personal communication) showed me how to find hidden words much more efficiently, and a search of KJV Genesis at *all* possible steps for my list of 25 names came up with over ***one million*** additional matches. These include six hits for "Clinton," fifteen for "Gardner," three for "Hillary" and "Einstein," and two for "Kennedy." McKay's algorithm allows for much faster searches, and I quickly incorporated it into my own code programs. By being tens of times faster, it allows me to search for all possible step sequences. It is faster than my brute-force approach (checking all possible equidistant letter sequences) because it's more like the way you can find short words by inspection of the puzzles. You focus on those letters of the text that match the first letter of the desired hidden word, and then find letters matching the second letter of the desired word. For each two-letter pair, check the location of the third letter in the pattern; if it matches your desired word, keep going, otherwise move on to the next pair.

Further Developments

My first report on "Hidden Messages and the Bible Code" in the November/December 1997 *Skeptical Inquirer* was only the beginning. There have been several interesting developments in the Bible-code saga since then.

At the suggestion of a *People* magazine reporter, I downloaded the chapter excerpt of Michael Drosnin's book, *The Bible Code*, from Simon and Schuster's Website and began searching. Even though the chapter was only about 4,000 characters in length, I was able to produce a number of hits. One puzzle held a lunar theme: "space," "lunar," "craft," and several instances of "moon"—all authentic hidden words. I found the ubiquitous "Hitler/Nazi," even though the excerpt did not mention those words directly, talking instead mainly about the Rabin assassination. One puzzle contains the hidden message, "The code is a silly snake-oil hoax." And I even found, "The code is evil," hidden in Drosnin's book (he's sending us a mixed message here). The two-page article on the debunking of the Bible code appeared in *People* in the November 3, 1997, issue.

Reporter Eric Zorn of the *Chicago Tribune* had me look in his old editorials for the name of a very recently disgraced Chicago alderman. Sure enough—the alderman's demise had been predicted years before. The "Zorn code" was announced on October 27, 1997, in the *Tribune*.

Drosnin went on the stump in Australia and around the world, flattering code-buster Brendan McKay with compliments such as "clown," "liar," "fraud"; and me with, "Thomas appears not to understand the Bible Code at all." Drosnin accuses us of "counterfeiting" codes, even though McKay and I do not need to alter even one letter of various texts—either the puzzles are there, or they're not. (And to Drosnin's dismay, the puzzles continue to turn up everywhere).

Drosnin is also attacking us because our puzzles allegedly do not have "minimality." Not only must hidden words appear close together in a puzzle, they must also be the shortest skip distances for the given word in a fair-sized portion of the text. Drosnin only mentions minimality in passing, buried in the chapter notes at the end of his book: "All of the Bible code print-outs displayed in this book have been confirmed by statistics to be encoded beyond chance. The word combinations are mathematically proven to be non-random.... The computer scores the matches between words, using two tests—how closely they appear together, and whether the skips that spell out the search words are the shortest in the Bible. (For a more detailed explanation see Appendix.)"

Interestingly, some of Drosnin's prize puzzles are not "minimal."

His match for "Clinton" has the largest step of all four "Clinton's" found in the Hebrew Torah, and the other three occur entirely within the chosen match. Each of these three serves to give the chosen "Clinton" a "domain of minimality" of zero. (In contrast, the close matches of "Hitler" and "Nazi" I found in Drosnin's own book are both minimal over the entire chapter, and the mention of "Roswell" I found in the King James Bible is minimal over the complete text of the Book of Genesis.) In other words, Drosnin's prime "Clinton" puzzle is invalid because it breaks official Code Rules.

As mentioned previously, I modified my program to handle the Hebrew characters via the Michigan-Claremont transliteration scheme (in which, for example, the Hebrew letter "Shin" is represented as "$"), using a download of the Torah (Koren edition) from McKay's Website. I have since reproduced a number of Drosnin's puzzles to the letter, including his non-minimal "Clinton/President" match. I also contrived a method for printing the puzzles in the actual Hebrew characters. (Pretty good for someone who doesn't "understand the Bible Code at all.")

Amazingly, Drosnin found "Shoemaker-Levy" (transliterated as $WMKRLWY, eight characters), not in the five books of the Torah, but in *Isaiah*. Eliyahu Rips used Isaiah as a control, an example of an ancient Hebrew text without the "code," and found no unlikely codes therein. Drosnin also found "computer" in the book of Daniel. Perhaps he forgot that the code is supposed to occur only in the five books of Moses: Genesis, Exodus, Leviticus, Numbers, and Deuteronomy.

A book titled *Cracking the Bible Code* by Jeffrey Satinover appeared recently. It is not nearly as sensationalized as Drosnin's book, but it still strongly supports the code phenomenon. Interestingly, most of the true-blue code promoters despise Drosnin as the proverbial bull in the china shop—Satinover alludes to him, but won't even mention him by name.

In the September 1997 *Notices of the AMS* (American Mathematical Society), Harvard mathematics professor (and Orthodox rabbi) Shlomo Sternberg blasted the code phenomenon. In particular, he pointed out that the elaborate "codes" found by both Rips and Drosnin would collapse even if just a few letters were added to or dropped from the text they used.

Sternberg notes that "any serious student of the Talmud knows that there are many citations of the Hebrew Bible which indicate a differing text from the one we have.... One of the oldest complete texts of the Bible, the Leningrad codex (from 1009) (also available electronically) differs from the Koren version used by Rips and Witztum in forty-one places in Deuteronomy alone. In fact, the spelling in the Hebrew Bible did not become uniformized until the sixteenth century with the advent of a printed version that could provide an identical standard text available at diverse geographical locations."

The search for the truth about equidistant letter sequences goes on. One thing I am looking at is how "clumpiness" of letters in real texts sometimes produces many more or fewer matches than would be expected for a purely randomized text. I found one 934-letter chunk of a book about science by Isaac Asimov that produced an amazing seven matches for the word "Nazi," even though only one was expected. This result is apparently "beyond chance," with odds of at least 2,000 to one against. But it is not really that surprising—the chunk of text happened to contain several instances of the word "generalization." And inside every instance, at a step of three, lurks a Nazi: ge**N**er**A**li**Z**at**I**on.

It looks like we have to be more careful about what we write!

Bible Code: The Movie

The 1999 movie *The Omega Code*, starring Michael York, was a millennial thriller based on the premise that the Bible code is real. The movie had a good first weekend in mid-October, with $2.4 million in sales, and an average of $7,700 per screen. It had been advertised mainly through churches and word of mouth. But by the next weekend, only two more screens were added, and earnings fell 32 percent (25 percent is considered normal). "Mr. Showbiz" predicted that the film would be lucky to break even; the production cost $7.2 million. Mr. Showbiz also noted that the producer of the film wanted to have it playing in 450 theaters by the end of November. But by then, *The Omega Code* was only in a few theaters. Once it came to video, I broke down and rented the film. After building around several plot threads, the final code turned out to be simply, "Y2K=Armageddon." The Rapture sucked away all the characters in the most emotionally unsatisfying conclusion to a film I have ever seen.

David Thomas in the Torah

Recently, a nice lady from Louisiana asked me if I had ever looked for my own name in the Torah. "There's an idea," I thought. So I resurrected my trusty code programs, and consulted with experts on how to spell "David Thomas" in Hebrew. I launched the search, and found several instances of my name encoded in the Torah itself. One of these was located entirely within the first book, Genesis; this appears below. Here, the Hebrew letters spelling "David Thomas" run from bottom to top.

ש	מ	ה	פ	י	צ	מ	י	ה
א	מ	ל	כ	ס	ד	מ	ו	מ
ת	ע	ו	ל	מ	ו	ע	ר	ל
י	מ	ב	ל	ו	ט	ל	א	מ
ה	י	ב	ע	ת	ה	ה	ו	א
ו	א	ש	ר	ד	ב	ר	ל	י
ט	ו	ר	ה	ו	י	ת	נ	א
י	ל	א	י	ד	ע	ת	י	י
ל	מ	ל	ו	ז	ש	מ	ה	ע

Of course, I didn't stop with the Torah. I looked for myself in Charles Darwin's epic *Origin of Species*, and found my name in there, too! When I told my Louisiana correspondent about that, she replied, "Maybe that's just how Jesus says, 'Look, even here.'" I then told her about a Muslim who found coincidences with the number 19 in the Koran, and how he felt those proved that only the Koran is divine. I told her I had found mysterious 19 coincidences, not just in the Koran, but also in Ted Kaczynski's *Unabomber Manifesto*. I asked her how she would respond if my Muslim correspondent dismissed the Unabomber's number-19 coincidences by simply claiming, "It's Allah's way of saying, 'Look, even here.'" I did not hear back from her.

The End of the Bible Code, Part I

As my wife and I were driving through New Mexico on Sunday, June 14, 1998, we listened to game six of the Chicago Bulls/Utah Jazz National Basketball Association (NBA) playoffs. As the game drew to a close, we heard the Utah crowd groan as Michael Jordan sank the winning basket. And then and there, a chill went down my spine. "Oh my God...," I thought to myself. "The Tolstoy code is real."

Fifty days (more than seven weeks) before, on April 27, I had undertaken a search for NBA teams and players using the Bible code technique of equidistant letter sequences. (One of Drosnin's strongest claims in support of the Bible code was that his code-based prediction of the assassination of Israeli Prime Minister Yitzhak Rabin was made a year *before* the event took place.) Unlike Drosnin, however, I wasn't searching in the Hebrew Torah—instead, I was looking in Book 1 of an English translation of *War and Peace*.

I had wondered if the NBA playoff winner could actually be predicted in advance. What did my April search reveal? "Chicago" was found encoded just once in *War and Peace*, at a step of 8,891 characters (and therefore 100 percent "minimal," i.e. having the shortest step for that word). Ominously, "Jazz" was not encoded at all.

But there was more! "Bulls" was also encoded 32 times in Book 1 of *War and Peace*, and of these, five matches had non-zero domains of minimality. Amazingly, "Chicago" and one of the minimal (shortest-step) "Bulls" appeared close to each other in a classic Bible-code crossword puzzle. I also found fourteen hidden occurrences of "Jordan," and one of these (minimal step, of course) made an excellent, small puzzle with one of the minimal "Bulls."

With all these "Bible code" indicators flashing—matching of long words, proximity of paired matches, and strict use of "minimal" matches—I rushed to send my prediction to several reporters and scientists. I thought about trying to warn Karl "the Mailman" Malone of the Jazz—but I decided to let history run its course. When I made my prediction, there were sixteen teams in the playoffs. And the Bulls, while favored, almost lost it all on more than one occasion. In fact, the Indiana Pacers came very close to defeating them, but Tolstoy's Bulls clung to their destiny.

And on June 14, my prediction came to pass. Not only had Tolstoy predicted the victors would be the Chicago Bulls, but Jordan's key role in the victory had been forecast—almost two months in advance.

And now, we are left to ponder the somber truth.

Either the "Bible code" nonsense is just a general, arcane mathematical technique, which can be employed to find any desired messages or predictions, hidden in any book or text...

...or Leo Tolstoy is the Supreme Being who created the Universe.

The End of the Bible Code, Part II

One of the chief arguments employed by proponents of the Bible code is to mention that the original code proponents—Witztum, Rips, and Rosenberg—published a paper supporting the phenomenon in the journal *Statistical Science* in 1994, and that, to date, no rebuttal has ever been published there.

But just such a paper, authored by Brendan McKay, Dror Bar-Natan, Maya Bar-Hillel, and Gil Kalai, has finally been published in the May 1999 edition of *Statistical Science*. The authors show definitively that the secret of the codes lies not in any special properties of Genesis, but rather in methods by which the lists of modern names and dates were chosen. In other words, the data (the text of Genesis) was not altered or modified, but the choice of the experiments (e.g. the list of famous rabbis and measures of closeness) completely determines the results.

McKay and his coauthors also show that several very reasonable measures of code effectiveness, much less convoluted than the complicated one chosen by Witztum and Rips, show no trace of the alleged "encoding" in Genesis or other books of the Torah. The article, and many others, is available on the Web at McKay's excellent site <cs.anu.edu.au/~bdm/dilugim/torah.html>. McKay's article, at almost 40 pages, is much more detailed and rigorous than the original paper by Witztum, Rips, and Rosenberg, and contains a detailed bibliography.

Drosnin's claims are so sensational that they can be dismissed rather easily. The claims of the original Israeli mathematicians are much more difficult to understand, and also to disprove. We are indeed fortunate that McKay and colleagues have published their extensive and devastating research on the codes of Rips and Witztum.

Conclusion

The promoters of hidden-message claims say, "How could such amazing coincidences be the product of random chance?" I think the real question should be, "How could such coincidences not be the inevitable product of a huge sequence of trials on a large, essentially random database?"

Once I learned how to navigate in puzzle-space, finding "incredible" predictions became a routine affair. I found "comet," "Hale," and "Bopp" linked in KJV Genesis, along with "forty" and "died," which could be interpreted as an obvious reference to Heaven's Gate. I found "Trinity," "Los Alamos," "atom," and "bomb" encoded together in *Edwards*, in a section containing references to "security," "test," and "anti-fascist." And I found "Hitler" linked to "Nazi" dozens of times in several books. When I set out to engineer a "hidden code" link of "code" and "bogus" in KJV Genesis, I was able to produce 60 closely-linked pairs. And every single one of these pairs could fit inside a reasonably sized puzzle.

Perhaps my most elaborate puzzle to date is this one, from Tolstoy's *War and Peace*: "Guilty Lee Oswald shot Kennedy, Both Died."

The source of the mysterious "Bible code" has been revealed—it's *homo sapiens*.

Now somebody go tell Oprah.

Endnotes

1. Drosnin, Michael. (1997). *The Bible code*. New York: Simon and Schuster, pp 50-51. **2.** Hewitt, V. J., & Peter Lorie. (1991). *Nostradamus: The end of the millennium*. New York: Simon and Schuster. **3.** Begley, Sharon. (1997). Seek and ye shall find. *Newsweek*, June 9, pp. 66-67. **4.** Gardner, Martin. (1997). Farrakhan, Cabala, Baha'i, and 19. *Skeptical Inquirer* 21 (2), pp 16-18, 57. **5.** *Op cit.*, Drosin, p 26.

Further References

McKay, Brendan, Dror Bar-Natan, Maya Bar-Hillel & Gil Kalai. (1999). Solving the Bible code puzzle. *Statistical Science* 14 (5), May.

Thomas, David E. Hidden messages and the Bible code. *Skeptical Inquirer*, November/December 1997

Thomas, David E. Bible code developments. *Skeptical Inquirer*, March/April 1998

Van Biema, David. (1997). Deciphering God's plan. *Time*, June 9, p 56.

Witztum, Doron, Eliyahu Rips, & Yoav Rosenberg. (1994). Equidistant letter sequences in the Book of Genesis. *Statistical Science* 9 (3).

Mystics and Messiahs

Mythkiller Philip Jenkins Unravels the Gospel about "Cults"

Interview with Philip Jenkins

> *"Extreme and bizzare religious ideas are so commonplace in American history that it is difficult to speak of them as fringe at all."*
> *—from* Mystics and Messiahs: Cults and New Religions in American History

Russ Kick: Since your book *Mystics and Messiahs* is about new religious groups in America, I thought it would be a good idea to start out by asking what a new religious group is, what features it typically has, etc. Also, what are your feelings of the words/phrases "new religious group" vs. "cult" vs. "sect"?

Philip Jenkins: Originally there were churches and sects, a division which developed in early twentieth-century European sociology. It's not terribly applicable to the US anyway, because in Europe "churches" were established and state-supported, and we don't have that here. Basically, churches are large and respectable and you're born into them; sects are small, fiercely active, and people join by conversion. In Europe today, what we call "cults" are called "sects," so there is a lot of confusion.

"New religious group," or "new religious movement" (NRM), is intended as a nice neutral term, partly to replace the word "cult," which had become almost unusable because of its cultural baggage. I use the word "cult" always in quotes, just to indicate a small, unpopular religious group, with no necessary reason for it to be unpopular. Having said this, some groups certainly do look more "cultish" than others. There is a nice definition of some small religious groups as "highly authoritarian, charismatically led, puritanical, and intolerant." This is useful because it avoids the need to accept all the mythology about brainwashing, mind control, etc.

An excellent criterion is how easy it is to leave the group. If you can walk out without recriminations, it's not a cult. I'd also add that if they can laugh at themselves, you're not dealing with a terribly pernicious group.

New Religious Groups Aren't Very New

RK: In *Mystics and Messiahs*, one of your themes—probably the overarching theme—is that new religious groups are not a creation of the 1960s and 1970s but have been in the US throughout its entire history, even in colonial times. What were some of these sects from the early days of America and what became of them?

PJ: Think of it in market terms. Two people set up businesses. One is (say) Pam's Candle Store, and it lasts six months; the other is Microsoft, and it rules the world. The colonial groups are like this. The Methodists are a classic bizarre and extreme sect that goes on to become the mainstream of the mainstream (just as bizarre in the eighteenth century as Baptists and Quakers were in the seventeenth). In other words, they go on to be Microsoft.

There are a hundred other groups, including all sorts of communal sects, which were often mystical, celibate, or occult, and they lasted maybe ten years or a century. We see the remains of their settlements as tourist attractions around the country, like the Harmony settlements in Pennsylvania and Indiana, or the Ephrata commune in Pennsylvania, or the Shaker communes in New England. Wonderful, magical, evocative places.

> America had Rosicrucians and alchemists before it had Methodists.

RK: I was fascinated by two related points you made: Most, if not all, mainstream religions started out as what could be called "cults." Similarly, many of today's "cults" have what you term "respectable lineages." Please elaborate.

PJ: One criterion that people try to use to differentiate cults from churches is that cults have no roots in a given society, that they are new outbreaks of alien ideas. By those standards, there are no cults. The example I use is that America had Rosicrucians and alchemists before it had Methodists, so the occult is nothing new—we have groups organized by the 1690s. We have also had Hindus and Buddhists longer than we have had Pentecostals.

Also, virtually all the so-called "cults" grow out of mainstream organizations—the People's Temple (of Jonestown fame) developed from a respectable evangelical denomination, the Christian

Church/Disciples of Christ, and Jim Jones was ordained in that group. Incidentally, the same group gave rise to the International Churches of Christ, which is today the main target of anti-cult critics. Another example I use in the book is Jeffrey Lundgren, whose group undertook several ritualistic slayings in the late 1980s: His origins lay in the Reorganized Church of Latter Day Saints, a sober and conservative branch of the Mormon tradition.

Virtually all the so-called "cults" grow out of mainstream organizations.

RK: Asian sects and gurus have been in America since way before the 1960s. When did they first make their mark on America?

PJ: This goes back at least to Thoreau and the Transcendentalists, basically the 1840s. In literally every generation since then, there have been new infusions of Hindu and Buddhist thought, often disguised in American mode—the New Thought movement of the late nineteenth century, Theosophy in the 1870s. With its cults, health fads, and wandering gurus, Boston in the 1880s looks a whole lot like San Francisco in the 1970s.

With its cults, health fads, and wandering gurus, Boston in the 1880s looks a whole lot like San Francisco in the 1970s.

The Anti-Cult Attitudes, Then and Now

RK: You've noted that it's not only new sects that have been around since day one, but anti-cult groups as well. Every period has it opponents of new religions, and their basic charges and allegations have remained constant. Please elaborate.

PJ: The best account of an anti-cult movement I know is found in a work called the New Testament, where literally every single charge familiar today is made, specifically against Jesus. Take a look. Jesus is accused of being a drunkard and a crazy man, his family tries to drag him away from his group, and in return he insists that his followers have to *hate* their wives, parents, children etc. You can make a striking list of the New Testament passages calling believers to separate from the world, break from their families, separate from darkness, etc. In other words, cult scares and anti-cult reactions go back a very long way. Today, most of the issues concern Europe, where we are seeing the same kinds of panic that we saw in the US in the 1970s.

RK: I found it very interesting that a "Satanic Panic" occurred in the US before the famous one of the 1980s and early 1990s. Please tell us about the Satanic Panic of the 1930s.

PJ: I originally discovered this back in the late 1980s when I was trying to test the claims made by anti-satanic theorists that there were these old, established cults and covens in the US. I found that claims went back a long way, but in virtually every case, they could be associated with sensationalistic tabloid media, pulp fiction, etc. Interestingly, too, there has been a pattern whereby most anti-satanic claims originate as fiction and then find their way into the media as claims of facts. Most of the claims of the 1980s can be traced back to two fictional works, namely Herbert S. Gorman's novel *The Place Called Dagon* (1927) and the British thrillers of Dennis Wheatley, above all *The Devil Rides Out*.

RK: Another theme of your book is that the threat of "cults" is often extremely overblown. First of all, talk to me about the numbers of people involved in new religions in different periods, and how and why the "anti-cult" forces, the media, and the sects themselves often inflate their membership and influence.

PJ: Without trying to evade the answer, it's almost impossible to know how many people are "involved" because it depends what we mean by "involved." If we include everyone who ever read a leaflet, bought a book, or attended a meeting, probably tens of millions of Americans now alive have been involved in "cults" of different kinds, but of course they didn't give up their lives and go join a commune.

Anti-cult people give ludicrously high estimates for this sort of activity, obviously to make the issue look as threatening as possible. The common figure in the 1980s was that two million Americans were full-time cult members at any given time, which is absurd. Probably, the proportion of Americans generally interested and active in cults and new religions—though not fully committed activists—was roughly the same at any given time in the twentieth century, whether we are looking at 1920, 1945, or 1980. That is of course counterintuitive, since we believe this all started in the 1960s. It didn't. The proportion of people living in cult communes was probably far less at any given moment in the twentieth century than in the nineteenth.

The proportion of people living in cult communes was probably far less at any given moment in the twentieth century than in the nineteenth.

RK: Continuing on the theme of demonizing new religious groups, you say that although there are a few cases of sects and/or their leaders doing harmful things in every era, the vast majority are sincere and well-behaved. How and why is it that the few "bad apples," so to speak, are used to smear all new religions?

The idea of gullible, hysterical women is perhaps the commonest single strand in anti-cult fears over the centuries.

PJ: It's an obvious tactic, which we all use to some extent. If you want to attack the Christian Right, say, we focus on the bad apples, like Jim Bakker or Jimmy Swaggart. Such rhetoric is all the more important in religious matters, where we are setting claims of purity and morality against a sinful reality. Nobody was too surprised or shocked when Bill Clinton turned out to be a prize lecher, but if you could make the same claims against someone who was a great moral activist, it would be much more effective. Finding Hugh Grant with a hooker was a national joke; finding Jesse Helms with one would be a moment of ineffable joy for liberals across the nation.

RK: You make a point that mainstream organized religions often have the same problems (e.g. child abuse, misused funds) as some new religious sects, yet the former often get off the hook. Although there may be some outcry about the specific incidents, no one in the mainstream uses these occurrences to smear organized religion as a whole. Why is that?

PJ: Things are changing here. Prior to 1980 or so, nobody but nobody published bad stories on mainstream religion, mainly because it was felt to be in atrocious taste, partly because of a well-substantiated fear of boycotts. Things changed with new media standards in the 1980s and the weakening of respect for church authority by believers. Hence the Catholic clergy scandals of the last few years. But generally, if (say) a rabbi sins, he is seen as a bad rabbi, not as proof of the evils of Judaism; if a "cult leader" sins, that is proof of the evils of cults. Jews (and other mainstream believers) buy newspapers and will complain if their religion is abused; whereas cults are not seen as a serious constituency.

RK: In *Mystics and Messiahs*, you wrote, "Racial factors are also significant in sculpting cult fears." Please explain that and give some examples.

PJ: Think of anti-cult charges over the years, which can be neatly divided into two categories: African stereotypes (primitivism, violence, sexual excess, savagery) and Asian stereotypes (passive obedience, mind control, brainwashing, slavish submission). These twin patterns run over the last century or so, back to the 1890s when the whole language of cult was invented. The same images emerge very strongly in the 1970s—the myth of brainwashing is a direct consequence of American nightmares of encounters with supposedly "Asian" mind-control and brutality in Korea and Vietnam. The fact that some of the most visible new cults were Asian—or even Korean, like the Moonies—was the icing on the cake.

RK: You also noted that gender politics plays a role in new religions. Please explain and show how that plays into anti-cult fears.

PJ: The idea of gullible, hysterical women is perhaps the commonest single strand in anti-cult fears over the centuries, and again I look at the charges against the early Christians, the myths about Mary Magdalene (hooker, crazy woman, etc). It emerges against literally every new religion, including Methodism and Pentecostalism, and the camp meetings in US history. Critics are quick to point out that emotional excesses in religion often look very much like orgasmic experiences. Equally, women frequently emerge as leaders of cults—Ann Lee of the Shakers, Elizabeth Claire Prophet, Mary Baker Eddy, and so on. The critics charge that any movements so led must be neurotic, fanatical, irrational, and unfit for rational believers. Though they don't overtly use words as coarse as "pussy whipped," that idea is strongly in the background.

Reality Check

RK: Do you feel that certain new religious movements are problematic in any way? What are your thoughts on charges of brainwashing, member abuse, etc.? Are they ever valid? If so, what can be done (and what should be done) about them? Obviously, the answer is not to fly into hysterics and slander new religions across the board, but how can a real problem be handled in a sane way?

PJ: Absolutely, many fringe (and not-so-fringe) religions oppress and abuse their members. We can cite examples of fraud, rape, illegal imprisonment, and so on. In many cases, such instances fall under what should be the constitutional right to fall victim to one's own stupidity. If you choose to give all your money to a religious fraud, there's not much anyone can or should do to protect you. If you choose to go through Marine Corps training when no one is making you, that's your choice, and you have a right to do it. The problem, of course, is where we are dealing with children, who can't give legitimate consent to be exploited.

Normally, I feel that the battery of laws we already have is more than sufficient to deal with these problems: Just enforce them in a way that does not discriminate against religious groups, and within that broad category, just against new or fringe religious groups.

In many cases, such instances fall under what should be the constitutional right to fall victim to one's own stupidity.

Religious Laboratories

RK: Finally, another major theme of your book is that new sects play an important and often positive role in the development of religion in the US. How has this occurred in the past, and how do you see it playing out in the future?

PJ: I cite lots of examples of cults and fringe religions serving as laboratories for mainstream religion or social thought. In religion, ideas like racial and gender equality were commonplace long before they got into the mainstream. Other ideas become mainstream without anyone realizing they are religious in origin, like 12-step groups or vegetarianism. And let's not forget washing machines and labor-saving devices! They began as a means for commune members to have enough time for prayer and religious exercises.

In religion, ideas like racial and gender equality were commonplace long before they got into the mainstream.

Next Up: The "Hidden Gospels"

RK: Your next book, which should be available by the time *You Are Being Lied To* is out, is titled *Hidden Gospels: The Modern Mythology of Christian Origins*. What is the main theme/focus of this book?

PJ: Over the last 20 years or so, we've heard a lot about supposed "hidden gospels" which have been recently discovered, like the Gospel of Thomas, which turned up in Egypt in 1945. The common belief is that these texts contain lost or suppressed secrets about the "real" Jesus, and this theme shows up a lot in popular culture, in movies like *Stigmata*, even in *The X-Files*.

I am arguing that nothing about these "new" texts is likely to be accurate or authentic. They are much later and more derivative than many people think, and most of their ideas have been known by scholars at least for well over a century. As a constructionist, what I am doing is trying to understand how and why these myths developed about these amazing "hidden gospels," and I try and explain it in terms of power shifts in Christianity, the rise of feminist scholarship, changes in the universities, etc.

Who's Who in Hell

His Secular Holiness Reveals the Hidden Legacy of Non-Belief

Interview with Warren Allen Smith

During my last semester in college, I took a course on science fiction. Early on, the guy beside me said that he was sickened to find out that Isaac Asimov was an atheist. He had been reading *Foundation* at the time, and when he discovered Asimov's beliefs, he quit reading the book and vowed never to read anything by the prolific science and science-fiction author again.

That knucklehead dropped out of the class soon afterwards, but my nameless former classmate came to mind recently. I'd really love to call him on his bluff. If he refuses to read a book because the author is a non-believer, then I assume he refuses to read all books by non-believers. On top of that, following this principle, he should never again listen to music, watch a movie, look at art, or use an invention that was created by a non-believer. "Fine," he might say, thinking this only rules out a few minor things. Actually, he wouldn't be able to read a lot of science fiction, including *Brave New World*, *2001: A Space Odyssey*, *Stranger in a Strange Land*, *The Hitchhiker's Guide to the Galaxy*, *The Handmaid's Tale*, or *Fahrenheit 451* (how appropriate). For that matter, he couldn't read *Tom Sawyer* or *Huckleberry Finn*, "Kublah Khan," *Robinson Crusoe*, *Oliver Twist*, *A Tale of Two Cities*, *Les Miserables*, *The Three Musketeers*, *The Great Gatsby*, *Ulysses*, *The Call of the Wild*, *Moby Dick*, *Death of a Salesman*, *Winnie-the-Pooh*, "The Raven," *Frankenstein*, "Ode on a Grecian Urn," *Prometheus Unbound*, *The Grapes of Wrath*, *Walden*, *Candide*, *Slaughterhouse Five*, *The Color Purple*, *Leaves of Grass*, "My Luve Is Like a Red, Red Rose," *Don Juan*, *For Whom the Bell Tolls*, or the poetry of William Wordsworth, Emily Dickinson, and E.E. Cummings. Naturally, he also couldn't watch movies based on any of these works.

Speaking of movies, he won't be able watch *The African Queen*, *The Godfather*, the first *Star Wars* trilogy, the *Superman* trilogy, the *Die Hard* trilogy, *Butch Cassidy and the Sundance Kid*, *The Sting*, *One Flew Over the Cuckoo's Nest*, *The Shining*, *Jurassic Park*, *The Silence of the Lambs*, *Chinatown*, or any of the films of Charlie Chaplin, W.C. Fields, Ingmar Bergman, Marlene Dietrich, or Uma Thurman.

According to his own rules, he couldn't enter a building designed by Frank Lloyd Wright, attend a ballet starring Baryshnikov, or gaze at *The Thinker*, "*Whistler's Mother*," or the paintings of Delacroix, Picasso, Wyeth, and Frida Kahlo. He wouldn't be able to listen to the music of Beethoven, Brahms, Debussy, Haydn, Mahler, Mozart, Verdi, or Wagner, not to mention R.E.M., the Beatles, or, um, Barry Manilow.

He can't look at any pictures sent back from the Hubble telescope, go to a Barnum & Bailey Circus, fly in a hot-air balloon, drink pasteurized milk, or use the services of the Red Cross.

And he wouldn't be able to watch CNN or an Atlanta Braves game. Or the original *Twilight Zone* series. He'd better be using a Mac, because Windows and DOS—not to mention Word, Hotmail, and Internet Explorer—are all owned by an agnostic. Of course, he wouldn't need to use Internet Explorer, because he couldn't surf the Web, which is the creation of a Unitarian. Come to think of it, he can't use a telephone or incandescent lighting, either. On top of all that, he'd have to leave the US, whose principal founders were deists.

The point of my little thought exercise, of course, is that nonbelievers of all stripes—atheists, humanists, naturalists, agnostics, deists, transcendentalists, Unitarians, and other freethinkers—have contributed an awful lot to civilization. It's easy to overlook this fact, though, since the beliefs of many famous freethinkers are not widely known. Once in a while, one of them—such as John Lennon or Jesse Ventura—will cause a shit-storm by bashing religion, but mostly the uncomfortable fact that these achievers don't believe in a god or gods is conveniently overlooked. Except by Warren Allen Smith, who has spent over 50 years compiling information on non-belief. The fruits of this effort have finally been borne in the form of the gargantuan, cheekily-titled *Who's Who in Hell: A Handbook and International Directory for Humanists, Freethinkers, Naturalists, Rationalists, and Non-Theists*, from which I gleaned all of the above info. Cleverly designed to look like a standard *Who's Who* volume, this weighty tome is the first large-scale effort to catalog information on non-belief in 50 years and just might be the largest ever. I interviewed the author via email in August 2000.

Mostly the uncomfortable fact that these achievers don't believe in a god or gods is conveniently overlooked.

Russ Kick: You mentioned to me that Christians try to claim Charles Darwin as one of their own, to the point of burying him in Westminster Abbey. This hits on the topic of historical individuals whose belief systems have been lied about. Tell me a little about this regarding Darwin, as well as other non-believers whose belief systems have been posthumously "revised."

Warren Allen Smith: Darwin was clearly an agnostic. "For myself," he wrote, "I do not believe in any revelation. As for a future life, every man must judge for himself between conflicting vague probabilities." In my book I cite his son's account of the last

Friends have found that provisions written in some freethinkers' wills were not carried out, because their families were believers.

moments: "He seemed to recognize the approach of death, and said, 'I am not the least afraid to die.' All the next morning he suffered from terrible nausea and faintness, and hardly rallied before the end came."

As for any last-minute conversion, Francis Darwin told T.H. Huxley in 1887 that any such allegations were "false and without any kind of foundation," calling such stories "a work of imagination." He affirmed that his father died an agnostic. Of his sons, Sir Francis became a leading botanist, Sir George Howard a distinguished astronomer at Cambridge, and two others became successful engineers. All, stated Joseph McCabe [one of the greatest, most prolific writer-scholars of freethought], were agnostics.

Off the top of my head, I only recall one deathbed conversion (although there must have been many more): novelist Kay Boyle's. In her final months the elderly writer of short stories was tenderly treated by a kindly monk, and she agreed to becoming a Catholic as a special favor to him. Her son, Ian Franckenstein, wrote me the details, however, and confirmed that her entire life had been lived as a non-believer.

Also, Sinclair Lewis was rumored to have converted, but his wife Dorothy Thompson and I could point to a 1950 postcard in which he wrote to me, "Just back from Italy. I find your letter. Yes, I think naturalistic humanism—with dislike for verbalistic philosophy—is my category."

Also, friends have found that provisions written in some freethinkers' wills were not carried out, because their families were believers.

RK: On a related note, we have a case in which an entire nation's religious heritage has been lied about. Christians insist that the United States is a Christian nation, but the facts don't bear this out. Please tell me about this.

WAS: In my book I show how the Founding Fathers, no longer agreeable to having King George III their spiritual head, came up with a deistic solution: a Constitution that separates church and state and favors no one church. To deny this is to admit one's prejudging the facts.

RK: Who are some famous people of the past and present who most of us would probably be surprised to learn are non-believers?

WAS: At the end of the book, I include over a dozen pages which organize many of the listees by occupation. In parentheses are some who surprised me that they are agnostics, Unitarians, rationalists, or some kind of freethinker: Actors (Charles Chaplin, George Clooney, Marlene Dietrich, Phyllis Diller, Carrie Fisher, Katharine Hepburn, Paul Newman, Jack Nicholson, Christopher Reeve, Peter Ustinov); anthropologists (Carleton Coon, Weston LaBarre, Richard Leakey, Bronislaw Malinowski); architects (Buckminster Fuller, Cesar Pelli, Frank Lloyd Wright); artists (Marie Bonheur, Lucian Freud, Henri Matisse, Pablo Picasso, Auguste Rodin, James Whistler, N. C. Wyeth); astronauts (R.M. Bonner; Yuri Gagarin, Robert Jastrow); astronomers (Alan Hale, Edmund Halley, Fred Hoyle, Edwin Hubble, Carl Sagan, Harlow Shapley); authors (two entire pages!). And that's just the A's!

Other extensive listings of occupations include biologists, business executives, critics, dancers, economists, educators, encyclopedists, explorers, feminists, historians, humorists, inventors, journalists, jurists, mathematicians, musicians, Nobel Prize winners (over 50 of them), philosophers, physicians, physicists, playwrights, poets, psychiatrists, publishers, reformers, revolutionaries, satirists, scholars, science fiction writers, scientists, sexologists, soldiers, statesmen, television producers, and zoologists.

Who's Who in Hell is an A-to-Z listing of individuals who, over the centuries and all over Earth, have not been attracted to the concept of a personal God.

RK: Tell me about your book.

WAS: *Who's Who in Hell* is an A-to-Z listing of individuals who, over the centuries and all over Earth, have not been attracted to the concept of a personal God. Admittedly, they are in a minority now and have been over the ages.

Corliss Lamont's *The Philosophy of Humanism* lists some of the early freethinkers: Protagoras, the fifth-century B.C.E. agnostic;

Lucretius and Spinoza, the naturalists; and Epicurus, who neither believed that deities intervene in human affairs nor that there is an afterlife after death. Then Voltaire, the Encyclopedists, and the deists; Kant, Coleridge, Emerson, and the transcendentalists. And today there are the existentialists, pragmatists, secular humanists, and other non-theists. My intent has been to name every freethinker I could find, including officers of atheist and humanist chapters or staff members of freethought publications.

My intent has been to name every freethinker I could find.

Theism admittedly has been more popular than non-theism. As a result, most people use words that, according to the Principle of Verifiability, rationalists say are meaningless. In short, if something cannot be verified, it is considered meaningless. It is easy to verify, for example, that Prague is not the capital of Czechoslovakia—no such nation now exists. But theists come up with meaningless, or unverifiable, concepts such as sin, grace, baptism, God, Christ, Heaven, atheism, angel, transubstantiation. Philosophers, on the other hand, speak of logic, ethics, morality, epistemology (the nature of knowledge), and naturalism (as opposed to supernaturalism).

In addition to listing over 10,000 freethinkers by name, the book also lists, again alphabetically, hundreds of subjects of interest to freethinkers. Cannibalism, for example, is related to Christian communion and therefore to theophagy (the eating of god). The book lists as many international freethought organizations as I could find, so by looking under Nepal or New York, one can locate humanist chapters, often with their officers and snail-mail or email addresses.

The 1,237-page tome weighs over six pounds. I like to point out that it's "bigger than the Holy Bible...and far funnier." For example, a "fairy" was once linguistically connected with the god that vanquished a demon, and the Celts shrank the old gods into fairies, brownies, or "little people." Today, I quote a wag who said, "Large numbers of fairies have been seen in the rest rooms of churches, libraries...and even skirting about in offices of the most prestigious philosophy departments." Footwashing is a rite for Christians, a fetish for freethinkers. Although both a lama and a llama are wooly, the latter is pronounced YAH-ma in Spanish and is not a "superior one," whereas the former "is neither a beast of burden nor a ruminant." The only humor I could find in the entire Holy Bible—this says much about people who are attracted to its contents—was the verse alluding to a geographical location, "And Noah looked from the ark and saw..."

Footwashing is a rite for Christians, a fetish for freethinkers.

In 1990 when I purchased an Apple Macintosh computer, I started alphabetizing all this. A year ago, when I submitted the proposed manuscript to Beacon Press, Open Court, Prometheus Books, and the Rationalist Press in England, I got immediate rejections. But when I approached Lyle and Carol Stuart of Barricade Books, I was signed up almost immediately and was even allowed to edit my own work using their QuarkXPress.

Theists who have corresponded included Faith Baldwin, Paul de Kruif, Alan Dowling, E.L. Mayo, Reinhold Niebuhr, J.B. Priestley, Dorothy Sayers, Karl Shapiro, and Richard Wilbur. Although some non-theists advised me not to include them, I not only did but also in the handbook attempted to define some of the strange terminology used by theologians. Not many humanists, for example, are aware that a theologoumenon is a theological statement or concept that is an individual opinion, rather than authoritative doctrine. Or that theodicy refers to a defense of God's goodness and omnipotence in view of the existence of evil; if bad things occur, in other words, God may have done them to illustrate His mysterious ways—rationalists are more apt to spell the word "idiocy." In addition, I have defined philosophic terms for the average layman, terms such as epistemology, metaphysics, logical atomism, pragmatism, evolution, Darwinism, process philosophy, phenomenalism, instrumentalism, and realism.

The book challenges creationism, homophobia, anti-abortionism, anti-euthanasia, and hatred in general. It is science-, feminist-, gay-, and rationalism-friendly. As Paul Edwards, editor-in-chief of *The Encyclopedia of Philosophy* has already noted, "Religious fanatics will hate it."

RK: I noticed that you've actually corresponded with many of the famous people covered in your book.

WAS: While I was studying with Lionel Trilling at Columbia University in 1948, Thomas Mann wrote me his ideas about "humanism," and to my surprise I later talked with or received correspondence about humanism over the years from James Truslow Adams, Conrad Aiken, Van Meter Ames, Maxwell Anderson, Isaac Asimov, Margaret Bourke-White, Paul Cadmus, John Cage, Brock Chisholm, Sir Arthur C. Clarke, George Counts, Norman Cousins, E.E. Cummings, John Dewey, Paul Edwards, Albert Ellis, Royston Ellis, James T. Farrell, Erich Fromm, Allen Ginsberg, Emily Hahn, Nat Hentoff, Julian Huxley, Horace Kallen, William Heard Kilpatrick, Paul Kurtz, Corliss Lamont, Sinclair Lewis, Walter Lippmann, Vashti McCollum, Archibald Macleish, Butterfly McQueen, Cesar Pelli, Charles Francis Potter, James Randi, Ned Rorem, Alan Ryan, Charles Smith, Gordon Stein, Rob Tielman, Norman L. Torrey, Sir Peter Ustinov, Gore Vidal, Kurt Vonnegut Jr., Eva Ingersoll Wakefield, Ibn Warraq, Glenway Wescott, William Carlos Williams, and Edwin H. Wilson.

Many people, I have found, do not like to be labeled. Playwright Arthur Miller, for example, when asked what kind of humanist he is, replied that it depends on the day. "I'd call myself a secular humanist, excepting when the mystery of life is overwhelming and some semi-insane directing force seems undeniable." Thomas Mann granted me the right to label him whatever I wished. "Humanism is the most precious result of rational meditation upon our existence and that of the world," wrote Albert Schweitzer, avoiding my question. Robert Frost simply told me his mother was a Swedenborgian.

RK: What about your own beliefs?

Playwright Arthur Miller, for example, when asked what kind of humanist he is, replied that it depends on the day.

WAS: I personally was raised a Methodist, but upon leaving Iowa's Bible Belt for college I moved progressively from nihilism to agnosticism to deism to Emersonianism to pantheism to transcendentalism to the Unitarian humanism of the John H. Dietrich-Curtis W. Reese vintage to freethought to rationalism, and then to naturalistic humanism and secular humanism. As the result of my 50 years of research, I now feel more comfortable being described as a "humanistic naturalist," which implies that naturalism (not supernaturalism) is paramount but that my inspiration (not in any way connected to spiritualism) comes from the humanities (music, art, novels, poetry, drama, essays).

For theists to accuse non-theists of being atheists is analogous to soccer players accusing baseball players of lacking goal posts. When asked if I am an a-theist, I can honestly respond that I am and also that I am an a-vegetarian, an a-Texan, and an a-transgendered person. In short, I am *not* many things, although it escapes me why anyone should be interested in what I am *not*.

During the past five decades I also have experienced being on Omaha Beach, rioting in June 1969 at the Stonewall Inn, teaching several thousand teenagers, founding the recording studio in which Liza Minnelli made her first demo record, cremating after our 40 years of companionship a Costa Rican lover who founded the studio with me, writing a syndicated column in West Indian journals, and publishing numerous materials for skeptics and freethinkers.

For theists to accuse non-theists of being atheists is analogous to soccer players accusing baseball players of lacking goal posts.

Do I go to church? No, but on my way to Omaha Beach I left Fort Knox long enough to join the Unitarian Society in Louisville, Kentucky. I have since been a Unitarian in Des Moines, Iowa; Cedar Falls, Iowa; Nassau County, New York; and Westport and Stamford, Connecticut. The present leader of the Fourth Universalist Society of New York, which I attend with my present lover, knows that as a member I am active in various freethought, non-theist, rationalist, and humanist groups. Anyone who does not know me very well probably thinks I'm a left-of-center liberal, and I would not initiate litigation if so accused.

RK: Who are some of your heroes?

WAS: Well, Bertrand Russell is high on the list. A.J. Ayer, Antony Flew, and David Hume all rejected the gods and held that we only die once. In Sir Bertrand's words, we become "food for the worms." Historian Priscilla Robertson, Bangladesh physician Taslima Nasrin (upon whose head the Muslim fundamentalists have placed a *fatwa*, so whoever assassinates her will achieve Allah's approval and gain entry to Paradise once they die), Susan B. Anthony, and Elizabeth Cady Stanton are also high, because they are activists, not just theorists. I also prize the close friendship of freethinkers such as Taslima Nasrin, anthropologist H. James Birx, editor Timothy Madigan, and economics professor Robert Shirley.

RK: What are some of your thoughts on religion?

WAS: Well-known and apparently rational individuals ironically use opposite facts to reach conclusions. The Pope and Mother Teresa "believe" in the Holy Bible, in the supernatural, and in life after death. Freethinkers by the thousands do not make such "leaps of faith," and others such as Christopher Hitchens find the "presumably virgin" Teresa egregiously evil because of her views on India's caste system, her holding that the Inquisition was right and Galileo was wrong, her having buddied with dictators, and her views on how to treat HIV by preaching penance through suffering. Readers of American journals exalt the Pope and Teresa, but in Sri Lanka the former was snubbed when he last visited, and the latter was described by rationalists in Calcutta as a Nobel Prize winner "who is not at all any better than all the other godmen and godwomen, because she helps to place a more kindly mask on the overall exploitation in our society."

As for "belief," entertainer Steve Allen makes the point that he does not "believe" that 2 + 2 = 4. He knows it. Rationalists tend to avoid using "belief" and any words which are theological inventions.

RK: Do you think non-belief will ever become more accepted? Can we ever expect to see an atheist president, for example?

WAS: According to Sir Arthur C. Clarke's *3001*, anyone showing symptoms of religiosity in the year 3001 will be sent to a booby hatch for observation. Meanwhile, so long as the Religious Wrong holds sway in the United States, I see no atheist becoming president for a long, long time. The present President of Brazil, Fernando Cardosa, I've just learned (too late to include him) is a non-believer.

Other contemporary non-believers who are statesmen or stateswomen are Ms. Shulamit Aloni in Israel, Manuel Avila Camacho (president of Mexico in the 1940s), Fidel Castro of Cuba (whom many humanists find inhumane), Dobrica Cosic (a former President of Yugoslavia and a signer of the Humanist Manifesto 2000), Senator Alan Cranston of California (who also signed the Humanist Manifesto 2000), William Hayden (a Governor General of Australia), Lionel Jospin (a French Prime Minister), Neil Kinnock (former member of Britain's House of Commons), Aleksander Kwasniewska (the atheistic politician in Poland who defeated Lech Walesa), Eliot Richardson (a Unitarian who has served in more Cabinet positions than any other person in US history), Simone Vail (who was President of the European Parliament), and Jesse Ventura (the Minnesota Governor who has said, "Organized religion is a sham and a crutch for weak-minded people who need strength in numbers. It tells people to go out and stick their noses in other people's business.").

Atheists, humanists, and all other freethinkers have never received good press, of course.

What alarms me these days is how difficult it is to find disinterested facts and opinions. I have to read several newspapers, including my mainstay *The Economist*, to figure out what is really going on. Corporations swallow newspapers, book publishing concerns, Internet concerns, show-business organizations, television programs, and magazines, and as the global corporate influence grows, it is questionable who is behind what a person is seeing or reading.

Atheists, humanists, and all other freethinkers have never received good press, of course. If tomorrow a VIP dies, cameras will pan in on the church ceremony, implying that death and organized religion are in cahoots (except that freethinker François Mitterand's funeral featured not only his non-belief but also his wife and his mistress; and Isaac Asimov's memorial at the New York Ethical Society and Carl Sagan's memorial at St. John's Episcopal Cathedral in New York City both cited their non-theism).

Ted Turner may once have described Christianity as "a religion for losers," but where is this viewpoint dramatized, described, and written about by the mass media? Usually, it's a story about a lesbian atheist who gives birth and the father is unknown.

RK: What reactions has your book gotten so far? What do you hope to accomplish with *Who's Who in Hell*?

WAS: Like Topsy, the book just grew, so I never compiled the work for money. It clearly has been a labor of love. I have already been interviewed by Brazilian, British, Ecuadorian, and Indian journalists—I am pleased that already it is considered a handy international reference book.

Frank DiGiacomo of the *New York Observer* wrote a page-one story (August 14, 2000) complete with my caricature and a photo. CNN correspondent Jeanne Moos not only televised an interview but then followed it up wittily by going to St. Patrick's Cathedral and inquiring of parishioners on camera if they were aware of the book and what they thought about the title. Various radio talk-show hosts have interviewed me, and I am being asked to travel for book-signings around the country. *Publishers Weekly* came out with a 101% favorable review. I've frankly been overwhelmed by the praise but, realistically, am expecting the brickbats to follow.

The bottom line? What I hope to accomplish is to have written something that will be consulted for decades to come, to gain the recognition that the work is in a category with Pierre Sylvain Maréchal's *Dictionnaire des Athées* (1798), J.M. Wheeler's *Biographical Dictionary of Freethinkers of All Ages and Nations* (1889), and Joseph McCabe's *Biographical Dictionary of Ancient, Medieval, and Modern Freethinkers* (1945). If this is accomplished, I will settle for having made a little footnote in the study of intellectual history.

Meanwhile, I'm happy to report that having long since discarded Heaven and Hell, I almost never experience hell in my personal relations and, in fact, am enjoying this moment's heaven.

BLINDED BY SCIENCE

Environmentalism for the Twenty-First Century

Patrick Moore

As we start the twenty-first century, environmental thinkers are divided along a sharp fault line. There are the doomsayers who predict the collapse of the global ecosystem. There are the technological optimists who believe that we can feed twelve billion people and solve all our problems with science and technology. I do not believe that either of these extremes makes sense. There is a middle road based on science and logic, the combination of which is sometimes referred to as common sense. There are real problems, and there is much we can do to improve the state of the environment.

I was born and raised in the tiny fishing and logging village of Winter Harbour on the northwest tip of Vancouver Island, in the rainforest by the Pacific. I didn't realize what a blessed childhood I'd had, playing on the tidal flats by the salmon spawning streams in the rainforest, until I was shipped away to boarding school in Vancouver at age fourteen. I eventually attended the University of British Columbia, studying the life sciences: biology, forestry, genetics; but it was when I discovered ecology that I realized that through science I could gain an insight into the mystery of the rainforest I had known as a child. I became a born-again ecologist, and in the late 1960s, was soon transformed into a radical environmental activist.

I became a born-again ecologist, and in the late 1960s, was soon transformed into a radical environmental activist.

I found myself in a church basement in Vancouver with a like-minded group of people, planning a protest campaign against US hydrogen bomb-testing in Alaska. We proved that a somewhat rag-tag-looking group of activists could sail a leaky old halibut boat across the North Pacific Ocean and change the course of history. By creating a focal point for opposition to the tests, we got on national news and helped build a groundswell of opposition to nuclear testing in the US and Canada. When that bomb went off in November 1971, it was the last hydrogen bomb ever detonated on planet Earth. Even though there were four more tests planned in the series, President Nixon canceled them due to public opposition. This was the birth of Greenpeace.

Flushed with victory and knowing we could bring about change by getting up and doing something, we were welcomed into the longhouse of the Kwakiutl Nation at Alert Bay near the north end of Vancouver Island. We were made brothers of the tribe because they believed in what we were doing. This began the tradition of the Warriors of the Rainbow, after a Cree legend that predicted one day when the skies are black and the birds fall dead to the ground and the rivers are poisoned, people of all races, colors, and creeds will join together to form the Warriors of the Rainbow to save the Earth from environmental destruction. We named our ship the *Rainbow Warrior*, and I spent fifteen years on the front lines of the eco-movement as we evolved from that church basement into the world's largest environmental activist organization.

I spent fifteen years on the front lines of the eco-movement as we evolved from that church basement into the world's largest environmental activist organization.

Next we took on French atmospheric nuclear testing in the South Pacific. They proved a bit more difficult than the US Atomic Energy Administration. But after many years of protest voyages and campaigning, involving loss of life on our side, they were first driven underground and eventually stopped testing altogether.

In 1975 we set sail deep-sea into the North Pacific against the Soviet Union's factory whaling fleets that were slaughtering the last of the sperm whales off California. We put ourselves in front of the harpoons in little rubber boats and made Walter Cronkite's evening news. That really put Greenpeace on the map. In 1979 the International Whaling Commission banned factory whaling in the North Pacific, and soon it was banned in all the world's oceans.

In 1978 I was arrested off Newfoundland for sitting on a baby seal, trying to shield it from the hunter's club. I was convicted under the misnamed Seal Protection Regulations that made it illegal to protect seals. In 1984 baby sealskins were banned from European markets, effectively ending the slaughter.

Can you believe that in the early 1980s the countries of Western Europe were pooling their low- and medium-level nuclear wastes, putting them in thousands of oil drums, loading them on ships, and dumping them in the Atlantic Ocean as a way of "disposing" of the wastes? In 1984 a combined effort by Greenpeace and the UK Seafarer's Union put an end to that practice for good.

I had been against at least three or four things every day of my life for fifteen years; I decided I'd like to be in favor of something for a change.

By the mid-1980s Greenpeace had grown from that church basement into an organization with an income of over US$100 million per year, offices in 21 countries, and over 100 campaigns around the world, now tackling toxic waste, acid rain, uranium mining, and drift-net fishing, as well as the original issues. We had won over a majority of the public in the industrialized democracies. Presidents and prime ministers were talking about the environment on a daily basis.

For me it was time to make a change. I had been against at least three or four things every day of my life for fifteen years; I decided I'd like to be in favor of something for a change. I made the transition from the politics of confrontation to the politics of building consensus. After all, when a majority of people agrees with you, it is probably time to stop hitting them over the head with a stick and sit down and talk to them about finding solutions to our environmental problems.

All social movements evolve from an earlier period of polarization and confrontation, during which a minority struggles to convince society that its cause is true and just, eventually followed by a time of reconciliation if a majority of the population accepts the values of the new movement. For the environmental movement this transition began to occur in the mid-1980s. The term "sustainable development" was adopted to describe the challenge of taking the new environmental values we had popularized, and incorporating them into the traditional social and economic values that have always governed public policy and our daily behavior.

We cannot simply switch to basing all our actions on purely environmental values. Every day six billion people wake up with real needs for food, energy, and materials. The challenge for sustainability is to provide for those needs in ways that reduce negative impact on the environment. But any changes made must also be socially acceptable and technically and economically feasible. It is not always easy to balance environmental, social, and economic priorities. Compromise and cooperation with the involvement of government, industry, academia, and the environmental movement is required to achieve sustainability. It is this effort to find consensus among competing interests that has occupied my time for the past fifteen years.

Every day six billion people wake up with real needs for food, energy, and materials.

Not all my former colleagues saw things that way. They rejected consensus politics and sustainable development in favor of continued confrontation and ever-increasing extremism. They ushered in an era of zero tolerance and left-wing politics. Some of the features of this environmental extremism are:

- Environmental extremists are anti-human. Humans are characterized as a cancer on the Earth. To quote eco-extremist Herb Hammond, "Of all the components of the ecosystem, humans are the only ones we know to be completely optional." Isn't that a lovely thought?

- They are anti-science and -technology. All large machines are seen as inherently destructive and unnatural. Science is invoked to justify positions that have nothing to do with science. Unfounded opinion is accepted over demonstrated fact.

- Environmental extremists are anti-trade; not just free trade but anti-trade in general. In the name of bioregionalism they would bring in an age of ultra-nationalist xenophobia. The original "Whole Earth" vision of one world family is lost in an hysterical campaign against globalization and free trade.

- They are anti-business. All large corporations are depicted as inherently driven by greed and corruption. Profits are definitely not politically correct. The liberal democratic, market-based model is rejected even though no viable alternative is proposed to provide for the material needs of six billion people. As expressed by the Native Forest Network, "It is necessary to adopt a global phase-out strategy of consumer-based industrial capitalism." I think they mean civilization.

- And they are just plain anti-civilization. In the final analysis, eco-extremists project a naive vision of returning to the supposedly utopian existence in the garden of Eden, conveniently forgetting that in the old days people lived to an average age of 35, and there were no dentists. In their brave new world there will be no more chemicals, no more airplanes, and certainly no more polyester suits.

Let me give you some specific examples that highlight the movement's tendency to abandon science and logic and to get the priorities completely mixed up through the use of sensationalism, misinformation, and downright lies.

The *Brent Spar* Oil Rig

In 1995, Shell Oil was granted permission by the British Environment Ministry to dispose of the North Sea oil rig *Brent Spar* in deep water in the North Atlantic Ocean. Greenpeace immediately accused Shell of using the sea as a "dustbin." Greenpeace campaigners maintained that there were hundreds of tons of petroleum wastes on board the *Brent Spar* and that some of these were radioactive. They organized a consumer boycott of Shell, and service stations were firebombed in Germany. The boycott cost the company millions in sales. German Chancellor Helmut Kohl denounced the British government's decision to allow the dumping. Caught completely off guard, Shell ordered the tug that was already towing the rig to its burial site to turn back. They then announced that they had abandoned the plan for deep-sea disposal. This embarrassed British Prime Minister John Major.

Independent investigation revealed that the rig had been properly cleaned and did not contain the toxic and radioactive waste claimed by Greenpeace. Greenpeace wrote to Shell apologizing for the factual error. But they did not change their position on deep-sea disposal despite the fact that on-land disposal would cause far greater environmental impact.

During all the public outrage directed against Shell for daring to sink a large piece of steel and concrete, it was never noted that Greenpeace had purposely sunk its own ship off the coast of New Zealand in 1986.

During all the public outrage directed against Shell for daring to sink a large piece of steel and concrete, it was never noted that Greenpeace had purposely sunk its own ship off the coast of New Zealand in 1986. When the French government bombed and sunk the *Rainbow Warrior* in Auckland Harbour in 1985, the vessel was permanently disabled. It was later re-floated, patched up, cleaned, and towed to a marine park where it was sunk in shallow water as a dive site. Greenpeace said the ship would be an artificial reef and would support increased marine life.

The *Brent Spar* and the *Rainbow Warrior* are in no way fundamentally different from one another. The sinking of the *Brent Spar* could also be rationalized as providing habitat for marine creatures. It's just that the public relations people at Shell are not as clever as those at Greenpeace. And in this case Greenpeace got away with using misinformation even though they had to admit their error after the fact. After spending tens of millions of dollars on studies, Shell recently announced that it had abandoned any plan for deep-sea disposal and will support a proposal to re-use the rig as pylons in a dock-extension project in Norway. Tens of millions of dollars and much precious time were wasted over an issue that had nothing to do with the environment and everything to do with misinformation and fundraising hysteria.

To make matters worse, in 1998 Greenpeace successfully campaigned for a ban on all marine disposal of disused oil installations. This will result in hundreds of millions, even billions, of dollars in unnecessary costs. One obvious solution would be to designate an area in the North Sea for the creation of a large artificial reef and to sink oil rigs there after cleaning them. This would provide a breeding area for fish and other marine life, enhancing the biological and economic productivity of the sea. But Greenpeace isn't looking for solutions, only conflicts and bad guys.

Exotic Species

There has been a recent flurry of sensationalist warnings about the threat of exotic species. Zealous cadres of conservation biologists descend on wetlands to rip foreign weeds from the bog, declaring that "a rapidly spreading invasion of exotic plants and animals is destroying our nation's biological diversity." It's amazing how a word that was so good, as in "exotic paradise" and "exotic pleasure," is now used to describe an alleged biological holocaust.

I was inspired to write about exotic species when I heard a news story from Washington, D.C., in the spring of 1999. The citizens of the Capitol were distressed to find that a family of beavers had taken up residence there and were busy felling the Japanese cherry trees that adorned the banks of the Potomac River. It became a national emergency of sorts, and a great effort was made to trap every last beaver; only then were the townspeople put at ease. There was no mention made of the fact that the beaver is a *native* North American species whereas the cherry trees are exotics, imported from Japan. Yet there was no question which species the public favored.

In fact, the reason we dislike certain species and like others has nothing to do with whether or not they are exotic. By playing on people's natural suspicion of all things foreign, environmentalists confuse the issue and give the public a misleading picture. There are actually thousands of exotic species that are not only beneficial, they are the mainstays of our daily lives. Food crops like wheat, rice, and cabbage are all exotics when grown in North America. Vegetables that originated in the Americas such as beans, corn, and potatoes are exotics when they are grown in Europe. All around the world, agriculture is largely based on species that originated somewhere else. This is also the case for domestic animals, garden plants, and street trees.

There are also hundreds of native species of plants and animals that we consider undesirable. For centuries we have referred to them as weeds, pests, vermin, and disease. There are also many exotic species that fall into this category. And, of course, there are many native species that are considered extremely beneficial, especially those that provide food for a growing population. The point is, both exotic and native species can be desirable or undesirable from a human perspective, depending on how they affect our lives. Our almost innate dislike of rats and spiders has nothing to do with whether or not they are native or exotic; it is due to the possibility of deadly disease or a fatal bite. And even though dandelions in the lawn are hardly a life-and-death issue, millions are spent each year to rid lawns of these "weeds."

Certain exotic species have resulted in severe negative impacts. The most notorious case involved the introduction of European species of animals to Australia, New Zealand, and the Pacific Islands when Europeans colonized these regions beginning about 225 years ago. Many native species—flightless birds and ground-dwelling marsupials in particular—were not able to survive the introduction of predators such as rats, cats, and foxes. As a result, hundreds of native species were eliminated. Another well-known exotic is Dutch elm disease, a fungus that actually originated in Asia, came through Europe and on to North America, where it has resulted in the death of many native elms in the US and Canada.

The point is, both exotic and native species can be desirable or undesirable from a human perspective, depending on how they affect our lives.

There can be no doubt that we should always be careful when considering the introduction of a new species, and that regulations are needed to prevent undesirable accidental introductions. At the same time, we must not lose sight of the fact that introduced species play a vital, indeed essential, role in modern society. Each species must be evaluated on its own merits. The introduction of some species may be desirable in one region and yet undesirable in others. Islands are particularly susceptible to introductions because they are isolated and their native species are not subjected to as wide a variety of predators and diseases. When rats are introduced to islands that support large bird rookeries, there is often a precipitous decline in bird populations due to predation on eggs and nestlings.

There is really no difference when considering the use of an exotic species of tree for managed forests. The main reason we tend to use native species of trees for forestry in North America is because they are the best available in terms of productivity and wood quality. In other regions this is not the case. Radiata pine from California has been very successful in New Zealand, Australia, and Chile. Eucalyptus from Australia is the forestry species of choice in many parts of Brazil, Portugal, and South Africa. Douglas-fir from Oregon has become the number-two species of softwood produced in France. And Chinese larch is a favorite for reforestation in Scotland, where forest cover was lost centuries ago to sheep farming.

The Invisible Poisons

Beginning with the Natural Resources Defense Council's scare tactics about the use of the pesticide Alar on apples, the environmental movement has been very clever at inventing campaigns that make us afraid of our food. They conjure up invisible poisons that will give us cancer, birth defects, mutations, and otherwise kill us in our sleep. We will all soon be reduced to a hermaphroditic frenzy by endocrine-mimicking compounds as we approach the Toxic Saturation Point.

Meanwhile, the National Cancer Institute of Canada conducted a joint study with US counterparts beginning in 1994 to investigate the possible relationship between pesticide residues in food and cancer in humans. The findings published in the peer-reviewed journal *Cancer* in 1997 concluded that it could not find "any definitive evidence to suggest that synthetic pesticides contribute significantly to overall cancer mortality," a careful way of saying they found zero connection. And yet, the article pointed out, over 30 percent of cancers in humans are caused by tobacco, a natural substance. And another 35 percent are caused by poor diet, mainly too much fat and cholesterol and not enough fresh fruit and vegetables. The main effect of the environmental campaign against pesticides is to scare parents into avoiding fresh fruit and vegetables for themselves and their children.

The same kind of scare tactics are now being employed in the campaign against biotechnology and genetically-modified foods. Even though there is no evidence of negative human health effects, and environmental concerns are blown completely out of proportion, great fear has been whipped up in the public. Large corporations are in retreat and governments are scrambling to get control of the issue. Unfortunately, some biotechnology companies and associations continue to belittle public concerns and resist disclosure of food ingredients. There is no escaping the fact that this is a new technology and that it must be introduced carefully and sometimes slowly.

In response to the fact that there is no evidence of negative impacts, environmentalists invariably resort to the so-called "precautionary principal," which is actually not a principal at all. If it were, we could do virtually nothing because we never know all future outcomes of actions taken today. It would be better if it were called the "precautionary attitude" or the "precautionary approach." While it is perfectly legitimate to be cautious, we cannot allow that to freeze us in our tracks. It is sobering to consider that the terrible side effects of DDT,

The main effect of the environmental campaign against pesticides is to scare parents into avoiding fresh fruit and vegetables for themselves and their children.

now largely corrected, are not a sufficient argument to ban pesticides altogether, any more than those caused by Thalidomide are sufficient to ban all pharmaceuticals.

Climate Change

Global climate change is another area where extreme statements are made, in this case on both sides of the debate, when there is little in science to defend them. Some things are quite certain. Carbon dioxide levels are rising, and our consumption of fossil fuels and deforestation in the tropics are probably the main causes. There is a lot of evidence that the earth's climate is warming: The glaciers in Alaska are retreating, and great egrets are visiting northern Lake Huron. But here the consensus ends.

Climate change is a wonderful example to demonstrate the limitations of science.

Climate change is a wonderful example to demonstrate the limitations of science. There are two fundamental characteristics of climate change that make it very difficult to use the empirical (scientific) method to predict the future. First, there are simply too many uncontrollable variables—the empirical method works best when you can control all the variables except the one you are studying. Second, and even more significant, is the fact that we have only one planet to observe. If we had 50 planet Earths and increased the carbon dioxide levels on 25 of them, leaving the other 25 alone, we might be able to determine a statistical difference between the two samples. With only one Earth, we are reduced to complex computer models of questionable value, and a lot of guesswork.

Climate change is not about scientific certainty; it is about the evaluation and management of risk. I think it is fair to say that climate change poses a real risk, however small or large. When faced with the risk, the logical thing to do is to buy an insurance policy. Unfortunately we have no actuarial science on which to base the size of the insurance premium; this is where the guesswork comes in. Is it worth reducing fossil fuel consumption by 60 percent to avoid global warming? Should we add the risk of massive nuclear energy construction to offset carbon dioxide emissions? What does "worth doing away" really mean? Is it possible that global warming might have more positive effects than negative ones?

Biodiversity and Forests

The Rainforest Action Network, an eco-political group based in San Francisco, stated on their Website that, "[T]he International Botanical Society recently released the results of an extensive study showing that, at current rates, two-thirds of the world's plant and animal species will become extinct by the year 2100." The International Botanical Society is nowhere to be found on the Internet.

More seriously, in March 1996, the World Wildlife Fund held a media conference in Geneva during the first meeting of the UN Panel on Forests. They stated that there are now 50,000 species going extinct every year due to human activity, more than at any time since the dinosaurs went extinct 65 million years ago. Most significantly, WWF stated that the main cause of these extinctions is "commercial logging." This was largely due, according to WWF director-general Claude Martin, to "massive deforestation in industrialized countries." The statements made at the media conference were broadcast and printed around the world, giving millions of people the impression that forestry was the main cause of species extinction.

I have tried to determine the basis for this allegation, openly challenging the WWF to provide details of species extinctions caused by logging. To date it would appear that there is no scientific evidence on which to base such a claim. WWF has provided no list of species that have become extinct due to logging. In particular, the claim of "massive deforestation" in industrialized countries runs counter to information provided by the Food and Agriculture Organization of the United Nations. According to the FAO, the area of forest in the industrialized world is actually growing by about 0.2% per year, due to the reforestation of land that was previously cleared for farming.

In May 1996, I wrote to Prince Philip, the Duke of Edinburgh, in his capacity as President of WWF. I stated in part:

> Myself and many colleagues who specialize in forest science are distressed at recent statements made by WWF regarding the environmental impact of forestry. These statements indicate a break with WWF's strong tradition of basing their policies on science and reason. To the best of our knowledge, not a single species has become extinct in North America due to forestry.

Prince Philip replied:

> I have to admit I did not see the draft of the statement that (WWF spokesperson) Jean-Paul Jeanrenaud was to make at the meeting of the Intergovernmental Panel on Forestry in Geneva. The first two of his comments (50,000 species per year and the dinosaur comparison) are open to question, but they are not seriously relevant to the issue. However, I quite agree that his third statement (logging being the main cause of extinction) is certainly contentious and the points that you make are all good ones. All I can say is that he was probably thinking of tropical forests when he made the comment.

Since this exchange of correspondence, WWF has changed the way they characterize the impact of forestry in relation to species extinction. At their "Forests for Life" conference in San Francisco in May 1997, there was no mention made of forestry being the main cause of species extinction. Instead, WWF unveiled a report stating that "three quarters of the continent's forest ecoregions are threatened with extinction, showing for the first time that it is not just individual species but entire ecosystems that are at risk in North America." The word "extinction" is normally used to mean that something has been completely eliminated. It is entirely beyond reason to suggest that three quarters of the forested areas of North America will become 'extinct,' yet this is what WWF is proclaiming to the public.

I have been a subscriber to *National Geographic* since my father first gave it to me as a gift when I was in school. I have always looked forward to the latest edition, with all the wonders of the world between its covers. Lately, however, even this stalwart of objective science has fallen prey to the prophets of doom who believe a human-caused "mass extinction" is already underway.

The February 1999 special edition on "Biodiversity: The Fragile Web," contained a particularly unfortunate article titled "The Sixth Extinction." This refers to the fact that there have been five main extinction events during the past 500 million years, the two most severe of which are believed to have been caused by meteor impacts. It may well be that all five were of extraterrestrial origin. During the most recent mass extinction, 65 million years ago, 17 percent of all the taxonomic families of life were lost, including the dinosaurs. An even greater extinction occurred 250 million years ago when 54 percent of all families perished, including the trilobites. ("Family" is a term used in taxonomy, two levels up from individual species; for example, the cat family, the lily family, and the hummingbird family. Each family contains many, sometimes hundreds, of individual species.)

The first two pages of the article contain a photo of Australian scientist Dr. Tim Flannery looking over a collection of stuffed and pickled, small, extinct mammals. The caption under the photo reads: "In the next century half of all species could be annihilated, as were these mammals seen in Tim Flannery's lab at the Australian Museum. Unlike the past five, this mass extinction is being fueled by humans." To be sure, mention is made later in the article that the Australian extinctions were caused by the introduction of cats and foxes when Europeans colonized the region over 200 years ago. This resulted in the loss of about 35 animal species, mainly of flightless birds and ground-dwelling marsupials that were not able to defend themselves against these new predators. This is hardly a "mass extinction," and the cause was a one-time introduction of exotic species.

The rate of extinction of Australian mammals has slowed considerably in recent decades, partly because the most vulnerable species are already extinct, and partly because people started caring about endangered species and began working to prevent them from going extinct. In Australia today there are programs to control wild cats and foxes, some of which have resulted in the recovery of native animal populations.

The use of the Australian example to justify claims that we are experiencing a mass extinction is put into focus by Brian Groombridge, editor of the IUCN Red List of Threatened Species, when he states, "[A]round 75% of recorded extinctions...have occurred on islands. Very few extinctions have been recorded in continental tropical forest habitat, where mass extinction events are predicted to be underway." It is clearly misleading to point to the specific and exceptional case of extinctions caused by the introduction of new species to islands as evidence of a worldwide mass extinction. The *National Geographic* article goes on to quote biologist Stuart Pimm: "It's not just species on islands or in rain forests or just birds or big charismatic mammals. It's everything and it's everywhere. It is a worldwide epidemic of extinctions." Yet nearly every example used in the article involves islands such as Australia and Tasmania, Mauritius, Easter Island, and the many islands of the South Pacific.

On pages 48 and 49 of the "Sixth Extinction" article, there is a graph depicting the number of taxonomic families that have existed on Earth for the past 600 million years. The graph shows that despite the five great extinctions that have occurred during this period, the number of living families has risen steadily, from around 200 families 500 million years ago to over 1,000 families today. This tendency to diversify over time is one of the major features of evolution. The line of the graph is a thick, solid one until it reaches the present day, whereupon it turns abruptly downward as if to indicate a loss of families due to the "mass extinction" now underway. But the line does not remain thick and solid; it turns fuzzy right at the point where it turns down. I wrote to *National Geographic* and asked, "Why does the line turn fuzzy? Is it because there are actually no known families that have become extinct in recent times? I do not know of any families of 'beetles, amphibians, birds, and large mammals' that have become extinct as implied in the text."

In other words, there is no evidence that a mass extinction is actually occurring now, even though the article plainly implies that it is.

The reply to my inquiry came from Robin Adler, one of the researchers who worked on the article. She thanked me for "sharing my thoughts on this complicated and controversial issue" but offered no answer to my question about the graph. Instead she asked me to, "Rest assured that...the many members of our editorial team...worked closely with numerous experts in conservation biology, paleobiology, and related fields. The concept of a 'sixth extinction' is widely discussed and, for the most part, strongly supported by our consultants and other experts in these areas, although specific details such as the time frame in which it will occur and the number of species that will be affected continues to be debated."

Nowhere in the *National Geographic* article is there any mention that the "sixth extinction" is a controversial subject; it is presented as if it is a known fact. It is clear from the reply that the "mass extinction" is actually in the future ("the time frame in which it will occur"). In other words, there is no evidence that a mass extinction is actually occurring now, even though the article plainly implies that it is. The reply also refers to the sixth extinction as a "concept," implying that it is just an idea rather than a proven fact. Perhaps a better title for the article would have been "No Mass Extinction Yet, Maybe Someday."

It is very frustrating when a trusted institution such as *National Geographic* resorts to sensationalism, exaggeration, and misleading illustrations. There is enough bad science and misinformation in the popular press as it is. One can only hope that the present tendency to ignore science and logic, rightly referred to as a "bad intellectual climate" by environmental philosopher Henry H. Webster, will eventually come to an end.

If trees are the answer, you might ask, what is the question?

Trees Are the Answer

If trees are the answer, you might ask, what is the question? I believe that trees are the answer to a lot of questions about our future. These include: How can we advance to a more sustainable economy based on renewable fuels and materials? How can we improve literacy and sanitation in developing countries while reversing deforestation and protecting wildlife at the same time? How can we reduce the amount of greenhouse gases emitted to the atmosphere, carbon dioxide in particular? How can we increase the amount of land that will support a greater diversity of species? How can we help prevent soil erosion and provide clean air and water? How can we make this world more beautiful and green? The answer is, by growing more trees and then using more wood, both as a substitute for non-renewable fossil fuels and materials such as steel, concrete, and plastic, and as paper products for printing, packaging, and sanitation.

When the world's leaders met in Rio de Janeiro in 1992 at the Earth Summit, they agreed that three issues are at the top of the international environmental agenda. These are climate change, biodiversity, and forests. Of course there are many other important issues, including toxic chemicals and nuclear waste, but they are secondary compared to these "Big Three," all of which are global in nature. Unfortunately, most scientists, activists, and policy-makers have specialized in one or the other of these critical areas of concern, and have not focused as strongly on the profound interrelationships among them. This has resulted in a situation where most of the environmental movement has adopted a position on forests that is logically inconsistent with its positions on climate change and biodiversity. The risk of climate change is mainly due to fossil fuel consumption and the emission of CO_2. The risk to biodiversity is mainly due to the loss of forests caused by clearing for agriculture and cities. A large part of the solution to both these issues involves growing more trees and using more wood. The environmental movement has adopted a policy that is the opposite of this approach.

By considering forests in isolation from the other major issues, it may seem logical that we can save them by reducing wood consumption, that is, by cutting fewer trees. Greenpeace has appealed to the members of the United Nations to reduce wood consumption and use "environmentally appropriate alternatives" instead. The Rainforest Action Network is campaigning for a 75 percent reduction in wood use in the United States through its "wood use reduction program." The Sierra Club has adopted a formal policy called "zero cut" that would put an end to commercial forestry on federal public land. All these campaigns can be summed up as "cut fewer trees—use less wood."

There are two problems with this approach. First, just because people stop using wood for fuel or building houses doesn't mean they will not need warmth or shelter. The fact that six billion humans wake up every morning with real needs for energy, food, and materials must be taken into account. All the likely substitutes for wood—steel, concrete, plastic, and fossil fuels—have far higher emissions of CO_2 associated with their production and use. Using less wood will automatically result in the use of more of these non-renewable resources and an inevitable increase in CO_2 emissions.

Second, much of the land that is used to grow trees could just as well be cleared and used for grazing, farming, and housing. If there is less demand for wood, there will be less economic incentive to grow trees and retain forests. It is unrealistic to expect people to retain vast areas of the landscape in forests if they cannot use them. The best way to encourage people to retain and expand forests is to make the resources they provide, including wood, more valuable.

All the likely substitutes for wood —steel, concrete, plastic, and fossil fuels— have far higher emissions of CO_2 associated with their production and use.

Environmentalism for the Twenty-First Century

It's easy to see that the mainstream of the environmental movement has fallen prey to misguided priorities, misinformation, dogmatism, and self-interest. Soon after I left Greenpeace in 1986, I found out that they had initiated a pension plan. I knew I had gotten out just in time. In the early days many of us realized that our job was to work ourselves out of the job, not to give ourselves jobs for life. I feel the same way about my efforts to promote sustainability, sustainable forestry, and the application of science and logic to environmental issues. I am sometimes amazed by the fact that this seems more difficult than my original work to promote awareness of ecology and the environment. Perhaps this time I do have a job for life. Still no pension plan, however!

What are the main features of a rational environmental policy for the twenty-first century? Some points to consider are as follows:

- Wherever possible, we should move towards an economy that is based on renewable energy and material resources. Sustainability is not synonymous with renewability, but it is strongly linked to it. Where we do use non-renewable resources, they should be used wisely and recycled whenever practical.

- We should learn to manage our population voluntarily. The UN Conference on Population, held in Cairo in 1994, concluded that the most effective way to manage population growth is the education and empowerment of women. This leaves no place for patriarchy, religious fundamentalism, or dictatorships.

- We should develop a more globally unified analysis of the relationships among land use, energy and resource consumption, forests and biodiversity, and population. Policies that have global implications must not be logically inconsistent one with the other.

- We should learn to be better gardeners at both local and global scales. With six or eight billion mouths to feed, this will require more intensive agricultural production, including the use of fertilizer, synthetic pesticides, and biotechnology. It is a simple fact of arithmetic that the less land we need to grow our food, the more is available for forest and wilderness.

- Urban sprawl must be brought under control. We have allowed the automobile to determine urban form by default. 300,000 hectares of forest are lost in the United States every year, all of it due to 200 cities spreading out over the land. Denser, more livable cities must be designed if population continues to grow.

- Deforestation in the tropics must eventually be stabilized or reversed. This can be accomplished by the transfer of intensive agricultural practices, the establishment of fast-growing, sustainable fuel-wood plantations, and the management of population growth.

As an ecologist and environmentalist, not a political scientist or political activist, I have always shied away from strong opinions on poverty and class. But it seems unacceptable to me that so many hundreds of millions of people live at a material standard that we in the industrialized countries would not consider acceptable for a dignified life. I believe there is a great deal to be learned by exploring the relationships between ecology and politics. In some ways politics is the ecology of the human species. The two subjects have developed such completely different disciplines and terminologies that it is hard to think of them together. But I believe we must if we are to gain a truly holistic understanding of the relationship between ourselves and our society, and the Earth upon which we ultimately depend.

Policies that have global implications must not be logically inconsistent one with the other.

"MAY THE FOREST BE WITH YOU"

www.greenspirit.com

Humans Have Already Been Cloned

Russ Kick

It's now routine to see news stories about various mammals being cloned. Almost always, these reports mention that this "brings us one step closer to cloning humans," "human clones are right around the corner," and other clichés. What every last one of these insightful stories fails to mention is this: Humans have already been cloned.

I'm not talking about the "artificial twinning" experiments performed in 1993 at the Washington University Medical Center.[1] Although newspapers were quick to trumpet this as human cloning, it was soon revealed that in reality this was a relatively primitive procedure in which an already-fertilized egg was split into two fertilized eggs. A nice party trick, but Mother Nature already does it thousand of times a day when she creates twins, triplets, etc.

Unbelievably, only a few small newspaper stories weakly revealed one of the most important biotechnology developments of all time.

The real cloning took place two years later, in 1995, although it wasn't revealed until mid-November 1998.[2] Unbelievably, only a few small newspaper stories weakly revealed one of the most important biotechnology developments of all time. In fact, it's probably one of the most important developments in the history of science and technology, period.

Working under the auspices of the private company Advanced Cell Technology and using the facilities of the University of Massachusetts at Amherst, scientists James Robl and Jose Cibelli created a human clone. They took cells from Cibelli's leg and cheek, put them alongside a cow's ovum with the genetic material stripped out, and added a jolt of electricity. One of Cibelli's cells fused with the cow's ovum, which acted as though it had been fertilized, and the cells began dividing. This is the same process used to create Dolly, the famous cloned sheep from Scotland, only this was done *before* Dolly was created.

A small story in the *Boston Globe* reported the following about this achievement:

> The experiments were privately funded, and therefore aren't bound by government regulations on embryo research....
>
> The researchers fused a human skin cell with a cow egg stripped of its nucleus because that avoided using a scarce human egg to nurture the genetic program of the new embryo, they said.[3]

So what happened to the clone? The scientists destroyed it when it reached the 32-cell stage. In other words, the zygote had already gone through five divisions and was on its way to becoming a human being. Scientists aren't completely certain what would've happened if the zygote had been allowed to develop in a womb or in vitro, since such a thing has never been attempted (as far as we know), but Dr. Patrick Dixon has an educated guess:

> If the clone had been allowed to continue beyond implantation it would have developed as Dr. Cibelli's identical twin. Technically 1% of the human clone genes would have belonged to the cow—the mitochondria genes.
>
> Mitochondria are power generators in the cytoplasm of the cell. They grow and divide inside cells and are passed on from one generation to another. They are present in sperm and eggs.
>
> Judging by the successful growth of the combined human-cow clone creation, it appears that cow mitochondria may well be compatible with human embryonic development.[4]

Dixon is the author of ten books, including *The Genetic Revolution*, which in 1993 predicted many of the cutting-edge advances in biotech that have since come to pass. He was also responsible for catapulting Dolly to international stardom, convincing the first two newspapers that ran the story that this was indeed a newsworthy development.

As for why the experiment was performed, CEO Michael West said that it was strictly to harvest stem cells, not to create a human being. As the *Boston Globe* article explained:

> The embryos would be allowed to develop for only a few days, at which time they would be stripped of their "embryonic stem cells" that would be grown in laboratory dishes.
>
> These stem cells, the primordial cells in every human embryo from which all of the hundreds of different types of cells are descended, would be kept in their undifferentiated state for as long as needed. Then, presumably, they could be directed to develop into one or more of a long list of tissues and organs to treat human illnesses, among them diabetes, heart failure and Alzheimer's disease. However, the means to order stem cells down particular developmental paths are in their infancy.
>
> Each patient's own cells—scraped from a cheek or a piece of skin—would be used to make the human-cow embryo. The resulting donor tissues could then be transplanted back into the patient without the body's immune system rejecting them, because they would be genetically identical.[5]

West explained why the zygote was destroyed at the 32-cell stage: "'We wanted to take a timeout,' said Michael West, chief executive officer of Advanced Cell Technology Inc., 'and get input from ethicists and public policy-makers' before committing more time and money to the project."[6]

In other words, the zygote had already gone through five divisions and was on its way to becoming a human being.

One month after this startling development, scientists in South Korea said that they, too, had cloned a human:

> Researchers at the infertility clinic of Kyunghee University Hospital in Seoul said they had grown an early human embryo using an unfertilised egg and a cell donated by a woman in her 30s....
>
> Lee Bo-yon, a researcher with the hospital's infertility clinic, told Reuters that the human embryo in the Kyunghee University experiment divided into four cells before the operation was aborted. "If implanted into a uterine wall of a carrier, we can assume that a human child would be formed and that it would have the same gene characteristics as that of the donor."[7]

Unlike the Advanced Cell Technology experiment, all cells involved in the Kyunghee experiment were human, and they all came from the same woman.

These stories would've probably created more of a stir if the embryos had been allowed to mature into full-fledged babies. It would make "great television" to show a gurgling baby while a voice-over explains that it's a clone. Still, the silence is inexplicable. If the budding embryos hadn't been destroyed at the 32-cell and 4-cell stages, they certainly had a good chance of becoming humans. Naturally, lots of embryos self-abort (i.e. miscarriages), and cloned animals have a higher-than-average rate of lethal mutations, so there are certainly no guarantees that the babies would've made it to term. Despite that, though, the cloning of a human has already been accomplished. The ova were fertilized for all intents and purposes, and they were going through the normal divisions and growth that every one of us went through in the womb.

Yet these red-letter days in science have been forgotten. Articles since then have utterly ignored these accomplishments. For example, on August 5, 2000, an article in the *Washington Post* noted: "Since the 1997 birth of Dolly—the first animal cloned from an adult cell—scientists around the world have announced successful clonings of mice, cows and most recently pigs."[8]

My heart skipped a beat when I saw this Associated Press headline on August 13, 2000: "Research on Human Cloning Hushed." I thought that perhaps the media had remembered their own tiny reports in late 1998. No such luck. Amazingly, the article talks only about the possibility that humans probably could be cloned sometime in the indeterminate future, neglecting to mention that it's already happened. Here are some representative excerpts:

> Dolly's creators at Scotland's Roslin Institute boasted she embodied the promise of animals that could produce drugs and organs for humans. But from the moment her birth was announced February 23, 1997, many interpreted her arrival as confirmation that cloning of humans lurked around the corner—despite the institute's careful attempt to downplay that prospect.
>
> "I'd be absolutely flabbergasted if we saw it in my lifetime," Grahame Bulfield, Roslin's chief executive, reiterates more than three years later. "It's a nonsensical bit of hype."
>
> Still, scientists say some of their colleagues are undoubtedly working on it, encouraged by further success with cloning animals such as cows and pigs.
>
> ....
>
> [Dr. Severino Antinori, the head of the International Associated Research Institute in Rome] said many fertility clinics are beginning to take more seriously the idea of cloning babies.
>
> ....
>
> Biologist Brigitte Boiselier, the Montreal-based scientific director of Clonaid, a company set up the month after Dolly's birth was heralded with banner headlines worldwide, said her lab is trying to perfect cloning in humans.
>
> ....
>
> Eric Schon, a molecular biologist at New York's Columbia University, believes the creation of cloned babies could be two to five years away.
>
> "If it can be done, it will be done," he said. "The moment it could be done in sheep and mice and cows, it was only a matter of time for human cloning."[9]

I suppose this reporter could've missed the brief acknowledgements in the *New York Times*, the *Boston Globe*, the *Wall Street Journal*, Knight Ridder, Reuters, the BBC, and Dr. Dixon's heavily-trafficked Website that discussed the fact that humans have already been cloned, but how to explain the ignorance of the people quoted in the article? Several theories spring to mind. Since the idea of cloning humans is so controversial, they don't want to admit that it's already happened. Given the fact that Advanced Cell Technology didn't admit its research for three years, this seems quite possible. It also seems that some scientists don't feel that these accomplishments qualify as their definition of cloning, apparently because the embryos weren't allowed to mature. They want to see a mewling infant; the fact that the ova were dividing and in the process of creating a human being doesn't count for some reason. Do I sense professional jealousy?

Finally, owners of companies engaged in cloning obviously want to be credited with being the first to clone a human, so they're not going to let the cat out of the bag. In the above AP article, notice that Brigitte Boiselier of Clonaid "said her lab is trying to *perfect* cloning in humans." That's a very telling word. She's not trying to develop it, create it, devise it, pioneer it, or anything like that—she's trying to "perfect" it, which leads me to believe that she knows it's already been done, and Clonaid may have done it themselves.

You have to wonder what other human cloning news has been kept from us.

Given the secrecy in this area—not only did Advanced Cell Technology keep the lid on for three years, but even the announcement of Dolly was delayed until she was eight months old—you have to wonder what other human cloning news has been kept from us. After all, the Americans created their clone in 1995, and the Koreans in 1998. What's happened in the years since then? For all we know, there might be babies and toddlers out there who are clones.

But that is speculative, while the achievements of the American and Korean scientists are not. The next time some news report breathlessly announces that human clones could possibly be created sometime soon, just remember that you're being lied to. They already have been.

Endnotes

1. Anonymous. (1993). "Embryo experiment succeeds." *New York Times*, Oct 24. **2.** Saltus, Richard. (1998). "News of human-cow cell raises ruckus." *Boston Globe*, November 14; McFarling, Usha Lee. (1998). "Bioethicists warn that human cloning will be difficult to stop," Knight Ridder, November 18; anonymous. (1999). "First cloned human embryo revealed," BBC News, June 17. **3.** *Op cit.*, Saltus. **4.** Dixon, Patrick, Dr. "Human cloning from cow eggs and human cells." Global Change Website <www.globalchange.com>. **5.** *Op cit.*, Saltus. **6.** *Ibid.* **7.** Dixon, Patrick, Dr. "Human cloning: First embryo made in Korea or Britain?" From original article by Reuters. Global Change Website <www.globalchange.com>. See also anonymous (1998). "Human cloning?: Cloning research in South Korea." *MacLean's*, Dec 28, p 110; anonymous. (1999). "Human cloning research proceeds in South Korea." *The Christian Century*, Jan 20, p 48; Schuman, Michael, et al. (1998). "Korean experiment fuels cloning debate; more work is needed to prove a live birth is possible." *Wall Street Journal*, Dec 21, p B7; WuDunn, Sheryl. (1998). "Koreans clone human cell." *New York Times*, Dec 20. **8.** Chea, Terence. (2000). "Going whole hog for cloning." *Washington Post*, Aug 5. **9.** Anonymous. (2000). "Research on human cloning hushed." Associated Press, Aug 13.

Thanks to David McGowan for alerting me to the American Cell Technology clone.

NutraFear & NutraLoathing in Augusta, Georgia

Alex Constantine

Mr. X of Augusta, Georgia, is unable to discuss a death he witnessed inside a local processing plant because he signed a secrecy oath. His silence has nothing to do with protecting state secrets or the "sources and methods" of the CIA. He was coerced into signing the agreement because the manufacturer of a common "food additive" does not want the public to know it is a potent toxin.

Mr. X made the grave error of walking into Augusta's NutraSweet plant "without a 'space suit,'" says Betty Martini, an anti-aspartame activist in Atlanta. (Workers at the plant wear protective clothing.) "It almost completely destroyed his lungs. A man who entered the plant with him—also without a suit—dropped dead."

The company attempted to discredit Mr. X by publicly dismissing the death as alcohol-related. NutraSweet executives offered him a settlement if he signed a secrecy agreement. He turned them down. He was shadowed for two years by corporate spies. He went to a local television station. A pair of reporters taped the interview.

"A week later the reporters were fired and NutraSweet somehow obtained the tapes," Martini recalls. Mr. X signed the secrecy agreement "to prevent the persecution of friends at the plant. He has little lung function left and probably won't live long.[1]

"We're used to stories like this," she reports with a shrug.

The company often contracts work to local engineers to spare NutraSweet the public embarrassment of admitting there is a high mortality rate among employees. Trucks idling up with incoming cargo do not dock to unload; an employee drives the trucks in. Visitors to the complex must don protective clothing to avoid contact with lethal waste.

Exactly what is aspartame (commonly known by its brand name, NutraSweet)? The aspartame molecule has three components: aspartic acid, phenylalanine, and methanol amino acids swimming in petrochemicals. Searle, Inc.—the developer of aspartame—was founded in 1888 on Chicago's North side and is a mainstay of the domestic medical establishment. The company's products range from prescription drugs to advanced medical technology. And, formerly, artificial sweeteners. In 1983 Denise Ertell, a public affairs director at Searle, offered: "Phenylalanine is a fermentation byproduct of soybeans and corn, and aspartic acid is a total synthesis from hydrocarbons, petrochemical derivatives." A petrochemical, like gasoline.

Monsanto—until recently, the producer of NutraSweet—is one of the leading chemical manufacturers in the country, based in St. Louis. The company has contracted with the US government in the past to produce chemical warfare agents in collaboration with I.G. Farben, a cartel that supported the rise of the Nazi Party under Hitler and manufactured Zyklon B, the gas used to decimate much of Europe's Jewish population. Another bridge to Farben and the Nazis was Monsanto's acquisition of American Viscose in 1949—20 years earlier, the US Commerce Department identified this company as a Fascist front. Monsanto's board of directors has long included officials of the CIA. The company claims on its Website that their concoction is "made from peaches."

"It is a powerful metabolic poison," Martini laments, "a witch's brew of breakdown products."

"It is a powerful metabolic poison," Martini laments, "a witch's brew of breakdown products. The methanol—wood alcohol—converts to formaldehyde and finally formic acid (ant sting poison). The breakdown product of diketopiperazine, DKP, is a tumor agent.

"I was lecturing one afternoon on NutraSweet," Martini recalls, "and a gentleman in the audience stood up and said he had prepared legal papers for a man who was killed at the plant. 'The papers are sealed,' he told me. 'I can't find anything out and it does no good to ask. That product is a poison.'"[2]

Many medical activists have arrived at the same conclusion. *Prescription for Nutritional Healing*, by James and Phyllis Balch, lists aspartame under the "Chemical Poison" category. Dr. Russell L. Blaylock, a professor of Neurosurgery at the Medical University of Mississippi, drew upon some 500 scientific references to demonstrate, in *Excitotoxins: The Taste That Kills*, how a surplus of free excitatory amino acids, such as aspartic and glutamic acids, results in serious chronic neurological damage and a score of adverse reactions.

Dr. Walton wrapped up: "Individuals with mood disorders are particularly sensitive to this artificial sweetener; its use in this population should be discouraged."

Dr. Ralph G. Walton conducted an independent, double-blind study of subjects with mood disorders in 1993. NutraSweet Co. stonewalled, refusing to sell Dr. Walton the aspartame needed for his study. He was forced to turn elsewhere for the supply. He noted a sharp rise in symptoms among volunteers on aspartame. Some of the side-effects were so severe that the Institutional Review Board terminated the research project to safeguard the health of test subjects—three of whom complained they'd been "poisoned." Martini: "One [subject] was bleeding from the eyes (conjunctival bleeding) and one had a retinal detachment, common with aspartame."[3] Dr. Walton wrapped up: "Individuals with mood disorders are particularly sensitive to this artificial sweetener; its use in this population should be discouraged."[4]

"The Pepsi Generation is ill," says Carol Guilford, author of *The New Cookie Cookbook* and *Carol Guilford's Main Course Cookbook*. "Aspartame poisoning mimics MS [multiple sclerosis] and rheumatoid arthritis. Fibromyalgia is a catchall term for the excruciating joint pain endured when aspartame dries up the lubricating synovial fluid and turns the joints into plastic."[5]

Monsanto spokesmen swear the sweetener is no more toxic than a glass of orange juice: "The overwhelming body of scientific evidence establishes that aspartame is not associated with side effects. Specific research has been conducted in each of these areas. The results support the safety of NutraSweet brand sweetener," the company boasts.[6] On September 13, 1995, a Congressional environmental committee reported that of all food additive complaints filed with the FDA, "more than 95 percent have been about two products: the sweetener aspartame and sulfite preservatives. No firm evidence exists to prove that aspartame actually causes many adverse reactions."[7] This is dangerous rhetoric, obscuring the risks not only of aspartame, but also of scores of drugs allowed on the market by the Food and Drug Administration.

In February 1994, one study reported that 51 percent of all drugs approved by the agency had serious or fatal side effects.[8] But the FDA has received more complaints of aspartame poisoning than all other food additives combined, about 75 percent. In 1995 the FDA tabulated 10,000 consumer complaints, listing 92 documented symptoms, including death—so many, incidentally, that the FDA pulled the plug on its complaint lines and referred complainants to the AIDS Hotline.[9]

The FDA has received more complaints of aspartame poisoning than all other food additives combined, about 75 percent.

NutraSweet is an addictive drug. At its inception, scientists for Searle acknowledged that it was a drug (corporate revisionists have labeled it a "food additive"). Martha M. Freeman, M.D., from the FDA division of metabolic and endocrine drug products, wrote in an August 20, 1973, memo to Dr. C. J. Kokost, division of toxicology:

> **Conclusion:**
>
> 1. The administration of aspartame, as reported in these studies at high dosage levels for prolonged periods, constitutes clinical investigational use of a NEW DRUG SUBSTANCE.
>
> 2. The information submitted for our review is inadequate to permit a scientific evaluation of clinical safety.
>
> **Recommendations:**
>
> 1. An IND (notice of claimed investigations [exemption for a new drug]) should be filed, to include all required manufacturing controls, pharmacology and clinical information.
>
> 2. Marketing for use as a sweetening agent should be contingent upon satisfactory demonstration of clinical safety of the compound...

A quarter-century later, the complaints that have come Betty Martini's way are a grim commentary on the FDA's "regulatory" integrity. ("The FDA conveniently puts death in their report under 'symptoms,'" she points out, aghast):

William Reed, Pullman, Michigan:

I'm a diabetic. I used Equal in my coffee, a lot of diet soft drinks, and NutraSweet in many foods. I started having headaches all the time... seizures, up to eight seizures, one right after the another. I couldn't sleep, my mouth was dry all the time. I had sores on my tongue, I started having trouble with my memory. I had muscle spasms in my legs almost every night which cause my legs to be sore all day long, and my back was sore from seizures...

Alicia Morris, Doraville, Georgia:

I'm a 29 year old athletic female.... I began using it in the spring of 1990, and soon afterwards my condition began to deteriorate.... My eyesight began to fade until I was almost blind in one eye. Next my hearing became dull and my legs, feet and torso lost sensation and became numb...

Mark Motluck, Chicago, Illinois:

My wife wrote to you last year (Kelli Motluck). She told you her story about her use of aspartame and the subsequent onset of brain tumors. She died on April 21, 1998 at the age of 37. She left behind a grieving husband and an eight-year-old daughter. Our lives will never be the same. Tonight, the Chicago NBC affiliate ran a story on the ten o'clock news about the controversy surrounding aspartame. A spokesman for Monsanto spewed their garbage about aspartame's safety and the like. Fortunately, the reporter also mentioned that every report which showed aspartame as being safe to use was funded directly by Monsanto. Quite a coincidence. The FDA refused to comment, which is no surprise either.

And it's not as though the marketers of aspartame are insensible to the side-effects despite 20 years of specious denials. (Monsanto: "Formaldehyde has been implicated as a possible carcinogen when inhaled, but this hasn't been shown to be the case when it's taken by mouth..."). Jonathan Leake, science editor of the *London Times*, reported in February 2000 that a suppressed report written in the early 1980s by researchers for the National Soft Drink Association (NSDA) "condemned" NutraSweet as a "dangerous" and "potentially toxic" neurochemical.

The same soda bottlers who suppressed the report on aspartame "now buy tons of it to add to diet drinks." They were warned at the outset that aspartame "can affect the workings of the brain, change behavior and even encourage users to eat extra carbohydrate, so destroying the point of using diet drinks. The documents were unearthed last week under freedom of information legislation. It follows a decision by researchers at King's College in London to study suspected links between aspartame intake and brain tumors." The NSDA's own scientific advisors stated, "We object to the approval of aspartame for unrestricted use in soft drinks." Their 30-page report listed the means by which aspartame was believed to affect brain chemistry directly, including the synthesis of serotonin and other crucial neurotransmitters. "Other papers obtained with the NSDA documents show the Food and Drug Administration also had misgivings. Despite this, it approved aspartame."[10]

Aspartame has become a staple of the American diet. And yet flies won't touch it.

"Coke knew," Martini observes, "and knowing, broke their good faith contract with customers, a breach exhibited by the recent plot to program vending machines to raise the price with the temperature. Dissatisfied with selling flavored sugar water plus phosphoric acid, they switched to pushing an addictive formula called 'Diet.' Addictive substances multiply markets, so Diet Coke soared off the sales charts."

Aspartame has become a staple of the American diet. And yet flies won't touch it, as a health columnist at the *Boston Globe* reported:

> Q. Are insects attracted to artificial sweeteners as much as to sugar? — J.M., Boston
>
> A. Linda Kennedy, assistant professor of physiology at Clark University in Worcester, says her studies indicate that flies have no reaction to aspartame, the basic ingredient in NutraSweet, although they are attracted to sugar. For more information on this tasty subject, she suggests you read Vincent Dethier's *The Hungry Fly*, published by the Harvard University Press in 1976.[11]

NutraDeath Comes for Santiago

The same lobbying group, the NSDA, now insists that aspartame is safe. So how, many consumer activists wonder, to account for the Niagara of complaints pouring into the FDA, the blindings, neurological symptoms, the abrupt rise in chronic fatigue, the headaches and memory loss—the swollen desk reference of adverse reactions associated with aspartame?

The most extreme case histories are warning flares in the night, sporadically reported by the corporate press. A rare exception was Janet Soto of Brooksville, Florida, who recently appeared on a local television news program to accuse the NutraSweet company of responsibility for her father-in-law's gradual decline.

The victim, Santiago "Chago" Echiverria, struggled with diabetes for fifteen to twenty years. Upon his retirement from the railroad, he moved from Ashtabula, Ohio, to Puerto Rico, where he continued his habitual swigging of diet cola and copious intake of coffee sweetened with Equal.

When Soto received word of Echiverria's death in June of 1994, she and her husband made arrangements to fly to Puerto Rico for the wake. The funeral director informed them that a surfeit of formaldehyde in the body made it necessary to close the casket.

The putrid chemical seeped through the cadaver's skin.

"His sisters, Minerva Ortiz and Nydia Colon, told me that the funeral director said he had never seen a body deteriorate as quickly, and was puzzled by the formaldehyde content even before embalming," Soto says.[12]

In a letter to Mission Possible, a registered nurse in Florida tells her own grim horror story of formaldehyde poisoning—diagnosed as the cause of death of a patient—from daily aspartame use. A physician at the hospital learned that the deceased had stored cases of diet drinks in his garage, and was poisoned by the petrochemical byproducts of heated aspartame released in the cola.

"The formaldehyde stores in fat cells," Martini explains. "Some undertakers tell me that bodies sometimes come to them reeking of formaldehyde." The chronic ingestion of formaldehyde at very low doses has, according to medical activist Mark Gold, "been shown to cause immune system and nervous system changes and damage as well as headaches, general poor health, irreversible genetic damage and a small medical grimoire of severe health problems. One experiment (Wantke, 1996) showed that chronic exposure to formaldehyde caused systemic health problems (i.e. poor health) in children at an air concentration of only 0.043 - 0.070 parts per million. Obviously, chronic exposure to an extremely small amount of formaldehyde is to be avoided. Even if formaldehyde adducts did not build up in the body from aspartame use, the regular exposure to excess levels of formaldehyde would still be a major concern to independent scientists and physicians familiar with the aspartame toxicity issue."[13]

Every single morning, millions wake up to a steaming cup of coffee, RNA derivatives, and petrochemicals.

Aspartame is a drug. It interacts with other drugs, alters dopamine levels and can cause birth defects. It has been known to trigger seizures.[14]

Nevertheless, as the tobacco industry soft-peddles the hazards of smoking, so do NutraSweet executives insist that aspartame is safely absorbed. But intake standard comparisons alone write another commentary: The EPA safety standard for methanol intake is 7.8 mg. a day. A liter of diet soft drink contains 550 mg. of aspartame, 55 mg. of methanol.[15] The methanol ingested by heavy consumers could easily exceed 250 mg. daily—32 times the FDA's suggested limit.

The late Dr. Morgan Raiford, a specialist in methanol toxicity, circulated a fact sheet in 1987 deploring the sweetener's adverse effects on eyesight and the central nervous system. He found "toxic reactions in the human visual pathway, and we are beginning to observe tragic damage to the optic nerve, blindness, partial to total optic nerve atrophy. Once this destructive process has developed there is no visual restoration." (Mission Possible refers patients going blind on aspartame to the National Eye Research Foundation, a diagnostic lab outfitted to detect toxic reactions to methanol.) He described a second side-effect "related to phenylalanine levels in the central nervous system.... Over the past year the writer has observed the fact that any portion of the central nervous system can and is affected." The chemical feast caused "sensations of dullness of the intellect, visual shadows, evidence of word structure reversing and some hearing impairment. This can and will in time cause problems in learning."[16]

Lennart Hardell, M.D., Ph.D., in 1999 reported in Sweden that both cell phone use and heavy aspartame use correlate with increased brain cancers.[17] Normally, the blood/brain barrier shields the user from excess aspartate and accompanying toxins—but is not fully developed during childhood, so the young are particularly at risk. Further, it does not fully protect all areas of an adult brain, so damage with chronic use is a distinct possibility. The barrier allows seepage of excess glutamate and aspartate into the brain even when intact, and gradually destroys neurons. Most of the neural cells, better than 75 percent, in one area of the brain are depleted before clinical symptoms of chronic disease are detectable. Some of the many illnesses attributable to long-term exposure to excitatory amino acid damage include MS, Lou Gehrig's Disease, memory loss, hormonal problems, hearing loss, epilepsy, Alzheimer's, Parkinson's Disease, hypoglycemia, AIDS dementia, brain lesions, and neuroendocrine disorders.[18]

Laboratory rats turn their noses up to any food with aspartame in it. Yet every single morning, millions wake up to a steaming cup of coffee, RNA derivatives, and petrochemicals.

Pass the ant poison, please. Splash of formic acid?

Endnotes

1. Betty Martini, Mission Possible, private correspondence forwarded to author, July 9, 1996. **2.** Martini, correspondence with author, July 9, 1996. **3.** Martini, letter to Robert Cohen, August 30, 1996. **4.** Ralph G. Walton, et al, "Adverse Reactions to Aspartame: Double-Blind Challenge in Patients from a Vulnerable Population," *Biological Psychiatry*, 1993:34:13-17. **5.** Carol Guilford, "No Hoax, Crime of the Century," Internet posting. **6.** Company public relations release. **7.** Committee for the National Institute for the Environment, "Food Additive Regulations: A Chronology," Congressional Research Service, Updated Version, September 13, 1995. **8.** See *Omni* magazine, February 1994. **9.** Martini correspondence. **10.** Jonathan Leake, "Top sweetener condemned by secret report," *London Times*, February 27, 2000. **11.** *Boston Globe*, July 16, 1988. **12.** Janet Soto, letter to Martini, April 3, 1995. **13.** Mark D. Gold, "Scientific Abuse in Methanol/Formaldehyde Research Related to Aspartame," <www.holisticmed.com/aspartame/abuse/methanol.html>. **14.** *Ibid.* **15.** Dr. H.J. Roberts in a letter to Martini. Also see, H.J. Roberts, *Aspartame: NutraSweet, Is It Safe?* (Charles Press). **16.** "Nutrasweet Factsheet," original in possession of the author. **17.** <www.medscape.com/MedGenMed/braintumors>. **18.** Life Sciences Research Office, FASEB, "Safety of Amino Acids," FDA Contract No. 223-88-2124, Task Order No. 8.

Forbidden Archaeology

Michael A. Cremo

A couple of years ago, in the middle of my talk about my book *Forbidden Archeology* to students and professors of earth sciences at the Free University of Amsterdam, a professor stood up and said, "What you say is all very interesting, but how can we accept something that goes against what thousands of archaeologists and geologists and other scientists are telling us?"

Forbidden Archeology documents evidence for extreme human antiquity. Actually, over the past 150 years archaeologists have found abundant evidence showing that human beings like ourselves have existed for hundreds of millions of years. This evidence, practically unknown to both scientists and members of the public, radically contradicts the picture of human origins that is presented to us by Darwin's modern followers, who say that we evolved fairly recently—within the past 100,000 years or so—from some more apelike ancestors.

So the professor was correct. I was indeed asking my audience to consider something that goes against what all the conventional experts are saying.

"You know," I responded, "it must have been quite interesting to have been a Darwinist in 1860, when hardly anyone accepted it. Even though I disagree with the Darwinists, I have a lot of respect for the early ones, because it must have taken a considerable amount of courage to stand up for Darwinism in the face of heavy opposition and disagreement from what was then the scientific establishment."

I then added, "I am especially surprised to hear such an objection from you, because Dutch scholars have an historic reputation for intellectual independence, and now you are saying that we can only accept ideas that have already been endorsed by thousands of experts."

At that point, sensing that the mood of the audience was against him, the professor bravely said, "I can also stand up against thousands," and sat down.

I returned to the Netherlands for another series of lectures to students and professors of archaeology, anthropology, and biology at the universities of Amsterdam, Utrecht, Leiden, Groningen, and Nijmegen, among others. After the lectures, during the question sessions, there were many kinds of reactions from my listeners. Sometimes they were shouting at me; sometimes they sat in shocked silence, not knowing what to say or think; sometimes they asked deep questions about the nature of our knowledge of humankind's hidden history.

Yes, the audiences were tough, unsympathetic, and skeptical, but that is to be expected when you present ideas as radical as mine. Nevertheless, despite all this, I did win some admissions that the case I was presenting was interesting, well-argued, and worthy of serious consideration. This reaction mirrors that of the scientific world in general, where *Forbidden Archeology* has attracted a great deal of attention. The book has been reviewed in most of the major journals of archaeology, anthropology, and history of science, not always unfavorably. I have also had the chance to speak about the book at international conferences, such as the World Archaeological Congress, held in New Delhi in 1994, the Twentieth International Congress for the History of Science, held in Liege in 1997, the World Archaeological Congress, held in Cape Town in 1999, and the European Association of Archaeologists annual meeting, held in Bournemouth, England, in 1999.

Over the past 150 years archaeologists have found abundant evidence showing that human beings like ourselves have existed for hundreds of millions of years.

Not all of my audiences in the Netherlands were unsympathetic. I spoke about *Forbidden Archeology* at a lecture in Amsterdam organized by Herman Hegge of the Frontier Sciences Foundation, which publishes the bimonthly Dutch-language journal *Frontier 2000*. I also had the chance to talk to Theo Paijmans and his listeners on Talk Radio 1395 AM (Theo's show, *Dossier X*, focuses on scientific anomalies). But although I do like to speak to people who are already inclined to agree with me, I especially enjoy attempting to change the minds of people who are not so inclined.

My research into humanity's hidden history was inspired by my study of the ancient Sanskrit writings of India, collectively known as the Vedas. Among these Vedic writings are the Puranas, or histories, which tell of human civilizations existing on this planet for tens of millions, even hundreds of millions of years. My interest in India's Vedic writings is more than intellectual. For 25 years, I have been practicing the *bhakti* (devotional) school of Indian spirituality as a member of the International Society for Krishna Consciousness. Sometimes people are surprised to learn that the gray-haired person of over 50 years of age, lecturing before them in suit and tie, is a member of what is popularly known as the Hare Krishna movement. But indeed I am, and during my stay in Amsterdam, I took the chance to join the young local members in one of their Thursday evening chanting processions through the shopping streets of the city center. This clash of images—science and street religion—is nothing new. For ages, the *bhakti* tradition in India has always been a mixture of two seemingly contradictory elements—the emotional expression of *bhakti* through public chanting and profoundly deep scholarship.

One thing that such scholarship reveals is that time proceeds in cycles rather than in linear fashion. According to the Puranas, the basic unit of these time cycles is the day of Brahma, which lasts 4.3 billion years. The day of Brahma is followed by the night of Brahma. During the day of Brahma life is manifest, and during the night of Brahma life is not manifest. If we consult the ancient Sanskrit calendar of cosmic time, we learn that we are about two billion years into the current day of Brahma.

Now let's imagine that we have a "Vedic archaeologist." Based on the information given above, he or she would expect to see signs that living things have been present on earth for about two billion years. Interestingly enough, modern science says that the oldest signs of life on earth do indeed go back two or even three billion years. These signs of life include fossils of algae and other single-celled creatures. But our Vedic archaeologist would not be surprised to also find signs of more advanced life forms, including the human form. A conventional archaeologist, however, would not expect to find any such thing. According to conventional views, human beings like ourselves have appeared fairly recently on earth, within the last 100,000 years or so.

Taking all this into consideration, our Vedic archaeologist would make two predictions: First, scientists digging into the earth should find signs of a human presence going back hundreds of millions of years. Second, this evidence will largely be ignored because it radically contradicts the ideas of human origins currently held by the scientific community.

This leads us the concept of what I call the knowledge filter. The knowledge filter represents the dominant ideas of the scientific community regarding human origins and antiquity. Evidence that conforms to these ideas passes easily through the filter. Evidence that varies slightly from these ideas may pass through the filter with some difficulty. But evidence that radically contradicts these dominant ideas will not pass through the filter. Such evidence is forgotten, set aside, or, in some cases, actively suppressed.

The existence of the knowledge filter is something that scientists themselves will admit. When archaeologist Wil Roebroeks of the University of Leiden visited me in Amsterdam, we had a long talk about it, and he shared with me some of his own personal experiences with knowledge filtration in treatment of evidence for the earliest occupation of Europe, particularly northern Europe. Of course, it goes without saying that I think the filter operates differently and to a greater extent than he would accept. For example, Roebroeks thinks the filter operates to unfairly include evidence for a very early occupation, whereas I believe it operates to unfairly exclude it.

In *Forbidden Archeology,* I document two things:

1. Hundreds of cases of scientifically-reported evidence for extreme human antiquity, consistent with the account of human origins given in the ancient Sanskrit writings of India.

2. The process by which this evidence has been filtered out of normal scientific discourse.

Let's now look at some particular cases.

In the last century, gold was discovered in the Sierra Nevada mountains of California, and miners came from all over the world to extract it. At first they simply took the gold from streams, but afterwards they began to dig mines into the sides of mountains. Inside the tunnels where they were digging into solid rock, the miners found human skeletons, spear points, and numerous stone tools. These finds occurred at many different locations. One of them was Table Mountain in Tuolumne County, California.

According to modern geological reports, the rock in which the miners found the bones and artifacts at Table Mountain is about 50 million years old. Our Vedic archaeologist would not be surprised at this. But our conventional archaeologist would be very surprised, because his textbooks say that no humans (or even apemen) existed at that time.

The California discoveries were very carefully documented and reported to the scientific world by Dr. J. D. Whitney, a geologist for the state of California. His work (*The Auriferous Gravels of the Sierra Nevadas*) was published by Harvard University in 1880. So why do we not hear anything about these discoveries today?

In other words,
if the facts do not agree with the favored theory,
then such facts,
even an imposing array of them, must be discarded.

Whitney's work was dismissed by Dr. William H. Holmes, a very influential anthropologist who worked at the Smithsonian Institution in Washington, D.C. He said in the Smithsonian Institution's annual report for 1898-99: "Perhaps if Professor Whitney had fully appreciated the story of human evolution as it is understood today, he would have hesitated to announce the conclusions formulated [that humans existed in very ancient times in North America], notwithstanding the imposing array of testimony with which he was confronted." In other words, if the facts do not agree with the favored theory, then such facts, even an imposing array of them, must be discarded. This is a good example of the operation of the knowledge filter.

And the knowledge filtration process continues to influence the California gold mine discoveries even today. I appeared on a television show called *The Mysterious Origins of Man,* produced by BC Video and broadcast by NBC, the largest television network in the United States. This show was based in part on my book *Forbidden Archeology.* The show also featured the work of other researchers who challenge the current ideas of human prehistory.

Among them was Graham Hancock, author of *Fingerprints of the Gods.* Earlier this year, Graham and his wife Santha stopped to visit me in Los Angeles, on their way to Japan, where they were going to investigate some underwater pyramids, *apparently* of human construction. In the course of our conversation, we agreed that a lot of the really exciting scientific research is going on outside the normal channels.

In any case, when the producers were filming *The Mysterious Origins of Man*, I asked them to go to the museum of natural history at the University of California at Berkeley, where the California gold mine artifacts are stored.

The producers asked the museum officials for permission to film the artifacts. The museum officials, assuming that the producers were working on a tight deadline, said they could not bring out the objects on short notice. The producers then explained that they had six months time to finish their work. The museum officials then said they had another problem—a shortage of staff and money. They would have to pay their workers "overtime" to bring out the objects and could not afford to do it. The producers replied that they would pay the museum workers any amount of money required. But at that point the museum officials simply said they were not going to bring out the artifacts for filming. Finally, the producers just used some nineteenth-century photographs of the objects in the show.

When the show finally aired in February 1996, it inspired extreme reactions from the orthodox scientific community in the United States. This was the first time that a major American television network had ever broadcast a show that seriously questioned the Darwinian account of human origins.

Why was the scientific community so angry? One reason is they did not like anti-Darwinian ideas reaching American schoolchildren through the popular medium of television. The president of the National Center for Science Education, as reported in the journal *Science,* complained that after *The Mysterious Origins of Man* was broadcast, the phones in his organization's headquarters were ringing constantly. Science teachers from all over the country were calling, saying that their students who saw the show were asking them difficult questions. Meanwhile, on the Internet, scientists wondered what effect such television programs might eventually have on government funding for certain kinds of scientific research.

Most of the opposition to the program came from what I call the fundamentalist Darwinian group within the scientific community. This group adheres to Darwinism more out of ideological commitment than scientific objectivity. If this group was disturbed when NBC showed *The Mysterious Origins of Man* in February 1996, they became even more disturbed when they learned that NBC was going to show it again, despite their protests. After the show aired the second time, Dr. Allison R. Palmer, president of the Institute for Cambrian Studies, sent an email message (dated June 17, 1996) to the Federal Communications Commission (FCC) of the United States government, asking the FCC to punish NBC for showing the program to the American people. This letter was circulated on scientific discussion groups by Dr. Jere Lipps, a paleontologist at the University of California at Berkeley, in order to generate more pressure from scientists on the FCC. Palmer and his supporters wanted the FCC to censure NBC for showing the program, compel NBC to repeatedly broadcast a public apology, and compel NBC to pay a substantial fine. Fortunately, this effort did not succeed.

At that point the museum officials simply said they were not going to bring out the artifacts for filming.

What all this shows is that science does not always operate according to its high ideals. The way science works, we are normally told, is on the basis of free and open discussion of evidence and ideas. But in the case of *The Mysterious Origins of Man,* we see elements of the scientific community restricting access to evidence and preventing open discussion of it. Yes, there is in fact a knowledge filter. I have fully documented the reactions to *The Mysterious Origins of Man,* along with other reactions to *Forbidden Archeology,* in a book titled *Forbidden Archeology's Impact.*

Now let's consider a case from the more recent history of archaeology. In 1979, Mary Leakey found dozens of footprints at a place called Laetoli, in the East African country of Tanzania. She said that

Scientists who find things that should not be found sometimes suffer for it professionally.

the footprints were indistinguishable from those of modern human beings. But they were found in layers of solidified volcanic ash that are 3.7 million years old. According to standard views, humans capable of making such prints should not have existed that long ago. So how do scientists explain the Laetoli footprints?

They say that there must have existed in East Africa 3.7 million years ago some kind of apeman who had feet just like ours. And that is how the footprints were made. That is a very interesting proposal, but unfortunately there is no physical evidence to support it. Scientists already have the skeletons of the apemen who existed 3.7 million years ago in East Africa. They are called *Australopithecus*, and their foot structure was quite different from that of a modern human being.

This question came up when I was speaking at the World Archaeological Congress in Cape Town, South Africa. Also speaking there was this scientist, Ron Clarke. In 1998, Clarke discovered a fairly complete skeleton of *Australopithecus* at a place called Sterkfontein, in South Africa. This discovery was widely publicized all over the world as the oldest human ancestor. It was 3.7 million years old, the same age as the Laetoli footprints. But there was a problem.

Clarke reconstructed the foot of his Sterkfontein *Australopithecus* in an apelike fashion, as he should have, because the foot bones were quite apelike. For example, the big toe is very long and moves out to the side, much like a human thumb. And the other toes are also quite long, about one and a half times longer than human toes. Altogether the foot was not very humanlike. So after Clarke gave his talk, I raised my hand and asked a question: "Why is it that the foot structure of your Sterkfontein *Australopithecus* does not match the footprints found by Mary Leakey at Laetoli, which are the same age, 3.7 million years old, but which are just like those of modern humans?" You see what the problem was for him. He was claiming to have the oldest human ancestor, but there is evidence from elsewhere in Africa that human beings like us were walking around at the exact same time. So how did he answer my question? He said that it was his *Australopithecus* who made the Laetoli footprints, but he was walking with his big toes pressed close in to the side of the foot, and with his other toes curled under. I did not find that to be a very satisfactory explanation.

Scientists who find things that should not be found sometimes suffer for it professionally. One such scientist is Dr. Virginia Steen-McIntyre, an American geologist whom I know personally.

In the early 1970s, some American archaeologists discovered stone tools and weapons at a place called Hueyatlaco, in Mexico. They included arrowheads and spear points. According to archaeologists, such weapons are made and used only by humans like us, not by apemen.

At Hueyatlaco, the artifacts were found in the bottom layers of the trenches. Of course, the archaeologists wanted to know how old the objects were. So when archaeologists want to know how old something is, they call in some geologists because the geologists will be able to tell them, "The layer of rock in which you found these objects is so-and-so thousand years old." Among the geologists who came to date the site was Virginia Steen-McIntyre. Using four of the latest geological dating methods, she and her colleagues from the United States Geological Survey determined that the artifact-bearing layer was 300,000 years old. When this information was presented to the chief archaeologist, the chief archaeologist said it was impossible. According to standard views, there were no human beings in existence 300,000 years ago anywhere in the world, not to speak of North America. The current doctrine is that humans did not enter the Americas any earlier than 30,000 years ago. So what happened? The archaeologists refused to publish the date of 300,000 years. Instead they published an age of 20,000 years for the site. And where did they get that date? It came from a carbon-14 date on a piece of shell found five kilometers from the place where the artifacts were found.

Steen-McIntyre tried to spread the word about the true age of the site. Because of this, she began to get a bad reputation in her profession. She lost a teaching position she held at a university, and all of her opportunities for advancement in the United States Geological Survey were blocked. She became so disgusted that she went to live in a small town in the Rocky Mountains of Colorado and remained silent for ten years, until I found out about her case and wrote about it in *Forbidden Archeology,* giving her work some of the attention it deserves. Partly because of this, the Hueyatlaco site is now being studied by more open-minded archaeologists, and hopefully before too long her original conclusions about the age of the site will be reconfirmed.

An anatomically modern human skull was found by the Italian geologist Giuseppe Ragazzoni at Castenedolo, near Brescia, northern Italy, in the late nineteenth century. Ragazzoni found not only this skull, but the skeletal remains of four persons, in layers of rock which, according to modern geological reports, are about five million years old.

Sometimes when Darwinist scientists hear of modern-looking skeletons being found in very ancient layers of rock, they say: "There is nothing mysterious here. Only a few thousand years ago, someone died on the surface, and his friends dug a grave and placed the body down fairly deep. And that is why you think you have found a human skeleton in some very ancient layer of rock."

Such things, technically called intrusive burial, can certainly happen. But in this case, Ragazzoni—himself a professional geologist—was well aware of the possibility of intrusive burial. If it had been a burial, the overlying layers would have been disturbed. But he checked very carefully during the excavation, and found that the overlying layers were perfectly intact and undisturbed. This means that the skeletons really are as old as the layers of rock in which they were found, in this case five million years old.

Early in the twentieth century, the Belgian geologist A. Rutot made some interesting discoveries in his country. He found hundreds of stone tools and weapons in layers of rock 30 million years old. I mentioned in connection with the California gold mine discoveries that sometimes we are not allowed to see the ancient objects in the museum collections. In this case I was able to see the artifacts. Once when I was in Brussels for some newspaper interviews, a friend of mine was driving me around, and I suggested that we go to the Royal Museum of Natural Sciences, because that is where I thought Rutot's collection should be. The first museum officials we spoke to had denied having any knowledge of the collection, but finally we found an archaeologist who knew the collection. Of course, it was not being displayed to the public.

This archaeologist took me into the storerooms of the museum, and there I took photographs of Rutot's collection of hundreds of 30 million-year-old stone tools and weapons from Belgium.

Up to this point, all of the finds we've discussed were either made by professional scientists or were reported in the professional scientific literature. But if this evidence for extreme human antiquity really is there in the layers of the earth, then we might expect that people other than professional scientists might be finding it. And their reports, although they might not appear in the pages of scientific journals, might appear in the pages of more ordinary literature. I think we can predict that this should be happening. And in fact it does happen.

I learned that the layers of the earth in which the skeleton was found are about 300 million years old.

Let us consider an interesting report from the *Morrisonville Times,* a newspaper published in the little town of Morrisonville, Illinois, in the year 1892. It tells of a woman who was putting a big piece of coal into her coal-burning stove. The piece of coal broke in half, and inside she found a beautiful gold chain, ten inches long. The two pieces of coal were still attached to the ends of the chain, demonstrating that the chain had been solidly embedded in the coal. From the newspaper report we were able to determine the mine from which the coal came. According to the Geological Survey of the State of Illinois, the coal from that mine is about 300 million years old, the same age as the human skeleton found in the same state.

Lets go back to the scientific literature. In 1862, a scientific journal called *The Geologist* (volume 5, p 470) told of a human skeleton found 90 feet below the surface in Macoupin County, Illinois. According to the report, there was a two-foot thick layer of unbroken slate rock directly above the skeleton. From the government geologist of the state of Illinois, I learned that the layers of the earth in which the skeleton was found are about 300 million years old, making the skeleton the same age as the gold chain found in the same state. In 1852, *Scientific American* reported that a beautiful metallic vase came from five meters deep in solid rock near the city of Boston. According to modern geological reports, the age of the rock at this place is 500 million years old.

The oldest objects that I encountered in my research were some round metallic spheres found over the past 20 years by miners at Ottosdalin, in the Western Transvaal region of South Africa. The objects are one or two centimeters in diameter. Most interesting are the parallel grooves that go around the equators of the spheres. The spheres were submitted to metallurgists for analysis before they were filmed for the television program *The Mysterious Origins of Man.* The metallurgists said they could see no way in which the spheres could have formed naturally in the earth, indicating they are the product of intelligent work. The spheres come from mineral deposits over 2 billion years old.

We are nearing the end of this brief review of evidence for extreme human antiquity. I have given you only a small sample of this evidence. I could go on for quite some time, because there are hundreds of such cases from the scientific literature of the past 150 years.

I will end by saying this. We have been told by the Darwinists that all the physical evidence ever discovered by scientists supports their picture of human origins, which has human beings like us coming into existence about 100,000 years ago. I think we can safely say that is not true. There is a chain of discoveries going from 100,000 years ago all the way back to 2 billion years. I did not find any evidence older than that. I think it is, at the very least, an interesting coincidence that the ancient Sanskrit writings say humans have been present on earth for two billion years.

What does all of this suggest? It means we need an alternative picture of human origins, and I intend to present one of my own in my next book, *Human Devolution.* In that book, I will suggest that we have not evolved upward from the apes on this planet, as modern science tells us, but that we have devolved from an original spiritual position in higher levels of reality.

There Is So Much That We Don't Know

Selections from the *Science Frontiers* Book and Newsletter

William R. Corliss

From the Preface to *Science Frontiers: Some Anomalies and Curiosities of Nature*

The primary intent of this book is entertainment. Do not look for profundities! All I claim here is an edited collection of naturally occurring anomalies and curiosities that I have winnowed mainly from scientific journals and magazines. With this eclectic sampling I hope to demonstrate that nature is amusing, beguiling, sometimes bizarre, and, most important, liberating. "Liberating?" Yes! If there is anything profound between these covers, it is the influence of anomalies on the stability of stifling scientific paradigms.

My view is that anomaly research, while not science per se, has the potential to destabilize paradigms and accelerate scientific change.

My view is that anomaly research, while not science per se, has the potential to destabilize paradigms and accelerate scientific change. Anomalies reveal nature as it really is: complex, chaotic, possibly even unplumbable. Anomalies also encourage the framing of rogue paradigms, such as morphic resonance and the steady-state universe.

Anomaly research often transcends current scientific currency by celebrating bizarre and incongruous facets of nature, such as coincidence and seriality. However iconoclastic the pages of this book, the history of science tells us that future students of nature will laugh at our conservatism and lack of vision.

Such heavy philosophical fare, however, is not the main diet of the anomalist. The search itself is everything. My greatest thrill, prolonged as it was, was in my forays through the long files of *Nature*, *Science*, *English Mechanic*, *Monthly Weather Review*, *Geological Magazine*, and like journals. There, anomalies and curiosities lurked in many an issue, hidden under layers of library dust. These tedious searches were hard on the eyes, but they opened them to a universe not taught by my college professors!

The Incorruptibility of the Ganges

The Ganges is 2,525 kilometers long. Along its course, 27 major towns dump 902 million liters of sewage into it each day. Added to this are all those human bodies consigned to this holy river, called the Ganga by the Indians. Despite this heavy burden of pollutants, the Ganges has for millennia been regarded as incorruptible. How can this be?

Several foreigners have recorded the effects of this river's "magical" cleansing properties:

- Ganges water does not putrefy, even after long periods of storage. River water begins to putrefy when lack of oxygen promotes the growth of anaerobic bacteria, which produce the telltale smell of stale water.

- British physician C.E. Nelson observed that Ganga water taken from the Hooghly—one of its dirtiest mouths—by ships returning to England remained fresh throughout the voyage.

- In 1896 the British physician E. Hanbury Hankin reported in the French journal *Annales de l'Institut Pasteur* that cholera microbes died within three hours in Ganga water but continued to thrive in distilled water even after 48 hours.

- A French scientist, Monsieur Herelle, was amazed to find "that only a few feet below the bodies of persons floating in the Ganga who had died of dysentery and cholera, where one would expect millions of germs, there were no germs at all."

More recently, D.S. Bhargava, an Indian environmental engineer measured the Ganges' remarkable self-cleansing properties:

> Bhargava's calculations, taken from an exhaustive three-year study of the Ganga, show that it is able to reduce BOD [biochemical oxygen demand] levels much faster than in other rivers.

Quantitatively, the Ganges seems to clean up suspended wastes fifteen to twenty times faster than other rivers.[1]

Underwater Thumps

Scientists based on the central California coast are trying to identify the origin of a mysterious underwater sound that disturbed surfers and divers for three weeks—and then just as mysteriously disappeared.

> The sound, made up of thumps occurring at 10-second intervals, was compared by one diver to five or six giant bongo drums going off simultaneously. Most experts have concluded that it was of human origin.

As usual in such cases, no governmental or military sources knew anything about the thumps.[2]

The Earth Is Expanding and We Don't Know Why

Let us taunt the geologists now with an idea that many of them consider to be nonsense. The expanding earth hypothesis goes back to at least 1933, a time when the continental drift hypothesis was accorded the same sort of ridicule. Now, continental drift is enthroned, and many of its strongest proponents are vehemently opposed to the expanding earth theory, ignoring the lessons of history.

The data that suggest that the earth has expanded significantly over geological time come from the pleasant pastime of continent-fitting. If one takes the pieces of continental and oceanic crust and tries to fit them together at various times over the past several hundred-million years, taking into account the production of crust at the mid-ocean ridges, the fit gets worse and worse as one works backward in time. Great gaps (or "gores") appear between the pieces of crust which geologists believed existed at these periods. (Of course, one can play this puzzle-piece game only at passive continent-ocean boundaries where the oceanic crust has not slid under the continental crust. The South Atlantic is a good place to work.)

These embarrassing, grotesque gaps can be made to disappear almost as if by magic by assuming that the earth was smaller in the past. This seems, on the surface, to be a crazy idea. Why would an entire planet swell up like a balloon? Hugh Owen answers in this way:

> The geological and geophysical implications of such Earth expansion are so profound that most geologists and geophysicists shy away from them. In order to fit with the reconstruction that seems to be required, the volume of the Earth was only 51 per cent of its present value, and the surface area 64 per cent of that of the present day, 200 million years ago. Established theory says that the Earth's interior is stable, an inner core of nickel iron surrounded by an outer layer that behaves like a fluid. Perhaps we are completely wrong and the inner core is in some state nobody has yet imagined, a state that is undergoing a transition from a high-density state to a lower density state, and pushing out the crust, the skin of the Earth, as it expands.[3]

Reference. For more on the expanding earth hypothesis, see category ETL6 in *Carolina Bays, Mima Mounds, Submarine Canyons* (Sourcebooks, 1988).

About as Anomalous as Mounds Can Get

The title refers to a circle of eleven earthen mounds located near Monroe, Louisiana—the Watson Break site. Local residents have known about the mounds for years, but archaeologists weren't attracted to them until clear-cutting of the trees in the 1970s made the size and novelty of Watson Break all too obvious.

"It's rare that archaeologists ever find something that so totally changes our picture of what happened in the past, as is true for this case."

Just how anomalous is Watson Break? Archaeologist V. Steponaitis, from the University of North Carolina, opined:

> It's rare that archaeologists ever find something that so totally changes our picture of what happened in the past, as is true for this case.

On what does Steponaitis base such a powerful statement?

- Watson Break is dated at 5000–5400 BP (Before Present), some three millennia before the well-known mound-builders started piling up earthen structures from the Mississippi Valley to New York State. In other words, the site is anomalously early.
- Indications are that Watson Break was built by hunter-gatherers, but no one really knows much about them; there's an aura of mystery here.
- Watson Break consists of eleven mounds—some as high as a two-story house—connected by a peculiar circular ridge 280 meters in diameter. The back-breaking labor required to collect and pile up all this dirt is incompatible with the lifestyle of mobile bands of hunter-gatherers.
- The purpose of the Watson Break complex escapes us. Why the mounds? Why the circular ridge? Can we just shrug it off as a "ritual site"?[4]

Mysterious Swirl Patterns on the Moon

In at least three lunar locations, enigmatic bright-and-dark swirl patterns drape craters and mar terrains. Ranging from ten kilometers across to less than 50 meters, they may be ribbon-like, open-looped, or closed-looped. The swirls are sharply defined but do not appear to scour or otherwise disturb the terrains where they occur. Similar swirl patterns have been recognized on Mercury. Two intriguing characteristics of the lunar swirl patterns are that (1) they coincide with strong magnetic anomalies, and (2) they appear to be very young, being superimposed on top of essentially all lunar features of all ages. Schultz and Srnka suggest that recent cometary impacts created the patterns.[5]

Comment. The terrestrial implications are obvious: Our earth must have been hit, too. Perhaps at the Tunguska site there are similar swirl patterns—now obliterated by vegetation.

In at least three lunar locations, enigmatic bright-and-dark swirl patterns drape craters and mar terrains.

Reference. Lunar swirl patterns are cataloged in Section ALE5 of *The Moon and the Planets* (Sourcebooks, 1985).

Ten Strikes Against the Big Bang

T. Van Flandern, editor of the *Meta Research Bulletin*, has compiled a list of big bang problems—and it is not a short list. Can the big bang paradigm be *that* shaky? Like evolution and relativity, the big bang is usually paraded as a proven, undeniable fact. It isn't.

- Static-universe models fit the data better than expanding-universe models.
- The microwave "background" makes more sense as the limiting temperature of space heated by starlight rather than as the remnant of a fireball.
- Element-abundance predictions using the big bang require too many adjustable parameters to make them work.
- The universe has too much large-scale structure (interspersed "walls" and voids) to form in a time as short as 10 to 20 billion years.
- The average luminosity of quasars must decrease in just the right way so that their mean apparent brightness is the same at all redshifts, which is exceedingly unlikely.
- The ages of globular clusters appear older than the universe.
- The local streaming motions of galaxies are too high for a finite universe that is supposed to be everywhere uniform.
- Invisible dark matter of an unknown but non-baryonic nature must be the dominant ingredient of the entire universe.
- The most distant galaxies in the Hubble Deep Field show insufficient evidence of evolution, with some of them apparently having higher redshifts (z = 6-7) than the faintest quasars.
- If the open universe we see today is extrapolated back near the beginning, the ratio of the actual density of matter in the universe to the critical density must differ from unity by just one part in 1,059. Any larger deviation would result in a universe already collapsed on itself or already dissipated.[6]

Einstein's Nemesis: DI Herculis

DI Herculis is an eighth-magnitude eclipsing binary about 2,000 light years from earth. These two young blue stars are very close—only one-fifth the distance from earth to our sun. They orbit about a common center of gravity every 10.55 days. So far, no problem!

The puzzle is that, as the two stars swing around one another, the axis of their orbit rotates or precesses too slowly. General relativity predicts a precession of 4.27°/century, but for DI Herculis the rate is only 1.05°/century. This does not sound like a figure large enough to get excited about, but it deeply troubles astronomers. D. Popper, an astronomer at UCLA, says:

> The observations are pretty clear. I don't think there's any question there's a discrepancy and, frankly, it is an important one and it's unresolved.

Accentuating the challenge to general relativity is the discovery that a second eclipsing binary, AC Camelopardalis, also violates general relativity in the same way. It *seems* that wherever gravitational fields are extremely strong and space-time, therefore, is highly distorted, general relativity fails.

Ironically, it was a very similar sort of astronomical observation that helped make general relativity a pillar of the scientific edifice early in the twentieth century. The orbit of Mercury precesses a bit faster than Newtonian physics predicts. The application of Einstein's general relativity corrected the calculation of Mercury's rate of precession by just the right amount. Now we may need a new theory to correct Einstein—at least where time-space is sharply bent![7]

Where Have All the Black Holes Gone?

Like the big bang, black holes are an astronomical staple. Most scientists and laymen assume that black holes are proven, well-observed denizens of the cosmos. Certainly the media entertain no doubts! Let us take a skeptical look.

Does theory require black holes? In 1939 R. Oppenheimer and H. Snyder showed on paper that a massive star could collapse and create a black hole, *assuming* the correctness of stellar theories and General Relativity. Initially, scientists were skeptical about black holes because of their bizarre properties: They emit no light and inhale unwary starships. Black holes are also singularities, and singularities make scientists nervous. In the black-hole singularity, thousands of stars are swallowed and compressed into an infinitesimally small volume.[8] This grates against common sense.

All objects previously proclaimed to be small black holes have instead turned out to be neutron stars.

The philosophical uneasiness about black holes is worsened by the discovery that they:

> ...threaten the universe with an irreversible loss of information, which seems to contradict other laws of physics.[9]

Adding to these problems are nagging doubts about General Relativity, which underpins black-hole theory. Recently, some theorists have shown that General Relativity requires that two bodies of approximately equal size not attract one another![10]

Despite all these qualms, black holes have become a fixture of astronomy because they promise to explain the incredibly powerful energy sources seen in the cores of galaxies.

Do astronomers really observe black holes? The answer is: *maybe*. And even if yes, there are not nearly enough of them to satisfy theory.

To illustrate, according to present theory, when stars weighing in at less than three solar masses collapse, they become neutron stars; if larger, the stars turn into *small* black holes. Theoretically, there should be one small black hole for every three neutron stars. But with some 500 neutron stars already pinpointed, only three "possible" small black holes have been given votes of confidence; namely, Cyg X-1, LMC X-3, and AD 620-00. All objects previously proclaimed to be small black holes have instead turned out to be neutron stars.[11]

The case for *massive* black holes weighing in at millions of solar masses is not overwhelming either. These are supposed to lurk in the centers of galaxies. To find them, astronomers look for intensely bright spots in galaxies, around which stars swirl at speeds approaching the speed of light as they are sucked into the black hole's maw. Such fantastic celestial maelstroms *do* seem to exist, as evidenced by "something" in the giant elliptical galaxy M87.[12]

New claims for massive black holes are always being put forward. The spiral galaxy NGC 4328, for example, is thought to harbor a super-massive black hole weighing in at 40 million solar masses![13] However, claims for massive black holes are also being shot down all the time. Several have thought they had found a massive black hole at the center of our own galaxy. This no longer seems likely.[14]

> **Conclusion**. Don't be too quick to accept such bizarre constructs as black holes, whether small or massive.

More Quantum Weirdness

You have probably already heard how a change in one subatomic particle can cause an instantaneous change in another, even if the second particle is cruising along in another galaxy. That's quantum weirdness all right, but this weirdness can also produce effects we can see and hear.

All you have to do is cool helium down to almost absolute zero. It will liquefy but, unlike most other gases, it will not freeze. You are surprised at this, of course. Now, if you spin a bowl of this liquid helium around, you will be astounded. The liquid remains absolutely stationary in its spinning container—no centrifugal effects, no friction with the contained wall, *nada*! However, the strangest part comes when you:

> Draw a cupful out of the bowl, suspend it a few centimeters above the remaining liquid, then stand back and rub your eyes—the fluid in the cup will cheat common sense by pouring itself, drop by drop, back into the bowl. A drop climbs up the inside of the cup, then runs down the outside. When it falls, another begins climbing, and the magic continues until the cup is dry.[15]

The First Digit Phenomenon

Back in 1881, Simon Newcomb, the renowned Canadian-American scientist, published a provocative conjecture that was promptly forgotten by everyone. Newcomb had noticed that books of logarithms in the libraries were always much dirtier at the beginning. Hmmm! Were his fellow scientists looking up the logarithms of numbers beginning with 1 more frequently than 2, 3, etc.? It certainly seemed like it. He formalized his suspicions in a conjecture:

$p = \log 10\ (1 + 1/d)$

where p = the probability that the first significant digit is d.

This (unproven) equation states that about 30 percent of the numbers in a table or group will begin with 1. Only about 4.6 percent will begin with 9. This result certainly clashes with our expectation that the nine digits should occur with equal probability.

Fifty-seven years later, F. Benford, a GE physicist who was unaware of Newcomb's paper, observed the same dirty early pages in the logarithm tables. He came up with exactly the same conjecture. Benford didn't stop there. He spent several years collecting diverse data sets—20,229 sets, to be exact. He included baseball statistics, atomic weights, river areas, the numbers appearing in *Reader's Digest* articles, etc. He concluded that his (and Newcomb's) conjecture fit his data very well. There were notable exceptions, though. Telephone directories and square-root tables didn't support the conjecture.

Interestingly, the *second* digits in numbers are more equitably distributed; the third, even more so.

Mathematicians have never been able to prove the Newcomb-Benford conjecture. How could they if it doesn't apply to all tables? Nevertheless, it works for most data sets, and that's still hard enough to explain.[16]

All Roads Lead to 123

> Start with any number that is a string of digits—say, 9,288,759—and count the number of even digits, the number of odd digits, and the total number of digits it contains. These are 3 (three evens), 4 (four odds), and 7 (seven is the total number of digits), respectively. Use these digits to form the next string or number, 347. If you repeat the process with 347, you get 1, 2, 3. If you repeat with 123, you get 123 again. The number 123, with respect to this process and universe of numbers, is a mathematical black hole.

We have a black hole because we cannot escape, just as spaceships are doomed when captured by a physical black hole! You end up with 123 regardless of the number you start with. Other sorts of mathematical black holes exist, such as the Collatz Conjecture, but we must not fall into them because our printer awaits.[17]

Poets at Sea: Or Why Do Whales Rhyme?

We found the following in *Newsweek*:

> When scientists talk about whales singing songs, they're not talking about mere noise. They're talking about intricate, stylized compositions—some longer than symphonic movements—performed in medleys that can last up to 22 hours. The songs of humpback whales can change dramatically from year to year, yet each whale in an oceanwide population always sings the same song as the others. How, with the form changing so fast, does everyone keep the verses straight? Biologists Linda Guinee and Katharine Payne have been looking into the matter, and they have come up with an intriguing possibility. It seems that humpbacks, like humans, use rhyme.

Guinee and Payne suspect that whales rhyme because they have detected particular subphrases turning up in the same position in adjacent themes.[18]

Comment. This is all wonderfully fascinating, but why do whales rhyme at all, or sing such long, complex songs? Biologists fall back on that hackneyed old theory that it has something to do with mating and/or dominance displays. Next, we'll hear that human poets write poems only to improve their chances of breeding and passing their genes on to their progeny!

Reference. Whale "communication" is the subject of BMT8 in *Biological Anomalies: Mammals I* (Sourcebooks, 1995).

Eight Leatherback Mysteries

Our subject here is the leatherback turtle. Weighing up to 1,600 pounds, it is the largest of the sea turtles. It is also the fastest turtle, hitting nine miles per hour at times. But weight and speed are not necessarily mysterious; here are some characteristics that are:

- The leatherback is the only turtle without a rigid shell. Why? Perhaps it needs a flexible shell for its very deep dives. What looks like a shell is its thick, leathery carapace—a strange streamlined structure with five to seven odd "keels" running lengthwise.

- These turtles are *warm-blooded* and able to maintain their temperatures as much as 10°F above the ambient water, just as the dinosaurs apparently could.

- The bones of the leatherback are more like those of the marine-mammals (dolphins and whales) than the reptiles. "No one seems to understand the evolutionary implications of this."

- Leatherbacks dive as deep as 3,000 feet, which is strange because they seem to subside almost exclusively on jellyfish, most of which are surface feeders.

- Like all turtles, leatherbacks can stay submerged for up to 48 hours. Just how they do this is unexplained.

- Their brains are miniscule. A 60-pound turtle possessed a brain weighing only four grams—a rat's weighs eight!

- Leatherbacks' intestines contain waxy balls, recalling the ambergris found in the intestines of sperm whales.

- The stomachs of leatherbacks seem to contain nothing but jellyfish, which are 97 percent water. Biologists wonder how the huge, far-ranging leatherback can find enough jellyfish to sustain itself.[19]

The Ubiquity of Sea Serpents

Public interest is usually focused (by the media) upon the supposed monsters in Loch Ness, Lake Champlain, the Chesapeake Bay, etc. Actually, an immense body of sea-serpent reports also exists. B. Heuvelmans collected many of these in his 1965 classic *In the Wake of the Sea-Serpents.*

P.H. LeBlond, a professor at the University of British Columbia, is extending Heuvelman's work, concentrating on the thousand miles of Pacific Coast between Alaska and Oregon. Since 1812, there have been 53 sightings of sea serpents or other unidentified animals along this narrow strip of ocean. Some of these are very impressive. Take this one for example:

> In January 1984 a mechanical engineer named J.N. Thompson from Bellingham, Washington, was fishing for Chinook salmon from his kayak on the Spanish Banks about three-quarters of a mile off Vancouver, British Columbia, when an animal surfaced between 100 and 200 feet away. It appeared to be about eighteen to twenty feet long and about two feet wide, with a "whitish-tan throat and lower front" body. It had stubby horns like those of a giraffe, large ("twelve to fifteen inches long") floppy ears, and a "somewhat pointed black snout." The creature appeared to Thompson to be "uniquely streamlined for aquatic life," and to swim "very efficiently and primarily by up and down rather than sideways wriggling motion..."

LeBlond and biologist J. Sibert have analyzed all of the 53 sightings in a 68-page report entitled "Observations of Large Unidentified Marine Mammals in British Columbia and Adjacent Waters," published by the University of British Columbia's Institute of Oceanography. Of the 53 sightings, 23 "could not definitely or even speculatively be accounted for by animals known to science." The authors of the report emphasize that the reports are of high quality, made by people knowledgeable about the sea and its denizens.[20]

Facing up to the Gaps

The textbooks and professors of biology and geology speak confidently of the fossil record. Darwin may have expressed concern about its incompleteness, but, especially in the context of the creation-evolution tempest, evolutionists seem to infer that a lot of missing links have been found. Some scientists, however, are facing up to the fact that many gaps in the fossil record still exist after a century of Darwinism. One has even despaired that "the stratigraphic record, as a whole, is so incomplete that fossil patterns are meaningless artefacts of episodic sedimentation."

D.E. Schindel, Curator of Invertebrate Fossils in the Peabody Museum, has scrutinized seven recent microstratigraphical studies, evaluating them for temporal scope, microstratigraphical acuity, and stratigraphical completeness. His first and most important conclusion is that a sort of Uncertainty Principle prevails such that, "a study can provide fine sampling resolution, encompass long spans of geological time, or contain a complete record of the time span, but not all three." After further analysis he concludes with a warning that the fossil record is full of habitat shifts, local extinctions, and general lack of permanence in physical conditions.[21]

One scientist has even despaired that "the stratigraphic record, as a whole, is so incomplete that fossil patterns are meaningless artefacts of episodic sedimentation."

Comment. This candor makes one wonder how much of our scientific philosophy should be based upon such a shaky foundation.

Polar-Bear Bones Confound Ice-Age Proponents

Given the unquestioning fealty accorded the Ice Ages, it is not especially odd that the information reported below has not received wider circulation.

In 1991 construction workers at Tysfjord, Norway, 125 miles north of the Arctic Circle, accidentally dug up polar-bear bones that were later radiometrically dated as at least 42,000 years old, probably 60,000. R. Lie, a zoologist at the University of Bergen, and other scientists subsequently found the bones of two more polar bears in the area. These were dated as about 20,000 years old. An associated wolf's jaw was pegged at 32,000 years.

The problem is that Norway and many other northern circumpolar lands are believed to have been buried under a thick ice cap during the Ice Ages. In particular, northern Norway is thought to have been solidly encased in ice from 80,000 to 10,000 years ago. Polar bears could not have made a living there during this period. Clearly, something is wrong somewhere.[22]

Single cells taken from multicellular organisms tend to inch along like independent amoebas—almost as if they were looking for companionship or trying to fulfill some destiny.

An associated conundrum. Some authorities have stated that polar bears evolved *recently*—only 10,000 years ago! Polar bear evolution is discussed in more depth in *Biological Anomalies: Mammals II* (Sourcebooks, 1996).

Artificial Panspermia on the Moon

A colony of earth bacteria, *Streptococcus mitis*, apparently survived on the moon's surface between April 1967 and November 1969. The organisms were discovered in a piece of insulating foam in the TV camera retrieved from *Surveyor 3* by Apollo astronauts. [Note: Panspermia is the idea that life—particularly primitive life—does or at least can survive in outer space.][23]

Blebs and Ruffles

Single cells taken from multicellular organisms tend to inch along like independent amoebas—almost as if they were looking for companionship or trying to fulfill some destiny. This surprising volition of isolated cells becomes an even more remarkable property when the individual cells are fragmented. Guenter Albrecht-Buehler, at Cold Spring Harbor Laboratory, has found that even tiny cell fragments, perhaps just a couple percent of the whole cell, will tend to move about. They develop blebs (bubbles) or ruffles and extend questing filopodia. They have all the migratory urges of the single cells but cannot pull it off. Cell fragments will bleb or ruffle, but not both. Why? Where are they trying to go?[24]

Subversive Cancer Cells

It has been generally believed that most cancers originate in a single founder cell, which then multiplies to create the tumor. But cancer is more insidious than expected. A *pre*cancerous founder cell may actually subvert nearby *non*cancerous cells and turn them into cancerous cells. In this sense, the first precancerous cell recruits and transforms healthy cells, enlisting them in its destructive operations, and thereby turning them against the body that produced them. No one yet knows how this subversion is effected or how it evolved. (Why is there cancer anyway?)

The basis for this claim involves a few rare human *mosaics*, whose bodies are built of cells with two different genetic complements. Cancers in human mosaics have been found to contain *both* types of cells and, therefore, did not grow from a single cell alone.[25]

Comments. Curiously, some "primitive" animals, such as sharks, seem to have evolved defenses against cancer that mammals lack.

Tobacco and Cocaine in Ancient Egypt

The current newsletter of the New England Antiquities Research Association has flagged an important anomaly that appeared on a 1997 TV program:

> In January [1997] the Discovery Channel broadcast a program stating that cocaine and tobacco had been found in Egyptian mummies known to be at least 3,000 years old. Tests used modern forensic methods and were repeated many times under carefully controlled conditions. Since coca and tobacco are not known to have grown anywhere other than the Americas, the evidence points to trade routes across the Pacific or Atlantic in those remote times. The program seemed to favor a Pacific crossing and then delivery via the Silk Route.

This news item continued with a reference to Dr. Balabanov's supporting tests on bodies from China, Germany, and Austria, spanning the years 3700 BC to 1100 AD. These bodies contained incredibly high percentages of nicotine.[26]

Comment. In *Science Frontiers* #7/48, back in 1978, we reported that the mummy of Rameses II contained anomalous traces of nicotine.

American Pygmies

Today's anthropological texts say little about pygmies populating ancient North America, but a century ago, when tiny graves replete with tiny skeletons were discovered in Tennessee, controversy erupted. Were they the bones of pygmies or children of normal-sized tribes? The latter choice was made, and we hear no more on the subject—at least on the standard academic circuits.

But a few reverberations are still detectable elsewhere. V.R. Pilapil, for example, asserts that the disputed Tennessee graves *really* did contain pygmy remains. Not only that, but he hypothesizes that the pygmies arrived in ancient times from southeast Asia, probably the Philippines, where today's diminutive Aetas live.

To support his case, Pilapil recalls B. Fell's examination of the Tennessee skeletal material. Fell noted that:

- The skulls' brain capacity was equivalent to only about 950 cubic centimeters, approximately the volume of a non-pygmy seven-year-old.

- The teeth were completely developed and showed severe wear characteristic of mature individuals.

- The skulls were brachycephalic with projecting jaws. Fell had, in fact, described skulls very much like those of today's adult Philippine Aetas.

Another line of evidence adduced by Pilapil involved the traditions of British Columbia tribes, which recognized a tribe of very small people called the Et-nane. More significant is the oral history of the Cherokees, which mentions the existence of "little people" in eastern North America.[27]

When Humans Were an Endangered Species

At one point during the last 400,000 years, the human population worldwide was reduced to only about 10,000 breeding men and women—the size of a very small town. What caused this population "bottleneck"? Did a population crash engulf the entire globe? If not, who was spared?

Such questions arise from a surprising observation: Human DNA is remarkably uniform everywhere humans are found. This hidden genetic uniformity is difficult to believe if one strolls through a cosmopolitan city like New York or Paris. Nevertheless, compared to the DNA of the great apes, whose mutation rates *should* be close to ours, human genes on the average show far fewer mutations. Human DNA from Tokyo and London is more alike than that from two lowland gorillas occupying the same forest in West Africa. Harvard anthropologist M. Ruvolo has commented: "It is a mystery that none of us can explain."

At one point during the last 400,000 years, the human population worldwide was reduced to only about 10,000 breeding men and women—the size of a very small town.

The clear implication is that humans recently squeezed through a population bottleneck, during which many accumulated mutations were wiped out. In a sense, the human race began anew during the last 400,000 years. Unfortunately, DNA analysis cannot say where the very grim reaper came from.[28]

Comment. The hand that wiped the slate clean, or nearly so, might have been a meteor impact, a pandemic, the Ice Ages, a flood, volcanism, etc. Whatever it was, it seems to have largely spared Africa. The chimps and gorillas there apparently did not pass through the bottleneck. Even more interesting is the observation that the DNA of Subsaharan Africans does show more variability and therefore *seems* older than that from humans elsewhere on the planet. (See *Biological Anomalies: Humans III* (Sourcebooks, 1994).) Or perhaps Subsaharan DNA only seems older because it was not forced through that bottleneck. There are implications here for the African Eve theory.

Our Genes Aren't Us!

Almost without exception, biology textbooks, scientific papers, popular articles, and TV documentaries convey the impression that an organism's genes completely specify the living animal or plant. In most people's minds, the strands of DNA are analogous to computer codes that control the manufacture and disposition of proteins. Perhaps our current fascination with computers has fostered this narrow view of heredity.

Do our genes really contain all the information necessary for constructing human bodies? In the April 1994 issue of *Discover*, J. Cohen and I. Stewart endeavor to set us straight. The arguments against the "genes-are-everything" paradigm are long and complex, but Cohen and Stewart also provide some simple, possibly simplistic, observations supporting a much broader view of genetics:

- Mammalian DNA contains fewer bases than amphibian DNA, even though mammals are considered more complex and "advanced." The implication is that "DNA-as-a-message" must be a flawed metaphor.

- Wings have been invented at least four times by divergent classes (pterosaurs, insects, birds, bats); and it is very unlikely that there is a common DNA sequence that specifies how to manufacture a wing.

- The connections between the nerve cells comprising the human brain represent much more information than can possibly be encoded in human DNA.

- A caterpillar has the same DNA as the butterfly it eventually becomes. Ergo, something more than DNA must be involved. (This observation **does** seem simplistic, because DNA could, in principle, code for metamorphosis.)

Like DNA, this "something more" passing from parent to offspring conveys information on the biochemical level. This aspect of heredity has been bypassed as geneticists have focused on the genes.

Cohen and Stewart summarize their views as follows:

> What we have been saying is that DNA space is not a map of creature space. There is no unique correspondence between the two spaces, no way to assign to each sequence in DNA space a unique animal that it "codes for." Biological development is a complicated transaction between the DNA "program" and its host organism, neither alone can construct a creature and neither alone holds all the secrets, not even implicitly.[29]

Comment. If "genes aren't us," the billion-dollar human genome project cannot fulfill its promises.

You May Become What You Eat

When we scarf down a hamburger, we ingest bovine DNA. The textbooks say that this alien DNA is destroyed during digestion. Otherwise, it might "somehow" be incorporated into our own DNA, leading in time to our acquisition of some bovine characteristics! You'll recall that cannibals thought to acquire the virtues of their slain enemies by grabbing a bite or two. But this all sounds pretty far-fetched, doesn't it?

Maybe not. When W. Doerfler and R. Schubbert, at the University of Cologne, fed the bacterial virus M13 to a mouse, snippets of the M13's genes turned up in cells taken from the mouse's intestines, spleen, liver, and white blood cells. Most of the alien DNA was eventually rejected, but some was probably retained. In any event, alien DNA in food seems to make its way to and survive for a time in the cells of the eater.[30]

Comment. We are only half-kidding when we ask if food consumption could affect the evolution of a species. After all, our cells already harbor mitochondria, which are generally admitted to have originally been free bacteria that were "consumed" by animal cells. The process even has a name: "endosymbiosis."

Organ Music

Your doctor is understandably concerned if he finds your heartbeat is irregular. But it turns out that the healthy heart does *not* beat steadily and precisely like a metronome. In fact, the *intervals* between normal heartbeats vary in a curious fashion: In a simple, direct way, they can be converted to musical notes. When these notes (derived from heartbeat intervals) are heard, the sound is pleasant and intriguing to the ear—almost music—and certainly far from being random noise. In fact, a new CD entitled *Heartsongs: Musical Mappings of the Heartbeat*, by Z. Davis, records the "music" derived from the digital tape recordings of the heartbeats of fifteen people. Recording venue: Harvard Medical School's Beth Israel Hospital! This whole business raises some "interesting" speculations for R.M. May:

> We could equally have ended up with boring sameness, or even dissonant jangle. The authors speculate that musical composition may involve, to some degree, "the re-creation by the mind of the body's own naturally complex rhythms and frequencies. Perhaps what the ear and the brain perceive as pleasing or interesting are variations in pitch that resonate with or replicate the body's own complex (fractal) variability and scaling."[31]

Monogrammic Determinism

About two years ago (*Science Frontiers* #108), we succumbed to the lure of "nominative determinism." The Feedback page of the *New Scientist* had been printing case after amusing case in which a person's occupation was described or suggested by his or her surname. A classic example is seen in a paper on incontinence published in the *British Journal of Urology* by J.W. Splatt and D. Weedon! Does a person's name exert a psychological force of the choice of a career? We have seen no formal studies of nominative determinism, but we have just discovered a closely-allied phenomenon that *has* been scientifically investigated. We call it "monogrammic determinism."

An individual's monogram does not seem to be associated with his or her occupation but rather with longevity. People with monograms such as ACE, WOW, or GOD tend to live longer than those with monograms like PIG, RAT, DUD, or ILL.

The study was conducted at the University of San Diego, where 27 years' worth of California death certificates were examined. Only men were chosen, because their initials did not change with marriage. They were divided into three groups: (1) those with "good" monograms, (2) those with "bad" monograms, and (3) a control group with "neutral" monograms. Those men bearing "good" monograms lived 4.48 years *longer* than those in the control group; those with "bad" monograms, 2.8 years *less*.

Manifestly, being called DUD or PIG all your life can shorten it. Being addressed as ACE or GOD can give one a psychological boost that prolongs life.[32]

But it turns out that the healthy heart does *not* beat steadily and precisely like a metronome.

The Birthday: Lifeline or Deadline?

"Women are more likely to die in the week following their birthdays than in any other week of the year."

The following abstract is from a paper in *Psychosomatic Medicine*:

> This study of deaths from natural causes examined adult mortality around the birthday for two samples, totaling 2,745,149 people. Women are more likely to die in the week following their birthdays than in any other week of the year. In addition, the frequency of female deaths dips below normal just before the birthday. The results do not seem to be due to seasonal fluctuations, misreporting on the death certificate, deferment of life-threatening surgery, or behavioral changes associated with the birthday. At present, the best available explanation of these findings is that females are able to prolong life briefly until they have reached a positive, symbolically meaningful occasion. Thus the birthday seems to function as a "lifeline" for some females. In contrast, male mortality peaks shortly before the birthday, suggesting that the birthday functions as a "deadline" for males[33]

Addictions to Placebos

A 38-year-old married schizophrenic was in psychotherapy for severe depression and multiple suicide attempts. She was addicted to methylphenidate, taking 25 to 35 ten-mg pills per day. She was incredibly adept at persuading pharmacists to refill old prescriptions. With the help of her husband and a drug company, placebos were gradually substituted for the real pills to the point where only two real pills and 25-30 placebos were taken each day. The patient never noticed, indicating that the placebos satisfied the patient's real need—something to fill an inner void.[34]

Lacrima Mortis: The Tear of Death

It must be a heart-wrenching experience to see a single tear roll down the cheek of a person at the moment of his or her death. I. Lichter, medical director of the Te Omanga Hospice, in New Zealand, wondered how often this phenomenon occurred and why. Working with the Hospice nursing staff, Lichter followed 100 patients nearing death.

> The results showed 14 patients shed a final tear at the time of death, and a further 13 within the last 10 hours of life.
>
> In 21 of the 27 cases, the dying person was unconscious at the time of the last tear. And in all but one case the tear was shed by patients whose death was expected rather than sudden.

Lichter and colleagues wondered if the death-bed tears were emotional in origin or perhaps caused by a reflex action. Notes made by the nursing staff were inconclusive on this matter. Lichter thought of chemically analyzing some of the last tears, because emotional tears have a different chemical composition from those produced by irritation. Unfortunately, a single tear was insufficient for the analysis.[35]

Evolvable Hardware

First, you must envision a computer chip as an evolvable entity—an array of logic gates that can be connected in an almost infinite number of ways. A software instruction becomes the equivalent of a biological gene. Software instructions can be changed to achieve certain hardware goals just as genes can be rearranged to modify an organism. Furthermore, human operators can specify a hardware goal to the chip and let it evolve on its own, something it can do in microseconds rather than millions of years.

This is not a frivolous subject. D. Fogel, chief scientist at Natural Selection, Inc., in La Jolla, California, asserts:

> Eventually, we will need to know how to design hardware when we have no idea how to do it.

A few demonstration devices have already been built, and in them we see something worthy of note for *Science Frontiers*. One such device, built by A. Thompson, University of Sussex, was tasked to identify specific audio notes by certain voltage signals. Given 100 logic gates, the device needed only 32 to achieve the result. The surprise was that some of these working gates were *not even connected* to others by normal wiring. Thompson admitted that he had no idea how the device worked. Something completely unexpected had evolved. Perhaps, thought Thompson, some of the circuits are coupled electromagnetically rather than by wires. Human engineers would never have tried this stratagem; it is not even in their computer-design repertoire.[36]

Comments. Evolvable hardware, like God and Nature, works in mysterious ways! As the above type of hardware evolves, it will probably leave a "fossil record" full of mysterious transitions.

What shall we call the units a cyberheredity? "Cyberenes" is too cumbersome. How about: "bytenes"?

Computers Can Have Near-Death Experiences!

When HAL, the treacherous computer of *2001: A Space Odyssey*, was being slowly disconnected, it began singing "A Bicycle Built for Two." In other words, the cutting of the computer's interconnections did not result in gibberish, but rather memories that were previously stored flashed through its data processors. Something similar seems to happen with nonfictional computers.

When a type of computer program termed an "artificial neural network" is "killed" by cutting links between its units, it in effect approaches a state which might be something like biological "death."

When a type of computer program termed an "artificial neural network" is "killed" by cutting links between its units, it in effect approaches a state which might be something like biological "death." S.L. Thaler, a physicist at McDonnell Douglas, has been systematically chopping up artificial neural networks. He has found that when between 10 percent and 60 percent of the network connections have been severed, the program generates primarily nonsense. But, as the 90 percent (near-death!) level is approached, the network's output is composed more and more of previously learned information, like HAL's learned song. Also, when *untrained* artificial neural networks were slowly killed, they responded only with nonsense.[37]

Endnotes

1. Kalshian, Rakesh. (1994). "Ganges has magical cleaning properties." *Geographic*, 66, April, p 5. **2.** Shurkin, Joel N. (1994). "Underwater thumps baffle ocean scientists." *Nature*, 371, p 274. **3.** Owen, Hugh. (1984). "The earth is expanding and we don't know why." *New Scientist*, November 22, p 27. **4.** Saunders, Joe W., et al. (1997). "A mound complex in Louisiana at 5400-5000 years before the present." *Science*, 277, p 1796; Pringle, Heather. (1997). "Oldest mound complex found at Louisiana site." *Science*, 277, p 1761; Stanley, Dick. (1997). "Finds alter view of American Indian prehistory." *Austin American Statesman*, September 19. Cr. D. Phelps. **5.** Schultz, Peter H. & Leonard J. Srnka. (1980). "Cometary collisions on the moon and Mercury." *Nature*, 284, p 22. **6.** Van Flandern, Tom. (1997). "Top ten problems with the big bang." *Meta Research Bulletin*, 6, p 64. (*Bulletin* address: P.O. Box 15186, Chevy Chase MD 20825-5186.) **7.** Naeye, Robert. (1995). "Was Einstein wrong?" *Astronomy*, 23, November, p 54. **8.** Parker, Barry. (1994). "Where have all the black holes gone?" *Astronomy*, 22, October, p 36. **9.** Flam, Faye. (1994). "Theorists make a bid to eliminate black holes." *Science*, 266, p 1945. **10.** *Ibid.* **11.** *Op cit.*, Parker **12.** *Ibid.* **13.** Cowen, R. (1995). "New evidence of a galactic black hole." *Science News*, 147, p 36. **14.** Goldwurm, A., et al. (1994). "Possible evidence against a massive black hole at the galactic center." *Nature*, 371, p 589. **15.** Brooks, Michael. (1998). "Liquid genius." *New Scientist*, September 5, p 24. **16.** Hill, T.P. (1998). "The first digit phenomenon." *American Scientist*, 86, p 358. **17.** Ecker, Michael. (1992). "Caution: Black holes at work." *New Scientist*, December 19/26, p 38. **18.** Cowley, Geoffrey. (1989). "Rap songs from the deep." *Newsweek*, March 20, p 63. Cr. J. Covey **19.** McClintock, Jack. (1991). "Deep-diving, warm-blooded turtle." *Sea Frontiers*, 37, February, p 8. **20.** Gordon, David G. (1987). "What is that?" *Oceans*, 20, August, pp 44. **21.** Schindel, David E. (1982) "The gaps in the fossil record," *Nature*, 297, p. 282. **22.** Anonymous. (1993). "Polar bear bones cast doubt on Ice Age beliefs." *Colorado Springs Gazette*, August 23. An Associated Press dispatch. Cr. S. Parker. (A COUDI item. COUDI = Collectors of Unusual Data, International) **23.** Anonymous. (1982). *Science Digest*, 90, April, p 19. **24.** Anonymous. (1981). "The blebs and ruffles of cellular fortune." *New Scientist*, 90, p. 87. **25.** Day, Michael. (1996). "Cancer's many points of departure." *New Scientist*, June 1, p 16. **26.** Ross, Priscilla. (1997). *NEARA Transit*, 9, Spring, p 5. **27.** Pilapil, Virgilio R. (1991). "Was there a prehistoric migration of the Philippine Aetas to America?" *Epigraphic Society, Occasional Papers*, 20, p 150. **28.** Gibbons, Ann. (1995). "The Mystery of humanity's missing mutations." *Science*, 267, p 35. **29.** Cohen, Jack, & Ian Stewart. (1994). "Our genes aren't us." *Discover*, 15, April, p 78. **30.** Cohen, Philip. (1997). "Can DNA in food find its way into cells?" *New Scientist*, January 4, p 14. **31.** May, Robert M. (1996). "Now that's what you call chamber music." *Nature*, 381, p 659. **32.** Anonymous. (1998). "Do initials help some live longer?" *San Mateo Times*, March 28. Cr. J. Covey. **33.** Phillips, David P., et al. (1992). "The birthday: Lifeline or deadline?" *Psychosomatic Medicine*, 54, p 532. **34.** Muntz, Ira. (1977). "A note on the addictive personality: Addiction to placebos." *American Journal of Psychiatry*, 134, p 327. **35.** Morrison, Alastair. (1993). "The mystery of the death-bed tear." *Wellington Dominion*, August 11. Cr. P. Hassall **36.** Taubes, Gary. (1997). "Computer design meets Darwin." *Science*, 277, p 1931. **37.** Yam, Philip. (1993). "'Daisy, Daisy'." *Scientific American*, 268, May, p 32

THE BIG PICTURE

Will the Real Human Being Please Stand Up?

Riane Eisler

What does it mean to be human? Is there really something terribly wrong with us? Or is the story about "human nature" we get from our education—both formal and informal—skewed toward a particular way of relating?

Our first inventions, we are told, were weapons, and the first human groups were organized by men to more effectively kill both animals and members of other human groups. Stanley Kubrick's film *2001: A Space Odyssey* (based on Arthur C. Clark's book) begins with a scene showing a hominid creature suddenly realizing that a large bone can be used as a weapon to kill another member of his species. The "innocent" cartoon (we think nothing of showing it to children) of a brutal caveman carrying a large club in one hand, dragging a woman around by her hair with the other, has this same message. Not only that, in a few "amusing" strokes it tells us that sex and male violence have always gone together, that this is just "the way it is."

The invention of tools does not begin with the discovery that we can use bones, stones, or sticks to kill one another.

Although this story of an inevitably flawed humanity is still embedded in prevailing religious and scientific narratives about "original sin" and "selfish genes"—which also present male dominance as justified by either God or evolution—scholars from many disciplines tell us a different story of our cultural origins.

In this story, the invention of tools does not begin with the discovery that we can use bones, stones, or sticks to kill one another. It begins much earlier, with the use of sticks and stones to dig up roots (which chimpanzees do) and continues with the fashioning of ways to carry food other than with bare hands (rudimentary vegetable slings and baskets) and of mortars and other tools to soften foods.

In this story, the evolution of hominid, and then human, culture also follows more than one path. We have alternatives. We can organize relations in ways that reward violence and domination. But, as some of our earliest art suggests, we can also recognize our essential interconnection with one another and the rest of the living world.

The Two Chimps

In most nature documentaries, as well as in a huge body of sociobiological literature, we are led to believe that we are prisoners of our "unfortunate" evolutionary heritage. Just look at other primates, we are told, and you see why men are violent and women are subordinate to them.

But that's actually not what we see if we look at our species' two closest primate relatives: the common chimpanzees and the so-called pygmy chimpanzees or bonobos. The DNA of bonobos (pygmy chimpanzees) and common chimpanzees (who are actually no larger) is basically the same. Moreover, it is not very different from that of our own species. However, observations of both these species in the wild indicate that there are marked differences between the behaviors and social organizations of bonobos and common chimps.

In many ways, bonobo chimpanzees prefigure much of what we find in humans. They have what primatologists call a more gracile (or slender) build, longer legs that stretch while walking, a smaller head, smaller ears, a thinner neck, a more open face, and thinner eyebrow ridges than most other apes. Of particular interest is that—also like humans but unlike most other species—bonobos have sex not just for reproduction but purely for pleasure, and even beyond this, pleasure-bonding.

In fact, this sharing of pleasure through the sharing of food as well as through sexual relations is a striking aspect of bonobo social organization. Just as striking is that even though theirs is not a violence-free social organization, their society is held together, far more so than among common chimps, by the exchange of mutual bene-

To maintain social cohesion and order, this species, so closely related to us, relies primarily on the sharing of pleasure.

fits characteristic of partnership relations. To maintain social cohesion and order, this species, so closely related to us, relies primarily on the sharing of pleasure—and not on the fear of pain (or violence) required to maintain rigid rankings of domination.

Equally striking is that, even though males are not dominated by females, in bonobo society females—particularly older females—wield a great deal of power. Moreover, it is through the association of females in groups that bonobo females seem to have avoided the kind of predatory sexual behavior that has been observed among common chimps, where males have been seen to force sexual relations on females.

In short, the bonobo chimpanzees rely more on bonds based on pleasure and the sharing of benefits than on rankings based on fear and force. (A good resource here is the article on the bonobos by the primatologist Takayoshi Kano in *Nature*. The difference between the bonobo chimps and common chimps is also discussed in detail in my books *Sacred Pleasure* and *Tomorrow's Children.*)

Were Women There?

Much of what is still written about the story of human evolution follows the old view that "man the hunter" was its main protagonist. Indeed, most of the scientists in this field have been men, although there are some notable exceptions, such as Mary Leakey, who found the first early human fossil in East Africa in 1959, and Adrienne Zihlman, who has proposed the bonobo chimpanzee as the most likely prototype for the "missing link" between hominids and earlier primates, and who has also helped to develop a theory about the origins of human tools in which women play an important role.[1]

These contributions present a view of our human emergence in which more stereotypically "feminine" human characteristics, such as nurturance and nonviolence, are highlighted —*whether they reside in women or men.*

Zihlman is among a growing number of scientists—most of them women in fields ranging from physical anthropology and biology to cultural anthropology, psychology, and sociology—who have over the last 30 years been developing a more gender-balanced narrative of early human evolution. As Zihlman notes, this has been an uphill struggle. No sooner are earlier male-centered accounts of human evolution contradicted by new evidence, than new theories are put forward to again render women invisible, or at best portray them as "handmaidens to men" and squarely place men—and with them an emphasis on aggression and competition—at the center of our human adventure.[2]

Not only that, these theories—which invariably portray male-dominance as natural—continue to be replicated in the vast majority of textbooks, as well as in visual representations of human evolution. Typical are museum dioramas where a male stands tall in the foreground while a group of females sits in the background, or where a male towers over a smaller crouching female, as in the dioramas of Neanderthals and *homo sapiens* at the American Museum of Natural History exhibit. (For a survey of such scenes in books, see Diane Gifford-Gonzales' "You Can Hide, But You Can't Run: Representations of Women's Work in Illustrations of Paleolithic Life," where she speaks of one classic pattern for depicting women sitting on or working with animal skins as the faceless "drudge-on-the-hide" distortion of women's roles as passive and peripheral).[3]

By developing more balanced, and accurate, narratives in which women, and not just men, play a major role in innovating and making hominid and human evolution happen, women scientists are making significant contributions to our understanding of how we became human. These contributions present a view of our human emergence in which more stereotypically "feminine" human characteristics, such as nurturance and nonviolence, are highlighted—*whether they reside in women or men.*

For example, Zihlman goes beyond earlier accounts about what distinguishes our species: Our upright posture, which freed our hands for tool use, and on our large brains, which give us our great capacity to learn, making possible our immense behavioral flexibility. Like other theorists, such as Glynn Isaacs, Nancy Tanner, Ralph Holloway, Paul MacLean, and Humberto Maturana, she emphasizes the role of communication and caring in human evolution. The theory she developed together with Nancy Tanner also emphasizes our enormous human capacity for creativity. Indeed, Tanner and Zihlman propose that we have even to some degree been co-creators of our own biological evolution—and that females played a key part in this process.

As Tanner writes in *Becoming Human*, not only is it more than likely that females developed and used some of the earliest tools, such as slings and other means of carrying infants, baskets to carry gathered plants, and possibly also tools to dig for tubers and roots; these tools, in turn, also affected our evolution. "Tools for gathering meant mothers could collect more food for offspring who, then, could be supported longer before becoming independent"[4]—a longer period of dependency being a salient characteristic of our species. This also made it possible for children to have a longer period to "learn social and technological traditions"—another key development in human evolution, as it lead to the much greater role of culture in shaping behavior found in our species.[5]

One could even speculate that as we increasingly relied not on teeth, but on the use of tools and cooking methods to soften food, the huge molars characteristic of most other primates became less necessary, leaving more cranial room for larger brains. As many scientists have noted, it is our larger relative brain-size of an average of 1,350 cubic centimeters—a quantum leap from even our first hominid ancestors, who had already attained a brain size of 450 cubic centimeters—that characterizes our human emergence.[6] One could further speculate that this reduction in molar size also left more room for the voice boxes required for the complex verbalizations of human language—leading to the much greater capacity for communication and symbolization that make possible the complex social, technological, and artistic development that we call human culture.

Indeed, as Paul MacLean also argues, it is highly probable that the most unique and important of human tools—our highly complex language—originated out of mother-child bonds; in other words, out of the bond of caring and love between mother and child.[7] Moreover, as Humberto Maturana and Gerda Verden-Zöller emphasize, writing about what Maturana calls the biology of love, one of the most important developments in our evolution is this human capacity for love.[8]

This kind of approach to the study of human evolution makes it possible for people to refocus from selfishness and violence as the main themes in our evolution to caring and creativity as equally, and in some ways more important, themes. It also makes it possible for us to see that these qualities are part of the nature of both women and men. And it makes it possible to see that our primary and most meaningful identity is as human beings, regardless of gender, race, religion, or nationality. At the same time, this approach also helps us appreciate, and respect, other life forms and our Mother Earth, thus better equipping us to responsibly deal with the environmental challenges we face.

It is highly probable that the most unique and important of human tools —our highly complex language— originated out of mother-child bonds.

Our Neglected Mythic Heritage

The period after the gathering/hunting so-called Old Stone Age is known as the Neolithic or New Stone Age. It marks the beginning of what is perhaps the most important human invention: agriculture.

Here we are taught another interesting story of cultural origins. It is completely inconsistent with the one about violence and male dominance being "human nature," but it still conveys a similar message. Now we are told that chronic warfare and male dominance were ushered in by the agricultural age. That is, war and the subordination of one half of humanity are unfortunately the price we have to pay for civilization.

But what we are today learning about the Neolithic does not support this view. For example, the belief that the Neolithic was a male-dominated period is inconsistent with the myths found in many cultures throughout the world. Stories about female deities with great power and importance, as well as functioning partnerships between priestesses and priests, are found in many traditions. Female deities are also in many world traditions associated with important inventions that most texts still credit solely to men. In Mesopotamia, the Goddess Ninlil was revered for providing her people with an understanding of planting and harvesting methods. The official scribe of the Sumerian heaven was a woman, and the Sumerian Goddess Nidaba was honored as the one who initially invented clay tablets and the art of writing—appearing in that position earlier than any of the male deities who later replaced her. Similarly, in India, the Goddess Sarasvati was honored as the inventor of the original alphabet.[9]

That we find basic human inventions—from farming to writing—credited to female deities suggests that women probably played a key part in their development. That female deities are attributed so much power, including the power to create the world and humanity, also suggests a time when women occupied positions of leadership in their communities. And that we find these powerful female deities in ancient stories of every world region suggests that this was once widespread.

We find clues to this earlier period in the traditions of many indigenous North American tribes. As Paula Gunn Allen writes in *The Sacred Hoop: Recovering the Feminine in American Indian Traditions*, many Indian myths revolve around powerful female figures.[10] Serpent Woman is one. Corn Woman is another. Earth Woman is another. Still another is Grandmother of the Corn. As Allen writes, "Her variety and multiplicity testified to her complexity: she is the true creatrix for she is thought itself, from which all else is born... She is also the spirit that forms right balance, right harmony, and these in turn order all relationships in conformity with her law."[11] Similarly, central to Keres Pueblo theology is a Creatrix called She Who Thinks, who is the supreme spirit, both mother and father to all people and to all creatures.[12]

From China, too, we have myths about a time when the yin or feminine principle was not yet subservient to the yang or male principle. This is a time that the Chinese sage Lao Tsu, who dates to about 2,600 years ago, reports was peaceful and just. Likewise, one of the earliest known European writers, the Greek poet Hesiod, who lived approximately 2,800 years ago, tells us that there was once a "golden race" who lived in peaceful ease before a "lesser race" brought with them Ares, the Greek god of war.

These stories were undoubtably greatly idealized folk memories of earlier times. Nonetheless, they tell us that, although most of the early agricultural era was not a violence-free utopian period, it was not the bloody time we have been led to believe.

That we find basic human inventions —from farming to writing— credited to female deities, suggests that women probably played a key part in their development.

The Metamorphosis of Myth—and Reality

Towards the end of the Neolithic period, however, we begin to see evidence of a fundamental social and cultural shift. In the Americas, even before the European conquests, there are indications that during a period of great drought there were incursions from warlike tribes. For example, such a drought is documented by dendrochronology in the western part of the American continent between approximately 1275 and 1290. There is also evidence of raiders who came down from the north and destroyed earlier Mogollan and Anasazi communities—highly developed cultures that represent a Golden Age of American Prehistory, the Anasazi later becoming the Hopi and Zuñi Pueblo Indians.[13]

In Europe and Asia Minor, this shift occurred much earlier, approximately 5,500 years ago. At that point there appear, in the words of the British archaeologist James Mellaart, severe signs of stress. There are natural disasters and severe climate changes. Here, too, during a period of severe drought we begin to see invasions by nomadic herders, who bring with them a more warlike social organization.[14]

In the area the archaeologist Marija Gimbutas calls Old Europe (the Balkans and Northern Greece) we now, for the first time, find large stores of weapons. Often these are in a new type of burial: "chieftain graves." Horses, women, and children were often sacrificed and placed in these graves to accompany their masters into the afterworld.

In China, scholars at the Chinese Academy of Social Sciences in Beijing have also traced this shift from more peaceful and egalitarian societies in which women do not appear to have been subservient to men and female deities seem to have played leading roles to a later time when Chinese society oriented more to the dominator model.[15] For example, in his article "Myth and Reality: The Projection of Gender Relations in Prehistoric China," Professor Cai Junsheng writes: "NuWa is the most important mythological female figure handed down from the prehistoric age. NuWa was long considered by the Chinese as the creator/creatrix of the world. However, a careful examination of Chinese myths shows how, at the same time that the social structure changed to a patriarchal one, NuWa lost her power until finally there are myths where she dies."[16]

As Junsheng puts it, "due to the elimination and misinterpretation of information during the subsequent long period of patriarchal society" available data have to be carefully analyzed.[17] However, as he also notes, a careful analysis of myths provides clues to a massive cultural shift.

There are mythical clues to this shift from every world region. In Africa, the female status in sacred mythology deteriorated over time. This seems to follow the pattern found in other world regions, were female mythological figures start out as the Creatrix, then become a wife or mother of a male god, first in an equal role and then in a subservient role, are next demoted to non-divine status, and finally are demonized as witches or monsters. African goddesses can be found which run the gamut of these roles. The South African Ma is the "Goddess of Creation" and Mebeli (of the Congo) is the "Supreme Being;" Haine is the Tanzanian Moon Goddess whose husband is Ishoye (the sun); Dugbo (of Sierra Leone) is an Earth Goddess, responsible for all plants and trees, married to Yataa, the Supreme Being. There are also La-hkima Oqla (of Morocco), a female "jenn" who inhabits a river and rules over other evil spirits, Yalode (of Benin) who causes foot infections, and Watamaraka (of South Africa), the "Goddess of Evil" who is said to have given birth to all the demons.[18]

Today all these female mythic representations are found side by side. But if we do a little detective work, we can trace their origins and situate them in a sequence from Creatrix to subservience to conversion to a male deity or to a demonic witch or monster. For example, in the iconography of old Europe, the figure Gimbutas, called the Snake Goddess, plays a prominent role, probably because the snake was viewed as one of the manifestations of the power of regeneration, since snakes shed and renew their skins. But in later Greek mythology, we have the monstrous Medusa, a terrible female with hair of coiled snakes. Significantly, she has been stripped of the power to give life, but still retains the power to take life, as she is said to turn men to stone.

Similarly, the Hindu Kali is noted for her bloodthirsty cruelty. Nonetheless there are also remnants in Hindu mythology of the female power to give life splintered off into a number of deities, including Parvati. Along a somewhat different trajectory, the early Greek Mother Goddess Demeter is first turned by Christian remything into Saint Demetra—and finally masculinized as Saint Demetrius. Following still another trajectory, female deities such as Athena in Greek mythology and Ishtar in Middle Eastern mythology are now goddesses of war and human sacrifice—reflecting the shift to a more violent, hierarchic, and male-dominated social structure.

Does this mean that societies ruled by women, matriarchies, are superior to societies ruled by men? Hardly. There is no evidence that these earlier societies were ruled by women.

But there is evidence that women and qualitities stereotypically associated with women, such as caring and nonviolence, were not excluded from social governance. In other words, rather than patriarchies or matriarchies, these societies seem to have oriented more to what I have called a partnership rather than dominator model of organizing relations with other humans and with our Mother Earth.[19]

A New Look at Modern History

When we look at the last 300 years, taking our hidden cultural heritage into account, we see that the struggle for our future is not between right and left, religious and secular, or even industrial and pre- or postindustrial. It is rather between the two basic ways of organizing relations that—because there were no names to describe the configurations I discovered—I named the partnership model and the dominator model.

Another important aspect of modern history that then becomes visible is that during the great technological and social disequilibrium of the industrial revolution and now the postindustrial revolution of electronic, nuclear, and biochemical technologies, has come the opportunity for another major cultural shift: this time from domination to partnership. For what is still seldom noted in conventional history texts and classes is that, as new technologies destabilize established institutional forms, there are opportunities to challenge entrenched systems of belief and social structures.

For what is still seldom noted in conventional history texts and classes is that, as new technologies destabilize established institutional forms, there are opportunities to challenge entrenched systems of belief and social structures.

This leads to a completely different, more interesting, and more meaningful picture of the last 300 years: one with important practical implications for what we can do today.

Certainly the Enlightenment was a period where we begin to see a massive questioning of entrenched patterns of domination. The so-called rights of man movement of the late seventeenth and early eighteenth centuries eventually led to both the American and French Revolutions and to a gradual shift from monarchies to republics. Paralleling the challenge to the supposedly divinely-ordained right of kings to rule was the feminist movement of the eighteenth and nineteenth centuries, which challenged the supposedly divinely-ordained right by men to rule over women and children in the "castles" of their homes, bringing about a gradual shift to less autocratic and male-dominated families.

During both the nineteenth and twentieth centuries there were movements against slavery and against the colonization and exploitation of indigenous peoples. We see the rise of organized labor and socialism, followed by the toppling of feudal monarchies and warlords by communist revolutions in Russia, China, and other countries. In the United States, there is a gradual shift from unregulated robber-baron capitalism to government regulations—for example, anti-monopoly laws and economic safety nets such as Social Security and unemployment insurance.

There is the nineteenth-century feminist movement demanding equal education and suffrage for women and the organized movement by blacks for the vote, followed by the twentieth-century civil rights and women's liberation and women's rights movements. There is the nineteenth-century pacifist movement followed by the twentieth-century peace movement, expressing the first fully-organized rejection of violence as a means of resolving international conflicts. There is the twentieth-century family planning movement as a key to women's emancipation as well as to the alleviation of poverty and greater opportunities for children.

In basic respects, however, the dominator system remained firmly entrenched. Colonialism and the killing and exploitation of darker-skinned peoples continued the tradition of conquest and domination on a global scale. There are also periodic backlashes; for example, Jim Crow laws passed after the abolition of slavery, anti-union violence during the first half of the twentieth century, and continuing anti-feminist agitation—from resistance to higher education and the vote for women in the nineteenth century to the defeat of the Equal Rights Amendment and renewed opposition to reproductive rights for women in the twentieth century.

The twentieth century also witnessed massive dominator regressions. In Europe, for example, we see Hitler's Germany (from the early 1930s to the mid-1940s) and Stalin's Soviet Union (the 1920s to the 1950s), in which the ideals of a more just society were coopted into a "dictatorship of the proletariat," creating still another version of a brutal dominator model.

And even after Western colonial regimes are overthrown in Africa and Asia, we see the rise of authoritarian dictatorships by local elites over their own people, resulting in renewed repression and exploitation, including the rise of so-called fundamentalist religious regimes that once again reinstate the domination of one half of humanity over the other as a cornerstone of a violent and authoritarian system.

During this modern industrial age we also see the use of ever more advanced technologies to more effectively exploit, dominate, and kill. Moreover, it is during the industrial age that high technology begins to be harnessed to further "man's conquest of nature"—wreaking ever more environmental damage.

Humanity at the Crossroads

Today the mix of the dominator model and advanced technology becomes increasingly unsustainable. The blade is the nuclear bomb and/or biological warfare and terrorism. Increasingly advanced technologies in the service of a dominator ethos threaten our natural habitat, as well as that of most species with whom we share our planet.

This postmodern period brings further challenges to traditions of domination. It brings a strong environmental movement: millions of people coming together to challenge "man's conquest of nature." It also brings a strengthening of the family-planning movement as integral to environmental sustainability; stronger movements against the domination and exploitation of indigenous peoples; a growing challenge by peoples in the "developing world" to its domination by the "developed world;" and thousands of grassroots organizations all over the world working toward political democracy, nonviolent ways of living, and economic, racial, and gender equity.[20]

Significantly, because these are foundational relations where we first learn and continually practice either domination or partnership, we now see a much more organized challenge to traditions of domination and violence in intimate relations. Child abuse, rape, and wife-beating are increasingly prosecuted in some world regions. A global women's-rights movement frontally challenges the domination of half of humanity by the other half, gaining impetus from the unprecedented United Nations conferences (1975-1995) that brought women from all world regions together around such pivotal issues as violence against women, equal legal rights and economic opportunities, and reproductive freedom.

However, precisely because the movement toward partnership is intensifying and deepening—for the first time focusing on the so-called private sphere of human relations that are the foundations for habits and attitudes we carry into all areas of life—the resistence to change stiffens. There is continued, and in some places increasing, violence against women and children. Some of the statistical increases are due to the fact that this violence was formerly unreported, as it was not prosecuted and was often instead blamed on the victims. But since violence is what ultimately maintains dominator relations, as women's and children's human rights are asserted, violence against them has also increased to literally "beat them back into submission." In some countries, this violence is perpetrated by government officials; for example, in Afghanistan, Algeria, Pakistan, Bangladesh, and Iran the stoning to death of women for any act perceived as countering male sexual and personal control—even a young woman exposing her ankles—is again being justified on "moral" grounds.[21]

There is also, under the guise of economic globalization, a recentralization of economic power worldwide. Under pressure from major economic players, governments are cutting social services and shredding economic safety-nets—"economic restructuring" that is particularly hurtful to women and children worldwide. In the developing world, this restructuring is enriching dominator elites through a shift from the production of food and goods for local consumption to products for the export trade. At the same time, it is contributing to the impoverishment of Third World people, who no longer produce what they need and are ever more dependent on jobs in urban centers.

Concurrently, high-paying jobs in postindustrial economies are shrinking, creating increased competition for low-paying jobs (generally without benefits) by workers in blue collar, pink collar, and middle management displaced by automation or corporate downsizing. Regions ranging from the former Soviet Union to countries in Asia, Africa, and Latin America are being forced into a replay of the robber-baron days of early capitalism, complete with sweatshops, forced child labor, rampant political corruption, and organized crime.[22] In short, there is a widening gap between haves and have-nots both within countries and between different world regions.

There is growing scapegoating of women (particularly single mothers living in poverty) and minorities, once again sometimes in the name of religious fundamentalism. There is an increase in terrorism, even in once supposedly impregnable nations such as the United States—some by its own citizens. There are "ethnic cleansings," such as those in Bosnia and Kosovo, and resurgent genocidal warfare, such as the carnage of Rwanda. In addition, in the name of entertainment, the mass media obsessively focus on violence—constantly emphasizing the infliction or suffering of pain that are mainstays of dominator politics and economics.

There is also burgeoning population growth. The world's population, which has doubled in the last 40 years—in only a few decades reaching more than 5 billion people, the vast majority in the poorest world regions—is projected to again double by the mid-twenty-first century, exacerbating hunger, violence, and other causes of human

Regions ranging from the former Soviet Union to countries in Asia, Africa, and Latin America are being forced into a replay of the robber-baron days of early capitalism.

suffering, straining the world's natural resources. This unsustainable population growth is in large part also due to dominator systems dynamics: the continued denial of reproductive freedom to women (or the loss of gains already made) and the efforts, often violent, to deny women access to life options other than procreation.

In sum, the outcome of the tension between the partnership and dominator models as two basic human possibilities is far from settled. We are now at what scientists call a bifurcation point, where there are two very different scenarios for our future.

One is *dominator systems breakdown*: the unsustainable future of high technology guided by the dominator model. This is where high technology in service of the domination of nature despoils and pollutes our natural habitat. It is a future where advanced technologies will be used not to free our human potentials, but to more effectively control and dominate. And ultimately, it is a future of environmental, nuclear, or biological holocaust.

The other scenario is *breakthrough to partnership*: the sustainable future of a world primarily orienting to the partnership model. Here advanced technologies are developed and used in ways that promote environmental balance and the realization of our species' great untapped potentials. International regulations ensure corporate accountability to workers, communities, and our natural habitat. New economic institutions and rules recognize the value of the work of caring and caregiving, and discourage violence, exploitation, and the despoliation of nature.[23]

Although in this world, too, nation-states may continue to break down, instead of leading to genocidal ethnic civil wars, diversity is valued and our shared partnership heritage binds cultures together. Although there is still some violence, it is not built into the system as a means of maintaining rankings of domination. Although there is still conflict, as is inevitable in human relations, young people have the tools to resolve it in creative ways.

Women and men are equal partners in both the "private" or family sphere and the outside or "public" sphere. And children are valued and nurtured not only by their biological parents, but by the entire community—which recognizes that children are our most precious resource.

To move toward this world, however, requires fundamental changes, including changes in our education that make it possible for today's and tomorrow's children to see that if we work together we can create a more equitable, peaceful, and sustainable future—once we acquire the knowledge and skills to do so.[24]

Endnotes

1. Zihlman, Adrienne L. (1982). *The Human evolution coloring book*, with illustrations by Carla Simmons, Wynn Kapit, Fran Milner, and Cyndie Clark-Huegel. New York: Barnes and Noble Books. **2.** Zihlman, Adrienne. (1997). The Paleolithic glass ceiling: Women in human evolution. In Hager, Lori D. (Ed.) *Women in human evolution.* New York: Routledge, pp 91-113, p 91. **3.** Gifford-Gonzales, Diane. (1993). You can hide, but you can't run: Representations of women's work in illustrations of Paleolithic life. *Visual Anthropology Review* 9, pp 23-41. **4.** Tanner, Nancy M. (1981). *Becoming human.* Cambridge, Mass.: Cambridge University Press, p 274. **5.** *Ibid.*, pp 274-275. See also Zihlman, Adrienne & Nancy Tanner. (1974). Becoming human: Putting women in evolution. Paper presented at the annual meeting of the American Anthropological Society, Mexico City. **6.** Leakey, pp 44-48. **7.** MacLean, Paul. (1995). *The triune brain in evolution: Role in paleocerebral functions.* New York: Plenum, p 544; MacLean, Paul. (Sept 1996). "Women: A more balanced brain?" *Zygon*, 31:3, p 434. **8.** Maturana, Humberto R., & Gerda Verden-Zoller. (1998). *Origins of humanness in the biology of love.* Durham, NC: Duke University Press. **9.** Stone, Merlin. (1976). *When God was a woman.* New York: Harcourt Brace Jovanovich, p 3. This book is an excellent source of information about ancient female deities, its only drawback being that it does not make a distinction—which is critical—between the character of the female deities before and after the shift to a dominator model, when they often became goddesses of war and sacrifice. For a discussion of this, see *The Chalice & the Blade* and *Sacred Pleasure*, both by Riane Eisler. **10.** Allen, Paula Gunn. (1986). *The sacred hoop: Recovering the feminine in American Indian traditions.* Boston: Beacon Press. **11.** *Ibid.*, p 14. **12.** *Ibid.*, p 15. Herb Martin and Terri Wheeler of California State University at Monterey Bay contributed material on Goddess myths from Native American traditions. **13.** Gibson, Arrell Morgan. (1980). *The American Indian: Prehistory to the present.* Lexington, Massachusetts: D.C. Heath and Company, pp 30-34. **14.** Chapter 5 of Riane Eisler, *Sacred pleasure* (San Francisco: Harper Collins, 1996) explores some of the reasons that the culture of these herding people, who came from arid environments, may have evolved in a dominator direction. **15.** Jiayin, Min. (Ed.). (1995). *The chalice and the blade in Chinese culture.* Beijing: China Social Sciences Publishing House. **16.** Junsheng, Cai. "Myth and reality: The projection of gender relations in prehistoric China," in Jiayin (1995), p 44. **17.** *Ibid*, pp 34-35. **18.** Herb Martin and Terri Wheeler of California State University at Monterey Bay contributed material on Goddess traditions from Africa. **19.** For a detailed description of these societies and the factors behind the shift, see Eisler, Riane (1987, 1988). *The chalice and the blade.* San Francisco: Harper & Row; Eisler, Riane. (1995, 1996). *Sacred pleasure.* San Francisco: Harper Collins. For a work that incorporates this information into education, see Eisler, Riane. (2000). *Tomorrow's children.* Boulder, Colorado: Westview Press. **20.** For examples, see chapters 18 and 19 of *Sacred Pleasure.* **21.** Women Living Under Muslim Laws, an organization of Muslim women with offices in Pakistan and France, is an excellent source of information here. They can be reached at Women Living Under Muslim Laws, Boite Postale 23, 34790 Grables (Montpellier) - France. Another excellent source is the quarterly *Women's International Network News*, which can be subscribed to by writing to Women's International Network News, 187 Grant Street, Lexington, MA 02173. **22.** Some good readings are Mander, Jerry & Edwin Goldsmith. (Eds.). (1996). *The case against the global economy and for a turn toward the local.* San Francisco: Sierra Club Books; Henderson, Hazel. (1991). *Paradigms in progress: Life beyond economics.* Indianapolis: Knowledge Systems, Inc.; Korten, David. (1995). *When corporations rule the world.* San Francisco: Barrett-Koehler; Peterson, The. Spike & Anne Sisson Runyan. (1993). *Global gender issues.* Boulder: Westview Press; Eisler, Riane, David Loye, & Kari Norgaard. (1995). *Women, men, and the global quality of life.* Pacific Grove, California: Center for Partnership Studies; *Human development report 1995.* (1995). Published for the United Nations Development Program (UNDP) by Oxford University Press (New York); *The world's women 1995: Trends and statistics.* (1995). New York: The United Nations. For a short piece that has some good statistics and could serve as a handout, see also Korten, David. (June 1997). A market-based approach to corporate responsibility. *Perspectives on Business and Global Change* 11: 2, pp 45-55. See also the Center for Partnership Studies' Website <www.partnershipway.org> to download "Changing the Rules of the Game: Work, Values, and Our Future," by Riane Eisler, 1997. **23.** See Riane Eisler, "Changing the Rules of The Game" on the CPS website <www.partnershipway.org>. **24.** These two scenarios are outlined in chapters 12 and 13 of *The Chalice and the Blade* and detailed in the closing chapters of *Sacred Pleasure.*

Adapted from Tomorrow's Children: A Blueprint for Partnership Education in the 21st Century *by Riane Eisler (Westview Press, 2000).*

You Are Being Lied To

Disinformation Books Roundtable

Compiled by Alex Burns

Get past Y2K and The X-Files*, and it's no secret that fringe subcultures, conspiriology, and emerging worldviews have been changed forever by global media vectors. One barometer of this seismic shift in consciousness is how people perceive their milieu and who controls relativistic 'information' and 'truth' in a chaotic era.*

"Are we being lied to, why, and by whom?"

Disinformation Books posed this predicament to social activists, media analysts, cutting edge scientists and philosophers, avant-garde artists, counterculture icons, and conspiracy theorists. The answers we received about "the Big Lie" ranged from sociopolitical critiques to personal reflections; they were always illuminating and provocative.

I'm the biggest liar I have to deal with, with my hopes, fears, biases, and psychological defenses subtly distorting the way I perceive the world and react to it.

▪▪▪▪▪▪▪▪▪▪▪

Of course! It's part of life on earth to be lied to by others at times, and part of our growth challenge is to find a reasonable compromise between being naively trusting and pathologically paranoid.

But it's not the lies of others that worry me the most, but rather our habit of lying to ourselves, with no conscious awareness of it. I'm the biggest liar I have to deal with, with my hopes, fears, biases, and psychological defenses subtly distorting the way I perceive the world and react to it.

That's why, in addition to my psychological research on others, I've devoted a lot of time to studying myself and trying out systems of self-knowledge. My current best understanding (subject, I hope, to further growth) of my and others' minds and ways of knowing them better is expressed in two published books, *Waking Up* (1986) and *Living the Mindful Life* (1994), and a new book, *Awakening Mind: Meditation Training for the Scientifically Inclined* (2000).

In them I try hard not to lie to myself or others and to share the best knowledge and methods I have.

Charles T. Tart <www.paradigm-sys.com/cttart/> is internationally known for his psychological work on the nature of consciousness (particularly altered states of consciousness), as one of the founders of the field of transpersonal psychology, and for his research in scientific parapsychology. His many books include *Waking Up: Overcoming the Obstacles to Human Potential* (Boulder, CO: Shambhala Books, 1986), *Living the Mindful Life* (Boulder, CO: Shambhala Books, 1994), and *Awakening Mind: Meditation Training for the Scientifically Inclined* (Boulder, CO: Shambhala Books, 2000).

▪▪▪▪▪▪▪▪▪▪▪

Being very self-centered, I never pay attention to what other people say! So let them be the judges of their own pronouncements.

Hans Moravec <www.frc.ri.cmu.edu/~hpm/> is director of the Robotics Institute, Carnegie Mellon University, and is cited as a key influence upon the "Extropian" philosophical school. His many books include *Robot: Mere Machine to Transcendent Mind* (New York: Oxford University Press, 1998) and *Mind Children: The Future of Robot and Human Intelligence* (Cambridge, MA: Harvard University Press, 1988).

▪▪▪▪▪▪▪▪▪▪▪

I lie all the time, don't you?

"How are you?" "Fine."

One of the scariest of lies is the politician or prospective mate who promises, "I'll never lie to you." The deeper message there is: "I lie about lying." And: "I'm completely irresponsible."

Stewart Brand is a member of the Global Business Network <www.gbn.org>, and founder of the Long Now Foundation <www.longnow.org>. He is author of over 20 books, including *The Clock of the Long Now* (New York: Basic Books, 2000) and *The Media Lab: Inventing the Future at MIT* (New York: Penguin USA, 1988).

▪▪▪▪▪▪▪▪▪▪▪

When Windows 98 was released, Microsoft paid strategically placed journalists to write favorable pieces about its new operating system. When this fact was leaked to other, possibly more upstanding press members, the Evil Empire covered by diverting the press' attention with a "Blue Screen of Death" at Win 98's unveiling. Ho, ho, ho. . . oops.

I don't know how high that particular story rates on the truth-scale, but I do know that after the Department of Justice announced its ruling in its anti-trust case against the Evil Empire, Bill Gates appeared almost immediately on NBC News to steer, counteract, and spread new memes. This is fishy because Microsoft and NBC are partners. Is the biggest network actually going to cover the facts of the case when it's in its best interest to make its Goliath business partner look good? The Emperor has a direct link to the minds of his minions because he's in bed with their media outlet.

How could an arrangement like that ever be conducive to an informed society? It couldn't, and more and more of these vertical alliances are forming: AOL and Time Warner, ABC and Disney . . . Hell, it's even happened in the Open Source community where VA Linux Systems owns the parent company of Slashdot—the major news outlet for the Open Source community.

If the news media and the corporations of this country are one and the same, we have been and will be lied to more and more.

Roy Christopher is editor of Front Wheel Drive <frontwheeldrive.com>, and one of the Internet's leading interviewers of subculture and new science icons.

▪▪▪▪▪▪▪▪▪▪

No, we are never lied to.

Politicians would never lie, because they are at our service, and not at the bidding of the richest financier. The CIA and intelligence establishment would never lie, because their sole job is to protect the national security and only do what is necessary to protect freedom throughout the world. The Pentagon and defense industry would never lie, because all they are interested in is securing the blessings of liberty, and are doing so altruistically. The FBI and police forces would never lie, because they are only interested in stopping evil,

If the news media and the corporations of this country are one and the same, we have been and will be lied to more and more.

predatory criminals who use the legal system that clearly is to their benefit. Businesses would never lie, because they are only interested in giving us more information about their products via commercials so we can make better purchasing decisions. And, of course, religious leaders would never lie either, because they are only interested in spiritually saving others and have a duty to God to tell the truth.

The funny thing is, most people take on faith these denials of deceit, and get really upset if someone points out how full of shit our given assumptions are. Which leads me to conclude that the biggest liars of all are ourselves.

As even Fox Mulder would put it, "I want to believe."

Robert Sterling is editor of the Konformist <www.konformist.com>, and a bona fide *agent provocateur*.

▪▪▪▪▪▪▪▪▪▪

"The Immortalization of Humanity"

The history of the world is the history of lies. It is probably true that no area of history, religion, politics, or science is free from fabrica-

The history of the world is the history of lies.

tion or deception. My mind is particularly tuned to scientific or medical hoaxes. Of course, the word "lie" may sometimes be too strong, because there are many viewpoints on truth, and there are many unreported stories that are not quite lies.

To me, the most unreported story deals with evolution of human lifespans and intelligence. Although we hear news reports about how humans will live longer in the future, we rarely hear reports that our children or grandchildren will be immortal by the end of the century.

Given the tremendous advances in molecular biochemistry that will take place by 2100, we will certainly uncover the molecular and cellular mysteries of aging, and therefore many humans will live forever, assuming they don't suffer a fatal accident. I am amazed that this obvious concept is not discussed more often or taken more seriously. Of course, the ecological, economic, political, social, and religious implications will be extreme. Imagine an immortal Pope discussing the afterlife with his followers—or the growth of two social classes, those that can afford immortality and those too poor to gain access to the required anti-aging "treatment."

Clifford A. Pickover <www.pickover.com> received his Ph.D. from Yale University and is the author of over twenty books, including *The Girl Who Gave Birth to Rabbits: A True Medical Mystery* (New York: Prometheus Books, 2000).

▪▪▪▪▪▪▪▪▪▪

The powerhouse Slovenian philosopher Slavoj Zizek introduces the important idea that truth can function as a lie.

What this means is that someone may well tell me the truth, but still they lie in the way they tell it. And I don't mean a white lie or something trivial like that. I mean that in a mediatized corporate culture, truth (sincerity, facts, disclosure) functions even more effectively than lies in trapping people into the system and making them complacent.

(Honestly, this is one of the things that irritates me about lots of conspiracy theorists. They write as if it were some big secret that corporations make deals, shoddy goods, pollute the environment, etc.)

I just saw a pathetic movie with Winona Ryder called *Boys* (1996). It's set in a boys' boarding school and one of the boys wants to hide the unconscious Winona Ryder in his room. He can't get his friends to leave and they keep bugging him, "What's the big secret," blah,

No one believes anything, so the actual content of a statement is not so relevant any more.

blah, blah. Finally, the kid says, "There's an unconscious woman in the car and I want to hide her in my room." At this point, the other guys laugh and walk off, sure that this is a crock.

Lies and truth today are more complicated than they've ever been because we live in a highly cynical culture. No one believes anything, so the actual content of a statement is not so relevant any more.

Think about this politically. We hear all sorts of things—yes, experiments were carried out on African American men in Tuskegee; yes, American military personnel and civilians were horribly exposed to radiation during US nuclear tests; yes, major players in the tech industry give loads of money to politicians of all shapes and sizes. These are true statements, but they function as a lie that makes us think that the system is fair, just, and inclusive.

Think about how information works (and this is one of the things that drives me crazy when I try to do political work). Before anything happens, everyone says, "Oh, well, first we need more information"—again, as if it were a mysterious fact to be documented that the police force is racist, for example. And then what happens, well, we get different kinds of information.

One kind would be confirmation of the obvious—but then wrapped in all sorts of explanations: "Things are changing," "We've hired new people," "The problem is under investigation." Another kind of information would be a horrible admission: "Oh yes, cigarettes are nicotine delivery systems"—but then the information is wrapped in an excuse: "People want nicotine delivery systems." Other excuses include deflections: "But isn't poverty really the big issue," and "What about the farmers?"

So anyway my point is simply that lies and truth are irrelevant. What is relevant is a strong understanding of the system, how power works, and how to change it.

Jodi Dean is professor at the Department of Political Science, Hobart-William Smith Colleges <www.hws.edu/PEO/faculty/dean/index.html>. She is author of several books including *Aliens in America: Conspiracy Cultures from Outerspace to Cyberspace* (New York: Cornell University Press, 1998).

■ ■ ■ ■ ■ ■ ■ ■ ■ ■

We are not being told the truth about quantum physics by most of the physicists writing for the general public. Not so much that they are lying, but rather, they are not aware of David Bohm's solutions to many of the key problems they present as unsolved mysteries.

A good case is Julian Barbour's book *The End of Time: The Next Revolution in Physics* (New York: Oxford University Press, 2000). Julian is a good man, a brilliant man, a good writer, and a serious thinker. He does an admirable job within the mainstream quantum metaphysics that simply assumes that the quantum wave function is a complete description of reality at the individual level with no additional "hidden variable." Julian's solution to the problem of time in quantum gravity falls apart when one applies Bohm's ontology to the problem. His book is actually a good indirect argument for Bohm's ontology.

From what I hear we are being lied to about the existence of real mechanical flying saucers from advanced intelligence not from our time. I could be wrong about this. But my best Baysean estimate based on imperfect, incomplete information is that our military has such captured alien machinery but has not been able to reverse engineer them, in any fundamental way, because of really stupid security restrictions that weed out the very people who could actually figure it out as "loose cannons," such as myself as the prime example.

I have been told this by various intel types for the past 30 years or so. My suspicion, based on my own probably direct contact with them in 1953, is that there are dormant conscious nanocomputers in the thin skin of the fuselage. They will respond, "wake up" as it were, when touched, I mean literally touched, like the finger of the ape touching the Black Monolith in the film *2001: A Space Odyssey* (1968), by the right people. This may just be my teenage fantasy of course. On the other hand it might be the reality. A simple test will decide.

Jack Sarfatti <www.stardrive.org> is senior consulting scientist to the International Space Sciences Organization <www.isso.org>. Founder of Esalen Institute's legendary "Physics Consciousness Research Group," he would make a great script-writer for *The X-Files*.

These days, everyone's speaking the truth, or at least they've managed to convince themselves and their followers that they are.

■ ■ ■ ■ ■ ■ ■ ■ ■ ■

Are we being lied to? No, we're not. Not any more.

We've moved beyond that, at least in Australia and, I suspect, in most other countries of the Western world.

These days, everyone's speaking the truth, or at least they've managed to convince themselves and their followers that they are. Whether you believe that AIDS isn't related to HIV, that air pollution doesn't cause the greenhouse effect, that tobacco smoke isn't carcinogenic, that there are no stolen generations of Aborigines and Torres Strait Islanders, that Microsoft benefits the world economy, that Bill and Monica only discussed debt reduction policies for the Third World, you can now find people who agree with you, and you can find—or buy—a scientific study to back you up.

No, we're not being lied to any more. We're being told the truth, and nothing but the truth, in the same way that religious fanatics all through the ages have told people the truth and rejected outright any even minor attempts to correct their points of view. Only now it's not fanaticism any more: it's politics.

And that's the truth. Pure and simple.

Axel Bruns is an Internet researcher at the University of Queensland and Production Editor of *M/C - A Journal of Media and Culture* <www.api-network.com/mc/> and *dotlit: The Online Journal of Creative Writing* <www.dotlit.qut.edu.au/>.

■ ■ ■ ■ ■ ■ ■ ■ ■ ■ ■

Of course we are. Daily/hourly, by the whores of the New World Order agenda (One World Government, Global Governance, "the Third Way," Globalism... monikers change, but the song remains the same).

If you really want a thorough background on this Grand Design, which will incorporate all sovereign nation-states into a bloated, socialistic Oligarchy—one-currency, one-military, redistribution of wealth (like the white-owned farms in Zimbabwe—theft, by any other name), go no further than these texts:

America's Secret Establishment: An Introduction to the Order of Skull & Bones, Chapter 322 by Dr. Antony Sutton (Bundaberg, QLD [Australia]: Veritas Press, 1986); *Tragedy & Hope* by Carroll Quigley (Palos Verdes, CA: GSG & Associates, 1975); *The Fearful Master: Inside the United Nations* by G. Edward Griffin (Boston MA: Western Islands, 1964); *The Unseen Hand* by A. Ralph Epperson (Tucson, AZ: Publius Press, 1985), and *Proofs of a Conspiracy* by John Robison (Appleton, WI: American Opinion Books, 1967).

Or ask yourself this question: If every Secretary of State in the US Government, and every President (with the exception of Ronald Reagan), since about 1913, as well as the heads/producers/senior editors of CNN, ABC, CBS, NBC, Gannett, yaddayadda, were all members of, say, the National Rifle Association or the John Birch Society, do you think there'd be a shit-storm of protest? Damned straight there would be.

But when the so-called "Right" (or even concerned Libertarians) questions having such high-power slots filled consistently, as if by birthright, by members of the Council on Foreign Relations and Trilateral Commission (the two prime-movers of NWO-schemes), "we" (as I count myself of the Right/Libertarian axis) are called "kooks," "crackpots," "wearers of tin-foil hats" for daring to cast light on such schemers.

Remember folks: A Conspiracy cannot stand to see its own shadow.

Todd Brendan Fahey is founder of Far Gone Books <www.fargone-books.com>, and one of America's most illuminating renegade minds. His novels include *Wisdom's Maw: The Acid Novel* (Los Angeles: Far Gone Books, 1996) and *Hell Bottled Up!: Chronicles of a Late Propaganda Minister* (Los Angeles: Far Gone Books, 2000).

■ ■ ■ ■ ■ ■ ■ ■ ■ ■ ■

We are being lied to all the time, but not all lies are conscious or deliberate. Some of the worst lies may come from our trusted friends because they themselves may have picked up the lies from a trusted source. Misinformation spreads like a virus without regard to the underlying truth of the news. Juicy gossip involving sex, power, and celebrities carries much more viral spreading power than mundane facts. Simplistic explanations are much more satisfying that truthful ones. The seeker of truth must sit awake in a lonely tower, prepared to question everything and anything that comes his or her way, or risk succumbing to the soporific comfort of the common wisdom.

Richard Brodie <www.memecentral.com> is author of several books, including *Virus of the Mind: The New Science of the Meme* (Seattle: Integral Press, 1996). In a previous incarnation, he was the original author of Microsoft Word, and PA to Gates of Borg.

■ ■ ■ ■ ■ ■ ■ ■ ■ ■ ■

The seeker of truth must sit awake in a lonely tower, prepared to question everything and anything that comes his or her way, or risk succumbing to the soporific comfort of the common wisdom.

Do I feel we are being lied to? I think we are lying to ourselves. We want to believe someone is piping some sort of untruth into our brains so that we can release ourselves from the responsibility of taking care of ourselves and those around us.

I don't believe that some group of people is "in charge" of our world, and disinforms the greater population. I believe that we find people and institutions on whom we can project our own powerlessness, and then they rise to the occasion.

I believe that when a group or individual has monopoly over the technology of communication—be it language, television, or the Internet—then he or they can maintain an unfair advantage in promoting a particular worldview. The Catholics did it with religion, the British did it with language, Hitler did it with radio, the Americans with TV and now the Internet. It's not lying, exactly—it's just presenting magic tricks as reality. Usually, though, it's our greed that is exploited by such trickery.

I think we lie to ourselves that this situation has existed throughout history, and is essentially unchangeable.

I think we can stop lying to ourselves any time we choose, that we

I believe that when a group or individual has monopoly over the technology of communication—be it language, television, or the Internet—then he or they can maintain an unfair advantage in promoting a particular worldview.

are afraid to do so, and that many people have learned to gain power by exploiting this fear.

Douglas Rushkoff <www.rushkoff.com> is professor of media culture at New York University's Interactive Telecommunications Program, an Adviser to the United Nations Commission on World Culture, on the Board of Directors of the Media Ecology Association, and a founding member of Technorealism <www.technorealism.org>. He is author of eight books, including *Coercion: Why We Listen To What 'They' Say* (New York: Riverhead Books, 1999) and *The Ecstasy Club: A Novel* (New York: Riverhead Books, 1998).

■■■■■■■■■■■

Lying is such a touching, all-too-human quality. Let's not get rid of that one. Or pretend we can erase this evil aspect. No more healing, please. We can expect the worst, in this respect, with the human DNA having been mapped. Some mega-Christian American scientist will discover the "lying sequence" and push for "global treatment." Staged by organized goodwill.

Praise the Liar, blast the Truth agent!

In the news media context it is becoming more and more easy to deconstruct, and even more effective, ignore propaganda. I would not call it lying what CNN is presenting us. We could accuse some Pentagon officials of that. The news media are just sheep. One can attack them for being tame. Behaving like a herd.

Of course there are hardly any courageous dissenters within the mainstream media, with the exception of, let's say John Pilger, Germaine Greer, and a few others. It is bloody hard to be an investigative journalist. Most people working in the news industry are rewriting press releases from wire agencies and other firms.

News is a commodity like any other. And there is amazingly little of it. Surprise, surprise. The reprocessing of news worldwide, on television, radio, in print media, on the Net, is a fascinating process. With amazing speed a news meme is traveling through the Networks, replicating and mutating along the way. See all these poor bastards, hooked on their screens, doing their copy-paste thing. Are they lying? No. This is clear case of finding one's self beyond, or beside the borders of Good or Evil. *Information im aussermoralischen Sinne.*

The war in Kosovo could be a good example. There was enough information about the dreadful situation there, before 1998, when the armed conflict really started. By the end of 1998, things started getting blurred. It became obvious that the Serbian army, warlords, and media manipulators very well knew how to deal with the Western media industry. So did the Kosova-Albanian side and their UCK army.

Then, by the end of March 1999, the Western media jumped on it, without having possibilities to check facts on the ground. There was little else for them to do then but become slaves of the Pentagon.

The reason for this is a simple one: time. Facts need to be checked. In the realtime 24/7 news economy there is no time for this. Everything has to be reported, instantaneously. If you don't, others will report it first.

Paul Virilio has already pointed at this mechanism. It might take at least five, ten years to reconstruct what really happened there. Who killed who. Who fooled which news organization. The War Tribunal in the Hague will play a role in this, so might some documentary video makers, NGO researchers. The amount of information these people will produce about Kosovo will be overwhelming. The truth might be hidden there, somewhere, under a pile of self-replicating complexities.

Geert Lovink <thing.desk.nl/bilwet> is a co-founder of Amsterdam's Digital Cities project <www.dds.nl>, the *Next Five Minutes* conference series <www.n5m.org>, and the Nettime discussion list <www.nettime.org>. He was previously editor of *Mediamatic* <www.mediamatic.nl> for four years.

■■■■■■■■■■■

Everyone is always being lied to, all the time. All communication lies. It is always in some way *different* from that to which it refers. It can even refer to things that don't or can't exist. This fundamental, inescapable nature of all communication is the real conceptual core of the experience of paranoia.

Paranoia is the partial realisation of the truth of the lie. Partial, because doomed to the futile illusion that, "the truth is out there." Of course most people, most of the time, prefer to accept the lie, rather than accept the truth of the inescapability of the lie.

This was Nietzsche's great insight. We lack the strength to live with lies, determine what are good lies to live by, bad lies to fight. We want what we can't have—the unmediated truth. We accept some lies as more true than others on the most spurious grounds. Because they conform to our desires, our weaknesses, our interests. Or we lie to ourselves about the fact that we see through the lie, and pretend we believe it.

There is a whole pathology of the lie. There are good and bad lies, ethical and unethical lies, useful and harmful lies, and it behooves us to tell the difference, deploy them with cunning, read them with subtlety. But there are only lies. And that's the truth of it.

McKenzie Wark <www.mcs.mq.edu.au/~mwark> is a senior lecturer in Media Studies at Macquarie University (Australia). He edits Pluto Press, Australia's media.culture book imprint <socialchange.net.au/pluto>, and is author of four critically acclaimed books, including *Sensoria* (Sydney: Pluto Press Australia, 2000) and *Virtual Geography: Living with Global Media Events* (Bloomington, IN: Indiana University Press, 1994).

■ ■ ■ ■ ■ ■ ■ ■ ■ ■ ■

We are all lied to all the time about drugs. In this deceitful atmosphere few people dare to discuss the spiritual experiences some drugs can induce, the insights they can provide, or simply the pleasure of taking them. We hear a lot about drug "abuse," which is certainly something to be discouraged, but almost nothing about drug "use."

Worse still, our children are lied to at school. They are told that all illegal drugs are dangerous and are given no useful information on how to use drugs carefully and with respect. They stand no chance of developing a healthy (let alone sacred) relationship to powerful drugs and as a consequence are likely to follow only one of two courses—avoid them altogether (the minority), get mired in abuse and confusion.

Let's get the drugs out of the hands of criminals and into the hands of a controlled marketplace (with lots of tax gained for our governments as a side effect). Then, I believe, we might hear the truth.

Susan Blackmore <www.memes.org.uk> is senior lecturer in psychology at the University of the West of England. She is author of seven books, including *The Meme Machine* (New York: Oxford University Press, 1999) and *Dying to Live: Near-Death Experiences* (New York: Prometheus Books, 1993).

■ ■ ■ ■ ■ ■ ■ ■ ■ ■ ■

Corporate public relations (PR) is the art and science of presenting information in such a way as to maximize profit. Sometimes it is proactive, like advertising.

We want what we can't have—the unmediated truth.

The promotion of the Gulf War is a particularly dramatic example—Iraqi atrocities were concocted and promoted by Hill & Knowlton, on the payroll of the Kuwaiti government, to convince US taxpayers to support the war.

Other times it is defensive, and intended to defuse criticism and prevent erosion of corporate liberties. "Black Websites," for example, are employed by companies engaged in dangerous or reprehensible pursuits, in anticipation of a disaster or public outcry. When an oil spill or embarrassing discovery finally occurs, the "black Website," prepared months or years in advance, communicates the company's essential innocence, heartfelt shock, and commitment to future improvement.

Corporate PR is always one form or another of lying—from the "white lie" to the worst kind of disinformation. It is protected in the US as free speech.

This is because in the 1870s corporations succeeded, with the help of lots of PR, in getting themselves defined as "persons" under the law, with all the Constitutional rights thereto attendant.

Because the direction of corporate PR is always to maximize profit, and because it is so astoundingly powerful and widespread, its cumulative effect is to conform public consciousness, democratic processes, and even the Constitution to the corporate pursuit of gain. Next to corporate PR, all the lying in the media and government combined vanishes into near insignificance.

Ray is part of ®™ark <www.rtmark.com>, a shadowy company at the forefront of twenty-first century corporate consulting. Just ask George W. Bush <www.gwbush.org>.

■ ■ ■ ■ ■ ■ ■ ■ ■ ■ ■

The answer is "yes," of course we are lied to, over and over. Truth has become a very rare commodity in our culture. The most obvious example faces the American voter every day now in this election year: the lie that the two candidates represent a choice, when both are the pure products of the corporate oil and military industry. With politicians so bought and paid for, every false "issue" of contention between the two, trotted out and tracked through stilted polls by the compliant media, serves as another lie.

Media even present the evidence of extra-electoral manipulation as merely convenient coincidence. For instance, fires near the Los Alamos national laboratories drew the attention of the country to that area, followed shortly by the mysterious disappearance and reappearance of computer hard drives at the Los Alamos facility. Just coincidence, the voter/viewer was told.

Coincidence also that fallout from the event tarnished the reputation of Energy Secretary Bill Richardson, until then a top contender for the vice presidency on the Gore side of the military party. Richardson is now passing nuclear weapons plants contracts out as fast as he can to the likes of Bechtel National, Inc., just to hold on to his job.

Religion, the classic liar of history (see: Acharya S., *The Christ Conspiracy*), also remains one in current affairs. The Vatican, for instance, recently proclaimed that the "Third Secret" of the Fatima visions of the Virgin by three children in 1917 was a prediction of the 1981 assassination attempt against Pope John Paul II.

In reality, the sole survivor of the Fatima visions, Sister Lucia, working from notes she jotted in 1944, had said the vision showed the Pope "killed by a group of soldiers who fired bullets and arrows at him, bishops, priests and nuns and other people, who died one after the other."

It fell to Mehmet Ali Agca, the man who fired the shots at John Paul, to issue a statement from prison about the extent to which the Vatican had distorted its interpretation of the third secret. Agca also claims that the Vatican itself set up the assassination.

In parapolitical history, someone named Michael Ledeen, identified by Danny Casolaro as a peripheral player in the Octopus conspiracy, planted a story that the assassination attempt against JPII had a Bulgarian/Stasi/Soviet link, but no one believes that now. If the Vatican did indeed have this information 64 years prior to the assassination, one would think it would have re-routed the papal parade that day, or at least would have told the Pope to duck.

Kenn Thomas is founder of Steamshovel Press and editor of *Steamshovel Review* <www.steamshovelpress.com>. He is author of over ten books including the two-volume *Cyberculture Conspiracy: A Steamshovel Press Reader* (Book Tree Publishers, 1999-2000), *Maury Island UFO: The Crisman Conspiracy* (Atlanta, GA: IllumiNet Press, 1999), *The Octopus: The Secret Government and Death of Danny Casolaro* (Los Angeles: Feral House, 1996).

■■■■■■■■■■■

"Popsicle Lies"

The Popsicle Index is the % of people in a community who believe a child can leave their home, go to the nearest place to buy a popsicle, and come home alone safely.

When I was a child, the Popsicle Index was 100%, the Dow Jones Index was around 500, and debt per person was almost nothing. Today, the Popsicle Index is reaching new lows, the Dow Jones is reaching new highs, and debt per person just went over $100,000 in the US.

I used to work at the US Department of Housing and Urban Development <www.hud.gov>. HUD's deeper mission was to shift control of community resources to outsiders. It made the Dow Jones go up.

We lied about what we were doing. We lied to ourselves, each other, the press, the people. Every effort was made to make sure information was not integrated, accessible. We were lost in a mapless world. Data at HUD was like cigarettes in a prison.

When I left, I started a company that helped Web users make money maps—graphic-like comic books of how all the money worked where they lived. The money map tool, Community Wizard, was destroyed when the Department of Justice and HUD targeted and destroyed the company and seized our digital systems and databases.

Catherine Austin Fitts is president of Solari <www.solari.com>, a progressive investment advisory company. She was formerly Assistant Secretary of State for Housing and Urban Development under President George Bush from 1989 to 1990.

■■■■■■■■■■■

Lies are the *koine*, the common tongue of the world. I know the counter person at the copy store is lying about having done my order—so I lie about when I brought it in.

What a small thing. Yet, here is how it works. Ten million small rain drops fill up a pond. The people that are looking for the big lies from Big Brother or whoever, miss the point, they are looking at waves and thinking that's what's keeping them from seeing the Real. (A little Chaos Theory might help here.) It's the whole pond, and none of us even cares that we are filling it.

When I wrote this note back to Alex Burns I started to tell him I that I had misfiled the e-mail so it was late. Well, one less drop for today.

Don Webb is an award-winning author of over 200 short stories and articles. His novels include *The Double: An Investigation* (New York: St. Martin's Press, 1998) and *Essential Saltes* (New York: St. Martin's Press, 1999). In another life, he was contributing editor for *FringeWare Review* <www.fringeware.com>.

■■■■■■■■■■■

Of course, I feel like I'm being lied to all the time by 3M—the Multinational Military Media mouthpiece that I wrote about in my first novel, *The Kafka Chronicles*, a story that partly dealt with the Big Lies being broadcast during the Gulf War. It's such a strange sensation, being glued to the tube as a kind of willing media victim, a casualty of the propaganda wars, quite literally allowing all of that top-down disinformation to enter my bloodstream like a language virus gone out of control.

Lying is an art form. Take it from me, a fiction writer (i.e. one who manipulates language to try and re-tell the Truth so that the word actually has meaning again). At one point in my novel, in a section called "Our & We," the narrator says:

Lying is an art form. Take it from me, a fiction writer.

"Language: ultimate strategy: get the lingo: then turn on the jingo spectacle: turn on the vid: then ransack the id."

In those glory days of a kindler, gentler nation reaching out to an orgasmic convergence of a thousand points of light, there was nothing but the promise of a lackluster Vision Thing—and endless news polls telling us that "we" actually wanted to be lied to, that "we" preferred it that way.

Again, from *The Kafka Chronicles*:

"**We** be the ones: **we** be the ones who die for them: who them?: turn on the t.v. and find out: they ain't ashamed to show they face: they got us support: they say **we**: they say ours: they say us: **we** deliver on command."

Mark Amerika is one of America's most important and acclaimed experimental novelists. He is publisher of the Alt-X Network <www.altx.com>, described by *Publishers Weekly* as "the publishing model of the future." His novels include *The Kafka Chronicles: A Novel* (Tallahassee, FL: FC2, 1993) and *Sexual Blood* (Tallahassee, FL: FC2/Black Ice Books, 1995).

■ ■ ■ ■ ■ ■ ■ ■ ■ ■ ■

Can we blame Big Business and Government for lying to us—when lying is integral to our culture?

First thing in the morning, find in the mailbox envelopes consciously designed to look like utility bills or cheques: Tear them open and find that they're advertisements, junk mail. They lied.

Turn on the television, commercials tell us a product makes us younger, more attractive: It's a famous old lie, yet that's the point: We accept it.

We accept ads for "psychic hotlines" that take advantage of stupid people, though everyone but that stupid person knows that these are con artists. We know that government-sponsored TV ads lie about how buying a state-lottery ticket will change your life. But we accept the lie.

Many years ago, as an executive assistant in a New York City public relations firm, I was startled when PR press releases I'd typed up for the local papers were reprinted almost verbatim. The articles, in many instances, were giddy reports on the wonders of new drugs, diets, and health "systems," with no mention of possible contraindications. When I questioned this, I was fired.

The same thing happens in our newspapers every day: PR is published as news....We accept that political TV ads lie—we shrug it off. Recently here in California the pharmaceutical industry ran a TV ad "warning" people that legislation making it possible to buy cheaper prescription drugs from, say, Canada would endanger them: They implied the drugs would be impure. Drugs from Canada? Impure? The ad was ripely deceptive.

But it's okay, it's permitted. That's our culture. We're a culture of liars. It extends to everything we do so naturally our acceptance of lies is perfected in government.

John Shirley <www.darkecho.com/johnshirley> was once described by William Gibson as "Cyberpunks' Patient Zero, first locus of the virus, certifiably virulent." He was the original script-writer of *The Crow* (1994). He is author of the radical, prophetic cyberpunk trilogy *Eclipse*, *Eclipse Penumbra*, and *Eclipse Corona* (Northbridge, CA: Babbage Press, 2000).

■ ■ ■ ■ ■ ■ ■ ■ ■ ■ ■

Well, shit, when are we *not* being lied to? What's that phrase from *The X-Files*, "I want to believe"? Think how mind-numbingly easy it is just to believe, not to question the information bombarding us every day. Our minds fill in the cognitively dissonant spaces. Most of us spend so much mental and spiritual time and effort just to stay alive and well and possibly happy that there is little room left to question lies, but they surround us like an acrid fog. Any group, company, or institution with a vested interest in the economic and social status quo is suspect, and invariably guilty.

The word from the conspiracy crowd (and certain of their friends shirking about the shadows of the military and bowels of government) is that people will start to care about the lies when there are three colors and styles of clothes, cars, and personal computers, and stops on every highway (online and on land) to check I.D.s. If this is true, then disinformation and spin control will never end. It is far easier and more profitable to let us *think* we have a choice than through any jackbooted door-smashing tactics. It is insidious and will continue to be so. Probably the best hope right now is a simple awareness that guides our perception. Keep the early-warning system alive.

Well, shit, when are we *not* being lied to?

A quick scan of the available "conspiracy" literature is a real head-spinner. If you read too many of these stories (and who ever stops at just one?), the paranoid mindset is guaranteed to take over. What was that noise on the phone? Who is that in the rearview mirror? Why is there tape over the envelopes in my mailbox? The paranoid style will become part of your life, like eating and breathing and looking for someone to get naked with.

Ever since the first time that doctor smacked you on the butt, you have been lied to. You're a grown-up now.

Greg Bishop is editor of *The Excluded Middle* <www.excludedmiddle.com>, an influential conspiracy magazine, and coauthor of *Wake Up Down There!: The Excluded Middle Reader* (Kempton, IL: Adventures Unlimited Press, 2000).

■ ■ ■ ■ ■ ■ ■ ■ ■ ■ ■

We are certainly being lied to every day, especially by government and the media, who work hand in hand to create imaginary Menaces, usually to "children," which they say can only be prevented by repressive legislation.

The Child Molester Menace, the Drug Menace, the Assault Rifle Menace, the School Shooting Menace—all are imaginary Menaces created by the media, assisted by government.

I remember recently seeing a TV news broadcast about some teenagers in Connecticut who stole some prescription drugs from their parents' medicine chest, and had to be hospitalized. As footage ran of the zonked-out kids being loaded into ambulances, a giant marijuana leaf was displayed prominently on the screen.

On the extremely rare occasions when some little psycho shoots up a school, every TV station runs the same story for weeks, when in fact more kids are struck by lightning on the playground than are shot by other students.

And always, the "solution" is more repressive, civil-liberties-eroding legislation, or lawsuits.

So, the next time your TV set warns you about a Menace, remember, the real menace is their lies.

Mike Hoy is president of Loompanics Unlimited <www.loompanics.com>, described as "the best book catalog in the world."

▪▪▪▪▪▪▪▪▪▪▪

Are we being lied to? The answer is on an almost inconceivably huge scale, the size of which is indicated by two books, the well-known *The Chalice and the Blade* (1987) by Riane Eisler, and the newly published *Darwin's Lost Theory of Love: A Healing Vision for the New Century* (2000) by myself. (This new book can be browsed in its entirety on iUniverse.com <www.iuniverse.com>, or purchased from same, Amazon.com, or your local bookstore).

In brief, it shows how for over a century the completing half for Darwin's theory of evolution was shoved out into Never Never Land by the dynamics of the prevailing dominator paradigm for science as well as politics and economics.

In plain language, the scientific and biography-writing establishment, by and large a brilliant and well-meaning bunch, wholly the captives of paradigm, for a century sold us the Big Lie about Darwin and who we really are and can become.

They tried to convince us that in the holy pursuit of survival of the fittest, our species is driven by "selfish genes" to tromp over the rights of all others in a meaningless world run by a "blind watchmaker," thereby requiring huge armies to protect us from one another and offering consumption of everything in sight as our only salvation.

What Darwin actually said was that what drives evolution at the level of emergence for our species is primarily moral sensitivity, love, cooperation, and above all the drive of MIND, (i.e. consciousness, education, and learning).

David Loye, Ph.D. <www.partnershipway.org> is author of many books, including *Darwin's Lost Theory of Love: A Healing Vision for the New Century* (Lincoln, NE: iUniverse.com, 2000), and *An Arrow Through Chaos: How We See into the Future* (Rochester, VT: Inner Traditions International, 2000). He coauthored *The Partnership Way: New Tools for Living and Learning* (2nd edition, Brandon, VT: Holistic Education Press, 1998) with Riane Eisler.

▪▪▪▪▪▪▪▪▪▪▪

"The Genetic Theology Movement"

Many scientists portray their ideas as products of serenely dispassionate analysis, even when strong religious sentiments are involved. Recently, the language of genetic evolution theory has provided new ways to cloak religious faith behind the veneer of serene dispassion. While unbelievers may formulate these newfangled mixes of science and religion, the ideas themselves are very much funded and publicized according to their popularity in a world of believers.

A prime example is the notion that evolution has produced a genetically innate "God module" in the brain. Superficially, this thesis arises from observations that specific regions of the brain are associated with some kinds of religious experience.

Yet the reasoning is about as sound as observing that specific brain regions are associated with differential calculus, and then concluding that genetic evolution has given us a "calculus module."

One can easily envision how a "calculus module" would help early hunter-gatherers compute the trajectory of a spear, enhancing survival and reproduction. Yet neither the "God module" nor the "calculus module" corresponds to the actual history of human thought. No gene has ever been identified for these "modules" either.

Instead, the "God module" belief infects new minds by connecting to monotheistic religions that have been around for the past few thousand years. It especially harkens to the notion of a "God-shaped vacuum" in the hearts of unbelievers. Thus, the "God module" idea spreads as a religious thought contagion in its own right, exquisitely adapted to an environment filled with impressive technologies and scientific jargon.

Aaron Lynch <www.thoughtcontagion.com> is author of *Thought Contagion: How Belief Spreads Through Society* (New York: Basic Books, 1996), and recently contributed "The Memetic Mind: Natural Selection in Mental Software" to Robert J. Sternberg and James C. Kaufman's collection *The Evolution of Intelligence* (Mahwah, NJ: Lawrence Erlbaum Associates, Inc, 2001). He is an editor of the *Journal of Memetics: Evolutionary Models of Information Transmission* <www.cpm.mmu.ac.uk/jom-emit/>.

▪▪▪▪▪▪▪▪▪▪▪

We tend to think of conspiracies of disinformation as deliberate, conscious efforts by a cabal of evil people. But my multi-disciplinary research over the last several decades shows that we are all to various degrees implicated in perpetuating disinformation.

Why? Because there are aspects of what we have all been taught as knowledge and truth that are not true—or are at best half-truths. For example, we are taught that human nature is inherently bad: We are evil due to original sin or selfish genes. So the debate between fundamentalist religious dogma and sociobiological scientific dogma is not a substantive one. Indeed, it serves to conceal the fact that both camps perpetuate the belief that there is something inherently wrong and evil about humans—and that hence we need to be rigidly controlled.

My books, *The Chalice and the Blade* (1987), *Sacred Pleasure* (1995), *The Partnership Way* (2nd edition, 1998), and most recently *Tomorrow's Children* (2000), re-examine these kinds of myths. They show that they are a very important part of the belief system that has for most of recorded history maintained the configuration of what I have identified as a dominator model of human relations. This is a way of relating based on ranking of "superiors" over "inferiors"—men over women, men over men, race over race, religion over religion, and man over nature.

Even the most sincere of those around us try their best to approximate reality and never quite succeed.

These books also show that over the last several centuries there has been strong movement toward a social organization that orients more to what I have identified as the core configuration of a partnership model. This is a way of structuring relations based not on hierarchies of domination ultimately backed up by fear of pain and violence, but rather based on linking and what I call hierarchies of actualization (where parents, teachers, leaders, and managers exercise power in ways that facilitate rather than inhibit the realization of our great human potentials for caring, creativity, and consciousness).

Moreover, they show that these movements challenging entrenched patterns of domination—from the challenge to the "divinely ordained" right of kings to rule over their "subjects" and of men to rule over the women and children in the "castles" of their homes to today's social justice, human rights, and environmental movements—have deep roots in prehistoric partnership traditions we are today beginning to reclaim.

How are we to counter the disinformation about "human nature" still contained in much of what we are taught? My new book *Tomorrow's Children: A Blueprint for Partnership Education for the 21st Century* provides detailed and practical answers to this question.

Riane Eisler <www.partnershipway.org> is an influential cultural and feminist studies scholar. Her books include *The Chalice and the Blade: Our History, Our Future* (New York: Harper & Row, 1987), *Sacred Pleasure: Sex, Myth, and the Politics of the Body* (San Francisco: HarperSanFrancisco, 1995), and *Tomorrow's Children: A Blueprint for Partnership Education in the 21st Century* (Westview Press, 2000). She coauthored *The Partnership Way: New Tools for Living and Learning* (2nd edition, Brandon, VT: Holistic Education Press, 1998) with David Loye.

■ ■ ■ ■ ■ ■ ■ ■ ■ ■

The biggest lie of the moment is that we are constantly made the target of conspiracies—attempts by global corporations, by governmental agencies, by local salesmen, and by an infinity of others to manipulate our minds.

The conspiratorial mindset is, like most statements about reality, both true and false. Even the most sincere of those around us try their best to approximate reality and never quite succeed.

> Artists, poets, scientists, prophets, professors, all are trying to feel their way through the fabric of appearance to the essence within. They are doing their best to communicate what they find. So, in fact, am I. But truth-telling is a process.

We hope that each probe of "reality" takes us closer to an understanding that is accurate and helps improve our lives. Yet everything we say contains its elements of error, its accidental lies.

To top it off, each of us lives in a different world with different problems, different gifts, and different sensibilities. What's downright true for me may be utterly false for you. Am I trying to influence you with these words? Of course, or I wouldn't be writing them. Am I part of a conspiracy to manipulate you? If I am, I'm not aware of it.

What worries me is this. Postmodernists have taught a generation to believe that almost every utterance is a falsehood used by massive powers to mislead. Yet even television advertising, so full of efforts to persuade and change our minds, is often filled with wonders of visual artistry.

We can choose to loathe a 30-second bit of magic because Mitsubishi or Buick brought it to us. Or we can forget the sponsor and appreciate the marvel of the cinematography. Wonder or the lack of it is up to you and me. We are lied to when we're told there is no wonder, and that all we see around us is conspiracy.

Howard Bloom <www.howardbloom.net> is founder of the International Paleopsychology Project <www.paleopsych.org>, and a Visiting Scholar at New York University. He is the author of *Global Brain: The Evolution of Mass Mind From the Big Bang to the 21st Century* (New York: John Wiley & Sons, 2000) and *The Lucifer Principle: A Scientific Exploration into the Forces of History* (New York: The Atlantic Monthly Press, 1995).

■ ■ ■ ■ ■ ■ ■ ■ ■ ■

The easy answer would be to point to someone who is obviously lying, like Bill Clinton, Al Gore, George W., Barry McCaffrey, or someone of that ilk. Professional liars.

But I hate easy answers, and I have an unusual way of approaching "other people." I think the real lie is that there are "other people." The boundaries of self and not-self are a convenient illusion that we use to perpetuate the game of consciousness. With a little nudge, "your" consciousness could be centered in your computer, your desk, your refrigerator, or a thousand miles away (if you don't believe that, then either present yourself for a demonstration, or count me in your own list of liars). It could be centered in [US Drug Czar] Barry McCaffrey.

The most pervasive lie is that our personalities, our personas, our egos, are something separate from everyone/everything else. The tough part here is the "whom." Who made this lie? Did we create it for ourselves? Did our parents and social institutions create it for us when we were children? Did "God" make the Big Lie?

If you are a believer in "truth," it might be uncomfortable to accept that everything you perceive is part of a spectrum of relative lies, but the ramifications are intriguing. What kind of really creative whopper can you convince yourself to believe that will make "your" life more fantastic?

Phil Farber <members.aol.com/pstuart> is editor of *Paradigm Shift* <www.paradigmshift-zine.com>, an online journal about magick, music, hypnosis, media, NLP, and consciousness. He is author of *FutureRitual: Magick for the 21st Century* (Chicago, IL: Eschaton Productions, 1997).

▪▪▪▪▪▪▪▪▪▪

I believe that I am being lied to by the American dieting industry.

The industry holds out the promise that there is a program, food, dietary supplement, or piece of exercise equipment or some combination of these that will produce a lifetime of thinness for most fat people.

During the last 30 years huge sums of money have been spent on dieting programs, foods, supplements, and exercise equipment. During the same period of time the average American has been getting fatter. What other proof is needed that, for most people, most of the time, these things do not work?

Russell Williams, self-described as "23 year member of the leadership of the fat acceptance community." He is vice president of the International Size Acceptance Association <www.size-acceptance.org>.

▪▪▪▪▪▪▪▪▪▪

The public is not being told the truth about our federal criminal justice system. They're being lied to, mostly by Republicans and centrist Democrats like Clinton who have helped dismantle Fourth and Fifth Amendment protections, as well as make the system increasingly retributive and decreasingly humane.

For example, most people have no idea that federal parole was eliminated in 1987. Most people think that federal prisoners get paroled and run out and commit crimes, but this is completely untrue. Most people think that federal prisoners only serve a small portion of their sentences. They don't know that *all* federal prisoners must serve at least 85 percent of their sentences, and with some crimes—not necessarily violent ones—100 percent must be served.

Many people think you can get probation for a first-time offense for all kinds of crimes and are completely unaware of the mandatory sentencing requirements that take any discretion away from sentencing judges to assess, for example, an offender's social and personal situation, both of which may be good reason to be lenient, or not.

I believe that I am being lied to by the American dieting industry.

Most people think that the police can't use illegally-seized evidence. This is also untrue. Illegally-seized evidence can be used to obtain legally-seized evidence, or to impeach your defenses at trial. For example, the police illegally tap your phone and find out that someone is bringing you a few ounces of marijuana. They go talk to the supplier, get him to name you, then get him to cooperate and soon, based on an illegal wiretap, you are arrested. The charges stick.

Where is this system that coddles the accused? I haven't seen it in my professional career. And if you're ever arrested for a federal crime, you won't see it either.

Lawrence Stanley is a defense attorney specializing in the First Amendment and intellectual property.

▪▪▪▪▪▪▪▪▪▪

Anybody who labels the ongoing centralization of political power and the increasing tax burden in this country as "progressive." "Medieval" is more like it!

While their motives may be well-intentioned, and the term "progressive" has such a benign ring to it, I wish they would acknowledge that they are perfectly comfortable with wielding a system that orders men with guns (i.e. armed federal agents) to force other people to submit to their bidding. Never in their wildest dreams would they personally extract money from their neighbors at gunpoint to achieve a social goal. What makes it right, then, to send a surrogate to do so?

Ultimately, it is never a wise idea to entrust the possession of firearms and the sole legal authority to use them in the hands of a small class of legislators and bureaucrats. Such a concentration of power historically attracts unsavory, ambitious people whose agenda will most assuredly be different from what is considered "progressive" these days.

Perhaps Supreme Court Justice Louis Brandeis put it best in *Olmstead v. United States* (1928): "The greatest dangers to liberty lurk in insidious encroachment by men of zeal, well meaning but without understanding."

Jon Ford is editorial director at Paladin Press <www.paladin-press.com>, one of America's most provocative independent publishers.

Self-proclaimed right-thinking minds drive off alternatives and limit the channels to truth by silencing the wisdom of soft voices.

▪▪▪▪▪▪▪▪▪▪▪

Are "we" being lied to? Easy answer: by (a) broadcast media that pander to quarter-minute attention spans and focus on profitable infotainment while pretending that glib pronouncements intoned by inbred talking heads actually contribute to informed decisions; (b) economic analysts wearing blinders who take the NASDAQ and S&P figures as reliable indicators of the well-being of an at-risk, interconnected ecosystem; (c) political image spinners who adroitly conceal the puppet strings attached to their clients while their corporate handlers trot out phony ethics and faux-environmentalism; and (d) rose-colored glasses vendors who insist the present system is actually sustainable if we just get the global marketplace opened up, create more niches for laborers edu-doctrinated into First World thinking, and allow geo-corporatism to prove Marx the fool.

But the heavy-duty liars are the paradigm mongers—left and right—who sell quick-fix, end-state, absolute ideas wrapped in hype and hope. It's the finders of simplicity which is not there who are the most dangerous liars of all because they believe their own deceits. Self-proclaimed right-thinking minds drive off alternatives and limit the channels to truth by silencing the wisdom of soft voices. In an era of image over substance, the most adroit, convinced, and convincing liar wins in a delusion that fantasies are facts. They look into mirrors of their own imaginings and see "truth, the whole truth, and nothing but the truth." Because it is their delusion, it fits. The big lie is that there is only one path to truth, and the liars are those who brilliantly deceive themselves.

Chris Cowan is coauthor of *Spiral Dynamics: Mastering Values, Leadership, and Change* (Cambridge and Oxford: Blackwell Business Publishers, 1996). He is a founder of the National Values Center, and a partner with National Values Center Consulting <www.spiraldynamics.org>.

▪▪▪▪▪▪▪▪▪▪▪

I think that the most serious lying that takes place occurs when people lie to themselves. This is well-documented in the field of social psychology. People typically hold a distorted perception of the world—based on their pre-existing belief systems. Somehow, mysteriously, all events seem to confirm what they have already known all along. This is true, oddly enough, across the whole spectrum of belief systems.

Jeffrey Mishlove, Ph.D. <www.mishlove.com> is currently director of the Intuition Network <www.intuition.org>. He was host of *Thinking Allowed* <www.thinking-allowed.com>, a syndicated weekly PBS series exploring humanistic psychology, and has authored several books, including *The Roots of Consciousness* (New York: Marlowe & Co, 1997).

▪▪▪▪▪▪▪▪▪▪▪

I'm not interested in the "lie" question, so I'll pass.

Kevin Kelly <www.well.com/user/kk> is editor-at-large for *Wired* magazine. His latest book is *New Rules for the New Economy* (New York: Viking Press, 1998).

▪▪▪▪▪▪▪▪▪▪▪

With all respect—no. The question is silly . . . in my view. Too silly for me to facilitate.

Michael Albert is editor of *Z Magazine* and ZNet <www.zmag.org>, founder of South End Press, and one of America's most influential progressive social activists.

"Howard, you sound like you're on coke. A lot of it."

I Have Met God and He Lives in Brooklyn

Or how the arch-skeptic,

dark lord of Disinformation becomes convinced,

and tries to convince you the reader,

that Howard Bloom is next in a lineage of seminal

thinkers that includes

Newton, Darwin, Einstein, Freud,

and Buckminster Fuller

and how he is going to change the way

we see ourselves and everything around us

Richard Metzger

"Yes, hello?"

"Richard? Howard Bloom."

"Hi, Howard, how are you?"

"Well, not so good. Not too good at all. [Pauses.] Richard, as you are a curator of the extreme, I have a very extreme situation that I would like to propose to involve you in. Does this seem like the kind of thing that you would want to hear about right now? Do you have anything planned for this evening? I have a weird idea and you're the first person I thought of calling."

I'd been corresponding with Howard Bloom, legendary music business publicist and author of the mind-blowing book, *The Lucifer Principle*, for about five weeks now, since we both were interviewed for Alex Burns' upcoming book, *Mind Kampf*. Alex, knowing that my own violently rejected religious upbringing in West Virginia closely resembled his similar boyhood in Australia, brought me into an email discussion he was having with Bloom that ranged from why Christians try to censor other social groups to how much we all admired Jello Biafra to Satanic cults Alex had either joined or at least obsessively researched. It was a lot of fun.

But I'd not yet met Bloom in person, so I wasn't prepared for the crazed energy that came leaping out of the phone line, practically grabbing me by the throat. (As I type this I wonder what *could've* possibly prepared me for the human tornado that is Howard Bloom, and I must confess, I'm drawing a complete blank.) It was an eccentric (and amusing) performance to be sure, but since I hadn't the vaguest notion of what his scene consisted of and he sounded like he'd just snorted *a few fucking pounds* of crystal meth, I mumbled a few syllables of positive encouragement and committed to nothing. I wasn't exactly in the mood for an Abel Ferarra kind of night, if you know what I mean, but since I'd been calling the guy a genius to all my friends and anyone who'd listen for a month now, I thought I'd at least listen to what he had to say.

And then it occurred to me: Didn't Howard Bloom develop such a bad case of Chronic Fatigue Syndrome in the late 1980s that he had to suddenly retire from running his top rock and roll PR company? Wasn't the über-publicist of the rock era unable to move his jaw for longer than ten minutes without completely wearing himself out? But this is a force of nature on the line. Hadn't he been *horizontal* for the better part of the last decade? Robin Williams himself would sit down and shut up if forced to share the same *country* with this guy!

"Howard, you sound like you're on coke. A lot of it."

"That's what people used to always say to me when I was in the music industry. But I am a bit manic tonight, yes. Well, two weeks ago (January 14) I tried to commit suicide when the divorce proceedings with my wife, Linda, became too much for me. I ate 80 Valium, fourteen Chlorpromazine, and gave myself an intramuscular injection of five cc's of Lidocaine Hydrochloride, which according to my copy of the *Physician's Desk Reference* was an unequivocally fatal dose. I actually was so close to dead that the Grim Reaper had digested my soul and was burping up the remains.

"For two and a half days I lay in bed like a corpse, the blood pooling in my body and breaking out through the skin, almost like stigmata. When I woke up I'd lost the use of three limbs and 40 percent of my circulatory system. I've been experiencing the highest spiritual and intellectual highs and the lowest of the lows in roughly fifteen-minute cycles ever since. As a scientist, it's an incredible thing to witness, but being the person experiencing it, it really sucks. So I tried to kill myself. Yes, you could say I'm a little on edge, that's for sure.

"Anyway what I want to propose is this: You come out here to Brooklyn and baby-sit me. You keep me company and keep me distracted from thoughts of killing myself, and I, for my part, will keep you entertained and be witty and funny and be a genius and, well, uh, that's the job if you choose to accept it. Let me entertain you, in other words. I guarantee it'll be pretty interesting. I really need human contact now. I could die and I'm afraid. I don't want to die. Not tonight. Not for a long time. But I need help. I need a baby-sitter to keep me from killing myself. Does this sound like anything you'd be interested in participating in?"

It's difficult here to get across how utterly persuasive and yet how deeply desperate Bloom sounded that night. His rap was equal parts sheer force of personality, deft (even unfair) cajoling, and flat-out emotional blackmail, skills no doubt honed during his tenure as the top publicist in the music industry. It was a preposterous position to be put in. Resistance wasn't only futile, it wasn't even an option.

I laughed. "Well, Howard, what you propose is indeed extremely extreme, so, yeah, why not? I'm game. When do you want me to come over?"

"Eleven. I need you to keep me company in the worst hours which are from 4:00 to 6:00 AM."

Howard Bloom's 1995 sleeper masterpiece, *The Lucifer Principle* (Atlantic Monthly Press), is now in its eighth printing, and he's putting the final touches on a new book, *Global Brain*, that furthers his startling and controversial new theories of evolutionary psychology. Armed with vivid examples combined with meticulous documentation from several scientific disciplines, *Lucifer* (and Bloom's embryonic science of paleopsychology) takes its cue from Thomas Hobbes' *Leviathan*, theorizing that evolution has organized mankind (and every other life form) into "super organisms" (think ant colonies *and* cell cultures *and* capitalism *and* devotion to a cause or religion and you'll be in the Bloomian ballpark) that compete with each other in an eternal biological conflict closely resembling something akin to St. Paul's conception of "original sin." War, death, hatred, violence, and even racism are necessary underpinnings of the genetic *plan*—integral components of creation and of life itself. *The Lucifer Principle* asks why "our finest qualities often lead us to the actions we most abhor—murder, torture, genocide, and war" and answers it with the cold and clammy facts: Evil, according to Bloom, is an evolutionary imperative. In other words, we're genetically *hardwired* for it.

Far from being an apologist for hate crimes and ethnic cleansing, Bloom wants us to understand hatred, racism, and genocide, to understand our evolutionary development—ourselves, who we are *down to the microbial level*—so we can outwit the script that an apparently insane programmer, God himself, wrote into our genetic code.

Yup. Whatever Bloom has in store for me tonight, I doubt that I'll be bored.

The "D" train to Bloom's Park Slope neighborhood leaves me off at Flatbush Avenue, but the normally bustling open-air hip-hop culture shopping mall is utterly deserted. A healthy fog blanketing the area makes things very much like a Sherlock Holmes story. Brooklyn has transformed itself into Victorian London. It was a nice dramatic touch. As I walked the nearly fifteen blocks to his home, I tried to imagine what Bloom's apartment would look like. He'd spoken about his medical condition and the women who "watched" him, and I was imagining, I suppose, a Stephen Hawking sort of figure in a somewhat ambulatory setting.

But when I got there, Bloom himself answered the door. Wait a minute. Hadn't he been paralyzed since the suicide attempt two weeks ago? In fact wasn't he crippled just three hours ago when we spoke on the telephone?

"A lot of weird things are going on right now inside me. I'm walking around in a body that is a bunch of barely-connected parts. I'm getting feeling in my legs that hasn't been there for two weeks—I'd given up thinking I'd ever walk again—and I just walked 5.6 miles around this apartment." He glanced at a pedometer hooked on the belt of his jeans. "Yeah, 5.6 miles. Do you mind walking around with me so I can get the blood flowing?"

War, death, hatred, violence, and even racism are necessary underpinnings of the genetic *plan*—integral components of creation and of life itself.

And so it was that I first met Howard Bloom. We talked (and walked, in a makeshift track around his apartment) into the wee hours about *everything*, or more precisely, Howard talked and I listened. He badly needed an audience, badly needed to perform, to be witty and special and a genius, and as promised, he put on quite a show. It was like having a private conversation with Krishnamurti or Buckminster Fuller. If you've ever seen film footage of either of these men, you know what I'm saying here: Remarkable figures and geniuses like Bloom don't seem to exist in any great number, but they are unmistakable once you've met them. You'll know when you've met the real thing. Trust me, you'll just know.

Here then is a transcript of a conversation between Howard Bloom and myself that took place a few days after our initial meeting on January 28. Also present was our mutual friend, Naomi Nelson. As soon as we arrived, Howard informed us that the suicide attempt, he has now figured out, was primarily the result of severe Valium withdrawal (I'm sure the divorce didn't help matters), and he's been feeling much better lately. He seemed almost a different person, calmer, *much* calmer, but the edgy energy was still there. He sat in his bed, propped up by pillows, surrounded by books, six computers, wires, televisions, VCRs, notepads, pens, magazines, keyboards, and lots of little bottles of vitamins, amino acids, and prescription medicines.

Richard Metzger: Okay, let's get started. Since we only have a few hours, there are a few basic themes I wanted to explore and—

Howard Bloom: Let's start with this: You need to tell them why in the world they should be interested in me. Let's start out with the credentials.

RM: All right, well what I was going to propose is: Since I have no need to impress either you or Naomi with my interviewing prowess and suave Roger Moore-like talk-show host "stagecraft" [laughs], I was thinking that—

HB: Well let me do this for you, let me write your lead for you—

RM: Hang on, let me finish. It's more interesting for me to get your take on yourself, you know, you are this legendary publicist and consummate modern mythmaker and memetic engineer, so I'd love to know how you would, uh, handle your own account, I suppose. How would you sell yourself to the public if I was a publisher approaching you to handle my newest author, the controversial genius author of *The Lucifer Principle*, Howard Bloom?

HB: All right, sure. So why should they be interested in this absolutely anonymous character named Howard Bloom? Why be interested in Bloom? Hmmm.... Bloom's got a book called *The Lucifer Principle*. *The Lucifer Principle* was endorsed by 22 major scientists, none of whom had ever met Bloom or heard of Bloom. None of them. They said things like it's a seminal book, it's monumental, it's brilliant, it's gonna change the way we see human nature, it's gonna change the way we see the world around us, it's going to scratch holes in our illusions about ourselves and force us to face realities we never saw. These are major scientists saying that this book is revolutionary.

It's become a textbook in universities from Germany to Australia, but it comes from this person who everybody thought: Who is this person? He can't write a book about science. He's a music publicist. He established Prince; he worked closely with Michael Jackson, John Cougar Mellencamp, Joan Jett, who had 23 record companies turn her down. He worked with Kiss. Publicized Simon and Garfunkel's Central Park reunion concert.

He started the "heavy metal magazine," according to the grad-school thesis written by Chet Flippo; used to be the East Coast editor for *Rolling Stone*. Howard Bloom, who occupies eight pages in this book, invented a new genre called the "heavy metal magazine," which became the dominant form of rock and roll magazine until the 1990s. From the early 1970s to the 1990s. I didn't want to do it, the task was dumped in my lap. I did this without knowing a damn thing about rock and roll. I listened to Mozart, Bartok, and Vivaldi, but I took *Time* magazine apart like a biologist dissecting a fetal pig. I came to understand all of its nuances, and then I was able to reproduce it as a heavy metal rock and roll magazine [*Circus*]. I tuned my guts to what the kids wanted—I was 28 at the time—and then used every marketing trick in the book, every marketing survey technique I could invent, to sell it back to them. I was doing statistics and correlational studies using ideas I'd picked up from reading Martin Gardner's column in *Scientific American*.

"Well the tribe that has interested me is the entire human race, especially the heart that beats at the center of mythology and the worldviews that surround us every day and give us our concept of what we think of as reality, the central core that gives us everything from our tall tales, to our movies, to our fantasies."

Through a series of misadventures I ended up as a rock and roll publicist, and I started my own company, with a fairly high-minded corporate ethos. It wasn't bullshit. I sold these artists' souls to the public. I sold truth. You don't make the kind of mass connections with the hearts of human beings—millions of them—that you make when you work with Prince or Michael Jackson and fake it. It has to be real, and that's what I did when I worked with these artists. I pulled their souls out of them. I wasn't selling cornflakes—I was selling soul.

Now why should anyone care about this ? It's because I'm a scientist, and this is how I was doing my "Margaret Mead" fieldwork. Margaret Mead had to become a chieftainess among the tribes of Samoa and then again among the tribes of New Guinea in order to get the inside scoop on how these tribes operated. Well the tribe that has interested me is the entire human race, especially the heart that beats at the center of mythology and the worldviews that surround us every day and give us our concept of what we think of as reality, the central core that gives us everything from our tall tales, to our movies, to our fantasies. How could I get to the heart of this? By getting to the heart of the entertainment industry.

Was I *prepared* for the entertainment industry? No! I was called the "sickly scientist" when I was a little kid. I was shunned by every human being around me. I was busy working with a professional microscope when I was in the seventh grade. I was the pale kid who isolated himself in his room with 50 animals. Lab rats that kept multiplying, Guinea pigs that kept multiplying, guppies, lizards that I raised from eggs. I lived in this little environment, as sealed off as if it were a sealed-off capsule traveling through outer space on its way to another galaxy.

RM: When I look at your present surroundings, with all these computer screens, TVs, and phone lines around you—

HB: They're my windows on the world—

RM: Your illness put you back in that capsule hasn't it?

HB: Which has given me a totally different perspective. It's outsiders that, as Thomas Kuhn will tell you in his theory of scientific revolutions, it's outsiders who perceive the big picture in a way that no one else could see it. Like Erwin Schrödinger in his book, *What Is Life?* He was a physicist, and he came up with this seminal book that started all the modern biology we know, right down to genetics. He did it about 40 years ago or so. He was a total outsider. Outsiders can see what insiders cannot see. Being an outsider is an incredibly lonely proposition—I tried to kill myself two weeks ago—that's how lonely it gets, but it is an incredibly fruitful proposition, because of what you can see.

RM: That reminds me of something you'd said last week about the Jewish tradition of prophets who stand at the gates in rags, utterly socially unacceptable, like Isaiah shouting at the gates of the city, this outsider who can shake the walls and the people inside because he is armed with truth, with the "truth." Why is the Jewish rebel-philosopher such an important intellectual archetype?

HB: Well, it's the same thing. We're always outsiders. We are always outsiders no matter how assimilated we are.

RM: But why does the tribe still cohere? Why is it even still identifiable?

HB: Because we know damn well that whether we identify ourselves as Jews or not, whether you're an atheist like I am, even people like me who are thoroughly assimilated and—hey, Western culture is *my* culture—we are still outsiders. If a Hitler comes along—and a Hitler comes around every few-hundred years for us—he doesn't give a damn if we identify ourselves as Jews or not. There have been versions of the ovens when the Babylonians threw us out of Jerusalem, when the Assyrians threw us out of Jerusalem, when the Persians under Haman wanted to hang 70,000 of us. There are Hamans right now all over the Islamic world, a world of a billion people, who are busy reading *The Protocols of the Elders of Zion*. It's one of the most popular books they sell there. They have books in Iran with titles like *Would You Rather Have Bedbugs or Jews?* and *Get Rid of the Jews*.

RM: Let me ask you this, using your theories about "super organisms" as the filter, why is anti-Semitism seemingly an ubiquitous component of the Arab super organism? Is it in the Arab DNA?

HB: It isn't the DNA, okay? And it's an Islamic thing, not an Arab thing. I wrote about this in *Global Brain*. It says basically that those groups which are the most similar to each other are the ones that fight the most. Why? Because this is what creates the kind of differentiation that drives evolution. Jews and Arabs are *brothers*.

Here's an example. When I was in Hanover, Germany, I was there for meetings. It's a wonderful place, very democratic, a great place to walk around. Lovely. But after two days I realized, "Hey, there's nobody here with dark, curly hair. I'm the only one with dark, curly hair in this whole city. What's going on here?" And then I realized they killed off all the people with dark, curly hair! I'm the only one!

And then I got on a plane and my flight had a layover in Frankfurt, and there I suddenly saw this mob of people with dark, curly hair.

"It says basically that those groups which are the most similar to each other are the ones that fight the most."

Now after you've been isolated from people who look like you for several days, this is an experience that is utterly unreal. And who are these people? They are Jordanian guest workers; these are the people who want to exterminate me. These are my brethren. These are the people who carry my genes! These are my brothers, and the greatest battles of all are between brothers.

Why? Because that is how the separations are formed which create new groups and generate new ideas that are thrown into the vast melting pot of ideas from which it draws its new creations. Islam, according to Paul Johnson, the historian, is a Jewish heresy and so is Christianity. Who hates Jews more than Christians and Islamics? It's because we are brothers!

RM: So Cain and Abel is true?

HB: Yes. Metaphorically Cain and Abel is absolutely true. Cain had one way of life—hunting. Abel had another way of life—agriculture. The agriculturist killed off his brother and attempted to obliterate one alternative from the group mind—the hunter-gatherer way of life.

The weird thing is that in Japan, which has never had any Jews, anti-Semitic books sell in the millions. In the millions.

RM: It's true. I have a lot of Japanese friends, very close friends, and every once in a while, one of the most far-out and forward-thinking members of this, you know, elite, elite Japanese in-crowd, will say something to me that I find so gauche and unthinkable, and then it forces *me* to recalibrate, and then I realize, "Oh, this is the way it is there." The thing that clued me in was how casually it was dropped into the conversation.

HB: Well, you know Japanese racism is just astonishing—

RM: Especially against Koreans.

Naomi Nelson (herself Japanese-American): The things my grandmother says about Koreans are scandalous!

HB: Well you know that the Koreans and the Japanese are brothers, too, for all practical purposes. But the things the Japanese say about the Koreans are terrible. And the things the Koreans have to say about the Japanese are equally disastrous. Why? It's like the Arab-Israeli split. Because they're brothers! And we have to differentiate ourselves. It's called the "narcissism of minor differences," according to Sigmund Freud. It's called "character displacement" by population geneticists. There's a chapter in *Global Brain* that explains its evolutionary value. It throws new options into the group mind. As it says in the beginning of *The Lucifer Principle*, everything in this world that is creative has its destructive side.

"Germans are wonderful. They are wonderful people. A wonderful people tried to kill my people."

RM: Then how do you personally, as a scientist, as an individual Jew, react to the idea that the Arab world hates you and would like to see you and your type dead?

HB: I hate them. I respect them, I follow them like crazy. I'm a scholar of Islamic culture and history. When I am with my Islamic enemies, like the head of one of the major Islamic groups who I debated on television, I invite him out to lunch. I'm fascinated by him. He's a wonderful human being. It's like the good Germans who were running the concentration camps and listening to Mozart and Vivaldi and all the music that I listen to. And getting the same exhilaration out of it that I get out of it, while they had their Jewish woman who cleaned their houses and who they fucked. And who when they were finished with them, they threw into the ovens. They ran the ovens.

These were wonderful people if you were a part of their family and they liked you. But if they were determined to exterminate you, they did. You were *stucken*. Livestock. Jews and Slavs were livestock. To be eliminated. Hitler was a wonderful person if you spent time with him. He loved his dog. He loved Eva Braun, he loved nature. He loved many of the same things that you and I love. We'd love to spend time with Hitler on his "eagle's mountain" or whatever. He was a fucking genius. I study him like crazy.

But the fact is, if a person is determined to eliminate you, then you have to retaliate with all the power in you. It's tit for tat. I don't want to eliminate them, but I sure don't want to allow them to eliminate me. Not by a longshot. Germans are wonderful. They are wonderful people. A wonderful people tried to kill my people. A wonderful people exterminated my family in Europe, probably about 350 people.

A cousin of mine put together a magazine and assigned a story to a top journalist, who is Jewish, then sent him to Jordan. He tells in his article of dancing with a Jordanian girl and they had a wonderful time. They went clubbing until they were utterly blown and blissed out. Then he asked, "What would happen if you guys went to war with Israel?" and she said, "I'd have a knife in your back and you'd be dead in two seconds."

RM: What motivates that? What makes it so that the mind of the super organism takes over from the mind of an individual to the extent that a woman will kill her lover?

HB: The best way to explain these things is we are still operating on impulses not that we learned, not as hunter-gatherers, but the impulses we learned from our days as bacteria. The bacteria from 3.5 billion years ago are our ancestors, and we share something like 70 percent of our genes with them. You can consider yourself, from your feet up to your nipples, a bacterium.

And bacteria are processing organisms, thinking organisms, highly creative organisms. They operate in communities, in intelligent communities of a vastness that we cannot comprehend. A bacterial colony in a stromatolite has a population roughly a trillion times larger than all the human beings who have ever existed, and yet it operates as a single metropolis with a sense of singular purpose and a collective intelligence. These colonies last for billions of years.

Let's take the example of sea anemone, because I know their structure in battle better. Bacteria have not been studied enough in the wild to know what the nature is of their intergroup tournaments. But sea anemones have been. When you see a mass of sea anemones in tidal pools on the coast of Monterey, they look harmless. They are like plants. The only thing that we don't realize is that plants, if you watch them on their own time scale, are in *furious* competition with each other. Like the sea anemones, they are in battles for land and territory that last hundreds of years.

A sea anemone colony is set up in such a way that the ones in the center of the colony, the vast mass of sea anemones, are just there to basically eat and multiply. But there is a whole periphery of warrior sea anemones on the colony's border that are equipped with specialized weaponry, with poisonous tentacles, and their entire purpose is to make war on the colony next door and attempt to crowd it out of the territory and to take possession of its stretch of seabed.

These are behaviors we inherited. We got them not from our primate ancestors, but from our unicellular, microbial relatives of 3.5 billion years ago, who already had degrees of social sophistication and warfare that are unimaginable to us. They had a degree of complexity that went far beyond anything that we have ever achieved. They had information-swapping mechanisms that are beyond our newspapers, our magazines, and our Internet. They did it by swapping bits of genetic material. They still do it constantly.

And what is a piece of genetic material? It's a massive—it's like swapping out a fourteen-megabyte disk. In fact it's like swapping out a 14,000-megabyte disk. Yet they swap these things constantly. What's more, they generate new ones—when they run into problems, they reengineer their own genomes and add a new level or layer of learning and innovation which they can then swap around and trade with others. And of course when you put a new network together of these learning modules, you've got a larger "whole" that operates in an entirely different way.

But these colonies make war on each other. Some of them operate symbiotically, just like some of our groups do, and some of them make war on each other. Sometimes they're partners, sometimes they're our friends, just like the Vikings. Sometimes the Vikings were raiders, and sometimes the Vikings were traders. Sometimes the Vikings were symbionts, and sometimes they were genocidal.

RM: What makes one tribe genocidal and another traders?

HB: Opportunity. When the Vikings saw that they had the opportunity to steal all of the people in a tribe through warfare, well, for one thing, they loved warfare. It was their ideal. Their ideal of a heaven. The Viking idea of heaven was to go to a place, Valhalla, where men did nothing but make war, because *that* was paradise. Now why was it paradise? Because it was exhilaration. And why was it exhilarating? Because the pleasure of bloodlust is built into us as much as the pleasure of sugar is built into us!

RM: Yeah, I can see that in myself. I'm a friendly enough person, but I'm incredibly competitive. When my will is thwarted in any way, I become evil incarnate. It's sheer bloodlust. It's the adrenaline flow happening.

HB: Yes, and that adrenaline flow is built into us, not at a primate level, not at a level we got from our tribal hunter-gatherer days—it's built into us from our days as bacteria. Bacterial behavior explains our mass behavior. We are nothing but bacterial colonies. We are as primitive as that. Our behaviors go back 3.5 fucking billion years, and you happen to be talking to the only person who has been tracing those behaviors back that far right now. I'm the only person doing that in a systematic manner.

"Our behaviors go back 3.5 fucking billion years, and you happen to be talking to the only person who has been tracing those behaviors back that far right now."

RM: How long will it take to get a "meme" like that out and until it's firmly established in the culture?

HB: It's getting out there. It's already getting out there. If *Global Brain* follows the example of *The Lucifer Principle*, I designed these books to be around fifteen years minimum, and if I have the strength to do the promotion I need to do on this one, then this book *will* be around for fifteen years. You know what happens with *The Lucifer Principle*: One person tells another person who tells another person, and many of the people who read it say that it changed the whole fucking way they look at the world. They can't even watch the news the same way anymore.

RM: I'm sure I must've said that very thing to about 50 people. I can't rave enough about *The Lucifer Principle*. I was reading the bit that talks about the thuggish behavior of certain monkey tribes and flipping the channels, and the juxtaposition of seeing fat, old [Congressman] Henry Hyde and [Congressman] Bob Barr at a Monica-related press conference and then flipping past a scene from one of the *Planet of the Apes* films where an orangutan and a sanctimonious chimp were discussing the fate of a human in captivity awaiting trial, and I immediately saw Hyde as the haughty, puffed out, fatuous orangutan and Barr as the tight-assed, effete chimpanzee. One of those sublime intersections that modern culture so rarely affords. I even saw your thesis in between *those* cracks, if you take my point. It's hard to shake it, that's for sure.

HB: Well, here's one aspect of memetic penetration: Kids 18-years-old are reading *The Lucifer Principle* in their college classes. That means it's going to be guiding their perceptual framework for the rest of their fucking lives.

RM: But how long does it take? I've noticed that in the science reading that I do, and I try to read all the major books that come along, it's always ideas that have been around for 30 years, but before they could reach a mass audience, language had to evolve to the point where such concepts could be explained in a pop way before they really could have impact. You have a very, very readable style. I'd say that you made reading a dense scientific thesis no more difficult than reading a Kurt Vonnegut or Tom Robbins novel.

HB: The goal was to make the book conversational. But to answer your question, Thomas Kuhn said that a new paradigm doesn't take hold until the old generation has died off—

RM: The old generation *is* dying off and not just in science!

HB: Yeah, but fuck that! Look, what have I been practicing all these years? What have I been fascinated by? Behavior. What have I learned? The practicalities of mass behavior. And what did I invent? Something called perceptual engineering. And perceptual engineering is something that is designed to turn things around, *not* in 20 years, but in a year. You can be a total outsider and a year later you can be on the cover of the *New York Times*' science section. This is what I learned from selling rock and roll. This is what I learned from being a publicist. I can create a scientific and cultural revolution right here, right here from this bedroom, with the International Paleopsychology Project. Because I'm selling truth. I am possessed by it.

"Truth is my religion."

RM: You're very messianic, that's for sure. If I wasn't so 100 percent convinced that you're right and of the importance of your work, I would think that you were paranoid and delusional. But I don't. The worldview and the new perceptual framework provided by *The Lucifer Principle* could become a new religion. It's an all-encompassing worldview. It obligates the reader to agree with its central ideas using utterly passionate examples and arguments. Aren't you worried that you might be creating a new "ism"? Doesn't every new school of thought lead to a new orthodoxy?

HB: Max Weber says that any movement starts out with a charismatic leader who is in touch with "the Force," basically—a charismatic leader who is charged with energy and who is able to break through the boundaries of existing custom and let people's souls out. But within a generation after he's gone, everything that he laid down to liberate people is turned into a new bureaucracy, a new set of habits, a new set of clichés, and it is stripped of its essential meaning. It gets stripped of its soul.

When I entered the scientific world and became a part of the Human Behavior and Evolution Society, which is a group that's, well, they are *the* evolutionary psychologists right now, the fashionable scientists of the moment, they disgusted me. They were not scientists; they were religionists. They had dogma and they had heresy. Anyone who disagreed with their doctrine was a heretic. Now in science, you treat your own idea as a provisional hypothesis, always up for revision. So you treat other ideas as alternatives that must be considered seriously. Because without that there is no science. If you begin to treat other ideas as heresy and then treat the people who adhere to those ideas or dare speak them as heretics, if you eliminate their opportunities for tenure, destroy their careers, blackball them from publication, and punish them in an inquisitorial manner for holding an idea which disagrees with your theory, your dogma is no longer a science, it's a religion.

Evolutionary psychology has become a religion, and I couldn't stand that because the scientific ethic is my ethic. Truth is my religion. So I started the International Paleopsychology Project, and this is where the revolution is happening. With the International Paleopsychology Project's New Paradigm book series I'm working with scientists and science authors to pull forth ideas which will build the perceptual foundations for the next two generations down the road. There are bidding wars going on for these books. Not tell-all memoirs by Monica Lewinsky. Books of theory that hold your attention with the grip of a novel. And there are bidding wars for these books. The editors at several major publishing companies are starting to be able to see what's coming. They know this is important stuff.

I'm working to establish a new science so that the next generation can stand on our shoulders. Sir Isaac Newton said that he only saw what he saw because he was able to stand on the shoulders of scientific giants before him. The goal is to allow a generation ten years from now to see things that for us were almost impossible to understand and that we had to struggle to get a grip on. They'll no longer have to struggle to see what we tried to see, but they can struggle to comprehend what's beyond, things that would shock, surprise, and absolutely delight me, that would confuse me because they would be so alien. If I came to understand the insights that kids two generations down the road will wrestle into submission, that would be paradise for me. That's my job, to bring together the shoulders of these scientific giants who will lift the vision of generations to come. And that's what I'm *going* to do. With every last bit of strength that I've got left in this body.

Step One: Prepare the Test Subjects to Receive a New Meta-Program

"In the province of the mind, what one believes to be true either is true or becomes true, within limits to be determined by experiment."

Everything you see, everywhere, has an effect on you. Every bit of information you encounter changes you irreversibly. That's just the way it is; even if you closed your eyes against the words on this page, the waves of photons, washing over you, would leave an impression. You'll never leave this moment entirely behind.

From the moment that humans began to speak, spreading their infections this way and that, we have been in each other's heads, never entirely ourselves, mostly a pastiche of someone else's fears and dreams and Will to Power.

Yet humans suck seed because we are so gullible, so willing to imitate the idiotic and tragically successful behaviors of the other members of our species.

This virus of language has successfully inoculated us from any sort of ridiculous extinction—even as it leaves us more and more at each other's mercies. In this moment, at least, you have surrendered yourselves to my idea of high weirdness, busted out of your straightjackets, and left your cynicism and rationalism behind.

Which is right where I want you.

You are—for the next few minutes—in *my* hands, eager and willing to be programmed, ready to become the acolytes of the Church of the Motherfucker.

Step Two: Memetic Infection

In the Beginning, the Word emanated from *Ain Soph*, too brilliant to be directly perceived, except in the ever-increasing perfection of forms which populate the universe, the receiving antenna of the broadcasts of the divine current.

The Great Lie—perhaps once true—held that a singular recipient—Pharaoh, Melchizedeck, Moses—possessed the mysteries of revelation, keys to the kingdom.

And thus ever since: no way to the kingdom but through me; there is no god but Allah and Mohammed his prophet; Hear O Israel: I am that I am, I am one.

And this, then, the entry point of the divine current into the human space of being, to lift it up. But the lovers of power, transfixed by puissance, subtly deny the Bringer of Light, drape the Logos in different language, substitute black for white, heaven for hell. All things reversed, the temper tantrums of a blind idiot god Chaos the only possible release.

And this the first rule: Imposition of Order = Escalation of Chaos.

The lightning strike. Actualities revealed. Sight itself a blow against the Empire. A crack in the egg of perception, and through it, another truth. The Buddha. Lao Tzu, the "Old Boy." This current comes for AL; come swim in its waters and emerge anew.

But of course, we did not believe it. We could not believe it, too much trained to disregard the evidence of our own senses in favor of what we have been taught to believe.

The Great Lie—perhaps once true—held that a singular recipient—Pharaoh, Melchizedeck, Moses—possessed the mysteries of revelation, keys to the kingdom.

Then the prickly creatures of another Aeon who pronounced the Word from lips so foul we knew not to linger on the speaker, but the spoken:

Love is the Law. Do as thou wilt.

You are your own High Priest. *This* is the greatest of all the mysteries, the greatest of heresies, that which must not be True if the Center—*their* center—is to hold.

It is all out there. Believe it. It has *all* been revealed. Believe it. Everything is known. *Believe it.*

So now the End begins.

Step Three: Subjugation of the Will

Falling into a global mind, increasingly the gravity of the situation threatens to overwhelm any commentary that can be made about the process; at some point we cross the Schwartzchild radius of the

Noosphere, an Eschaton of sorts, the moment of irreversibility when everything becomes both true and trite, absolute and certain as air, safe as milk and the very pillar of family values.

The lines of simulation—imagination electrified, and the engines of creation—the ultimate articulation of Will—seem intent on a transhuman convergence, one which will not free us from entropy nor upload us into eternal, meaningless silicon, but will place us squarely where our boundaries are dissolved; between I and thou, this and that, us and them. The Eschaton is an emotional event, transcendent even in its expectation.

Every word spoken by every one of us brings us ever closer, another necessary iteration as the fabric of reality twists itself into a hypersurface, then disappears into the ultraviolet catastrophe of a single point. In a moment, our words will take control of us; just as the stuttering codes of our genes spell out the actualities of our bodies, so our memes will dictate the interiors of our being.

There is no escape, except this: "The way down is the way up."

It can not be very far. It doesn't feel very far. And you can go there and see for yourself.

Step Four: Teach Them the Rituals

There is only one ritual in the Church of the Motherfucker; a sacrament we take very seriously. Our only common practice. As is the case in *all* earlier mystery cults, it involves the ingestion of a sacred substance, an entheogen, to infuse the earthly body with the divine spirit.

During the initiation ritual, an incredibly powerful and fast-acting psychedelic is inhaled, producing an ecstatic out-of-body experience which can only be compared to a thermonuclear communion with the divine. An appearance on the other side of the Eschaton.

I will not threaten the legal status of this true Soma, this Philosopher's Stone, by mentioning its name, but I am prepared to tell you this: It is both perfectly legal and freely available. I buy it on the Web.

The passage through initiation is the shamanic journey from death to rebirth, a tsunami striking down the fragile walls of ego, carrying the shattered planks of being to a distant shore....

■ ■ ■ ■ ■ ■ ■ ■ ■ ■ ■

The wave recedes, and the universe has changed. You are back. But you *were* gone. You *had* passed from this world. And you are back.

I cried like a child at my own initiation, with the beauty and wonder of the World, and my gratitude to be back within it.

Shortcuts to gnosis invariably draw the ire of those who have tirelessly sacrificed to receive the same benefits as those bestowed by pineal grace. For those souls there is no truth except by the path of suffering. But for those who can receive it, the Church of the Motherfucker offers instantaneous grace, a guarantee of gnosis, and a sure-fire path to illumination.

No dogma, just ritual and love.

But he who seeks illumination is like an arrow flying directly into Hell.

Step Five: Pronounce Them Members. Make Them Feel Involved, Special

For this reason, we need community; to hold us together when everything falls apart. No one can take the trip with you, but they can hold your hand and focus their love. Nothing more is required. No dogma, just ritual and love. Go there!—to that place *after* the End of History—and when you've come back to us, make up your own mind. Do as you will: Join us—or don't.

But if you find something so extraordinary, so beyond expectation, so utterly surprising, then let us know. We've been there. I'd say, "We understand," but we don't. No one does. But it is possible to share our confusion—and our wonder. Together.

We may not be able to offer much in the way of conventional religion: no festivals, no fasting, no bingo games, but we do have a Pope. She pronounced the word of the Aeon as only a Russian-born, Moscow-raised and New York City-dwelling bitch-goddess can.

"Motherfucker!"

When everything else has been stripped away, ground to dust before the Absolute, burnt away in Revelation, where no word but "Yes" is possible, then—*then*!—you will be a Motherfucker.

Until that blessed moment, you will wander in the courts of the Temple; afterward, you'll dwell in the Holy of Holies. Forever.

It is complete; it is complete; it is complete.

I pronounce you—all of you—acolytes in the Church of the Motherfucker.

> A nature found within all creatures
> but not restricted to them;
> outside all creatures,
> but not excluded from them.
>
> —*The Cloud of Unknowing*

A Sentient Universe

Peter Russell

What is consciousness? The word is not easy to define, partly because we use it to cover a variety of meanings. We might say an awake person has consciousness, whereas someone who is asleep does not. Or, someone could be awake, but so absorbed in their thoughts that they have little consciousness of the world around them. We speak of having a political, social, or ecological consciousness. And we may say that human beings have consciousness while other creatures do not, meaning that humans think and are self-aware.

The way in which I shall be using the word "consciousness" is not in reference to a particular state of consciousness, or a particular way of thinking, but to the faculty of consciousness—the capacity for inner experience, whatever the nature or degree of the experience.

> For every psychological term in English there are four in Greek and forty in Sanskrit.
>
> —A. K. Coomaraswamy

The faculty of consciousness can be likened to the light from a video projector. The projector shines light on to a screen, modifying the light so as to produce any one of an infinity of images. These images are like the perceptions, sensations, dreams, memories, thoughts, and feelings that we experience—what I call the "contents of consciousness." The light itself, without which no images would be possible, corresponds to the faculty of consciousness. We know all the images on the screen are composed of this light, but we are not usually aware of the light itself; our attention is caught up in the images that appear and the stories they tell. In much the same way, we know we are conscious, but we are usually aware only of the many different perceptions, thoughts, and feelings that appear in the mind. We are seldom aware of consciousness itself.

Consciousness in All

The faculty of consciousness is not limited to human beings. A dog may not be aware of all the things of which we are aware. It does not think or reason as humans do, and it probably does not have the same degree of self-awareness, but this does not mean that a dog does not have its own inner world of experience.

When I am with a dog, I assume that it has its own mental picture of the world, full of sounds, colors, smells, and sensations. It appears to recognize people and places, much as we might. A dog may at times show fear and at other times, excitement. Asleep, it can appear to dream, feet and toes twitching as if on the scent of some fantasy-rabbit. And when a dog yelps or whines, we assume it is feeling pain—indeed, if we didn't believe that dogs felt pain, we wouldn't bother giving them anesthetics before an operation.

If dogs possess consciousness then so do cats, horses, deer, dolphins, whales, and other mammals. They may not be self-conscious as we are, but they are not devoid of inner experience. The same is true of birds; some parrots, for example, seem as aware as dogs. And if birds are sentient beings, then so, I assume, are other vertebrates—alligators, snakes, frogs, salmon, and sharks. However different their experiences may be, they all share the faculty of consciousness.

Consciousness does not arise from some particular arrangement of nerve cells or processes going on between them, or from any other physical features; it is always present.

The same argument applies to creatures further down the evolutionary tree. The nervous systems of insects are not nearly as complex as ours, and insects probably do not have as rich an experience of the world as we do, but I see no reason to doubt that they have some kind of inner experience.

Where do we draw the line? We usually assume that some kind of brain or nervous system is necessary before consciousness can come into being. From the perspective of the materialist metaparadigm, this is a reasonable assumption. If consciousness arises from processes in the material world, then those processes need to occur somewhere, and the obvious candidate is the nervous system.

But then we come up against the inherent problem of the materialist metaparadigm. Whether we are considering a human brain with its tens of billions of cells, or a nematode worm with a hundred or so neurons, the problem is the same: How can any purely material process ever give rise to consciousness?

Panpsychism

The underlying assumption of the current metaparadigm is that matter is insentient. The alternative is that the faculty of consciousness is a fundamental quality of nature. Consciousness does not arise from some particular arrangement of nerve cells or processes going on between them, or from any other physical features; it is always present.

If the faculty of consciousness is always present, then the relationship between consciousness and nervous systems needs to be rethought. Rather than creating consciousness, nervous systems may be amplifiers of consciousness, increasing the richness and quality of experience. In the analogy with a video projector, having a nervous system is like having a lens in the projector. Without the lens there is still light on the screen, but the images are much less sharp.

In philosophical circles the idea that consciousness is in everything is called *panpsychism*, from the Greek *pan*, meaning all, and *psyche*, meaning soul or mind. Unfortunately, the words "soul" and "mind" suggest that simple life-forms may possess qualities of consciousness found in human beings. To avoid this misunderstanding, some contemporary philosophers use the term *panexperientialism*—everything has experience. Personally, I prefer the term *pansentience*—everything is sentient.

Whatever name this position is given, its basic tenet is that the capacity for inner experience could not evolve or emerge out of entirely insentient, non-experiencing matter. Experience can only come from that which already has experience. Therefore the faculty of consciousness must be present all the way down the evolutionary tree.

We know that plants are sensitive to many aspects of their environment—length of daylight, temperature, humidity, atmospheric chemistry. Even some single-celled organisms are sensitive to physical vibration, light, and heat. Who is to say they do not have a corresponding glimmer of awareness? I am not implying they perceive as we do, or that they have thoughts or feelings, only that they possess the faculty of consciousness; there is a faint trace of sentience. It may be a billionth of the richness and intensity of our own experience, but it is still there.

According to this view, there is nowhere we can draw a line between conscious and non-conscious entities; there is a trace of sentience, however slight, in viruses, molecules, atoms, and even elementary particles.

Some argue this implies that rocks perceive the world around them, perhaps have thoughts and feelings, and enjoy an inner mental life similar to human beings. This is clearly an absurd suggestion, and not one that was ever intended. If a bacterium's experience is a billionth of the richness and intensity of a human being's, the degree

What emerged over the course of evolution was not the *faculty* of consciousness, but the various qualities and dimensions of conscious experience—the *contents* of consciousness.

of experience in the minerals of a rock might be a billion times dimmer still. They would possess none of the qualities of human consciousness—just the faintest possible glimmer of sentience.

The Evolution of Consciousness

If the faculty of consciousness is universal, then consciousness is not something that emerged with human beings, or with vertebrates, or at any particular stage of biological evolution. What emerged over the course of evolution was not the *faculty* of consciousness, but the various qualities and dimensions of conscious experience—the *contents* of consciousness.

With mammals the limbic system appeared, an area of the brain associated with basic feelings such as fear, arousal, and emotional bonding.

The earliest living organisms, bacteria and algae, had no sensory organs and detected only the most general characteristics and changes in their environment. Their experience might be likened to an extremely dim, almost imperceptible hint of light on an otherwise dark screen—virtually nothing compared to the richness and detail of human experience.

With the evolution of multicellular organisms came the emergence of specific senses. Some cells specialized in sensing light, others in sensing vibration, pressure, or changes in chemistry. Working together, such cells formed sensory organs, increasing the detail and quality of the information available to the organism—and enhancing the quality of consciousness.

In order to process this additional information and distribute it to other parts of the organism, nervous systems evolved. And, as the flow of information became more complex, central processing systems developed, integrating the different sensory modalities into a single picture of the world.

As brains grew in complexity, new features were added to the image appearing in consciousness. With mammals the limbic system appeared, an area of the brain associated with basic feelings such as fear, arousal, and emotional bonding. With time the mammalian brain grew yet more complex, developing a new structure around it—the cerebral cortex. With this came better memory, focused attention, greater intention, and imagination.

The picture appearing in consciousness had by now reached the richness of detail and diversity of qualities that we associate with our own experience. But this is not the end of the story. With human beings another new capacity emerged—speech. And with this, the evolution of consciousness took a huge leap forward.

For a start, we could use words to communicate experiences with each other. Our awareness of the world was no longer limited to what our senses told us; we could know of events occurring in other places and at other times. We could learn from each other's experiences, and so begin to accumulate a collective body of knowledge about the world.

Most significantly, we began to use language internally. Hearing words in our minds without actually saying them allowed us to talk to ourselves. An entirely new dimension had been added to our consciousness—verbal thought. We could form concepts, entertain ideas, appreciate patterns in events, apply reason, and begin to understand the universe in which we found ourselves.

Then came the most important leap of all. Not only could we reflect upon the nature of the world around us, we could also reflect upon thinking itself. We became self-aware—aware of our own awareness. This opened the door to a whole new arena of development. We could begin to explore the inner world of the mind and, ultimately, delve into the nature of consciousness itself.

"A Sentient Universe" is chapter 3 of *From Science to God: The Mystery of Consciousness and the Meaning of Light* by Peter Russell.

A Lost Theory?

Introduction to *Darwin's Lost Theory of Love*

David Loye

A "lost theory" of Charles Darwin's? How could this be? Don't we by now know Darwin from A to Z?

Certainly few other figures have been so comprehensively covered by biographies. And surely the story is one which we must by now know every detail. The amiable, indifferent student, cowed by a domineering father. The fervent collector of beetles. The year of trying out medicine at Edinburgh. The three years of tentative commitment to the ministry at Cambridge. How he then went off to sea in the *Beagle*. And how, transformed by this journey of journeys—which was also to transform the lives of every one of us living today—he became Darwin the ruminating, troubled, but ever steadily ascendant man of science.

We know seemingly everything about the long years of his immersion in the development of his theory of evolution—only to be nearly upstaged by Alfred Wallace. If we happen to be interested in the family life of the great figures of the past, we know of the sunny and quirky charm of the Down household and what at times seems to have been dozens of children and pets. If we are interested in medical details, we also know that he was mysteriously sick for much of his working life.

If we are interested in science, we also know of the incredible range of his experiments with pigeons, barnacles, wild ducks, and lizard and snakes' eggs. Also: cabbage, lettuce and celery seeds, orchids, passion flowers, purple loosestrifes, wild cucumbers, Venus fly traps, and on and on. We may even have chuckled over the story of how he sought evidence of the roots of intelligence in earthworms, once even assembling a family orchestra—his wife Emma on the piano, son Francis on the bassoon, grandson Bernard with a whistle—to play to a dish of earthworms to see how they might respond to this form of cultural advancement.

Thereafter, it is true, to all but the most devout of Darwinians, the story fades away into the pleasant mush of a few more books after the pivotal *On the Origin of Species by Means of Natural Selection,* then death and a ceremonious burial in Westminster Abbey. But where in all this well-plowed ground could anything like a lost theory have been hidden?

Theories do not leap into being overnight. Indeed, the story of Darwin's development of what we know today as his theory of evolution has become the favorite story of how long theories take to build—at least eighteen years, in this case. It just does not seem possible to tuck away in all those years a lost theory that amounts to anything.

And yet there was such a theory, and for over 100 years it was ignored—a theory that might have changed the course of the twentieth century in countless ways for the better. Could we have gone to war so often, or tolerated being globally inundated with television violence, had we believed we were not incurably selfish and vicious by nature? This, we were told, Darwin's theory proved.

Or could this theory—the core of modern science—have been attacked so successfully by right-wing religious forces as to endanger not only the teaching of science itself but also our hard-won heritage of free inquiry in a democracy?

It goes in and out of the news so fast as to hardly register, but the theory of evolution has been on trial again not only in Tennessee but elsewhere in the US. The decision in 1999 of the Kansas State Board of Education to drop the requirement that evolution be taught in schools sent out a shock wave that circled the educated world.[1] A few months later Oklahoma followed suit with a requirement that all new textbooks carry a disclaimer saying that evolution is a "controversial theory." This after more than 100 years of science to establish evolution theory as the floor under modern mind. Could this have happened had Darwin's theory been seen after all this time not merely as the "godless" plaything of "pointy head" scientists, but rather as something of practical value that could provide the growing child, as well as the rest of us, with some sense of dignity, purpose, direction, and meaning to life?

The fact is that, buried for 100 years within the lost theory, has been the proof that the beliefs of *both* regressive religion and reductionist science are gross distortions of what Darwin really believed.

The fact is that, buried for 100 years within the lost theory, has been the proof that the beliefs of *both* regressive religion and reductionist science are gross distortions of what Darwin really believed.

Most meaningful today, as we emerge—still shellshocked—from the twentieth century, this lost theory is astoundingly attuned to both our deepest yearnings socially and our most advanced scientific probing. It is a theory, moreover, that in a time of increasing doubt and fear of the future offers a new burst of hope for the twenty-first century.

The Old Theory and the New Theory

How can I most quickly convey the nature of this "new" theory, or the startling story that lies ahead? Perhaps the best way is to briefly characterize Darwin's theory as it is known to us today and then go to the largest chunk of his writing, long ignored, in which he so radically departed from what we have been told.

One of the great difficulties holding back both advances in evolution theory and, I believe, the advance of humanity globally is the immense gulf between the social "footprint" and the scientific "head trip" of Darwinism. In other words, most scientists interested in evolution theory today are aware of many refinements, shadings, and qualifications of the prevailing Darwinian story line.[2] But what gets "out there" to us—or what we are generally told—has the raw psychological impact of the footprint of a King Kong. Everywhere the story is that science tells us that evolution is basically a matter of the great predatory force of natural selection that feeds on the wild output of random variation in order to pick out only the very best of organisms or efforts and discards the rest. This "footprint" theory is dressed up in much biology and paleontology, but at the core it seems to work very much like a giant motorized threshing machine moving through a wheat field. Through the front end it swallows up sheaf after hapless sheaf of wheat, and out the rear end it spews mountainous piles of the rejected straw and a thin stream of the precious grain.

In classrooms throughout our world, in an unending stream of beautifully packaged books, and routinely over television, we are shown what is further pursued here in chapter two—how this combination of forces has not just shaped every living thing prior to the emergence of the human, but also ourselves: our species, we humans, and everything about us. This theory is dressed up in ways to make it more palatable, and summaries such as this are always attacked as exaggerations. But basically we are told that this is why by necessity we are so aggressive and violent, or why by necessity we are driven by selfish genes, or why by necessity we must be ruthlessly competitive and exploitive. We are told that only in this way can our species evolve according to the sacred Darwinian principle of survival of the fittest.

We are also told that, with a few modern improvements, this was and is Darwin's one and only theory. But what happens if, with an open mind, we move from *Origin of Species*, where he first articulated this theory, to *The Descent of Man*, or to the early notebooks he filled out just after getting back from the famous voyage of the *Beagle*?

What became for me many years of exploration can be condensed into a simple bit of research toward the end of this process that I believe reveals it all in one fell swoop, as they say. In *The Descent of Man* Darwin moves on from the world of the "lower organisms" supposedly to show how the great threshing machine operates among us, at the human level. Now, for over 100 years the index at the back of the book—dutifully put to use by scholars as a guide to what is of importance in *Descent*—has shown but a single listing for "love." This, of course, is not unusual. Until quite recently, this simple word, which not only fills our songs but also our minds much of the time, was considered not only suspect but wholly outside the realm of science. "Love" was just not what science was all about. Yet through the use of a modern computerized search of the whole book, I discovered that in *Descent* Darwin is actually exploring the usage and evolutionary meaning for "love" 95 times![3]

What is going on here, one wonders? What could account for such a massive contradiction? And why should the discrepancy involve a concept that in a world everywhere now torn apart by hate has become of increasing scientific as well as popular interest?

I then tried searches for what we should, with more certainty, expect to find in *Descent.* According to what we have been told is Darwin's binding theory for us at the human level, we would, for example, expect to find much about the survival of the fittest. The computer found only two entries. And in one of the two he tells us he exaggerated its importance in *Origin of Species*! Or what about competition? Nine entries. From all we have been told, we would certainly *not* expect to find anything about cooperation. Yet for the nearest equivalent to this word for Darwin's time, "mutuality"—as in *mutual aid*, which Darwin coined as a phrase—there were 24 entries.

And if what primarily operates at our level is only the impersonal grinding of the great machine of natural selection and random variation, why do we find Darwin talking so often not of the power of the great machine? Why, instead, is he so often talking about the powers of the supposedly hapless organism at the heart of this process—that is of ourselves, of you and me? Why does he speak so often of the powers of our minds to perceive, and puzzle over what is going on, and decide what to do, and thereby make our way so effectively in this world? Why does he speak so often, for example, of our power of reasoning—24 entries? Or of imagination—24 entries? Or of sympathy for one another—which jumps to *61* entries?

And why do we find 95 entries for "habit," a concept explored by psychologists, as against 95 entries for "instinct," which used to be the biological equivalent for habit but was more often probed by psychologists than by biologists?

I discovered that in *Descent* Darwin is actually exploring the usage and evolutionary meaning for "love" 95 times!

And why, if science has nothing to do with values, and what happens to us is up to the random action of a fate in which we supposedly have little voice, do we find the entries for Darwin's use of the word "moral"—or how we decide what is right and what is wrong for us to do—skyrocketing to a number just short of that for "love," *90* in all?

Why, in short, do we find this overwhelming interest on Darwin's part in what in actuality most interests and concerns every one of us about ourselves at our level—not that of barnacle, finch, or amoeba? In contrast to what we have been told, why does he seem to find love, sympathy, reason, and morality of overriding importance for evolution at *our* level? Why do we find so much about the mind and the future for our species in this book that for over 100 years has been written off by evolution theorists as of little interest other than for its passages on sexual selection?

The Challenge for Twenty-First Century Science

The answers I found to these and many other questions can be put quickly and bluntly. Although present evolution theory represents a considerable and, I believe, an enduring achievement, because of a purblind immersion in a theory overwhelmingly fixated at the biological level we have overlooked something huge and meaningful for over 100 years. Through the research over a number of years reported in this book, I discovered there were actually two halves to Darwin's theory. There is the first half, or foundation, of a biological base for his theory, with which we are somewhat familiar. **But then Darwin went on to complete his theory with the superstructure of a psychological, systems scientific, humanistic, and morally-grounded "higher" half—of which today we know almost nothing**.

Moreover, the understanding of the lost Darwinian superstructure casts a wholly new and more hopeful light on the biological foundation. The biological picture, to put it quickly, looks more like a slate upon which each organism writes its own brief message than like the heedless rolling among us of first-half Darwinism's beloved threshing machine.

What this discovery can mean for science is a jolt of the earthquake proportion that is needed to speed up the all too slow-moving rearrangement of thinking and priorities for all scientific fields as we enter the twenty-first century. Within the comfortable, snail's-pace world of academia—and often plans to here, now, and ever after be—this matter of a so-called "lost theory" of Darwin may not seem to be of earthshaking importance. But what it can mean for every one of us—scientist, and layman and lay woman alike; that is, for every one of us with children and grandchildren or larger hopes for humanity—is something of exceptional urgency and meaning. In a world increasingly desperate for guidance out of science, it can mean that at last there may emerge an adequate theory of who we really are, and how to get from here to the better world we want to build.

It can mean that out of the science that gave us atomic bombs and pesticides and acid rain there might at last emerge a unified theory not of atoms, quarks, and strong and weak fields but of what accounts for what is *best* in us, rather than of excuses for what is *worst* in us. It can mean that out of science can emerge a theory that soars beyond so much that is secondary, trivial, and wasteful to show us how to achieve what is of first-rate importance and our highest aspirations. Of increasing importance in a world everywhere involved both in massive breakdown and the drive for the hopeful breakthrough, it can show us how to build the radically better world that we human beings have sought for thousands of years.

We hear much of chaos, complexity, or the abiding mystery of the cell these days, but in reality there are far more pressing challenges for science. As an evolutionary scientist myself, I express the conviction of increasing numbers of us about the one most urgent task today for all scientists. This is to find and advance whatever their field can do to better serve the needs of humanity as we enter a century in which, in terms of evolution, it seems evident we face a threat to the survival of our species.

What other conclusion can we come to? It does not take a scientist to read the handwriting on the wall. Who but the most blind among us can fail to see the warning in the widening global gap between rich and poor, the proliferation of nuclear and all other forms of superbomb, the polluting of sky, land, and water already beginning to silence the voices of the birds and frogs?

Yet at the same time—if we can find the vision and the courage of leadership—there opens before us a great new opportunity for long-term improvement of the human condition. It is here that the most unexpected thing of all rises out of the past here recovered—for in the pages that lie ahead we are to encounter not only the revolutionary implications of Darwin's lost theory, but also the grandeur, majesty, and humanity of Darwin's lost vision of the real nature and destiny of our species.

How urgent is the need for an updating of Darwin's theory of evolution can be seen from the cry for something better out of the very fields of biology and physics to which the task of building a modern theory of evolution was mainly relegated.

Those who are aroused—for example, the thousands of us responsive to the purpose of the Union of Concerned Scientists and similar professional bodies—write and speak out of a jolting recognition of the incredible danger our species faces at this juncture. Of the many questions that press upon us, one I believe is of overriding and inescapable meaning. After nearly 150 years since Darwin set the whole thing going, shouldn't we by now have a theory of evolution good for something more than scholarly squabbles and dubious mass entertainment? Shouldn't we by now have a theory of evolution that might provide us with *a source of guidance through these difficult years?*

A theory that can find a place for love as well as violence in our development? A theory offering hope rather than despair at the end of the line?

But instead we have this great, slick, gleaming, and entrancing package of a one-sided story of the past and the prehuman. We have the half-truth of this story out of which, pumped up by a global orgy of media feeding on fear, we are given the vision of killer apes, selfish genes, blind watchmakers, and an incurably violent species that continues to drive us toward destruction.

The main news of this book is the surprising new voice that has been added to the ignored voices of those who have been trying to reach their scientific peers and everybody else with a larger and more hopeful vision of human evolution—the voice of none other than Darwin himself.

In page after page out of his own long-ignored writings, he returns here to disavow much of what has been attributed to him by what is today known as the Darwinian tradition. He reaffirms the basic theory of his *Origin of Species*, of the centrality of natural selection and variation. But to this he now adds two startling departures.

One is his leap beyond biology and natural science into the psychology and the social and systems science that are the main focus for this book. We find ourselves able at last to marvel at the wonder of his lost leap to identify something far more important than natural selection and random variation at the human level. It is the power of moral sensitivity, he tells us—of love, mutuality, reasoning, imagination, habit, and education.

The other departure is even more surprising from the scientific standpoint. For I have brushed away the cobwebs from how Darwin discovered what is only today beginning to be explored as the possibility for a *new* major principle for evolution. As we enter the twenty-first century, in addition to natural selection and random variation, the focus is on *self-organizing* processes as a third candidate for being a prime shaper of our lives. This idea animates the new evolutionary theories of thermodynamacist Ilya Prigogine, biologists Stuart Kauffman and Humberto Maturana, and many others. And Darwin was already there more than a hundred years ago!

And what emerges in his vision of the completed theory? Very much what progressive science—as well as progressive spirituality—has long dreamed of. It is very much what humanistic psychologists as well as humanistic biologists, systems theorists, chaos theorists, general evolution theorists—and moral and spiritual theorists, mothers, fathers, grandmothers, grandfathers, uncles, aunts, and everybody else concerned with how our species is to get better before it wipes itself out—have wished that his theory *could* have been.

The story, ramifications, and explanation of how all this was buried for over 100 years is covered in Part I: The Story. Part II: The Theory provides the reconstruction of his lost theory made possible by an editing that frees Darwin's own extremely readable and engaging writings from the murk of their long-time burial. Part III: The Vision then briefly explores the implications of what the story and theory have uncovered for the betterment of our lives during the twenty-first century.

A brief appendix takes the reader behind the scenes into the exciting new world of the advanced exploration of evolution theory for a glimpse at some of many new groups involved in this vital venture. In particular, I focus on the one I am best acquainted with. Drawn together by systems philosopher Ervin Laszlo, this is the General Evolution Research Group, of which I was a cofounder. This is a group composed of biologists; physicists; astrophysicists; mathematicians; systems, brain, social, and computer scientists; psychologists; historians; philosophers; and chaos, feminist, and management theorists. Working toward the development of an evolution theory that might better fit the needs of our time, these heirs and heiresses of the new Darwin live in or are from Germany, Italy, England, France, Sweden, Belgium, Chile, China, Finland, Hungary, Russia, Sri Lanka, Switzerland, and the United States.

After nearly 150 years since Darwin set the whole thing going, shouldn't we by now have a theory of evolution good for something more than scholarly squabbles and dubious mass entertainment?

This book is an independent work, representing my own research and my own conclusions. But I owe the inspiration, the perspective, and key aspects of the data out of which I write to some of the members of the General Evolution Research Group, as well as to others among the much larger group of scientists trying to build a better and more useful evolution theory.

Increasing numbers of us in these groups look to this new century as not only one of the very greatest of challenges but also of the greatest of opportunities—as something really special for our species. As I sketch in the last chapter, beyond its inevitable horrors, we look to the twenty-first century for the opening of windows and doors into springtime after a long winter.

In this regard, however fierce the howls or the drubbing of the brickbats this book may raise in certain quarters now, I feel confident that over time it will be met with increasing appreciation—and much relief.

Endnotes

1. See Sommerfeld, Meg. (June 5, 1996). "Lawmakers put theory of evolution on trial." *Education Week*; Johnston, Robert. (March 13, 1996). "70 years after Scopes, evolution hot topic again." *Teacher Magazine*; and Beem, Kate. (June 13, 1999). "Debates over evolution in the classroom rage country-wide." *Kansas City Star*. **2.** For good summaries of the varieties of evolution theory, see references for Ervin Laszlo's *Evolution*, and particularly for biologically-oriented questioning of the gross social "footprint," Peter Corning's "Holistic Darwinism," Stanley Salthe's *Development and Evolution*, or David Depew and Bruce Weber's *Darwinism Evolving*. **3.** A fascinating new resource for the researcher is *Darwin 2nd Edition*, a CD-ROM produced by Pete Goldie for Lightbinders, Inc., 2325 Third Street, Suite 324, San Francisco, CA 94107. Not only are the texts beautifully accessible but the reproductions of the original engravings and color plates in Darwinian works are amazing. Besides *The Descent of Man*, this CD-ROM offers *Origin of Species*, *The Voyage of the Beagle*, *The Expression of Emotions in Man and Animals*, and many other useful items.

Excerpted from *Darwin's Lost Theory of Love: A Healing Vision for the New Century* (iUniverse.com, 2000).

APPENDICES

Appendix A: More Lies, Myths, and Manipulations

Russ Kick

The Book Monopoly

A slightly modified excerpt from my interview with Kevin Segall of Essential Media <www.essentialmedia.com>:

"It's not discussed much, but there is a corporate oligarchy that controls the American book publishing and bookselling industries, just as there are oligarchies (often overlapping) that control music, movies, and the news media. The major book publishers are owned by huge parent corporations, such as Viacom and Time Warner. In 1998 the German conglomerate Bertelsmann bought Random House, which also includes Knopf, Ballantine, and Bantam Doubleday Dell. That one company now controls 30 percent of the nonfiction market in the US. Add in Simon & Schuster and Penguin Putnam, and the three of them control 54 percent of the market. In all, the seven major corporate publishers make up 73 percent of the nonfiction market. The news is even worse for fiction: Random House controls just over a third of the fiction market; three other publishers added together control just under a third; and everyone else combined makes up 33 percent of the fiction market.

"The German Bertelsmann megacorporation has entered a deal with Barnes & Noble to run their online bookselling efforts together. This one company now has a lot of power over book publishing and selling in the US. And speaking of Barnes & Noble, which is the biggest bookseller in the country—they attempted to buy Ingram Book Group, which is the largest book distributor in the country. Luckily, they were thwarted by antitrust regulations, but the attempt shows the mindset that's at work here. How would most booksellers fare if their biggest competitor were also their biggest supplier?

"Fewer executives are making more decisions about what gets published."

"All of this centralization means less choice for us. Fewer executives are making more decisions about what gets published. And it's not just the publishers who are shooting down books. The major chain stores have a say in whether some books get published. There have been cases where they've said they're not wild about a particular upcoming book, so the publisher shitcanned it. Also, the pricing practices of the chain bookstores and big online booksellers are affecting independent booksellers. The big publishers know that the big booksellers automatically discount most books 10 percent to 30 percent, sometimes more, so they price their books higher to adjust for this. The indie booksellers that charge retail get screwed because they have to charge $24.95 for a hardcover that isn't particularly thick."

The Chase Legacy

"Even as Chase Manhattan prepares to take over J.P. Morgan, the bank's past is returning to haunt it. Recently revealed documents show that Chase, which was already known to have helped the Nazis, aided slavery here at home as two of its predecessor banks worked with an insurance company to insure slave owners against loss. Chase is, as far as can be determined, the first company whose forerunners have been identified as aiding both the perpetrators of the destruction of the Jews in Europe and those who enslaved Africans and their descendants in America."[1]

Cowboys

"In the old days the word cowboy was synonymous with thief. Cowboys were drifters—laid-back, mostly illiterate, unwashed ne'er-do-wells, whom President Arthur likened to 'desperadoes.' It may be that the cowboy's myth was directly disproportionate to his lowly state."[2]

Disappearing Food

"Monocultures and monopolies are destroying the rich harvest of seed given to us over millennia by nature and farming cultures....

"Traditionally, 10,000 wheat varieties were grown in China. These had been reduced to only 1,000 by the 1970s. Only 20 percent of Mexico's maize diversity survives today. At one time, over 7,000 varieties of apples were grown in the United States. More than 6,000 are now extinct. In the Philippines, where small peasants used to cultivate thousands of traditional rice varieties, just two Green Revolution varieties occupied 98 percent of the entire rice-growing area by the 1980s."[3]

"Architect Kyosho Izumi's LSD-inspired design for the ideal mental hospital won him a commendation for outstanding achievement from the American Psychiatric Association."

Drugs Fry Your Brain

"Architect Kyosho Izumi's LSD-inspired design for the ideal mental hospital won him a commendation for outstanding achievement from the American Psychiatric Association. His plan has been used in the construction of several mental health centers.

"Herman Kahn, a civil defense planner for the Department of Defense, used acid to contemplate complexities of bombing strategy. Ralph Abraham, professor of mathematics at the University of California in Santa Cruz, is a pioneer of new 'chaos mathematics' that includes the equations used to generate the swirling fractal images so popular among people enthused about psychedelics. Abraham has publicly attested to using acid for insight in developing this revolutionary new branch of mathematics."[4]

Electroshock

"'People like to say forced electroshock doesn't happen in the United States,' said ect [electroconvulsive therapy] activist Juli Lawrence of St. Louis. 'It happens much more than we'd like to believe. In the last year, I've stepped in on several forced electroshock cases. In every case, the patient was perfectly competent, aware, and able to make an informed decision. But because these doctors made up their minds to forge ahead, they weren't allowed to have a choice.'

"The federal Center for Mental Health Services and the President's National Council on Disability (NCD) have both released reports admitting that, from time to time, some individuals in the USA do receive the controversial electroshock procedure *against* their expressed wishes. Earlier this year, the NCD issued a call to end electroshock all together. Lawrence said that people are encouraged to contact her organization via her Website, <www.ect.org> or by email at <juli@ect.org>."[5]

Entrapment

"Y'know, if you ask someone if they're a cop, then they *gotta* tell you they are or else it's entrapment." You might've heard this from one of your stoner friends, and you've undoubtedly seen it in the movies. It isn't true. According to Bruce Margolin, director of Los Angeles NORML (National Organization for the Reform of Marijuana Laws): "Undercover cops DO NOT have to tell or admit that they are police. Even if directly asked, they can legally deny it." Margolin is an attorney who has defended his clients from drug charges for over 30 years, so if anybody knows first-hand, he does.[6]

Fertility

An article in *Psychology Today* says: "Contrary to popular belief, there is no infertility crisis sweeping the nation. We've just lost all conception of what it takes to conceive. Reproductive technology has made us impatient with nature.

"Rather than an infertility crisis, what we have is a society that's allowed technology to displace biology in the reproductive process, in effect dehumanizing the most human of events. At the very least, this means stress replaces spontaneity as women become tied to thermometers—constantly checking to see when they're ovulating—while men stand by waiting to give command performances. At the most, it involves women and men subjecting themselves to invasive procedures with high price tags. Whatever happened to love and romance and the idea of letting nature take its course? Instead, we seem to have embraced the idea that science, not sex, provides the best chance for producing biological children. Technicians have stolen human reproduction. And there are some 300 fertility clinics—with annual revenues of $2 billion—to prove it."[7]

While we're on the subject, it looks like underwear choice doesn't have an effect on male fertility. For decades, the accepted wisdom has been that wearing briefs leads to sterility because they hold the testicles too close to the body, causing the temperature to rise and short-circuiting sperm production. An article in the *Journal of*

"Contrary to popular belief, there is no infertility crisis sweeping the nation."

Urology indicates that this untrue. There is what the researchers call "a paucity of data measuring scrotal temperature as a function of underwear type," so they conducted their own study at the State University of New York. The bottom line: "In our study there was no difference in scrotal temperature depending on underwear type."[8]

Ford's Bottom Line

If anyone insists that corporations aren't heartless greed machines that only care about the bottom line, they've obviously never heard of (or have forgotten about) Ford's handling of the fuel-leakage problem of the early 1970s. By 1973, Ford knew that some of its models leaked fuel when they turned over—leading to fires and explosions—and that this could be fixed by installing an $11 valve. So Ford immediately told all vehicle owners to drive to their nearest Ford dealer for a quick replacement, right? Well, no. First they did a little number-crunching.

They figured that if they did nothing, the fuel leakage would result in 180 deaths, 180 serious injuries, and 2,100 burned vehicles. So *then* they issued a recall, right? Surely it would be worth it if they could save just one person from burning to death in an inferno of gas and metal. Not exactly. They figured that each death would cost them an average of $200,000 in legal fees, settlements, etc.; each serious injury would set them back $67,000; and each burned vehicle would result in a $700 tab. Therefore, the total cost would be $49.5 million.

It was much cheaper to do nothing and let an estimated 180 people get immolated and an equal number spend the rest of their lives recovering from severe burns.

Then they figured the other side of the equation. If they spent $11 to replace the valve on 11 million cars and 1.5 million light trucks, it would cost them $137 million. *It was much cheaper to do nothing and let an estimated 180 people get immolated and an equal number spend the rest of their lives recovering from severe burns.* So that's exactly what they did—nothing. (There was never a recall, though *eight* years later, Ford did make the necessary minor modifications to new cars being assembled.) This case is still taught as an example of cost-benefit analysis in many college business textbooks.

And then Ford wonders why we don't believe them when they claim they didn't realize the Firestone/Bridgestone tires used on many of their vehicles are faulty and cause rollovers.[9]

"In the nearly two years following the complete banning of firearms, Australian homicides increased 29 percent with gun deaths in the state of Victoria up more than 300 percent."

Gas Prices

According to a 1999 study by the International Center for Technology Assessment, a gallon of gas in the US costs $15.14. If you factor in billions upon billions of dollars per year in federal and state tax breaks, federal subsidies, regulation, pollution clean-up, and other factors, each gallon has cost taxpayers over $15 by the time it gets to our tanks.[10]

Guns

Defending yourself. The e-book *Gun Facts* summarizes the findings of an article in the *Journal of Criminal Law and Criminology*: "Every year people in the United States use a gun to defend themselves against criminals an estimated 2,500,000 times—more than 6,500 people a day, or once every 13 seconds."[11]

Rape. Of these 2.5 million incidents, approximately 192,500 are women defending themselves against rape. In fact, the Department of Justice found that while rape against unarmed women was successful one-third of the time, it was only successful 3 percent of the time when the woman was armed with a gun or knife.[12]

Guns and crime in Washington, DC. Based on the FBI Uniform Crime Statistics: "In 1976, Washington, D.C., enacted one of the most restrictive gun control laws in the nation. Since then, the city's murder rate has risen 134 percent while the national murder rate has dropped 2 percent."[13]

Guns and crime in Australia. What would a total gun ban accomplish? Fortunately, the Second Amendment has so far prevented the US from finding out, but Australia provides our answer. Jim Marrs writes: "In the nearly two years following the complete banning of firearms, Australian homicides increased 29 percent with gun deaths in the state of Victoria up more than 300 percent. Assaults increased 17 percent and armed robberies increased more than 100 percent despite having continually dropped in the 25 years preceding the weapons ban. Property crimes, assaults and muggings are now more than twice as high as in America."[14]

Concealed carry. A national survey performed in 1996 at the University of Chicago found that rates of violent crime drop when states allow citizens to carry guns outside of their homes. "States which passed concealed carry laws reduced their murder rate by 8.5 percent, rapes by 5 percent, aggravated assaults by 7 percent and robbery by 3 percent. If those states not having concealed carry laws had adopted such laws in 1992, then approximately 1,570 murders, 4,177 rapes, 60,000 aggravated assaults, and over 11,000 robberies would have been avoided yearly."[15] The reason is obvious: If criminals—who have guns regardless of whether or not they're allowed to—aren't sure if a potential victim also has a gun, they're less likely to attack.

"Assault rifles." To be an "assault rifle," a gun must be capable of firing in automatic mode (meaning that keeping the trigger pulled results in a stream of bullets being fired). The "assault rifles" that the media wring their hands about are not capable of auto fire. These so-called assault rifles, or assault weapons, are functionally no different than hunting rifles; they just look more "military." On top of that, "Over 100,000 police officers delivered a message to Congress in 1990 stating that only 2 to 3 percent of crimes are committed using a so-called 'assault weapon.'"[16] And that was four years *before* Congress banned "assault weapons."

What about the children? "In espousing their agenda, the Million Mom March web site cites the Centers for Disease Control and Prevention and the National Center for Health Statistics on gun deaths from children 0-19. Although they correctly observe that '4,223 young people aged 0-19 were killed by gunfire in 1997,' they fail to divulge that 70 percent of these deaths occur among 'children' between the ages of 17-19, most of whom die as a result of gang violence.... While 110 children aged 1-14 died from gun accidents in 1998, 200 suffocated from ingested objects, 570 died from burns, 850 drowned, and 2,600 died in car accidents."[17]

Media bias. Brian Patrick of the University of Michigan studied the news media's treatment of the National Rifle Association for a year and found that there was an undeniable bias against them. "The ACLU [American Civil Liberties Union] will typically be labeled a 'civil liberties group,' 'abortion rights group,' or 'leading liberal champion.' Handgun Control Inc. is usually identified as a 'citizens' lobby,' 'nonprofit organization,' or 'public interest group.' The NAACP [National Association for the Advancement of Colored People] is referred to as a 'national civil rights group,' 'venerable civil rights organization,' or 'the nation's oldest and largest civil rights organization.'

"But when the NRA is in the news, the tone and terminology are often very different.

"'Semi-automatic caucus.' 'Lobbying juggernaut.' 'Powerful gun lobby.' 'Gun organization.' 'Radical gun lobby.' 'The classic Washington superlobby.' 'Arrogant lobby.' 'The gun lobby consisting of everything from neo-Nazis to nature-loving hunters.' 'Most feared lobby.' 'The Beltway's loudest lobby.' 'A rich and paranoid organization.'...

"When information comes from the AARP [American Association of Retired Persons], the papers use verbs like 'reported,' 'indicated,' 'concludes,' 'documents.' When the NAACP is quoted, the stories note that it 'spoke out,' 'vowed,' 'declared,' 'announced.' But when the NRA speaks, the papers often choose verbs that imply doubt: 'claims,' 'asserts,' 'likes to portray,' 'contended,' 'alleging.'"[18]

Furthermore, another media study showed that on network news broadcasts over the course of two years, 91 percent of stories on gun policy pushed an anti-gun view.[19]

The Second Amendment's "militia." "Report by the US Senate Subcommittee on the Constitution (1982): 'In the Militia Act of 1792, the second Congress defined "militia of the United States" to include almost every free adult male in the United States. These persons were obligated by law to possess a [military-style] firearm and a minimum supply of ammunition and military equipment.... There can be little doubt from this that when the Congress and the people spoke of the "militia," they had reference to the traditional concept of the entire populace capable of bearing arms, and not to any formal group such as what is today called the National Guard.'"[20]

~~Overp~~ Underpopulation

For the past few decades, the dire (and unfulfilled) warnings of overpopulation have been ringing in our ears. Strange, then, that the United Nations, the US Census Bureau, the Population Research Institute, and Eurostat are now saying we should brace ourselves for *underpopulation*. The birthrates of 61 countries (and counting) are in negative territory, meaning that their populations are dying faster than they're being replenished. "With growing elderly populations and a declining number of workers ages 15 to 65, those countries will depend on large-scale immigration of younger people to provide not only goods and services but also the tax base on which the older population depends for social services.

The United Nations, the US Census Bureau, the Population Research Institute, and Eurostat are now saying we should brace ourselves for *underpopulation*.

"The U.N. study says the numbers of immigrants needed to offset declines in the working-age population are significantly larger than those needed to offset total population decline. It adds that the levels of immigration needed to offset population aging are extremely large and in all cases entail vastly more immigration than has occurred in the past."[21]

Additionally: "Recently the United Nations Population Division estimated that 44 percent of the world's people live in countries where the fertility rate has already fallen below the replacement rate, and fertility is falling fast almost everywhere else."[22]

In the short term, though, we will see an overall rise of the world's population. The number of people in the world will probably peak at 8 to 9 billion in 2050. (It's interesting to note that some of the doomsday prophesiers of the 1960s and 1970s predicted that there would be over 10 billion people on the planet right *now*. "We were all supposed to be eating our dogs and children by now, and wishing we lived on the moon, according to forecasts of Paul Ehrlich, author of the best-selling 1968 book, *The Population Bomb*."[23])

Many countries (including the US) will peak before 50 years, though. "In the U.S. by 2050, the number of people over 65 will outnumber people under 15 by 2.5 to one."[24] As for Russia, "The Russian Academy of Science has compared the anticipated population decline from 147 to 121 million by 2050 to catastrophes on the scale of famine and war."[25]

The UN's study also predicts that—if trends continue—the world's population in the twenty-second century will fall *below* its current level of six billion, and that's just the beginning.[26] "Unless people's values change greatly, several centuries from now there could be fewer people living in the entire world than live in the United States today."[27]

Panama Canal

From an article in NewsMax.com: "A Chinese company with close ties to the Beijing communist government was planning to take over the operation of the Panama Canal, a secret government report revealed.

"And according to Adm. Thomas Moorer, with facilities at both ends of the canal and an agreement with the Panamanian government, Hong Kong-based Hutchison Whampoa Ltd. has the ability to all but control the strategic waterway.

"The company has long-term 25-year leases on the ports at each end of the Canal. They are run by the Panama Ports Co., a Hutchison Whampoa subsidiary.

"Last November President Clinton almost let the Chinese cat out of the bag when he appeared to agree that the Chinese firm would be running the canal, but after his staff realized the extent of what he'd revealed, he pulled back, saying that he'd 'misstated this.'

"Asked by a reporter, 'You're not worried about the Chinese controlling the Canal?' Mr. Clinton replied: 'I think the Chinese will, in fact, be bending over backwards to make sure that they run it in a competent and able and fair manner.... I would be very surprised if any adverse consequences flowed from the Chinese running the canal.'...

"Internal documents show that in 1990, Lilly scientists were pressured by corporate executives to alter records on physicians' experiences with Prozac, changing mentions of suicide attempts to 'overdose' and suicidal thoughts to 'depression.'"

"According to the April 22, 1998, intelligence report, an article from the Defense Intelligence Agency intelligence information service headed 'Panama: China Awaits U.S. Departure' stated 'Li Ka-shing, the owner of Hutchison Whampoa Lt. (HW) and Cheung Kong International holdings Ltd. (CK) is planning to take control of Panama Canal operations when the U.S. transfers it to Panama in December 99.'

"'Li is directly connected to Beijing and is willing to use his business influence to further the aims of Chinese government,' the report states."[28]

PR as News

From an interview with John Stauber—editor of PRWatch <www.prwatch.org> and coauthor of *Toxic Sludge Is Good for You!* and *Trust Us, We're Experts!*—conducted by Derrick Jensen:

Stauber: "Half of everything in the news actually originates from a PR firm. If you're a lazy journalist, editor, or news director, it's easy to simply regurgitate the dozens of press releases and stories that come in every day for free from PR firms.

"Remember, the media's primary source of income is the more than $100 billion a year corporations spend on advertising. The PR firms are owned by advertising agencies, so the same companies that are producing billions of dollars in advertising are the ones pitching stories to the news media, cultivating relationships with reporters, and controlling reporters' access to the executives and companies they represent. In fact, of the 160,000 or so PR flacks in the US, maybe a third began their careers as journalists. Who better to manipulate the media than former reporters and editors? Investigative journalist Mark Dowie estimates that professional PR flacks actually outnumber real working journalists in the US."[29]

Prozac

An investigative report by the *Boston Globe* uncovered many unsavory facts about the alarmingly popular antidepressant Prozac and its maker, the pharmaceutical giant Eli Lilly.

"Internal documents show that in 1990, Lilly scientists were pressured by corporate executives to alter records on physicians' experiences with Prozac, changing mentions of suicide attempts to 'overdose' and suicidal thoughts to 'depression.'...

"Lilly's own figures, in reports made available to the *Globe*, indicate that one in 100 previously nonsuicidal patients who took the drug in early clinical trials developed a severe form of anxiety and agitation called akathisia, causing them to attempt or commit suicide during the studies....

"Using figures on Prozac both from Lilly and independent research, however, David Healy, an expert on the brain's serotonin system and director of the North Wales Department of Psychological Medicine at the University of Wales, estimated that 'probably 50,000 people have committed suicide on Prozac since its launch, over and above the number who would have done so if left untreated.'"[30]

Also in the report: A 1984 document from Lilly shows that it knew akathisia appears in a minimum of one in 100 people who take the drug, which means that it must be listed as a "frequent" side effect on Prozac's literature and package inserts. However, in the US literature for Prozac, akathisia is listed as just one of many "infrequent" side effects, and its link to suicide is left unmentioned.

"The patent for the new Prozac or R-fluoxetine (U.S. Patent No. 5,708,035), which Lilly will market after the existing patent expires in 2001, contains a wealth of information about the original Prozac.

"According to the patent, the new Prozac will decrease side effects of the existing Prozac such as headaches, nervousness, anxiety, and insomnia, as well as 'inner restlessness (akathisia), suicidal thoughts and self-mutilation'—the same effect Lilly has contended has not occurred in any substantial way in some 200 lawsuits against it over the past decade. Most of the suits were settled out of court and the terms kept confidential."[31]

Rainforests

According to Philip Stott, a professor of biogeography at London University's School of Oriental and African Studies and the editor of the *Journal of Biogeography*: "One of the simple, but very important, facts is that the rainforests have only been around for between 12,000 and 16,000 years. That sounds like a very long time but, in terms of the history of the earth, it's hardly a pinprick. Before then, there were hardly any rainforests. They are very young. It is just a big mistake that people are making.

"The simple point is that there are now still—despite what humans have done—more rainforests today than there were 12,000 years ago....

"This lungs of the earth business is nonsense; the daftest of all theories. If you want to put something forward which, in a simple sense, shows you what's wrong with all the science they [i.e. most environmentalists] espouse, it's that image of the lungs of the world.

"The simple point is that there are now still—despite what humans have done—more rainforests today than there were 12,000 years ago."

"In fact, because trees fall down and decay, rainforests actually take in slightly more oxygen than they give out. The idea of them soaking up carbon dioxide and giving out oxygen is a myth. It's only fast-growing young trees that actually take up carbon dioxide.

"In terms of world systems, the rainforests are basically irrelevant. World weather is governed by the oceans—that great system of ocean atmospherics. Most things that happen on land are merely blips to the system, basically insignificant."

He adds: "If the rainforest in Amazonia was being destroyed at the rate critics say, it would have all vanished ages ago."[32]

A Russian "Atrocity"

In early March 2000, the world was incensed by news footage showing a pit filled with mutilated bodies. The bodies, we were told, were those of Chechen civilians who had been interrogated, tortured, and killed by Russian troops. The US State Department, European Parliament, and human rights activists went ballistic. More sanctions against Russia were introduced.

Trouble is, the Moscow correspondent for Germany's N-24 Television—the original broadcaster of the footage—admitted that he actually got the film from a Russian journalist, who told him the bodies were of Chechen rebels who had been killed in *combat* against Russian troops. The Russian reporter said he plans to sue N-24.[33]

Sanctions Against Iraq

According to legendary investigative reporter John Pilger: "Under economic sanctions imposed by the United Nations Security Council almost ten years ago, Iraq is denied equipment and expertise to clean up its contaminated battlefields, as Kuwait was cleaned up. At the same time, the Sanctions Committee in New York, dominated by the Americans and British, has blocked or delayed a range of vital equipment, chemotherapy drugs, and even painkillers....

"Britain and the United States are still bombing Iraq almost every day: It is the longest Anglo-American bombing campaign since the second World War, yet, with honorable exceptions, very little appears about it in the British media. Conducted under the cover of 'no-fly zones,' which have no basis in international law, the aircraft, according to Tony Blair, are 'performing vital humanitarian tasks.' The Ministry of Defence in London has a line about 'taking robust action to protect pilots' from Iraqi attacks—yet an internal UN Security Sector report says that, in one five-month period, 41 percent of the victims were civilians in civilian targets: villages, fishing jetties, farmland, and vast, treeless valleys where sheep graze.

"This is a war against the children of Iraq on two fronts: bombing, which in the last year cost the British taxpayer £60 million, and the most ruthless embargo in modern history. According to Unicef, the

United Nations Children's Fund, the death rate of children under five is more than 4,000 a month—that is 4,000 more than would have died before sanctions. That is half a million children dead in eight years"[34]

"That is half a million children dead in eight years."

The US and UK like to claim that exceptions to the sanctions are made for food or medicine, but that is demonstrably false. Among some of the things that the UN sanctions committee has refused to let Iraq have, usually because of a veto by the US and/or the UK: vaccines for tetanus and diphtheria, insulin, epilepsy medication, baby food, rice, incubators, stethoscopes, water purification chemicals, toilet paper, children's clothes, and school notebooks.[35] Remember, sanctions *never* hurt the leaders and other elite of a country; the only people who end up suffering are the common people, with children and the sick bearing the brunt of it.

Textbook Errors

Earl Lee's article, "School Textbooks: Unpopular History vs. Cherished Mythology?" discusses many things that are wrong with textbooks. Add to the list that they are also shot through with errors. The Textbook League and other watchdogs have found an alarming number of mistakes in the books that kids are supposed to be learning from. Among the current mistakes pointed out by a *Reader's Digest* article: the Korean War ended when Truman dropped the atomic bomb; Napoleon was victorious at Waterloo; Corpernicus thought the earth was at the center of the Solar System; Columbus sailed in 1942; an incorrect definition of "perimeter;" incorrect classifications of landforms; and tons of math errors. Also, they found textbooks which said "that Richard Nixon resigned rather than face impeachment by the Senate (it was the House), that fish have scales so they won't leak (huh?), that the nose controls the sense of smell (it's the brain), that Jimmy Carter was the first Democratic President since Harry Truman (what about Kennedy and Johnson?)." Even when textbook publishers are alerted, the mistakes often stay in the books in subsequent editions.[36]

TWA 800 Eyewitnesses

From a full-page ad[37] placed in the *Washington Times* (Aug 15, 2000) by the TWA 800 Eyewitness Alliance:

"Eyewitness Michael Wire, described by the CIA as a key eyewitness, saw what he at first thought was a 'cheap firework' ascending from behind a house near the beach, arching over, speeding out to sea, and culminating in an explosion so powerful that it shook a 70-ton bridge on which he was standing."

"Eyewitness Dwight Brumley, an excellent witness according to the CIA, was in a plane going north when he noticed a fast-moving light at a lower altitude also going north. Its flight ended with two explosions a short distance ahead. He said another passenger told him he had seen the cabin lights of eastbound TWA 800 before the explosion."

"Eyewitness Paul Angelides, an engineer, from the deck of his beach house saw a red glowing object quite high in the sky. At first it moved slowly, leaving a short white smoke trail, but it picked up speed, streaking out to sea. He lost sight of it when it was about ten degrees above the horizon. He then saw a series of flashes followed by a fireball falling into the ocean. He heard a prolonged boom like thunder followed by three loud bursts of sound, the last so long that it shook the house."

"Eyewitness Maj. Frederick Meyer was in an Air Force National Guard helicopter when he saw a streak of light 10 or 15 miles away. He lost it for about a second, and then further to the left he saw two bright, white explosions, which he identified as ordnance, followed by a fuel explosion that was bright orange."

The independent TWA Flight Investigation Website contains all 755 witness statements taken by the FBI.[38] Below are just a few of the highlights they selected:

Witness 8: "saw a red object flying upward." "described the object as a flare"..."but that it was actually much bigger than any flare he had ever seen." "As the 'flare' lifted into the sky he next saw a big explosion of a large red color."

Witness 72: "She thought it was a flare." "When she first observed the object, it appeared cylindrical in shape and was rising up in an arc like direction." "The red streak was leaving a light gray smoke trail."

Witness 73: Watched the aircraft for approximately 10 seconds. She then noticed a "contrail that appeared to come from an object which was flying toward the plane she was watching." "This object approached the aircraft from behind." Described the "contrail as a long elongated tail." "She replied that she believed that she witnessed a missile, which was fired from a boat which was located somewhere on the Atlantic Ocean."

Witness 88: "observed what he thought was a firework ascending into the sky." "originally felt this firework emanated form the shoreline." "this object which was ascending left a wispy white smoke trail." "observed an airplane come into the field of view." "the object ran into the airplane....and then exploded."

Witness 108: "in southwest he saw what appeared to be a flare rise up from below the tree line." "rising at a 65 degree angle at a steady speed." "the flare left behind a smoke trail which was bluish/gray in color." "The flare rose upward and then arced downward." "the flare descended from the arc for approximately one second and exploded into an orange ball."

Witness 145: "stated that she saw a plane and noticed an object spiraling towards the plane." "The object, which she saw for about one second, had a glow at the end of it and a grey/white smoke trail." "she saw the object hit the plane."

Witness 150: "noticed an unusual object traveling at high speed from north to south." "described the object as cylindrical, tubular and bullet shaped. Having no apparent wings, except perhaps, a small vertical shape at the rear." "moved more quickly than any plane." "almost flat trajectory." "she followed the object for 2 or 3 seconds when she then noticed a large commercial airliner which appeared to be traveling at the same altitude." "the object headed toward the side of the plane."

Witness 151: "he described what he thought was a flare." "he described the flare as a white wispy trail that went straight up." "he followed the flare for about 5 seconds, then the flare turned into an orange burst."

"Witness 465: 'saw a reddish/orange object projecting in an upward southern position.' 'the object looked like a flare.' 'maintained a view of the object until he saw an explosion in the air.'"

Witness 174: "saw a skyrocket type object streak up into the night sky from behind Sheffield Island. The skyrocket had an orange contrail which had a continuous brightness." "A few seconds later, after the skyrocket contrail disappeared, he saw a large orange fireball appear."

Witness 465: "saw a reddish/orange object projecting in an upward southern position." "the object looked like a flare." "maintained a view of the object until he saw an explosion in the air."

Witness 493: "saw a firework/rocket go up from his car." "said the rocket was orange in color and had fire coming from its tail. He realized it was not a firework but a rocket. He saw the plane explode."

Witness 539: Witness was taking photographs over the ocean. When they were developed she "noticed a small white streak." The FBI requested the negatives and "contacted her three days later to inform her that the negative was clear and there was nothing wrong with her camera."

Witness 550: saw "a plane coming from the west to east and then what looked like a 'smaller' plane coming from the northeast on a dead course toward the nose of the larger plane."

UFOs and Astronauts

It's widely believed that astronauts have never seen UFOs, even though they would be the most likely people to have encountered inexplicable crafts. Almost all astronauts publicly claim that they and their colleagues have never seen UFOs. But that's not entirely true. As Jim Marrs reveals: "According to transcripts of the technical debriefing following the Apollo 11 mission, astronauts [Neil] Armstrong, Edwin 'Buzz' Aldrin and Michael Collins told of an encounter with a large cylindrical UFO even before reaching the Moon. Aldrin said, 'The first unusual thing that we saw I guess was one day out or pretty close to the Moon. It had a sizable dimension to it.' Aldrin said the Apollo crew at first thought the object was the Saturn 4 booster rocket (S-IVB); but, he added, 'We called the ground and were told the S-IVB was 6,000 miles away.' Aldrin described the UFO as a cylinder, while Armstrong said it was 'really two rings. Two connected rings.' Collins also said it appeared to be a hollow, tumbling cylinder. He added, 'It was a hollow cylinder. But then you could change the focus on the sextant and it would be replaced by this open-book shape. It was really weird.'

"Even more strange was the experience of Aldrin and Armstrong, after they reached the Moon. According to an Associated Press story of July 20, 1969 (my file copy is from the *San Bernardino Sun-Telegram*), the astronauts sighted eerie lights inside a crater near the point on the Moon where their lunar lander was due to touch down the next day.

"On their first sweep around the Moon, Armstrong described a mysterious bright light on the inner wall of the crater Aristarchus, located north of their flight path. 'It seems to have a slight amount of fluorescence to it. The area in the crater is quite bright,' he reported.

"'That area is definitely brighter than anything else I can see. There doesn't appear to be any color involved in it...It looks like an eerie sight,' confirmed Aldrin."[39]

The year 2000 saw the publication of *Leap of Faith: An Astronaut's Journey into the Unknown* (HarperCollins), by Mercury 7 astronaut Gordon Cooper. Again, Jim Marrs comments: "Cooper first puts to rest the long-repeated rumor that he observed UFOs while orbiting in his Mercury capsule. 'I saw *no* UFOs from space,' he states succinctly (emphasis in the original). But he saw plenty of UFOs from Earth, beginning in 1951 when he flew F-86 Sabrejets against Russian MIGs in unpublicized Cold War encounters.

"After being scrambled to intercept what was believed to be a Soviet incursion of allied air space, Cooper reported, 'We reached our maximum ceiling of around 45,000 feet, and they were still way above us, and traveling much faster. I could see that they weren't balloons or MIGs or like *any* aircraft I had ever seen before. They were metallic silver and saucer-shaped. We couldn't get close enough to form any idea of their size; they were just too high.

"'For the next two or three days the saucers passed over the base daily.'...

"On May 3, 1957, Cooper was a captain in charge of a film crew within the Air Force's Experimental Flight Test Engineering Division at Edwards Air Force Base. His crew reported that while they were filming the landing of a test plane that morning, a 'strange' silver saucer-shaped craft flew over them, hovered and landed about 50 yards away after extending three landing gear. The crew filmed the entire event."[40]

Violent Behavior

One of our few self-deprecating cultural myths is that humans are the only animal that kills for fun, pleasure, sport, etc. Solid evidence that this is hogwash has existed at least since January 1974, when members of Jane Goodall's research team in Tanzania watched a group of eight chimpanzees gather, purposely walk out of their territory and into that of another chimp community, and proceed to brutalize a lone male they found in a tree. One chimp held him down while the others savagely beat him almost to death for ten minutes. Having had their fun, the chimps left. Their victim crawled away and was never seen again.[41]

On a related note, humans don't have a monopoly on rape either. Males of several species—including primates (especially orangutans), elephant seals, scorpion flies, and several types of duck—have routinely been observed violently forcing themselves on females who have expressed no interest in mating with them.[42]

The World Economy

According to a paper coauthored by Russell C. Kick—a professor of MIS (management information systems) and head of the e-commerce program at National University, as well as the father of this book's editor—and G.A. Swanson—a professor of accounting at Tennessee Technological University:

"The world's economic activities are more centrally controlled and more overwhelmingly huge than most people realize. A new supranational system, a product of the information and financial revolutions, has come into existence relatively suddenly. Over $1.4 *trillion* daily—equivalent to over $250 for every man, woman, and child on Earth—is moved by real-time computer systems into the seamless worldwide electronic financial marketplace solely for the purpose of speculation. On the other hand, only about $20 billion daily—representing 1.5 percent of the speculative funds—is employed for actual economic trade. For every $1 that is put into economic trade, $66 are put into high-risk speculation. Less than three decades ago, the ratio of speculation to trade was 4 to 1. When economic trade transactions are deducted from economic and financial transactions, what remains is the reality of speculative transactions creating debt for nations while amassing tremendous hordes of wealth for the few....

"The Society for Worldwide Interbank Financial Telecommunications (SWIFT), the primary system for sending international payments, was installed in 1973. A cooperative owned by over 2,200 banks worldwide, including 150 from the US, it operates in 190 countries with the US accounting for more usage than any other nation. Over 7,000 institutions worldwide use SWIFT 24 hours a day, seven days a week.

"SWIFT is technically a message system, rather than an Electronic Funds Transfer system (EFTS). However, for many purposes it is considered an EFTS because it provides the instructions to move money's ownership from bank to bank around the planet. Its activities are crucial. Messages from SWIFT instruct a bank to make payment, and the bank then transfers from one account to another on its books. Approximately $5 trillion was transferred *every day* during 1999, and annual message volumes rose from 3.2 million in 1977 to 604 million in 1995 to over a billion in 1999.

"For every $1 that is put into economic trade, $66 are put into high-risk speculation."

"The Clearing House for Interbank Payments Systems (CHIPS) is the central clearing system in the United States for international transactions, handling over 95 percent of all dollar payments in the world. It is an online, electronic payment system that transfers funds and settles transactions in US dollars, the common currency of international business. CHIPS—which is privately owned and operated by its member banks—began operations in 1970. As of July 2000, there were 80 CHIPS participants representing financial institutions from over 20 countries.

"CHIPS is the focal point and facilitator of the global economy and world financial marketplace. In 1997 CHIPS handled, on the average, $1.4 trillion daily, an amount equal to approximately 22 percent of the United States' money supply. On November 28 of that year, CHIPS set a single-day record by processing over $2.2 trillion. The amount of money processed dipped a little in the two subsequent years, but the amounts for 2000 are back at 1997 levels."[43]

World Hunger

World hunger is not caused by the inability of the earth to provide enough food for the teeming billions. Instead, it is caused by economic and political power structures.

"Perhaps one of the most fallacious myths propagated by Green Revolution advocates is the assertion that high-yielding varieties [of food crops] have reduced the acreage under cultivation, therefore preserving millions of hectares of biodiversity....

"A study comparing traditional polycultures with industrial monocultures shows that a polyculture system can produce 100 units of food from 5 units of input, whereas an industrial system requires 300 units of input to produce the same 100 units. The 295 units of wasted inputs could have provided 5,000 units of additional food. Thus the industrial system leads to a decline of 5,900 units of food. This is a recipe for starving people, not for feeding them."[44]

According to another source: "Japan, Hong Kong and Singapore are extremely densely populated, but do not suffer from any shortage of food. In fact, heavily industrialized Japan, where farmland is at a premium, nevertheless produces as much rice as Burma, which is twice as large and entirely rural, while France produces more wheat than Argentina and Australia combined. Meanwhile, Cuba, Honduras and Angola have food shortages but have plenty of arable land....

"In Honduras, multinational corporations own most of the arable land and use it to raise export crops. In Cuba, Castro imposes a communist-style agricultural system on his society, fearing that if farmers were allowed to freely market their food it would weaken his control....

"During the famine in Ethiopia in the mid-1980s, Western countries contributed vast amounts of food. Rock musicians held Food-Aid concerts and produced a hit song to raise funds for relief. The effort

World hunger is not caused by the inability of the earth to provide enough food for the teeming billions.

seemed to go for nothing—food rotted on the wharves as people continued to starve. It became clear that the Ethiopian government was using starvation to break the Eritrean insurgency."[45] It should also be noted that gangs in developing countries often steal entire shipments of food sent as relief.[46]

Endnotes

1. Friedman, John. (2000). "Chase's historical ledger." *The Nation*, Oct. 9. **2.** Steiner, Stan. (1984). "Cowboy: The enduring myth of the wild West." *Natural History*, Feb, pp 84-8. **3.** Shiva, Vandana. (2000). *Stolen harvest: The hijacking of the global food supply*. Cambridge, MA: South End Press, pp 79-80. **4.** Cloud, Cam. (1999). *Acid trips and chemistry*. Berkeley, CA: Ronin Publishing, pp 38-9 **5.** Dendrite alert, August 23, 2000. <www.mindfreedom.org> **6.** Unsigned. (2000). "Police drug bust secrets" (interview with Bruce Margolin). *Ectacy: Journal of Divine Experience* #3, p 33. **7.** Rutter, Virginia. (1996). "Who stole fertility?" *Psychology Today*, March/April, p 48-9. **8.** Boyles, Salynn. (1998). "Study finds underwear choice makes no difference." *Impotence & Male Health Weekly Plus*, Dec 28. **9.** Dowie, Mark. (1977). "Pinto madness." *Mother Jones*, Sept/Oct. <www.motherjones.com/mother_jones/SO77/dowie.html>. The figures come directly from Ford's internal memorandum, "Fatalities Associated with Crash-Induced Fuel Leakage and Fires." You can view it online at <www.motherjones.com/mother_jones/SO77/death.html>. **10.** International Center for Technology Assessment. (1988). "The real price of gasoline." <www.icta.org/projects/trans/> **11.** Smith, Guy. (2000). *Gun facts*, version 2.1. Self-published, p 26. Available at <members.home.net/guys/guns.html>. **12.** *Ibid.*, p 27. **13.** *Ibid*, p 18. **14.** Marrs, Jim. (2000). "A tale of three countries: A glimpse into our future?" AlienZoo Website, Aug 31. <www.alienzoo.com/features/m/200008310001.cfm>. **15.** Gun Owners of America. (1999). "Firearms fact-sheet, 1999." <www.gunowners.org>. **16.** *Ibid.* **17.** Sneider, Jaime. (2000). "Calling shots for the march." *Washington Times*, May 10. **18.** Jacoby, Jeff. (2000). "The media's anti-gun bias." *Boston Globe*, Jan. 17. **19.** *Ibid.* **20.** *Op cit.*, Gun Owners of America. **21.** Rodriguez, Paul M. (2000). "U.N. Now Fears Underpopulation." *Insight on the News*, May 15, p 6. **22.** Singer, Max. (1999). "Demographics: The population surprise." *Atlantic Monthly*, August, p 22. **23.** McGovern, Celeste. (2000). "The bomb that didn't explode." *Alberta Report*, Feb 28, p 39. **24.** *Ibid.* **25.** *Ibid* **26.** Easterbrook, Gregg. (1999). "Reproductivity: Overpopulation is no problem—in the long run." *New Republic*, Oct 11. **27.** *Op cit.*, Singer. **28.** Unsigned. (2000). "Is China in control of the Panama Canal?" NewsMax, April 5. <www.newsmax.com/articles/?a=2000/4/5/80227> **29.** Jensen, Derrick. "War on Truth: The Secret Battle for the American Mind." *The Sun*, no date. <www.ratical.org/ratville/PRcorrupt.html>. **30.** Garnett, Leah R. (2000). "Reports link Prozac, suicide." *Tampa Tribune*, May 9. **31.** *Ibid.* **32.** Wigmore, Barry. (2000). "Eco-scientists deny Amazon's in danger." *New York Post*, May 30. <www.nypost.com/05302000/4951.htm> **33.** Shrurenko, Igor. (2000). "War crimes—or faked 'news'?" *News & Observer*, March 10. **34.** Pilger, John. (2000). "Squeezed to death." *The Guardian*, March 4. **35.** The Mariam Appeal Website <www.mariamappeal.com>, referencing Simons, Geoff. (1988). *The scourging of Iraq: Sanctions, law and natural justice* (second edition). London: Macmillan. **36.** Ecenbarger, William. (2000). "Textbooks that don't make the grade." *Reader's Digest*, September, pp 165-70. **37.** The ad can be viewed at <twa800.com/images/times-8-15-00.gif> **38.** <twa800.com/witnesscd/witnesscd.htm> **39.** Marrs, Jim. (2000). "Something on the Moon beyond rocks and dust." AlienZoo Website, <www.alienzoo.com/features/m/200003020001.cfm>. **40.** Marrs, Jim. (2000). "Who says astronauts have never seen UFOs?" AlienZoo Website, Aug 10. <www.alienzoo.com/features/m/200008100001.cfm>. **41.** Wrangham, Richard & Dale Peterson. (1996). *Demonic males: Apes and the origins of human violence*. New York: Houghton-Mifflin. **42.** *Ibid.* **43.** Kick, Russell C., Ph.D. & G.A. Swanson, Ph.D. "A World on the edge: Is the new supranational system propelling the world towards socioeconomic chaos?" **44.** *Op cit.*, Shiva, p 13. **45.** Kirchner, Paul. (1995). *Everything you know is wrong*. Los Angeles: General Publishing Group, pp 123-4 **46.** *Ibid.*

The News Media and Other Manipulators

A Mathematician Reads the Newspaper by John Allen Paulos
In this follow-up to his classic *Innumeracy: Mathematical Illiteracy and Its Consequences*, mathematician John Allen Paulos uses verve and short, punchy chapters to demonstrate how numbers are used to mislead, beguile, and otherwise influence us. Such diverse topics as voting, economic forecasts, war casualties, various biases, SAT scores, death rates, health risks, ads, fads, circulation figures, calories, sports scores, religion, and frequency of reporting are affected by facile analogies, interactive variables, inverted pyramid structures, randomness, benchmark estimates, ambiguity, regression, correlation, S-curves, self-reference, scale, anecdotes versus statistics, and other such things. Paulos reveals that the number of cellphone users who developed brain tumors and the number of women with breast implants who developed connective tissue disorders don't appear to be any higher than would normally be expected in any population of people. He also talks about a 1993 poll which showed that a quarter of the population doubted the reality of the Holocaust. However, it was later revealed that the question was confusingly worded as a double negative. When it was later asked with unambiguous phrasing, the number of people who thought it was possible that the Holocaust never happened was one percent.

Quote: "It is by turns amusing and depressing to track the way descriptions of numerical relations depend on their authors' intentions. To make a quantity appear large, for example, a consumer group, political group, or business advertiser might stress a linear measure of its size. To make it appear small, it might stress its volume. Thus, although a single tower of nickels stretching from sea level to the height of Mount Everest would contains more than four million coins, you can easily verify that this pile would fit comfortably in a cubicle box about 6 feet to a side. And spacious cubicle apartments (20 feet on a side) for every human being on Earth could fit comfortably into the Grand Canyon. By contrast, if all living humans were placed end to end, they would extend to the moon and back more than eight times." [p 79]

Anchor Books/Doubleday (Bantam Doubleday Dell) • 1995 •
212 pp • softcover • $12.95 • ISBN 0-385-48254-X •
<www.randomhouse.com/anchor/>

Lies We Live By: Defeating Double-Talk and Deception in Advertising, Politics, and the Media by Carl Hausman
Lies We Live By is presented as a practical toolkit for beefing up your bullshit detector. Journalism professor Carl Hausman starts off by showing how to spot deceptions presented through words, numbers, or graphs and other visuals. He then takes a chapter to look at lies, exaggerations, and half-truths in each of ten areas that affect us to some degree on a day-to-day basis: government, politics, the media, finance, retail stores, car sales, phone rates, junk mail, Net scams, and sports rankings. There's also a lengthy section providing lists with guidelines for how to read a newspaper, watch TV news, makes sense out of a poll, evaluate a "scientific breakthrough," and otherwise sift through nonsense and hype. With zippy writing and a sense of humor (the chapter on junk mail is titled, "You May Already Be a Sucker!"), Hausman brings the fight against lies to the workaday world.

Lies We Live By is presented as a practical toolkit for beefing up your bullshit detector.

Quote: "Reaction shots are used in TV news to cover edits. The on-the-scene interview is usually done with one camera, and the shots of the reporter nodding or re-asking the question are taken later, sometimes even after the subject of the interview has left. Sometimes reporters spruce up their original questions to make them appear more aggressive, to indicate that they forcibly extracted information from a villain, when that information was, in reality, offered up quite willingly." [p 129]

Quote: "One of the most heavily advertised '10-10' numbers offers 99 cents for calls up to twenty minutes. And that's actually a good buy under certain circumstances. But there's a Veiled Variable lurking in the circuits. The 99-cent charge is a blanket price, you pay 99 cents regardless of whether you talk for one minute or nineteen. So a one-minute call—a connection, perhaps, to somebody's answering machine—is going to cost you roughly a dollar a minute." [p 97]

Routledge • 2000 • 229 pp • hardcover • $24.95 •
ISBN 0-415-92280-1 • <www.routledge.com>

How to Lie with Maps (second edition) by Mark Monmonier

A map must inherently lie to some degree because it can never completely represent the reality of the terrain it is purporting to show. But a lot of maps lie more than they need to, and sometimes they lie for specific reasons, whether an unconscious bias or a Machiavellian manipulation. They aren't as obvious as newspaper articles or corporate press releases, but maps are another tool in the arsenal of propagandists. In this updated version of the classic book on the subject, a distinguished professor of geography at Syracuse looks at the myriad ways maps mislead.

If you look strictly at black men *of college age* (18 to 24), you'll find that almost three times as many are in college as are in prison.

Scale, symbols, projection, shading, color, simplification, smoothing, and many other aspects of maps can intentionally or unintentionally cause problems. Maps in advertisements can make a store or office look as conveniently located and easy-to-find as possible. Maps are often used for manipulation in city/regional planning, giving the illusion that a proposed project wouldn't negatively affect its surroundings. Two possible ways to use a map for political purposes are to display certain countries/areas as part of another country or at least as a disputed territory, and to use bold arrows to "dramatize an attack across a border, exaggerate a concentration of troops, and perhaps even justify a 'pre-emptive strike.'" Epidemiological maps showing clusters of illnesses can be partitioned in various ways to inflate or minimize the appearance of a pandemic. Color is an emotionally manipulative tool, and features that a cartographer wants you to like may be colored blue or red, while features you're not supposed to like may be in a displeasing hue, such as orange or greenish-yellow.

Quote: "No projection has been as abused in the pursuit of size distortion as that devised by sixteenth-century atlas publisher and cartographer Gerardus Mercator. Designed specifically to aid navigators, the Mercator projection vastly enlarges poleward areas so that straight lines can serve as *loxodomes*, or *rhumb lines*—that is, lines of constant geographic direction.... Yet for decades the John Birch Society and other political groups intimidated by Communist ideology and Stalinist atrocities have reveled in the Mercator's cartographic enhancement of the Soviet Union. Birch Society lecturers warning of the Red menace commonly shared the stage with a massive Mercator map of the world with China and Russia printed in provocative, symbolically rich red...." [pp 94-6]

Quote: "...American maps often omit information that might embarrass industrial polluters or local officials.... The 1946 map [of Love Canal, New York] which shows the canal as a long, straight vertical feature, fails to indicate use of the canal since 1942 as a dump for chemical waste. The 1980 map not only shows no trace of the filled-in canal but ignores the area's tragic history..." [p 121]

The University of Chicago Press • 1996 • 209 pp • softcover • $15 • ISBN 0-226-53421-9 • <www.press.uchicago.edu>

Politricks

Fortunate Son: George W. Bush and the Making of an American President by J.H. Hatfield

Fortunate Son, a biography/exposé of George W. Bush, was originally published by St. Martin's Press, a large corporate publisher, in October 1999. Its most controversial part was its afterword, which, based on three unnamed sources, said that Shrub "had been arrested for cocaine possession in 1972 but had his record expunged after his father arranged for him to perform community service." Almost 90,000 copies had been shipped to bookstores when St. Martin's made the almost unheard-of move of *recalling* the book and turning it into "furnace fodder," to quote the company's own press release. Luckily, whatever scared the shit out of that corporate publishing house so badly that they burned their own book, it didn't rattle Soft Skull Press. A highly independent publisher, Soft Skull saw to it that not only was the book republished, but their edition includes even more damaging information than the original.

Now you can read all about the allegations of coke use, Shrub's arrests during his Yale days, his defense of branding pledges at the fraternity that he headed, getting out of service in Vietnam, his disastrous oil business, his born-again conversion, his role as hatchet man in his father's presidential campaigns, his engineering of a sweet government deal for a small oil company that hired him as a "consultant," his fishy stock selling, his gubernatorial campaign against Ann Richards, his real record as governor, his earnings of almost $15 million on a $606,000 investment, his penchant for executing people, his shaky record on crime, his allegiance to the Christian right, the first stages of his run for President in 2000, and more.

Quote: "Bush, who vowed to make significant strides in increasing the number of minority appointments to state boards and commissions as governor, actually decreased minority choices by 15 percent, compared to his predecessor's tenure in office....

"Allegations of racial prejudice by the governor were raised at the end of his first term in office when a report was issued noting that of the fourteen pardons he granted, all but one (a Hispanic convicted of a 1961 burglary) had been given to white males." [pp 211-2]

Quote: "In 1998, before departing on a high-profile trip to the Middle East, Bush sophomorically joked with U.S. reporters that the first thing he would say to his hosts in Israel would be that they were all 'going to hell.'" [p 3 of photo insert]

Quote: "When President Clinton's extramarital affairs made headlines in in 1998, Bush announced—without being asked by the media—that he'd been faithful to Laura, his wife of more than twenty years. He had also repeatedly recited his story of a 'young and irresponsible' early life of excessive drinking followed by sobriety at age forty. Unlike drinking and infidelity, cocaine use is illegal and

Bush testily refused to say whether he had experimented with the drug, stating at each campaign appearance that he was not going to participate in the 'politics of personal destruction.'" [p 300]

Soft Skull Press • 2000 • 414 pp • softcover • $16.50 •
ISBN 1-887128-50-6 • <www.softskull.com>

The Social Fabrication

Don't Believe the Hype: Fighting Cultural Misinformation About African-Americans by Farai Chideya

We're constantly bombarded with statements about African Americans that are at best misleading, and at worst, simply wrong. We're also not told some important facts. In *Don't Believe the Hype*, Farai Chideya—a syndicated columnist and the anchor of *Pure Oxygen* (on Oprah Winfey's Oxygen Channel)—aims to correct the situation. She shows that, although the picture isn't exactly rosy and sunny, neither is it nearly as bleak as we've been led to believe. A good example is the oft-stated fact that there are more black men in prison than in college. Unfortunately, if you're comparing both groups as a whole, this is true, but it's disingenuous. If you look strictly at black men *of college age* (18 to 24), you'll find that almost three times as many are in college as are in prison.

Similarly, it's a fact that in 1990 67 percent of black children were born out of wedlock, while 20 percent of white children were. But the statistic you're not likely to hear is that the gap is narrowing: "Between 1980 and 1990, the birth rate for white unmarried women climbed nearly 100 percent, while the black rate rose by only 12 percent." And although a black woman is twice as likely to have an abortion as a white woman, black teenagers are *less* likely to have abortions than their white counterparts.

There is also unmitigated good news. The percentage of welfare recipients who are African American has fallen since 1973. Also since that year, high school graduation rates for black students have increased dramatically. And, "The number of black elected officials at all levels of government rose from fewer than 300 in 1965 to more than 8,000 by January 1993."

Chideya also points out underreported facts that are troubling. No African Americans received doctorates in cell biology, applied math, physics, or comparative literature in 1992. Although racial segregation in housing is sometimes declared to be a class issue, rather than a racial issue, some stats put this in doubt: "African-Americans earning over $50,000 per year are more likely to be segregated than an Hispanic-American earning just $2,500 per year."

Chideya brings up lots of good points and overlooked stats, with the book's main problem being that is was published in early 1995 and desperately needs updating. (The author has told me that she's preparing a new edition, but her publisher is ambiguous about when or if it will be released.)

Quote: "Northwestern University professor Robert Entman found that black experts only showed up as experts in fifteen of 2,000 minutes not specifically covering racial issues. (They were half of the experts on race-based stories.)" [p 4]

Quote: "One of the biggest 'affirmative action' programs on campus is not for minorities but for 'legacies'—the privileged children of alumni. A 1992 study by the U.S. Department of Education (looking into complaints by Asian-Americans that they were being rejected for less-qualified whites) uncovered some unexpected information. Children of alumni, as well as athletes, consistently received 'special preference' over other applicants at some of the nation's top schools, including Harvard, Yale, and Stanford. While the average combined SAT score of Harvard legacies was thirty-five points lower than for all those admitted, legacies were more than twice as likely to get in." [p 83]

Quote: "Team leadership positions like football quarterback are overwhelmingly white. In 1990, for example, 93 percent of NFL quarterbacks were white, in a league where 60 percent of all players were black. That was an improvement from 1983, when the figure was an astonishing 99 percent."

Plume (Penguin) • 1995 • 277 pp • softcover • $13 •
ISBN 0-452-27096-0 • <www.penguinputnam.com>

The Myths That Divide Us: How Lies Have Poisoned American Race Relations by John Perazzo

John Perazzo has concocted one bitter pill with regard to race relations. Luckily, he made the pill out of high-quality ingredients known as "facts." A lot of people won't like what he has to say, but it'll be hard to refute him on the basis of fact rather than ideology and name-calling. Perazzo seems to genuinely desire peaceful relations between black and white people, but he's disturbed by the direction the civil rights movement has taken since the death of Martin Luther King Jr. Whereas King wanted a color-blind society, he says, today's black leaders are divisive and bitter; they race-bait, blame, and tell lies, thus betraying King's vision of a civil rights movement.

After an introductory chapter, he shows that some prominent African Americans fan the flames of racial hatred in numerous ways, from contending that white people's attitudes are no better now than during the days of slavery, all the way to supporting the random killing of white people (*a la* Sister Souljah and Amiri Baraka, aka LeRoi Jones). From there, Perazzo discloses startling facts about black-on-black crimes, black-on-white hate crimes, the Rodney King incident and the resulting riots, brutality of black cops towards whites and Hispanics, hate crime hoaxes (especially Tawana Brawley), institutional racism, affirmative action, Afrocentrism, Africa, preferential policies, the fates of other minorities in America, the slave trade, black church burnings, and the largely unacknowledged strides that African Americans as a group have made since the 1950s.

Perazzo presents numerous surprising facts that counter prevailing opinion. Despite the collective blame for slavery that is sometimes forced on the white people of America, the majority of whites never owned slaves, and in 1830 more than 3,500 free blacks owned slaves. For every white man who rapes a black woman, over 100 black men rape white women. America's top law schools admit African American students at 17.5 times the rate that they would if the system were color-blind. Despite the fact that Africa has abundant natural resources—including 50 percent of the world's gold, eight percent of its petroleum, and most of its diamonds—the entire continent's Gross Domestic Product is equal to that of tiny Belgium, and 95 percent of black Africa's population lives in poverty. While the people starve, millions of acres of farmland go unused. This is because of the political tyrants and guerrilla gangs that run the countries.

Quote: "Nor do many people realize that [Rodney] King had two black companions in his car on that fateful night, both of whom cooperated with the police, and neither of whom was harmed. Shortly after the incident, in fact, King himself expressed his belief that race had *not* been a factor in the treatment he had received—a most significant statement that journalists chose to *ignore*. (Of course, King would later change his story and claim that the officers had used racial epithets against him during the beating.)" [p 115]

Quote: "Those who criticize the West for its historical participation in the transatlantic slave trade rarely mention that the abolition of slavery was a uniquely Western idea originating in eighteenth-century Great Britain, the largest slave-trading nation of its time.... Thus after thousands of years during which people everywhere had simply accepted slavery as a natural part of the social order, it was eradicated from the entire Western hemisphere in less than a single century." [pp 372-3]

Quote: "While there is no white-ruled nation on earth today where slavery is considered anything but an abomination, there are currently hundreds of thousands of black slaves held captive in several African countries.... For even the slightest infractions, these slaves [in Mauritania] are subjected to beatings, denial of food, or prolonged exposure to the sun with their hands and feet bound together." For serious infractions, the slave's genitals are scorched with hot coals, or insects are put into their ears, which are then sealed. [pp 343-4]

Quote: "In 1995 the yearly median income of black families nationwide rose by 3.6 percent, far more than the 2.2 percent gain of white families. Between 1993 and 1996, black family incomes rose by 13.4 percent, while white earnings grew by just 5 percent. In fact, blacks are the only racial or ethnic group whose current, inflation-adjusted income exceeds its 1989 level." [p 450]

World Studies Books • 1999 • 630 pp • softcover • $24 •
ISBN 0-9651268-1-1 • 1858 Pleasantville Rd, Suite 131,
Briarcliff Manor, NY 10510

Who Stole Feminism?: How Women Have Betrayed Women
by Christina Hoff Sommers

Almost all attacks against feminism, not surprisingly, come from the right. But Christina Hoff Sommers is herself a feminist, which makes her a spy in the house of estrogen. Sommers draws some crucial distinctions within feminism, though. The feminists of the 1800s and early 1900s were the admirable "classically liberal feminists," who based their ideas on the principles of the Enlightenment and fought to get women the rights men took for granted. The New feminists, or "gender feminists," as Sommers calls them, are "divisive," "gynocentric," and "chronically offended." They don't think of women and men as equal members of the human race working for the same goals; rather, women are a constantly attacked, suppressed class who must be hostile to the brutal, selfish patriarchal system that victimizes them.

Although several chapters show how intolerant the gender feminists are and how they've taken over academia to the detriment of all other viewpoints, the book's most powerful parts are the ones that utterly destroy the supposed facts that are touted by mainstream feminism. In fact, Sommers opens the book by immediately showing one claim to be outright false. The statistic that 150,000 women and girls die of anorexia each year in the US has become accepted wisdom after being trumpeted by Gloria Steinem, Naomi Wolf, and Ann Landers, among others. Sommers decided to do what none of them did—actually check the facts behind this "hidden holocaust" against females. She finally traced it back to the American Anorexia and Bulimia Association. She personally talked to the group's president, who flatly said that they had been misquoted. The statistic came from a newsletter they published in 1985 which said that 150,000 to 200,000 females *suffer* from the disorder. Government stats show that, in reality, around 100 females die each year from anorexia. Of course even one death from self-starvation is upsetting, but something that causes 100 deaths annually is hardly comparable to something that cause 150,000 deaths annually.

From there, Sommers plows through the other commonly-quoted "facts" and "figures" that mainstream feminism uses. She eviscerates the two heavily-flawed, hard-to-find studies that are the source for the idea that girls have their self-esteem crushed at school. Among the other things she reveals regarding the claims of feminism: Domestic abuse of pregnant women is not responsible for more birth defects than all other causes combined; Super Bowl Sunday is not "the biggest day of the year for violence against women;" the phrase "rule of thumb" did not originate because of an English law that allowed men to beat their wives with a stick no bigger around than their thumb; the claim that one of four women will be raped is undoubtedly way too high; the idea of a "backlash" (as espoused by Susan Faludi and Naomi Wolf) is unfounded; and 40 percent of women do not suffer from severe depression.

Sommers looks at the claims of domestic abuse, noting that the guesstimates range from the Department of Justice's figure of 626,000 women (married and single) per year to 18 million married women per year (cited by the National Coalition Against Domestic Violence). Furthermore, few outlets are willing to relay the fact that women are physically abusive (in minor and major ways) towards their partners at a rate equal to men. And when it comes to rates of psychological abuse against women, some statistics include heated exchanges between couples. (For more of Sommers' work, be sure to read her second book, *The War Against Boys: How Misguided Feminism Is Harming Our Young Men* (Simon & Schuster, 2000).)

> Of course even one death from self-starvation is upsetting, but something that causes 100 deaths annually is hardly comparable to something that cause 150,000 deaths annually.

Quote: "The Wellesley study [on self-esteem] gives lots of attention to how girls are behind in math and science, though the math and science test differentials are small compared to large differentials favoring girls in reading and writing....

"Almost twice as many girls as boys participate in student government, band and orchestra, and drama or service clubs. More girls work on the school newspapers and yearbooks. More are members of honor and service societies. Boys far outnumber girls in sports, but that gap is narrowing each year." Boys are also more likely to cut classes, not do homework, and drop out of high school. Although girls are more likely to *attempt* suicide, boys are equally more likely to actually kill themselves. [pp 160-1]

Quote: "Recently several male students at Vassar were falsely accused of date rape. After their innocence was established, the assistant dean of students, Catherine Comins, said of their ordeal: 'They have a lot of pain, but it is not a pain that I would have necessarily spared them. I think it ideally initiates a process of self-exploration. "How do I see women?" "If I did not violate her, could I have?" "Do I have the potential to do to her what they say I did?" These are good questions.' Dean Comins clearly feels justified in trumping the common law principle 'presumed innocent until proven guilty' by a new feminist principle, 'guilty even if proven innocent.'" [p 44]

Touchstone (Simon & Schuster) • 1994 • 320 pp • softcover • $13 • ISBN 0-684-80156-6 • <www.simonandschuster.com>

When She Was Bad: How and Why Women Get Away with Murder by Patricia Pearson

Yet another myth that doesn't hold up to scrutiny is the belief that women are inherently much less violent than men. Self-described feminist crime journalist Patricia Pearson snuffs that assumption, showing that some women can be as brutally violent as the worst men and that women as a whole are as violent as men as a whole. So why doesn't it seem that way? Because of a circular definition: Men almost always commit violence because what we think of as violence is the actions that men usually commit. If we expand our definition of violence, we see that women engage in lots of it. Whereas men typically are thought to engage in public violence against strangers, women are usually violent towards family—children (including infants), siblings, elderly parents, and significant others—although there are more female serial killers than you'd think. Female gang members and terrorists, of which there are many, are known to be especially vicious. Women also participate in organized violence—warfare, vigilante mobs, massacres (such as the slaughter of Tutsis in Rwanda)—more than has been suspected. Though we know Joan of Arc and Cleopatra, history has forgotten most of the great female militarists. Women also engage in indirect violence, such as encouraging their boyfriends/husbands to assault or kill someone.

Pearson also makes the argument that while men direct their anger outwards at other people, women are more likely to direct it against themselves through self-mutilation and suicide or suicide attempts. This is somewhat speculative, and the author doesn't dwell on it, instead giving chapters over to mothers who kill their babies, mothers who hurt and kill their older children, women who attack their spouses and lovers, female serial killers, women as partners in violent crime (think Bonnie and Clyde), and female prisoners.

Besides looking at these women and their crimes, Pearson compares their methods and motives to those of men, and she talks about the cultural dynamics that let women get away with murder. Because both sexes conceive of women as naturally passive and innocent, they are often not suspected in violent crimes, and if they are accused, they can offer all kids of excuses, from PMS to, "I'm too small and weak to have done that," to saying that they meant to commit suicide but got confused and killed someone else (I'm not making this up). Another strange dynamic is that we tend to forget the female psychos while remembering the male ones. Jack the Ripper is a household name, but there are no legends or lore surrounding Belle Gunness, who killed at least 40 men and four children in Chicago in the first decade of the 1900s. The fairer sex, indeed.

Quote: "Women commit the majority of child homicides in the United States, a greater share of physical child abuse, an equal rate of sibling violence and assaults on the elderly, about a quarter of child sexual abuse, an overwhelming share of the killings of newborns, and a fair preponderance of spousal assaults." [p 7]

Quote: "Reviewing the nicknames given to multiple killers by media and law enforcement over the century, criminologist Eric Hickey has found that, while men are referred to as 'The Ripper,' 'The Night Stalker,' 'The Strangler,' or 'The Slasher,' women receive names that make light of their crimes—and by extension, of their victims. Comical monikers like the 'Arsenic and Old Lace Killer,' and 'Giggling Grandma' and 'Old Shoe Box Annie' are utterly undescriptive of the brutality of murder, while sexual monikers like the 'Beautiful Blonde' and 'Black Widow' hook almost jocularly into men's sexual fear of women." [p 153]

Quote: "Our collective amnesia about female serial killers is so pronounced that when Aileen Wuornos was arrested in 1992 and charged with the shooting deaths of seven men along I-75, she was immediately proclaimed America's first serial killer. Only four years earlier, ten female serial killers had been arrested across the United States." [p 156]

Penguin • 1997 • 296 pp • softcover • $13.95 • ISBN 0-14-024388-7 • <www.penguinputnam.com>

Male on Male Rape: The Hidden Toll of Stigma and Shame
by Michael Scarce
Given society's fascination with violent crime and the media's glee in reporting it, it seems impossible that there is a violent phenomena which has gone unrecognized. But there is. As it turns out, men are raped by other men with stunning regularity. It's no secret that this activity is par for the course in prison, but only one chapter in

> Jack the Ripper is a household name, but there are no legends or lore surrounding Belle Gunness, who killed at least 40 men and four children in Chicago in the first decade of the 1900s.

Michael Scarce's groundbreaking and exhaustive book *Male on Male Rape* deals with sexual violence in all-male environments, which includes not only jails but also military organizations, athletic organizations, and fraternities. The rest of the book looks at man-rape in the day-to-day world by examining the scant literature on the subject, its appearance in pop culture, how it relates to HIV and sexual orientation, its effects on survivors, the motivations behind it, and the often ignorant and shameful attitudes of law enforcement, courts, medical practitioners, the anti-rape movement, and society in general. Scarce offers many suggestions regarding how doctors, police, the survivors themselves, and others can more effectively deal with this hidden occurrence. Scarce interviewed 24 men who were raped, and several of them contributed essays to the book. A guide to organizations, state statutes, books, and articles concerning male on male rape rounds out the proceedings.

Quote: "In terms of incidence, studies of male rape in the United States and United Kingdom indicate that somewhere between 5 and 10% of all reported rapes in any given year involve male victims. The number and percentage of rapes involving male victims is presumably much higher than this, however, as this estimate reflects only reported rapes. Several researchers...have indicated that male rape survivors are much less likely to report their rape victimization than are female survivors....

"The sexual orientation of men who rape other men tends to be heterosexual (either self-identified or as later identified by the men they assault). The rapists are usually in their early to mid-20s at the time of the assault, and are primarily white. Virtually every study indicates that men rape other men out of anger or an attempt to overpower, humiliate, and degrade their victims rather than out of lust, passion, or sexual desire." [pp 16-8]

Insight Books (Plenum Press) • 1997 • 323 pp • hardcover • $27.95 • 0-306-45627-3 • <www.plenum.com>

Forbidden Relatives: The American Myth of Cousin Marriage
by Martin Ottenheimer
Marriage of first cousins is legally prohibited in the majority of US states and socially frowned upon throughout the entire country. Currently, the main reason for this attitude is the belief that cousin marriage will result in physically or mentally disabled children. Anthropologist Martin Ottenheimer shows that, based on the findings of modern genetics, this belief is false; children of cousins are at no special risk. In this academically oriented book (read: dry and detailed), he also presents a history of the attitudes toward cousin marriage in US and European history, overviews the changing legal status of cousin marriage in both societies, and shows why the current American legal and cultural prohibitions are wrongheaded (and, thus, the laws represent the State's interference with individual liberty (i.e. the right to marry)).

Quote: "This biological, sociocultural, historical, and theoretical study of the forbidden relatives in American culture and law has made it clear that an ancient aversion to marriage between close consanguineal relatives [i.e. blood relatives] emerged in U.S. civil law during the nineteenth century because of a myth. This myth—cousin marriage is a form of inbreeding that threatens the well-being of offspring and the civilized status of the country—led to the passage of laws against the marriage of first cousins in a majority of states. Thirty-one states still maintain injunctions against cousin marriage today in spite of the fact that empirical data do not support the need for any prohibition. In contrast, no European country has civil laws prohibiting cousin marriage. Europeans have viewed cousin marriage as a sociocultural institution that engendered social evolution through the formation of alliances.... The new view proposed here posits cousin marriage as a means on maintaining cultural continuity." [p 151]

University of Illinois Press • 1996 • 180 pp • softcover • $14.95 • ISBN 0-252-06540-9 • <www.press.uillinois.edu>

The Way We Never Were: American Families and the Nostalgia Trap
by Stephanie Coontz
One of the most pervasive and swallowable social myths is that American families today are radically different than in the past, and usually worse off because of it. At least until the first half of the 1960s, the male-headed, picket-fenced, 2.5-children family was the model of *Leave It to Beaver* bliss, right? As Stephanie Coontz meticulously shows, we've idealized the notion of the family, creating a

"golden age" of the family when, in fact, there was no such thing. By examining the *real* forms and functions of families from the days of the Founders to the early 1990s, she shows that, while some things are changing (such as the higher divorce rate), families were never as homogenous, perfect, or "nuclear" as we've been led to believe. Colonial families, frontier families, Victorian families, turn-of-the-century families, families of the 1920s and 1950s—all were systematically wracked with problems and were often no better or worse than families of today.

Quote: "Today's diversity of family forms, rates of premarital pregnancy, productive labor of wives, and prevalence of blended families, for example, would all look much more familiar to colonial Americans than would 1950s patterns. The age of marriage today is no higher than it was in the 1870s, and the proportion of never-married people is *lower* than it was at the turn of the century. Although fertility has decreased overall, the actual rate of childlessness is lower today than it was at the turn of the century; a growing proportion of women have at least one child during their lifetime.... Even though marriages today are more likely to be interrupted by divorce than in former times, they are much less likely to be interrupted by death [because of increasing lifespans], so that about the same number of children spend their youth in single-parent households today as at the turn of the century, and fewer live with neither parent....

"America's Founding Fathers were not always married: In Concord, Massachusetts, a bastion of Puritan tradition, one-third of all children born during the twenty years prior to the American Revolution were conceived out of wedlock...

"What one author calls 'the myth of the abstinent past' stems in part from lower fecundity and higher fetal mortality in previous times, making early sexual activity less likely to end up in pregnancy or birth....

"It is also estimated that there was one abortion for every five live births during the 1850s, and perhaps as many as one for every three in 1870." [pp 183-4]

BasicBooks • 1992 • 393 pp • softcover • $16.50 •
ISBN 0-465-09097-4 • <www.basicbooks.com>

Framing Youth: 10 Myths About the Next Generation
by Mike A. Males
Fretting about the recklessness, shallowness, and general inferiority of the younger generation is a time-honored tradition stretching back at least to ancient Greece. Yet somehow the younger generation grows up, the world keeps going, and then its their turn to kvetch about "these damn kids nowadays." In his second book on the subject (the first was *Generation Scapegoat*), social commentator Mike A. Males uses truckloads of statistics to show that, as the Who said, "The kids are all right." He demonstrates that today's young people are not nearly as violent, homicidal, suicidal, self-destructive, drunk, stoned, knocked-up, or immoral as they are generally painted as being, and that the rates of these activities among the young have been generally declining since the mid-1970s. He also shows that the media lie about this situation and that young people are policed and impoverished at alarming degrees.

Today's youth are less criminal than the kids of the 1970s and 1980s. Their rate of serious crime has dropped at the same time as the rate among people in their thirties and forties has increased dramatically. To pick just a few of many statistical examples: The felony arrest rates in California from 1976 to 1997 decreased by 32 percent among non-white youths, while at the same time increasing *160* percent among white adults over 30. Today's kids are more likely to get murdered at home by a parent than at school by their peers. Across the country, studies show teens use less alcohol and illegal drugs than their parents currently do. Of the 1100 people who died of drug-related causes in Los Angeles County in 1995, a mere seven were teenagers.

Quote: "The press headlines recent shootings in Pearl, West Paducah, Jonesboro, Edinboro, Springfield, which killed a total of 11 youths over an eight-month period. None of the anguished commentaries on these school tragedies mentioned that is the average number of children murdered by their parents in *two days* of domestic violence in the United States. In a society in which Simi Valley, Daly City, Riverside (California), Weston (West Virginia), Kerrville (Texas)—a few examples of many communities where multiple killings of children (totalling 16 dead in these cases) recently occurred—were as well known to the public and deplored by officials as Jonesboro or Springfield, what we call 'youth violence' would be better understood." [pp 3-4]

Quote: "Since 1979, fourteen juvenile executions have occurred worldwide. The enlightened democracies of Pakistan, Rwanda, Barbados, and Bangladesh accounted for five. The U.S., nine." [p 82]

Common Courage Press • 1999 • 391 pp • softcover • $18.95 •
ISBN 1-56751-148-1 • <www.commoncouragepress.com>

Condemned to Repeat It

War Before Civilization: The Myth of the Peaceful Savage
by Lawrence H. Keeley
The idea that prehistoric times were not marred by warfare appeals to both the general public and even the scientific establishment (especially the archaeologists and anthropologists). We like the Romantic notion that civilization has ruined the once pure and peaceful human race, but there is a crushing load of physical evidence that shows that this is untrue. Anthropologist Lawrence H. Keeley has investigated much of this evidence himself, as well as drawing together the research that appears scattershot in obscure academic articles and monographs. After looking at how and why scientists have twisted themselves into knots to explain away the obvious evidence, Keeley looks at the reality of the situation. Wars, battles, raids, "feuds," etc.

were actually more common and more vicious among primitive tribes and chiefdoms than among modern nation-states. The Maya, the Kung, Eskimos, Mbuti Pygmies, Australian Aborigines, Vikings, the Apache, the Pueblo—almost all past and recent non-nation-state societies regularly engaged in warfare. Kelley details the evidence, showing the weapons, tactics, casualties, reasons, contexts, etc. of precivilized warfare. It is not a pretty picture.

Quote: "Historic data on the period from 1800 to 1945 suggest that the average modern nation-state goes to war approximately once in a generation. Taking into account the duration of these wars, the average modern nation-state was at war only about one year in every five during the nineteenth and early twentieth centuries.... Compare these with the figures from the ethnographic samples of nonstate societies discussed earlier: 65 percent at war continuously; 77 percent at war once every five years and 55 percent at war every year; 85 percent fighting more than once a year; 75 percent at war once every two years."

Quote: "It is extremely uncommon to find instances among nonstate groups of recognizing surrender or taking adult male prisoners....

"A few cultures occasionally took men captive only to sacrifice them to their gods or torture them to death later. Among the Iroquoian tribes of the Northeast, captured warriors were often subject to preliminary torture during the return journey of the war party. When the party arrived at the home village, the prisoners were beaten by running the gauntlet into the village. At a council, the warrior prisoners who survived these initial torments were distributed to families who had recently lost men in warfare. After these prisoners were ritually adopted and given the name of the family's dead member, they were usually tortured to death over several days.... When the prisoner was dead, some parts of his body were eaten (usually including his heart) by his murderers."

Oxford University Press • 1996 • 251 pp • softcover • $14.95 • ISBN 0-19-511912-6 • <www.oup-usa.org>

Day of Deceit: The Truth About FDR and Pearl Harbor
by Robert B. Stinnett
The debate over whether or not Franklin Roosevelt knew in advance about the attack on Pearl Harbor has generated numerous books and articles. The establishment view, of course, is that he knew nothing about it, that it's beyond crass to suggest that a president would sacrifice American lives in order to give the US a pretext to enter World War II, something the Roosevelt Administration wanted very much to do. In his article (and book) *Saving Private Power*, Michael Zezima presents numerous quotes showing that upper level executive and military officials obviously knew, but now WWII Naval veteran Robert B. Stinnett has found the smoking gun. Not only does this document show that FDR and his foremost military and policy advisors knew Pearl Harbor would happen, it shows that they deliberately *provoked* it.

After seventeen years of research, including an untold number of Freedom of Information Act requests, Stinnett managed to shake loose an eight-point memo, dated October 7, 1940, written by Lieutenant Commander Arthur H. McCollum, the head of the Far East Desk of the Office of Naval Intelligence. He outlined the eight steps the government needed to take in order to push Japan into making war on the US. He sent the memo to FDR's two closest advisors, and almost immediately the President began implementing the steps. Soon after the eighth, final step was taken (i.e., "Completely embargo all trade with Japan...") in November 1941, Japan attacked.

As if that weren't enough, Stinnett provides a second bombshell. It's well-known that the military broke Japan's diplomatic codes, but through his research (including interviews with cryptographers of the period), Stinnett found that Japan's *military* code for messages to its Navy had been cracked in the early fall of 1940. FDR was constantly briefed on the contents of these intercepts, and therefore he knew exactly where and when the attack was coming. The belief that Japan maintained radio silence is also shown to be a myth—they broadcast their plan several times.

The silence surrounding these revelations has been deafening. Stinnett has produced definitive evidence that FDR and his advisors provoked Japan and knew about its pending attack on Pearl Harbor, yet no one is paying any attention. Add to this the fact that *Day of Deceit* was published by the giant Simon & Schuster—which has marketing and publicity capabilities to burn—and the silence becomes downright inexplicable.

Quote: "By provoking the attack, Roosevelt accepted the terrible truth that America's military forces—including the Pacific Fleet and the civilian population in the Pacific—would sit squarely in harm's way, exposed to enormous risks. The commanders in Hawaii, Admiral Husband Kimmel and Lieutenant General Walter Short, were deprived of intelligence that might have made them more alert to the risks entailed in Roosevelt's policy, but they obeyed his direct order: 'The United States desires that Japan commit the first overt act.' More than 200,000 documents and interviews have led me to these conclusions." [p xiv]

The Free Press (Simon & Schuster) • 2000 • 390 pp • hardcover • $26 • ISBN 0-684-85339-6 • <www.thefreepress.com>

Wars, battles, raids, "feuds," etc. were actually more common and more vicious among primitive tribes and chiefdoms than among modern nation-states.

Tripping

Marijuana Myths, Marijuana Facts: A Review of the Scientific Evidence by Lynn Zimmer, Ph.D. and John P. Morgan, M.D.

If Paul Armentano's article, "Drug War Mythology," whetted your appetite for suppressed truth regarding drugs, then be sure to check out *Marijuana Myths, Marijuana Facts* for further revelations. Written by a pharmacologist and a sociologist, it is the definitive statement on what science—not the hysterical misconceptions and propaganda of the Drug Warriors—has to say about pot. Drawing on studies in the *Journal of the American Medical Association* (which praised the book highly, by the way), *Pharmacological Reviews*, *Psychopharmacology*, the *Journal of Substance Abuse Treatment*, and other respected medical journals, they show that pot is not addictive and that it does not

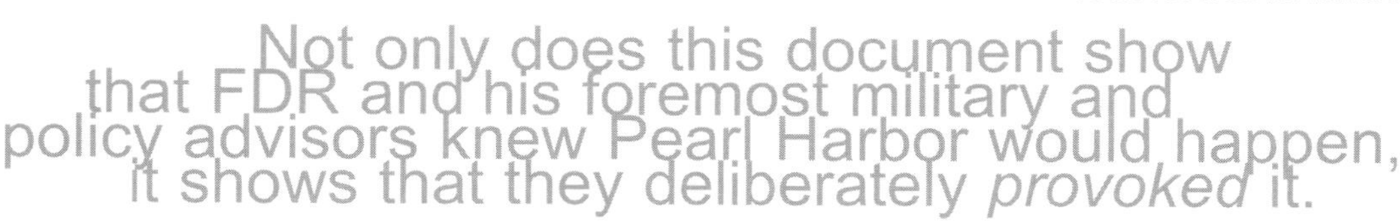

kill brain cells, cause psychological harm, interfere with sex hormones, impair the immune system, or do other terrible things that it's rumored to do (almost all of which *are* effects of tobacco and/or booze). They also demonstrate pot's medicinal value, show that grass is not more potent than it used to be, and undermine the laughable idea that marijuana use can be prevented.

The only psychological impairment marijuana causes is trouble with short-term memory, and even that only lasts during the time that you're stoned. Despite the fact that as recently as 1995 a book claimed that a joint has as many carcinogens as fourteen to sixteen cigarettes, the scientific evidence shows that pot smoke is no more likely to cause cancer than tobacco smoke, and pot smoke doesn't appear to cause emphysema. Also, because the amount of pot smoked by a stoner is degrees of magnitude less than the amount of tobacco smoked by nicotine addicts, marijuana users are much less likely to develop any lung disease.

Quote: "In 1995, based on thirty years of scientific research, editors of the British medical journal *Lancet* concluded that 'the smoking of cannabis, even long term, is not harmful to health.'" [p 6]

Quote: "In 1972, after reviewing the scientific evidence, President Nixon's Shafer Commission said it was of 'unanimous opinion that marihuana use is not such a grave problem that individuals who smoke marihuana, and possess it for that purpose, should be subject to criminal persecution.' Between 1969 and 1977, government-appointed commissions in Canada, Britain, Australia, and the Netherlands issued reports that agreed with the Shafer Commission's conclusions. All found that marijuana's dangers had been greatly exaggerated. All urged lawmakers to drastically reduce penalties for marijuana possession, or eliminate them altogether." [p 151]

The Lindesmith Center • 1997 • 247 pp • softcover • $13.95 •
ISBN 0-9641568-4-9 • <www.lindesmith.org>

Holy Rolling

The Christ Conspiracy: The Greatest Story Ever Sold by Acharya S

Drawing together an amazing amount of research, Acharya S—a classically-trained archaeologist and historian—utterly demolishes the facade of Christianity, showing that is 100 percent mythology. Not only was Jesus not the Messiah/Son of God with supernatural powers, she contends, but such an historical figure never existed at all. Jesus, Mary, the Wise Men, the Disciples, the Patriarchs, the Saints—all are amalgamations of gods and other characters that have existed in the mythologies of almost every culture on earth. The savior-figure, Jesus, is merely a personification of the Sun, which has been revered for millennia for its ability to chase away darkness and bring light and warmth (and, thus, life). Among Acharya's many other points are that early Christians were not persecuted to nearly the degree that today's Christians say they were; Christianity spread much later and more slowly than is generally believed; the four Gospels did not appear until 150 A.D. at the earliest (and perhaps much later than that); the books of the Bible have been repeatedly altered and even outright forged; the canonical Bible was not assembled until after 1000 A.D.; and the Hebrews did not develop monotheism and were actually latecomers to the concept. Acharya brings in secular history, church history, archaeology, theology, mythology, linguistics, and other disciplines to provide plenty of backing for her theses. This is an essential book for anyone who wants to know the reality behind the world's dominant religion.

Quote: "Thus, we find the same tales around the world about a variety of godmen and sons of God, a number of whom also had virgin births or were of divine origin; were born on or near December 25th in a cave or underground; were baptized; worked miracles and marvels; held high morals, were compassionate, toiled for humanity and healed the sick; were the basis of soul-salvation and/or were called 'Savior, Redeemer, Deliverer'; had Eucharists; vanquished darkness; were hung on trees or crucified; and were resurrected and returned to heaven, whence they came." [pp 105-6]

Quote: "St. Athanasius, bishop and patriarch of Alexandria, was not only aware of the allegorical nature of biblical texts, but he 'admonishes us that "Should we understand sacred writ according to the letter, we should fall into the most enormous blasphemies."' In other words, *it is a sin to take the Bible literally!*

"Christian father Origen, called 'the most accomplished biblical scholar of the early church,' admitted the allegorical and esoteric nature of the Bible: 'The Scriptures were of little use to those who understood them literally, as they were written.'"

Adventures Unlimited Press • 1999 • 434 pp • softcover • $14.95 •
ISBN 0-932813-74-7 • <www.adventuresunlimited.co.nz>

Papal Sin: Structures of Deceit by Garry Wills

Papal Sin presents a steely-eyed look at the obfuscations, omissions, and other Clintonian bullshit tactics used by the Catholic Church over the last 100 years or so. The fact that it was written by a Catholic—Garry Wills, the Pulitzer Prize-winning author of *Lincoln at Gettysburg*—makes it all the more interesting...and damning. It's impossible for Catholics to brush aside this attack as coming from some heathen who wants to see the Church destroyed. This time the charges are leveled by an insider who wants to see reform, not destruction. As such, Wills naturally doesn't question the fundamental nature of the institution. It's not organized religion, Christianity, or even Catholicism that is at fault, it's just the *way* the leaders have been handling things. Nonetheless, it's very instructive to read Wills' criticisms of the Church's "evasions, the disingenuous explainings, outright denials, professions, deferences, pieties, dodges, lapses, and funk" of recent times.

The four chapters of the first section are entirely devoted to the Holocaust—one chapter looks at how the Church rolled over and played dead during the Holocaust; another looks at the Church's attempts to wash its hand of its passive duplicity in the Holocaust; and two reveal the Church's efforts to convince the world that the Nazis also specifically targeted Catholics, when in fact they didn't. These chapters also contain material on anti-Semitism in the Church.

The book's longest section, "Doctrinal Dishonesties," contains eleven chapters looking at the zig-zagging and hypocrisy regarding the Church's views on contraception, female clergy, priestly celibacy and nonmarriage, the alleged superiority of the clergy, the nature of marriage, annulment (aka "Catholic divorce"), child molestation by clergy, gay priests, Mary, and abortion. The three chapters in "The Honesty Issue" take a chronological look at how the modern mechanics of deceit were formed in the Church, and the final trio of chapters examines some of the great truthtellers of Catholicism. Along the way, Wills unearths many troubling facts: Priests *were* allowed to marry into the fourth century; the sacrament of penance didn't exist until after the fourth century; in all of his voluminous writings, St. Augustine never says or even implies the alleged fact that the wafer and wine become the literal body and blood of Christ during communion; and although Catholics claim that a fetus is a person with a soul, they do not baptize miscarried fetuses.

Priests *were* allowed to marry into the fourth century.

Quote: "The church has no power to ordain women, that document [*Inter Insigniores* (1976)] said, because Christ made only men his original apostles. Despite an official position that now welcomes scriptural scholarship, the Vatican can revert, when that is useful, to biblical fundamentalism of the most simpleminded sort. The twelve apostles were men, so all priests must be men. But the twelve apostles were married, and the church authorities decided they could change that—in fact, John Paul [II] says that the church cannot go back to the original situation on this point. Saint Peter had a wife, but no modern Pope or priest can. Are we to say that all priests must be converted Jews? The twelve were. Are they all to speak Aramaic? For that matter, if we are to make the gospel situation binding now, we should observe that the apostles were not priests (see below). And there was at least one woman apostle in the New Testament, Junia (Rom 16:7)." [pp 104-5]

Doubleday (Random House) • 2000 • 326 pp • hardcover • $25 • ISBN 0-385-49410-6 • <www.randomhouse.com>

Blinded by Science

The Conscious Universe: The Scientific Truth of Psychic Phenomena by Dean Radin, Ph.D.

It seems to me that one of the most important discoveries of our time has gone basically unnoticed. Dean Radin has managed to pull it all together into one book, and still it's been ignored by society at large. At the time *The Conscious Universe* was published, Radin was the director of the Consciousness Research Laboratory at the University of Nevada, Las Vegas. As such, he led one of the three most important parapsychology programs in academia (Princeton and the University of Edinburgh house the other two). He has also done parapsychological research for corporations and the US government. Radin's message is this: Psi phenomena have been scientifically proven to exist.

Addressing each aspect of psi separately, he shows that decades' worth of controlled, replicable scientific experiments have yielded positive, significant results for telepathy, perception at a distance, perception through time, mind-matter interaction, mental interactions with living organisms, and field consciousness (which is basically mind-matter interaction on a large scale). For each phenomenon, he carefully shows how the experiments have been constantly redesigned, often ingeniously, to control for confounding factors and otherwise make them as rigorous and unassailable as possible. He then reviews the meta-analyses and performs his own meta-analyses on these experiments, boiling all the results from thousands and thousands of trials down to the bottom line.

For example, to analyze the results of people trying to mentally influence a random number generator, Radin crunched the results of 832 studies performed over almost 30 years. He found that for the controls (i.e. people who weren't trying to influence the numbers), the results were right at the chance level of 50 percent. But when people tried to influence the numbers, the numbers did indeed change. So much so, in fact, that the odds of those results happening by chance are more than a *trillion* to one.

Similarly, Radin crunched the numbers from 148 experiments in which people tried to influence the toss of dice. These experiments were done over a 50-year period and involved more than 2,500 people trying to influence 2.6 million dice throws. Overall, the dice throws in the control group matched chance (specifically, 50.02 percent). However, among people trying to influence the dice, the hit rate was 51.2 percent. As Radin says, "This does not look like much, but statistically it results in odds against chance of more than a billion to one."

Radin also addresses and refutes the criticisms that have been leveled against the experiments and meta-analyses, including charges of selective reporting. He goes on to discuss some theoretical aspects of psi phenomena and what all this implies for biology, psychology, medicine, business, and other areas. Interestingly, he looks at all the corporate research that's being directed toward parapsychology. Such giants as Sony, Bell Labs, AT&T, and the gambling industry have poured money into it, not to mention the research of governmental entities, including the CIA, FBI, the US military, the British Army, and Japan's Science and Technology Agency.

Quote: "The evidence for these basic phenomena is so well established that most psi researchers today no longer conduct 'proof-oriented' experiments. Instead, they focus largely on 'process-oriented' questions like, What influences psi performance? and How does it work?" [p 6]

Quote: "Honorton and Ferrari surveyed the English-language scientific literature to retrieve all experiments reporting forced-choice precognition tests. They found 309 studies, reported in 113 articles published from 1935 to 1987, and contributed by sixty-two different investigators. The database consisted of nearly two million individual trials by more than fifty thousand subjects. The methods used in these studies ranged from the use of ESP cards to fully automated, computer-generated, randomly presented symbols....

Psi phenomena have been scientifically proven to exist.

"The combined result of the 309 studies produced odds against chance of 10^{25} to one—that is, ten million billion billion to one. This eliminated chance as a viable explanation.... Further analyses showed that twenty-three of the sixty-two investigators (37 percent) had reported successful studies, so the overall results were not due to one or two wildly successful experiments. In other words, the precognition effect had been successfully replicated across many different experimenters." [p 114]

HarperSanFrancisco (HarperCollins) • 1997 • 366 pp • hardcover • $25 • ISBN 0-06-251502-0 • <www.harpercollins.com>

The UFO Enigma: A New Review of the Physical Evidence
by Peter A. Sturrock
As I look at *The UFO Enigma*, something occurs to me: *You Are Being Lied To* is filled with articles by some of the greatest investigative journalists and political commentators of our time, and I'm going to talk about *flying saucers*? I must be out of my mind. Well, I'm certainly not going to argue *what* UFOs are, but I want to point out the evidence that a certain, tiny number of flying objects just cannot be explained (away) by any "rational" explanation.

The UFO question is highly polarized. On one end you have the skeptics, who would say that a mile-long metallic craft that shows up on radar facilities and is seen by 1,000 trained observers is merely swamp gas and the planet Venus. On the other hand you have the true believers who think that every twinkling star is the mother ship coming to deposit loving Space Brothers or nefarious Grays. It would be nice if a panel of dispassionate scientists would objectively examine the evidence. In *The UFO Enigma*, that's exactly what we get.

The panel is headed by Peter A. Sturrock—an emeritus professor of applied physics and emeritus director of the Center for Space Science and Astrophysics at Stanford University—who has won awards from the National Academy of Sciences, Cambridge University, and other equally prestigious institutions. He is the epitome of mainstream respectability. The panel he selected is equally sober: an electrical engineer from Stanford, a space scientist from the National Center for Atmospheric Research, an expert in radiation injuries from the Institute for Aerospace Medicine in Germany, a plant biologist from the University of Bordeaux, and other intellectual heavyweights in the areas of astronomy, geophysics, geology, photographic analysis, and atmospheric phenomena. They examined photographic evidence, luminosity estimates, radar evidence, vehicle interference (e.g. car motors dying), aircraft equipment malfunctions and sightings by pilots, gravitational effects, ground traces, injuries to vegetation, physiological effects on witnesses, and analyses of debris.

To cut to the chase: The panel concluded that it is obvious that there are phenomena occurring in the sky that are not readily explainable to the observers. The vast majority of these sightings, however, can be explained by ordinary phenomena. Some might involve rare natural phenomena but not anything that is currently unknown to science. Tellingly, the panel did say this in its formal conclusion: "A few cases may have their origins in secret military activities." In other words, some cases do appear to involve strange aircraft under intelligent control. The panel also displays a surprising amount of concern regarding people who see UFOs and then have physical problems, often severe, due to being exposed to high levels of radiation that civilians should not be able to encounter.

The panel is unequivocal in its call for science to seriously study the question of unidentified flying objects. They are routinely observed and filmed, yet they are not fully understood, to say the least—in other words, the kind of subject science was made to handle. Sturrock's group calls for regular contact between the UFO community and the scientific community, the support of universities, labs, and other institutions in studying the phenomenon, and the creation of a modestly-sized governmental agency to collect info, study, and report on UFOs.

Quote: "The UFO problem is very complex, and it is quite impossible to predict what might emerge from research in this area. But the same is true of any really innovative and exciting area of scientific research. As the panel remarked, 'Whenever there are unexplained observations, there is the possibility that scientists will learn something new by studying those observations.' What is learned may bear no relation to the concepts that were entertained when the research was undertaken. We venture to hope that more scientists will take an interest in this curious subject so that there will be more progress in the second half century [of modern UFO sightings] than there has been in the first half century. There could hardly be less." [p 127]

Warner Books • 1999 • 407 pp • hardcover • $23.95 •
ISBN 0-446-52565-0 • <www.twbookmark.com>

Alternative Medicine: What Works by Adriane Fugh-Berman, M.D.
My blood boiled when I recently read a book in which a biochemist flatly declared that there is no scientific evidence that any alternative medical therapies work. What evidence there is, he intoned, was all anecdotal; controlled studies are nonexistent. Bullshit. In *Alternative Medicine: What Works*, Adriane Fugh-Berman—an M.D. who works for the US government and has been published in *Lancet*, the *Journal of the American Medical Association*, and other bastions of mainstream medicine—assembles an impressive survey of all the studies that have shown significant positive results for various forms of healing. Many of these studies are clinical trials, including blind and double-blind controlled trials, and almost every one of them was published in the peer-reviewed journals of the medical establishment, such as *Lancet*, the *JAMA*, the *New England Journal of Medicine*, the *Journal of Internal Medicine*, the *International Journal of the Addictions*, the *British Medical Journal*, *Nose and Throat Journal*, *Annals of Internal Medicine*, and *Cancer*.

The author divides the book by modality, giving a chapter each to ayurveda and yoga, chiropractic, vitamins and minerals, homeopathy, mind/body interaction (music, attitude, living alone, etc.), and many other therapies. Exercise has one of the most impressive records against heart disease, adult-onset diabetes, cancer, depression, and more. Acupuncture has done well at relieving lower back pain, neck pain, and menstrual cramps in trials. Biofeedback is impressive for circulation and some types of headaches, and fish oil eases the symptoms of arthritis. The herb feverfew helps prevent migraines, ginger is great for nausea (except when caused by motion sickness), and St. John's Wort is more effective than a placebo at alleviating depression. Massage and other forms of bodywork significantly reduce pain and anxiety and do wonders for premature babies.

Cranberry juice halved the amount of bacteria in the urine of women in a placebo study. Hypnosis on pregnant women with severe, all-day vomiting resulted in improvement in 88 percent of the subjects. Even when the news isn't good, the author still mentions studies that didn't yield positive results and studies that were equivocal or flawed. She absolutely lambastes the faulty studies on prayer and directed healing.

Quote: "Another double-blind study of 40 patients with high cholesterol found that after four months, total cholesterol fell 21% in the group taking garlic, compared to a 3% reduction in the control group. Triglycerides also fell 24% in the garlic-treated group vs. a 5% reduction in the control group." [p 111]

Quote: "A trial of artemisinin (the active ingredient of sweet wormwood) in 638 malaria patients in Vietnam showed a dramatic success rate—parasites in the blood decreased more than 98% within 24 hours and were completely gone in 48 hours." [p 120]

Quote: "In a similar study of 24 epilepsy patients, PRT [progressive relaxation training] reduced seizure frequency by 29%. In a control group that practiced quiet sitting, seizure frequency dropped only 3%." [p 168]

Quote: "Electrical stimulation may also help ankle sprains. In a randomized, double-blind study of 50 active-duty troops with Grade I or II (mild to moderate) sprained ankles, one treatment with pulsed electronmagnetic energy resulted in a statistically significant decrease in swelling." [p 191]

Williams & Wilkins • 1997 • 254 pp • softcover • $14.95 •
ISBN 0683-30407-0 • <www.lww.com>

Sacred Cows and Golden Geese: The Human Cost of Experiments on Animals by C. Ray Greek, M.D., and Jean Swingle Greek, D.V.M.
As a doctor and a veterinarian, both authors of *Sacred Cows and Golden Geese* have used animals in medical experiments. Now they are against the practice and have marshaled persuasive evidence that it is useless or worse. The authors don't discuss the cruelty of the procedures, the pain inflicted on the animals—they take that as a given. Instead, they show that animal experimentation is expensive, unnecessary, and even detrimental to the human race. Most advances in medicine and health have come from a variety of non-animal procedures ranging from clinical research, autopsies, and postmarketing drug surveillance to serendipity, mathematical modeling, and the specialization of medical care. And the few advances that were based on animals could have been done without their use.

Furthermore, the authors contend that the extrapolation of results of animal experiments to humans is worthless, dangerous, and downright unscientific. Although there are some similarities between us and non-human mammals, there are just too many complex differences on the macro and micro levels to be able to generalize results across species. Legal drugs kill around 100,000 people in the US every year, yet those drugs were extensively tested on animals for "safety." (For example, birth control pills cause blood clots in some women, but the animal studies didn't show this, and the dog studies even showed *less* clotting.) Not only do drugs and other treatments that are not harmful to animals end up killing humans, but the reverse is also true, meaning that treatments that hurt animals often don't get used on humans, even though they could help us *homo sapiens*. (Aspirin triggers birth defects in mice and rats, and ibuprofen causes kidney failure in dogs.) There are many other problems with animal experimentation, including the infection of humans by viruses in animals tissue used as culture.

The case against animal experimentation on strictly scientific/medical grounds is made in detail. The authors look at the role of animal testing in diabetes, cancer, AIDS, organ transplants, etc. They show case after case that proves animal testing is scientifically meaningless, and they look at alternative methods that can be and have been used to get much better results. In a revealing chapter, they expose the extremely wealthy, powerful interests that fight hard to keep animal experimentation afloat. They also show that many people involved in animal experimentation have admitted that it doesn't mean diddly. Dr. Arnold D. Welch of the department of pharmacology at the Yale University School of Medicine wrote, "In part because of possible major differences in responses to drugs in animals and man, the knowledge gained from studies in animals is often not pertinent to human beings, will almost certainly be inadequate, and may even be misleading."

Quote: "As the incidents of deformity [of human newborns] increased, scientists frantically attempted to reproduce teratogenesis [i.e. birth defects] from thalidomide in animals of all varieties. They gave thalidomide to scores of animals looking for proof in animals of what they already *knew* occurred in humans—that thalidomide could cross the placenta and drastically damage unborn offspring—and they could find none. Since animal testing had not indicated a problem with thalidomide, its use persisted. Hence, animal testing delayed the recall of this highly teratogenic drug." [p 45]

Birth control pills cause blood clots in some women, but the animal studies didn't show this, and the dog studies even showed *less* clotting.

Quote: "Total money spent on animals and animal support products is difficult to estimate since frequently the companies are private and unwilling to divulge figures. By estimates, the industry grosses between one hundred billion and one trillion dollars per year worldwide. This includes the direct employment of hundreds of thousands of individuals. Indirectly, the industry affects thousands if not millions of people who manufacture steel, plastics, and other materials. Animals experimentation does nothing for your health but it does help keep the economy going." [p 93]

Continuum International Publishing Group • 2000 • 256 pp • hardcover • $24.95 • ISBN 0-8264-1226-2 • <www.continuumbooks.com>

Biological Exuberance: Animal Homosexuality and Natural Diversity by Bruce Bagemihl, Ph.D.
My own observations lead me to believe that a lot of people are confused about whether or not animals engage in homosexual behavior. A lot are either not certain or think that if it does happen, it's only when the animals are in the unnatural state of captivity. I've even read one Christian claiming that reports of same-sex animal humping have been completely fabricated by scientists who want to advance the "homosexual agenda."

Now biologist Bruce Bagemihl has written a gigantic book that definitively answers the question. Yes, animals in the wild routinely engage in homosexual behavior. Males mount other males in more species than you can name, from elephants to hummingbirds. This doesn't always result in anal penetration, but sometimes, as in the case of American bison, it does. Female pygmy chimps (aka bonobos) rub their genitals together in a face-to-face position, and lionesses sometimes take turns mounting each other. Male bonnet macaques give each other handjobs and sometimes eat the resulting semen. Around one-third of gay encounters between killer whales involves incest. Female kob perform oral sex on each other and even stroke each other's vulvas with their forelegs. They're also into watersports—during sex, one female will urinate while the other sticks her nose in the stream. Giraffes are especially gay, often engaging in male-male sex much more than male-female sex. Group sex among four or five males has repeatedly been observed. It's also fascinating to note that two members of some species (such as flamingos, penguins, and red squirrels) sometimes form committed same-sex relationships—lasting years or even a lifetime—that involve sex, traveling and living together, and raising young together.

And gay sex isn't the only "alternative lifestyle" wild critters engage in. Bagemihl notes many other non-reproductive forms of sex. Sometimes females mount males (up to 40 percent of the time among golden monkeys, for example). At least one half of pregnant rhesus macaques continue to have sex. Some male bighorn sheep are "behavioral transvestites," meaning that they act in every way as if they were female instead of male. Red deer stags have been observed ejaculating from the pleasure of rubbing their antlers against vegetation. Female American bison seem particularly horny, often having sex multiple times with a partner (up to eight times in half an hour). Orangutans have been known to engage in heterosexual anal sex, and cattle egrets have threesomes.

The second half of the book examines the behaviors of a large number of mammals and birds, and is very detailed and repetitive. The first half is more readable, grouped into sections on the frequency of homosexual behavior, a comparison between gay male and lesbian behaviors, the relationship to human homosexuality, two centuries of studying gay animals (including "Homophobia in Zoology"), various (usually ridiculous) explanations that zoologists have offered for same-sex activity, and the developing new paradigm of animal sexuality, which is obviously more diverse and "exuberant" than has generally been recognized. In the chapter section "Anything But Sex," Bagemihl deflates the notion that most homosexual behavior is actually just a form of establishing social dominance. He points out, among other things, that such behavior is sometimes mutual or reciprocal, and that it is often the subordinates in the hierarchy who mount their superiors.

Biological Exuberance also contains dozens of remarkable photographs and drawings, the most memorable of which include photos of a female hyena nuzzling another hyena's swollen clitoris, a male bonobo giving a blowjob to another chimp, two male giraffes getting it on, and a walrus stroking his hard-on with his flipper.

Giraffes are especially gay, often engaging in male-male sex much more than male-female sex.

Quote: "The traditional view of the animal kingdom—what one might call the Noah's ark view—is that biology revolves around two sexes, male and female, with one of each pair. The range of genders and sexualities actually found in the animal world, however, is considerably richer than this. Animals with females that become males, animals with no males at all, animals that are both male and female simultaneously, animals where males resemble females, animals where females court other females and males court other males—Noah's ark was never quite like this!" [p 36]

Quote: "Male Botos [Amazon River dolphins] participate in a wide variety of homosexual interactions, including mating with each other using fully three different types of penetration: one male may insert his erect penis into the genital slit of the other, into his anus, or into his blowhole.... Pairs of males who interact sexually also display a great deal of affection toward one another, swimming side by side while touching each other's body, flippers, or flukes, surfacing to breathe simultaneously, or playing and resting together." [pp 339-40]

St. Martin's Press • 1999 • 754 pp • softcover • $21.95 • ISBN 0-312-25377-X • <www.stmartins.com>

The Myth of Human Races by Alain F. Corcos
Biologist Alain F. Corcos confronts us with a challenging idea: "Race is, and always has been, a social concept without biological foundation." Scientists, as well as human beings in general, have an urge to classify, but the classifications applied to humans don't hold up. Just the fact that there are a large number of conflicting classification systems for human races indicates that something is wrong. Corcos explains why some physical characteristics tend to show up in certain groups of people, and demonstrates that sets of characteristics are not bound together. There are times when Corcos fails to argue a point convincingly, not providing enough detail or explanation, but most of the time he seems to hit the mark. His explanation of why sickle cell anemia mostly (though not exclusively) strikes people of African descent is fascinating. (Basically, it's because sickle cells provide resistance to malaria and are thus an evolutionary advantage that helped Africans.) There's much food for thought in this challenging book.

Quote: "First, as mentioned in chapter 2, if we can perceive several main groups, there are millions of people who cannot be pigeonholed into them because they have one characteristic of one group and another characteristic of another group. Second, there is extreme diversity among individuals of the same group. For example, not all Africans have dark skin. Not all Asians have skin flaps (scientifically called epicanthic folds) over their eyes. Third, no 'racial' trait is restricted to one specific human group. For example, take skin color. There are many individuals in the world with dark skin. Some live in Africa, others in Australia, and still others in India. Take another trait, the epicanthic fold. It is very frequent among the populations of East Asia, but it is also frequent among some native dark-skinned inhabitants of southern Africa. It also occurs in some European children, but disappears once they are adults. This common trait is part of our human heritage and is expressed more strongly in some individuals than in others.

"However, the most glaring problem in 'race' categorization is that not all the individuals in a particular group have the combination of traits that they are supposed to have. For example, there are many dark-skinned Africans who do not have thick lips, whose hair is not thick and curly, and whose noses are not broad. There are many individuals in Asia with epicanthic folds who do not have small noses and/or medium lips." [p 46]

Michigan State University Press • 1997 • 218 pp • softcover • $17.95 • ISBN 0-87013-439-6 • <www.msu.edu/unit/msupress>

The Big Picture

The Secret Parts of Fortune: Three Decades of Intense Investigations and Edgy Enthusiasms by Ron Rosenbaum
Ron Rosenbaum is unique among journalists and writers, which naturally makes his work hard to describe in a short review. In his earlier days, when he still wrote for the *Village Voice*, he was nicknamed "the Dostoevsky of the *Voice*," which should give you some idea of the literary talent and approach that he brings to his reporting. His style has been labeled "literary journalism," which feels quite accurate, though he prefers the term "narrative nonfiction." Whatever the case, Rosenbaum always manages to pick fascinating, strange topics for his investigations, which he reports with a mixture of related undercurrents, thoughtful reflections, and enlightening tangents, all presented in his beautiful prose. When he's not investigating, he's bringing his trademark style to social or literary commentary. All of which makes this collection of 56 pieces written over a span of 30 years quite diverse, to put it mildly.

It is held together, more or less, by an overarching theme hinted at in the book's title: hidden patterns, lost knowledge, cryptic meanings that could be understood if only we could find the key, the lost Rosetta stone. Rosenbaum may or may not believe such things exist in any particular instance, but *somebody* doggedly believes they exist, and it's often their story that he's telling. Even when he's investigating conspiracy-oriented material, his aims are slightly off-center. He's not interested as much in whether or not Lee Harvey Oswald was a patsy as he's interested in deciphering who the hell Oswald was. He's not as concerned with what the Dead Sea Scrolls say as he is with the often horrible effects they've had on obsessed researchers. His take on Danny Casolaro—the writer/journalist who died under suspicious circumstances while investigating a unified conspiracy theory—is that he was not murdered in a way that was supposed to look like suicide; he actually killed himself in a way that was supposed to look suspiciously like murder. He wanted his death to be "the corroboration for a conspiracy, the corroboration he couldn't find in life."

Readers who enjoy *You Are Being Lied To* will most likely resonate with the articles on Oswald, Casolaro, the Dead Sea Scrolls, Watergate, Henry Lee Lucas, spymaster Kim Philby, phone phreaks, cancer cures, the system for launching a nuclear attack, murdered JFK mistress Mary Meyer, Hitler, J.D. Salinger, Thomas Pynchon, the occult overtones of some get-rich-quick literature, and, of course, Rosenbaum's groundbreaking sleuthing on the Skull & Bones secret society at Yale. In an article you won't want to miss,

"Race is, and always has been, a social concept without biological foundation."

Rosenbaum hunts down the whispered-about nude "posture photos" of Ivy League students from the 1940s to the 1960s—a timeframe that includes the student days of George Bush, Bill Clinton, Hillary Rodham, Bob Woodward, Diane Sawyer, and Meryl Streep, among many other famous people.

Some of his literary investigations peer into Nabokov's butterfly obsession, the hidden meanings of Hart Crane's poetry, and Borge's metaphysical labyrinths. Rosenbaum also offers up some pointed observations about Bill Gates and *Life Is Beautiful*, among other pieces of popular culture, digging out their deeper meanings. Even articles that could have become worthless puff pieces, such as Rosenbaum's look at Robin Leach (host of *Lifestyles of the Rich and Famous*), become something else in his hands. For example, during an interview over lunch he asks Leech, "Don't you feel that in some ways *Lifestyles* is a little bit like porn for the wealth-obsessed...?" Leach can't compute what Rosenbaum is getting at, and is obviously shaken for the rest of the article.

Quote from "The Subterranean World of the Bomb": "...I am invited into the capsule simulator to look around. It is exactly like the working missile capsule I had been permitted access to a few days ago in every respect but one: the keys. In the working missile capsule the keys are locked securely in a fire engine-red box that is to be opened only in time of high-level nuclear alert. But as soon as I walked into the simulator that morning I caught site of the now-familiar bright red box with its little red door wide open. And then I saw the keys. They gleamed brassily, each of them inserted into their slots in the two launch consoles, just as they will be in the last seconds before launch. Apparently the keys had been left there from a launch-procedure problem. I looked at the key closest to me. It had a round brass head and looked like an old-fashioned apartment key. It was stuck into a slot with three positions marked upon it: SET on top, and LAUNCH on the right. This particular key was turned to OFF at the left.

"I asked one of the crewmen if I could get a feel of what it would be like to turn the key." [p 66]

Random House • 2000 • 824 pp • hardcover • $29.95 • ISBN 0-375-50338-2 • <www.randomhouse.com>